ROCKIN' LAS AMÉRICAS

Illuminations: Cultural Formation of the Americas
John Beverley and Sara Castro-Klarén, Editors

Rockin' Las Américas

The Global Politics of Rock in Latin/o America

EDITED BY DEBORAH PACINI HERNANDEZ,
HÉCTOR FERNÁNDEZ L'HOESTE, AND ERIC ZOLOV

University of Pittsburgh Press

Published by the University of Pittsburgh Press, Pittsburgh, Pa., 15260

Copyright © 2004, University of Pittsburgh Press

All rights reserved

Manufactured in the United States of America

Printed on acid-free paper

10 9 8 7 6 5 4 3 2 1

Library of Congress Cataloging-in-Publication Data

Rockin' las Américas : the global politics of rock in Latin/o America / edited by Deborah Pacini Hernandez, Héctor Fernández L'Hoeste, and Eric Zolov.
      p.   cm. — (Illuminations)
Includes bibliographical references and index.
  ISBN 0-8229-4226-7 (cloth : alk. paper) — ISBN 0-8229-5841-4 (pbk. : alk. paper)
   1. Rock music—Political aspects—Latin America. 2. Rock music—Social aspects—Latin America I. Pacini Hernandez, Deborah. II. Fernández L'Hoeste, Héctor D., 1962– III. Zolov, Eric. IV. Illuminations (Pittsburgh, Pa.)
  ML3917.L27R63 2004   2003027604

To *rockeros* and *rockeras* everywhere, who over the years have defied the idea that rock is a crime.

Para todos los rockeros y rockeras, quienes, a través de los años, han desafiado la noción de que el rock sea un crimen.

Para todos os roqueiros e roqueiras em todo mundo, que, através dos anos, tem desafiado a idéia de que o rock seja um crime.

CONTENTS

Acknowledgments ix

Mapping Rock Music Cultures across the Americas 1
Deborah Pacini Hernandez, Héctor Fernández L'Hoeste, and Eric Zolov

La Onda Chicana: Mexico's Forgotten Rock Counterculture 22
Eric Zolov

Between Rock and a Hard Place:
Negotiating Rock in Revolutionary Cuba, 1960–1980 43
Deborah Pacini Hernandez and Reebee Garofalo

Black Pau: Uncovering the History of Brazilian Soul 68
Bryan McCann

Boricua Rock: Puerto Rican by Necessity! 91
Jorge Arévalo Mateus

The Politics and Anti-Politics of Uruguayan Rock 115
Abril Trigo

"A contra corriente": A History of Women Rockers in Mexico 142
Julia Palacios and Tere Estrada

"Soy punkera, ¿y qué?": Sexuality, Translocality, and Punk in Los Angeles and Beyond 160
Michelle Habell-Pallán

On How Bloque de Búsqueda Lost Part of Its Name: The Predicament of Colombian Rock in the U.S. Market 179
Héctor D. Fernández L'Hoeste

Let Me Sing My *BRock*: Learning to Listen to Brazilian Rock 200
Martha Tupinambá de Ulhôa

Guatemala's Alux Nahual:
A Non-"Latin American" Latin American Rock Group? 220
Paulo Alvarado

My Generation: Rock and *la Banda*'s Forced Survival Opposite
the Mexican State   241
Héctor Castillo Berthier

Neoliberalism and Rock in the Popular Sectors of
Contemporary Argentina   261
Pablo Semán, Pablo Vila, and Cecilia Benedetti

A Detour to the Past: Memory and Mourning in Chilean
Post-Authoritarian Rock   290
Walescka Pino-Ojeda

The Nortec Edge:
Border Traditions and "Electronica" in Tijuana   312
Susana Asensio

Esperando La Última Ola / Waiting for the Last Wave:
Manu Chao and the Music of Globalization   332
Josh Kun

Afterword: A Changeable Template of Rock in *Las Américas*   347
George Yúdice

Appendix: Rock in Latin America, 1940–2000   357
Notes   363
Selected Bibliography   395
Contributors   405
Index   409

ACKNOWLEDGMENTS

First and foremost, we wish to express our profound gratitude to the Rockefeller Foundation for providing the funds, setting, and logistics that permitted us to realize the *Rockin' Las Américas* authors' seminar that immeasurably improved this book. On behalf of all participants at the Bellagio meeting, our sincere thanks to Susan Garfield, Director of the New York Office of the Bellagio Conference Center, and to Gianna Celli, Director of the Center in Bellagio, Italy, for all their help in making sure that the seminar ran smoothly. The staff at the Bellagio Conference Center did everything possible to maximize our efforts during the two weeks of our meeting, and did so in an extraordinarily hospitable and welcoming atmosphere. This book would not have been the same without the Bellagio conference.

We also want to acknowledge a number of people who contributed to this project by commenting on prospectuses, proposals, and/or various sections of the manuscript. These include Emmy Bretón, John Coatsworth, Christopher Dunn, Juan Flores, Reebee Garofalo, Bryan McCann, Lauri McKain-Fernández, Charles Perrone, George Yúdice, and anonymous reviewers for the University of Pittsburgh Press. Other assistance came from Lori Oxford and Daniel Richardson, who worked on the translations from Spanish and Portuguese, and David Rains, who helped in the final assembly of the manuscript.

Special thanks go to the editorial staff at University of Pittsburgh Press, and especially to our editor Nathan MacBrien and series editor John Beverley for their unwavering enthusiasm for this project. The immense challenge of copyediting fell to Ruth Steinberg, who worked diligently from her post in Guanajuato, Mexico, to provide consistency and flow to the final manuscript.

Finally, we want to express our gratitude to our home institutions for supporting us during the various stages of the project: Georgia State University's College of Arts and Sciences, its Center for Latin American and Latino Studies, and the Georgia State University Foundation; the Provost's Office at Franklin and Marshall College; and the Dean's Office of Tufts University.

ROCKIN' LAS AMÉRICAS

Los Angeles
UNITED STATES
Tijuana
New York City
Ciudad Juárez
ATLANTIC OCEAN
Monterrey
MEXICO
Miami
THE BAHAMAS
Guadalajara
Havana
Mexico City
HAITI
DOMINICAN REPUBLIC
CUBA
BELIZE
JAMAICA
Belize City
PUERTO RICO
Tegucigalpa
GUATEMALA
HONDURAS
Santo Domingo
Guatemala City
NICARAGUA
San Juan
San Salvador
EL SALVADOR
Barranquilla
Cartagena
Caracas
Manugua
San José
VENEZUELA
GUYANA
COSTA RICA
Georgetown
PANAMA
Panama City
Paramaribo
Medellín
Cayenne
Cali
Bogotá
FRENCH GUIANA
COLOMBIA
Quito
SURINAME
ECUADOR
BRAZIL
Recife
PERU
Lima
Salvador
BOLIVIA
Brasília
La Paz
PACIFIC OCEAN
PARAGUAY
Asunción
Rio de Janeiro
São Paulo
CHILE
Córdoba
Santiago
Buenos Aires
URUGUAY
Montevideo
ARGENTINA
0
800 km
0
500 mi

Mapping Rock Music Cultures across the Americas

DEBORAH PACINI HERNANDEZ, HÉCTOR FERNÁNDEZ L'HOESTE, AND ERIC ZOLOV

"**R**ock is not a crime." This graffiti on a wall in Puerto Rico only makes sense when one understands that, for decades, Latin American rock fans and performers have been subject to a systematic pattern of harassment and abuses, under all forms of government—from Castro's Cuba to Pinochet's Chile—and ranging from outright government repression, to intellectual demonization and social ostracism. In Mexico, one of the first countries in Latin America where rock 'n' roll took hold, the government closed down the *cafés cantantes* (youth clubs) throughout the early 1960s, claiming that they fomented "rebellion without a cause" and encouraged the "distortion of local customs."[1] In mid-1960s Brazil, the avant-garde rock project called Tropicália had to defend itself both from nationalists on the right, who feared its potential for subversion, and from critics on the left, who loudly asserted that rock was a deformation of traditional musical forms.[2] When, in 1967, the young Cuban guitarist Silvio Rodríguez (who would shortly become a principal figure of the left-leaning Nueva Trova song movement) mentioned on government television that the Beatles were an important influence on his work, he was promptly fired.[3] During the "Dirty War" period in Argentina (1976–82), the police routinely disrupted concerts and beat up rock followers for the sole offense of gathering to listen to music considered threatening to the military regime. Those in public office who supported local rock could also find themselves vulnerable to attack. In 1971 the mayor of Medellín, Colombia, lost his post after having allowed a major rock festival to take place in the town of Ancón, just outside of the city. Following a similar massive outdoor festival of national rock bands in Mexico in 1971, commercial rock venues and large concerts were effectively banned for more than a decade.

Rock in Latin America has by now been "decriminalized." Five decades after its initial arrival in Latin America, rock's long-contested status has finally given way to social acceptance: it is now recognized as a legitimate form of popular music and has been incorporated within nationalist cultural discourses. Today, no nation—from revolutionary Cuba to indigenous Ecuador—is exempt from the cultural impact of rock. And, as vigorous, nationally identified rock 'n' roll scenes have developed throughout the Americas, following similar yet divergent trajectories, the region's cultural landscape has been transformed in profound ways.

Nevertheless, in spite of a growing literature examining the impact and spread of rock music cultures throughout Europe and the former Soviet Union, little has been written on the history and contemporary presence of rock in Latin America (or, for that matter, other developing nations).[4] This lacuna has tended to reinforce assumptions that rock is somehow a distinctively North American and European phenomenon, and moreover, that musicians and fans need to be "developed," not only to appreciate rock's aesthetics, but also to create original rock sounds. The essays here intend to challenge these misconceptions and, at the same time, broaden the understanding of rock's global impact by addressing fundamental questions regarding the spread of rock and roll to Latin America: Why is it that rock became such a controversial cultural force in Latin America? Given the highly contested nature of Latin American nationalism, in what ways has rock served as a medium for expressing national identities? How has rock, a transnational musical practice originating in the United States and Great Britain, been resignified in Latin American contexts? How are questions of race, class, and gender that are specific to Latin America inscribed in rock music and performance? How are the tensions between desires for local belonging (to the nation, region, or neighborhood) negotiated with desires for cosmopolitan belonging—especially given that "local" often means dealing with the everyday politics of poverty and repression, while "cosmopolitan" means engaging, in one form or another, with the influence of the United States or Western Europe? Ultimately, can there be a *national* rock in a transnational era, and if so, what exactly makes Latin American rock truly Latin American?

These questions guided the intense collaboration that resulted in this book, a collaboration among scholars and practicing *rockeros/as* (*roqueros/as*)[5] from diverse disciplines and from throughout the Americas (and Spain). With the exception of Reebee Garofalo, most of us were not "rock scholars" per se; rather, we had migrated to the study of rock and its associated musical forms from a wide range of disciplines in the humanities and social sciences—from ethnomusicology (Ulhôa, Asensio, Arévalo Mateus), history (Zolov, McCann), and literature (Fernández L'Hoeste, Pino-Ojeda, Trigo) to sociology (Castillo Berthier, Séman, Palacios, Vila), anthropology (Pacini Hernandez, Benedetti), and ethnic studies (Habell-Pallán, Kun). Two rock musicians—Tere Estrada and Paulo Alvarado—provide the crucial perspective of practitioners. The essays in this volume represent the geographical diversity of the Americas—from Chile to Chicano Los Angeles. In our choice of authors, we also strove to be balanced with respect to both gender and generation, including both those who witnessed the birth of rock and those whose musical frames of reference are punk, techno, and the new wave of *rock en español*. This introductory essay, then, is largely the result of the intellectual ferment generated by this encounter of contrasting positions, cultures, gender perspectives, and ages.[6]

Despite the diversity embodied in this book, any collective discussion of rock music cultures must face an acute awareness of the inherently unreliable and vexing nature of "representation." We cannot adequately describe the totality of rock practices in the Americas. First, such a task is physically impossible, given the immensity of the region. But in recognizing this impossibility, in choosing this or that musical culture or form for discussion, we run the risk of legitimizing and codifying certain sounds and styles as paradigmatic of rock, both historically and culturally, thus establishing a canonical (official) narrative that might exclude other histories. Furthermore, as mostly middle-class professionals, we cannot presume to speak for those whose lived experiences have shaped these practices, and of whom we often have only snapshot glimpses and understanding. This creates a particular challenge for the editors of this volume, situated in privileged locations within U.S. academia, in assuming roles as observers and enunciators, as interpreters and translators of a phenomenon largely occurring outside of the United States. While we are aware of these dilemmas, there seems to be no practical way to avoid them, other than to make very clear at the outset that, while each author speaks *from* one of many possible social as well as geographical locations, none speaks *for* anyone but themselves; and, moreover, our interpretations, although formed by attending as best we can to the methodologies of our chosen fields, are just that—interpretations. This caveat is particularly pertinent to the authors of this Introduction, which seeks to place the fifteen essays within a broader historical framework. Despite what we would like this book to accomplish, we do not—and cannot—claim the exclusive power to define.

Other crucial definitional issues bear addressing at the outset. The terms

"America" and "American," and their usurpation by the United States to refer to itself alone or to its presumed Northern European–derived culture, pose immediate problems for any book that conceives of Latin American culture transnationally. And, in a related problem, where does one locate rock music produced by U.S. Latinos/as—for example, by Chicanas in the United States (discussed in this volume in Habell-Pallán's essay) or by Puerto Ricans (discussed in Arévalo's essay)? If the term "Latin America" encompasses all the speakers of Romance languages in the hemisphere, then it follows that the United States, which has become the fifth largest Spanish-speaking country in the world, must also be included in any analysis of Latin American rock.[7] We resolve these difficulties by employing the term "Américas," in its original meaning—that is, to refer to the entire hemisphere, a usage that has been articulated most eloquently by the Cuban poet José Martí. In this way, we hope to add this volume to the body of work aiming to restore the terms "America," "Americans," and "Americas" to their rightful owners: the totality of nations and peoples that lie within the hemisphere.

A far thornier problem is the definition of rock itself, and what it means within a Latin American context. It is important to remember that early rock 'n' roll was a hybrid musical form, performed by black, white, and Latino musicians (for example, Ritchie Valens), which foregrounded African American aesthetics and performance styles.[8] As it moved into the mainstream, however, the music industry increasingly privileged white performers, such as the Philadelphia teen idols, the West Coast surfers, and the folk-rockers, over darker and more "ethnic" artists. Later, with the arrival of the Beatles and the rest of the British Invasion, musicians of color were virtually wiped off the U.S. pop charts.[9] As the marketing term "rock and roll" was shortened to simply "rock" around 1964–65—with black artists relegated to the categories of "soul," "funk," and/or "r&b"—many Latin Americans, especially younger fans who had come of age in the 1960s and thereafter, remained largely unaware of rock's original hybrid characteristics and their cultural implications. As a consequence, "rock" within most of Latin America tends to exclude those styles originated by African Americans. Thus, as Ulhôa and McCann have pointed out to us, black Brazilian funk is *not* usually categorized under the rock umbrella; similarly, Pacini Hernandez and Garofalo note in their essay that the black Cuban doo-wop group Los Zafiros occupies a marginal place at best in reconstructions of that nation's rock history. As for rap, its aesthetics have permeated rock throughout Latin America, but it remains to be seen how rap per se will figure within Latin American rock genealogies. While Trigo's essay hints at the traces of African influence in Uruguay's rock tradition, it is clear that one of the more significant and underexplored areas of research is precisely the question of how "black music" has been understood by youth throughout Latin America, both in those areas that are still characterized by large black and mulatto populations, such as Brazil, Colombia, and the Caribbean, and in regions whose African populations have largely disappeared, such as Uruguay, Mexico, and Argentina.

There are additional reasons for problematizing the term "rock." Asensio, for example, does not consider Nortec, the new category of Tijuana-based techno music analyzed in her essay, to be a form of rock. And given the range of styles and sounds that exist under the rock umbrella, it is reasonable to question whether "rock" should be used solely to refer to a form of music, or whether it more accurately refers to a more general complex of cultural practices, including fashion, hairstyle, dance, and that indefinable quality known as "attitude." In other words, are we discussing rock cultures rather than a particular type of music? These, of course, are the same definitional problems that rock scholars in the United States and Europe have been arguing about, without solution, for decades. Following Garofalo, who has participated in many of these debates, we find it most useful to consider rock as a template within which a variety of sounds and behaviors can be located and still be understood as a coherent category. Such a broad and flexible description thus accommodates all music that is mass-mediated, self-consciously "contemporary," makes at least some use of electric or electronic instrumentation, is associated primarily (but not exclusively) with youth, and whose aesthetics are hybrid, that is, reflecting multiple cultural sources. This "definition" brings rock into more visible relief, especially when contrasted with other, similarly inclusive (and imprecise) categories, such as "traditional music" or "classical music." Although true to its hybrid nature, rock can and does borrow from both of these domains. For all its imperfections, the idea of a rock template allows us to properly include musical forms such as funk and techno that otherwise might be excluded from consideration.

Although these terminological and taxonomical quandaries are necessary (if unresolvable), the more important and interesting question is historical: Why has rock been so problematic in the Latin American context? This discussion is impossible without first considering the intrinsic association of rock music with the United States, and thus with the history of unequal power relations between the United States and other countries of the Americas. Set against the dismal realities of U.S. economic and military interventions in Latin America, it is no wonder that for many, especially those on the left end of the political spectrum, rock was seen as an unwanted export of the Colossus to the North—at best, a distracting influence from the more urgent task of revolution, and at worst, the cultural component of what was perceived to be a blatant imperialist offensive. Indeed, the era of rock 'n' roll coincided with the end of the "Good Neighbor Policy," as the United States came to identify reformist and more radical policies in Latin America through the narrow lens of Cold War struggle. The juxtaposition between the seemingly frivolous fads associated with a foreign youth culture and the brutal reality of military-backed repression, sanctioned and often orchestrated by the U.S. State Department, situated rock music, from the start, at the center of a polemic over national identity and sovereignty that was largely, if not wholly, absent from parallel controversies unfolding in the Anglo-European world. This juxtaposition can be gleaned, albeit somewhat crudely, through the following encapsulated narrative highlighting key moments in rock culture. The narrative begins with Bill Haley. As Haley was "Rockin' Around the Clock," Latin Americans were still coming to terms with the consequences of the CIA's direct role in the 1954 overthrow of Jacobo Arbenz, Guatemala's first democratically elected president and a symbol for many Latin Americans of the possibilities for a nonviolent path to reform. While young people were twisting to Chubby Checker, CIA-trained forces were landing on the beaches of Playa Girón in Cuba, seeking to topple Fidel Castro's new, revolutionary regime. Soon after, as the Beatles were instigating young people to let their hair hang down, the U.S. government was openly expressing support for a military coup in Brazil that had put an end to democracy in that country and that would keep the military in control for the next two decades. In 1965, as the Beach Boys were pining after "California Girls," the United States was sending twenty thousand troops to the Dominican Republic in order to squelch the reform-minded democratic regime of Juan Bosch, perceived by the State Department as a possible "second Cuba." And, as the hippie counterculture was reaching its apogee in the United States, the CIA was plotting with rightist elements in Chile to overthrow the elected socialist government of Salvador Allende, which in turn unleashed a brutal, fifteen-year-long repression under General Augusto Pinochet. In short, it is quite understandable that the Left in Latin America so closely identified rock with the United States and perceived it as a reflection, if not also an embodiment, of imperialism. As a result, the Left was reluctant to recognize rock's progressive potential. At the same time, rock was also being attacked by right-wing conservative sectors of society, who abhorred the music because, to them, it signified the breakdown of traditional patriarchal institutions and values. Thus, rock found itself in an isolated position, literally caught between *la espada y la pared* (the sword and the wall)—the "sword" of ideological purity and the "wall" of the old order; or, in U.S. terms, and excusing the pun, between "a rock and a hard place."

Another fundamental issue that needs to be addressed is how and why rock music was embraced by Latin American (and U.S. Latino) youth in the first place—especially in countries, such as Mexico and Cuba, that already had extraordinarily vibrant and commercially successful national forms of popular music. Most often, credit (or blame) is given to the U.S. entertainment industry, an explanation that reflects the "cultural imperialism" thesis,[10] which holds that "a culture, usually that of a powerful society or group in a society, is imposed on another in a more or less formally organized fashion."[11] Popular music scholar Dave Laing has shown that the idea of cultural imperialism "depends on an analogy between the historical colonizing role of Western nations in politically subjugating the Third World and the current role of transnational media and electronics corporations."[12] To be sure, simultaneously with rock 'n' roll's inception in the United States during the 1950s the music and youth culture it spawned was transported to other English- and non-English-speaking countries. Thus, major recording companies like RCA Victor and Columbia Records (CBS) worked in tandem with U.S. film and television production companies to promote commodified versions of youth rebellion that made their way around the globe via transnational channels. By 1960, virtually every urban, middle-class youth throughout the Americas (if not globally) knew who Elvis Presley was, what his music sounded like, and what his gestures looked like, even if access to that music and imagery was unequal.[13]

While the cultural imperialism thesis at least partially explains the spread of rock 'n' roll to Latin America, the sociocultural processes that allowed for rock's acceptance within Latin countries were far more complex. In fact, Latin Americans were especially receptive to these transnational processes. By the late 1950s, as rock 'n' roll was gathering steam in the United States, the largest countries in Latin America were already well advanced upon programs of intensive, state-directed industrialization, which, under the intellectual and policy-making rubric of *desarrollismo* (Import Substitution Industrialization), were focused on breaking the dependency on foreign imports. These programs aimed to stimulate domestic production of manufactured goods (through the protection of local industries), while at the same time meeting the consumption demands of a growing middle class—itself an outgrowth of the industrialization process.[14] Even the smaller countries of Central America, or those that were still predominantly agricultural, such as Colombia, were caught up in the inexorable trend toward urbanization.[15] In short, Latin America was becoming increasingly urbanized and "the middle sectors"—those who would become the first and most avid consumers of rock 'n' roll—were on their way to becoming important political, economic, and cultural actors in Latin American society.[16]

Associated with the urbanization process was a "push-pull" dynamic that simultaneously forced peasants from their lands while at the same time drawing them to the cities, where they ended up swelling the ranks of the largely under- or unemployed. These newly urbanized and marginalized folk would, in due time, also become important consumers of rock. Thus, the 1960s was not only a decade of increasing middle-class growth but also one of rapid urban expansion in general. Mexico, for example, which had always been characterized by its enormous (largely indigenous) rural population, was 50 percent urban by 1960, and by 1970 the nation's capital had become one of the largest cities, in terms of population, in the world. The same promise of modernization that had vastly expanded middle- and working-class populations also exacerbated social and economic inequalities between, as well as within, urban and rural communities. Addressing this unequal economic development became an imperative for U.S. and Latin American policymakers after the Cuban revolution, which introduced the prospect of a revolutionary approach to resolving the question of underdevelopment. In response to this challenge, the United States made Latin American economic progress a priority of its foreign policy.[17] Unlike U.S. policymakers, many Latin Americans, particularly left-wing intellectuals, saw the Cuban model as a sensible response to oligarchic regimes. In the context of the Cold War, then, the ideological struggle over the very terms of modernization—whether it should occur through the private investment of capital, through state-directed capitalist expansion, or through socialist redistribution of accumulated wealth—raised the stakes for everyone: policymakers, intellectuals, and, of course, the emerging middle class.[18]

As envisioned by both Latin American and U.S. policymakers, modernization was a powerful cultural as well as economic process. To counter the appeal of socialist revolution, with its promise of a vibrant cultural nationalism, the middle classes were in effect offered a more tangible promise—that of achieving a certain level of cosmopolitanism by means of capitalist consumption, which came in the form of both domestically produced and imported goods. An integral component of this cosmopolitan promise was access to mass-mediated forms of popular culture, which had quickly become an influential—and profitable—U.S. global export. For middle- and upper-class consumers in Latin America, rock 'n' roll represented the quintessential experience of modernity: its appeal was precisely its cosmopolitanism, which was increasingly interpreted as being synonymous with U.S. culture. Hence, unlike in the United States, where rock 'n' roll emerged as an expression of working-class culture (and was thus antithetical to a construct of cosmopolitanism based on white, middle-class hegemony), rock 'n' roll in Latin America was initially embraced by the upper and middle classes as one manifestation of their modernizing aspirations. This direct association between rock 'n' roll and the upper strata of Latin American society held true until the mid- to late 1960s, after which the lower and working classes also began to claim rock as their own.

Ironically, in self-identifying with modernity by listening and dancing to imported and domestic cover versions of rock 'n' roll, young people in Latin America were subverting the traditional patriarchal values, or *buenas costumbres,* of their elders. For boys, this often meant defying one's father by mocking (or, arguably, simply rewriting) the prevailing standards of machismo, for example, by growing long hair "like a girl." For girls, rock could be especially liberating. In socially and (often) religiously conservative societies, women face enormous pressures to conform to patriarchal value systems that subsume their desires and ambitions to the authority of men—often including their "liberated" boyfriends. The rock revolution thus offered new possibilities for women to manifest their rebellion against parental and social ideologies that kept women subservient to male dominance. An important paradox here, of course, is that by the end of the 1960s rock 'n' roll coincided with the ideals of capitalist modernization while at the same time challenging the very social and ideological foundations of those capitalist hegemonic projects. For example, in the mid-1960s, the television program *El Club del Clan,* Colombia's equivalent of *American Bandstand,* featured domestic rock groups like Los Flippers, who performed cover versions of top-40 U.S. hits. However, at the same time that these bands were being promoted by the mass media to Colombian youth, they were also provoking outrage within the historically traditional society of Bogotá. Something similar was occurring in Mexico, where Telesistema (later, Televisa), the monopoly television conglomerate, promoted groups such as Los Yaki on their program, *Yeah Yeah Yeah a Go Go,* often to the consternation of religious conservatives.

Indeed, this was a common pattern that was evolving throughout Latin America. By the end of the 1960s virtually every country could boast of homegrown rock bands and an accompanying countercultural milieu. In some cases, such rock scenes would culminate in local rock festivals, patterned after Woodstock and featuring local bands, in which tens of thousands of mostly middle-class youth would openly flout their parents' cultural values: examples include Avándaro (Mexico, 1971), Ancón (Colombia, 1971), Caracas (Venezuela, at various moments in the early 1970s), and Guatemala (1969). The fact that the local mass media were seen as collaborating with transnational corporations in promoting youth countercultures only highlighted, for nationalists on the right and left alike, the inherent dangers of unbridled capitalist modernization. The music was often regarded as a sign of imperialist attack, moral collapse, or worse. In fact, rock *was* empowering—even if in contradictory ways (such as singing in English).

If rock 'n' roll (and later, rock) coincided with, and simultaneously subverted, ideologies of capitalist consumerism across Latin America, the ramifications of the Cuban revolution on rock music's reception were considerable. Cuba's revolution offered a competing vision of modernization, one that not only sought to redistribute economic wealth (through the expropriation of private property), but also approached culture as a domain that could and should be utilized in the service of revolutionary goals. The idea of constructing a "national culture" was not in itself new; since the 1930s, throughout Latin America, many regimes had understood the utility of protecting and promoting autochthonous forms of cultural expression as central to their elite hegemonic projects. Indeed, the objective of fomenting an (imagined) national culture was itself inherent to the Import Substitution Industrialization (ISI) project, then approaching its apogee in many Latin American countries. The Cuban revolution, however, sought an even more radical (if ultimately unsuccessful) cultural outcome for the ISI project: to extirpate all traces of extra-revolutionary consumption. (Thus, Fidel Castro's famous dictum "Within the Revolution, everything; outside the Revolution, nothing.") The clear association of rock 'n' roll with capitalist consumerism—patently evident during the 1960s—was logically anathema to the Left's revolutionary project, in Cuba and elsewhere, not only because of its association with U.S. imperialism but, more fundamentally, because rock—as a reflection of "bourgeois decadence"—threatened to deplete the virile energies of (potentially revolutionary) youth. This ideological paradigm, embraced—often uncritically—by many within the Latin American Left, stimulated support for a new vision of popular music, one intended to counter the perceived hegemony of the mass-mediated, commercial, popular music that was being disseminated throughout Latin America by multinational culture industries. By the end of the 1960s, music inspired by this vision, known variously as *nueva canción, nueva trova, canción protesta/política,* and *canción folclórica,* could be heard throughout the hemisphere.

Popular music under this formulation differed from its commercialized counterpart in four principal ways. First, it was linked explicitly to a revolutionary consciousness. In contrast to commercialized music, which was viewed as stupefying and alienating, "authentic" popular music had an intrinsic didactic intent: to raise social and political awareness. Second, the logical outcome of this didacticism was that the music was disassociated from the expression of bodily gratification; this music was for listening, not dancing.[18] Third, this music was envisioned as linked to the fulfillment of the Bolivarian dream of a pan–Latin American solidarity. This was expressed musically by the adoption of acoustic instruments autochthonous to Latin America, in opposition to the electronic instrumentation that characterized commercial music. Finally, the new music disputed the very definition of the term "popular." "Politicized songs" championed the concept of *música popular,* music that was produced by artists who used native instruments to reproduce traditional melodies and rhythms from the rural (read, authentic) countryside, though ironically many if not most of these performers were themselves from the urban middle classes. *Música popular* was meant to contrast with *música pop,* which was attacked for its explicit commercialism and thus identified with urban (read, transfigured) cultural practices. To some extent, our description of the new music as celebrating the "rural" is an overgeneralization intended to underscore a point; many instances of *nueva canción* songs, those of Silvio Rodríguez (of Cuba) and Piero (of Argentina), for example, were actually meditations on modernity and urban life. Still, it is fair to say that the heroic cultural vision of the Left invoked the full recovery and protection of rural, "native" culture as a bulwark against the onslaught of urban, "foreign" culture (that is, culture linked to capitalist consumption). Given the music's explicit links with a utopian ideology, and its promotion (sometimes institutionally) by left-wing regimes (viz., Luis Echeverría in Mexico [1971–76]; Salvador Allende in Chile [1970–73]; General Juan Velasco Alvarado in Peru [1968–75]; and Fidel Castro in Cuba [1959–present]), it was all but impossible for socially conscious youth to disregard it. Indeed, the proponents of this new music were all too successful in achieving their goal of pitting *música popular* against *música pop*, in the process putting enormous pressure on young people to embrace the former and reject the latter. For instance, Julia Palacios, whose essay with Teresa Estrada on the history of women rockers in Mexico appears in this volume, ruefully recalls how in the early 1970s she almost threw away her entire collection of rock records, not only because she felt pressured to do so (by her socially conscious peers), but also because she herself had come to believe that her political convictions required her to do so. Indeed, Eric Zolov argues in his essay on La Onda Chicana that Mexico's rock countercultural movement of the early 1970s disappeared after the Avándaro music festival, in large part because the middle class, exposed to the strong leftist critique of rock as cultural imperialism (a criticism that would be sustained by the incoming populist regime of Echeverría), had come to disparage even home-grown rock. In effect, the political song movement itself became a hegemonic construct, one that later generations would confront—musically, if not also ideologically. Walescka Pino-Ojeda addresses precisely this issue in her essay, which asks why young Chilean rockers in the 1990s rejected the *"charanguito"*—a disparaging reference to the small acoustic guitar popularized by Chile's *nueva canción* performers as a symbol of liberation across the Americas. For a new generation of Chilean youth, the *charango* had become a symbol of cultural dogmatism.

Beginning in the late 1960s, in response to the ideological backlash mounted by the Left against rock, some Latin American rockers sought to strategically reposition themselves, by incorporating elements of political song and by attempting to redefine the rock genre so as to demonstrate that it was not necessarily opposed to a revolutionary paradigm. By adopting syncretic musical forms, rock artists (some more successfully than others) tried to show that a "dialogue" between rock and politicized song was possible, both at the aesthetic and ideological level. The Chilean group Los Jaivas, for example, fused indigenous instruments and rock styles, creating an original variant of rock whose sound helped bridge the polemic that separated rock from political song. Even in Cuba, as Deborah Pacini Hernandez and Reebee Garofalo show, there were efforts to create a syncretic form that would embrace both the political and the popular. There, the Grupo Experimental Sonora del ICAIC (which included the musicians Silvio Rodríguez and Pablo Milanés, who would later become renowned promoters of Cuba's Nueva Trova movement) insisted, despite the official opprobrium of the Castro regime, that revolutionary music could and should experiment freely using all available styles, including rock—and that such music could still be socially progressive.

These indications that the polemical divide that had plagued rock since the early 1960s was being transcended, coincided, to a greater or lesser extent, with the transition to repressive military regimes across the region. For the same reasons the Left had supported the political song movement, the new military governments now viewed political song as subversive. While the few remaining populist-revolutionary regimes (Cuba, Mexico, Peru) continued to support political song for their own political ends, elsewhere in Latin America the movement came under attack and went underground. Most notoriously, in 1973, the musician Víctor Jara had his hands broken before being executed by the Chilean military and the *charango* (as well as other native instruments) was virtually proscribed.[20]

Unfortunately, despite their progressive intentions, proponents of the political song movement of the late 1960s and 1970s did not take into account the ideological implications of celebrating (and romanticizing) Latin American indigenous music and culture. They could not transcend one of the region's most troubling historical legacies—that of "whitening."[21] In their eagerness to champion marginalized native peoples, political song artists tended to overlook Latin America's African musical heritage, thus perpetuating preexisting racial hierarchies that had long privileged *mestizaje* over blackness.[22] Consequently, blackness was largely displaced in musical representations of the pan–Latin American imaginary that was heralded in the political song movement (once again, there are important exceptions to this generalization, notably the music of Pablo Milanés, who is himself Afro-Cuban, and that of Gilberto Gil, who is Afro-Brazilian). For example, the Left's reification of Andean music as the embodiment of a commitment to indigenous political struggle typically ignored the popularity of African-derived dance musics from the Caribbean basin, such as *cumbia*.[23] *Cumbia* (which paradoxically contains indigenous influences), along with other Caribbean dance musics such as merengue, was perceived as "party" music and therefore unsuitable for transmitting the intellectual and artistic seriousness of political song's cultural and revolutionary project. Similarly, in the Dominican Republic, the Nueva Canción–inspired group Expresión Joven incorporated the Andean panpipe into their music, but not the accordion, an instrument that was integral to the country's most representative popular musical style, merengue. Ironically, many practitioners and fans of popular dance styles, such as salsa and merengue, held equally critical views of rock; they and their political-song counterparts both used the same anti-imperialist language to denounce it. However, in the prevailing climate, even salsa and merengue could be perceived as problematic since these musical forms were at the same time patently commercial and primarily associated with urban, working-class black festivity. All of this is notwithstanding the efforts of such Nueva Canción–inspired *salseros* as Rubén Blades, who sought to infuse a greater degree of political content into salsa.

It is a sad coincidence that Latin America's historical predisposition to privilege whiteness by associating it with higher-class cultural values, and thus with modernity, coincided with a similar process of racial "whitening" of the rock 'n' roll genre in the United States. As previously touched upon in this introductory essay, in the United States this process was responsible for the transfiguration of rock 'n' roll into just plain "rock," a process that was accelerated in the 1960s, owing to the innovations of Bob Dylan and the Beatles, whose compositions helped rock achieve the status of "Art." This new development established an important distinction between music for dancing and music for listening; its attendant mind/body split was further reinforced when rockers began to use hallucinogenic drugs. In this sense, rock music was situated in opposition to soul music (for example, the Stax and Motown sounds), which was clearly music for dancing. Art rock took rock into a symphonic and highly intellectualized (read, European) direction, separating it still further from its African American roots. If rock was Art, soul was entertainment, which relegated it to a lower level in the hierarchy of cultural practices and excluded it from serious consideration by the press, both in the United States and Latin America.²⁴ In Brazil, in the 1970s, as Bryan McCann discusses in his essay, black and mulatto youth favored African American soul and funk, whereas their white counterparts were experimenting largely with avant-garde rock musical styles that followed in the wake of the Tropicália movement. (It should be noted, however, that because of the influence, especially, of Gilberto Gil, an Afro-Brazilian founder of the Tropicália movement, African-derived rhythms—including samba and reggae—were in fact integrated into various aspects of the Tropicália repertoire; Gil would later play a key role in the legitimization of Brazilian funk and soul.²⁵) It was the Tropicália style that came to "represent" the Brazilian countercultural rock vanguard throughout the hemisphere, whereas Brazilian soul continues to be denigrated by rock critics and excluded from the nation's rock historiography (and musical canon). During the 1970s, then, both Latin American art rock music and political song effectively subordinated African-derived music and dance forms, particularly in countries where whites, mestizos, and Amerindians constituted the majority.

By the late 1970s, those rock bands that had survived the earlier period, as well as those bands that had distanced themselves (for whatever reasons) from the polemic over rock versus political song, now became the vehicle for youth resistance to political as well as social repression. In authoritarian contexts, such as in Argentina, Brazil, Chile, and Guatemala, bands' lyrics were usually not politically explicit but rather contained encoded narratives of opposition, often expressed metaphorically, to avoid military censorship. For example, during the Dirty War in Argentina (1976–82), "Canción de Alicia en el País" (Alice's Song in the Land) by the rock band Serú Girán conveyed the idea that, under the military junta, "wonder" had been supplanted by "terror." In this same period, the very name of the Guatemalan rock band Alux Nahual conveyed their implicit identification with that nation's Mayan population, at a time when the Guatemalan military was engaged in a scorched-earth policy against Amerindians suspected of abetting the guerrillas. The lyrics of "Hombres de Maíz," a song which romanticizes rural life, are otherwise benign, but they contain a single, veiled reference to the civil war that was engulfing Guatemala: "I don't care for the government / or for the revolutionaries / but if this is what it is to be alive / I'd sooner die while singing."²⁶ In Argentina, by the 1980s, in a process of self-identification by rock critics and fans alike, bands such as Serú Girán were seen as constituting a coherent national movement, which came to be referred to as *rock nacional*.²⁷

This process of "nationalizing" rock occurred simultaneously elsewhere in Latin America in the same period, although in different ways. The common denominators, however, were threefold. First, rock musicians began using original Spanish or Portuguese lyrics. Second, they began to incorporate local youth slang—reflecting the increasingly diversified class origins of rock musicians and their publics. Third, rock bands began adopting local and national topics into their songs. In order to appreciate the significance of this shift at the textual level—a musical shift would also occur, as we explain below—it is important to understand that the choice of language had been politicized from the moment rock 'n' roll arrived in Latin America. In the early days, a combination of marketing considerations, nationalist sentiment, and a lack of familiarity with English had led to the rise of the *refrito* (from the verb *refreír,* "to refry"). The term was originally used in Mexico to describe the production of Spanish-language covers of imported hits, but it could easily be used to describe similar practices throughout the region. In Brazil, the media baptized the fledgling rock 'n' roll/youth movement the Jovem Guarda (Young Guard), while in Spanish-America it was generally referred to as La Nueva Onda/Ola (the New Wave). Beginning in the mid-1960s, however, as rock 'n' roll evolved into rock in the wake of the British Invasion, Latin American rock musicians (and their fans) concluded that "authentic" rock needed to be sung in English—that only English conveyed the essential feeling of the rock original.[28] (An important exception is the case of Brazil, where in 1964 Ronnie Cord inaugurated a *fase nacional* with his original song "Rua Augusta," sung in Portuguese; this trend was later cemented by the Tropicália movement after 1967.[29]) The shift to incorporating English (Mexican groups, for example, would at one point write exclusively in English) naturally fed into the indictment of rock by its nationalist critics.

Nevertheless, the politics of language choice was always more complex than the cultural imperialism thesis might suggest. For example, rock musicians of La Onda Chicana (Mexico's countercultural movement of the late 1960s–early 1970s) employed English to endow their music with a legitimacy they believed had been lacking from the earlier period of *refrito* rock. An alternative manifestation of the politics of language choice occurred during this same period in Cuba, where some young rockers used the original English-language lyrics of foreign tunes to establish the authenticity of their performances. By singing in English they were simultaneously showing their capability (and courage) to break through the cultural blockade, imposed from without by the United States and from within by the island's Communist regime, which forbade the use of such lyrics as imperialist. This pattern of adopting English, within a variety of local contexts and with varying political and cultural implications, held true for many countries.

By the end of the decade of the 1960s, however, most Latin American bands were breaking away from a dependency on this linguistic artifice. Pioneers in this trajectory away from English included Luis Alberto Spinetta's group Almendra in Argentina (1967–70), and the group Three Souls in My Mind (later, the TRI) in Mexico (after 1971). The move toward Spanish also brought with it the use of local vernacular, which reflected the increasingly diverse class composition of rock musicians and their fans. As Pablo Semán, Pablo Vila, and Cecilia Benedetti show in their essay, in Argentina the lyrics of *rock nacional* included the *lunfardo* street slang of the Argentine lower classes. In Mexico, Héctor Castillo Berthier points out, such groups as the TRI led the way in introducing the *caló* (slang) of the *chavos banda* (economically marginalized youth of the capital) to rock. Ironically, in spite of its new emphasis on Spanish or Portuguese lyrics and on local themes, in its early stages *rock nacional* often *sounded* like a close replica of its U.S. and British equivalents. Recovering indigenous musical forms had been central to the ideological mission of political song, but what made *rock nacional* "national" was not necessarily expressed at the level of musical style. Indeed, *rock nacional*'s musical aesthetic was often closer to the formerly demonized sound of imported rock. Its musical template could range from symphonic rock, as with Guatemala's Alux Nahual (see the essay by Paulo Alvarado), to Colombia's punk-rock group La Pestilencia (see the essay by Héctor Fernández L'Hoeste), to the New Wave sound of Argentina's Soda Stereo. Although their music often duplicated the sound of foreign rock, these new bands had clearly advanced beyond their predecessors' direct emulation and dependency on covering foreign hits: now performing original, musically and lyrically sophisticated songs in vernacular Spanish, they could no longer be simplistically characterized as mere imitators of foreign models.

The rise of *rock nacional* also coincided with the advent of neoliberal economic policies, initiated during the 1980s, which set in motion the systematic privatization of national infrastructures throughout Latin America. These policies, largely imposed by U.S. and international lending agencies, signaled the collapse of the nationalist projects (encompassed under the rubric of ISI) that had defined the economic policy of Latin American governments since the 1930s. In addition, this radical economic transition was accompanied by the return, after decades of military rule, of democratically elected governments all across Latin America. In this new environment, local rock not only thrived but for the first time also began to receive open approval by leftist intellectuals. These former critics, who had once shunned rock for its presumed cultural imperialism, now embraced *rock nacional* as an authentic movement of cultural resistance to the devastating economic marginalization and political repression that was accompanying the structural shift toward neoliberalism.

Abetting this intellectual rapprochement was a concurrent shift in academic discourse toward a reappraisal of the term *cultura popular*. Once used to refer exclusively to rural cultures, the term was now broadened to incorporate urban cultural practices as well, including those which were mass-mediated.[30] Latin American rock was now seen as a legitimate form of expressive culture, akin to literature and cinema, which clearly opened up new possibilities for narrating and performing nationality. The fact that intellectuals (and music critics) were ready to recognize this reality thus heralded an important new era in the legitimization of locally produced rock as an authentic form of cultural expression.

By the late 1980s, the middle and upper classes had lost their exclusive claim to rock. Rock's fan base was now increasingly diverse with respect to race, ethnicity, and class. This new generation of rock musicians and their fans had come of age listening to the *rock nacional* genre—both locally produced and imported from other Latin American nations, especially Argentina, Chile, and Mexico. No longer interested in the outdated polemic over rock's "politics," they rejected the heroic discourse of an earlier revolutionary moment. Musically and lyrically, they enacted a politics of *anti*-politics, repudiating at the level of sound and performance not only the old hegemonic ideology of the socialist Left but the ascendant ideology of neoliberal capitalism as well. The disintegration of the Soviet Union (and in its wake, the increasing dollarization of Cuba's economy), on the one hand, had rendered the goal of communist revolution obsolete, while the rise of neoliberalism had created severe social disruptions that were disproportionately shouldered by the poor. As the title of the 1989 Colombian punk-rock film *Rodrigo D No Future* signaled, there would be "no future" for marginal sectors of society—that is, for the majority of Latin America's urban and rural populations.

Unlike their predecessors, this new generation of rockers assumed their right to listen to and make rock music, whether in Spanish, Portuguese, or English, whether domestically produced or imported, and whether incorporating "foreign" formulas or "traditional" musical elements. Like the Puerto Rican rockers discussed by Jorge Arévalo Mateus, rockers throughout Latin America were saying, in essence: We have a right to express ourselves without being socially ostracized, accused of being a *vendepatria* (a "sell-out"), and, more fundamentally, without having our heads cracked by the police. Totally uninterested in participating in the construction of a master narrative of the nation as a uniform imagined community (as pursued by the political song movement, for example), they put into practice a more flexible and inclusive discourse— one in which they actually claimed some protagonism—that articulated the complex (if often violent) textures of *lo cotidiano* (everyday life) in urban Latin

America. Examples of such rockers include Rodrigo González, who is discussed by Héctor Castillo Berthier in his essay on Mexico, and Patricio Rey y Sus Redonditos de Ricota, members of the *rock chabón* movement that Semán, Vila, and Benedetti discuss in their chapter on Argentina. Many of these groups employed a punk and heavy-metal aesthetic, as well as a "do it yourself" approach to making music, reflecting not only their marginalized economic and political situation but also their limited access to production and distribution facilities.

During the 1990s, as Latin American governments sought to reinsert their nations into global circuits of capital, culture, and media—transformations collectively recognized as "globalization"—they found themselves newly open to outside cultural and economic influences. In response, some rock bands turned inward, incorporating popular and indigenous musical traditions that originated within Latin America and that would distinguish them within the global marketplace. Rock groups such as Café Tacuba (Mexico), Los Fabulosos Cadillacs (Argentina), Aterciopelados (Colombia), and Los Amigos Invisibles (Venezuela), for example, all freely incorporated regional genres and transnational styles as diverse as salsa, tango, *cumbia, vallenato,* reggae, ska, rap, and hip-hop.[31] This trend toward hybridity was facilitated by new local media infrastructures, which were connected to (but not dependent upon) the dominant transnational cultural industries, and which, in turn, opened up new markets for these musical expressions. Paradoxically, while this eclecticism did indeed mark such music as "local" and distinguish it from rock that originated elsewhere around the globe, it simultaneously served to internationalize the groups' fan bases, as consumers from widely disparate regions of the Americas and beyond heard, understood, and embraced these novel sonic mixtures. As a result, many of these groups came to enjoy a global exposure unimagined by their predecessors. But, more importantly, as was not the case in earlier decades, when rock was produced and consumed in isolation from other musical genres, these new musical forms articulated both local and transnational styles and thus could be understood as truly cosmopolitan—a cosmopolitanism no longer narrowly associated with a triumphant U.S. consumer culture but, rather, one which retained a place for the local within the global.

Significantly, this new strain of hybrid rock, by incorporating diasporic musics from within and beyond the nation, also opened up the possibility for new ways of re-imagining the region's African heritage, which had long been undervalued or ignored. For decades, dance musics from the predominantly black Caribbean basin and Brazil—for example, *cumbia,* salsa, samba, and merengue, generically referred to as *música tropical*—had circulated throughout the Americas and had held their own against rock, particularly among the lower classes.[32] Indeed, salsa in particular was perceived by many Latin/o Americans as a bulwark against the encroachments of rock.[33] Given the widespread perception among middle-class rockers of dance music as music of the lower classes—literally "darker" and thus less sophisticated—it should come as no surprise that the audiences for *música tropical* tended to remain distinct from those for rock. The *rockero/cocolo* split, described by Arévalo Mateus, was an outgrowth of such perceptions. This distancing held true until the mid-1980s, when the impact of lower-class musicians and fans whose musical *habitus* had always included *música tropical* finally began to be reflected in rock music throughout Latin America. Thus, by the 1990s, rock was not only consumed among the working class, but working-class preferences for dance musics also began to seep into the hardcore aesthetics of such music as punk and heavy metal, reflecting a new musical (and narrative) sensibility. Indeed, one might venture to say that the relationship of contemporary Latin American rock to popular dance styles, and its blending of these aesthetics, go a long way toward explaining what makes Latin American rock Latin American.

Despite the Latinization of rock via the use of Spanish or Portuguese vernacular language and themes, and the incorporation of regional/national musical aesthetics, *rock en español* has not fit easily within the pan-national category of "Latin music." The terms *rock en español* and *rock en tu idioma* first appeared in Latin America during the 1980s as part of a strategy by regional subsidiaries of the transnational recording industry, who hoped to distinguish a local rock product within a growing market for popular music. Today, well-established recording industries located in major urban centers throughout the Americas—Mexico City, Caracas, Buenos Aires, Bogotá, and Rio de Janeiro, as well as New York City, Los Angeles, and, more recently, Miami—constitute multiple nodes of a transnational circuit of production and distribution, and are led by Spanish- and Portuguese-language media conglomerates such as Univisión, Telemundo, Globo, and Venevisión and supported largely with Latin American capital. These conglomerates generate most of their content in—and primarily for—audiences in major urban hubs such as Mexico City, Buenos Aires, and Caracas. And while these conglomerates maintain important offices in (now Latinized) Miami, as well as in Los Angeles (where much Mexican and Chicano/Latino rock is recorded),[34] it is important to note that they develop their media strategies with Latin Americans in mind, as does MTV Latin America and its Latin American equivalent, HTV (also based in Miami). If Latin Americans now "share the power" with the U.S. culture industry, this fact does not obviate the problem of exclusion and erasure. Instead, what we find are certain sounds and images that have been elevated as the dominant tropes of *latinidad*, or "Latinness," which supposedly encompass the diversity of Latin Americans and Latinos.[35] Indeed, as Alvarado points out, in this construction the musical practices of Latinos residing within the United States are virtually excluded, as are those from smaller countries such as Guatemala.

Thus, while Miami's growing importance as a music center continues to facilitate economic and cultural flows along a North-South axis, the larger picture reflects a multidirectionality that is far more complex. On the one hand, we find that the different media conglomerates are quite attentive to local music scenes. On the other hand, the marginal place to which bands in under-represented geographic regions are relegated points to a politics of exclusion, an observation made by Héctor Fernández L'Hoeste in his analysis of David Byrne's "discovery" and marketing of the Colombian rock group Bloque de Búsqueda.

In the face of these problems, the coalescence of domestic rock scenes has also forged new social spaces and created alternative narratives of belonging. In repressive societies, where the state seeks to monopolize political discourse (either through authoritarian practices, outright military rule, or the narrow participation of a limited sector in democratic politics), rock has served as a vehicle for participatory action and a site for expressing a political discourse or agency that is either too dangerous or impossible to express through other means. However, even the most apolitical, commercialized rockers have presumed—demanded—the right to speak (to narrate through song and gesture) and to associate (to occupy space through performance and dance). Rockers have assumed their right to belong to the nation and thus to have their voices heard as citizens.

What remains problematic, however, is the way that self-conscious youth music, with all its abstract cries for freedom, liberty, and justice, and its critique of power relations, can often end up reproducing conservative, or status quo, embodiments of masculinity.[36] Women have always been present in Latin American rock. In fact, the very first "rock 'n' roller" in Mexico was a woman (Gloria Ríos), and women have played a central role in that nation's rock history. In short, rock created new possibilities for female empowerment, as well as enabling a critique of the dominant patriarchal hierarchy. The simple act of attending a rock concert unchaperoned, for example, or of using fashion to assert an act of stylistic rebellion, indicates the presence of a profound paradigmatic shift occurring in society. The essay by Palacios and Estrada, discussing the history of *rockeras* in Mexico, demonstrates this important aspect. Yet the sounds of rock, its genres, performance spaces, and performance gestures, have always been defined in masculine terms, and these have seldom been examined critically. Michelle Habell-Pallán addresses this question in her essay on how Chicana punk-rockers enacted new, less limiting gender identities in East Los Angeles.

Looking back on the past fifty years of rock music in Latin America, what conclusions can we draw? The essays in this volume only begin to scratch the surface of the complexities involved in understanding rock's trajectory in Latin America, although we do believe that collectively they illuminate a number of themes that are significant for rock studies both in the United States and in Latin America. For one, any lingering doubts about whether rock is an exclusively U.S. phenomenon—the idea that developments in rock that take place beyond the Anglo world are merely imitations of the "original" rock product—should be laid to rest once and for all. These essays confirm the validity of local rock projects, while also demonstrating the commonalities and disjunctures between them. Second, conventional notions of a U.S.–Latin American cultural axis that is defined by U.S. cultural hegemony no longer hold true (if they ever did): music, images, and ideas now circulate via multiple nodal points of production and reception, severely complicating any simplistic dichotomy of a North-South divide. Moreover, there are peripheries within the "core," and "cores" within the periphery, and these latter cores also exercise their own forms of hegemony (such as with the preeminence of Argentine and Mexican rock, to the exclusion of other national groups). Finally, it is clear that while rock may be impossible to define, it is quintessentially hybrid and characterized both by its musical porosity and semiotic flexibility. It is these qualities that have made rock the music of choice for generations of young people from widely varying socioeconomic classes and cultural contexts throughout the Americas. They have found in rock an effective and powerful vehicle for articulating their particular experiences and visions of modernity—and postmodernity. We hope this volume contributes to the legitimization of Latin American rock as a cultural practice and as a serious object of scholarly study, not only in the United States, where it still remains outside of the academic canon (as well as off the English-only mainstream airwaves), but especially in Latin America, where in spite of an emerging corpus of research and personal memoirs, it still bears the stigma of decades of condemnation. Rock, we insist, is not a crime.

La Onda Chicana

Mexico's Forgotten Rock Counterculture

ERIC ZOLOV

Mexican rock music has come a long way since the late 1960s, when the first indications of a truly original movement (La Onda Chicana) became evident. Contemporary groups such as Café Tacuba, Maldita Vecindad y los Hijos del Quinto Patio, Molotov, Tijuana No, El Gran Silencio, and others have all achieved what their predecessors only dreamed of, namely, gaining respectability as part of a musical vanguard both within Mexico and abroad. Today, moreover, Mexican rock is an integral aspect of left-wing student politics and has gained more than a grudging respect from intellectuals, not to mention politicians. The question of rock as "cultural imperialism"—a rallying cry of the Latin American Left in the late 1960s—is no longer relevant, which has as much to do with the impact of a postmodernist discourse on the social sciences as it does with the fact that today's rock seems light-years away from that of La Onda Chicana. Yet, strangely, although this earlier movement paved the way for today's diverse and vibrant rock scene, a collective memory of La Onda Chicana has been all but lost. For a number of reasons, La Onda Chicana marks a period which is literally difficult to access, and which, at any rate, many seem eager to forget.

This essay explores three important themes related to this formative period in Mexican rock, which will hopefully help to highlight both the similarities and uniqueness of Mexico's rock history in the Americas. The first theme I examine is the irrelevancy of native rock to the 1968 student movement, an event that shook the political and cultural foundations of Mexican society.

Whereas rock and politics began to merge by the mid-1960s in other national contexts (despite a familiar polemic with protest song), in Mexico the opposite was more the case: native rock was denigrated by most students for being a "bourgeois" copy of foreign rock and thus roundly denounced as "imperialist." A second theme explored here is the unusual situation of La Onda Chicana as an original rock movement that was written and performed almost exclusively in English. While rock in other Latin American contexts had evolved during this same period with songs written in Spanish (or in the case of Brazil, Portuguese), Mexican rock turned *away* from Spanish—which had characterized the movement in its initial years—to embrace English as the language of youth revolt. A final theme explored is that while Mexico's present-day youth culture is indebted in key respects to La Onda Chicana, little popular memory of the movement or epoch itself has survived. The music, images, and, more essentially, enthusiasm for La Onda Chicana remain for the most part closeted away in private collections or encountered in a haphazard fashion in the rock underground. It took thirty years, for example, before the first professionally produced documentary on Mexico's rock history was made, and to this day few images (much less music) exist from the controversial Avándaro festival, the so-called Mexican Woodstock, which marked the climax of La Onda Chicana in 1971.[1] Recently, there have been new efforts at appreciating and cataloguing this period of Mexican rock history, but the fact remains, its significance has been all but forgotten; more often than not, enthusiasm for La Onda Chicana bounces into a void of collective amnesia and lack of interest. By addressing these three themes, this essay aims to establish a framework for understanding Mexico's unique position as a consumer and producer of rock music during this foundational period, as well as an appreciation for how the Mexican situation speaks to other contexts of rock's reception and performance in Latin America.

Era of the *Refritos*

Mexico's proximity to the United States has long established the basis for its ambivalent and often politically charged relationship with U.S. culture and society. As with other revolutionary societies in Latin America, a xenophobic nationalism in reaction to foreign influences constituted an important element of national reconstruction in the aftermath of Mexico's decade-long period of violent revolution (c. 1910–20). The Partido Revolucionario Institucional, or PRI, the political party that (through different name changes) held power in Mexico for more than seventy years after the revolution, took an active role in the reshaping of a shared nationalist culture. This process began in the 1920s under the auspices of Mexico's Secretaría de Educación Pública (SEP) and involved a range of state-sponsored cultural activities that embraced music, dance, art, and education. From the start, the revolutionary state cultivated a close relationship with students and intellectuals as collaborators in a nationalist discourse. By the late 1950s, the institutional reach of the PRI had become omnipresent in the realms of politics, economics, and culture. The heroes of Mexican history had become the PRI's heroes, absorbed into the pantheon of a patriarchal revolutionary nationalism. At the same time, various intellectuals and artists had begun to distance themselves from the ideological grasp of the ruling party. But, arguably, the greatest rupture within official culture came not from the intellectual critique (inspired by the heroic nationalism of the Cuban revolution) but from the rock 'n' roll craze and its challenges to patriarchal authority embodied in the youth counterculture that quickly followed.

When rock 'n' roll first took hold in Mexico in the late 1950s, the United States was already deeply mired in its own debates over juvenile delinquency and the "moral crisis" induced by Elvis Presley, Little Richard, and others. Given that the two countries are neighbors, perhaps it should not be surprising to learn that the rebel icons of U.S. youth culture had also drifted south across the border. One of the principal avenues by which rock 'n' roll culture was introduced into Mexico was through films, such as Bill Haley's *Rock Around the Clock* (1957) and those of Elvis Presley. In fact, Presley's *King Creole* (1958) sparked a riot at a Mexico City theatre in 1959 and led to a de facto ban on imported youth-rebellion films for years to come. Even earlier in the decade of the 1950s, however, Marlon Brando's mocking of authority in *The Wild One* (1953) and James Dean's destructive youth angst in *Rebel Without a Cause* (1955) had also been especially scandalous. The editorial pages of the country's government-dominated press expressed the mounting fear that imported rebel idols were displacing the country's *own* revolutionary heroes. The nation's youth were allegedly succumbing to *rebeldismo sin causa,* a phrase invented by the press that captured the public's disgust and fear of a wanton challenge to patriarchal authority. "James Dean is the mirror where today's youth look," lamented one editorialist in describing the breakdown of patriarchal respect within the family.[2] For a generation that had grown up under the repressive stability and ideological conformity of a one-party state, the outlaw appeal of James Dean was stronger than that of the twentieth-century revolutionaries Pancho Villa or Emiliano Zapata, not to mention the nineteenth-century former president (and radical in his own time) Benito Juárez, all now eclipsed by new heroes imported from the United States. Carried to Mexico on the wings of transnational capital and in the suitcases of upper-class teenagers who traveled abroad, rock 'n' roll threatened to subvert the very ideological foundations of the nation, at least as far as its most vocal opponents were concerned.

Even as rock 'n' roll was being scandalized for its association with a disruptive foreignness, the new youth culture also embodied a sense of modernity that appealed to the cosmopolitan aspirations of the middle and upper classes—both youth and adults alike. As a result of this discursive tension, the late 1950s witnessed an impassioned debate over the meaning of rock 'n' roll and the role of the mass media more generally in Mexican society. At stake was not only a concern about the future direction of youth, but, with rock 'n' roll serving as an apt metaphor for the tensions and contradictions of the modernizing experience, of the nation itself.

Following a public outcry and nationalist backlash against the dangers of "foreign influence," the Mexican Congress passed a sweeping communications bill in early 1960, designed to protect the nation's *buenas costumbres*—"proper family values"—and safeguard the state's revolutionary project. The film and television industry would now be required "to avoid noxious or disturbing influences on the harmonious development of children and youth" while "contribut[ing] to the cultural elevation of the population, the conservation of its national characteristics, customs, and traditions, the propriety of the language, and exalt[ing] the values of Mexican nationality."[3] Strict rules of conduct delimited the boundaries of propriety that film producers and distributors would now have to follow to avoid harassment or worse by the authorities. The new law had the effect of censoring the distribution of certain foreign films (such as those by Elvis Presley) while at the same time sanitizing the representation of "rebel youth" depicted in the numerous Mexican films that emulated the genre.

A second important measure was the implementation, in mid-1961, of a restrictive tariff on record imports. The tariff was ostensibly aimed at protecting the flagging native record industry and thus safeguarding the popularity of traditional Mexican performers, who had been hurt by cheap imports and the growing presence of transnational companies. But the tariff clearly was also meant to keep out the noxious influence of rock 'n' roll. Still, the belief that the nation's youth had now "turned their backs on the rabid 'rock-roll' [*sic*]" in favor of more "sentimental melodies" was merely wishful thinking.[4] Within a matter of months, scores of local bands—now ironically protected by tariff restrictions on imports—emerged on the scene. The era of Mexican *rocanrol* had begun.

The period of the early 1960s in Mexican rock 'n' roll was called the era of the *refritos* (from the verb *refreír,* "to refry"). The term conjured up notions of appropriation—the "refashioning" of foreign music by imposing local standards. Mexican bands with names such as Los Locos del Ritmo, Los Loud Jets, Los Crazy Boys, Los Hooligans, and others recorded Spanish-language cover versions of original, foreign rock tunes, keeping as true as possible to the songs' original rhythms while cleaning up their lyrics (at the behest of the recording companies) so as to conform to the conservative ideological standards set by the state. By popularizing Mexican *rocanrol* throughout Latin America, the best of these groups gained national and even international fame, as their music was heard as far afield as Western Europe and Japan.[5] Yet the bands themselves had little control over the lyric content of these "refried" covers, much less over their public image. All production and marketing of records was tightly controlled by the record companies, which were careful not to let the music become too provocative lest the government find a pretext to react.

An example of this type of control can be seen with the Little Richard tune, "Good Golly Miss Molly," recorded in 1960 as a *refrito* titled "La Plaga" by Los Teen Tops, who were under contract to CBS Records. The English lyrics by Little Richard convey an unabashed sense of wild abandon—"sure likes to ball"—and an implicit challenge to parental authority—"can't hear your mamma call." In the *refrito* version, however, this challenge is transformed into a simple affirmation of youthful ebullience. Miss Molly becomes La Plaga (although that Spanish term, meaning both "gang of friends," and, literally, "plague," was certainly also ambivalent), who "sure likes to dance." La Plaga is "queen of the place" (the lyric which was substituted for the original "can't hear your mamma call"), which implied proper place, style, and hierarchy. The lyrics of both songs end with implications of marriage, although La Plaga more explicitly references traditional Catholic values: Little Richard sings about "buying a diamond ring"; Enrique Guzmán (lead singer for Los Teen Tops) urges, "Let's go see the priest." Even more important, in the final lyric of the English version there is an implication of sexual expectation: "Pardon me a-kissin' let me ting-a-ling-a-ling." In the Spanish-language *refrito*, this finale is translated as "It's not that you're good lookin' but you sure know how to dance!" In other words, in the Mexican version the provocation of the original, with its implicit challenge to parental control and outright celebration of sexual rebellion, is contained. As a record company official later explained, "We made it clear to the public that [*rocanrol*] was not doing anything to [youth], that they kept being good *hijos de familia* [family-oriented children] who paid attention to their parents—that the girls were not getting pregnant or anything."[6] Rock critic Víctor Roura later summed up this contradiction of a youth culture that was inoffensive to parents: "The bourgeoisie imposed the beat [on *rocanrol*]."[7]

The mass media thus promoted the *rocanrol* movement as one that reflected Mexico's own middle- and upper-class aspirations. This was an effort to deflect the criticism—from the Right as well as Left—that *rocanrol* was an imperialist import that threatened to subvert national cultural values. In its Mexican incarnation, then, rock 'n' roll epitomized the very essence of modernity: speed, youth, technology, consumerism. Mass-distributed fanzines with clear connections to the culture industry, like *México Canta* and *Notitas Musicales,* offered up gossip items about Mexican rockers. Such magazines even published the original English-language lyrics of some songs, but they stayed well clear of publishing either images or editorial content that might be construed as challenging *buenas costumbres* or parental authority. Many bands also found an outlet on television, through *American Bandstand*–style programs such as *Orfeón a Go G*o and *Yeah, Yeah,* sponsored by national and transnational record companies. Finally, an entire genre of *rocanrol* cinema emerged as a key commercial vehicle for promoting the new bands and, in particular, their handsome male lead performers. Although several of these films dealt with themes such as divorce and juvenile delinquency, all of them ended with their youthful protagonists respecting the values of family and patriarchal authority. In the early 1960s, then, it appeared that the Spanish-language domestication of a potentially disruptive youth culture had successfully contained any possible rebellion by conforming to parental concerns while staying within the boundaries of a conservative, yet "revolutionary" propriety. Arguably, Mexican youth could still carve out a space to express their own identity; after all, this was music to be listened to at full volume, even if the lyrics no longer offended adult sensibilities. And "knowing how to dance" clearly encoded a sense of incipient youth rebellion. Yet the containment of *rocanrol* restrained musicians from developing a more explicitly radical critique of patriarchal authority and of the government's oppressive nationalism that a more independent rock 'n' roll movement might have achieved.[8]

Rise of a Mexican Counterculture: La Onda

After 1964, this style of sanitized youth performance was increasingly displaced by a more aggressive sound influenced by the evolving British and U.S. rock scenes. Yet because of tariff restrictions, only those who were able to travel abroad, or who knew someone who did, were able to keep up, more or less, with the latest trends. Personal collections "were like treasures," as one youth from the period later commented.[9] For the majority, however, the new sounds were introduced more indirectly—by Mexican bands who immigrated to the capital from the northern part of the country, where they had enjoyed greater access to music from across the border. The story of Los Dug Dug's, a musical group that originated in the northern state of Durango, exemplifies the influence of the United States in the formation of Mexico's own rock revolution, and the relationship between the Mexican capital and its northern borderlands.

Armando Nava, founder and leader of Los Dug Dug's, had been raised on the sounds of Los Locos del Ritmo, Los Teen Tops, and other *refrito* groups of the early 1960s. The band he and his friends formed in high school—Los Xippos—in fact often played covers of these same *refritos* (covers of covers, in effect). In the early 1960s Nava had the opportunity to visit Tijuana, and that experience convinced him that the possibilities for playing rock 'n' roll were far better there than in the remote provincial city of Durango (which is the capital of the Mexican state of the same name). Nava convinced the members of his band to return with him to Tijuana in 1965. En route to that border city, he changed the band's name to Los Dug Dug's, to reflect the band's origins in Durango, Durango. More importantly, his inclusion of the apostrophe (nonexistent in Spanish orthography) was meant to convey a more "modern" sensibility. The group's experience in Tijuana dramatically changed its musical direction. Initially, the band performed at an all-night striptease joint, from 7 p.m. to 10 a.m., earning a mere $3 a day. Unsurprisingly, their audience was composed largely of U.S. tourists and sailors on shore-leave, there to take advantage of Mexico's cheap liquor prices and the lack of a curfew on drinking. These paying customers did not want to hear Spanish-language *refritos* (what Los Dug Dug's were playing), but rather hits in English by groups such as the Beach Boys, the Zombies, and especially the Beatles—all then in vogue in the United States. To survive, Los Dug Dug's learned to play the songs their audience demanded. To do so, of course, they first had to gain access to the music itself, which required crossing into Southern California to buy records. Although no one in the band spoke English, they were quickly able to transform their repertoire by learning to play the latest rock sounds and, more importantly, by learning to phonetically sing the English lyrics. Soon, they gained a solid reputation as a first-rate bar band and found a permanent gig at a different club, where they were able to play a straight rock show performing covers in English. Recognizing that Mexican youth were dying to hear the songs they now were able to play so well, Nava took the band to Mexico City with dreams of making it big.

For Los Dug Dug's the capital offered not only the prospect of a recording contract and media exposure, but an audience of their peers, primed to hear what the band now had to offer. Middle-class youth had tired of *refritos*, yet they had little or no opportunity to hear the originals of new songs by groups they could only read about. Los Dug Dug's arrived in Mexico City in 1966 (having replaced two of the original band members along the way) and quickly established a following. As Nava recalls, "The market [in Mexico City] was virgin in terms of the music we brought with us. . . . They hadn't heard this music before. For example, we started [our first concert] with the Beatles' 'You've Got to Hide Your Love Away' and the crowd went nuts. Nobody played those things."[10] In 1965, most of the *cafés cantantes*—live-music cafes where an earlier generation of rock 'n' rollers had performed—had been closed down in a repressive crackdown by the capital's law-and-order mayor Ernesto Uruchurtu. Perhaps by default, other venues, including the more upscale hotels and bars in the posh Zona Rosa district (which catered to foreign tourists) and an outdoor ice-skating rink located near the National University, became key gathering points for the new generation. Within a short time, Los Dug Dug's attracted the attention of RCA Records, which had introduced Mexican youth to Elvis Presley a decade earlier. Although their first LP would not be released until 1971, soon Los Dug Dug's were performing on television and were even featured in two 1967 films: *El mundo loco de los jovenes* (*The Wild World of the Young*) and the semi-underground cult film *Cinco de chocolate y uno de fresa* (*Five of Chocolate and One of Strawberry*), which featured the ballad singer Angélica María in the role of a cloistered-Catholic-girl-turned-psychedelic-hipster (the screenplay had been co-written by the young experimental novelist José Agustín). Los Dug Dug's were not alone in transforming the sound and performance style of rock in the capital. Other bands, several of which also came from the northern frontier and whose performance experience was similar to that of Los Dug Dug's, also descended on Mexico City. One of those groups was Los Yaki, "Yaki" being an Anglicized spelling of "Yaqui." (The Yaqui are an indigenous people from Mexico's Northwest who gained a reputation for combativeness when they stood up to the Spanish colonial and later national governments in disputes over land and cultural integrity.) Los Yaki were known for their energetic performances of songs by the Rolling Stones and the Doors. Like Los Dug Dug's, they too had mastered English as the language of live rock performance.[11]

This shift in musical practice pushed at the boundaries that had characterized an earlier moment in Mexican rock 'n' roll and thus coincided with and, in its own way, contributed to the emergence of a native youth counterculture, called La Onda. La Onda (literally "the wave," slang, synonymous with "groovy") began as a small, middle-class movement around 1966 and was identified with the creation of a new youth argot, the birth of a literary genre of "literature written by youth and for youth,"[12] changes in clothing and hair styles, and, of course, the new rock sound. Writing at the beginning of 1968, the young cul-

"La onda pesada está en Radio Juventud . . . ¿Cuál es la onda?" (The heavy vibe is found at Radio Juventud . . . What's the vibe?) Advertisement, *POP*, 8 October 1971, 17. Author's personal collection. (Readers should note that the caption text is a play on the word *onda*, which literally means "wave" or "wavelength," yet is also slang, synonymous with "vibe," "cool feelings," etc.)

tural critic Carlos Monsiváis described La Onda as "a new spirit, the repudiation of convention and prejudice, the creation of a new morality, the challenging of proper morals, the expansion of consciousness, the systematic revision and critique of the values offered by the West as sacred and perfect."[13] Ironically, however, although the new wave of Mexican rock bands helped to disseminate the sound and style of the "authentic" rock revolution found abroad, critics such as Monsiváis had little tolerance for Mexico's own native rock movement, which was viewed by most intellectuals and students on the Left as little more than an act of rote imitation. The fact that native rock was inextricably tied to the national and transnational mass media further discredited the movement in the eyes of those who otherwise considered themselves part of La Onda. Indeed, although Mexican rock bands reflected (stylistically) many of the countercultural values increasingly shared by the nation's middle-class youth—for which foreign rock had become a central reference point—these bands had yet to break out of the mold of performing covers. In short, the movement appeared overly submissive to the paternalistic hold of the cultural industries. Indeed, it seemed to exist in a parallel universe, one altogether separate from progressive politics. Thus, Mexican rock groups such Los Dug Dug's never embraced the emergent sociopolitical critique of students who spoke out against the PRI. That critique would later explode in the mass pro-democracy street protests of 1968.

La Onda Chicana

The new values and aesthetics of La Onda—long hair on men and pants on women, the questioning of authority, a celebration of youth as the vanguard of a radical social transformation—unsettled many adults, who began to view such changes as dangerous byproducts of the capitalist modernization process they otherwise embraced. Shortly, the new consciousness that underlay the otherwise stylistic aspects of La Onda took on political hues as well. In the summer of 1968, sparked by the example of youth in Paris, Berkeley, New York, Prague, and other cities around the world, Mexican students took to the streets. On the surface, marching students were protesting the huge sums of state funds that were being spent for the construction of tourist and athletic facilities for the Mexico City Olympic Games (scheduled for the fall of 1968), especially when so many Mexicans remained impoverished. But beyond this critique, something more profound was at stake: the youth were calling into question the anti-democratic and corrupt system behind one-party rule by the PRI itself. As youth discovered their solidarity in numbers, street protests turned into carnivalesque celebrations. La Onda provided the new language for this political revolt. Now, adults were forced to choose between supporting the student-led movement, which flouted authority in the name of democracy, or backing the wave of repression that was designed to put an end to it.

The mass media, subsidized and censored by the long reach of the government, unleashed a barrage of negative reporting aimed at denigrating the students' cause. The demonstrators were accused not only of being "subversives," but perhaps more importantly, of being "delinquents" and "rebels without a cause." One anti-movement broadsheet distributed by the government combined these elements by characterizing the movement as a "Beatle-Bolshevik Revolution": "The real students repudiate these [protesters] as opportunists directed by foreigners and whose members include 'pop professors' and pseudo-student 'hippies' who don't comprise or represent the true student body."[14] In reality, the Mexican students were far less radical than other student protestors (such as those of the Paris student movement, for example). Indeed, a U.S. State Department analysis concluded that "at least some of the student demands do not appear to be excessive."[15] But the media attack on the students also appealed to the concerns of many adults about the insolence of

Mexican youth—a form of rebelliousness already experienced by many parents in the home that now was appearing on the streets as well. One adult summed up the cause of the movement by stating: "It's the miniskirt that's to blame."[16]

While the fashions, language, and sounds of La Onda were in fact an integral element characterizing youth protest (and shaping the irreverent tone that protest often took), there was no merging of Mexican rock bands and the student movement itself. This contrasted with the way rock, countercultural politics, and student protest movements coalesced elsewhere, not only in the United States and Western Europe, but also in many Latin American nations as well.[17] At Mexico City's National University (UNAM), one of the principal centers for student activism, a carnival-like atmosphere mixed all-night political debates with impromptu mural art and folk music. Recorded rock music could also be heard, but it was not the sound of Mexican rock that protesting students listened to. Mexican rockers were thought to be mere cheerleaders for the Mexican economic "miracle," having been co-opted by bourgeois ideology and thus directly beholden to the very system the students were demonstrating against. Student protest culture was not hostile to rock per se (although there was a more radicalized element that viewed all rock as imperialist), but there was little common cause between protesters and Mexican rock bands. Despite the fact that many rock groups had managed to bring otherwise inaccessible music to Mexican listeners, they had done so at the expense of their own musical evolution. Discouraged by the record companies from recording their own tunes and trapped in a cycle of performing covers in English, Mexican rockers were easily scorned by university youth.[18] Mexican rock literally and figuratively had no place in the student movement of 1968.

The movement came to a dramatic end with the army massacre of unarmed students and supporters at the Plaza of the Three Cultures (Tlatelolco) on October 2, 1968, ten days before the opening ceremonies of the Olympic Games. The massacre left the majority of the student population numb, defeated, and frightened by the repressive powers of the regime. Marcelino Perelló, a student activist, described the impact of the massacre on the previously free-wheeling spirit at the UNAM campus: "On the morning of October 3rd we went to the UNAM. . . . We thought we would either find a great number of people there or no one. As it turned out, it was deserted. Fear had triumphed. They had screwed us."[19] Many youth sought an escape from their own despair by delving further into the countercultural movement, La Onda, where they tried to rebuild the sense of community that had been shattered at Tlatelolco. Yet, as youth from the middle classes increasingly "dropped out" to become *jipis*, the country's native rock movement benefited in the process.

The rise of Mexican *jipismo* was a complicated process. Middle-class youth began to appropriate the fashion styles of foreign hippies, but, ironically, foreign hippies were themselves appropriating the styles of Mexican indigenous peoples—whose huaraches, serapes, and beaded necklaces marked these rural Mexicans as "authentic" elements of the land. In emulating the hippies, the Mexican *jipitecas* (as they were also called) were in fact simply *re*-appropriating elements of their own culture previously viewed as "backward." Initially, the fact that indigenous culture had suddenly become fashionable—dressed up as countercultural protest—deeply disturbed many intellectuals, who viewed the *jipis* not as embodying a new critical discourse but as once more acting out through rote imitation. Linked as they were with the emergence of a native rock movement whose music was unabashedly sung in English, it is no wonder that many critics regarded the youth counterculture as mere dupes of imperialism—a generation of "foreigners in their own land," in Carlos Monsiváis's oft-cited phrase.[20]

A new rock movement that became known as La Onda Chicana was central to youth protest precisely because it offered a vehicle for the continued transgression of public space and the reconstitution of community in the wake of the government's repression. The rise of La Onda Chicana directly coincided with the collapse at Tlatelolco of a credible discourse of nationalist belonging, whereas the demise of this short-lived rock movement coincided with official efforts at rejuvenation of such a discourse under the subsequent populist regime of President Luis Echeverría (1970–76). In effect, the imagined community created by La Onda Chicana filled a discursive (and participatory) moment during which Mexico's political regime had lost its credibility with the nation's middle-class youth. Intellectuals, however, naturally viewed English-language Mexican rock with deep suspicion and cynicism, and, in turn, attacked the movement as inauthentic and imperialist. This disconnect between native rock enthusiasts and Mexican intellectuals contributed to the failure of La Onda Chicana to remain vibrant as a vanguard cultural force into the 1970s and played an important role in the suppression of cultural memory in subsequent generations. Still, for the first time, however briefly, native rock now resonated with a broad and growing segment of the population, not only in Mexico City but throughout the provinces. Hundreds of thousands of youth discovered a sense of empowerment through La Onda Chicana's music and the discourse of a reinvented sense of community.

While several rock bands from the earlier era now formed part of La Onda Chicana, the crux of the movement was the emergence of new groups (many from outside of Mexico City) whose credibility rested on original performance. Among the most important of these new bands were La Revolución de

"Psychedelize Your Guitar—Make It Different." Advertisement, *POP,* 14 January 1972. Author's personal collection.

Emiliano Zapata, La División del Norte, Bandido, Peace and Love, Nuevo México, La Máquina del Sonido, and Three Souls in My Mind. All of these groups wrote their own music and lyrics; bands no longer saw themselves as subservient to a recording industry that had tailored the music (and thus the message) of a previous generation of artists. It short, it was no longer acceptable for bands to perform covers. At the same time, the transnational recording companies, in particular, were newly eager to expand their own boundaries beyond the earlier containment of youth culture. For a brief period, then, the companies succeeded in commercializing the language and gestures of a middle-class generation in revolt.

The originality of the new rock movement, however, was compromised by one glaring contradiction: the music of La Onda Chicana was written almost exclusively in English. In order to understand the role of English and the broader significance of La Onda Chicana for its participants, as well as its detractors, it is necessary first to unravel the term itself. By 1969, "La Onda" had come to stand for cultural revolution, rebellion against patriarchal authority, self-discovery, and solidarity. The term "Chicano," on the other hand, was more contested. In the United States, "Chicano" was identified with a type of

Mexican-American activism, especially in the Southwest, that pushed not only for greater political and economic rights but for a cultural nationalist agenda as well. In its most extreme form, Chicano activism reflected a separatist ideology that pursued a reunification of territories captured by the United States from Mexico in 1848. But even in its less radicalized version, Chicano activism revealed a romanticized identification with Mexican revolutionary and pre-Hispanic culture. Chicano youth in the United States, in other words, repudiated the racism of Anglo society as they pursued an idealized conception of Mexican cultural identity tied, ironically, to the official nationalism of the PRI.

For Mexican youth, however, the term *"chicano"* had an entirely different set of meanings. Although Mexican-American activism introduced a new understanding of the word, for most Mexicans *"chicano"* was associated with a *loss* of national identity. The term conjured up images of a half-breed, cultural nomad who did not fit in, either in Anglo society or in Mexican society. A *chicano* was someone "outside" of Mexican culture and society: a *pocho*. However, in the same way that Chicano activists in the United States had redefined the term from an earlier, derogatory meaning, Mexican youth now also reappropriated the term. The sense of cultural nomadness embodied in the word was newly valorized; the transgression of national borders, once associated with loss, was now viewed as empowering. As a movement, La Onda Chicana, then, celebrated "in-betweenness" (simultaneously repudiating old markers of national identity while embracing new ones), but also embodied a sense of cosmopolitanism—an association with the avant-garde style and language of rock rebellion emanating from the United States, now resignified within the Mexican context. Mexican youth had not "gone American"—as certain intellectuals feared—although singing in English and "dressing like hippies" seemed to suggest as much. Rather, for a generation that had come of political age with the collapse of a credible discourse of revolutionary nationalism, the older, officially prescribed boundaries of Mexican identity were no longer held to be sacred. English now served as a weapon against an oppressive nationalism which ruled in youth's name, but also was a tool in the reformulation of identity, as youth struggled to define what it meant to be "Mexican" in a country whose social, political, and cultural boundaries were no longer clear.

English song lyrics symbolized the "cultural fusion" at the heart of La Onda Chicana and the use of English worked as a weapon against official nationalism, but there were other reasons as well for its usage. For one, English was the evident lingua franca of rock throughout the world. As one U.S. journalist sought to explain: "The Spanish language was simply too formal, or too steeped in tradition to convey nuances dictated by the counter-culture's attitudes."[21] Mexican bands were especially aware of this hegemonic role of English, and Mexico's location bordering the United States no doubt had a stronger influence on musical trends than, say, in Argentina or Chile, both relatively sheltered by distance. But the towering presence of the United States also offered the realistic possibility of Mexican bands reaching an English-language audience. In this sense, writing in English had a pragmatic, marketing component for bands that aspired to international stardom.[22] The fame of Carlos Santana, with his "Latin-rock" sound (emulated in the songs of several Mexican bands), and the success of other Mexicans (such as Fito de la Parra, drummer for Canned Heat) in the Anglo rock scene pointed to the potential opportunities for Mexicans. Indeed, several bands traveled and even recorded in the United States, though few achieved any degree of fame on that side of the border. Nevertheless, these were possibilities that their counterparts in the Southern Cone never envisioned. Another factor that is often cited to explain the use of English includes the role of state censorship in Mexico, since use of a foreign language for song lyrics might arguably mask subversive content.[23] Musicians in the Southern Cone, however, also faced censorship (arguably, even more so than in Mexico, at least during certain periods), and that did not lead them to write in English. For critics such as Víctor Roura, the fact that Mexicans insisted on playing rock in English was a major disappointment. "Is English the only medium for rock?" he asked prophetically at one point. "Just because rock was born sung in English, does this mean one can't sing in Spanish, German, French, etc.?"[24] He was right, of course, but it would take a new wave of government repression that essentially forced Mexican rock underground before Spanish would become the language of choice for Mexican rockers.

A band that neatly encapsulates the essence and contradictions of La Onda Chicana is La Revolución de Emiliano Zapata. The group's first album appeared in early 1971, and its cover featured an image of the 1910 revolutionary peasant leader superimposed over a burlap-textured background. Zapata's image had long been utilized by the PRI to bolster the regime's revolutionary credentials, and so his recontextualization through rock directly challenged the regime's monopoly on Zapata's representational power. La Revolución de Emiliano Zapata recorded for the transnational recording company Polydor Records, which featured a growing list of Mexican and international rock bands. With the help of their record label, the group's hit single "Nasty Sex" became known as far away as Chile and West Germany. The lyrics to "Nasty Sex" were an obvious allusion to the upsetting of traditional family values— "Somebody told me that she was sleeping / with a tricky guy"—but like the rest of the songs on the album, the music had nothing to do with Zapata's agrarian politics or with memories of 1968. *México Canta,* a fanzine which dated to the earliest days of *refrito* rock 'n' roll and which now dedicated itself to promoting La Onda Chicana, announced the band's arrival with great fanfare—though it was obliged to offer readers a "full translation" of the album's songs.[25] Rock for the masses still needed to be translated.

The immediate appeal of La Revolución de Emiliano Zapata was, of course, in their name. As was true of several groups from this era, many band names referenced key icons of the Mexican nationalist state. La Revolución de Emiliano Zapata represented themselves as long-haired youth whose mission was to "revolutionize" personal values (rather than state politics), a stance that not only mocked the PRI's ritualized lionization of Zapata as an "official national hero" but challenged the very legitimacy of the party to speak in his name.[26] In another example of La Onda Chicana bands thumbing their noses at the state, the group Bandido flaunted an "outlaw" image to contest the "order and progress" promised by the PRI to foreign investors. Other bands looked for the source of their identity not in nationalist references but rather in international ones. The group Peace & Love, for example, took its name from a phrase that circulated within the jargon of La Onda, both in Spanish ("Paz y Amor") and in English. Adding to the band's semiotic ambiguity was the fact that while the peace sign had been used in 1968 by students to signify "victory" against the forces of government repression, by 1971 it was directly associated with being a *jipi* and with pursuing a countercultural lifestyle. One of Peace & Love's songs, "We Got the Power," emerged as a sort of anthem for the movement:

> When we're on stage and making music,
> there's something that you can't take away.
> 'Cause our feeling's our own creation.
> It's awfully groovy to play together,
> and that's why I say:
> We got the power.
>
> You've got the power.
> It's within you
> and somewhere you can feel it,
> communicate it.
>
> With our music we feel the power
> and all we want for all of you
> is to feel the same.
> Say it proud:
> We got the power.

Although sung in English, the refrain "We got the power" was also shouted live in concert in Spanish: "Tenemos el poder." Either way, the message was clear. Empowerment would come through the *desmadre* (literally, "un-mothering," that is, social chaos) of rock performance, rather than by marching in the streets—which only brought death and repression.

Exploring the Fate of La Onda Chicana

The culminating event of La Onda Chicana was the two-day rock festival known as Avándaro, which took place in September 1971. The concert was held at Valle de Bravo, Avándaro, in the state of Mexico, just a few hours' drive from Mexico City—in an area where the elite of Mexico City owned country properties. In fact, the concert was originally planned as a side show for an annual car race hosted by the town, but the sheer volume of youth that descended on the site overwhelmed organizers' expectations and led to the cancellation of the race. The large open field where the festival transpired was transformed into a virtual encampment by youth, a "liberated zone," albeit one that was policed by upward of a thousand armed soldiers and federal police. Although actual numbers are disputed, at least 150,000 youth attended, the majority from Mexico City. Many of the attendees were from the lower classes, suggesting that rock as a movement had broadened beyond the middle classes and elite. Most of the audience was male, although females were clearly present. (It was more difficult, of course, for girls to escape from the grasp of their parents in order to attend.) Without a doubt, the festival brought together the largest and, in many respects, the most diverse gathering of youth since the 1968 student movement. The concert featured virtually no anti-government political overtones—not even (in the public record, at least) a commemorative declaration of solidarity with the student movement of three years earlier or with the victims of more recent slayings of student protesters that had taken place previously that summer.[27] The music was performed virtually all in English, and many, though not all, of the principal groups of La Onda Chicana were in attendance. Signs of a generation in revolt could be seen everywhere: in the long-haired and Indian-beaded *jipitecas* whose makeshift tents littered the grounds; in the scores of national flags (some with the eagle-and-serpent replaced by a peace sign) that hung from tent poles, as if announcing the liberation of a once-colonized territory; and in the casual nudity of some of those in attendance. The festival itself was sheer *desmadre*—an open flouting of a hypocritical morality (from youth's perspective) that buttressed a repressive authoritarianism. Despite its seeming contradictions, the festival also revealed the potential of La Onda Chicana as a movement with a message, one that could compete with and also make common cause with the larger, global discourse of the rock counterculture. "We don't need *gabacho* [U.S.] or European groups," came a cry from the organizers at one point. "Now we have our own music."[28]

Yet if Avándaro furthered a sense of pride and empowerment in the face of adult hostility and government repression, why is it that a memory of the Avándaro concert and of the entire La Onda Chicana movement is virtually absent from Mexico's contemporary rock music scene? Indeed, Mexican youth are more likely to recall Woodstock than Avándaro when reflecting on the rock counterculture era. The memory of Mexico's own movement has not only been erased, it has been largely replaced by the memory of foreign rock from without. In trying to understand this apparent paradox, we need to consider three central issues. First, that repression against La Onda Chicana in the aftermath of Avándaro halted the flow of recordings and other marketable commodities essential for sustaining the memory of a phenomenon grounded in mass culture; memory of La Onda Chicana is thus attenuated by the literal lack of material references. Second, that the stigma of "cultural imperialism" attached to the movement by leftist intellectuals has never been fully transcended; compared to the martyrdom of 1968 protesters, there was nothing "heroic" about a rock movement rooted in English. And, finally, there is the question of the sound of the music itself: What did youth *hear* in this music, and were those musical referents familiar enough to them for the music to actually "take hold" of their consciousness—and their bodies—especially given the fact that the lyrics were not in their native language?

The backlash against La Onda Chicana was swift in the days following the Avándaro festival. Images of youth run amok, coupled with reports about the misuse of the Mexican flag (and the presence of foreign flags, especially from the United States), unified critics on the Right and the Left. From conservatives came concerns about the breakdown of *buenas costumbres*: the sex, drugs, and flaunting of traditional values that characterized La Onda. From the Left, however, came criticism of the inroads that had been made by cultural imperialism: rock was viewed as having "mentally colonized" (to paraphrase Monsiváis) a generation of youth cut adrift in the wake of Tlatelolco. President Luis Echeverría, the Minister of Internal Affairs under former president Gustavo Díaz Ordaz and thus the man held to be most responsible for the repression of students in 1968, used the public outcry to his advantage. Having campaigned as a populist in the mold of former Mexican president Lázaro Cárdenas (famed for his expropriation of foreign oil companies in 1938), Echeverría now unleashed a new crackdown—this time against La Onda Chicana and undertaken in the name of rescuing Mexican "national culture" from moral and ideological collapse. Rock concerts were cancelled, record contracts severed (or left to languish), and repression set in as native rock was eliminated from the airwaves. Most groups broke up, others hung on, at least in name, playing *cumbia* or other dance music to keep afloat. One group that survived the period was Three Souls in My Mind. Later renamed the TRI (a clever play on the official party's acronym, PRI), the band thrived by tossing aside its original English-language recordings and middle-class fans and embracing the language, culture, and everyday concerns of those on the margins of urban society. In the process, they gained a national and, eventually, international reputation as the voice of the *chavos banda*—Mexico's lumpen proletariat youth, the neglected byproduct of the country's quest for modernization.

Somewhat curiously, however, middle-class youth quickly abandoned their once ardent support for Mexican rock. In part, of course, this was due to government repression; it was now much more difficult to see and hear the music of bands that had once been superstars. There was, however, yet another factor at play: the Echeverría regime simultaneously repressed La Onda Chicana while at the same time supporting a Latin American protest-song movement. Mexican rock was repressed in the name of fighting "cultural imperialism." Meanwhile, the government's cultural nationalism was demonstrated by its explicit support for Latin American revolutionary struggles and Third World development issues. Middle-class youth were swept up in this rejuvenated discourse of nationalist belonging, not only because it "made sense" to them—by offering a sense of belonging, once again, to the nation-state—but also because there had been scant intellectual support for La Onda Chicana to begin with.[29]

Which brings us to a final consideration: Did the middle classes, native rock's primary fan base, abandon La Onda Chicana in part because the music's referents were ultimately too "foreign sounding"? Unique to La Onda Chicana, when compared with other rock movements in Latin America, was its overreliance on musical forms that had no prior foundation within Mexican musical consciousness. Adopting such referents undoubtedly lent a more "authentic" sound to rock performances, but largely (though not wholly) absent from Mexico's countercultural rock scene was any interest in looking inward to the country's own musical repertoire for sources of inspiration. By comparison, native rock scenes in countries such as Chile, Argentina, Uruguay, and Brazil all culled from their nation's (and region's) musical histories. Indeed, contemporary Mexican rock—which is among the best in Latin America—endeavors to rework regional dance music such as *huapango, cumbia,* and *norteño,* often integrating it with elements of ska, reggae, and hip-hop. But in the 1960s and early 1970s, La Onda Chicana looked almost exclusively northward to the United States for its sound. The fact that African American styles, such as blues and soul, were an integral aspect of certain La Onda Chicana performers (for example, Three Souls in Mind) further complicates this picture. Thus, perhaps despite its originality in other ways, La Onda Chicana was simply too overwhelmed by sounds and musical references whose connections with Mexican national traditions were tenuous at best. This "disconnect" would be dramatically changed by the intensified migratory flows that followed the collapse of the Mexican economy in the 1980s, which would help carry U.S. musical traditions south of the border on a scale greater than in any prior era. But during the 1960s and 1970s such musical border crossings were still limited to commodity—rather than personal—channels.[30]

After Avándaro, La Onda Chicana quickly fragmented. Part of the movement retreated to the barrios, where a harder-edged style, heavily influenced by punk, would develop. Other rockers began to experiment with a rock fusion that sought to incorporate native musical traditions (including protest song) into rock. During the mid-1980s, as Latin American economies faced their worst crisis since the 1930s, and with official Mexican nationalism once more veering into the abyss, these two musical trends—one emerging from the lower classes and the other from the middle classes—would reconnect, giving rise to Mexico's highly creative rock present.

The short-lived rise and fall of La Onda Chicana coincided with the collapse, after 1968, and recovery, after 1971, of a credible discourse of nationalist belonging emanating from the official party. Widespread student protests that culminated in massive government repression in 1968 generated a profound cynicism among middle-class youth toward the official party and its revolutionary rhetoric. La Onda Chicana filled a gap left in the wake of that repression by offering youth the possibility of carrying on social protest through other means. Yet, the credibility of La Onda Chicana as an "authentic" rock movement was always contradicted by its reliance on English, and by the general absence of Mexican musical referents. With the renovation of a leftist cultural nationalism during the 1970s, spurred by the regime and embraced by the Left, La Onda Chicana was barely mourned by the middle-class youth who once were its principal fans. Today, the dearth of commodity objects linked to the movement makes it difficult to even locate the sounds and images that were once so prevalent. Yet, curiously, Mexican intellectuals, music critics, and the rock public itself are all still reluctant to embrace the music of La Onda Chicana, which continues to bear a badge of "dishonor" when compared with the heroism of 1968. In Chile today, the late-1960s rock–Andean fusion of the music of Los Jaivos is commemorated on a CD by that country's National Symphony Orchestra; in Argentina, the albums of the 1970s rock group Sui Generis are widely available; and in Brazil, the late-1960s Tropicália movement has undergone a recent boom in popularity. But Mexico's rock past is barely recalled today. For a country obsessed with historical memory, this is truly an odd fate.

Selected Discography

Avándaro: Por fin . . . 32 años después. 2003. Ludell/Bakita 91047.

Los Dug Dug's. *Los Dug Dug's.* 2001. RCA-BMG DBR2 74321 901 4924.

Peace & Love. *Avándaro/1971.* 1992. Denver CD-DCD-3023.

Las raíces del rock mexicano. Various artists. 1999. Universal/Manicomio 546 415–2 23.

El Ritual: Colección Avándaro versiones en inglés. 1992. Disco y Cintas CD-DCD-3020.

Toncho Pilatos. *Toncho Pilatos.* 1997. Polygram 536 561–2–23.

Vibraciones de Avándaro (25 aniversario). Various artists. 1996. Polygram/Manicomio 23 534 207–2.

Between Rock and a Hard Place
Negotiating Rock in Revolutionary Cuba, 1960–1980
DEBORAH PACINI HERNANDEZ AND REEBEE GAROFALO

In the mid-1960s, singer/songwriter Silvio Rodríguez was fired from his job at the Cuban Radio and Television Institute for mentioning the Beatles as one of his musical influences on the air. Some thirty-five years later, on December 8, 2000, the anniversary of John Lennon's death, a statue of John Lennon was dedicated in a park located in the once-fashionable Vedado section of Havana. Present at the ceremony were not only Abel Prieto, Cuba's long-haired Minister of Culture, but Fidel Castro himself, who helped Rodríguez unveil the statue. Understanding these two events and the nature of cultural negotiations between rock fans and the state that had taken place in the intervening years is crucial to situating rock within the popular music landscape of post-Revolutionary Cuba.

As happened in many locations around the world, U.S. rock 'n' roll exploded throughout urban Latin America in the 1950s, propelled by radio, recordings, film, and in the more developed countries such as Cuba and Mexico, by the new medium of television as well, which only added to its innovative aura. In Latin America, rock 'n' roll was welcomed by some (primarily young) people as an expression of urban modernity, youthful exuberance, and liberated nonconformity, but more commonly, it was rejected vigorously (primarily by their elders) as a symbol of U.S. cultural decadence and the seemingly unlimited power of the United States to force its products on unwilling nations.

Nowhere was this view of rock 'n' roll stronger than in post-1959 Cuba, where the Revolution and rock—both erupting in the same decade—were seen as intrinsically antithetical. Desiring to establish its independence from U.S. cultural imperialism, Cuba's revolutionary government did everything in its considerable power to disrupt the economic and social mechanisms it held responsible for the spread of rock and to stimulate alternative musical practices based on autochthonous Cuban traditions. While state policies succeeded in driving rock underground, they could not eliminate the enthusiasm of urban young people—even those committed to the Revolution—for rock, for whom rock represented alternative but equally valid notions of liberation. The Beatles, and especially John Lennon, were potent symbols of this contestatory idea, and over time they have acquired a significance to urban Cubans unmatched elsewhere in Latin America.

Arriving in Cuba in the mid-1950s, rock 'n' roll foreshadowed global cultural flows that are commonplace today. Rock's entry into post-revolutionary Cuba, however, was not easy: the image of a cultural "flow" does not adequately describe what was more like smoke seeping under a closed door. Yet, while the Cuban Revolution is often thought of as a rupture with the ideology and economic systems of the developed capitalist world, in practice many of the changes associated with this political transformation occurred gradually. With the exception of a short period between 1964 and 1966—interestingly, the period of the first wave of the so-called British Invasion—rock was never completely absent from Cuban radio and rock bands continued to perform whenever musicians could negotiate spaces in which to play. As a result, Cuba's musical landscape during the early 1960s resembled an amalgam of pre-revolutionary cultural forms, including the familiar mambo, rumba, and cha-cha bands from the 1950s, as well as a steady if dwindling stream of rock. Rock's presence in post-1959 Cuba, given the absence of international market forces and their attendant mass media promotions, demonstrates once again that there is no simple equation between cultural globalization and cultural imperialism.

Before the Revolution

It is hard to imagine today, in the context of unabated hostilities between the United States and Cuba, that the relationship between the two countries was once exceptionally close—so close that historian Louis Pérez entitled his 1997 book on the subject *Cuba and the United States: Ties of Singular Intimacy.* By the end of the 1950s most Cubans were thoroughly familiar with U.S. popular music and culture, either through their own travels or the media, or through personal contact with the 6,500 U.S. residents in Cuba or the almost 300,000 tourists who were attracted each year by Cuba's highly developed entertainment industry, which included dozens of hotels, casinos, and cabarets. A good number of these venues were either owned or controlled by U.S. interests, including mafia organizations. They often hired major U.S. artists such as Frank Sinatra, Duke Ellington, and Nat King Cole as headliners—much to the dismay of Cuban musicians who felt excluded from these lucrative gigs.[1] Of the Cuban musicians who did play in tourist-oriented venues, many incorporated into their repertoires whatever U.S. musical styles were popular at the time.[2]

As Pérez has observed, travel between Cuba and the United States was facilitated by as many as twenty-eight flights a day between various U.S. and Cuban cities (for example, Santiago–Charleston, Camaguey–Miami, Havana–Tampa), as well as by sea train and automobile ferry services that linked the island with the U.S. mainland. Middle- and upper-class Cubans routinely traveled to the States—primarily Miami and New York—for business and as tourists, but most commonly to shop. These Cubans were insatiable consumers of U.S. products of all sorts that they could obtain more cheaply in the United States; indeed, they were such good customers that some California, New York, and Florida department stores advertised their sales in Havana's newspapers. Much to the dismay of Cuban nationalists, Cuban consumers of U.S. goods also embraced U.S. popular culture of all sorts. Indeed, one U.S. visitor observed in 1959: "The United States is mirrored in every phase of Cuban life. The modern Cuban eats hot dogs, hamburgers, hot cakes, waffles, fried chicken and ice cream. It has become almost impossible today in Havana to find native foods such as *malanga*, *yuca* or *ajiaco*."[3]

The Cubans who ate waffles and traveled to the U.S. to shop tended to be affluent, but working-class Cubans—many of them Afro-Cubans—had also been traveling since the turn of the century between Cuba and Florida, particularly Tampa and Key West, where they worked in the cigar-rolling industry.[4] As Pérez notes: "Cigarworkers on both sides of the Florida straits inhabited a single universe. . . . This was a world in which Cuban workers in Havana and Tampa traveled freely and frequently, as much the catalysts as the consequences of change."[5] Even those working-class Cubans who could not or did not travel were familiar with U.S. popular music, thanks to Cuba's extraordinarily well-developed mass-media infrastructure (constructed primarily with U.S. capital). Indeed, despite the island's small size and its appalling economic inequalities, Cuba's media infrastructure was unrivalled in Latin America, with the exception of such affluent nations as Argentina, Brazil, and Mexico. Cubans owned more televisions and telephones, and had more newspapers per capita than any other Latin American country, and were ranked third in the number of radios per capita (after Mexico and Brazil).[6] In 1950, nearly 90 percent of Cuban households had a radio, which could tune into at least one of Cuba's 140 radio stations.[7] Among these was Havana's Radio Kramer, which regularly played popular music from the United States.[8] Moreover, radio from the United States, especially from the South, could also be picked up easily.

Cuba imported records from the United States, but its domestic recording industry was also very well developed, with seven record companies and a pressing plant that manufactured records for such foreign firms as Odeón, Capitol, and EMI, as well as for local companies.[9] Records, whether domestic or imported, were played not only on home record players, but also on the approximately fifteen thousand jukeboxes located in cabarets, bars, and *bodegas* throughout the country, which gave Cuba's working classes access to current musical developments.[10] Cuba also had over four hundred movie theatres that routinely played U.S. films, including such rock 'n' roll classics as *Rock Around the Clock* and *Blackboard Jungle*.

Given the intensity of cultural contacts, it should come as no surprise that rock 'n' roll became very popular in Cuba in the 1950s, especially as a dance form. Elvis Presley, as well as black artists such as Fats Domino, Little Richard, and Chuck Berry were well known in Cuba in the 1950s.[11] Numerous Cuban rock and roll groups were also popular at the time, including Luis Bravo, Los Llópiz, Los Armónicos,[12] and Los Hot Rockers (who experimented with a rock/cha-cha version of Rafael Hernández's famous song "Cachita").[13] In addition to a vigorous domestic music scene and internationally famous popular dance bands, Cuba also had a well-established rock 'n' roll scene at the time of the Revolution. If white middle-class Cubans were its primary consumers, working-class Cubans were also familiar with it via travel to Florida or the media.

Going Underground: Rock in the 1960s

The Cuban Revolution inherited an extraordinarily advanced media and entertainment infrastructure, as well as a populace accustomed to having access to a wide variety of cultural forms, both domestic and foreign. Because this infrastructure was intended for an unregulated market economy based on patterns of individual consumption, after the Revolution Cuba was faced with the question of how to develop a cultural policy that utilized these mass media in the service of strengthening national identity and indigenous cultural forms. This was not an easy proposition: on the one hand, the state sought to consolidate political power and establish Cuban cultural hegemony; on the other, it had to deal with the long-standing—if now ideologically questionable—cultural practices of its populace, ranging from Afro-Cuban music forms among the black working classes to the preference for U.S. popular music forms—including rock 'n' roll—primarily among those sectors of the population that had once constituted the middle and upper classes. Many ordinary Cubans, even those fully committed to the Revolution, rejected the state's attempts to define and confine their musical practices, and in numerous instances the state either backed off or looked the other way when it encountered resistance or noncompliance. The 1960s, then, can be characterized as a decade of negotiated fits and starts, experimentation and retreat, as the state sought to centralize cultural policies while balancing the competing tendencies that comprised Cuban popular culture.

As the Revolution consolidated its control over private enterprise, all Cuban mass media came to be seen as powerful ideological instruments to be used in the service of state policy. As Cuban television and radio stations passed into the hands of the state, U.S. popular music came to be regarded as the music of the enemy. This response has to be appreciated not simply as a reaction to foreign musical styles sung in English, but also to rock's ethos of youthful rebellion and its accompanying stylistic elements of long hair, tight (later, bell-bottom) pants, and miniskirts, which appeared to some party stalwarts as dangerously individualistic and antithetical to the goals of the Revolution. With no commercial means for its dissemination, it was impossible for rock in Cuba to become a mass phenomenon; instead, it went underground.

The official status of rock in Cuba during the 1960s has been the subject of considerable debate. By most accounts, there was an official prohibition against playing English-language rock on radio and television only between 1964 and 1966 (although, interestingly, Spanish-language rock, mostly originating in Spain, was permitted). After 1966, rock occupied only a marginal place on Cuban radio and television. Memories of rock's status in the 1960s vary widely. Cuban media sociologist Alfredo Prieto recalls that "it was an arrestable offense to listen to rock music," although he also notes that "kids did [listen] anyway, picking up Miami stations on the Malecón or at an alternative beach, the Playita de la 16 in Miramar."[14] Cuban rock historian Humberto Manduley explained that when the Unión de Escritores y Artistas Cubanos (UNEAC) sponsored the first colloquium on the Beatles in 1996, the biggest polemic was whether the Beatles had been actually forbidden or whether people simply steered clear of them to avoid problems.[15] The conference proceedings contain a variety of opinions on the subject, ranging from Yolanda Valdez's statement that "the Beatles were absolutely forbidden," to Guille Villar's recollections of freely listening to rock in public places—and his charge that the U.S. embargo was responsible for the invisibility of the Beatles in Cuba.[16]

Perplexed by such different recollections, Castellanos undertook archival and oral history research and then penned an epilogue to the proceedings, which he entitled "The Censure of the Beatles: Myth or Reality"; he concluded that if extreme positions had indeed been taken by uninformed government functionaries, the Beatles had never actually been forbidden and that no one had ever been arrested for listening to them. Castellanos concedes that some rock fans were beaten up or had their heads shaved and their records broken by overzealous citizens, but he insists that these were unfortunate individual incidents rather than state-directed repression. Humberto Manduley concurs with this conclusion, arguing that there was never an official prohibition of rock, although there were, as he puts it, "personal positions based on a phantom idea that was created, and people reacted to that."[17] Nevertheless, frequent references to clandestinity by rock fans who lived through those years suggest that there did exist a pervasive climate of apprehension and fear. Indeed, young people with long hair were sometimes detained, not explicitly for being rock fans but for being "anti-social." Sometimes, they were sent to the "rehabilitation" camps, along with prostitutes, thieves, and gamblers.[18]

Even if Cuba's censorship policies were not codified, the Communist Party's insinuations that rock 'n' roll was unacceptable led to widespread self-censorship. As in other socialist countries, censorship operated as a process of negotiation, with individuals and organizations testing limits until the state perceived the need to intervene.[19] In the mid-1960s, the treatment of the Beatles was emblematic of this practice, which partially explains why they occupy such a significant place in the memories of those who lived through the early stages of the Revolution. A more pertinent issue is how this deeply suspect form of music, originating in the United States, managed to survive and to articulate with Cuba's other, more unambiguously national musical scenes.

Roll Over, Beethoven

The mid- to late 1960s coincided with a crucial moment in the international trajectory of rock—the advent of the Beatles and the antiestablishment, antiwar hippie movement that they helped to promote. Much of the rock produced in the U.S. and the U.K. during the politically tumultuous 1960s was explicitly oppositional, but the Cuban government did not alter its view of rock, nor acknowledge rock's progressive potential. As Cuban cultural organizer Rodolfo Rensoli put it, "Rock was much misunderstood here, being a genre that wasn't considered national, and it was associated with the so-called *diversionismo ideológico* [ideological diversionism], that supposedly brought with it capitalist influences, deviances of all sort, physical and moral."[20] Francisco López Sacha, the president of UNEAC, recalls: "The Beatles were virtually ostracized by the media. . . . We saw them only once in the splendor of their days of glory, when Santiago Alvarez [Cuba's renowned documentary filmmaker, recently deceased] had the courage and intelligence to include them in an ICAIC newsreel."[21] Interestingly, Alfredo Prieto remembers this documentary quite differently, recalling that Alvarez mocked the Beatles by cross-editing images of the group with images of apes and monkeys.[22] Regardless of the documentary's intent, it was clearly momentous for fans, who had never before seen broadcast images of the famed group.

Even during the most stringent years of the 1960s, it was still possible to hear rock 'n' roll in Cuba via U.S. radio stations broadcasting from Florida, as well as from clear channels that could be tuned in from as far away as Arkansas—albeit discretely, at low volume, to avoid attracting attention.[23] By 1966 the impact of the Beatles worldwide was so great that Cuban censors realized the futility of trying to enforce a ban on rock on Cuban airwaves.[24] In 1966 Radio Progreso began programming the occasional Beatles record (although initially without attribution), and in 1967 the group's name was mentioned for the first time on Chucho Herrera's program, *Sorpresa Musical*.[25] These gains were achieved via constant if subtle cultural negotiations on the part of deejays wanting to play rock. Deejay Pedro Cruz remembers how the Beatles's "Anna" became their first "hit" in Cuba: "I remember that it had a lot to do with the fact that back then it was a common practice to pay homage to the Federation of Cuban Women, or the International Day of Women with programs of songs that had as titles women's names, and this excuse was taken advantage of to its fullest. 'Anna' became the first Beatles song to enter the Cuban hit parade."[26] Not until 1971 did regular programming of Beatles music begin, with the advent of Pedro Cruz's radio program *De* on Radio Rebelde, which played Beatles songs for an hour every Monday morning and evening. While the station manager was frequently called to task for "Beatle Mondays," the show was allowed to stay on the air. As Cruz recalls, "I don't know how we did it. I imagine the reason was the incredible obstinacy of the director of the radio station and his immense pleasure in defying the impositions 'from above.'"[27]

If young Cubans managed to keep up with developments in rock via the radio, the 1960 U.S. embargo made it extremely difficult for them to obtain records and other paraphernalia such as magazines, posters, and record players—and, significantly, for aspiring musicians, musical instruments. Castellanos notes that even in 1962 rock 'n' roll records from the United States could still be purchased in Havana, but as the decade progressed, Cuban record stores were no longer able to stock them. Records brought into Cuba by travelers, however, would not be confiscated by customs.[28] Therefore, lucky individuals like Guille Vilar, whose father traveled on official business, were able to obtain recordings from abroad—which immediately became prized possessions and were shared widely.[29] Interestingly, it was still also possible to buy inexpensive pirated discs, called *placas,* of rock recordings at some of the same radio stations that were prohibited from playing them on the air. Some Cubans assert that these *placas* were legal and above board;[30] others refer to them as clandestine.[31] In either case, their availability demonstrates the porousness of state control over the circulation of rock from abroad. Thus, even after commercial records ceased to be available for purchase, many Cubans owned or had access to at least some rock records.

For most rock fans, staying current with musical developments—especially during the global wave of Beatlemania—demanded extraordinary perseverance, which encouraged a strong sense of community. Vilar recalls this collective spirit when it came to sharing records and information: "Way before they [the Beatles] were played on Cuban radio, we were up to date on their records. A week or two after a new record was out, everyone knew who had it and we would all go in procession to hear it, regardless of the place or time."[32] According to López Sacha, "The Beatles dropped like a bolt of lightning over the Motorolas and RCA Victors that had survived the blockade, and over those Czech record players that had begun to replace them."[33] These records were most often played in private gatherings and at a low volume, however, for fear of reprisals. According to Cruz, "That's why, when someone heard that the Beatles were going to be on some program, the news was spread to everyone, so that this way we could raise the volume and listen to the music real loud; and what was better, free of the static interference radio 'from the outside' had."[34]

It is worth noting that the character of the rock 'n' roll that entered Cuba followed the trajectory of its development in the United States, but due to the lack of contact between the two countries after 1960, Cubans had few ways of contextualizing the music they received. Following the triumph of the Revolution in 1959, the first generation of U.S. rock 'n' rollers—such as Chuck Berry, Elvis Presley, Bill Haley, and Little Richard, as well as doo-wop vocal groups, whose profoundly hybrid music foregrounded African American performance styles—gave way to a second generation of white rockers like Paul Anka, Frankie Avalon, and Fabian, who had few connections to these musical roots. Since these white artists, and those of the subsequent British Invasion, were the most likely to air on powerful Top-40 radio stations that could be picked up in Cuba, most Cubans were exposed to rock that was increasingly separated from its African American roots. Most Cuban rock fans were only dimly aware of the racial dimensions of these developments. "Curiously, at that moment," recalls Manduley, "the modes of rock and roll that were most popular were the ballads—Paul Anka—no longer the energetic, strong music of before."[35]

Despite the barriers to rock in the media, young Cuban musicians continued to play it, and rock fans enthusiastically attended any performances they could. Many of Cuba's 1950s rock 'n' roll musicians emigrated in the first exodus of artists from the island, but others—from the Elvis Presley imitators who still inhabited the nightclubs in the early stages of the Revolution to artists like Luis Bravo and Los Bucaneros—remained and continued to enjoy popularity among rock fans, even under the most trying circumstances.[36] Without the kind of state support for obtaining instruments and instruction available to musicians playing officially approved music, Cuba's early rockers had to improvise. They taught themselves how to play traps and electric guitars, which were not taught in music schools, and they often had to construct their own equipment, using telephone wires for bass guitar strings and making drums out of scrap metal and X-ray film.[37] Because commercial nightspots were oriented toward more traditional musics, rock musicians often played for free at neighborhood cultural centers that were willing to open their doors to rock (the most well known of these being Vedado's Patio de María), or at private parties such as birthday and *quinceañera* (fifteenth birthday) parties. Interestingly, the willingness of rock groups to play at adolescent birthday parties nurtured successive generations of rock fans.

In spite of rockers' resistance to revolutionary cultural policies, Cuban rock lyrics were not oppositional. Cuban players did, however, continue to perform English covers in defiance of official disapproval. González Moreno argues that this was a strategy for introducing young Cubans to new music they might not necessarily hear via other channels; Manduley confirms that Cuban youth usually heard domestic versions of rock songs well before hearing the original.[38] Los Pacíficos were Cuba's first Beatles cover band, performing Beatles music in English and wearing Beatles suits in a variety of Havana venues. While they never recorded, at the height of their career (which lasted from 1965 to 1970) a performance at the 5,000-seat Anfiteatro de Marianao was cancelled because of the size of the overflow crowd wanting to hear Beatles music performed live.[39]

The most successful rock 'n' roll group in Cuba throughout the 1960s was, notably, Los Zafiros, a group of young black men from Cayo Hueso, one of Havana's historically black neighborhoods, who are seldom mentioned in Cuban accounts of rock history. Los Zafiros began in 1962 as a quartet backed up by a single electric guitar that took its cue from U.S. doo-wop—complete with 1-6-4-5 chord progressions, nonsense syllable background choruses, and a soaring falsetto. In the 1994 Spanish language feature film *Los Zafiros—Locura azul,* as well as in numerous press accounts, the group is often compared to the Platters.

Los Zafiros began recording in the state-owned EGREM studios in 1963, and by the mid-1960s they were so popular they were referred to as "the Beatles of Cuba." In 1965 they were included in a traveling revue entitled the Grand Music Hall of Cuba, which featured various stars of Cuban popular music and which performed in Moscow, Poland, and East Germany. They made their biggest impression in Paris, where, it is said, they even received an offer from Berry Gordy to sign with Motown—which they declined.[40] Los Zafiros's success might appear to be an aberration, given the climate of hostility to U.S. influences, but mitigating circumstances help to explain this apparent contradiction. The group became popular at a time when Cuba was seeking to elevate the status of its Afro-Cuban cultural heritage, in part to foreground its sense of national pride, and, ironically, to counteract the influence of outside cultural forces, most notably rock. Los Zafiros, however, were Afro-Cuban, they sang in Spanish, and just as doo-wop was the most hybrid form of rock 'n' roll in the U.S., the music of Los Zafiros integrated outside influences into an overall sound that exuded Cubanness. Perhaps for these very reasons Los Zafiros tend not to be included as members of the Cuban rock pantheon by Cuban rock historians.

Reconstructing Cuban Popular Music

Rock was not the only musical genre affected by the transition to socialism. Many of Cuba's best dance-band musicians emigrated, while those who remained, such as the venerable Benny Moré, found themselves cut off from the musical developments and exchanges with their counterparts, in New York, Puerto Rico, and elsewhere, that had been so productive for musicians from both regions. To fill the vacuum created by the absence of music from abroad, the government tried to stimulate Cuban music by providing financial support and media access to all national music forms, the most well-known example being the highly regarded national folkloric companies that performed Afro-Cuban music and dance in theatrical settings. Hoping to revitalize Havana's dance scene, in 1963 the Communist Party also threw its support behind a local bandleader, Pedro Izquierdo, aka Pello El Afrokán, hoping that the Mozambique, a dance he had invented, would divert attention from the public's interest in rock. Pello was featured constantly on radio and television, and the Mozambique did enjoy a brief period of widespread popularity. Young urban Cubans, however, resented attempts to impose the Mozambique from above. At the same time, they were increasingly bored with Havana's older dance bands, which were still playing styles popular in the 1950s. As Manduley put it, "They sounded old, and the young public didn't want to listen to music that sounded old."[41]

While most Cubans tend not to think about culture and social relations in racial terms, it is difficult to discuss the decade of the 1960s without considering its racial dynamics. In 1960 the government began seizing U.S. properties, including many of Havana's nightclubs, subsidizing their operations and opening them to the populace for nominal fees. For the first time, black Cubans could enjoy music and dance in elegant venues such as the world-famous Tropicana. As the musician Pablo Menéndez recalled: "What happened was, instead of American tourism, now you had Cuban workers. If you were a poor black Cuban, you weren't allowed even near the Tropicana before the Revolution, so after the Revolution this was your major aspiration and it was possible for you to go there. So having the birthday party for your fifteen-year-old daughter at the Tropicana, with your whole family invited, and putting a bottle of rum at every table, was the thing being done at that time."[42] It comes as no surprise, then, that black Cuban musicians such as Los Zafiros and Pello El Afrokán hit the zenith of their popularity during the early to mid-1960s.

Even though the Cuban government actively discouraged English-language rock (just as it was becoming increasingly white) and proactively stimulating black Cuban culture, the state's support for black Cuban culture was uneven at times. It tended to be more enthusiastic about those forms, such as rumba, that could be presented as "folkloric" and displayed in theatres and museums.[43] Other forms of lived Afro-Cuban popular culture, however, from Santería practices to revelry in bars—both of which were considered undesirable vestiges of the past—were more problematic. Carlos Moore notes that in 1967, for example, the government harassed those black Cubans who wore dashikis and Afro hairstyles, and who listened to rhythm and blues, funk, and jazz—a clear parallel to the harassment of young rock fans sporting long hair and miniskirts.[44] We should note that Moore's reference to the preferences of black Cubans for U.S. rhythm and blues, funk, and jazz diverges from those of other Cuban rock historians, whose references, when recalling youthful tastes in the 1960s, tend more toward white U.S. and U.K. musicians and groups—suggesting at least some degree of racial divide between the musical practices of black and white Cubans.

Rockin' the Revolutionary Boat

In 1968, just as the restrictions on foreign rock in the mass media were being relaxed, the government embarked on what it called the "revolutionary offensive," which included a crackdown on all remnants of private enterprise and the closing of all Havana nightclubs for an entire year.[45] Pablo Menéndez interprets the closing of the nightclubs as reflecting the government's conclusion that it was time to "get serious and try to develop this country, go out and do some work!"[46] but it also indicates the effort to exert greater control over popular music and culture. Attempts to stimulate indigenous Cuban music by supporting groups such as Pello El Afrokán and the Zafiros had failed to turn the attention of Cuban youth away from musical developments that were happening elsewhere in the world, particularly in rock.

To be sure, some young people were too involved with revolutionary activities such as literacy campaigns to suffer nostalgia for Havana's former nightlife, or to be interested in international cultural trends that seemed irrelevant to a revolutionary society. Many of these youth, however, could see no contradiction between their revolution and rock. To them, rock should not be equated with U.S. cultural imperialism, but rather with the liberating musical, cultural, and political experiments that youth elsewhere were engaging in. Indeed, some young rock fans were convinced that the cultural liberation movements taking place in the capitalist West were, in spirit, closely linked with the Cuban Revolution. As Menéndez put it, "The young generation was looking for something new and exciting, and hooking into a rock revolution that was happening because of other dynamics in the world, that were actually inspired by the Cuban Revolution; it was this ping-pong thing, between the Cuban Revolution and the rest of the world. It looks like it's not connected, but it's all connected."[47]

These ideas about the role of music in a revolutionary setting were best expressed in the musical practices of young musicians who believed that one of the benefits of living in a revolutionary society was to be able to make new forms of music. Musicians such as Silvio Rodríguez and Pablo Milanés, who had come of age listening to and playing music influenced by rock, perceived no contradiction in incorporating rock influences into their music, especially those of socially committed U.S. musicians such as Bob Dylan. Such ideas conflicted with the increasingly dogmatic official position requiring that music in a revolutionary setting should not only be totally committed to the Revolution and accessible to the masses but also free of foreign influences. Even after his firing, Silvio Rodríguez remained deeply committed to the Revolution, but, like so many of his contemporaries, he continued to play music that included rock influences.

While restrictions on playing English-language rock on the radio had begun to loosen in 1967, the government continued to be suspicious of music that exhibited foreign influences. Haydée Santamaría, director of Casa de las Américas (one of Havana's premier cultural institutions), was concerned about the future of committed young musicians like Rodríguez, whose careers were not advancing because they were running afoul of party cultural policies.[48] Hoping to give these young musicians a sanctioned platform, Casa de las Américas sponsored the first Festival de Canción Protesta (Festival of Protest Song) in 1967, and invited other socially-conscious musicians from elsewhere in Latin America, such as Uruguay's Daniel Viglietti. Silvio Rodríguez and Pablo Milanés were among the participants performing original songs in Spanish, which included some rock influences. This historic concert drew hundreds of young people, leading some Party officials to realize that rock influences *per se* were not automatically counter-revolutionary; henceforth the participating musicians enjoyed a certain "official acceptance,"[49] although they were still banned from the media.

In 1968 Alfredo Guevara, director of ICAIC, traveled to Brazil, where he was struck by the popularity of Tropicália, a (short-lived) category of urban popular song pioneered by Caetano Veloso and Gilberto Gil within the larger genre called Música Popular Brasileira (MPB). Tropicália was characterized by an attitude, or stance, that accepted rock or decided to use it for its own ends; expressed musically, it was a hybrid of rock and various Brazilian styles that mixed traditional and modern aesthetics and it was enthusiastically embraced by many Brazilian youth—although its electric guitars and rock stylings also generated heated opposition from nationalists.[50] Guevara was also impressed by the milieu of social activism in which Tropicália and MPB were embedded, and the manner in which young musicians and their fans used popular music to resist the oppression of Brazil's authoritarian government. Believing the same confluence of musical experimentation and a socially progressive outlook could capture the attention of Cuban youth, in 1969 Guevara established a musical unit within ICAIC, under the mentorship of the classically trained composer Leo Brouwer, whose official purpose was to provide soundtracks for ICAIC's films, but whose real mission was to serve as both hothouse and refuge for creative and committed young musicians such as Silvio Rodríguez, whose professional development would be nurtured institutionally by ICAIC. Like Haydée Santamaría, Guevara was a former militant whose revolutionary credentials were impeccable; thus, according to Martins, Guevara was able to create a "privileged institution [using Raymond Williams's term] . . . incorporated into the system, but which nevertheless, presents a certain controlled level of contestation."[51]

Under Guevara's protection, Brouwer, who himself was *prohibido* because he had protested the banning of jazz, set about hiring like-minded young musicians (whether or not they were formally trained) who would study the roots of Cuban music but whose interests extended beyond Cuban forms, and who would participate in collective musical experimentation and contribute to theoretical dialogues about the role of contemporary music in a revolutionary society.[52] The first musicians to be invited were the acoustic singer/songwriters Silvio Rodríguez, Pablo Milanés, and Noel Nicola. Later, invitations were extended to Eduardo Ramos (bass), Leonardo Acosta (saxophone), Leoginaldo Pimentel (drums), Emiliano Salvador (piano), and Pablo Menéndez (electric guitar), among others. These additions expanded the group's ability to play a wider range of musical styles; the gender balance was also improved when Sara González was invited to join in 1972. Brouwer's goals for the study group/musical think tank that came to be known as the Grupo Experimentación Sonora del ICAIC (GESI) were "to reclaim song with social content, but with a high sense of poetics, impeccable construction, and a high degree of technology. . . . It was a group that was going to mark—I was sure of it and so it happened—a milestone in Cuban popular culture."[53] Menéndez recalls: "The concept was like a guerilla focus, start with this little group of rebels in the film institute and see how they could influence the rest of Cuban culture."[54] To this end, GESI members studied music theory and aesthetics with Brouwer, as well as with some of Cuba's most distinguished figures in music education. More a collective than a fixed musical unit, they played together constantly, forming impromptu configurations as the spirit moved them and experimenting freely with anything and everything they desired.

In addition to studying traditional Cuban music, these young musicians were encouraged to listen carefully to whatever popular music from abroad they could get their hands on, from Brazilian Tropicália and MPB to U.S. jazz and rock, so that they could incorporate it into their collective experiments. Interestingly, much of the foreign music they listened to came from ICAIC's extensive collection of recordings, which even included rock groups such as Iron Butterfly and Country Joe and the Fish.[55] Not all the musicians were equally committed to rock—some were more interested in song or jazz—but those who were rock fans were deeply interested in finding echoes of Cubanness in rock—noting, for example, that the Chambers Brothers used a cowbell on "Time," that the Four Tops had conga drumming in "Bernadette," and that the Beatles' "And I Love Her" used claves. They also searched for signs of hy-

This photo of the Grupo de Experimentación Sonora del ICAIC, more commonly known as GESI, was originally taken for an album produced in 1972, though it was never used. Original photo by María Eugenia (Marucha) García. Provided courtesy of Pablo Menéndez.

bridity in other musical sources, which allowed them to construct the counterargument (to official policies) that rock was an international hybrid rather than a U.S. musical form. As Noel Nicola wrote in 1979, "For the Cuban people and Cuban musicians, the musical complex known as rock or beat, is not something distant nor totally foreign. It doesn't take much effort to hear everything that comes from Africa, Brazil, the Caribbean and our own Antillean island."[56]

Pablo Menéndez occupied a particularly interesting role with respect to the group's knowledge of rock. Menéndez is the son of U.S. blues and jazz singer Barbara Dane, an accomplished and well-known artist in radical circles, who was the first U.S. musician to break the blockade in 1966 by performing in Cuba. After this act of solidarity by his mother, Menéndez was invited to study music at Cuba's prestigious Escuela Nacional de Arte.[57] Arriving in Havana in 1966 at the age of fourteen, he started a rock band called Los Gallos with two of his classmates, the drummer Leoginaldo Pimentel and the keyboardist Emiliano Salvador, who later recommended Menéndez to Brouwer after they had been invited to join GESI. Having been born and raised in the U.S., and thanks to his mother's musical and political influences, Menéndez brought to GESI not only his talents as an electric guitarist and a critical cultural observer, but also a deep knowledge of U.S. popular music, especially African American music. "I would say, forget the Beatles, listen to the Shirelles, Chuck Berry. I had this old Wollensack tape recorder and I brought down tons of tape. Because I knew nothing of Cuban music when I came here, I was preparing for being exiled, so I spent a couple of months raiding my mother's record collection, which had everything, from the latest Beatles, Otis Reading, Rolling Stones, Animals, everybody, to the blues classics, Ray Charles, and a lot of folk music—all sorts of stuff."[58] As Menéndez noted in an interview published on the thirtieth anniversary of GESI's founding: "My contribution to the group was that the music of the metropolis, in many colonized countries, had always been somewhat mystified, and because of where I came from, I could recognize its origins, above all the Afro-American mix which is the fundamental dynamic within North American culture, and I knew its inner workings. . . . The music industry outside the U.S. gives a soft-boiled impression, a colonized one, in which it presents it as an Anglo-Saxon product even though it is part of a mixed and Afro-American culture. Somehow I translated that reality."[59]

Menéndez's ability to enhance his contemporaries' understanding of the racial dimensions of U.S. popular music helped the GESI articulate its defense of rock as a legitimate musical source, arguing that, on the one hand, it was the product of an oppressed racial minority, and on the other, that its multiple sources and influences complicated its reduction to a mere product of U.S. cultural imperialism. Nevertheless, the primary interest of Brouwer and most of the GESI musicians remained focused on creating a new musical language drawing on what they considered to be more sophisticated, or "cultured," music—jazz and symphonic rock, rather than dance music—which necessarily directed their interests more toward styles played by whites. Leonardo Acosta recalls arguments within the group because some members wanted to include more Cuban percussion but Brouwer wasn't interested.[60] Brouwer has denied Acosta's characterization, insisting that the vast majority of GESI's recordings were made with Cuban instruments, but that in the revolutionary spirit of the group, they were simply used in new ways.[61]

Being under the aegis of a prestigious state institution like ICAIC did not prevent GESI musicians from being *prohibidos* because of their suspect musical inclinations, such as "electrification" and the fact that they drew on rock sources (not to mention their long hair). Silvio Rodríguez remembers the scrutiny they were subjected to: "They practically used microscopes to check songs to see if they had any rock cells, which they interpreted as penetration cells, and pro-imperialist cells. In other words, in those days there were imperialist musical rhythms."[62] Pablo Menéndez is more pragmatic about the state's disapproval of rock and other foreign influences: "We didn't take them seriously and we didn't think it would last. As young people we were sure it would disappear."[63] But being banned had a significant impact on the group, because in spite of their prodigious output none of their early recordings were released and they were not allowed to perform on the air; a few compositions, however, were heard anonymously, on film soundtracks. But as Brouwer recalls, GESI musicians persisted and continued to argue with the authorities until eventually the policies were modified: "At first we didn't do concerts because we were forbidden. . . . Later we did do public concerts all over the island, not only in the capital. . . . These concerts were not publicized, but they caused a commotion among adolescents and youth who agitated public opinion. . . . We may not have come out on radio or television, but we performed live, in a sort of counterattack, and we did it intentionally. . . . Later . . . simply by playing live on the street, they were forced to abolish the restrictions on disseminating the group and its music on the radio."[64]

In addition to having better access to foreign recordings than most ordinary Cuban rock fans, their privileged status facilitated GESI's connections to socially progressive *nueva canción* musicians from throughout Latin America, some of whom similarly incorporated rock elements in their music. Most of these were drawn to Cuba because of its revolutionary ideals; others were invited to participate in the numerous song festivals that the government began organizing in the 1970s. In the course of the 1970s such *nueva canción* luminaries as Chico Buarque, Milton Nascimento, Daniel Viglietti, Inti-Illimani, and Mercedes Sosa were invited to perform, creating opportunities for members of GESI to meet and perform on stage with the visitors. The results were not always harmonious. In 1970 the Chilean group Quilapayún performed at the Festival Internacional de la Canción Popular in Varadero. As Pablo Menéndez recalls, "We thought they were great, but they were doing prerevolutionary stuff, not the stuff you make after the revolution and you are building a revolutionary culture."[65] The musical differences were mutual. According to Silvio Rodríguez: "They did not approach us because they believed what they had been told: that we were an undisciplined group of political deviants because we liked rock. They also told them we were drug addicts. They went and repeated this in other countries. Out of this came their ironic statement that curiously, some people in Cuba made songs with revolutionary texts and imperialist music; and that instead of being a red culture, it was a pink culture."[66] Members of GESI were furious but were forbidden by ICAIC from publishing their written response, which, in retrospect, Rodríguez believes was a strategic decision by an ICAIC directorship already under official scrutiny.[67]

While not a rock band—they played all kinds of music from Cuban *guaguancós* to jazz—some of GESI's members were genuinely interested in rock and incorporated it into their music. One of its most famous tunes, "Cuba Va," a collectively composed song in which various members contributed verses, displays no attempt to hybridize or dissemble its straight-ahead rock aesthetic; it was, as Rodríguez puts it, *"rock a lo inglés."*[68] Their eclecticism and their embrace of rock (not to mention the outstanding quality of their music) made them enormously popular among rock fans. Equally significant for Cuba's rock scene was GESI's (relatively) privileged position, which gave them a stronger position from which to push back against government harassment than was available to ordinary rock fans. Moreover, their rhetoric, clearly equating revolution with human liberation, gave other rockers a language with which to contest the official disparagement of rock.[69]

In the early 1970s Cuba's cultural policies took a step backward in the wake of a series of conflicts with some leading intellectuals that generated international criticism even from allies. The government defensively renewed its attack on foreign cultural influences, insisting that artists abstain from criticizing the government and requiring all art to become a weapon in defense of the Revolution.[70] In 1972 the government sought to incorporate the growing popularity of young singer/songwriters such as those participating in GESI by creating an official entity called Movimiento Nueva Trova (MNT), under the aegis of the Unión de Jóvenes Comunistas (UJC), the community youth party, which formalized these musicians' relationship with the state. Silvio Rodríguez and Pablo Milanés, who had been playing that style of music since the mid-1960s, left GESI and affiliated themselves with MNT—although they continued to collaborate with their former musical partners.

Between 1972 and 1978—the year GESI officially ceased to exist—the group underwent a number of transformations: Brouwer stepped down as director and was replaced by Eduardo Ramos; some original members left, new ones were added; and the group gradually achieved a certain level of official acceptance. They began performing more frequently in concerts, and in 1976 were even sent on a European tour to represent Cuba. If GESI's second period was perhaps less exciting than its stimulating if more precarious earlier years, their importance in Cuba's popular music scene actually increased, because their music began to be heard by a wider audience. While GESI had been producing quantities of music since 1969, it wasn't until 1972 that the recordings made in ICAIC's studios—comprising over two hundred masters—began to be released. A total of six vinyl records were eventually released, some of which also contained songs commissioned for political events. Their first record, for example, was made for the Federation of Cuban Women to take to a women's conference in Chile.[71] Other songs selected for release were those determined to be "politically committed."[72] Since the singer/songwriters were overrepresented, while the more experimental and instrumental music characterizing the collective was not included, these recordings do not reflect the full range and complexity of GESI's musical activity.[73]

Rock in the Broader Cuban Music Landscape

While GESI's wide-ranging experiments were taking place under the protective umbrella of ICAIC and its fraternal connections with MNT, there was also an underground but thriving grassroots rock scene. Even the best-known bands, such as Los Dada, Los Kent, and Almas Vertiginosas, however, were unable to record because of official disapproval.[74] If most of their earlier output was in English, Cuban rock bands were beginning to experiment with lyrics in Spanish in the 1970s, inspired by the visit of rockers from Spain such as Los Bravos and Los Mustang. González Moreno notes that most Cuban rockers merely substituted Spanish-language models for English-language ones, rather than producing genuinely new forms of Cuban rock. Some, however, sought inspiration in the music of Silvio Rodríguez because the structure of his music facilitated a transfer to a rock format and his lyrics reflected local concerns. Another group, Los Dada, also experimented with ways to nationalize rock by adding a *chékere* to its percussion.[75]

Despite the fact that rock was an underground phenomenon, it articulated with the rest of Cuba's popular music landscape in significant, if subtle, ways. Several important dance bands emerging in the late 1960s and 1970s were influenced in one way or another by U.S. rock and jazz. They, too, had to proceed with caution as they pushed against the restrictive boundaries set by official orthodoxy, although they were able to more easily conceal their experiments under the cover of more overtly national sounds. One of these bands was the Orquesta de Música Moderna, founded in 1968. During the 1960s, the term *música moderna* served as a code word for jazz and rock, so the band's name alluded to forbidden influences. While primarily a jazz band, it was an older style jazz band, which was acceptable to the authorities because it sounded like prerevolutionary bands such as Benny Moré's. As Rodríguez ironically observes, "Since people weren't endangered by listening to this music or of being contaminated by imperialist microbes, they were permitted to make it."[76] While the band had to be circumspect about how it incorporated jazz, any increase in the range of allowable sounds was welcomed by popular music fans. Bandleader Carlos Alfonso recalls the impact of the band on young rock fans like himself: "They were the light!"[77]

The following year, 1969, another seminal Cuban dance band, Los Van Van, was established. Its bandleader, Juan Formell, had begun his career arranging for Elio Revé's *charanga* band, whose repertoire included a fusion called *changui-shake*.[78] With his own band, Formell was free to expand his innovations, such as adding the electric guitar and trap set (rock's signature instruments) to the Latin dance band format, and incorporating vocal harmonies characteristic of U.S. pop-rock groups popular at the time, such as the Association and the Circle. Alfonso recalls, "When Formell did his compositions he lived in a shabby house in Center Havana, and with his guitar, his compositions seemed to be a rock song, but when you heard it with an *orquesta*, he mixed all of that, and the result was something miraculous."[79] Los Van Van has been credited with restoring Cuban dance bands to their prerevolutionary vitality and stature, and Alfonso believes it was Formell's incorporation of a subtle rock groove that attracted young urban Cubans who had formerly rejected what they perceived as the warmed-over music of their parents: "A few years ago I talked to him [Formell] and asked him about his influence from rock, and he said, 'That's the base, the foundation of my music.'"[80] Over the years, Los Van Van gradually moved away from the rock aesthetics heard on their early recordings and toward a more characteristically Cuban sound, based on the traditional *son*, called *songo*. Nevertheless, Formell never abandoned electric guitars and traps, which distinguishes Los Van Van from most salsa bands in the U.S. and Latin America.

In 1973 Chucho Valdez, Arturo Sandoval, and Paquito d'Rivera left the Orquesta de Música Moderna to form another seminal group, Irakere, whose sound was much more experimental than that of its predecessor. While primarily a jazz band, it incorporated Cuban dance music and also rock. Alfonso notes, "Irakere was simply the Cuban version of Chicago and Blood, Sweat and Tears. When Blood, Sweat and Tears came out, Cubans loved the combination of brass, strong vocals, and rhythms. Irakere is our version of that, with *bata* drums and *tumbadores*, but it was the same, the same objectives."[81] Irakere's ability to play Latin jazz, jazz-rock, and Cuban dance music equally proficiently had a major impact on the next generation of *timba* bands.[82] All of this is not to suggest that rock can be credited with the revitalization of Cuban popular music in the 1970s, but rather, that many of the young musicians responsible for the renaissance of Cuban popular music were both familiar and comfortable with the rock idiom and they saw no reason to summarily exclude it for ideological reasons.

The spirit of eclecticism and musical experimentation that characterized GESI and bands such as Irakere and Los Van Van was expressed in the music of another important rock band that emerged in the 1970s, Síntesis. Síntesis evolved out of the vocal group Tema Cuatro, formed in 1972 by Carlos Alfonso, his wife Ele Valdés, and three other musicians associated with MNT and GESI. Experimenting with a number of vocal styles, from Nueva Trova to street vendors' chants, they even incorporated harmonies inspired by the Beach Boys. Alfonso was also attracted to English art-rock groups like Emerson, Lake and Palmer, Pink Floyd, and Yes, whose music had open structures, complex arrangements, and appropriations from European classical music. In 1978 he formed Síntesis, a nine-member group with synthesizer, piano, trap drums, electric guitar, six-string steel acoustic guitar, electric bass, and voices, which could approximate the symphonic qualities of the English bands he admired; Alfonso's original lyrics, however, were in Spanish. The group caused a sensation among rockers and intellectuals, although the press attacked them for using rock.[83] The liner notes to their first LP, *En busca de una nueva flor* (recorded in Mexico in 1978) were written by former GESI musician Noel Nicola. Recognizing the influence of Yes, Emerson, Lake and Palmer, Pink Floyd, Jethro Tull, and Cat Stephens, Nicola justifies these musical choices by using the same arguments GESI had employed in the past—that is, by emphasizing the universality of rock and insisting on the music's independence from U.S. influence:

> In Cuba there are no multinationals, nor are we inert under the cultural bombardment from any metropolis, nor under the pressure of large record companies, nor under the uncontrolled actions of any manipulating machinations of any empire. Under these conditions, there is no reason to be afraid of critical and conscious assimilation of any universal musical current corresponding with its real values and technical contributions. In Cuba we are free to choose, and Síntesis has made good use of this liberty. It is healthy and important that there be a good "heavy rock" group in Cuba, with good instrumentalists, free of cheap imitation, and committed to serious and creative work within this current. Taking this direction, Síntesis has incorporated selected themes in the lyrics and selected musical patterns which depart from a Cuban national sensibility.[84]

Around 1980, Pablo Menéndez joined Síntesis as its electric guitarist. Menéndez and Alfonso had separately considered something that hadn't been done before: mixing rock with Afro-Cuban elements. In spite of the public legitimization of Afro-Cuban music and culture, Cuban rockers had generally avoided using traditional music forms perceived as antithetical to the more cosmopolitan aesthetics of rock. Alfonso recalls, "I realized that African, U.S., and Jamaican music were related to each other, so we started to drop our prejudices against ourselves."[85] Menéndez got his inspiration from a Sergio Mendes record called *Primal Roots*, whose aesthetics—"Brazilian *santería* music in a pop setting"—he wanted to adapt to the Cuban context.[86] This confluence of interests took Cuban rock in a new direction: after Síntesis's first composition, "Melewo," was aired on the radio, the response was so positive that EGREM asked them to record an entire LP. Entitled *Ancestros,* it included vocals by the *santero* Lázaro Ros, who was the most distinguished member of the Conjunto Nacional Folclórico. While its contemporary use of original Santería material and Yoruba lyrics generated some controversy, it won the prestigious Disco de Oro prize. Síntesis made other "straight" rock recordings after that, but they have been most successful with their signature sounds of Afro-Cuban rock.

Despite the success of Síntesis with Afro-Cuban rock, few other rock bands were stimulated to emulate their experiments with traditional Afro-Cuban music. The exception is Pablo Menéndez's band Mezcla, which means "mixture," formed after he left Síntesis around 1982. Mezcla, like Síntesis and GESI before it, is based on the concept of mixture and synthesis, although Mezcla has a stronger base in U.S. rhythm and blues—which is not surprising, given Menéndez's background. Both Síntesis and Mezcla have released recordings that have circulated internationally, although the prominent Afro-Cuban influence in their music renders it closer to world beat than to rock.

Coda

While developments in rock in the 1980s are beyond the scope of this essay, we want to conclude by highlighting a few relevant events. In 1979, corresponding with a short-lived relaxation of tension between Cuba and the United States during the Carter administration, Columbia Records organized a joint concert of Cuban and U.S. musicians in Havana. The concert included the Fania All Stars, Weather Report, and Cuba's Irakere, as well as U.S. musicians Stephen Stills, Kris Kristofferson, Rita Coolidge, and headliner Billy Joel, whose electrifying performance at the Karl Marx Theatre reportedly brought the proverbial house down. By the mid-1980s the government had begun relaxing its attitude toward rock. A new generation of bands such as Venus were moving on to Spanish-language lyrics about local concerns. By referring to their music as *rock nacional,* they positioned Cuban rock as part of the nascent Latin American *rock nacional* movement emerging elsewhere in the hemisphere. We should also mention singer-songwriter Carlos Varela, generationally somewhere in between the old and the new guard, who emerged from and is still considered to be part of the Nueva Trova movement rather than a rocker. Nevertheless, aesthetically, much of Varela's music is unequivocally rock, and his lyrics, which contain thinly veiled criticisms of the government's cultural conservatism, give voice to the perennial concerns of young rockers.

BETWEEN ROCK AND A HARD PLACE • 65

With the collapse of the Soviet Union in 1989, Cuba was forced to adopt a mixed economy. As the country opened itself up to tourism, performance venues proliferated and the most oppressive constraints on artistic expression disappeared. Rock began to be heard more frequently on radio, television, and in public venues, and new record companies, established as joint ventures (primarily with Spain), offered new possibilities for recording. Even the government-owned EGREM, responding to growing international interest in Cuban music, began re-releasing long-unobtainable recordings on CD, including GESI's compilations. As the older, more conservative party stalwarts, who had so misunderstood Cubans' embrace of rock, have died or retired, they have been replaced by a younger generation of committed socialists, many of whom grew up listening to rock and roll. Abel Prieto exemplifies these changes: as president of UNEAC, Prieto made it possible for the first, 1996 conference on the Beatles, and three years after he was named Minister of Culture, in 1997, he brought to fruition the idea of erecting the statue of John Lennon in John Lennon Park, whose dedication was attended by Fidel Castro.

Today there are dozens, if not hundreds, of rock groups in Cuba, playing every imaginable sub-genre of rock, from grunge to death metal to punk, each with a devoted fan base. Additionally, rap made its appearance in Cuba in the 1980s.[87] Interestingly, rap's entrance in Cuba, while not without problems, was much smoother than rock's, since rock had already paved the way for the acceptance of music from the United States. We should note, however, that the young rockers and rappers we talked to (in 1999) still felt marginalized, although they did not experience the same levels of censure experienced by their predecessors. Only a few of the new generation of rockers had been able to record, most of them with Spanish labels rather than EGREM. One of these was Havana, an alternative rock group whose lead guitarist is Pablo Menéndez's son Osamu. Another example is Garaje H, whose rock/rap hybrid sound resembles that of Rage Against the Machine.[88] In contrast, Carlos Alfonso's extraordinarily talented and versatile son, X Alfonso, had not (until 2002) been able to record a solo rock album, although he has recorded Afro-Cuban rock with Síntesis. Rockers, as well as rappers, interpreted their continued marginalization as a lack of interest in Cuban rock by their government as well as by foreign record companies, correctly noting that traditional or national Cuban music is perceived as more commercially viable abroad.

Internally, the broader acceptance of rock and rap has brought to the surface another dimension of Cuba's rock movement, which appears to be characterized by something of a racial divide (similar but not identical to its counterpart in the United States), in which rock is more closely associated with whiter Cubans, while *timba,* and now rap, are more associated with darker

Cubans. In the 1980s U.S. researchers who visited Cuba noted that both white and African American musicians from the United States (for example, Billy Joel, Donna Summer, Earth, Wind and Fire, the Bee Gees, Michael Jackson) were very popular.[89] However, when Cubans were asked about their favorite music from the United States when they were growing up, they seemed to express preferences that correlated highly with race: black Cubans were more likely to mention African American musicians, and vice versa, for whiter Cubans. "Rock made by black people is more for dancing," said Guille Vilar, "but rock for white people is different in many ways. . . . I think that black Cuban people . . . will like Earth, Wind and Fire, and if you ask whites, they will say no. White rock is the one most liked in Cuba, that's my point of view."[90]

In terms of Cuban rock, most of the musicians and fans at rock concerts we attended in the 1980s were white, while most of the fans at popular dance music venues such as Havana's legendary Jardines de la Tropical were dark-skinned. When questioned, Cubans tend to explain this phenomenon in cultural, not racial terms—that is, they say that it reflects different musical preferences, not social divisions. In fact, Cubans generally do not think about themselves in racial terms: official discourse in Cuba has held, with some justification, that racial discrimination was eliminated by the Revolution and that only vestiges of personal prejudices remain. Moreover, to focus on racial differences rather than national unity could introduce an element of instability into Cuba's social fabric, especially in the context of continuing U.S. hostilities. Nevertheless, since the 1990s, Cubans have begun paying more attention to the importance of race—and, interestingly, rap has been one of the main social forces generating this new dialogue.

Meanwhile, the wider acceptance of rock has had a dramatic effect not only on the practice of rock, but also on the historical discourse of rock within Cuba. Until recently, very little was known about Cuba's rock scene, not just because very little was recorded, but because very little was written about it. Therefore, most people's universe of knowledge was based on their own experiences and those of their acquaintances. Beginning in the mid-1990s, scholarly articles and books about rock in Cuba began emerging at an astonishing rate: these include Humberto Manduley's articles on the history of rock in Cuba (1994, 1997) and his recently published book *El rock en Cuba* (2001); Ernesto Juan Castellanos's books on the Beatles in Cuba (1997, 2000); and, beginning around 1999, a veritable avalanche of interviews and articles on the subject of Cuban rock has been posted on Cuban Web sites. Written from Cuban perspectives, these invaluable materials have finally opened a window onto an important chapter in Cuba's cultural history. Recovered histories such as these have contributed to a very different climate for rock and roll than in the past. Indeed, at a 1999 official gathering of musicians in Havana, where young rockers and rappers defended their music as "positive, even revolutionary," Minister of Culture Abel Prieto agreed to bring these artists under the aegis of the same state agency that represents other popular musicians. Declared Prieto: "It's time we nationalize rock and rap."[91]

Imagine!

Selected Discography

Grupo de Experimentación Sonora del ICAIC. *Grupo de Experimentación Sonora del ICAIC. Vol. II.* 1997. EGREM CD 0264.

Mezcla. *Fronteras de sueños.* 1993. Intuition Records CD INT 3047 2.

Síntesis. *En busca de una nueva flor.* 1978. Sol & Deneb Records CD NCL4 P-0035.

———. *Ancestros.* 1994. Qbadisc CD QB 9015.

Zafiros. *Canción a mi Habana.* 1998. EGREM CD 0292.

Black Pau

Uncovering the History of Brazilian Soul

BRYAN McCANN

The Brazilian soul recordings most difficult to find at the moment are, without a doubt, Tim Maia's *Racional* and *Racional II,* from 1975 and 1976, respectively. Maia, the husky, incorrigible rogue with the magic voice, made these recordings not under the influence of his otherwise preferred drugs—whiskey, cocaine, and marijuana—but rather under the influence of the teachings of Universo em Desencanto, or Universe in Disenchantment, a transcendental cult centered in the suburbs of Rio de Janeiro. As an adept of Universo, and one rising fast through its forty-odd levels of enlightenment, Maia had traded in his hard-partying ways for clean living—meditation, abstinence, and preaching the word of the cult through song. This resulted in a curious musical mixture in which Maia maintained the powerful foundation he had developed over the previous five years, emphasizing soulful grooves and catchy melodies delivered in his rich, booming baritone, while adding lyrics pulled straight from the pages of Universo tracts, like "Rational Immunization: All are directed to the Rational World, for all are illuminated by the light of their own origin."[1] Polydor, the company for which Maia had recorded his first four albums, balked. Determined to spread the word, Maia founded his own label, recorded *Racional* and *Racional II,* and sold them primarily to other Universo followers.

In mid-1976, Maia renounced the cult and did his best to forget the albums, refusing to re-release them and discouraging other interpreters from recording the compositions. But since his death in 1998, they have become prized collector's items, fetching over $100 in the used-record stalls of Rio and São Paulo. The representatives of Maia's estate, apparently in doubt as to whether they should honor Maia's wishes or cash in, have not announced any plans for re-release.

While Maia was struggling through Universo's cryptic philosophy, the straightforward soul of his first four albums was attracting its own disciples. The sound of those albums was something fresh and surprising in the early 1970s, breaking musical taboos and bringing a new musical vocabulary to the Brazilian scene. Maia borrowed freely from the Motown and Stax models of American soul, building his tunes around heavy bass guitar lines, staccato horn fills, and kit drums pumping the backbeat of a 4/4 rhythm. Most importantly, Maia expanded the vocal palette of Brazilian music, ranging from *coloratura falsetto* to *basso* grunts and howls with assurance and relaxed flair. His music proved an inspiration to other devotees of American soul. The composer and vocalist Genival Cassiano had given Maia one of his first hits with "Primavera," in 1970. As Maia's career took off, Cassiano himself got the opportunity to record. If Maia took his vocal cues, for the most part, from the deep luxuriance of singers like Isaac Hayes, Cassiano channeled Curtis Mayfield, singing in a quirky but crystalline high pitch. Their friend Hyldon, meanwhile, brought a gritty romantic pleading reminiscent of Percy Sledge to his recordings. Instrumentalists like saxman Oberdan Magalhães and bassist Jamil Joanes shared their enthusiasm for soul and became the indispensable session players for the new sound.

Most of these young men were from the semi-suburban working-class neighborhoods north of Rio de Janeiro, and those who were not, soon moved there. In the social clubs and bars of this region, they overlapped heavily with another crowd of musicians, one interested in blending Brazilian instrumental music with the jazz funk of pioneers like Herbie Hancock and Miles Davis. In the early 1970s, pianist Dom Salvador led a band called Abolição, or Abolition, experimenting with this transnational blend. As the name of the group suggests, these musicians considered themselves exponents of racial as well as musical liberation. This attitude increasingly imbued the work of the vocal artists as well, encouraging a deeper adoption of not only the sounds of American soul music but some of its ethos as well—black is beautiful, black power, soul brothers united in common cause. Together, they were creating a multifaceted subgenre that can now be recognized as Brazilian soul—music that relied heavily on the influence of strong U.S. corollaries but never without adding its own innovations, ultimately turning it into something that is at once familiar to North American ears and intriguingly different.

By the time Maia left Universo em Desencanto, soul had become a mass phenomenon in Rio de Janeiro, particularly among the Afro-Brazilian youth of the northern suburbs. The black power rhetoric, in particular, had fallen on fertile ground. By 1976, tens of thousands of revelers showed up every weekend at soul dances in recreational clubs and danced to U.S. soul records spun by celebrity DJs. They wore platform shoes and leather dusters, styled their hair in ambitious Afros, and shook each other's hands in elaborate rituals of several stages. Despite the fact that films like *Shaft* (1974), *Black Samson* (1974), and *Wattstax* (1973) had never seen major theater distribution in Brazil, they knew the lines by heart. And they took tremendous pride in the fact that they were a mass of young black Brazilians creating their own cultural happenings separate from the institutions of the white elite.

In a country that had, for several decades, trumpeted racial democracy as part of its official ideology, black pride was at first a shock and then a puzzle. The soul crowd seemed to reject the very essence of what it supposedly meant to be Brazilian—to share in a multiracial community that drew its cultural vitality from the vigorous and harmonious mixture of indigenous, Portuguese, and African influences. In the context of a long military dictatorship, such a challenge to official thought was not to be taken lightly, and soul dancers found themselves constantly negotiating for more space within the long, slow process of *abertura*—the "opening" toward political democracy begun in the mid-1970s and only completed a decade later. Performers and adherents found themselves assailed from all sides. Musical traditionalists chastised Maia and cohort for slavishly imitating impoverished foreign models that had nothing to do with Brazilian reality. Believers in the rhetoric of racial democracy accused the soul dancers of importing the dangerous North American virus of bi-racial division and animosity to an inappropriate tropical climate. Even leftists critical of official ideology found much to criticize in the soul phenomenon—its commercialism, its apparent foreignness, its pop-cultural rather than political approach to confronting racism. For a brief period—from 1975 to 1978, roughly—such criticism seemed to have no effect whatsoever: the soul juggernaut rolled on, spreading from Rio to São Paulo to Bahia.

The musical and social aspects of this phenomenon were never coterminous. Musical experimentation with the sounds of U.S. soul preceded the self-consciously black dances and surfaced in manifestations completely unconnected to the idea of black consciousness. The dances, meanwhile, always favored U.S. soul records over Brazilian performers, which meant that if Brazilian soul artists could not appeal to a larger audience, they had no sustained commercial viability. But during the heyday of Brazilian soul, the music and the social phenomenon intertwined and overlapped in a way that left a strong mark on the popular culture of the 1970s and several legacies for subsequent cultural expression.

For twenty years, this heyday was largely forgotten. Suddenly, however, in the early twenty-first century, interest has revived. Artists who have not performed in decades find themselves sought after by an avid young public. Performers of a new generation and new styles—rap, primarily—pay homage to the soul pioneers and seek to reproduce the climate of the black soul dances. Black cultural consciousness is once again abuzz in the clubs of Rio and São Paulo. And the rarities of the soul heyday, the most curious offshoots of a curious phenomenon—works like Tim Maia's *Racional*—are sought after and treasured as the keys to understanding a different Brazil, one whose contours and mysteries were barely glimpsed before it disappeared.

Musical Roots

Sebastião Rodrigues Maia, known to all as Tim, was by no means the first Brazilian to experiment with the sounds of North American popular music. Since at least the 1920s Brazilian composers and performers had incorporated elements of jazz, blues, and show tunes into their work. Nor were Maia's albums of the early 1970s the first Brazilian recordings to adopt elements of North American genres deriving from rhythm and blues, such as rock 'n' soul. Indeed, by 1970, the year when Maia's first album was released, rock 'n' roll–derived genres in Brazil had already gone through several moments of crisis and evolution. As a result, when Maia burst onto the scene, what was unusual about his style was not his use of North American popular source material, but the particular material he used and the way he used it.

Rio de Janeiro in the late 1950s was not a hospitable terrain for the implantation of rock 'n' roll. *Samba-canção*, a lush, unrepentantly melodramatic variant of samba, dominated the airwaves. And hip young urbanites of the middle-class beach neighborhoods of the Zona Sul, or Southern Zone, began to experiment with a spare, sophisticated abstraction of samba that would become known as *bossa nova*. A couple of the local radio stations broadcast rock 'n' roll records, mostly on late-night programs, but hardly enough to spark a fashion for blue suede shoes.[2] It is no surprise, then, that no one who was not a member of the band paid any attention to Tim Maia's first group, the Tijucanos do Ritmo, or Tijucans of Rhythm, named after Tijuca, the sedate, middle-class neighborhood where Maia grew up. The experiments of this group, formed in 1956, when Maia was fourteen, have been lost to time. Slightly more is known about Maia's second group, the Sputniks, not so much because of Maia's own presence, but because of that of his bandmates Erasmo Carlos and Roberto Carlos, unrelated teenagers from other Rio neighborhoods. The Sputniks left no recordings, but by all accounts they played rock and roll as best they could, being amateurs with minimal musical experience. When the band split up, its members went off in radically different directions. At the invitation of his school's administration, Maia dropped out of high school and never went back. Instead, he wangled a student visa, raised money for a ticket through odd jobs, and took off on a pilgrimage to the United States with twelve dollars in his pocket. He did not return until 1963. By that time, Erasmo and Roberto Carlos were the emerging idols of a rock and roll fad that would soon become known as the Jovem Guarda, or Young Guard. Roberto Carlos, in particular, turned his penchant for aching pop melodies and disarmingly simple lyrics into superstardom, becoming by far the most consistently successful recording artist in Brazilian history. Decades later, still angry with Carlos for a perceived unwillingness to help him on his return to Brazil, Maia remarked, "I taught him three chords, G, C, and D, and he is still using those three chords to sell 10 million records a year."[3]

Roberto and Erasmo Carlos are white and of middle-class background. The rock 'n' roll fad they helped fashion was clean-cut, apolitical, and—at least initially—respectably middle-class. They could package themselves as teen idols without transgressing any social boundaries. Their music certainly inspired repugnance among those zealous of protecting Brazil's national cultural heritage, but there was nothing unsettling about seeing their faces on the covers of magazines or on the TV program they inaugurated in 1965. They were camera-ready.

In contrast, Maia, at various times in his career, identified himself as *mulato*, black (using the English word), *preto*, and *negro* (both of which mean black, but can have slightly different connotations). His family struggled to remain in the working class. His parents operated a *pension* boarding house. Maia, the eighteenth of nineteen children (of whom twelve survived infancy) delivered meals to neighborhood customers as a child, circulating barefoot through the streets of Tijuca. In the late 1950s, he undoubtedly would have been perceived by elite Brazilian society as a troublemaking, marginal *mulato*. He had slightly better chances of major media exposure than he had of piloting the real Sputnik.

The music of the Jovem Guarda became known as *iê-iê-iê*, the Brazilian phoneticization of "yeah, yeah, yeah," from the Beatles-inspired choruses of its lyrics. (Roberto Carlos, for the most part, sang in Portuguese, throwing in the occasional English phrase.) Its primary interpreters managed to eliminate all obvious traces of the music's African American roots from their performance. Instead, Roberto Carlos looked to the romantic Portuguese tradition of the *modinha* for his lyrical structures. More creative in his musical combinations was Jorge Ben, a young Afro-Brazilian guitarist from the working-class Rio neighborhood of Catumbi. He became the most important local precursor of Brazilian soul. (In 1989 Ben changed his last name to Ben Jor and is now listed under that name in most source material.)

Beginning in the early 1960s, Jorge Ben blended samba, bossa nova and *iê-iê-iê* in a way that no one could pin down and that proved palatable to diverse audiences. Later in the decade, for example, he was the only performer to appear on three separate TV shows pitched at bossa nova fans, Jovem Guarda fans, and fans of a new, more rebellious blend of Brazilian music and rock 'n' roll that became known as Tropicália.[4] His acoustic guitar work had the slashing inflections of rock 'n' roll, but never lost a swinging samba beat.

Ben's lyrics were colloquial, seemingly extemporaneous, snatches of overheard conversations and bits of popular slang. In 1969, attuned to the currents of American soul, he began to ground these lyrics more explicitly in the local black experience of Rio de Janeiro. "Charles Anjo 45," or "Charles Angel 45," of that year, is an invocation of an outlaw-hero from a local *favela,* or hillside shantytown. The title figure, a "Robin Hood of the hill," has been taken away by the police "to spend his vacation in a penal colony," but he will return to enthusiastic community celebration, for, without him, there is no order in the *favela*. In one sense, the composition descends from a tradition of sambas in praise of *malandros,* or roguish petty criminals—Charles is identified as the "rei da malandragem," the king of *malandro* techniques. But the hero's English name, and the English words incorporated into the lyrics ("como é que é, my friend?") indicate that there is something not entirely homegrown about Charles's power. The explicit links between violence and heroism, moreover (Charles will be greeted in a celebratory "hail of bullets," and seems to derive his very name from the caliber of his gun) are unprecedented in the *malandro* tradition, as is the control Charles seems to exercise over his territory. Instead, these recall contemporary American representations of the violent ghetto as both the result of exploitation of the black population and the center of black power.

Ben's style inspired several imitators who followed and extended his combination of samba with the instrumentation and affectation of rock 'n' roll—electric guitars, kit drums, reverb. Their sound became known as *sambalanço* (swing-samba) or *samba-rock,* and reached an enormous audience in the late 1960s. *Sambalanço* star Wilson Simonal was the first black Brazilian superstar to perform in a style with a clear debt to North American rock 'n' roll, and overcame deeply held public expectations tying black Brazilians to "traditional" genres. He did not, however, give any hint of the "black soul" consciousness that would characterize the mid-1970s. Indeed, he was seen by many as a toady to the military regime, inaugurated in 1964.[5] Simultaneously, the young Bahian iconoclasts Caetano Veloso and Gilberto Gil, the vanguard of Tropicália, poked holes in the nationalist cultural assumptions of the student Left with their aggressive combinations of Brazilian roots and international pop sounds.[6] More so than Ben or Simonal, the *tropicalistas* made interrogation of the meanings assigned to "national" versus "international" explicit and fundamental in their music.

By the close of the 1960s the Jovem Guarda, the *tropicalistas*, and the *sambalanço* crowd had borne the brunt of nationalist reactions against the supposed corruption of authentic Brazilian music by foreign influence. Jorge Ben, Wilson Simonal, and Gilberto Gil had made it safe for Afro-Brazilians to experiment with rock and roll. The musical groundwork for Brazilian soul had been laid. The missing ingredients were the arrangements, the attitude, and the voice: Tim Maia provided these.

Tarrytown and Back

No one knows precisely what Tim Maia was doing during his sojourn in the United States from 1959 to 1963, but making music and getting into trouble were the principal themes. In the U.S., Maia went by the name of Jimmy the Brazilian ("Jimmy," in fact, is closer to the Brazilian pronunciation of "Tim" than is the American "Tim"). He boarded initially with distant contacts from Brazil in the New York area, washing dishes to pay the rent. He enrolled in summer school at New York University but apparently never completed any credits. He briefly moved into his own apartment in Tarrytown, a middle-class town up the Hudson River from Yonkers, where he sang in a vocal quartet known as the Ideals. The other members of the group were two Italian Americans and one African American, making the Ideals one of the few, but not exceptionally rare, integrated doo-wop quartets of the early 1960s.[7]

Maia was seen as a black kid in the U.S., and he experienced the racial polarization of the civil rights era at first hand. Later in his career, he recalled confronting racism in the United States and spoke briefly of participating in a civil rights march, remembering his discomfort and his sense of his own foreignness.[8] He was more forthcoming about the importance of his musical experiences in the United States, about the magic of delving into the rich world of black American music. The early 1960s were an auspicious time for such investigation, as the velvety harmonies of doo-wop and the rolling cadences of rhythm and blues evolved into the more sophisticated arrangements and wider-ranging subject matter of soul.

He was equally candid about the growth of his legendary appetite for illegal drugs. As he described it later, "I took my course in *malandragem* and drugs in the U.S. I learned everything fast because there everyone snorts, everyone smokes pot, everyone screws, drinks booze and pops pills."[9] Maia earned his degree in this field when he got busted for possession of marijuana. He spent an undetermined period in jail before being deported late in 1963. From then on, he would remain officially banned from the birthplace of soul.

Back in Brazil, Maia struggled to reacclimate himself to a society in the midst of political crisis. Early in 1964 the fragile democratic government crumbled; the April 1st military coup then sent the Left reeling, struggling within itself to articulate a coherent response. Popular musicians found themselves defined predominantly by their political allegiances, and were compelled to choose between the populist Marxism of the student Left and the apolitical pop of the Jovem Guarda. The *tropicalistas* roiled the waters with their explosion of these categories in the period 1967–69. A rising sector within the military government grew increasingly critical of all popular dissent and shifted toward increasingly oppressive rule by the end of the decade. Throughout this period, Maia drifted in search of an opportunity. His English skills landed him a job as a tour guide, which his utter lack of interest in Brazilian history soon lost him. He sang with one or two Brazilian groups that failed to make a splash, while his former friends and colleagues Roberto Carlos and Jorge Ben climbed the charts. He finally found some success of his own with a single for Fermata Records in 1969, a simple samba-ballad of his own composition, with lyrics in English and Portuguese, entitled "These Are the Songs."

There was no bigger star at that moment in Brazil than Elis Regina, a powerful, engaging singer with her own successful TV show. Regina picked up "These Are the Songs" and recorded it in a duet with Maia on a 1970 album. On the strength of Regina's *colher de chá,* or "spoonful of tea"—Brazilian slang for assistance from a powerful patron—Maia gained a contract with Polydor, and recorded four albums for the company over the next four years.[10] The contract was a pivotal break in establishing Maia's career. The Brazilian affiliates of Polydor and Warner had become the most powerful labels in the country. Their rise depended to a large extent on the increasing popularity of American music, sold in Brazil by these local affiliates. The size of their multinational parent companies, moreover, gave them enormous leverage in purchasing airtime and advertising products. Maia later became vociferously critical of their tactics, but in the early 1970s he was a beneficiary.

His first four albums inaugurated Brazilian soul as a musical subgenre. All were entitled simply *Tim Maia* and thus are distinguished in the discography by their dates. They are not uniform—as an arranger and producer of his own recordings, Maia was far more consistent and sophisticated in 1973 than he had been in 1970—but they share a general approach to instrumentation, form, and production, and a brash enthusiasm that Maia would never quite recapture following his Universo experience. He subsequently made records with more polish, but none with more infectious charm.

Maia brought Brazilian music closer than ever before to U.S. soul, but he was by no means a slavish imitator. In compositions on his first two albums he combined the sounds of American soul with Brazilian folk elements, emerging with a hybrid of Northeast Brazilian rhythm and subject matter with U.S. arrangement and style. In theory, this was what the *tropicalistas* were up to as well. In practice, however, Maia's approach was completely different—and it should be emphasized that in contrast to the *tropicalistas* Maia had no theory, only practice. The contrast is clear in a consideration of "Padre Cícero," a hit from Maia's first album. It honors the eponymous priest from the Northeast hinterlands, a renegade of the Catholic Church, regarded with mystic fervor by much of the Brazilian population. One can imagine a Caetano Veloso composition about Padre Cícero: in symbolic imagery it would offer an ambiguous portrait of Cícero as a dubious prophet, while simultaneously deflating easy interpretations of folk religion as false consciousness, tossing together Northeast harmonies and electric guitars, and leaving the listener moved and perplexed at the same time. Maia's tune is nothing like that. To begin, he wrote it not as an inquiry into Brazilian popular consciousness, but at the request of the Globo television network, which needed a Northeastern theme for an upcoming soap opera. As Maia was well aware, inclusion on a soap opera was a failsafe recipe for a hit record—Globo's dominance of Brazilian television and its ability to market soundtrack compilations made it a powerful force in the creation of popular music trends. Maia jumped at the chance, fulfilling Globo's request by hastily writing new words for an existing tune. The resulting lyrics disregard all specificity of time and context, describing Cícero, more or less, as soul brother number one—a poor man from the harsh backlands who became a hero to his people.

The tune begins with a trio of backing vocalists singing a high lament over a background of muted organ chords and heavy bass guitar. The backing trio includes Cassiano, co-author of the tune, who sings in his trademark high pitch, wavering on the edge of dissonance. This offsets Maia's own majestic presence: when the lead singer kicks in on the fourth line of the first verse, the tune undergoes an immediate transformation from sorrow to celebration. On the bridge, the rhythm section doubles the time, kicking into an ersatz *forró*, a Northeastern dance genre. Triangle and shaker, traditional Brazilian percussion elements, add further regional accents. In the closing section, Maia bellows soulful, truncated incantations of Cícero's name, which grow in intensity as the band fades behind him.

In contrast to the *tropicalistas*, Maia's goal in creating a transnational hybrid was not to reveal the absurdity of Brazilian modernity but to create a hit by giving Brazilian youth something attractively new, along with something familiar they could grab onto. Although his portrait of Padre Cícero was incongruous, it was hugely successful: the tune became one of four top radio hits from the first album. The album itself sold 200,000 copies in its first two years, a huge success for the period.

Maia was at his best in more straightforward adaptations of American soul. His fourth album, released in 1973, revealed a composer and arranger utterly at home with both the Stax sound of artists like Eddie Floyd and the early Isaac Hayes and the "Philly Soul" sound of producers Kenny Gamble and Leon Huff. On most of the tunes on these albums, Maia gives only subtle Brazilian inflections to these models. "Réu Confesso" ("Admitted Guilty," roughly) is the leadoff cut on the album.[11] The biggest difference between the arrangement here and that of "Padre Cícero" is the addition of a horn section of two trumpets, three trombones, tenor sax, and baritone sax. Like classic Stax hits (Floyd's "Knock on Wood," of 1966, for example), the tune begins with a limited number of instruments and builds in complexity. The horn section enters at the close of the first bridge, playing a counter-melody in punchy, brief riffs. In the closing choruses, Maia extemporizes, unleashing his vibrato in sustained phrases. Aside from the Portuguese lyrics, this could plausibly be a Stax release from roughly the same period. Only on closer inspection does one notice the hand drums, apparently bongo and tambourine, adding a percussive flair evocative of samba. And at the beginning of each chorus, the horns play a five-note pattern over two measures more directly linked to orchestral samba.

"Compadre," the next tune, in contrast, is pure Philly Soul of the early 1970s—smooth and sweet as a Delfonics single. The backing vocal trio of the first album has been expanded here to a sextet, providing a lush harmonic bed for Maia's lead. The horn section sits out for the first 2:15 of a 2:45 song, only kicking in for the final drive, as Maia himself steps away from the microphone and sings distant contrapuntal phrases. This judicious use of the full band demonstrates a remarkable restraint in the arrangement and is part of what gives this tune its slow-burning power. Again, subtle percussive inflections are the only self-consciously Brazilian element.

The point of these elaborate arrangements was to showcase Maia's own rich voice, which was unlike any other in Brazil. Vocal prowess itself had long been a prominent feature of Brazilian popular music. As early as the 1930s, Orlando Silva and Francisco Alves made records designed to highlight the range and power of their tenors. Among Maia's contemporaries, Milton Nascimento had a voice equally commanding and multifaceted, and perhaps a better ear for harmonic shading. But whereas Nascimento pursued a sophistication more reminiscent of *bel canto* than of rock and roll, Maia adopted a rumbling sound that alternated syncopated interjections with trilling glissandos. He was not afraid to be down and dirty one moment and romantic the next. He simply blew other popular singers off the map. Jorge Ben, Roberto Carlos, and Erasmo Carlos all changed their vocal styles noticeably in the early 1970s, in response to Maia's influence.[12] Elis Regina also fell under Maia's spell. She had already been known for her impassioned delivery: what she and her musicians learned from Tim Maia was primarily arrangement and instrumentation. And she did not let her white skin stop her from recording a composition entitled "Black is Beautiful" late in 1970.

Vocalists like Cassiano and Hyldon were better positioned to settle into Maia's wake. Both singers chose to delve further into the smooth Philly Soul–inspired sound, recording with the accompaniment of strings and backing vocals. Cassiano recorded his first album as a lead singer in 1973. Hyldon came a bit later to the studio, recording his first album in 1975. Both made outstanding records and attracted followings, without achieving anything like Maia's success. Cassiano was perhaps too unusual a singer for mass popularity, and too great a perfectionist—there was no way he could keep up with Maia's pace of steady hits. And Hyldon lacked Maia's vocal mastery. Singer Toni Tornado also rode Maia's coattails to success in the early 1970s. Later in the decade, Tornado, more so than Maia, became an icon of the black soul dances in Rio and São Paulo.

Maia, meanwhile, found himself a star. He performed frequently in packed halls—particularly in the social clubs of Rio's northern suburbs, the epicenter of his fan base. Alluding to his popularity in this region, he termed himself the "ídolo dos guetos," the idol of the ghettos.[13] The terminology was loaded: in Rio, *favela* was the common name for the poor hillside neighborhoods of the city center, or for any other cluster of shacks. The working-class neighborhoods of the North Zone were simply called *subúrbios*. By describing them as ghettos, Maia imported the racially charged language of the United States. He cultivated an Afro—another unusual practice in Brazil—which seemed to grow along with his fame, although the style started to spread among his fans and imitators.

He was by no means, however, a spokesman for a Brazilian black power movement. On the contrary—while he spoke frequently on the importance of his apprenticeship in black musical circles in the United States, he was just as likely to attribute his success to his *mulato* origins, claiming he united white melodic sophistication with black rhythmic ability.[14] Such hackneyed stereotypes came from the elementary primer of the tired rhetoric of racial democracy. Maia's willingness to fall back on them suggests that he was overwhelmed by his own success and did not know how to respond to mainstream media, and also that he was discovering that inconsistency could be one of his greatest allies in maintaining independence from promoters and producers who wanted to control his career. What it shows clearly is that if the dark-skinned, working-class fan base of the North Zone constituted a reservoir of discontent awaiting mobilization, Maia was not going to be the mobilizer, except on the dance floor.

He grew increasingly erratic in his personal life. He took his experimentation with drugs to new levels, famously attempting to turn on the entire staff at Polydor to LSD.[15] He was arrested twice in the early 1970s, once for domestic violence, once for suspicion of involvement with a marijuana ring.[16] He failed to show up for scheduled performances, a pattern he would continue until his death. When he did show up, he invariably complained about the sound. Nonetheless, when he did take the stage, he left his audiences breathless with thrilling performances of several hours that left him nearly incapacitated with exhaustion and intoxication. In retrospect, it seems clear that his turn in 1975 to Universo em Desencanto, with its promises of stability and contact with the higher life forms, was a way to flee this turbulent existence.

Making Music Black

Other musicians of the early 1970s were more consistent in their attempts to link their music to a struggle against racism in Brazil. Foremost among these was Dom Salvador, whose band Abolição united the best musicians of the Rio suburbs, including Oberdan Magalhães on sax and J. Carlos Barroso on trumpet, in an exploration of samba/bossa nova/funk/jazz hybrids. Abolição's 1971 album, *Som, Sangue, e Raça* (*Sound, Blood, and Race*) had the hallmarks of both funk and samba—the slap electric bass guitar and the electric piano, the tambourine and the *cuíca* (a samba drum with an attached stick, rubbed to produce resonant squeaks)—but its arrangements and its improvisation recalled orchestral jazz. The influence of the albums of Miles Davis (*In A Silent Way*) and Herbie Hancock (*Bitches' Brew*) was clear. The title of the album, meanwhile, as well as the group's style—Afros and dashikis—implicitly linked this music to racial consciousness. Salvador extended this link with pronouncements on the importance of cultivating black music in Brazil. Abolição initiated the second crucial current of Brazilian soul music, that of instrumental soul-samba funk, a vein that would reach its high point with Banda Black Rio later in the decade.

In the Northeast Brazilian city of Salvador, a new type of carnival parade band known as the *bloco afro,* or African block, also sought to create a self-consciously black music. The group Ilê Aiyê, the first *bloco afro,* found musical inspiration in West and Central African drumming traditions. Subsequent *blocos afros* looked to Bob Marley and other Jamaican reggae artists for both musical and political inspiration. In 1975 Ilê Aiyê placed itself at the forefront of a racial consciousness movement in Bahia by refusing to allow white participants in its *bloco*. This racial separatism in Bahia, the supposed stronghold of harmonious miscegenation, provoked outraged opposition from local authorities. Ilê Aiyê refused to back down and became the center of a social phenomenon that would parallel events in Rio and in São Paulo. While the cities of the Southeast saw the birth of black soul dances, youth in Salvador looked to the *blocos afros* for self-consciously black music of social protest. The music of Ilê Aiyê and other *blocos* gradually became a hallmark of Salvador's popular cultural landscape.[17]

What these various manifestations had in common was not so much a spirit of common cause, but a disillusionment with the status quo. Their politics grew out of a deepening criticism of the fraudulent notion that Brazil was a racial democracy. In turn, they spread that criticism among a popular audience. This was particularly true of soul, which reached a far larger audience than the rest of black music combined.

Attacking the Myth

Brazil had not always prided itself on racial miscegenation. For most of the elite, miscegenation was merely an unfortunate consequence of a history of African enslavement. Racism ran deep and virulent, and black skin was seen as the de facto marker of marginality. The occasional Brazilians of African ancestry who rose to power were tolerable exceptions to this rule, and their assimilation proved a justification of, rather than a threat to, a racist structure. In the early twentieth century, influential Brazilians searching for keys to national cohesion began to reconsider their nation's racial legacy. They began to postulate that instead of miscegenation being Brazil's burden, it could be its strength. Gilberto Freyre became the most influential exponent of this new idea, particularly with his 1933 work *Casa Grande e Senzala* (*The Masters and the Slaves*).[18] Freyre suggested that among modern nations Brazil's strength was its cultural vitality, which had its origin in the mixture of races.

Over the ensuing decades, Freyre's ideas took root with the force of destiny—they seemed to answer a deep need, ratifying a Brazilian singularity. Getúlio Vargas's dictatorial Estado Novo, or New State, government (1937–1945), made the idea of racial democracy a linchpin of its efforts to unite Brazilians. But racial democracy was not merely an official ideology: it found manifestations in every form of popular expression, particularly in samba. The idea of racial democracy, however, tempered but did not eliminate ingrained racist attitudes and practices.[19] The economic expression of this was a class structure in which the lower classes, largely of African and mixed ancestry, were divided by an enormous gulf from the almost entirely white elite. The social expression was a tradition of whites-only society clubs, service elevators that separated white residents from black employees, and a marriage pool in which the idea of a white person marrying a black person was by no means unheard of, but was distinctly considered a step down.

Brazilians recognized this contradiction implicitly, even unconsciously, and internalized it to a degree that the contradiction itself became a facet of Brazil's cultural makeup. And if the idea of racial democracy was a thesis of modernity, responding to the need for a national ideology, it very early generated an antithesis. In São Paulo black movements arose as early as the 1920s, giving the lie to the notion that racism did not exist in Brazil.[20] (Whenever such movements arose, of course, they were accused of being racist and of importing inappropriate foreign ideas to Brazil.) Given the historical interaction of these two conflicting bodies of thought, the "myth of racial democracy" is itself perhaps a misleading term. Perhaps it is more useful to speak of a rhetoric of racial democracy, understanding that this rhetoric was used in different ways by different actors.

Beginning in the late 1950s, the rhetoric of racial democracy became the object of scholarly attack. Florestan Fernandes, the most influential of these scholars, sought to rebut Freyre on every point, arguing that nearly four centuries of slavery had left a legacy of endemic racial exploitation.[21] From the late 1960s through the 1980s, researchers took Fernandes's work in two directions, with some emphasizing quantitative analysis to demonstrate the falsity of the rhetoric and some emphasizing the cultural and historical triumphs of black resistance. These scholarly arguments did not eliminate the rhetoric of racial democracy, but they did circulate new ideas encouraging anti-racist activism. In the worst years of the military dictatorship (roughly 1969–1973) these ideas had little chance of spreading beyond a narrow scholarly community. As the regime began its slow *abertura* in the mid-1970s, however, it relaxed its censorship. The emerging soul stars and members of their cohort were perfectly poised to turn this *abertura* into an opportunity for black mobilization. The direction that mobilization would take seemed to be up for grabs.

Black Rio

It is impossible to pinpoint the inauguration of the black soul dances. The suburbs of the North Zone had grown rapidly since the 1940s, following the spread of commuter rail lines. Since that period of initial growth, the suburbs had been home to two types of social clubs—"tennis" clubs, largely patronized by the white, striving middle class, and "football" (that is, soccer) clubs largely patronized by the black and mixed-race working class. Both types of clubs offered a range of leisure options, including weekend dances: the distinction between them was not so much of sports, but of class. As a result, it is impossible to determine with any precision when the weekend dances at the football clubs evolved into the laboratories for a new popular racial consciousness. Certainly by 1972 several of these clubs were hiring DJs who played primarily American soul music, and by 1974 several of these dances had taken on explicitly black themes. The recurring "Shaft's Night" party at the Clube Renascença, for example, was inspired by the Gordon Parks film *Shaft* (1971) and its Isaac Hayes soundtrack.[22] (It should be noted that the Renascença was not a football club but a social club primarily for the black middle class.)

The DJs were usually part of an *equipe*, or team, which included anywhere from two to six people to set up the sound system and decorate the halls. The *equipes*, working under names such as Soul Grand Prix and Afro Soul, created the parties, gradually taking over from the social clubs capital risks and rewards. By 1976, there were hundreds of soul *equipes* working in Rio and São Paulo. In addition to choosing the music and setting the mood, they were responsible for animating the parties, running contests, and exhorting the audience to dance. In 1976, for example, one *equipe* held an Isaac Hayes look-alike contest. The prize, a savings account in a local bank, suggests the economic standing of the target audience—the aspiring working class.[23]

The leaders of the *equipes* became local celebrities. It was almost inevitable that they would gradually adopt the rhetoric of black pride from the records they were spinning. How many times could a DJ looking out at a mass of celebrating brown bodies listen to James Brown sing, "Say it out loud, I'm black and I'm proud!" *without* taking up the banner? The language gap was no barrier here. Totemic phrases from the soul records—black power, black is beautiful—became buzzwords in the soul dances. What they lost in specific meaning they gained in power, precisely because of their foreign allure. Not surprisingly, they often took on new shades of meaning. "Black power," for example, was often pronounced and understood as black *pau*, which literally means "stick," but in common slang means "dick." The conflation of meanings fit in perfectly with the mood of the parties: black soul was liberating because it was sexy. It also underlined the gendered nature of the phenomenon. While men and women appear to have attended the parties in roughly equal numbers, all the DJs were men. Until the 1980s, all the notable performers were men as well. Black pau was not going to be a feminist movement.[24]

Some *equipes* took the rhetoric of black pride more seriously than others. Carlos Alberto Medeiros was a university student and attended the seminars hosted by the Instituto de Estudo Afro-Asiáticos, or Institute of Afro-Asiatic Studies, at the Universidade Cándido Mendes. The Instituto was an important nucleus for both currents of post-UNESCO research into Brazilian race relations, the economic and the cultural. Medeiros and his peers often met in the seminars by day and at the soul dances by night. As an organizer of these dances, Medeiros sought to nurture and spread black activism among a wider population. He understood the limits of the dances in this regard—that they were festive and not political, that the dancers were more interested in displaying style than in exchanging ideas—but he was impressed by the growing understanding of the nature of racism in Brazil. For Medeiros and his cohort, the soul dances were the perfect arena for the dissemination of the ideas debated in the Instituto among a public without access to higher education.[25]

Equally indicative, however, was Ademir Lemos, a white DJ who had begun his career spinning records for the rock 'n' roll dances of Rio's predominantly white South Zone. He made the transition to soul in the mid-1970s in order to tap into the emerging market of the North Zone. Partly because he had the capital to invest in an imported sound system and to acquire the latest U.S. releases, his *equipe* became one of the most successful on the soul circuit, charging about $1,000 for a typical gig. Lemos's record deal was more lucrative. Import restrictions severely limited the ability of U.S. independent labels like Motown and Stax to penetrate the Brazilian record market, favoring instead multinationals like CBS and Philips, owner of Polydor. Taking advantage of these restrictions, the multinationals acquired the rights to distribute independent U.S. singles in Brazil, with an eye toward the local release of compilation albums. Lemos astutely marketed the brands of the top soul *equipes* to the record companies and then served as "producer" for collections of diverse U.S. soul singles sold under those brand names. In 1976, for example, Lemos "produced" a highly successful collection for CBS, sold under the name of Soul Grand Prix, a black *equipe*. Soul Grand Prix and Lemos both took a share of album profits. The soul dancers were a captive market for such albums. In the midst of this commercial success, Lemos happily adopted soul rhetoric, particularly the less militant "black is beautiful" strain.[26] One need not believe that his usage of such rhetoric was entirely cynical in order to understand that Lemos's interest in soul was primarily commercial.

Soul was thus a social phenomenon born with a struggle over its own meaning at its heart: would it be a vehicle for black political awareness or merely another pop fad enriching promoters? The nature of this struggle was particularly clear at a July 1976 event at Rio de Janeiro's Museum of Modern Art that was sponsored by the Instituto de Pesquisa das Culturas Negras (the Black Cultures Research Institute), or IPCN. The IPCN, founded in 1975, was a group of scholars dedicated primarily to black political mobilization through cultural programs. At the museum, the IPCN screened the 1973 Mel Stuart film *Wattstax,* hoping that the film would bring the growing soul public to an intellectual environment that might favor further politicization. *Wattstax* mixes coverage of a 1972 soul music festival in Los Angeles with documentary footage of life in the neighborhood of Watts, site of pivotal race riots in 1965. The emotional climax of the film shows the young Jesse Jackson, fist raised in a black power salute, intoning "I am somebody" before an enthusiastic crowd. The IPCN screening drew hundreds of young soul adepts, many of whom had seen the film before at soul dances. At the climax, they mouthed the words of Jackson's speech, experiencing the same ecstatic response as the audience in the film.[27]

Obviously, such an experience was politically inspiring for many members of the audience. Most, however, seemed primarily excited by the opportunity to show off their latest soul regalia, and to temporarily take over a South Zone cultural institution generally reserved for the white elite. To the degree that soul had political implications for them, those implications derived from the transgression of social boundaries. Above all, soul was—for the majority of its participants—a celebration of new popular cultural options afforded by growing market power.[28]

This new power was primarily the result of the so-called economic miracle provoked by the military regime's opening to international capital and its borrowing of international funds in the early 1970s. The debt crisis and hyperinflation of the 1980s eventually revealed the flaws in the dictatorship's accounts, but in the short term, the "miracle" increased capital circulation and raised employment in the North Zone. While growing employment gave Rio's black youth greater ability to purchase records and new clothes, it also helped reveal to them the dimensions of racism, as they discovered that their opportunities for advancement were greatly diminished in comparison with those of their white peers. It is not surprising that they chose to exercise their new market power in a way that emphasized apparent contestation of the prevailing social structure. By their very nature as market phenomena, however, such popular cultural choices were inevitably not "pure"—that is, they ended up enriching white DJs and producers at least as much as their black counterparts.

Another facet of this ambiguity was that, even as the soul dancers created a parallel black entertainment circuit in the North Zone, they took particular glee in occasional "invasions" of predominantly white spaces, such as the Modern Art Museum and South Zone nightclubs.[29] Such invasions, of course, can easily be construed as mere mainstream social climbing, negating any oppositional rhetoric. But such dilution is an inevitable fate of any pop fad as it evolves from a larval stage, when it is nurtured among a closed, homogenous community, to a mature stage, when it flutters and takes wing before a heterogeneous audience.

Transando Soul

Understanding the roots of this ambiguity helps explain why soul dancers and DJs alike seemed evenly divided in their opinions as to whether soul had a political meaning. Many participants described soul as a movement, without necessarily giving any political weight to the term. (Example: *Interviewer:* Why the *cabelo afro* [Afro hair]? *Soul dancer:* It's just a movement that started up, you know?[30]) Many adopted the rhetoric of black pride, frequently using English terminology, such as, "Tenho o maior orgulho de ser *black*" (I'm really proud of being black). But participants were also likely to temper such assertions with references to Brazilian racial harmony. In 1976 the DJ Santos dos Santos told one reporter, "If there is one thing I would like to be in the next life it is black all over again. Because from the moment I turned on to that [soul] sound . . . I felt fulfilled." Just a few sentences later, Santos reassured the reporter: "I don't think that *soul power* is a racist movement. This is a country where we shouldn't implant that type of thing, because here, whether you are white or black, we should all be together. There are a few little barriers, but they are very small."[31]

Such statements can be read in two ways—as a superficial masking of a movement with real political consequences, or as evidence that the rhetoric of racial democracy maintained some power even in soul circles. I am inclined to the latter interpretation. Its obfuscation of real racism notwithstanding, the rhetoric did offer Afro-Brazilians a powerful tool: for a black citizen, invoking the idea of an essentially Brazilian racial harmony can be a way of scolding white elites for their anti-Brazilian ways.[32] Rejecting the rhetoric of racial democracy entirely, therefore, carries a heavy price—that of being labeled a racist, and therefore anti-Brazilian, oneself. Few Brazilians have been willing to pay that price. The inconsistency of the soul dancers on this score, then, was an eminently sensible negotiation of shifting racial problems. The participants often alluded to this negotiation using the popular contemporary slang word *transar,* which in its most common usage means "to have sex," but in the mid-1970s could also mean "to check out, to dig, to groove on," without losing some of its sexual overtones. For a teenager from the suburbs, *"transando soul"* could be a way to try on a sexy weekend identity of black militancy in a circumscribed environment before returning to the workaday world and its charade of racial democracy.[33]

The most politicized participants greeted such inconsistency with disdain. In the words of one dancer interviewed in 1978, "If [soul] continues this way, it won't go anywhere, because the majority only come to dance and don't worry about the community. They don't worry about competing with whites, about achieving better conditions."[34] Others, however, considered any mass gathering of people asserting a black identity a step in the right direction. As Medeiros put it in a 1978 interview, "In the moment one realizes 'If we can get together to do this, we can get together to do something more positive,' then it becomes important. Of course, not everyone makes that transition."[35]

Enough dancers made the transition to nurture the initial growth of several anti-racist political groups, including the umbrella organization Movimento Negro Unificado (MNU), or Unified Black Movement. The MNU was founded in 1978 by black activists from São Paulo and Rio, many of whom communicated through the soul dances. Two São Paulo soul *equipes* were among the most prominent signatories of the MNU's founding manifesto.[36] This did not make for an easy relationship. In its early years, the MNU was led by a Trotskyist wing that disdained soul's willful capitalism.[37] Nonetheless, the soul dances proved a crucial arena allowing the MNU to spread to a broader public.

Such political implications guaranteed that many outsiders would react to soul with incomprehension. Soul seemed to be a rejection of Brazil's cultural bounty in favor of a slick U.S. substitute. The title of the first major media coverage of the phenomenon, a 1976 article in the Rio daily *Jornal do Brasil,* gives away the headline writer's skeptical assessment—"Black Rio: The (Imported) Pride of Being Black in Brazil."[38] The article ignited a broader media reaction to soul, with intellectuals of diverse backgrounds joining together to label soul a racist, foreign, commercial fad.[39] Not surprisingly, Gilberto Freyre prominently denounced soul's racial politics.[40] The attitude of the police was one of disdain and harassment more than outright repression. Soul dancers were frequently stopped and searched by police who mocked their granny glasses and their platform shoes. In 1977 a sixteen-year-old girl was expelled from a Copacabana high school because she refused to cut her Afro. If being black was by itself grounds for official suspicion, soul style was an aggravating circumstance.[41]

At the same time, major record labels were eager to cash in on soul's potential. The expanding audience of the second half of the 1970s enabled the *equipes* to rent out larger halls and sell more records. The *equipes* soon found that the only way to maintain the enthusiasm of an audience of five thousand over the course of a six-hour dance was by incorporating live performances. Their ambitious spectacles gave a shot in the arm to Brazilian soul performers. Tim Maia had already reached a broader public and was no longer dependent on the clubs of the North Zone—when Maia emerged from Universo in 1976, he was, amazingly, able to pick up where he had left off, establishing a turbulent but independent career. Other performers, however, began to work with the *equipes*, collaborating on shows. Toni Tornado experienced a brief revival of his career in the late 1970s, putting on shows with *equipes* like Soul Grand Prix. He was outdone in soul style only by Gerson King Combo, also known as Gerson Cortês, a performer who adopted his curious stage name in honor of the King Curtis Combo. In tunes such as "Mandamentos Black" ("Black Commandments"), King Combo sought to take Brazilian soul to a new level of militancy: "Assume your mind, *brother* . . . Walk like a *black* man walks, talk like a *black* man talks" (italics in English in the original).

The Banda Black Rio also emerged from the new soul spectacles. The band included Abolição alumni Oberdan Magalhães and Barros, and took that group's explorations to a new level. Its 1977 album *Maria Fumaça* was a combination of the percussive wealth of samba, the contrapuntal invention of *choro*, and the horn grooves of deep jazz funk. Not all the group's members, however, felt equally comfortable in the milieu of the soul dances. Several felt constrained by what they perceived as the audience's narrow range of musical appreciation. They particularly resented the fact that Warner Brothers, the group's record label, pushed them to emphasize soul style, taking advantage of the fad. In 1978 pianist Cristóvão Bastos and bassist Jamil Joanes dropped out, following other musical directions.[42] With replacement personnel, the rest of the band recorded another album and toured into the early 1980s.

At the peak of soul's popularity, mainstream performers sought greater proximity to the soul genre. Caetano Veloso toured with the Banda Black Rio in 1978. Gilberto Gil recorded two strongly soul-influenced albums in the late 1970s and collaborated with Chic Show, São Paulo's most popular soul *equipe*. Gil also adopted his own version of an Africanized soul style, braiding cowrie shells into his hair and wearing dashikis. There is no question that both Caetano and Gil were sincere in their musical experimentation with soul and their appreciation of the phenomenon's political overtones. Gil, in particular, was deeply influenced by a 1977 trip to Nigeria, and was searching for ways to express a cosmopolitan black identity in his music.[43] Soul offered one approach. Neither performer was merely taking commercial advantage of a lucrative phenomenon. Nonetheless, such incursions into the territory of soul on the part of established performers indicated that soul was fast reaching the stage of dilution and decadence.

The year 1978 was also when disco took off in Brazil. Many *equipes* adapted quickly to the new style, dropping James Brown from their playlists and adding Donna Summer. Even soul icon Tim Maia put out a commercially successful disco album. Unlike soul, disco attracted a cross-class, mixed-race crowd from the beginning, and became a fixture at South Zone nightclubs. Black pride did not make the transition. With the exception of a few *equipes* in São Paulo and in the neighboring city of Campinas, soul as a popular phenomenon faded quickly along with the decade.

Vou Chamar o Síndico: Legacies

Soul passed on two kinds of legacies—musical and social—for future decades. Musically, two notable performers emerged in the 1980s. Sandra de Sá became the first female soul vocalist in Brazil. Her vocal stylings earned her the nickname "Tim Maia in skirts," and she asserted pride in an explicitly black identity. Luiz Melodia, another singer from Rio de Janeiro, carried on his own investigations of rock/soul/samba hybrids in the 1980s. Melodia experienced significant popular success, but in contrast to Sá, has never been recognized primarily as a soul performer.

Tim Maia, meanwhile, pursued his own turbulent career. Musically, his 1980s work tilted into syrupy R&B. Following his fallout with Universo, Maia had once again taken to indulging his appetite for drugs and alcohol with gusto, adhering to an ambitious regimen of nightly intoxication. He became notorious for his erratic performances and for his absenteeism, and his popularity ebbed to a low point by 1991. In that year, Jorge Ben recorded a samba-funk entitled "W/Brasil," which turned on the inexplicable refrain "Vou chamar o síndico . . . Tim Maia!" (I'm going to call the concierge . . . Tim Maia!). The tune took off as a dance single in 1993, reviving the careers of both Ben and Maia, and earning the irresponsible Maia the ridiculously inappropriate nickname of "O Síndico."

Maia's politics never grew any more coherent. He frequently accused radio stations and record companies of running a regime fueled by *jabuculê*, or payola, and claimed that the Brazilian copyright authority had defrauded him of millions of dollars. At the same time, he often refused to pay royalties to other composers and was at one point or another sued by eight former backup musicians for breaking contracts. In the late 1990s he vowed to run for senator as a candidate of the Socialist party, touting the need for a black university as his principal platform. Before he had the chance to fulfill his promise, he suffered an edema while onstage in a March 1998 performance. He died several days later.[44]

At the time of Maia's death, his nephew, Ed Motta, was just coming into his own as the best soul singer of a younger generation. Motta recorded an influential soul album in 1988, when he was still a teenager. After several less successful ventures, he released *Manual prático para festas, bailes e afins* (*Practical Handbook for Parties, Dances, and Such*) late in 1997, demonstrating a level of vocal expression that exceeded that of his uncle. Motta has since recorded a follow-up album, experimenting with a lighter sound featuring acoustic instrumentation, within the same soul and disco paradigm. But he has not been limited by soul. In recent years, he has collaborated with composers and performers of sophisticated instrumental music rooted in the Brazilian genres of samba, *choro,* and bossa nova. At the same time, he has become a historian of Brazilian soul. His Web site includes the best extant discography of the genre, along with opinionated and enlightening descriptions of the music.[45]

Soul as a social phenomenon went through lean years in the 1980s. In São Paulo, two of the most successful soul *equipes*, Chic Show and Zimbabwe, managed to persist and adapt, essentially evolving into the hosts of weekly parties. They gradually phased out soul in favor of R&B and, eventually, hip-hop, but they never lost their association with black community identity.[46] They were paralleled in that regard by the *bailes funk,* or funk dances, that became popular in Rio in the mid- to late 1980s. I have generally used the word funk in this article in its American sense, referring to the kind of sound developed by musicians like James Brown and George Clinton. In Brazil, however, the word has different connotations, referring to a variety of rap with heavy bass and drum machine. Funk, associated with Rio, has generally been distinguished from the rap and hip-hop of São Paulo, which usually has more political lyrics and more ambitious instrumentation and production. The *bailes funk* became associated with violence and the cocaine trade, generating an enormous amount of fear among outsiders. In reality, while many *bailes funk* have certainly served as an opportunity for drug trafficking, the majority have been no more violent than one would expect from a relatively unsupervised party of hyped-up teenagers.[47]

Brazilian soul is currently in the midst of a revival. Gerson King Combo has come out of retirement to play packed houses in Rio. Soul singers of a younger generation like Paula Lima have recorded successful albums. The albums of Toni Tornado and Hyldon have been re-released on CD. The French label Ziriguiboom and the American label Six Degrees collaborated on the recent release of *Samba Soul '70*, an excellent collection of early Brazilian soul and *sambalanço* recordings. A club in downtown São Paulo hosts a weekly soul night that seeks to reproduce the atmosphere of the 1970s dances, down to the décor and the attire. This soul revival also fits in with a renewed sense of black identity and criticism of the rhetoric of racial democracy. As in the mid-1970s, this criticism follows closely on the heels of an economic expansion that failed to alter economic inequality by race. Soul has again proved a useful vehicle for promoting a black cultural consciousness that holds a candle up to the ongoing reality of racism in Brazil. This explains why rap groups like Planet Hemp and Pavilhão 9 have become the greatest celebrants of figures like King Combo.

Like most popular cultural revivals, the current soul boom seems a distant echo of the louder concatenation of the 1970s. In a musical environment that has come to accept and adopt hip-hop, reggae, and rock, soul no longer seems like a threat to the national musical heritage. Far from it: Tim Maia is now remembered as a fallen hero. At the 2001 awards ceremony of the arts entertainment television network Multishow, Maia was given a posthumous lifetime achievement award. His former backup band (those members who had not sued him) took to the stage and played his 1973 hit, "Eu Gostava Tanto de Você" ("I Loved You So Much") while images of Maia singing the tune danced on an enormous screen. His ghostly presence seemed to reassure the audience, clapping along below him, that soul is now perfectly Brazilian, after all.

Selected Discography

Hoje é natal. Various artists. 1999. Mercury PHCW-1066.
Lima, Paula. *É Isso Aí, Sr.* 2002. Regata 260-002.
Maia, Tim. *Tim Maia*. 1971. Polygram 810515-2.
———. *Tim Maia*. 1973. Polygram 519660-2.
Maia, Tim, Cassiano, and Hyldon. *Velhos camaradas.* 1992. Polygram 517885-2.
SambaSoul 70. Various artists. 2001. Ziriguiboom/Six Degrees 6570361047-2.

Boricua Rock

Puerto Rican by Necessity!

JORGE ARÉVALO MATEUS

Latin rock, *rock en español*, Ñ, or as it is most recently called by the music industry, "Latin alternative music," has become a definitive marketing trend. It has enjoyed its greatest popular acceptance among young Mexican immigrants living on the West Coast, but on the East Coast as well, young Latinos and non-Latinos alike are becoming more involved with this pan-Latin musical movement. Replete with social, symbolic, and culturally laden messages and meanings, Latin alternative music draws from multiple rock variants, and is being put to the task of representing distinct subcultural communities and their associated national identities. In the U.S. territory of Puerto Rico, recent and homegrown acts such as Robi Draco Rosa, Puya, Fiel a la Vega, Sol d'Menta, Vivanativa, and La Secta All Star are now claiming a place within this global pantheon and achieving a substantial measure of popular recognition and industry attention. In the case of rock in Puerto Rico, or Boricua Rock (BR), the term I will use here, this phenomenon demonstrates Puerto Rican rockers' extraordinary creativity and cultural resilience in the face of music industry strategies to commodify Puerto Rican rock culture. BR rock is an active site of tension, conflict, and negotiation, as young musicians, resisting the island's neocolonial status, adopt internally and externally defined musical influences in order to assert their distinctive position as Latinos in a "nation" within a nation. This essay explores ways in which contemporary Puerto Rican rock musicians perceive their right to rock, on the island, in the New York City diaspora, and throughout the rock world, molding a collective identity as they draw from a broad repertoire of cultural forms to create distinctly Puerto Rican brands of rock within the international Latin rock movement.

While it is clear that the sort of national manifestations of rock discussed in this volume are the products of distinct sociopolitical and musical histories and environments, BR's evolution has been indelibly marked by Puerto Rico's unique political relationship with its "host" nation. Due to Puerto Rico's constant cultural intermingling with the U.S. mainland, the Boricua *rockeros*, in contrast to their Latin American counterparts, seem to stand outside of the industry's "alternative" Latin music circle, representing a different set of values, aesthetics, and social dynamics. More so perhaps than for other Latin American rockers, Puerto Rican *rockeros* have been subject to a U.S.-centric sociohistorical narrative that has regarded the development of Puerto Rican rock as merely imitative of North American and Anglo rock models. While musical genres are often regarded as "indigenous" only if they have distinctly local stylistic features, in the case of BR, I would argue that such elements need not be present. Puerto Rican rock does not need to be a fully synthesized hybrid in order to be Puerto Rican: it can contain foreign rock elements and still retain its Puerto Rican puissance. After having experienced intensive media infiltration for decades (and the emergence of MTV in the 1980s), present-day Boricua youth seem to have recognized the capacity for musical expression to contest and reject U.S. homogeneity while also embracing a heterogeneous Puerto Rican culture. Thus, a revitalized sense of a politicized Puerto Rican identity has found expression in the form of contemporary BR. It is important to emphasize, nonetheless, that the project for Boricua *rockeros* is fraught with obstacles. This is particularly so since they seek to assert Puerto Rican national and cultural identity without the benefit of a consensually agreed upon concept of either "state" or "nation."

Contemporary Boricua *rockeros* are, in fact, in a new phase of socio-musical and cultural development in which foreign and indigenous cultural forms are being fully accepted, and in which young musicians and audiences are participating in local, translocal, and transnational rock trends. These *rockeros* serve as a model of what Raymond Williams refers to as the "postmodern play of multiple identity positions, serving varying and sometimes conflicting ends, and manifesting elements of persistence, adjustment, unconscious assimilation, active resistance, [and] alternative effort."[1] By remaining cognizant of their own history, they are also challenging current music industry strategies, constantly negotiating the transnational and global media and music networks that can either ensure their success or perpetuate their marginalization. Within the highly charged social and political environment of present-day Puerto Rico, in which the lack of national autonomy stares the world in the face and conditions every aspect of Puerto Rican life,[2] the degree to which Boricua *rockeros* succeed or fail to overcome industry intervention and manipulation is directly related to the extent to which they either collude with industry marketing and distribution strategies or resist and reject them.

Rock, Nationalism, and Identity Politics

Rock has been an active musical form in Puerto Rico since the early 1950s, thanks to the concerted efforts of the North American music and media industry which gave island audiences easy access to U.S. rock. Local and mainland popular artists were also promoted via the entrepreneurial efforts of Puerto Rican music impresarios such as Alfred D. Herger, who revered U.S. music industry leader Dick Clark and replicated his teen television show format.[3] Musicians such as Chucho Avellanet, Bobby Capó, and Lucecita Benítez, initially performing Spanish-language covers of North American hits, helped to satisfy growing public demand for local performers, particularly among the white middle- and upper-class sectors of the island population. These sectors had more resources and better access to media and music industry products and technology, but they also (at least initially) tolerated rock's youthful articulation and even encouraged youth's active participation.

In Puerto Rico, the distribution of rock among island youths followed race and class distinctions. Lower-class Afro–Puerto Ricans generally embraced salsa, while young, white male teens were drawn to the ideologies of North American folk-rock singer-songwriters such as Bob Dylan; other middle- and upper-class Boricuas preferred Anglo and North American rock stars such as the Beatles, Rolling Stones, and, after Woodstock, the Mexican-born Chicano rocker Carlos Santana. Rock, as a result, became increasingly associated with the privileged class on the island, as well as with U.S. cultural dominance. Thus were sown the seeds for the intense cultural rift that would emerge in the late 1970s and early 1980s between *cocolos* (salsa fans) and *rockeros* (rock fans).[4]

By the early 1970s, a new breed of socially and politically aware Boricua *rockeros* emerged who were much less interested in achieving stardom and were suspicious of both the politics and the capitalist tendencies of the mainland. These rockers were attracted to the political messages of the Cuban *nueva trova* singers Pablo Milanés and Silvio Rodríguez, which served to encourage Boricua singer-songwriters to comment on Puerto Rico's struggles for national sovereignty and independence in their music. Harnessing the renewed sense of nationalism that grew out of the Puerto Rican *independentista* (Independence) movement, along with a growing political consciousness of the class and race issues of the time, singer-songwriters such as Roy Brown and Noel Hernández used folk-rock and *nueva canción* to express dissatisfaction with the status quo, providing a fresh nationalist vision of Puerto Rican identity and political awareness.

In some respects, their music paralleled that of their New York City *barrio* counterparts, who were mixing Latin and other Afro-Caribbean music with North American jazz and rhythm and blues, although their motivations differed. In the mid-1960s *barrio*-based Nuyorican musicians like Ray Barretto, Johnny Colón, and Joe Cuba had combined U.S. and Spanish Caribbean styles with African American rhythm and blues and rock. Despite obvious stylistic and aesthetic differences, both the experimental Nuyorican *salseros* and the island-based performers of *nueva canción* veered away from mainstream popular musical styles, choosing instead to retain the political inflection of their source genres. These syncretized forms informed and reflected the political views of large segments of the *puertorriqueño* community both on the island and on the mainland.

Today, there remains little evidence of the cultural antagonism that once existed between adherents of Latin and Puerto Rican "traditional music" and those eager to assimilate musically to the dominant culture.[5] Today, rock is regarded less of a political threat despite its power to express different ideas about nationality and nationalism.[6] In Puerto Rico, rock audiences are more representative of the island's mixed youth population than they were in the past, and even non-fans acknowledge that rock is a vital part of the Puerto Rican music scene. Quintero Rivera, for example, a fervent proponent of the social and cultural importance of salsa, recognizes that rock cannot be ignored as a Puerto Rican social phenomenon since it is a component of the island's "complex heterogeneous totality."[7]

In the following sections, I will discuss the present state of rock in Puerto Rico and in the diaspora. While there are literally dozens of bands performing throughout every corner of the island, making it difficult to establish a clear taxonomy, I have chosen to focus my analysis on four ensembles—Puya, Fiel a la Vega, Ricanstruction, and Konfrontazion. It is hoped that this representative sample will highlight similarities and differences in the social and political dynamics that have shaped the formation of BR.

Puya

Puya is the first Puerto Rican rock band to have achieved a high degree of music industry success, thanks to its association with MCA Records, a major

U.S. transnational with whom they signed in 1998. On their first major label release, *Fundamental* (1998), the band worked with the noted Argentine producer Gustavo Santaolalla. Well-known for his successful "crossover" projects with such Latin rock and *rock en español* artists as Mexico's Café Tacuba and Molotov, it appeared that Puya was destined to achieve success in the U.S. market.

In the band's early days in the 1980s (when they were known as Whisker Biscuit), Puya took no overt position on Puerto Rican political issues, aside from occasionally expressing a sense of Puerto Rican pride to the local music press. In 1992 the band relocated to Fort Lauderdale, Florida, which prompted a period of self-discovery that inspired the creation of their present sound. According to bassist Harold Hopkins, Puya's musical roots include the *música típica* of Puerto Rico, salsa, and U.S. and British rock and pop: "In the 1980s, we'd listen to the Fania All-Stars and all the rock and pop bands . . . Journey, Foreigner, Kiss, REO Speedwagon, Slayer, Metallica, Black Sabbath, and Van Halen. . . . Later, [the Brazilian metal band] Sepultura became one of our main influences."[8] Drummer Ed Paniagua claims that it was the competitive atmosphere of Florida's hard-core rock scene that ironically helped the band find its musical direction, along with a renewed sense of Boricua identity: "We wanted to go back to our roots, and it was interesting to find them musically in the United States."[9]

While the band has retained its hybrid rock formula, under Kevin Benson's management it has sought to infiltrate mainstream North American rock markets by presenting themselves as Latin rockers who can "rock as hard as any U.S. band."[10] Spanish linguistic and Latin cultural aspects of the music have been toned down in favor of emphasizing the alternative, hard-core, punk elements of the band's sound. Interestingly, Puya has been remarkably successful in the North American Midwest, which may be attributed to the band's image as young, white, alternative rockers—who sing largely in English although they just happen to be from Puerto Rico.[11] Touring regularly throughout Mexico and North America with major North American rock acts such as Red Hot Chili Peppers, Kiss, and Metallica, Puya has worked to build a wide audience base, participating in arena-scale rock fests such as Ozzfest, Tattoo the Earth, and Sno-Core.

While Puya's success suggests a large non-Latino/a fan base, the band also maintains close ties with their extremely loyal Puerto Rican fans, performing regularly on the island. Puya's position in the Latin alternative rock scene, however, requires a constant negotiation between their island status as "local heroes" and their mainland/mainstream objectives. Emphasizing the band's "eternal love for its homeland" and expressing ambivalence toward their role as "musical ambassadors," Paniagua credits the band for raising public awareness of Puerto Rico as a source of metal and hardcore rock: "I don't think there's any other rock bands that came out of Puerto Rico and were signed to an American label. There's a lot of big artists out of Puerto Rico, but not a hard band, we're the first."[12] Paniagua's comments draw attention to the wide recognition the band has achieved within the music industry, but they also emphasize Puya's unique position as a band that educates the public about Puerto Rican culture.

Most songs on *Fundamental* use instrumentals based on the prototypical power-rock trio of electric guitar, bass, and drums, blended with the requisite taunting lead vocals of punk and metal. Musically, "Sal pa'fuera" is typical of Puya's signature sound, reminiscent of Anglo heavy-metal icons Black Sabbath. While the highly compressed production emphasizes the band's aggressively loud, harsh, and distorted sonics, one can also discern the ease with which Puya migrates easily in and out of salsa-influenced sections in the bridge and chorus sections. In the song's lyrics, the band's once neutral stance gives way to expressing anger and frustration with the social and cultural environment in which they live. Singing in Spanish, the band loudly shouts in unison:

> Sal pa'fuera pa' la calle, sal pa'fuera coño
> Sal pa'fuera vamos, sal pa'fuera coño.
>
> (Get out to the street, get out damn it
> Come on get out, get out damn it.)

This rallying call against an unnamed power demands social action, as well as a collective political and spiritual awakening—the cleansing of a sick spirit ("la limpieza de un espíritu enfermo"):

> No es receta de derecha ni de izquierda
> es solo un proceso que
> despierta la conciencia
> que entiende las fuerzas que
> manipulan la mente.
>
> (It's not a recipe from the Left or the Right
> it's just a process that
> awakens the conscience
> that understands the forces that
> manipulate the mind.)

Like the cover art to *Fundamental,* which depicts a powerful male figure rising up out of the earth, Puya's collective cry for activism communicates a vigorous and urgent appeal for a self-actualized social conscience that emerges from reconnecting to the island and its traditional values. By denouncing the system of U.S.-imposed cultural values, notions of rebirth, cleansing, and healing are ground within the anthemic lyrics, revealing a perspective that is simultaneously proactive, positive, and self-determined.

On their follow-up release, *Union* (2001), Puya took a strikingly different musical approach. Still metal-edged but with an increased blending of styles and sounds, the band displayed greater confidence in its mixture of elements, made possible only after having established respectable record sales, sufficient radio airplay, and a solid fan base. According to Josh Norek, the band's publicist, *Union* reached the #1 position on *Radio & Records Magazine*'s Commercial Rock Radio Specialty Play chart, the first time an album from a bilingual band had ever done so.[13] While Puya's musical core remains anchored to the rap-metal-meets-alternative-*rock-en-español* formula (a sort of Spanglish "nü-metal"), the degree of musical synthesis has considerably increased. With *Fundamental*'s success, the band was encouraged to record material that would further push the boundaries of Latin rock and *rock en español,* as long as they maintained their mainstream rock appeal. Ever since the band's early years, Puya had been interested in pursuing this musical direction and responded by expanding the Boricua side of the equation. By restoring salsa and jazz elements, by increasing Afro–Puerto Rican and Caribbean influences (for example, *bomba, songo,* and *batá*) and the use of Spanish-language lyrics, and by hiring top Puerto Rican salsa session musicians for the recording, Puya enhanced their hybrid musical conception, creating a more densely "Latin" sound. Even Tito Puente, the "Mambo King" himself, agreed to record a timbale solo on *Union,* before his unexpected death. Only after having established a significant market presence, however, did Puya begin to exhibit increased political and social awareness in their song lyrics. *Union* prominently foregrounds environmental concerns along with increased social criticism and less vague nationalist sentiments. As Paniagua explains, their song "Pa' ti pa' mi" ("For You, For Me") "talks about the situation in Vieques," about "how the ecology of the island is being destroyed by these military practices and people are losing their lives"[14]:

> Mira que te está llorando
> Porque de ella se está abusando
> La máquina viene a destruir
> La marina fuera de Vieques.

(Look, she's crying to you
Because she's being abused
The machine is coming to destroy
Marines get out of Vieques.)

Opening with the standard 2–3 clave rhythm of salsa, the lyrics are performed in a rap-metal style over a hard rhythmic funk-rock groove, with a transitional middle bridge that references and shifts into world-beat-styled sung choruses. As the song ends, the "natural" sounds of a *coquí* and a tropical rainstorm are introduced in the mix, perhaps two of the most identifiable, symbolic, and autochthonous of Puerto Rican sound "images," used here metaphorically as aural signifiers to evoke the spirit of the island. With new song texts stressing Boricua self-awareness and spiritual freedom and the increased use of bilingual lyrics (drawing from a double cultural consciousness innate to many young Puerto Ricans), Puya's biculturality and increased politicized consciousness are now constitutive of their Boricua *rockero* self-image.

In 2002 MCA did not renew Puya's contract, reportedly because record sales for *Union* did not meet company expectations. Despite the setback, Puya regards their break with MCA as liberating. Constant negotiation in order to balance their creative needs with industry demands made it sufficiently clear that "MCA's route was to direct us musically toward the commercial."[15] Whether Puya can sustain the same level of public and media exposure it had while with the multinational, or whether they can continue to distribute their music as widely, remain doubtful. Aware of their past crossover success and present name recognition, however, Puya is determined to exercise control over their musical direction and reassert their hard-won position in the Latin alternative rock orbit. The band remains optimistic about the future of their brand of BR. Puya's commitment to addressing Boricua themes in their music remains prominent in spite of industry constraints. As the most visible and commercially accessible exponents of BR, Puya's Puerto Rican roots lie in their acknowledgment and adherence to processes of transcultural hybridization. As "master syncretizers,"[16] their accommodation to the transnational music industry's requirements has neither subordinated autochtonous Afro–Puerto Rican musical styles nor solely privileged North American rock models.

Fiel a la Vega

Fiel a la Vega is the most controversial and politically committed BR band in Puerto Rico; they are also commercially successful. Performing a hybrid mixture of classic American/Anglo blues-rock and *trova*-tinged *nueva canción*,

Fiel a la Vega represent a form of BR that is political and nationalistic in its working philosophy and textual/lyric content. Whether the band can achieve success outside the island remains doubtful, given certain music industry factors that impact their international marketability. The island-specific content of Fiel's songs, for example, limits their access to *rock en español* markets. In fact, Fiel is regarded as being particularly "Puerto Rican" by the island's music press—for their acute political sensibility and the distinctly Boricua manner in which it is expressed. Soto Torres explains that "although Fiel a la Vega is the BR group most associated with affirming Puerto Rican national identity, they are the ones who least incorporate Latin and Puerto Rican elements in their musical style."[17]

In 1989 and 1990 Tito Auger and Ricky Laureano each relocated to New Jersey from Puerto Rico in an effort to secure a record deal, but they were repeatedly frustrated. "After a few years of hard experiences, they understood that their essence was expressed in what they knew and who they are: Puerto Ricans."[18] Returning to the island, in 1995 Auger and Laureano formed Fiel a la Vega and subsequently released three self-produced recordings: *Fiel a La Vega* (1996), *El concierto acústico* (1997), and *A quien pueda interesar* (1998). Each release was successful, selling a total of nearly 200,000 units. On an island with a population of just over four million people, such figures are noteworthy even by music industry standards. By late 1999, Fiel a la Vega had signed with EMI Latino, the Latin subsidiary of the multinational, EMI Records. Despite the record company's lack of promotional support for *Tres* (1999), the band's only release on the label, the album sold more than 75,000 units. However, in 2002 Fiel a la Vega and EMI Latino severed their contractual ties; like Puya, Fiel de la Vega will most likely return to an independent island label.

With record sales generating substantial local press and media interest in 1998, island journalists and cultural critics alike discussed the topicality of the band's songs and the issues they raised. The impact of Auger's lyrics went beyond Fiel's generation-X audience, capturing a moment in Puerto Rican history in which almost forgotten political themes and sentiments were being renewed and rearticulated among young and old *puertorriqueños* alike. Juan García-Passalacqua, a self-proclaimed *viejo* (old man or elder) and former Luis Muñoz Marín cabinet member and political analyst, who has observed seven decades of Americanization and its consequences, declares that "many of our generation, admittedly, live in the past."[19] Quoting from Auger's "Salimos de aquí" (*Fiel a la Vega*, 1996), he adds, "We have to melt the jail cell of fears" and "affirm nationality with your flag of loyalty."[20] García-Passalacqua conveys a long-held nationalist ideology that emphasizes Puerto Rico's importance as a place to which all Puerto Ricans should be *fiel* (loyal).

While island writers like Melba Miranda and Edgardo Soto Torres continue to promote a Puerto Rican *rock nacional,* often focusing on Fiel a la Vega, their efforts have generally gone unnoticed by the international music press. Indeed, rock music critics in North America have at times been hesitant to consider BR beyond mainstream trends. Ed Morales, for example, a New York–based Puerto Rican music journalist and otherwise strong proponent for Latin rock, considers Fiel's music derivative of American rock, saying it contains a sense of *jíbaro* sentimentality.[21] Further suggesting that Fiel's success might be limited to the rock market in Puerto Rico because they are not "avant-garde enough in a European way," Morales privileges Anglo rock models over those of Boricua *rockeros.* Commenting on the marketing dilemma engendered by Fiel's juxtaposition of mainstream folk-rock and *nueva canción* with political song texts sung in Spanish, Soto Torres notes, "It's not the same to be a band *of Puerto Rican rock,* than *a Puerto Rican band* that plays rock."[22] Stressing the "Puerto Rican-ness" of BR as derived from its identification with Puerto Rican culture rather than from its association with rock per se, Soto Torres places greater emphasis on BR as a metaphorical site for *rockeros* to express Boricua identity. He notes, too, how Auger's lyrics often deal with Puerto Rican nationalist themes, maintaining this close identification and making Fiel a la Vega *puertorriqueño.*[23]

What is perhaps most significant about Fiel is their success at using rock music to communicate controversial political ideas to island audiences with little or no major label promotion or marketing, as well as the support they receive from their audiences and the local music press. Island radio and press have, in fact, been overwhelmingly supportive of Fiel's political views on Puerto Rican issues.[24] Moreover, Fiel's aesthetic attachment to the politically inflected *nueva canción* genre evinces Puerto Rico's long-standing appreciation of populist political songs that express national and cultural pride.[25] As for the political views that have come to define the band, Auger states that they are organically, and by necessity, constantly being transformed.[26] In fact, many of the ideas Fiel communicated on its earlier releases have changed dramatically as social and political circumstances and events have unfolded. For example, in a related side project, Auger and Laureano co-wrote and produced "Canción para Vieques" ("Song for Vieques") with the goal of demonstrating support for the sister island and its struggle to oust the U.S. Navy from its territory. This well-intentioned collaboration with a renowned group of artists—representative musicians and interpreters from Puerto Rico and Iberoamerica—proved problematic for Auger and Laureano: wishing to disseminate the recording free of charge, they sought an alternative means of distribution, which created tensions with their record company.

Perhaps because Fiel's success remains local to Puerto Rico, the implication is that their political ideas, in combination with a preference for singing exclusively in Spanish, presents something of a marketing problem for their record label. However, when a song such as Fiel's "Solamente" reaches the number-one spot off the island (as it did on a Bogotá, Colombia, rock radio station), it suggests that their music can appeal to international *rock en español* audiences. Soto Torres concludes that the record executives "still don't believe in BR," adding that "they still don't know how to deal with or sell independent [Latin] rock artists," particularly when "having a sociopolitical agenda doesn't make their careers easier."[27] Although it was Fiel's early recordings (that is, "Salimos de aquí" and "Un pueblo durmiendo") that sounded a chord of nationalist pride for many Puerto Ricans, which set the stage for how they would become a controversial Puerto Rican rock band, on *Tres* they continued to write songs with Puerto Rican social, political, and nationalist themes from a highly personal perspective.

Fiel a la Vega's song texts demonstrate how BR engages sociopolitical issues while maintaining a commercially viable format. Musically, there is notably little evidence of the strong political conviction or social outrage one might expect to hear in punk, rap, or roots rock. Instead, musical structures and themes are based on conventional folk-rock and *nueva canción* forms. However, the song texts are undeniably political. In "Indogmatización," for example, Auger opens with a personal statement about existing incompatibilities between Puerto Rican society's acceptance of an external colonial authority and the writer's own feeling of being marginalized:

> *Con certeza no eres mi ley*
> *Con franqueza tú mismo*
> *Me excluistes de tu gray* [sic].
>
> (It is certainly not my law
> Frankly you, yourself
> Have excluded me from your club.)

"Indogmatización" simultaneously serves as an indictment and challenge to an elite class hegemony that obstructs the "truth."

In the evocatively titled "Canción en la arena" ("Song in the Sand"), Auger uses irony to question *puertorriqueño* values. He first suggests that in Puerto Rico revolutionary ideology is simply fodder for marketing dollars. Then, the integrity of the island's political leaders is questioned. Finally, the adolescent and abusive patrimony of a metaphorical father figure is linked to artistic censure. "Canción en la arena" offers several viewpoints from which Puerto

Ricans can observe their place as social actors within a neocolonial and capitalist framework.

Soto Torres writes that by tackling social, political, and human themes in their songs, Fiel a la Vega reflect the concerns of young Boricuas; by remaining loyal to its roots, the group has been able to voice the anxieties of an entire generation.[28] In Fiel a la Vega's *trova-canción* substyle of BR, the topical nature of their narratives and its performance cannot be detached from long-standing Puerto Rican political issues. In their close identification with the island's cultural traditions, in their preference for Spanish, and in their use of protest song forms, Fiel a la Vega's hopes are linked to the primacy of Puerto Rican culture as the political foundation and source of radical projection.

KonFrontazion

KonFrontazion is a hard-core punk band from San Juan whose members are mostly still in their teens. They regard themselves as social outcasts and are generally not interested in commercial or popular success. According to Guillermo Echevarría, KonFrontazion's lead singer and songwriter, "We wouldn't like to see our music marketed . . . We aren't doing this for money."[29] As a prototypical Boricua punk band, KonFrontazion is part of the still relatively small, fragmented, and loosely structured punk "scene" that includes bands such as La Experiencia de Toñito Cabanillas, Actitud Subversiva, Ocinatas, Socialmente Muertos, and Rebelión. These bands create distinctively Boricua versions of punk rock and perform throughout the urban and rural *barrios* of Puerto Rico. Many of these young musicians move quickly in and out of numerous short-lived musical projects, and despite punk rock's growing presence, the underground nature of the scene is sustained, as bands perform in local bars, at informal parties, and on the circuit of strip clubs that cater to often underage audiences throughout the island.

Adopting punk fashion, imagery, and attitude, Boricua punks such as KonFrontazion perform for audiences for whom punk culture is a way to liberate themselves from oppressive and restrictive social mores and codes. True to punk aesthetics, the music is as loud and fast as its lyrics are militant and controversial. And while Konfrontazion's musical influences are wide-ranging, this does not mean that they identify with any particular locally, nationally, or internationally defined genre or style; rather, they are more interested in describing their daily personal struggles against social and political hypocrisy and oppression.

Selling their self-produced recordings at local shows and through their online Web site (www.Konfrontazion.com), KonFrontazion write and perform songs that are representative of the hard-core variety of the punk genre. Instrumental proficiency and technique are minimal and raw. Echevarría's vocals are screamed, in Spanish, while audiences react to abruptly changing rhythmic meters and accelerating tempos. In their signature song, "Soy el antirégimen" ("I Am the Antiregime"), KonFrontazion's indignant stance is readily apparent:

> Soy el antirégimen.
> El gobierno de esta nación quiere
> más posesión,
> imponiendo su ideal al pueblo
> sin razón.
> Ahora es el momento de que
> nuestra voz.
> No pidas derechos simplemente,
> tómalos.
> Dile no al tirano,
> dile no a la opresión
>
> (I am the antiregime.
> The government of this nation wants
> more possession,
> imposing their ideal(s) on the people
> without reason.
> Now is the moment for
> our voices.
> Don't simply ask for rights,
> take them.
> Say no to tyranny,
> say no to oppression.)

Puerto Rican teenage anger is often expressed in the anti-authoritarian tirades of Boricua punk bands such as KonFrontazion, whose questioning and rejection of Puerto Rico's leadership results in part from the island's political linkage and complicity with the United States. For KonFrontazion, their Puerto Rican-ness lies in the expression of unadulterated individuality and the desire to be free of social, political, and cultural domination. Drawing creative and musical strength from anti-fascist (read, anti-U.S.) sentiments, KonFrontazion's subcultural musical production captures Boricua youth thinking as well as their intense orientation toward independence and self-governance—what Juan Flores calls "moments of freedom."[30]

While some Boricua punks continue in the hard-core tradition of bands such as the Clash, the Sex Pistols, and the Ramones, many will eventually choose to perform in the style of any number of the more recent music trends entering and circulating throughout Puerto Rico. However, for the youngest segment of Puerto Rico's rockers, living with the ambivalence of a "multiple identity position,"[31] the adoption of punk culture represents the double-bind of rejection and the calculated accommodation of Anglo–U.S. and neotraditional Puerto Rican social norms and cultural values. Since many of the *puertorriqueño* teen musicians involved with the punk rock scene today have experienced the eclectic and rapid turnover of popular styles, the decision to perform punk rock appears to be a self-conscious rejection of the mainstream music that is imposed by the music industry and media networks. Viewed as the development of a meaningful local counterculture, the use of punk-influenced aesthetics provides the means for expressing attitudes not easily articulated within more marketable forms of rock and popular music.

These bands venture beyond the nihilistic tendencies of the genre, calling attention to Puerto Rican sociopolitical issues such as the Vieques controversy. There is more Vieques protest found in rock than in salsa or other Latin popular music. Although somewhat clichéd as a symbol of resistance and anti-U.S. authoritarianism, Vieques continues to provide a thematic narrative focus for Boricua punk *rockeros*. This is not to suggest that all *punkeros* engage in writing and performing political rock about Vieques, but combined with long-held *independentista* views and anger over U.S. governing policies and severe economic hardship throughout the island, Boricua teenagers have identified a germane musical language for expressing militant passion and social disillusionment. Given hardcore punk's limited socioeconomic and subcultural status, however, it seems unlikely that the Boricua punk movement will grow beyond its present state on the island (at least for the foreseeable future).

Nonetheless, the social and political self-positioning of young Boricuas has been of prime importance to the reconstruction of Puerto Rican identity, and punk rock as the medium of choice has helped to coalesce and galvanize them. For the youngest *rockeros,* participation in the neo-punk scene seems to cut across race, class, and gender lines. On the other hand, the gender politics associated with the BR phenomenon are displayed in the marked absence of women *rockeras,* the primacy of male perspectives in song texts, and the overwhelming degree of male-centric violence and angst that is physically acted out (for example, in the mosh pit). Soto Torres comments, "Apart from Alarma . . . girl bands or [those] with women singing [rock] are real 'lame.' The moment still hasn't happened in which a girl who likes rock and who understands what it's all about has gone up to sing."[32] Citing industry pressure, Soto Torres goes on to explain that in Puerto Rico they want women to sing only ballads and merengue. For example, although Melina León, one of the best *merengueras,* reportedly expressed an interest in singing rock, her record company convinced her she would have a hit sooner with merengue.[33]

Undoubtedly, gendered constructs regarding women's participation in BR relegates them to the role of passive consumers, as outdated hierarchies are maintained. Such notions are tacitly supported by music industry expectations and, perhaps inadvertently, by limitations imposed by some *rockeros* themselves. Although BR audiences include both young men and women, the social and cultural spaces that women occupy seem superfluous in the view of some *rockeros*. Whether the gender politics of BR serve to maintain or transcend stereotypes of Latino patriarchy, even the most politically oriented BR clearly seems to have much less to say about smashing sexism or *machismo* than it does about critiquing U.S. authoritarianism. Thus, the primary motivation of teen punk angst in BR remains the "us against them" clash.

Ricanstruction

"If Ricanstruction is about anything, we're about resistance," states Alano Baez, aka Not4Prophet, the New York band's vocalist and lyricist.[34] This young, hard-core, Porto-punk band from East Harlem's *barrio* participates in the discrete underground subcultures of the diaspora and Puerto Rico, imbuing their music with punk-rock aesthetics, urban street culture, and messages of a radical sociopolitical activism they claim is based on an Afro-Caribbean consciousness: "Our reality is also these inner-city streets, this cultural, spiritual and physical resistance. . . . This struggle is every second of every day. If Puerto Ricans are punks, it's probably by necessity and not always by choice."[35]

Defining themselves as aural anarchists orchestrating a head-on cultural collision, the members of Ricanstruction are strongly opposed to stereotypical notions associated with the term "Nuyorican." They deconstruct and reinvent their Boricua identity according to translocal and multicultural sensibilities, progressive social action, and political awareness. As Boricua *rockeros* voicing the consciousness of a colonized people of color trying to break free, the band aligns itself with aspects of Marxism, Black Nationalism, and Rastafarian ideologies, combining them with strongly felt *puertorriqueño* convictions. Not4-Prophet describes Ricanstruction's quasi-Rastafarianism as an example of neither strategic anti-essentialism, romantic idealization, or cultural confusion, but rather as the application of spiritual faith to radical activism: "Rasta helped

Ricanstruction poet and vocalist Not4Prophet (née Alano Baez) performing at CBGB, New York City, August 2002. Photograph by Sam LaHoz, © Sam LaHoz.

keep the spirituality [of religion] but combined it with the concept of resistance, enabling the band to further embrace a pan-African and Caribbean symbol of faith."[36]

Ricanstruction's music is a highly charged amalgam of contemporary urban styles: punk rock, rap, hip-hop, salsa, reggae, blues, and jazz are all present as musical sources to be deployed within the band's artistic framework. According to Not4Prophet, Ricanstruction does not consciously strive for Puerto Rican or Latin particularities in their music but freely uses *música folclórica (bomba, plena),* merengue, or salsa:

> We don't sit there saying, "We must sound like Andrés Jiménez now" [neo-*jíbaro* or traditional]. We're going to sound like Andrés Jiménez whether we try to or not. By the same token, we're going to sound like Bad Brains [hardcore punk], whether we try to or not.[37]

Along with their close identification with Puerto Rican music and culture, the band is deeply engaged in the complexities of the ethnic, racial, and class issues of New York City life. Not unlike Bad Brains, Living Colour, and other racially and ethnically mixed bands that draw upon punk rock's musical energy and anti-authoritarian stance, Ricanstruction considers its mission is to educate audiences about the meaning and impact of punk as a cultural practice of ritualized anarchy and subversion:

> The punk must know mainstream culture as well as . . . counterculture, so that they can know how to subvert it. Read their papers, their books, to understand their politics. Then resist. Read their magazines, listen to their music, to understand their co-opting of rebellion. Then make real rebellion.[38]

Contemporary urban music thus becomes a cultural tool used to disseminate anti-authoritarian rhetoric in what Ricanstruction views as a war against colonialism.

In the liner notes to their first independently produced release, *Liberation Day* (1998), Ricanstruction provides a list of their musical and political heroes, to whom special "praise" is given: Jah Rastafari, Pedro Albizu Campos, Bad Brains, John Coltrane, Marcus Garvey, Ernesto "Che" Guevara, Mumia Abu-Jamal, Last Poets, Bob Marley, Huey Newton, Miguel Piñero, Public Enemy, Carlos Santana, Betty Shabazz, and El-Hajj Malik El-Shabazz (Malcolm X). With the inclusion of *salseros* such as Willie Colón, Ray Barretto, and Héctor Lavoe, the potent symbol of cultural resistance that salsa represents for Ricanstruction, and other Boricua *rockeros*, is well represented.

The opening song on *Liberation Day*, "Pedro's Grave," begins with a spoken-word recording by Pedro Albizu Campos, founder of the Puerto Rican Nationalist party.[39] By emphasizing the spirituality of social activism rather than regarding themselves as "political," in the sense of being driven by idealistic or utopian goals such as social change or economic empowerment, Ricanstruction maintains a "revolutionary" stance by adhering to punk's nihilism and outright rejection of society at every level. Echoing Malcolm X's famous call for activism and African American solidarity "by any means necessary," Not4Prophet succinctly defines Ricanstruction's political identity and raison d'etre as Puerto Rican by necessity:

> We have to stay Puerto Rican or else we're wiped off the face of the earth. . . . It's the old case of the U.S. wanting the bird cage without the bird, Puerto Rico without the Puerto Ricans. . . . We don't have the privilege to be simply human, which is what we want to be. . . . We're forced to be political in order to survive.[40]

Ricanstruction's approach to "marketing" their music—a term they abhor for its capitalist connotations—focuses on a grassroots level of community participation and outreach. They independently produce and record their music, for which sole ownership is proudly claimed. Distribution is handled through alternative channels, such as leftist political organizations, bookstores, and involvement with other progressive groups with whom they sympathize or affiliate (for example, the National Committee to Free Puerto Rican Prisoners of War and Political Prisoners, La Resistencia, Refuse and Resist). Their recordings are made available, along with other revolutionary literature and paraphernalia, at live performances and on their Web site (http://www.ricanstruction.net).

Ricanstruction performs at political rallies, benefits, and Latino cultural centers throughout the New York metropolitan region, up and down the Eastern United States, and in Puerto Rico. In 1998 the band accepted an invitation to perform in El Salvador for the anniversary celebrations and party functions hosted by the FMLN. More recently, their involvement with the Vieques controversy included performances on the island, participation in protests against the U.S. Navy bombing exercises, and the production of the film "punkumentary," *Ricanstructing Vieques* (1999), highlighting the band's solidarity with island residents. Their audiences reflect a diversity of race, class, and ethnic social groups:

> If we courted anybody it was primarily street kids.... We had a lot of white punks, who simply came because they liked the music and then we gave them the message. So what ended up happening was that we started to have audiences that were mixed, white, black, Latino, non-Latino, homeless, male, and female.[41]

Not4Prophet's lyrics address topical urban issues such as racism, unemployment, and the shortage of affordable housing for Latinos in *el barrio*. "Breakfast in Amerika," for example, deals with squatting—the act of taking illegal residence in an abandoned or empty building. For Not4Prophet, this is a symbolic act of anticolonialism at the local level, one he encourages as a necessary strategy for undermining the gentrification of the *barrios,* which he considers a threat to the survival of New York's Puerto Rican communities:

> Barrio in barricades without a reason
> rounded up in midnight raids and shot for treason
> mothers, daughters, fathers, sons
> placed in detention bullets beatings
> torture guns too cruel to mention

Ricanstruction's Arturo Rodriguez (bass) and Not4Prophet (vocalist) onstage at CBGB, New York City, August 2002. Photograph by Sam LaHoz, © Sam LaHoz.

> sons of bitches wanted I to tell them my mission
> jury declared that I should die for sedition
> didn't they know that I was just sleeping?
> Oye hermano mi canción y siga p'alante la revolución
> coño despierta mi gente

One of the most salient aspects of Ricanstruction's music is also evident in "Breakfast in Amerika's" rhythmic complexity and exceptional musicianship. Beyond punk rock's strident power-chords and frenzied drumming, adherence to Latin musical elements is discernible in Ricanstruction's use of syncopation, anticipated beats, and rhythmic shifts. Song structures and durations are atypical of hard-core punk—which is more often brief and to the point—as the band injects a Latin-flavored "swing" that breaks away from the rigidity of the even, 4-beat, up-tempo meters found in most punk rock. The salsa-based call and response *soneo* section, in which Not4Prophet has the role of *sonero*, and shouts out the names of several Central and Latin American nations, with the responsorial chorus of the band members shouting back "Despierte!" (Wake up!), creates a distinctly modern *montuno* with a neo-punk rock feel that rallies forth pan-Latin solidarity.

Ricanstruction also performs cover versions of what Not4Prophet describes as "homage songs"; these include Bob Marley's "Redemption Song," Billie Holiday's "Strange Fruit," and "Independiente" by the highly regarded 1970s political salsa band La Protesta, as well as other politically inflected salsa songs by Willie Colón and Ray Barretto. In addition, the band attaches great importance to acknowledging and strengthening interracial bonds between themselves and African Americans; the identification with the militant pro–black power stance of rapper Chuck D of Public Enemy is particularly trenchant. In a recent collaboration between Ricanstruction and Chuck D, shared experiences of police brutality, economic poverty, and political disenfranchisement are expressed in the rap and punk diatribe "Love+Revolution":

> Cara, cuerpo, corazón, en la cuna de Babylon
> amor es tu conspiración y tú y yo revolución
> born in the bottom of Sodom another sling shot
> dropped in the rot and forgot blessed as a have not[42]

Drawing from a nexus of ideologies and Nuyorquino socio-musical experiences, Ricanstruction foregrounds island and world justice political struggles. Their musical and philosophical formulation is based on punk aesthetics and radical politics and reflects a syncretic model of multicultural and popular sources which inform current processes of Boricua identity formation in the diaspora.

The Politics of Marketing

Rock's increasing circulation on the island via intense mass-media promotion has enabled its gradual and widespread acceptance among young Puerto Ricans, who currently endorse both popular and alternative rock forms without the need to explain or reconcile ethnic, race, or class differences. Their musical tastes, however, are not segmented into distinct or clearly defined market categories, as previously assumed. This is particularly evident in current commercial radio programming, which consists primarily of salsa, *música tropical,* romantic *baladas,* and mainstream North American and English classic rock, along with a marked and steady rise in the amount of local, island-produced rock programming. "This past year [2001] has proved very positive for *rock nacional.* In radio, some stations have made space in their programming for *rock en español,* while another has dedicated itself completely to the genre."[43]

Music industry marketing strategies of BR vis-à-vis *rock en español* presents an interesting set of issues. Puya's manager, Kevin Benson, explains that the *rock en español* label is simply a marketing term that, after more than a dozen years of use by the U.S.-based recording industry, has finally gained widespread currency. He notes, however, that *rock en español* bands are limited to specific marketing regions by the music industry, resulting in sparse radio airplay of those bands within the United States. Jorge LaBoy, who has witnessed many of the transitions in rock on the island since the 1970s, describes the importance of *rock en español*'s advance into Puerto Rico:

> Rock is much more accepted now . . . because it started to sound a bit more right in Spanish. You have to remember that in Puerto Rico you have so much more of an American influence than in those other countries. It took all these years for the lyrics to kind of fit into the music. . . . In the 1970s I wouldn't dare to sing rock in Spanish, it sounded so weird. But since bands in Argentina, like Soda Stereo, and in 1983 when I went to Chile, and it was very big there, people like Charly García, Fito Páez, and all those guys were doing rock in Spanish . . . [in Latin America] they would just sing in Spanish no matter what . . . this style of singing was already developing.[44]

LaBoy's comments draw attention to the highly nuanced politics of language in the context of rock in Puerto Rico. Unlike their *rock en español* peers, for whom English is still a foreign language, Boricua *rockeros* use Spanish, English, or both, to convey Boricua identity in fluid yet unequivocal terms, even as intertextual readings are enhanced. The sociologist Juan Flores writes that "bilingualism as practiced by Puerto Ricans on both sides of *el charco* . . . constitutes an intricate tactic and strategy of response and assertion, with deep poetic and political implications."[45]

Ironically, the success of the most recent Latin pop wave (for example, Ricky Martin, Marc Anthony, Jennifer López), together with the demographics of growing Latino/a youth audiences, have made Latin rock an enticing commodity, ready to be packaged for mass-market consumption. The music industry, however, has been unable to cope with the complicated questions of language and nationality, and thus it is not surprising that it perceives two market segments: (1) the bilingual North American rock market, and (2) the Spanish-language Latin American rock market. In each, vastly differing degrees of politicized consciousness are either presumed, negated, or denied. Ed Morales feels that *rock en español* promoters should concentrate more on selling Latin rock to New York Latinos. He views excessive target market segmentation (for example, dividing MTV Latino into two separate programming regions) as an example of the music industry's narrow-minded and short-sighted strategy.[46] In efforts to develop industry networks and marketing strategies of their own, independent Latin rock musicians, record companies, producers, promoters, and booking agents have formed special-interest groups such as the Latin Alternative Music Conference (LAMC) and, in Puerto Rico, the Neo Rock Coalition (NRC).

Whether Boricua *rockeros* will be able to capitalize on the commercial success of mainstream Latin popular and rock artists remains to be seen, particularly since, according to music journalist Soto Torres, the industry remains largely uncommitted to marketing BR, either in Puerto Rico, a demographically inconsequential market by industry standards, or on the mainland. The role of BR within industry strategies to reach new pan-Latin international markets is still unclear: despite having made considerable inroads on the island, BR has not yet "proven" itself in international or mainland U.S. markets—certainly not to the extent that *rock en español* has in Mexico, Argentina, or Spain.

Conclusion

While rock is sometimes spoken of as an international language, a phenomenon not limited to a specific regional, national, or pan-Latin market or audience, in fact, BR is very much attached to place—the island of Puerto Rico, New York City, and other puertorriqueño diasporas—and to cultural politics. Boricua *rockeros* are aware that BR falls in between the cultural divide between Anglo–North American and pan-Latin rock markets (for example, "heartland" rock vs. *"rock en español"*). They understand industry marketing schemes, and that BR occupies an industry limbo, being neither sufficiently "Latin" nor "Anglo" in musical or narrative content. This problematic is consistent with a historical continuum that perpetuates Puerto Rico's marginalization based upon notions of national and cultural purity or authenticity. Thus, while *música jíbara* continues to hold a nostalgic sentimentality for many Puerto Ricans as the island's unofficial "national" music, and *músicas típicas* such as *bomba* and *plena* continue to be embraced as reflections and symbols of Puerto Rico's interracial and ethnic pluralism, *rockeros* such as Puya, Vivanativa, and La Secta All Star demonstrate the possibility for cross-cultural market appeal both within and outside the mainstream music industry.[47]

Despite the music industry's past failures to adequately market BR in the United States and beyond, young Boricua musicians have displayed a strong sense of autonomy, community, and political awareness, and they seem poised to participate within the international music industry and to establish a *rock nacional puertorriqueño.* Using conventional musical forms, as well as experimenting with hybrids—by drawing from punk and heavy metal to rap and salsa (or any of their many emerging variants)—BR is clearly performing a significant cultural function for young *puertorriqueños,* serving as a catalyst for contemporary Puerto Rican social and cultural change. As Susan McClary suggests, the self-conscious and unapologetic constructedness of music and images by today's artists does not signal artificiality or necessarily imply cynicism, but rather, "it can register confidence in the power of human signs to shape social reality."[48] Considering the musical production of contemporary BR bands in the context of *puertorriqueño* identity and its evolving relationship to rock and the music industry, it is easy to see the music's significance for articulating social and political realities, including ongoing tensions and conflicts. While not all BR can be described as political or nationalistic, sociopolitical messages specific to the Puerto Rican experience remain intensely meaningful for *rockeros,* for whom Puerto Rico's history and present development elicit powerful and diverse responses to questions of independence, nationalism, and colonialism.

The meanings we may be able to discern from the details and narratives depend on reading the formation of BR as connected in a practical way to real life.[49] Whether Boricua *rockeros* use the potent anger of thrash-metal-salsa of Puya, the hard-edged protest *trova* of Fiel a la Vega, the confrontational teen punk energy of KonFrontazion, or the extreme leftist denunciation of capitalism of Ricanstruction, BR's significance lies in its communication of a shared, vital sociopolitical and extralocal consciousness that contests and transcends dominant hegemonies as it reasserts and valorizes *puertorriqueño* identity. As Simon Frith put it, with reference to the "myth" of the rock community, "The sociological task is not to expose this myth or to search for its foundations, but to explain why it is so important."[50] Its importance lies in the capacity of Puerto Rican youth to explore and combine neotraditional Puerto Rican and contemporary musical elements in an effort to redefine community and re-create Boricua youth culture, thereby capturing a vision of daily life as it is experienced in a changing and increasingly homogenous and globalized worldscape.

Selected Discography

Canción para Vieques. Various artists. 2001. Produced by T. Auger and R. Laureano.
Fiel a la Vega. *Fiel a la Vega.* 1996. CPC Records 60401.
———. *A quien pueda interesar.* 1998. Joripatipe.
———. *Tres.* 1999. EMI Latin Records H2 7243 5 21809 2 9.

Konfrontazion. *Soy el antirégimen.* 1999. Produced by KonFrontazion.
Puya. *Union.* 2001. MCA Records 088 112 362 2.
———. *Fundamental.* 1999. MCA Records 11859.
Ricanstruction. *Abu Jamal.* 1998–2002. AWOL 001.
———. *Liberation Day.* 1998. CBGB Records 02.
———. *Operation: Bootleg, Live at CBGB, NYC.* 2001. Audiovisual Terrorism.

The Politics and Anti-Politics of Uruguayan Rock

ABRIL TRIGO

What is the difference between metropolitan rock and rock from the periphery? Is it just a matter of local tonality? Where does one locate a differential when the copy is as good as the original? These are key questions, whose many possible answers shed light on problems that have haunted Latin American thought and are situated at the center of Latin American cultural studies. If metropolitan rock, according to conventional definitions, is caught in a dichotomy of either repudiating or reproducing mainstream ideological values, of resisting or being co-opted by the "capitalist machine," of being marginalized from or assimilated to a hegemonic cultural system, then what is the *differential,* the *surplus,* the *excess* that makes peripheral rock "almost the same but not quite," as Homi Bhabha would put it? In other words, if English-language rock performed in the "centers" of global capitalism lies somewhere between pop and the pop*ular,* where is rock that is performed in the "peripheries" of global capitalism situated? Taking the case of Uruguay, this essay offers an historical analysis in an effort to address this fundamental, and perhaps irresolvable, question.

It has become a commonplace among cultural studies scholars to say that rock is "closer to the Unconscious," which explains why "sound would be the site of authenticity, for it is in sound that the very construction of identity takes place."[1] This essentialization has encouraged the mystification of rock as a countercultural apparatus, characterized by a rebellious, oppositional, and contentious politics of the body. Accordingly, rock is not always examined as a cultural product tied to specific social powers, geopolitical locations, technological centers, and modes of production, circulation, and consumption. Instead, it is generally celebrated either for its transgressive qualities and the democratic recovery of suppressed memories, or for its pathos of authenticity and open defiance of the culture industry apparatus.[2] In other words, rock is viewed as embodying an inherent resistance to capitalism. Yet this populist approach can also lead to a non-essentialist understanding of rock as a postwar musical culture "produced by a reconfigured music industry for an audience, self-consciously defined . . . by a system of generational and social differences. On this model, rock is music made explicitly for youth. . . . In either case, the socio-cultural field divided by youth's differences is always also divided by structures of class, race and gender. Out of this diversity, a variety of rock cultures are constructed."[3]

Although in the above quotation, Lawrence Grossberg is referring exclusively to the Anglo-Saxon world, he is aware that the strength of rock culture in part depends upon its ability to be articulated to specific locations. Moreover, he explains its oppositional character as a particular form of ideology, "often interpreted as rock's inextricable tie to resistance, refusal, alienation, marginality."[4] This ideology of authenticity "not only draws an absolute distinction between rock and 'mere' entertainment, it says that it is that difference that enables rock to matter," even though there are many forms of rock authenticity, "the center versus the margin, the mainstream versus the periphery, commercial versus independent, resistant versus co-opted."[5]

If metropolitan Anglo-Saxon rock has been historically imbued by an ideology of authenticity and opposition, this ideological tendency should be even more pertinent in the peripheries of global capitalism, where rock's class and generational tensions are magnified under acute conditions of social inequality, uneven and dependent modernization, and the clash with local and national cultural traditions. However, it is important to be cautious about this line of analysis, for it nurtures two opposing though complementary mystifications: on the one hand, the uncritical celebration of rock by neopopulists as a resistant cultural machine inherently clashing with the sociopolitical status quo; and on the other, the music's co-optation as a global ideological device produced by the transnational culture industry, as maintained by some heirs of the Frankfurt School. The consequences of these mystifications, which confuse the dynamics of capitalism with ideological or political agendas, are quite obvious: rock either endorses economic globalization and its ideological byproduct, the pseudo-egalitarian ideology of neoliberalism, or it is entrenched in national traditions that dismiss emergent modes of transculturation.[6] It is my contention here that rock, like other cultural phenomena in

Latin America, is a contested field of struggle for the symbolic reproduction of social reality, disputing and realizing, through cultural means, political hegemony. Consequently, rock does not have any intrinsic social, cultural, political, or ideological value per se. Rather, assigning such value always hinges on the intersection of local, national, and transnational economic, cultural, and political forces. To make rock in Latin America is, and has always been, an ambiguous, ambivalent, and agonizing experience; to make rock in Latin America is to place oneself, cynically or defiantly, in the center of the ideological and cultural maelstrom of globalization.

According to Marx, production implies the (objective) consumption of raw materials and the (subjective) consumption of the producer's faculties. This is called "productive consumption" or, simply, production. However, consumption is also production, for consumption implies the basic transformation of things. Consumption is production in two basic ways: objectively, it realizes the product by annihilating it ("the product . . . becomes a product only through consumption"), and subjectively, it creates the necessity for new products when it "posits the object of production as an internal image, as a need, as drive, and as purpose."[7] This moment in productive consumption (the reproduction of needs and desires) is the foundation of consumerism, inferred as the suspended satisfaction of desire. Thus, while productive consumption shows that the producer also consumes (for example, the omnivorous and homogenizing appropriation of local music by transnational world music), consumptive production demonstrates that the consumer is also a producer (for example, the selective adoption of world music and its transculturation to local heterogeneity). Concretely, though all varieties of rock in the periphery are necessarily produced from the consumption of globally rendered and distributed rock (that is, "consumptive production"), they display different degrees of productive autonomy (that is, "productive consumption"). Thus, the question becomes, if a certain degree of control over the means of production guarantees the local, national, or ethnic character of a cultural product, does a lack of control suggest a categorical indication of neocolonial dependence? And what is it that determines that rock, produced locally, can be distributed globally? In other words, what qualities should rock have in order to qualify for global consumption?

Beginnings (1960–1969)

There are three very different aesthetic trends in rock, all with an enduring impact, that originated in the period 1960–69 in Uruguay: the international melodic pop that is represented by the band Los Iracundos (Angry Men); the

Beatles-influenced style, sung in English, whose most outstanding example is Los Shakers; and the experimental *candombe*-beat of such performers as Eduardo Mateo, Rubén Rada, and El Kinto Conjunto.

Los Blue Kings (later to be called Los Iracundos) was formed in the provincial city of Paysandú in 1960 by a group of middle-class teenagers. In 1963 they participated in the Festival de la Canción de Parque del Plata, an international festival held at a beach resort forty miles from Montevideo, which also featured popular singers from the Argentinean TV program *El Club del Clan*, including Violeta Rivas, Palito Ortega, and Johnny Tedesco. There, the band was discovered by representatives of RCA Argentina, who brought them to Buenos Aires, changed their name, and modified the members' appearance by dressing them in black leather pants and jackets and dark glasses. These changes were utterly incongruous with the bland, melodic music and romantic lyrics Los Iracundos played, yet their first album met with amazing success. The band soon became an international hit, and since then, has been touring continuously throughout South America. They have released approximately forty albums and starred in several movies. In 1967 they went to Italy, where they recorded an album using more advanced technology and temporarily became part of the Italian pop scene. On their way back to South America, they performed in a show of Latin American music at Madison Square Garden in New York City. From 1967 to 1971, at the prime of their career, they released such major hits as "Es la lluvia que cae" ("It's the Rain That's Falling"), "Va cayendo una lágrima" ("Shedding A Tear") and "Puerto Montt" ("Port Montt"), which have since become classics of Latin American popular music. Forty years since they began, Los Iracundos have survived the death of lead singer and composer Eduardo Franco in 1989, as well as the retirement of two of their six founding members. Faithful to their original sound, they continue to play their old hits and to record new songs that carry on a familiar sound for their scores of aging fans, who, organized in clubs and by radio programs, still follow the band from the remote corners of Latin America.

The extraordinary success Los Iracundos enjoyed in the late 1960s and their lasting career since then are explainable by several reasons. For one, at the height of the youth rebellion that spread from Paris to Mexico, from Berkeley to Montevideo, Los Iracundos, despite their name, produced soft pop ballads related to what, back then, was called "international melodic music." The tempestuous Latin America of the late 1960s was criss-crossed by revolutions and military coups, fast-paced modernization and mass-media globalization, religious angst and political optimism, not to mention the rock invasion and rise of the folk protest song movement. In this climate, Los Iracundos offered to Latin American middle-class youth a professionally competent modern sound that fused the romantic melodies of a Charles Aznavour with the instrumental arrangements of a Ray Conniff, the beat of soft rock with the romantic treatment of youth's dilemmas. As Leonardo Franco, one of the original members, boasted in a 1999 interview: "There is no home in Latin America without a record of Los Iracundos. . . . We are not number one anymore because we're not fashionable, but our music is all around Latin America. What counts is that we sell many records and we fill stadiums."[8]

It was 1963 when the Fattoruso brothers (Hugo and Osvaldo), along with Caio Carlos Vila and Pelín Roberto Capobianco heard the Beatles for the first time on a record they received from a sailor. These very young musicians (Osvaldo was only thirteen) made up the Hot Blowers band, which played at local jazz clubs and bars in the Montevidean red-light district near the harbor. After they saw *A Hard Day's Night* (1964), the band was transformed and Los Shakers were born. Talented and seasoned musicians, well trained in playing different kinds of music and instruments, they were able to reproduce the Beatles' sound in competent renditions and thus led the wave of Beatlemania in Uruguay. Having performed at Punta del Este, they were invited to come to Buenos Aires by a producer for EMI-Odeón Argentina. Following their first recording session, they were offered a contract. At that time, 1964, the musical scene in Buenos Aires was dominated by the pop singers of the *Club del Clan* and the "new wave": not a single band was able to produce the kind of "foreign" sound with professional quality offered by Los Shakers. Yet their first recordings—cover versions of the Beatles—failed to sell, and true success came only after release of a single that featured two of their own compositions, "Break It All" and "More." Although the sound was still Beatles-like and they "didn't quite know what the 'shake' was, it was just a gimmick," the songs were very good indeed.[9] They were not mere imitation, but captured the flair of the Beatles while bringing to the surface a distinct style in a broken, tongue-in-cheek peripheral English. After the release of their first album in 1965 (all original songs), they led a hectic schedule, playing at several venues every night and starring in the weekly television show *Escala Musical*. Touring extensively in Latin America, they shortly became international rock stars and teen idols. In 1966, they recorded *Break It All*, which was released in the United States and Australia. Another album, *Shakers for You*, came out in Argentina. It followed the Beatles' evolution in *Rubber Soul* and *Revolver* but also reflected the influence of other British and U.S. bands, as well as a resurgence of the band's bossa nova roots.

Osvaldo Fattoruso remembers that the band soon got tired of "playing at being the Beatles" ("Estábamos cansados de jugar a los Beatles").[10] Despite their wide commercial success, the band felt they were reproducing a formula that was clearly an artistic dead end. Other bands had appeared both in Argentina and Uruguay who were singing in Spanish and were also experimenting with local rhythms and exploring other poetic forms. The band's final album, *La conferencia secreta del Toto's Bar* (*The Totos' Bar Secret Conference*)—whose title parodies the infamous conference of Punta del Este of 1962, in which Cuba was officially expelled from the Organization of American States—is considered a masterpiece of Latin American rock of the 1960s. Tired of being exploited by EMI-Odeón, at the time they recorded the album the band had already decided to split up. Perhaps it is for that reason, and despite the pressures of their record company to produce more surefire hits, that they felt freer to experiment with the music. The album's songs combine the band's old passions for bossa nova and jazz (what they called *calimbo*) with popular traditional local genres like tango, *candombe*, and *murga*, and includes some powerful arrangements à la John Coltrane and *bandoneón* solos à la Astor Piazzolla played by Capobianco. Before disbanding, the group performed some extraordinary rock renditions of traditional carnival themes from the 1930s for the popular Montevidean TV program, the *Discódromo Show*. Afterward, Pelín Capobianco went to Brazil to play classical music, Caio Vilas went to Venezuela to become a musical producer, and Hugo and Osvaldo Fattoruso went to the United States, where they formed Opa, a band that fused *candombe* and jazz. Opa eventually played with such musicians as Milton Nascimento, Chico Buarque, Fito Páez, and Luis Alberto Spinetta.

What is the legacy of the two bands chronicled here? Los Iracundos, despite their popularity across class and generational barriers, did not generate any progeny in Uruguay (although they did in other countries); Los Shakers, during their heyday, had many imitators. However, four decades later, Los Iracundos are still playing and they have fans in remote corners of Latin America, although their records are hardly played in Uruguay. Los Shakers, on the other hand, notwithstanding their disappearance from the music scene more than thirty years ago, are surrounded by a sort of aura, and the Fattoruso brothers played an active role in the renaissance of the local music scene after their return to Uruguay in the early 1980s. Despite considerable differences, both Los Iracundos and Los Shakers employed neocolonial mimicry (the counterpart of the latter were Los Mockers, who mimicked the Stones), which brought about an inevitable and necessary transculturation of the ultimate wave of modernity for a Europeanized but peripheral youth who desperately wanted to be modern. The bands' mimicry demonstrated that if modernity was imitable, it could be surpassed. Such mimicry squarely departed from consumptive production and the equalization of differences demanded by transnational corporations, and represented an ambivalent and ironic positionality "that is almost the same, but not quite." Although the bands did not sow the ground for this ironic stance, they did plow it, in turn closing the floodgates of a cultural inferiority complex. Only hard-line nationalists and traditional leftists were not able to understand how somebody could grow long hair or wear a miniskirt, sing tango by heart, dance to rock 'n' roll, love soccer, and belong to the Communist Youth—all in complete harmony.

A new aesthetic and an exploratory incursion into productive consumption was later opened by the experimental work of Eduardo Mateo, Rubén Rada, and the short-lived band El Kinto Conjunto. Mateo, a bohemian who stubbornly resisted the seductions of fame and money, died in 1990 in extreme poverty, yet he is considered by many to be the guru of contemporary Uruguayan rock and its truest transculturator. While Los Iracundos and Los Shakers were both promoted by transnational record companies, made movies, and toured Latin America, Mateo, whose music was difficult and esoteric at times, recorded almost reluctantly. His two albums, *Mateo solo bien se lame* (*Mateo Is Okay by Himself*, 1972) and *De cuerpo y alma* (*Body and Soul*, 1984), had limited local distribution. In his compositions, Mateo mixed rock with the local rhythms of tango, *milonga*, and Afro-Uruguayan *candombe*. His passions for bossa nova and bolero, Indian and African music, Miles Davis and Charlie Parker, led him to fuse every rhythm at hand. His anticonformist lyrics, sung in an intimate tangoesque style, brought poetry to the fore, in line with the new song lyricism of the 1970s. This lyricism is reflected, for example, in "Mejor me voy" ("I'd Better Go"):

> Más que ternura tienen tus ojos tristes, penas
> más que cansadas quedan tus manos chicas, muertas
> más que agotada quedas pensando triste, sola
> y en un rincón te quedas mientras un llanto asoma.
>
> (Your sad eyes have more than tenderness, pains
> your small hands remain more than tired, dead
> you keep thinking with sadness more than exhausted, lonely
> and stay in a corner while tears roll down.)

The band El Kinto brought together the very different talents of Mateo and Rubén Rada and became a transcultural machine that changed the music scene in Uruguay for years to come. This duo opened the path to a more political brand of rock while demonstrating the possibilities—though also the limitations—of a different, less dependent mode of cultural production. Although the group broke up in 1969 before finishing their sole album, their experimental interplay of poetic lyricism and polyrhythmic percussion laid the ground for many bands that later experimented with psychedelic rock, blues, and politics, including the *candombe*-rock that would come from Totem and the incomparable voice of Rubén Rada.

The Explosion of *Candombe*-Rock (1970–1973)

Candombe, a musical rhythm and dance that has evolved since colonial times, is the most significant contribution of the Afro-Uruguayan community, which makes up approximately 5 percent of the population, to Uruguayan popular culture. The term *candombe* can be traced back to the eighteenth century, when it designated all dances of African origin, as did the term *tango*. There are at least four stages in the historical evolution of *candombe*, each registering the progressive loss of original religious sources, until the emergence of *candombe*-rock. These are (1) the mythical and ritual dances brought by Afro-Brazilian slaves; (2) the choreographic pantomime of the coronation of the Congo kings, performed during the Christmas season; (3) *candombe*'s assimilation by the end of the nineteenth century into the modern urban carnival; and (4) *candombe*'s territorialization of national popular culture, which includes the emergence of *candombe*-rock.

The presence of blacks in Montevidean carnival can be traced back to the early 1800s, when *comparsas* (masquerades) are mentioned for the first time, including those of "the blacks and their tango."[11] This early phase of carnival lasted until the 1870s, when the *tablados* (street stages) and the *llamadas* (black parades) characteristic of modern carnival were definitively incorporated. The old characters of *candombe* still reign in the *llamadas*, as do the mesmerizing rhythms played by an ensemble of some twenty to forty drums of a barrel-like design arranged in three voices: *chico, repique,* and *piano*. Despite its staging and containment by carnival regulations, *candombe*'s natural habitat continues to be the narrow streets of the traditional black neighborhoods of Palermo and Sur, where the *llamadas* originated in the mid-1800s. In carnival, however, *candombe*'s energies are constrained because the stage imposes a certain discipline, a scenic formation which emphasizes elements that were borrowed from the variety show, such as the *vedettes* (sumptuous women dancers) and the Caribbean rhythms imported in the 1950s. In reality, the climax of carnival *candombe* takes place offstage, when the *comparsa* parades from the stage into the audience and the sound of drums fills the air. Although *candombe* made some inroads in tango orchestras in the 1940s and 1950s, it was only in the late 1960s that it began to be incorporated into popular music, alongside other musical genres, by folk protest singers and the emergent *candombe*-rock.

Rubén Rada, the most famous Afro-Uruguayan entertainer, was a carnival performer when he was an adolescent and is considered the founder, with Eduardo Mateo, of *candombe*-rock. The experimental work of El Kinto was transformed into a full-fledged *candombe*-rock machine by the group Totem, which dominated the music scene of the early 1970s. Nowadays, under the economics of global "world music," we are accustomed to exotic sounds and strange rhythms; under the politics of multiculturalism, we are trained to appreciate them. Thirty years ago, however, one had to be pretty audacious to believe it might be possible to market a local and peripheral sound internationally. It could only be done as part of a larger economic and cultural enterprise, and with the full support of international distribution. Totem's *candombe*-rock was a mature, perfectly balanced production of danceable music, locally inspired though full of worldwide connotations, reminiscent of diverse cultural landscapes, and politically committed to current events. But it did not achieve the kind of international success—beyond some popularity in Argentina and the admiration of critics and connoisseurs—that its members expected. After 1968, a spiral of economic, political, and social crises made for a very difficult and hazardous rock environment: worker strikes and student demonstrations that were violently squelched, and the emergence of the Tupamaro guerrilla movement, brought about a military coup that put an end to Uruguay's democratic system. Somewhat spellbound by a feeling of historical urgency, as well as by a generational sense of duty, many youth channeled their political energies into the folk protest song movement rather than rock. Yet, *candombe*-rock embraced what was in reality a complex and polymorphous cultural revolt, simultaneously socialist and nationalist, Latin Americanist and internationalist: countercultural sensibilities fused with the utopian revolutionary politics of the times. *Candombe*-rock synthesized the vision of the Left and the cosmopolitan and modern demands of youth. By effecting the shift from English to Spanish, incorporating the treatment of local and social subjects, and experimenting with local—folk, traditional, or simply popular—rhythms, *candombe*-rock reflected the nationalization of Uruguayan rock. "Biafra," by Rubén Rada, became a sort of anthem of the genre that helped to forge the anti-colonial identity of a generation while simultaneously recovering an erased Afro-Uruguayan identity:

> Quiero darle un tirón de orejas al hombre
> que piensa en la política y no responde,

que están muriendo niños a borbotones,
que olvide las banderas, piense en el hombre.
Ese que es hoy tu amigo, mañana no será,
porque confía en el lema que vos odiás.
Mientras que Biafra estaba muerta,
muerta de sol y sin pan,
sus crías estaban blancas,
blancas de peste mortal.
Biafra estaba muerta,
nadie allí quizo llegar.
Por unos negros que mueran,
a quien le puede importar . . .[12]

(I want to pull man's ears
because he only thinks in politics and is oblivious
to the mounds of children who are dying.
He should forget about flags and think of manhood.
Your friend today will be your enemy tomorrow
because he believes in what you hate.
Meanwhile Biafra was dead
under the sun, with no bread,
their kids were white,
white of a mortal plague.
Biafra was dead,
and nobody wanted to go there,
who cares about
a few blacks dying . . .)

Listening to *candombe*-rock and folk protest song, a politically and socially committed generation became fully national by feeling international, fully modern by recovering and renewing traditional, popular local culture, and fully committed to rock as a genre by nationalizing and politicizing local rock sounds. Despite the failure of the revolutionary dream, the political mistakes, and the hard times to come, *candombe*-rock helped shape a utopian, generous, and naive counter-imaginary, the closest Uruguay would come to a *rock nacional* similar to Argentina's, where rock was nurtured in its resistance to military dictatorship. After *candombe*-rock, the local and the national cultural scenes were transformed forever; the residual was transcultured through international forms, and new ways of feeling, experiencing, and making culture emerged.

The Politics of Exile and Inxile:
Murga-Rock and Carnival Resistance (1973–1985)

The neofascist military coup of 1973 crushed the dreams of a generation and an entire country. It also brought economic impoverishment, social inequality, and political repression. Incarceration, disappearance, and exile became daily events in everybody's life. Uruguayans became either exiles or inxiles, that is, exiles *within* their own country—socially alienated and politically annulled as citizens by the terror of the regime.[13] Although, under different circumstances, both inxiles and exiles might nurture a counterculture of political resistance, psychological endurance, and social survival, in Uruguay, both resisted cultural and psychological dissociation by taking refuge in cultural memory, endangered by the regime's politics of compulsory amnesia. The preservation, cultivation, and passing on of cultural memory to youngsters cut off from it became the most important task of the times. It was in this milieu that the *canto popular* (popular song) movement emerged. Though linked to the Latin American *nueva canción* (new song), which is characterized both by its "stylized, urban rendition of folk genres rather than the commercial, international pop styles fashionable in industrialized societies" and by its socialist, nationalist, and populist lyrics, *canto popular* differed from *nueva canción* in that it did not originate under the auspices of a progressive political regime, but rather under the most adverse conditions of repression and censorship.[14] Therefore, it did not convey a rousing or propagandistic political message, but instead created a shared discursive space for young people. Since most of the rock musicians had gone into exile, and those who stayed were under constant harassment, rock, in its many forms, tended to masquerade as *canto popular*. In its turn, *canto popular* evolved into an aesthetically heterogeneous, eclectic movement and an experimental compendium of genres, where diverse variations of vernacular jazz and rock, rural folklore, tango, *candombe*, and *murga*, as well as atonal music, had a place, always under the aegis of politically relevant lyrics.

Of all the folk urban rhythms transcultured in *canto popular*, those stemming from carnival, especially *murga*, were most successful in capturing the zeitgeist. *Murgas* are groups of about twenty members who perform satirical sociopolitical songs and dance, using a coded choreography, accompanied by a percussion ensemble composed of drums, cymbals, and bass drum. A few protest songs of the 1960s were based on *murga*, but around 1980, *murgas* went beyond the confines of carnival, selling records and performing at regular theaters year-round. Some reached a highly sophisticated professional quality, which fed a heated argument inside traditional carnival circles about *murga*'s "authenticity." But *murga*'s success was due mostly to its iconoclastic, parodic, and aesthetic malleability. As Mauricio Ubal states, "Carnival fascinates due to its unprejudiced, critical, and satiric language, and its permanent dynamic which brings together in itself almost all art forms and because it has been both a witness and a scourge for Montevideo's conservative cultural system."[15]

The 1979 song "A redoblar" ("Roll the Drums") by Ubal and Rubén Olivera, situated between rock and *canto popular*, became a hymn of resistance to the dictatorship and established new political and aesthetic foundations for the future development of *murga*-rock:

> Volverá la alegría
> a enredarse con tu voz
> a medirse en tus manos
> y a apoyarse en tu sudor.
> Borrará duras muecas pintadas
> sobre un frágil cartón de silencio
> y un aliento de murga saldrá.
> A redoblar muchachos esta noche
> cada cual sobre su sombra
> cada cual sobre su asombro
> a redoblar, desterrando
> desterrando la falsa emoción, el la-la-la
> el beso fugaz, la mascarita de la fe.
> A redoblar muchachos la esperanza,
> que su latido insista en nuestra sangre
> para que ésta nunca olvide su rumbo.
> Porque el corazón no quiere
> Entonar más retiradas . . .[16]

> (Joy will come again
> to entwine itself around your voice
> to be measured in your hands
> to be sustained by your sweat.
> It will erase frozen grimaces painted
> on the fragile mask of silence
> and a breath of *murga* will emerge.
> Roll the drums, guys, tonight
> each one over his shadow
> each one over his astonishment

roll the drums banishing
banishing the false emotion, the la-la-la
the fleeting kiss, the masquerade of faith.
Roll the drums, guys, and redouble hope
so that its beat keeps insisting in our blood
so that it never forgets its way.
Because the heart doesn't want
to intone any more farewells . . .)

Sung almost entirely to the accompaniment of a single, sober, hypnotic bass drum, "A redoblar" reflects in its own structure the carnival *murga* staging: introduction, couplets, and farewell. The introduction, written in the future tense, stresses the certainty of joy or, in other words, the proximity of carnival, in contrast to the political masquerade. The couplets are patterned in three stanzas reiterating the title's motif: "Roll the drums, guys . . ." This is a summons, an exhortation, a shout in an absolute present ("tonight") projected onto the future. The verb *redoblar* has three possible—and metaphorically interrelated—meanings: "to roll the drums," "to redouble" (as in efforts), and "to bend something over." The first stanza combines the meanings of rolling the drums and bending over (their shadows, their astonishment) in order to banish the present (oppressive, spurious) reality. A second stanza concentrates on the beating of drums (carnival drums, war drums?), but imagery of trucks in the night alludes to the nocturnal, political, and clandestinely written graffiti as well as to the itinerary of the *murgas* from one neighborhood stage to another. In the third stanza, the meaning is to redouble hope, accentuated in the beating of blood and heart, as drums in the city. The three meanings of *redoblar* oscillate and combine to empty out into the farewell, where two voices (the soloist and the chorus), two parts (the introduction and the couplets), and two times (the dystopian past and the utopian future) converge and superimpose over the explosive entrance of the entire percussion ensemble, redoubling the meanings while, supposedly, the *murga* departs.

While "A redoblar" seeks to reconstruct the collective imaginary in favor of the future, Jaime Roos's songs of this period, recorded originally in Holland and France, and later released in Uruguay, expressed feelings of estrangement and nostalgia in the culture of exile. Roos's lyrics are catalogs of reminiscences around the theme of *Ubi sunt?* (Where are they?)—memories of the neighborhood, trees in the streets, breezes from the sea, smells of the city, and ghosts from the past. The songs are an elegy and a eulogy to those absent and defeated protagonists, the most accomplished example of which is, perhaps, "Brindis por Pierrot" ("A Toast for Pierrot"). This song was included in a compilation released in Montevideo in 1985, which coincided with the restoration of democracy and established Roos as a major figure on the Uruguayan music scene:

> ¿No lo vieron a Molina
> que no pisa más el bar?
> ¿Dónde está la Gran Muñeca
> que no trilla el bulevar?
> Esta noche es de recuerdos,
> este brindis por Pierrot.
> ¿Volverás Mario Benítez
> con tu Línea Maginot?
> Me voy
> me voy me vivo yendo
> esta noche me hizo vista el tiempo
> en las copas me dieron changüí.
> Me llevo
> como un capricho burdo
> la esperanza escondida en el zurdo
> que el diablo se apiade de mí.
> Se van
> se van se siguen yendo
> cuesta abajo los sacude el viento
> como hojas de un sueño otoñal.
> Levanto
> mi vaso por las dudas
> a veces la suerte me ayuda
> nadie golpea al zaguán . . .[17]

> (Didn't you see Molina,
> who doesn't come to the bar anymore?
> Where is Big Doll
> who no longer walks the boulevard?
> Tonight is for remembering,
> this toast is for Pierrot.
> Mario Benítez, will you come back
> with your Maginot Line?
> I'm leaving
> I'm leaving, I keep on leaving.
> Tonight, time looked me right in the eye

in the drinks they cut me a break.
I'm taking
like a stupid whim
hope hidden in my heart
may the devil have mercy on me.
They're leaving
they're leaving, they keep on leaving,
the wind blows them downhill
like leaves in some autumnal dream.
I raise
my glass just in case
sometimes luck helps me out
no one knocks at the door . . .)

"Brindis por Pierrot" evokes characters, events, and places in the Montevidean geocultural landscape and the mythology of carnival with tangoesque nostalgia. It alludes to exile and the loss of referents in a disrupted society: those who have left and are about to leave the country are invoked by Pierrot in a toast for a mythical past, vanished forever. Thus, the text operates on the deep layers of a dormant cultural memory, entrenched in minuscule events from the tabloids and obscure neighborhood characters. The musical component meanwhile recalls a carnival atmosphere, which in turn evokes the symbolic recuperation of life through carnival stages. By making use of the cyclical ritual of carnival and its popular urban mythology, Roos reconstructs the shadows of a past lost forever in the folds of memory, where utopia keeps on living. While Roos's music updates the traditional, his lyrics traditionalize the present; while his sound carnivalizes pop music, his lyrics sublimate carnival as paradise lost; while his music deploys an irreverent carnivalization of rock and rock-and-rollization of carnival, his lyrics spin around a melodramatic nostalgia for an idyllic past. From this internal contradiction between the melodramatic and the spectacular, the satirical and the solemn, the traditional and the modern, the local and the global, all kept in suspense through the interplay of lyrics and music, *murga*-rock's characters keep on coming to us.

The Restoration of Democracy and the Anti-Politics of *Rock del Arrabal* (1985–1990)

With the demise of the dictatorship and the restoration of democracy in 1985, the countercultural and oppositional politics played by *canto popular* were no longer needed. In the interstices, despite or even against *canto popular*, a new kind of rock, produced for and sometimes made by unemployed youth from the lower urban sectors, broke onto the scene. This post-dictatorial rock, a de-territorializing machine of cultural banditry, appropriated cultural icons and regurgitated them mixed with trash, to the horror of traditionalists, as in the version of "Cambalache"—a classic tango by Enrique Santos Discépolo, itself an emblem of bohemian existentialism in the River Plate—by Los Estómagos (the Stomachs). Despite their aggressive antinationalism, the rockers' stance with respect to hegemonic culture is ambiguous, inasmuch as the profanation of national symbols always implies an explicit recognition of cultural heritage. This shows an accommodating, subcultural stance, in contrast to the politically contentious, countercultural strategy of *canto popular*. Although both countercultures and subcultures do oppose hegemonic cultures, the first poses a strategic, alternative opposition; the latter resists hegemony from within, by means of erratic, subversive tactics.

Given its subcultural strategy, *rock del arrabal* (rock of the slums) is simultaneously an ideological coming to terms with the counterculture of exile and inxile, a subversion of national culture, and a cannibalization of transnational pop culture. It is a triple articulation and questioning of hegemonies expressed as style in the expropriation and re-signification of equivocally hegemonic cultural texts. *Rock del arrabal* cannibalizes and regurgitates all sorts of music, from tango to reggae, from *milonga* to ska, from the Beatles to the Shakers, thus practicing a transculturation realized at the instant and in the act of consumption of whatever is at hand, as consumptive production. Aware of their own relationship to transnational pop culture, these songs produce a culture of consumers, an aesthetics of recycling, and a politics of bricolage. The back cover of the album *Las berenjenas también rebotan* (*Eggplants Bounce, Too*), by La Chancha Francisca, reads:

> La Chancha Francisca come porquerías
> y las convierte en el salame tan exquisito
> que ustedes mastican.
> La Chancha Francisca no es idiota.
> La Chancha Francisca vende lo que produce
> pero no se vende a sí misma,
> y como es un animal,
> por más que esté domesticado,
> hace caca, pichí y fornica a la vista del público,
> y eso es un escándalo
> porque la ley lo prohíbe.[18]

(Francisca The Sow eats garbage
and changes it into that exquisite salami
you all chew.
Francisca The Sow isn't an idiot.
Francisca The Sow sells what she produces
but doesn't sell out,
and since she is an animal,
no matter how tame she is,
she shits, pees and fornicates in full public view,
and that is a scandal
because the law forbids such behavior.)

The aggressiveness of groups like Los Estómagos and Los Traidores (the Traitors) produced a clashing, "busted-up" combination of heavy metal and punk rock in open contrast to *candombe*-rock and *murga*-rock. Unlike the eclectic fusion music that called on a traditional middle-class public, "'80s rock convey[ed] a lived experience without precedent . . . a frontal, purposeful break" with everything associated, no matter how loosely, with the status quo.[19] Its uglifying aesthetic (melodic minimalism, frenetic and syncopated beat, conceptual lyrics, monotonous and shouted vocals drowned out by the instruments' volume) is a praxis of clash scorning any ideological discourse; a trash-heap aesthetic for semi-marginal youths, blue-collar workers, and students from impoverished middle classes, who feel themselves represented by this "self-absorbed," psychotic, "cracked" rock. It would be wrong, however, to interpret *rock del arrabal* as skeptical disregard for politics and an individual surrender to neoliberal consumerism.[20]

Estoy viviendo en un sueño
una dulce pesadilla
corremos sin movernos
huimos y no hay salida.
Y éste es hoy su lugar
su tan querido basural.
Aquí he muerto una vez más
ya no me atraparán.
Pero a pesar de todo
de algo estoy todavía muy seguro
si es por mí al Uruguay
pueden metérselo en el culo.[21]

> (I'm living in a dream
> a sweet nightmare
> we run without moving
> we flee and there is no exit.
> And nowadays this is your place
> your beloved garbage heap.
> Here I have died once again
> you can't trap me anymore.
> But in spite of everything
> I'm still very sure of one thing
> if it's up to me
> you can take Uruguay and stick it up your ass.)

This brutal state of awareness by groups such as Los Traidores does not lead to apoliticism, as proven by innumerable stands taken on torture, support for human rights offenders, opposition to the foreign debt, and denunciations of poverty and political corruption. Rather than a formal party politics, *rock del arrabal* carries out a critique of everyday life, a negative politics, an excremental politics, a politicization along the edge of politics: an anti-politics. (One notable instance of the intersection between politics and anti-politics is the Luca Prodan Brigade, a group arising from within the Socialist Party that takes its name from an Argentine punk rocker who overdosed.) *Rock del arrabal*'s anti-politics destabilizes politics—the ideological and institutional apparatuses related to the state—by working at the level of the political, "a mobile, nomadic, ubiquitous dimension that can arise in the interior of any social sphere . . . wherever and whenever social identities based on division, enmity and real or potential confrontation are built."[22] *Rock del arrabal* is thus not only a seismograph of hegemonic culture at the global crossroads, but also its lucid questioner. When even the socially progressive of yesteryear are reborn as cynical neoliberals, youth, cornered by frustration, unemployment, migration, and anger, replies with the most corrosive strategy, *rock del arrabal*, as defined by Tabaré Rivero:

> Digo rocanrol cuando estoy caliente,
> cuando quieren hacerme creer
> que la vida es una mierda,
> cuando quieren venderme
> el último grito de la moda.
> Digo rocanrol del arrabal tercermundista,
> el que te pega en el forro,

el que no podés bailar.
Digo rocanrol cuando estoy repodrido,
y digo el de acá, el más pobre,
el que te vuela la tapa de los besos,
el que no podés parar.[23]

(I say rock 'n' roll when I'm mad,
when they want to make me believe
that life is shit,
when they want to sell me
the latest fashion.
I say third world slums rock 'n' roll,
the one that sticks in your craw,
the one you can't dance to.
I say rock 'n' roll when I'm fed up to here,
and I say rock from here, the poorest,
the one that blows the lid off kisses,
the one you just can't stop.)

This "rock from the slums of the world" radicalizes the neoliberal globalization of the periphery, flaunting its marginality, its acculturated culture, its sloppy, trashy, recycled production.[24] If simulacrum and pastiche are the modalities peculiar to postmodernism, parody and satire, despite their rituals of inversion, cannot begin to describe this frizzed *rock del arrabal*, which adds to its fully modern, satirical component an ironic supplement that converts its texts into something like pasticherodies: parodies of postmodern pastiche perched between entertainment and subversion. This is clearly the case of the decadent and nihilist production of Cuarteto de Nos, whose parodic lyrics, ironically sexist humor, soccer choruses, tropical escapades, and gimmicks of global pop, have made them extremely popular. Cuarteto de Nos terrorizes and destabilizes society from its guts, as in the disquieting love story "Eres una chica muy bonita" ("You're a Very Pretty Girl"), which ends up in (a) burlesque (of) tragedy:

Y ahora viene la parte divertida,
no sólo me pica el pito, tengo SIDA.
Maldita pervertida,
me cagaste la vida,
mi vida va en bajada y no en subida.
Y al fin y al cabo todo ha terminado,
lo que en polvo empezó,

en polvo ha acabado.
Pero aunque me ha matado
un polvo bien echado,
polvo seré, mas polvo enamorado.²⁵

(And now comes the funny part,
besides the itching in my dick, I have AIDS.
Damned and perverted woman,
you fucked up my life!
My life goes down, not up.
After all, everything is over,
what started with a dust [an orgasm],
in dust has ended.
But, though a good dust
has killed me,
Dust I will be, but enamored dust.)

Heirs to the satirical tradition of carnival, the sophisticated literary allusions of *canto popular*, and the baroque minimalism of the musician and satirist Leo Masliah, Cuarteto de Nos uses whatever is at hand to parody the culturally sacred, from sexual norms to family values, from ideologies to nationalism, from canonical literature to mainstream popular music. One of their songs, which referred to Uruguayan founding father José Artigas as a bisexual drunkard, provoked an impassioned debate amid charges of pornography, racism, poor taste, and anti-patriotism, until its final censure, despite the Cuarteto's tremendous popularity. They are cultural provocateurs whose music not only deconstructs the status quo, but also their own artistic practice and their musical and literary roots, cooked in black humor, delicious scatology, and the absurdity of everyday life. Born out of an outrageous cannibalization of transnational pop culture, *rock del arrabal* puts forward a local transculturation that overcomes the straitjacket of the national without being caught up in the consumption trap of the global. Made from residues, *rock del arrabal* is simultaneously an excess of transnational pop culture and a black hole in the peripheral nation.

Migrant Rock and New Patterns of Globalization (1990s)

The rock of the 1990s is the outcome of two dissimilar but interrelated phenomena: the side effects of exile and migration, and the new forms that globalized culture adopts in Latin America. I am referring, on the one hand, to the cultural impact of the returnees, particularly of the young people who spent most of their life abroad and who brought with their return a unique cultural baggage. On the other hand, I also speak of the new role that "Latino" music plays as a bridge between global cultural industries and the Latin American markets. Indeed, as a consequence of their increasing weight, the Spanish-speaking migrant communities in the United States were reified at the beginning of the 1980s as "Hispanics" or "Latinos," an imaginary construct with racial connotations, first deployed as a containment device, later employed as marker for a growing consumer market, and, finally, as a potential political electorate.[26] The expansion and rising buying power of the "Latino" consumer market in the United States, in tandem with the attraction—not devoid of exoticism—of U.S. society for the piquant *"sabor latino"* and the expansion of Spanish TV, caught the attention of the large media conglomerates, always in search of new segmented markets. By conflating the aesthetic preferences and cultural traits of certain communities of Latin American migrants with those of other communities, the "Latino" rubric provided for a more homogeneous consumer market. In turn, these same aesthetic preferences and musical tastes were later attributed to the whole of Latin America on the same assumption. In this way, the "Latino" U.S. market became the prototypical testing ground for the production and distribution of so-called "Latino" pop music on a global scale: "Latino" superstars came to represent "Latinidad amid globalization."[27] Through their enormous power of distribution, transnational media conglomerates not only sell "Latino" music to Latin America, but also sell Latin American music that they deem adequately "Latino" in the "Latino" U.S. market. In other words, they contribute to the construction of a "Latino" imaginary and influence, according to strictly marketable criteria, what is "Latino" and what is not.

Two partially convergent trends stem from this dual process of globalization: the playful *rock de agite,* or agit-rock, best represented by the band La Vela Puerca, and the *chilango-charrúa* hip-hop rock of Peyote Asesino (*chilango*, meaning someone from Mexico City, in popular jargon; *charrúa*, meaning natives adopted as imaginary ancestors of modern Uruguay). Despite their different aesthetic and communicational approaches, both bands work through a mode of transculturation which operates from productive consumption, propped up once again from the moment of consumption of, mostly, global culture. However, instead of attempting a parodic synthesis through the fusion of dissimilar components, they arrange these components in a juxtaposed, non-hierarchical, successive manner: "We catch whatever we like. . . . We make our songs from small chunks, which is characteristic of hip-hop, music made of elements from other sources."[28] Indeed, Peyote Asesino, a band named after the character of a Mexican comic strip, in allusion to the fact that half of its members were exiled with their parents in Mexico for several years, produces a brand of hard-core, funky rap whose texts, full of transcultural references, local slang, and global idioms, are composed from recycled scraps following phonetic associations and internal rhymes, rather than according to semantic or syntactic rules. Besides the "normal" psychological and cultural scissions caused by migration, which in the case of these young people has occurred twice, they experience a twofold sense of global aloofness, whose expression matures in the form of a bicultural collage. Interestingly, although their first album is called *Terraja,* their fans in Uruguay are *"chetos,"* middle-class, well-to-do youngsters, and not *"terrajas,"* lower-class youngsters from the *arrabales* (outer-city, working-class neighborhoods). Accused of being "scarcely Uruguayan" and a little snobbish, they answer: "Since we live here, we reflect what happens in this country. You don't need to do anthropology in Barrio Sur to be more Uruguayan."[29]

Likewise, the brand of agit-rock produced by La Vela Puerca and its immediate forerunner, La Abuela Coca, is a mixture of funk, ska, rap, and punk. Also coming from affluent middle-class neighborhoods, they show the influence of Mano Negra and Los Fabulosos Cadillacs, and a special attraction for Caribbean and Brazilian rhythms like merengue, salsa, calypso, samba, *batuque* and *forró*. Agit-rock, despite its anti-political lyrics, is a hot, festive, and danceable music, whose explicit purpose, in sharp contrast to the proletarian or marginal stance of *rock del arrabal*, is to agitate the spirits of the audience and stir their participation. Their live performances are set up like a fiesta, a circus show which starts with a parade of jugglers, flamers, torches, and flags, and ends up in a collective dance to the music of a *candombe* drum ensemble:

> Pará hermano, pará un poquito que estamos de la mente
> mente que busca enroscarse con la gente,
> gente que humilde camina por la calle, calle, calle.[30]
>
> (Stop brother, slow it down 'cause we're out of our mind
> mind that tries to link up with the people,
> simple people who walk in the street, street, street.)

While some thirty people are involved in the show, the band itself has eight or nine musicians, including a brass section composed of alto and tenor sax, flute and trumpet, in order to reproduce the "Latin" mimicry they call *tuco* (red pasta sauce), the cumulative juxtaposition of different genres characteristic of agit-rock. A single song, for example, can alternatively shift from funk rapping to salsa, then samba, calypso and *batuque*, all of them interspersed by jazz tenor sax and rockable guitar solos. The lyrics, similarly, juxtapose local idioms to global motifs, with particular references to U.S. Latinos, as in "Después te explico" ("I'll Explain Later"), by La Abuela Coca: "Listen Latin Boy mi Murderer Sound," or "Común cangrejo" ("Like a/Common Crab") by La Vela Puerca:

> Como un latino envenenado,
> que va diciendo que el futuro es hoy,
> va caminando de costao,
> común cangrejo en plena Nueva York.
>
> (Like an enraged Latino,
> who goes on saying that the future is now,
> he's walking sideways,
> like a crab in the middle of New York.)

This recurrent reference to the "Latinos" in the U.S. is done by Peyote Asesino through linguistic shifts that ambiguously locate and dislocate the subject and its object in the faults between the locus of enunciation and the epistemological locus: "montevideo no es l.a. city / ni vos sos negro, chicano o inmigrante" (Montevideo is not L.A. / nor are you black, chicano, or immigrant)[31]; or, "i warn ya esto no es california . . . this is not for the raza / but for the grasa and the jaterra / from general flores y Guerra.[32] If Spanglish reproduces (or reconfigures?) the shifting between Montevideo and Los Angeles, symptom of a vertical globalization, the shifting between the *lunfardo* Spanish of Montevideo and the *chilango* Spanish of Mexico City would produce a horizontal internationalism against the grain of economic globalization:

> afanamos música negra
> en forma honesta y brutal
> blanquitos
> de mierda
> rapeando y tocando funk
> el Peyote Asesino está acá
> sácate de aquí
> hijo de la chingada
> estoy hasta la madre de tus mamadas
> pinche güey
> ojete ora sí te la mamaste
> ya ni se te para
> de tanto que la jalaste
> órale cabrón no que muy chidín

mejor te sientas bien
que se te arruga el chiquitín
eres un
culero y tu a mí me la pelas
y si no te gusta
chingas a tu abuela.[33]

(We steal black music
in an honest and brutal way
fucking
white boys
rapping and playing funk
Peyote Asesino is here
get out of here
son of a bitch
I'm up to here from your shit
Asshole,
you really fucked up
you can't have a hard-on
after so much jerking off
come on "cabrón" weren't you all that
you better sit up
'cause you are chickening out
you are
a pussy and you're nothing against me
and if you don't like it,
you better fuck your grandma.)

This distasteful and abusive outburst of profanities uttered in *chilango* Spanish expresses a generational malaise across national boundaries and a horizontal internationalism that goes against the grain of globalization. It is a performance style intricately connected to a renewed feeling of Latin Americanism well suited to their festive anti-political denunciations, as illustrated by La Vela Puerca's versions of Latin American folk tunes, their quotations from José Martí, or their furious demand for justice, as in the song "Pinochet" ("death for Pinochet / death for the dictator"), but more clearly so in "El bandido Saltodemata" ("The Bandit-on-the-Run"):

Latinoamérica de colores
yo más me acerco y más huelo olores
Latinoamérica confundida

por los caminos llenos de vida.
Si un latino se esconde
me dicen adónde
para que lo pueda traer
y si el bandido aparece
la gente enloquece
no seas el primero en caer.
Gente bien gente humilde
cansada de palo
no vamó a dejarnó arrastrar.
No te asustes mujer
no te ponga a correr vida mía
esto va a terminar.[34]

(Colorful Latin America
the closer I am the stronger the smells
Latin America, confused
in the roads full of life.
If a Latino is hiding
please tell me where he is
so I can bring him back
and if the bandit shows up
and people panic
don't be the first to fall.
Good people, simple people
tired of being beaten
don't let ourselves be pulled down.
Don't panic woman,
don't run my love,
this is going to end.)

The ambivalent amalgamation of somber anti-politics and frivolous re-politicization, of anti-global mass-mediation and post-nationalistic re-Latin Americanization, reaches its climax in El Peyote Asesino's "UR Gay," a convoluted commentary on national and gender identities, neo-imperial hierarchies, and global disdains inspired by an episode of *The Simpsons*, when someone points to a globe and says "Uruguay" and Bart asks, "You are gay?" Expectedly, the song ends with the hilarious chorus, "Such is life in a tropical country / such is life en el trópico / such is life in a tropical country / such is life en Uruguay."[35]

It is not surprising, therefore, that La Vela Puerca later signed a contract with Sony and Peyote Asesino with Universal Music Latina. With records produced by Gustavo Santaolalla, both bands have enjoyed transnational success in Argentina, Chile, Mexico, Spain, and the United States. This is particularly so in the case of Peyote Asesino, whose video "Mal de la cabeza" ("Sick in the Head") figured among the best of 1998 in MTV Latin America, while "UR Gay" was included in *Spanglish 101,* a compilation of Latin American rock by Kool Arrow Records. Peyote Asesino also appeared on the 1998 cover of the annual review of *Rolling Stone,* Argentina, "From Charly García to Peyote Asesino."

Does the rock of the 1990s close the circle that started in the 1960s? Does Peyote Asesino reproduce the neocolonial mimicry of Los Shakers, this time mediated by *lo latino*? It is not, of course, the same kind of mimicry: the upbeat music and naive lyrics of Los Shakers, full of self-confidence and modernizing optimism, have given way to the ironic music and somber lyrics of Peyote Asesino and La Vela Puerca, fully aware of the folding traps of global dependence and disenchanted with modernity. Similarly, the ambivalent masquerading of Los Shakers' broken English has been replaced by the travesty of Peyote Asesino's Spanglish: once again, the meaning of the lyrics is based more on phonetics than semantics, more in speech than in language. The full circle demonstrates indubitably that economic globalization saturates in an expansive manner practically every instance of cultural production in the periphery. However, it also demonstrates that precisely because of its ominous omnipresence, the paradigm of globalization cannot give by itself a full account of the complexity of cultural phenomena in the periphery, which can only be adequately understood by paying close attention to local historical circumstances in the global scenario. For example, the trajectories of Uruguayan and Argentine rock, though parallel and in dialogue due to their geographical and cultural proximity to one another, nevertheless reveal enormous differences. Today, despite its social and aesthetic affinity to *rock del arrabal*, the Argentine equivalent (*rock chabón*) deploys a completely different kind of politics in accordance with Argentine historical conditionings. As I wrote at the beginning of this article, rock does not have any inherent cultural or ideological value, but rather its meanings depend on historically contingent conditions of possibility. As the rock group Tabaré Riverock Banda reminds us, "He aquí la moraleja" (Here is the moral of the story), like any other cultural product and in its deepest sense, "El rock también es mentira" (Rock is a lie, too).[36]

Selected Discography

La Chancha Francisca. *Las berenjenas también rebotan.* 1989. Orfeo 90897-1.
Los Estómagos. *Tango que me hiciste mal.* 1985. Orfeo 90792-1.
———. *Los Estómagos.* 1987. Orfeo 90886-4.

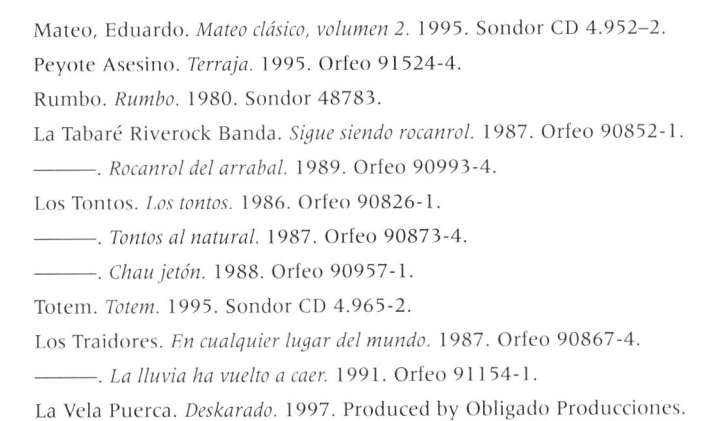

Mateo, Eduardo. *Mateo clásico, volumen 2*. 1995. Sondor CD 4.952–2.
Peyote Asesino. *Terraja*. 1995. Orfeo 91524-4.
Rumbo. *Rumbo*. 1980. Sondor 48783.
La Tabaré Riverock Banda. *Sigue siendo rocanrol*. 1987. Orfeo 90852-1.
———. *Rocanrol del arrabal*. 1989. Orfeo 90993-4.
Los Tontos. *Los tontos*. 1986. Orfeo 90826-1.
———. *Tontos al natural*. 1987. Orfeo 90873-4.
———. *Chau jetón*. 1988. Orfeo 90957-1.
Totem. *Totem*. 1995. Sondor CD 4.965-2.
Los Traidores. *En cualquier lugar del mundo*. 1987. Orfeo 90867-4.
———. *La lluvia ha vuelto a caer*. 1991. Orfeo 91154-1.
La Vela Puerca. *Deskarado*. 1997. Produced by Obligado Producciones.

"A contra corriente"

A History of Women Rockers in Mexico

JULIA PALACIOS AND TERE ESTRADA

Latin American *rockeras* are hot. Finally, the social spaces of rock have seemingly opened, and women have encountered a privileged place inside. The phenomenal popularity of Colombians Shakira, Soraya, and Andrea Echeverri (lead vocalist for Aterciopelados) is one indication of this success. But Mexican *rockeras* have also begun to make their mark, both within the country and abroad. One early forum for female rockers has been the tour De Diva Voz, a small-scale version of Lilith Fair that nevertheless traveled throughout Mexico and parts of the United States, and that helped to launch *rockeras* such as Julieta Venegas and Ely Guerra. Calling Julieta Venegas the Frida Kahlo of rock and roll, Tim Padgett wrote in *Time* that it was "her music, painful but color-splashed, raw and enigmatic, [that] makes Venegas a uniquely Mexican *rockera,* or female rocker." Venegas, the article continued, "has helped turn rock music from a marginalized form into a prominent Mexican idiom."[1] However, despite the fame that Venegas has achieved, the story of *rockeras* in Mexico is not a new one. Since rock's introduction over four decades ago, female *rockeras* have played an important, though often undervalued or unacknowledged role in the history of rock music in Mexico. This essay offers a partial recounting of that often invisible story. We propose here a counternarrative to the dominant narrative of rock in Mexico: the role and place of its *rockeras.*

In a traditionally conservative society such as Mexico, a generalized expectation is that a woman's destiny is to marry, become a mother, and dedicate herself to the care of a husband and home. Despite the growing insertion of middle-class women into the labor market (lower-class women, of course, have long worked for wages), many professional activities are still considered the exclusive domain of men. Rock has been one of them. Indeed, by the 1990s women comprised a mere 10 percent of the musically active rock population.[2] Being a *rockera* implies incorporating oneself into a predominantly masculine world, in which women often are forced to become "one of the boys." By coming into contact with electric instruments, *rockeras* are able to challenge a stereotypical perception of their physical and emotional fragility. Yet in general, female performers are viewed first as women and only secondarily as performers. Given women's underestimation in the music industry, their virtual absence from the histories, biographies, anthologies, and other analyses of the genre in Mexico comes as no surprise.

Mexicans first began dancing to rock 'n' roll around 1955 when the imported rhythm was incorporated as a new musical style within the existing musical traditions of *danzón*, rumba, mambo, merengue, bolero, and cha-cha and performed by the well-known orchestras and dance bands of the time. The audience for these dance bands, however, was still mostly adults. At the same time, *vedettes* (exotic female dancers) performed in cabarets, nightclubs, and burlesque halls, incorporating rock 'n' roll into their own repertoires, which at that time featured many Afro-Caribbean dance styles. One of these young *vedettes* was Gloria Ríos. Often billed as the "creator of rock and roll" in Mexico, she played an important role in popularizing the new rhythm during the second half of the 1950s. According to José Gutiérrez Maya, Ríos "adapted perfectly to fashionable rhythms. . . . She knew how to assimilate rock and roll's new rhythm and introduce it in Mexico."[3] She was the first to record a Spanish-language cover of a rock 'n' roll song—"Hotel de los corazones rotos" ("Heartbreak Hotel"); while in another song, "La mecedora" ("Rocking Chair"), she combined both Spanish and English in the lyrics. She also participated in films that helped to popularize the new rhythm.

During this same period, Mexico was undergoing a rapid transformation in which old conservative values were converging, not without some tension, with new values and fashions that were imported along with the so-called American Way of Life. Women were expected to faithfully preserve their virginity until marriage; amid such strong sexual repression, an unchaste woman was considered almost a prostitute. In a moralization campaign that permeated all levels of Mexican society, the Church and conservative watchdog groups such as the Mexican League of Decency denounced "that modern dance" which appeared to be corrupting youth. Ela Laboriel, a solo singer and the sister of Johnny Laboriel, the lead vocalist of the 1960s rock 'n' roll band

Los Rebeldes del Rock, remembers how she felt supervised and controlled by her parents, and criticized by friends and neighbors because of her participation in the youth environment:

> The rock and roll atmosphere didn't please parents. For them, rock and rollers were monsters with big hairdos and electric guitars. The opinion of the mothers was the deciding factor; in fact, they considered parties in record shops a waste of youth, so they organized themselves and got rid of them. My dad cut Johnny's hair and ran him out of the house. . . . Johnny used to tell me my place was at home and that I should be knitting or sewing. "You were born to be married, to see to your husband and children; until then, have fun playing the little singer," he would warn me. . . . In those days, *machismo* was very deep-rooted. My friends from school or from childhood stopped talking to me because I was an artist and that meant being a whore, and to make matters worse, being black meant being easy.[4]

As Parménides García Saldaña would write several years later, women carried the family's honor between their legs and were expected to uphold that honor.[5]

But from the start, women were an integral (if later, overlooked) element of the burgeoning rock 'n' roll youth scene. One important group was the female quintet Las Mary Jets (1956–1961). Wearing satin dresses with deep necklines and stiletto heels for their performances, they were unique perhaps anywhere in the world as a band of five women who played rock 'n' roll with electric guitar, electric bass, and drums. They alternated onstage with Bill Haley when he came to Mexico City in 1960 and later performed abroad, where they were presented as the Swinging Señoritas or Las Cinco Marías.[6] Another important band from a slightly later period was Las Chics (1964–67). Reflecting a more youthful look typical of the era, the group often donned wigs or hair curls, used eyeliner extended beyond the eyes, and tweezed their eyebrows. "They wanted us to look like little girls, well-dressed, modest, neat, and decent," recalled Silvia Garcel about the group's experience with RCA. "We wore miniskirts, but only as part of the show. In real life, we didn't wear them." Instead, they defied social conventions by wearing blue jeans.[7] For Las Chics, the Beatles were gods, and they imitated them even to the degree of dressing in suits and ties à la Beatlemania. One of their songs was a cover of the song "We Love You Beatles," originally performed by the Vernon Girls. Like Las Mary Jets, Las Chics also played all of the instruments in the band, but as Silvia Garcel recalls, "When we appeared, some assistants didn't believe

Las Mary Jets (known abroad as The Swinging Señoritas or Las Cinco Marías), in a publicity photo, circa 1960. Photo courtesy of Martha Agüero.

that we played our own instruments. They thought that we had pre-recorded music and they would yell at us, asking where we kept the record player."[8]

Some of the most important performance spaces during the early 1960s were the so-called *cafés cantantes* (singing cafes) that were meeting places for youngsters and, within Mexico City, a key to the development of the rock 'n' roll scene. Young people, mostly belonging to the middle class, gathered to smoke, listen to music, and enjoy soft drinks, lemonade, coffee, shakes, and cappuccino. Since the sale of alcoholic drinks was outlawed in the cafes, the most daring attendees would bring their little bottle of rum to drink just outside. Despite the "proper and correct" behavior of most of the public, the cafes suffered from ongoing crackdowns by the police. A great number of rock 'n' rollers and balladeers paraded through these cafes. As Silvia Garcel recalls:

> With the money that we were getting from the shows in the *cafés cantantes*, we got a Rickenbacker guitar for backup, a Fender for the entourage, and a used drum set, which I later sold off to buy myself a

> Ludwig, like the ones used by the Beatles. We learned to play by watching musicians. Besides, we visited the *cafés cantantes* and we would try to imitate all of the men's finger, arm, and wrist movements. Sometimes, we would ask for tips from the musicians about what equipment to buy or how to play some songs.[9]

Another important place for youths to meet were the record shops, as Ela Laboriel remembers:

> On our way to school, we would pass by the shop El Disco Rayado [The Scratched Record], which was a block away from the Sacred Family Church, in the Roma neighborhood, where some of the rock and roll band members lived. It was fun to put on the headphones and listen to Elvis Presley, Little Richard, Fabian, or Ricky Nelson.[10]

Rock 'n' roll also spread out in the city by way of the popular burlesque theaters, like the Iris and Follies, which opened their doors for many of the new bands. Among these first rock 'n' roll bands, Los Spitfires featured a female vocalist named Julissa. In their song "Ven cerca" ("Come Closer"), Julissa sang in a provocative tone that stunned social conservatives. Although the song was banned from radio, teenagers nonetheless listened to it in secrecy.[11]

Another important forum for rock 'n' roll was television. There were several musical programs and a few specifically youth-oriented ones, but undoubtedly the most popular was the weekly show *Premier Orfeón*, later called *Orfeón A Go-Go*. In addition to performances by female artists, a new type of feminine participation in the rock scene was also featured: the *chicas a go-go* who danced alongside—or were literally encaged—on stage with the mostly male performers. The distinctive presence of the go-go girls set the pace for dance steps, fashions, and hairstyles, but they also positioned women as "ornaments" and sexualized objects.

It is important to remember, however, that a woman who sang and danced on stage always ran the risk of being taken as "easy" and "available." This devalued her image as a "proper woman" in the eyes of conservatives but, more importantly, made her vulnerable to verbal and even physical attacks. As Ela Laboriel recalls from her experiences touring within Mexico, "At one point when I passed close to the audience, I felt like I was being grabbed, and I spun around furiously and slapped the person behind me. 'What's wrong with you?!,' I screamed. Julissa, who was right behind me, yelled 'They got me too.'"[12] In another example, a critic, clearly disillusioned with the shift in style by the once "nice and very pleasant Jiménez Sisters," denounced them for having become "strong defenders of the abominable twist." "Quite frankly," he wrote, "their graceful figures lose quite a bit with those anti-aesthetic and morbid movements."[13]

Between 1962 and 1964 the record labels began to launch vocalists separately from groups, promoting soloists in other styles and, correspondingly, seeking out more manageable and commercially viable figures. As a result, for example, César Costa left Los Black Jeans, as did Enrique Guzmán leave Los Teen Tops. This conservative marketing trend to male crooners fit squarely within an ongoing popular tradition of romantic ballads, in which female vocalists also found a place. Perhaps best epitomizing this success was Angélica María, who became known as "Mexico's girlfriend." It was a social role which implied that she had preserved her chastity and thus transformed her into a mythical and idealized woman: the perfect girlfriend of whom all men ought to be enamored.[14] Daughter of the renowned producer Angélica Ortiz, she had participated as a child in theatre and films, successfully making herself a part of the youth scene of the 1960s. Together with Enrique Guzmán, Alberto Vázquez, César Costa, Julissa, and other young soloists, Angélica "built an imaginary universe inhabited by rebellious adolescents, in which passions were diluted by chaste kisses and strawberry ice cream."[15]

In contrast to this idea of sweet women and untouchable adolescent angels, who evoked images of Beatrice, Dante's platonic girlfriend, are the testimonies of other *rockeras* whose role was to be Eve, the woman associated with the fall, a detonator of the basest worldly instincts. Such was the case of the female singer Martha Ventura:

> I was always very rebellious. That's why they say that I didn't do anything. If I had been more docile and more accessible to some of the managers, it would have been entirely different. I used to say I was a lesbian. To get them out of my face, I would say, "The one I love is your wife. Can I have sex with her?" [laughs loudly] . . . My downfall was the fact that I'm very determined. I don't latch on to anything that doesn't depend on my own control. It's horrible to depend on thirty or forty people above you.[16]

Another woman who broke with the image of the tender, conservative teenager was "Baby" Bátiz, who arrived in Mexico with her brother Javier during the so-called invasion of the border bands.[17] Like many other border musicians, "Baby" Bátiz was directly influenced by U.S. rock, blues, and soul. She brought the music of the entire school of black singers that included Aretha Franklin, Etta James, and Tina Turner with her to Mexico City. Her performances were quite different from those of the female ballad singers that were being pushed commercially by the Mexican record labels. Between 1964 and 1968, she went back and forth from Tijuana to Mexico City so that she could sing with her brother Javier when she had breaks from school. During that time, she worked in several *cafés cantantes,* including El Harlem and La Rue, as well as in bars, at parties, and in theatres. "My [musical] education was onstage, learning day by day." In Tijuana, she sang with her brother's blues band at school dances, as well as with other border-area groups that integrated blues and other contemporary rock sounds.[18] In 1965, when "Baby" was fifteen, she recorded her first LP as a soloist, *Aconséjame mamá* (*Give Me Advice, Mom*), for the Mexican label Peerless, with Spanish covers of U.S. and Italian ballads. She was warned by the record label not to "sing with *'mucha onda'* because that doesn't sell," but performing live in the *cafés cantantes,* she could sing freely and fill the atmosphere with rhythm and blues.[19] Just as her brother was a head man for this new batch of *rockeros* descending from the border, "Baby" was the link between the balladeers and the *rockeras* with hoarse throats full of soul.[20]

The countercultural period of La Onda, beginning in the late 1960s, also had its female representatives. One of the most important was Mayita Campos, a singer who some described as a cross between Grace Slick of Jefferson Airplane and Janis Joplin. Mayita began her musical career in 1965 by winning a contest organized by Radio Minería in Santiago, Chile, her birthplace. Her prize was serving as a presenter on a live program called *Savoy Hits*, as well as singing on rock shows. At that time, she performed songs by the Supremes and Connie Francis. Mayita's father, Enrique Campos—better known as El Chilote Campos, a cinema pioneer in Chile—passed on to her his tastes in music, above all, for gospel and blues, which he had learned to appreciate as a sailor living in the United States. Enrique had wanted his daughter to be an actress, so he convinced her to participate in the Teatro de Ensayo de la Universidad Católica (TEUC), with whom she traveled from Santiago to Mexico City in 1967. Because of political and economic problems in Chile, all of the Campos family migrated to Mexico's capital a short while later. Valentín Pimpstein, the famous Chilean producer, helped Mayita and her brother Kiko Campos to find work at Televicentro (Mexico's monopoly television network at the time). In 1968, they began to collaborate on the program *Operación Ja Ja* (*Operation Ha-Ha*), hosted by the comedian Manuel "El Loco" Valdez, who replaced her real name, Maggie, with Mayita. In 1969, Mayita and Kiko recorded an LP for RCA with four Spanish covers of songs by Bob Dylan and Joan Báez. When Mayita left Televicentro, she formed, along with Kiko, a five-voice group called Sonido 5, which sang tunes from the Beatles, the Rolling Stones, and the Mamas and the Papas. In 1970, she was invited to New Orleans by the bassist Benito Gómez to play alongside the group Los Esclavos, originally from Mexico City. New Orleans was an interesting experience for her, though since they played in segregated venues (she was considered "white") she was not able to attend many performances by black artists. "I arrived in New Orleans singing black music and I left singing white music," she comments with a certain irony.[21] Because of problems with her immigration status, however, Mayita needed to return to Mexico. A short while later, she participated in two key events in the countercultural scene in Mexico: she became part of the cast of the rock opera *Hair*, produced by Alfredo Elías Calles,[22] and she sang at the Avándaro musical festival in 1971.

The countercultural movement framed a series of changes that had an important impact for young people in general, and for women in particular. There was greater sexual freedom, a change that challenged the social pressures exerted on young women to preserve their virginity. Another important factor for sexual liberation was the growing commercialization of birth control pills. Young Mexican middle-class women were adopting a new attitude regarding their own bodies, challenging the dominant morals of their families. Unisex fashion took control of the market, and long hair and jeans were widely adopted by both sexes. This cultural revolution had a special impact on the role of women within the traditional Mexican family. As Carlos Monsiváis writes, "Many young people . . . had heated confrontations with patriarchal authoritarianism and chose to leave home."[23] For Chela Lora—who became the manager of El Tri in the 1980s, and the wife of the group's leader Alex Lora—her *rockera* tastes created enormous frictions at home:

> When I was young, I loved to buy the records of Savoy Brown, Janis, or the Doors. My father always hated rock—who would have known that he would have a rock star in the family years later? One day, when my sisters and I were singing and dancing in the living room, my father demanded that we stop being so scandalous, grabbed the record, and broke it to pieces. . . . My mother didn't want me to go to high school because it was full of "hopeless dope-smokers."[24]

The climax of La Onda counterculture took place at the Rock y Ruedas (Rock and Wheels) music festival at Avándaro. Ela Laboriel was twenty-four at the time and in charge of the press for the event. Yet, despite her own family's history of involvement in the earlier period of rock 'n' roll, she recalls how, after participating in the festival, "my brother, Johnny, stopped speaking to me for two years."[25] Her story was not atypical: many women who attended Avándaro had to invent ingenious stories or sneak away from home; only a few had their parents' permission. Although male bands predominated, two women also sang there: Mayita Campos, who performed with Los Yaki, and

Marisela Durazo, vocalist for the band Tequila.[26] As Durazo recalls, "For me, Avándaro revolutionized rock in Mexico. That marked us as a generation. We were part of the hippie movement; we wanted to try and experiment."[27] A central aspect of the festival was its sexual liberation, expressed in nudity and "obscene" language. Dozens of young people went skinny-dipping in a brook and invaded a golf course.[28] One of the more notorious moments was when Alma Rosa Gómez López, a native of Monterrey, disrobed while dancing, thereby becoming the mythical "encuerada de Avándaro" (the so-called Avándaro stripper) and providing editorial writers of the conservative press something to talk about for months.[29]

During the 1970s some musicians chose to live in communes, as was the case for the members of La Semilla del Amor (Love Seed), the group to which Mayita Campos belonged. They played spiritual Latin soul, and the songs' lyrics spoke of socio-ecological topics and spiritual searching. As Alfonso Miranda, a commune member, states:

> A return to nature and pollution of the planet were our concerns; we even separated organic and inorganic garbage. We lived off what we harvested and had our own orchards. Some of us made films or took naturism and Eastern philosophy classes and, while Margarita Bauche [a folk rock musician in the 1970s] did her songs, we organized concerts at the National University campus [in Mexico City] in which La Semilla alternated with her. . . . La Semilla del Amor was a family; we all considered ourselves brothers and sisters. One couple's children were not exclusively their responsibility; we all were parents and we participated in the support and education of the children. . . . "Money is the devil," we would say, and any profits from concerts were divided up for the maintenance of the house and instruments.[30]

La Semilla del Amor lasted until 1973, when some members moved to Ciudad Juárez on the border. In fact, their situation was exceptional, since few communes survived beyond the first few months.

Avándaro reflected the climatic peak of La Onda counterculture, but also its decline. The festival and rock in general were satanized by the Church, the government, and the Left. As contracts were dropped and performance outlets closed, the native rock scene, La Onda Chicana, quickly dissolved.[31] Only a few brave *rockeros,* now relegated to the margins, learned to survive in the underground. The new musical spaces for politicized, urban, middle-class youth were the *peñas.* There, one could listen to traditional Latin American folk songs and the so-called *protesta* compositions of heroes such as Violeta Parra, Víctor Jara, Atahualpa Yupanqui, Inti-Illimani, and Mercedes Sosa. The *peñas* were an important expressive space for many female singers and songwriters, some of whom would later become *rockeras*. However, the *peñas* also generated a purist ideological movement which refused to admit anything that had to do with electric instruments or perceptions of North American cultural imperialism. This was the situation encountered, for example, by Margarita Bauche and other musicians from the Semilla del Amor commune. They tried to play in various *peñas,* but even using acoustic instruments they managed only sporadic gigs: *peña* audiences wanted to hear Latin American folk music, not rock. Similarly, the singer and songwriter Laura Abitia was constantly arguing with the coordinators of *peñas* because only very rarely was she able to perform her own songs, much less material from the Beatles or from the Spanish composer and singer Joan Manuel Serrat, because they weren't allowed in those areas.[32] "The audience at the *peñas* was very strange," she recalled. "With the original material, sometimes they responded well. Other times they were perplexed. People honestly didn't care if you did your songs. After a while, this bothered me enormously, and I became a loner."[33]

After Avándaro, with the proliferation of *peñas* and the subsequent disappearance of rock's performing spaces, rock mostly found shelter in the *hoyos fonquis* (literally, "funky holes"). The *hoyos* were galleries, warehouses, cinemas, abandoned houses, parking lots, dance and multiple-use halls, all hardly equipped for concerts. Yet an important underground movement was generated in these spaces, in which many groups grew and developed. Some, like El Tri, proved to be survivors, while others had an ephemeral existence. The atmosphere in the *hoyos fonquis* was very different from what most of the musicians had experienced during the 1960s, above all because they were located in working-class neighborhoods and in the city's slum belts. Rock had been "appropriated" by the marginalized and working classes, who also demanded that it be sung in Spanish, which in turn forced the *rockeros* to write about their own surroundings and in their own language.

Some brave *rockeras* ventured to perform in these spaces, despite the risk of being sexually harassed. Regarding her participation in *hoyos fonquis,* Norma Valdez, Cosa Nostra's singer, explains how she was "always groped" and "even carried a whip to protect myself."[34] The concert organizers in the *hoyos fonquis* neither assumed responsibility nor provided security for the groups. If the audience started throwing things, the first thing an organizer most often did was to take off running with the money, leaving the musicians at the spectators' mercy. Groups were announced without prior contract arrangements; sound systems were deficient and anemic; and the beer-drinking audience was often under the influence of glue or some other drug. According to "Baby" Bátiz:

> For me, there was a big difference between the matinees of the sixties, which were well-organized and where the audience went to listen to music, compared to the concerts in the *hoyos,* where everything degenerated: drugs were rampant and they confused having a good time with getting wasted. Although I usually had someone to protect me, one day, singing a Janis Joplin blues song, a guy threw liquor in my face. It was so humiliating that I decided to stop doing shows in the *hoyos.* People don't appreciate what you're doing. You run the risk of getting yelled at, insulted, groped, and, ultimately, you're badly paid. Also, the air stinks, and your heart twinges when you see the kids get drugged up.[35]

Many *rockeras* chose not to perform in such contexts, but marrying or having children also influenced their careers. Martha Ventura is one example, who after becoming pregnant was subjected to pressures from producers and directors to quit performing. Her record label stopped promoting her in the media, using her marriage and pregnancy as an excuse. Just like many other *rockeras,* she had to decide between her personal life and her life with the band, and she chose the former. Another example is Ela Laboriel, who stopped singing in the mid-1970s because of her daughter's birth. "Maternity made me change many things. It was more difficult to work, so I thought about going back to my career until my daughter grew up. I changed my attitude toward my child. . . . There was a new way of doing things and I didn't want to repeat my parents' behavior with my daughter, so I allowed her to be herself."[36] Laura Abitia also comments on her role as a singer and a mother by remembering that "it was very complicated, going around with my baby at 11 or 12 at night, trying to see who in the world could give me a ride, or taking a taxi and spending half of what I had earned. For that reason, I decided to be a bureaucrat for a while."[37]

By the 1980s, the economic crisis, the disastrous earthquake in Mexico City (1985), massive youth unemployment, and the obsolescence of the Mexican political system, among other things, all spurred important sectors of Mexican society to organize politically at the grassroots level. Rock bands played an important role in these new social movements, despite the fact that they had few recording opportunities and often lacked a commercialized promotion. One central figure was Cecilia Toussaint, who rose to prominence alongside Jaime López in the midst of a *canto nuevo*–dominated atmosphere, when they created a new fusion of original rock in Spanish. As she explains, earning respect among musicians wasn't easy: "Sometimes, I would propose something, and they would look at me as though they were saying, 'Oh yes, sure . . .' without taking me seriously, but things have changed and since then, it's worked very well. Now, I have an excellent relationship with the musicians. I'm someone who's grown up around men, and I learned to deal with them since I was young."[38] Cecilia grew up in a propitious musical environment; her brothers are outstanding musicians, and her parents always supported her, giving her "the freedom to decide whatever I wanted to do, in every sense."[39] Cecilia Toussaint is a transition *rockera* who has helped generate a greater respect toward women. "Young people's attitudes have changed," she says. "Maybe other generations had it worse than we did, like Mayita or Baby. Yes, it was hard work, but it wasn't so pathetic, either. You can talk to the kids and say what you feel."[40]

Within the *rockera* genre of the 1980s, the group Kenny and the Electrics also stands out. Kenny, a Guadalajara native, is probably one of the most important women in Mexican rock. Her stage presence and attractive physique signaled her at the time as the Mexican Pat Benatar. She grew up in a totally musical environment, and she explains: "My brothers were all rock and rollers. As a child, I used to listen to Janis or Aretha Franklin, and I frequently attended concerts in the United States. I even had the privilege of seeing Jimi Hendrix live when I was fourteen."[41] She remembers the impact on her when, at the age of sixteen, she saw the Mexican group Peace and Love in Guadalajara. She fell in love with the group's guitarist, Ricardo Ochoa, and pretty soon ran off with him; in the end, they lived together for seventeen years. From 1977 to 1980 the couple lived in Los Angeles, where Kenny and the Electrics was born. She recollects: "Ricardo wanted it to be called just 'The Electrics,' but I stuck up for myself."[42] They played in clubs like the Whiskey a Go-Go, and when they returned to Mexico, as Kenny put it, "We looked like a *gringo* group." Initially, they sang in English, but by the mid-1980s, the group's name would be changed to Kenny y los Eléctricos and they began singing in Spanish, a shift in strategy that coincided with the beginning of the industry-led "rock en tu idioma" (rock in your language) movement. Soon they signed a deal with Melody Records, whose financial links with Televisa, the nation's media conglomerate, afforded them extensive marketing, something that had not occurred for many years with a rock group in Mexico.

During the 1980s rock also found an important space of dissemination on the radio. Commercial stations like Rock 101, Espacio 59, and WFM opened discussion to topics that might not have been possible before, such as sex or the political system. Equally important, female voices began to be heard as radio disk jockeys for the first time. "In the past, they wouldn't let a woman alone in the studio," Fernanda Tapia, one of the pioneering disk jockeys, re-

Kenny Avilés of Kenny y Los Eléctricos in a publicity photo, circa 1985. Photo courtesy of Melody Records.

calls. "They thought it would create conflict since a woman wouldn't listen to another woman."[43] However, these women disk jockeys convinced audiences that they had nothing to be afraid of and that they were trustworthy sources for information, entertainment, or debate. "You had to be strong-willed to survive in that world of *machitos*," remembers Dominique Peralta, another disk jockey. "In general, our attitude was aggressive. We had to be one of them, one of the boys."[44]

The 1980s also ushered in a new musical genre: punk. Although it implied an even more virile environment, some women succeeded at integrating and becoming accepted within the *chavos banda*, or punk, scene.[45] One was Ángela Martínez Texeiro, whose story also illustrates the growing link between rock and politics during this time. In 1973 she became a member of the Partido Mexicano del Proletariado (Mexican Proletariat Party), a left-wing party. At that moment of crisis and repression, along with other people from the organization, she was arrested, accused of links and cooperation with guerrilla groups. She recounts: "After three days, some of us were freed, but we never heard again about some other people."[46] After this experience, she returned to the music scene, singing and composing tunes with political content. In 1983 she began singing with TNT, a band that performed hard rock, heavy metal, punk, and trash. Ángela identified with TNT because of their social protest lyrics. They described their work as "music with lots of dynamite," hence the name of the band:

> My debut with TNT was in Salón Yáñez in the "La Blanca" neighborhood, near the Tenayuca pyramid. Since then, whenever I'm not singing, I get off the stage and dance with the kids.... One day, when we arrived at a concert in Barrio Norte, I saw a sign that said: "Ángela is the Mexican Janis Joplin." ... In 1985, the PRT (Partido Revolucionario de los Trabajadores, or Revolutionary Workers' Party) wanted me to be their candidate for representative. From the beginning, I knew that I wouldn't win; it's really hard for a *rockera* to get a spot. The party criticized me because I was vulgar and I would pass the microphone to potheads. I was in constant disagreement with people on the Left because they said that rock was alienating and imperialist. The only thing that the candidacy did for me was allow me to keep some kids from the Tianguis del Chopo [an outdoor rock "flea market"] from being *apañados* [that is, grabbed by the police]."[47]

Ángela sang with heavy makeup and the symbols for women, peace, and anarchy drawn on one cheek. She tinted her hair or wore extensions, and she usually dressed in tight-fitting leather. In the 1980s, Ángela and some punk girls formed a collective named Las Guerreras (the Warriors), which supported single mothers who had been rejected by their families because they were punks. She also launched several efforts to educate and aid *chavos banda*, marginalized kids who attended her concerts at the *hoyos fonquis*. Similarly, together with Father Chinchachoma, a priest who dedicated himself to aiding street children, she organized an anti-drug campaign, in which she told the *chavos:* "Get it together; we need to be full-blooded warriors to fight against this government which crushes us."[48]

Another punk woman was Patricia Moreno Rodríguez, better known as La Zappa Punk. In the late 1980s, she was the "screamer" of the hard-core group Secta Suicida Siglo Veinte (Twentieth-Century Suicide Sect), or SS-20. As the daughter of workers and shoemakers of lower-class urban origin, she notes: "My nickname comes from Frank Zappa and from *zapatos* [shoes], since my family has always worked with shoes and leather. It's a tradition; I make my punk clothes designs with leather." Between 1984 and 1986, La Zappa formed her own band, not with musicians, but with friends from the street, in which up to thirty-two girls, calling themselves Susy's Peleoneras Punks, came together.

> We took our name from a song by the Ramones called "Susy Is a Fighter [*peleonera*]." The band was like family; we were very close. Some were single mothers from the street, others came from neighborhood families. The *chavas* who ended up pregnant were helped according to whatever they decided. It was a form of resistance against marginalization and repression in a system as rotten as ours.[49]

For Zappa, "Rock is for people like us, from marginalized areas.... We hold it as a shield to defend ourselves from people who label us strange and from police repression." In 1985, by way of the Tianguis del Chopo, Zappa made contact with other *chavos banda* from working-class neighborhoods, meeting other girls with whom she would form Virginidad Sacudida (Discarded Virginity), her first punk group. "We were the first *punketas* to be rowdy and driven," she comments. "With the name, we wanted to poke fun at sex. Screw virginity; it doesn't work. Other things will do."[50] Still, it was difficult for her to face her family, especially because she was a woman. "My parents scolded me when I attended concerts and wore tight-fitting pants, or 'cause I had some design on them; I would always escape to the *reventón* [big party], even if Dad hit me. I was the black sheep of the family."[51] For the punk girls, breaking away from family morals was quite a challenge. In the song "Virginidad sacudida" Zappa expresses her refusal to follow patriarchal models:

> Pinche virginidad
> tu estás podrida
> a tu edad la tienes
> otras ya la pierden
> para qué presumes
> si de nada te sirve
> Te catalogan sexualmente
> escúpelos y exige
> que te cataloguen mentalmente
>
> (Fucking virginity
> you're rotten
> at your age you have it
> others lose it already
> why show off
> if it doesn't help
> they catalog you sexually
> spit on them and demand
> that they catalog you mentally.)

Patty Zappa (Patricia Moreno Rodríguez), better known as *La Zappa Punk*, performing in the street festival Tokín Callejero (1986). Photo courtesy of Fernando García.

For punk *chavas*, there is a key link between music and politics. Ana Punk, a follower of the movement, commented during the Primer Encuentro de Mujeres en el Rock (First Symposium of Women in Rock) at the Chopo Museum in November 1991 that a *chava banda* "should have a contestarian attitude and fight against *machismo* and sexism." In summing up the problem women had faced as *rockeras* since the history of the genre, she asked: "Why should we follow the pace imposed by men in rock? It is better to simply express ourselves as women."[52] In 1995 she came to the forefront of the movement known as the Colectivo Mujeres al Rescate de la Cultura de la Calle (Women to the Rescue of Street Culture Collective), which was made up of single mothers and women of the street. "Our intent," she explains, "was to demonstrate our repressed feelings, for our screams to come out of the deepest place, like our grandmothers might have wanted."[53]

Another important *rockera* is Rita Guerrero of the group Santa Sabina.

Born in Guadalajara, Rita is a woman whose theatre background has allowed her to develop a unique onstage presence. Santa Sabina's music is an interesting mix of gothic, jazz, soul, and funk elements; many have compared her to Nina Hagen and Diamanda Galas. "My exposure to rock was by way of theatre," she recalled, a fact about which many of her former drama teachers continue to question her.[54] The band was born in 1988 in the midst of the boom of *rock en español*. The name Santa Sabina came from a consideration of artistic creativity as a sacred element, and also as homage to the mushroom priestess of Oaxaca, the Zapotec Indian shaman María Sabina, an iconic figure for the Mexican counterculture. After a few failed attempts, their first record appeared in 1992, produced in Los Angeles by Alejandro Marcovich, then guitarist of Los Caifanes, for Discos Culebra, a label owned by BMG Ariola. Signing with a transnational label provided the group with support and promotion, as well as the opportunity of a greater market. "We have complete freedom to do what we please," Rita comments. "We aren't like so many other groups who are created, shaped, and thrown to stardom; we made ourselves."[55] In April 1997 Santa Sabina traveled to Miami to record "Unplugged" for the Latin version of MTV. Regarding her experience as a *rockera* of the 1990s, Rita claims: "There are a huge number of female singers in Mexico and the world. I think women face things better than men. I see men as expectant, as if they don't know how to act in the face of our strength."[56]

During the past few years, a wide range of possibilities for female expression has emerged, much of which succeeds despite a lack of diffusion by the mass media. At the same time, other women have shown up in an important way in the media. These include Alejandra Guzmán and, in her time, Gloria Trevi, who personified the archetype of the sexualized *rockera*.[57] On the other hand and distanced from this image of the *locochona* (wild woman), a new, younger generation of songwriters such as Frida, Ely Guerra, and Julieta Venegas have also broken into the market. Their success, however, has not been without criticism. Roberto Ponce, writing in the leftist newsmagazine *Proceso*, defined this new wave of female *rockeras* as "distanced from drugs, but also from feminism, politics, or Mexican recording studios. They prefer Anglo rock and are unfamiliar with the underground scene in Mexico."[58] But Julieta says, "We speak from our feminine point of view, from our way of making music, and I'm not talking about feminism. Ours is a different sensibility, a distinct way of saying things, and that's what is important."[59]

Currently, *rockeras* no longer live the same troubling experience as their predecessors; they are not forced to abandon their musical paths in favor of matrimony or motherhood. However, at work as well as onstage, they have had to be responsible for domestic labors and the care of their children. It's a double whammy, which sometimes becomes a triple, since their scant incomes as *rockeras* has forced them to take on other, better-paying jobs in order to contribute to family income. Thus, *rockeras* also work as music or voice teachers, speakers, actresses, managers, public-relations assistants, bar musicians, jingle singers, chorus singers for recording studios, or, in many cases, may even be involved in activities which have nothing to do with music.

After more than forty years, the road of the *rockera* in Mexico is still rocky. Despite a great number of achievements, *rockeras* haven't had sufficient impact to transform women's condition in rock, a territory that remains monopolized by men. When the myth is broken and more women are bold enough to play electric instruments, heed their musical calling, and write their own songs, in which they can express the condition of new generations of Mexican women, only then will their talents be acknowledged independently from their feminine condition. If women do not speak out with their own voices, no one will do it for them. This is the opportunity, as Zappa Punk said, of daring to yell what our mothers and grandmothers could not say.

Selected Discography

Angélica María. *Paso a pasito.* 1963. Musart D814 1963.

Bauche, Margarita. *Manos de tierra.* 1967. Cisne CI-1445.

Guerra, Ely. *Pa'morirse de amor.* 1997. EMI EAN 724353427523.

Kenny y los Elétricos. *Me quieres cotorrear.* 1985. Comrock/WEA LRM-2005.

Lucifer. *Lucifer.* 1974. RCA-Victor RCA-MKS-2020. (Mayita Campos sings here with the Popo Sánchez Orchestra)

Las Mary Jets. "Dulces tonterías"/ "Una encantadora chica anticuada." 1960. Columbia 4803.

Mexican Divas, vols. 1–3. 1998–2001. Opción Sónica. Subsello Eclécticas OPCD 77.

Ríos, Gloria. "El relojito"/ "Hotel de los corazones rotos." 1956. VIK-RCA 70-9980. (Ríos sings here with Jorge Ortega and Héctor Hallal, "El crabe")

Santa Sabina. *Santa Sabina.*1992. Discos Culebra, BMG Ariola EAN 7432 11191128.

Sirenas al ataque: Historia de las mujeres rockeras mexicanas, 1956–2000. Various artists. 2000. Ediciones Pentagrama RPCD 435. (CD accompaniment to book of same title by Tere Estrada)

Toussaint, Cecilia. *Cecilia Toussaint y Arpía.* 1987. Discos Pentagrama EAN 799 285200594.

Venegas, Julieta. *Aquí.* 1997. BMG Ariola EAN 7432 14718 223.

"Soy punkera, ¿y qué?"

Sexuality, Translocality, and Punk in Los Angeles and Beyond

MICHELLE HABELL-PALLÁN

> My theory had precedence. Stay with me on this. The Clash, for instance, jazzed up their music with this reggae influence—a direct reflection of their exposure to the Caribbean diaspora and its musical expression there in London. Nothing new—the usual white man appropriation of an exotic other story—anyway, the Sex Pistols, my theory went, were going to do the same with Norteño, el Tex-Mex. I was going on the assumption that the Pistols probably heard the *conjunto* on KCOR or Radio Jalapeño on the bus ride down from Austin. But the point is, it worked. Talk about your revisionist histories! Greil Marcus is gonna flip!
> —Molly Vasquez from Jim Mendiola's film, *Pretty Vacant*, 1996

> When Alice, lead singer for the Bags rock group, takes the stage in torn fishnet hose and micro-mini leopard-skin tunic, she explodes into convulsive, unintelligible vocals. The effect is a raw sexuality not for the fainthearted.
> —Flyer insert, *Los Angeles Times*, 1978

The xeroxed flyer advertising *Pretty Vacant,* Jim Mendiola's 1996 independent short film, depicts the much-loved figure of the Mexican Virgen de Guadalupe strutting, of all things, an upside-down electric guitar à la Jimi Hendrix.[1] As a U.S.-born Chicana who, in the 1980s, was rescued from the suburbs of Los Angeles by the Ramones, X, and Dead Kennedys, I must admit that I was captivated by this image and intrigued by the film's title, an obvious reference to the British Sex Pistols. A guitar jets out from La Guadalupe at a right angle, transforming the familiar oval shape of La Virgen's image into the shape of a cross, or an intersection of sorts. What was this flyer suggesting by

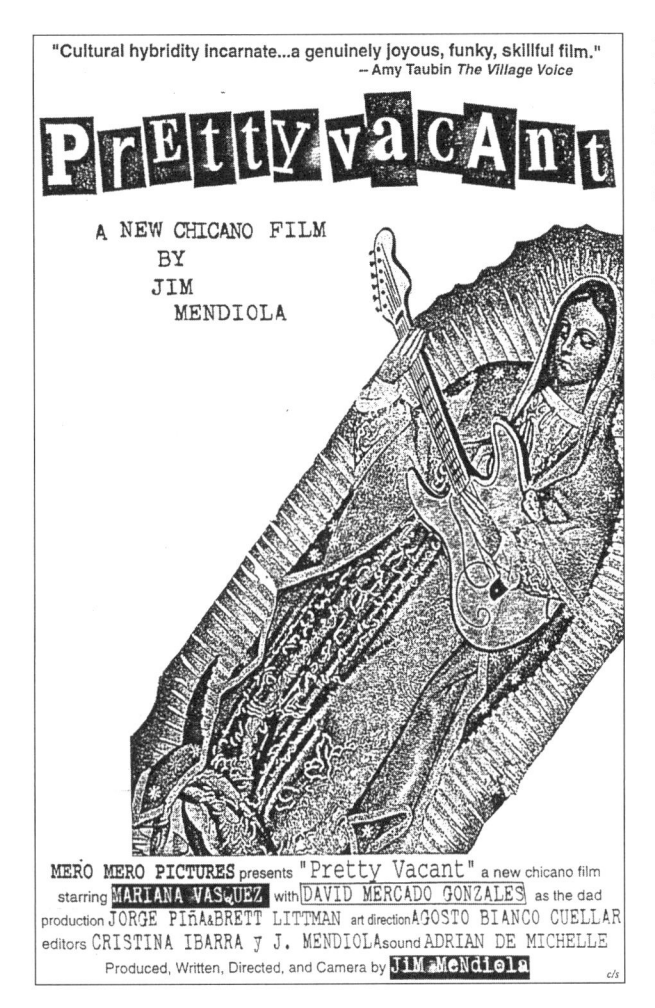

Flyer advertising *Pretty Vacant*, Jim Mendiola's 1996 independent short film. Here, the iconic figure of the Mexican Virgen de Guadalupe is repositioned holding an upside-down electric guitar à la Jimi Hendrix.

juxtaposing these deeply symbolic, yet seemingly unrelated cultural icons? How did the title relate? And why did this deliciously irreverent image prompt me to think of the critically acclaimed *photonovela*/comic series *Love and Rockets* by Los Bros. Hernandez?[2] And the title? *Pretty Vacant* is one of the "hit" songs of the infamous 1970s British punk band, the Sex Pistols. Again what is this flyer suggesting? With all due respect, what and who lie at the intersection of Guadalupe and punk?

It turns out that the main protagonist of *Pretty Vacant*, Molly Vasquez, the fierce Latina characters of the Hernandez Brothers' *Love and Rockets* comic book series, and, most importantly, the real-life Los Angelino Chicana punk musicians all live at that particular intersection. The film depicts a week in the culturally hybrid "do-it-yourself" world of "La Molly" Vasquez, the offbeat, twenty-something, English-speaking Chicana feminist, *artista,* bisexual *punkera* subject who lives in a working-class neighborhood of San Antonio, "Tejas." Her love of the Sex Pistols leads her to discover a well-kept secret that will allow her, as a producer of 'zines and a beginning filmmaker, to *re-write* rock 'n' roll history by inserting herself and Tejano culture into its narrative. All this while she prepares for a gig with her all-girl band, Aztlán-a-go-go.

My mention of *Pretty Vacant* serves as point of departure for my discussion of the emergence, during the late 1970s and early 1980s, of a punk "do-it-yourself" Chicana grassroots feminist cultural production that circulated co-terminously with other burgeoning Chicana activist and scholarly endeavors, as well as the East Los Angeles/Hollywood punk scenes, but which has yet to be examined in depth. The film shifts the paradigm that frames the reigning narrative of popular music produced in the U.S.[3] By disrupting the status-quo narrative of popular music production (in this specific case, that of U.S. punk), through granting a young Latina (more specifically, a Tejana) the authority to chronicle the history of punk, the film compels scholars to acknowledge the complexity of popular music and popular music studies in the United States. Ultimately it viscerally unsettles long-held assumptions that have unconsciously erased the influence of U.S. Latinos from popular music's sonic equation (and asks what is at stake in reproducing that erasure). It opens a discursive space for my own analysis of both the production of punk music by Chicanas in East Los Angeles and Hollywood during the 1970s and 1980s, and of that music's relationship to punk communities beyond the United States.

Las Punkeras

What is fascinating about the film *Pretty Vacant* is the overlapping of the fictional character's art practices with the underanalyzed artistic production of those Chicana musicians and visual artists who shaped the L.A.-area punk sensibility. In the late 1970s and early 1980s, Chicanas in local bands like the Brat (led by Teresa Covarrubias) and the Bags (led by Alicia Armendariz Velasquez) reconstructed the sound and subjects of British punk. In this essay, I will provide a brief context for the emergence of Chicana/o punk, followed by an analysis of the oral histories of these Chicana *punkeras,* in which they narrate their own artistic conditions of production and gender relations, as well as the punk aesthetic that emerged in the late 1970s and 1980s.[4]

Chicana/o punk, like punk everywhere, embodied a sonic response to the "excesses of seventies rock."[5] Rock chroniclers David Reyes and Tom Waldman note that "indulgent guitar solos, pretentious lyrics, and pompous lead singers went against everything that Chicano rock 'n' roll represented from Ritchie Valens forward."[6] The appeal of punk to rebellious Chicana and Chicano youth makes sense for two reasons: the DIY (do-it-yourself) sensibility at the core of punk musical subcultures found resonance with the practice of *rasquache*, a Chicana/o cultural practice of "making do" with limited resources[7]; and punk's critique of the status quo—of poverty, sexuality, class inequality, and war— spoke directly to working-class East Los Angeles youth.[8]

For all its familiar feel, punk's international sensibility also appealed to Chicanas/os, in spite of, or perhaps because of, the city's history of physically and economically segregating Chicanos from the wealthy West Side, which was thought to be Los Angeles's dominant locus of culture, where "worldly" culture was invented.[9] It goes without saying that Chicana/o punk did not exist in isolation. Reyes and Waldman observe:

> Chicano punk groups were much more deeply embedded in the Hollywood rock scene than were the 1960s bands from East Los Angeles. On any given weekend in the late 1970s and early 1980s, Los Illegals, the Brat, and the Plugs would be playing somewhere in Hollywood. Before they crossed the L.A. River, however, they played at the Vex, an East L.A. club devoted to presenting punk rock bands.[10]

Vex emerged as an attempt by Chicano youth in East Los Angeles "to eliminate the barriers that inhibited Chicanos from playing in other parts of L.A., and that kept outsiders from coming from the neighborhood." Willie Herron of Los Illegals remembers, "We wanted to bring people from the West Side to see groups from the East Side."[11] At a historical moment when the confluence of cultures began to accelerate in the wake of global demographic shifts, these Chicana/o youth transformed punk into a social site where popular music, national identity, sexuality, and gender dynamics were transformed. Bands like East L.A.'s Thee Undertakers used a "global" form of youth subculture to bring together local, if segregated, youth.

She Says

> Punk allowed people to just get up there, and even if you were not feeling confident—which was not a problem I ever had—but I think for women who felt like they weren't sure of themselves, it was very easy to get up and do it anyway, because you weren't being judged on how well you played.[12]

Working-class Chicanas such as Alicia Armendariz Velasquez, Theresa Covarrubias, Angela Vogel, and others shaped independent, non-commercial music communities and subcultures in Los Angeles and responded to the shrinking of the public sphere and the increased privatization of daily life in contemporary U.S. culture through their musical practices. Although these women impacted local independent music communities' sounds and concerns, almost no formal documentation of their participation exists. The fact that women disrupt categories of identity (such as singer-songwriter, Chicana, woman musician, punk, etc.) mitigates against recognition of their influence in discussions of subcultural musical practices and in discussions focused on countering the shrinking of the public sphere.

I am interested in the ways these women appropriated, reshaped, and critiqued imagery from unexpected sources such as British youth musical subculture to invent local cultural practices that allowed them to express their realities in a public context. Chicanas as producers transformed punk and New Wave aesthetics into sites of possibility for transnational conversations concerning violence against women and the effects of the shrinking public sphere. Given that punk-influenced musical practices and communities tend to be defined as male-dominated arenas, and almost never in terms of Latino social spaces, the advent of this subculture may seem an unlikely place for the development of a transnational conversation. Yet this punk subculture functioned as a site of possibility for individual expression by young Chicanas who participated in such spaces.

Las Gritonas / The Screamers

The Los Angeles bands I am interested in produced their own music, which circulated in grassroots and alternative distribution circuits, on independent labels. The bands had little access to major distribution networks for at least two reasons: most major record labels at the time could not imagine the market appeal of Chicano alternative music, much less the music of Latino rock inflected by a grassroots feminist ideology and a punk aesthetic; and the women's stated primary desire was not to make it within the mainstream music industry, but to create a place for public self-expression.

This context, in addition to larger social prejudices against women in rock, helps to explain why the innovative use by young Chicanas of alternative music to circulate critiques of social inequality and to express their rage against the domestic machine has often gone unrecognized: their recordings and visual images are extremely difficult to locate. This lack of distribution and exposure also occurred with other artists of the period, such as spoken-word performer Marisela Norte, who also articulated a grassroots critique of social inequality that circulated in and outside of the university setting.[13] The cultural production of these young Chicanas paralleled the efforts of Chicana feminist theorists of representation at the same time, even though their efforts rarely, if ever, intersected. As scholars of Chicana feminism wrote about multiple inflected subjectivity, the intersection of race, class, and gender, and the production of new Chicana subjects, these young women expressed those experiences in their music.[14]

Working-class Chicanas who helped create the local sound of the Los Angeles underground punk subculture were attracted to it for various reasons, but all of them experienced or witnessed violence against Chicanas at an early age and most had been violently sexualized. In a series of interviews I conducted with Alicia Armendariz Velasquez and Teresa Covarrubias, both women asserted that the visual and sonic language of punk subculture allowed them to express their private rage about restrictions placed on them and the violence done to their bodies and their mother's bodies. In addition, their narratives document the effects of the shrinking of the public sphere by forces of economic privatization that plagued the 1980s that continue to this day. In other words, theirs is a story of transnationalism told from the bottom up, from the point of view of working-class women, in the years leading up to accords like NAFTA. Though each woman's experience was different, each was attracted to the punk subculture because it was a place where they re-imagined the world they lived in, where they saw themselves as empowered subjects.

Despite the negative press the punk scene received (as extremely violent and racist), women experienced the punk scene as a liberating space where the lines between gender and race were easily if temporarily blurred. It was a place where class differences and racial divisions were held temporarily in suspension. In fact, all the interviewees attested to the fact that in Los Angeles, the scene was multicultural—it reflected the mix of Los Angeles's population. In an era when representation of Latinas was even more rare than today on English-language television and radio, the do-it-yourself attitude and aesthetic appealed to them.

In the Bag

Alicia Armendariz Velasquez, whose stage name was Alice Bag, of the Bags, is the daughter of Mexican immigrants. Growing up in East Los Angeles, she came of age in the late 1970s. She, like Teresa Covarrubias, described her engagement with punk as a way out of an environment she found too judgmental in terms of ethnicity and sexuality. She found no recourse within the mythic traditional Mexican family for discussion of the domestic violence she witnessed as a child. Her embrace of punk culture occurred in "a period when Chicanas were questioning their traditional roles, increasing their participation within the political arena, and inscribing a budding Chicana feminist discourse and practice."[15] Although Armendariz Velasquez's path diverged from most Chicanas of the day, so profound was her influence on the L.A. punk scene that she was recently featured in the photo exhibition and catalog entitled *Forming: The Early Days of L.A. Punk*. In fact, punk music chronicler David Jones calls Armendariz Velasquez the inventor of the West Coast hard-core punk sound.[16]

In 1978 Armendariz Velasquez was featured in a *Los Angeles Times* article, "Female Rockers—A New Breed," written by Kristine McKenna.[17] Then known as "Alice," Armendariz Velasquez, along with Diane Chai of the Alleycats and Xene of X, were considered groundbreaking women of the punk scene because their performances demolished narrow models of women in rock: "the wronged blues belter à la Janis Joplin or the coy sex kitten typified by Linda Ronstadt. In tune with New Wave's spirit of change, women punkers are rejecting the confining steoreotype and demanding more."[18] Although no explicit mention of Alice's ethnicity was made, McKenna describes her using code words reserved for ethnic Others: "Alice [is] an exotic beauty whose frenzied vocal seizures generate such chaos that the Bags has earned a reputation for closing clubs."[19] In retrospect, we note that McKenna, perhaps unknowingly, cites two Chicanas, Linda Ronstadt and Armendariz Velasquez, as wildly divergent models of women in rock.

Often accused of being too aggressive onstage, Armendariz Velasquez would perform in pink mini-dresses and severe makeup. In a clip from Penelope Spheeris's 1981 documentary film *The Decline of Western Civilization*, we witness Armendariz Velasquez exploding onstage and wrestling the boys who jump on stage during the show. The pink of her dress clashes with her performance and produces a complex statement about women's realities. Armendariz Velasquez did not reject femininity per se, but she rejected the equation of femininity with victimization and passivity. In fact, McKenna states, "Women punkers like Alice Bag and Xene project an oddly incongruous sexuality. While not exactly neuter, their shock-level redefinition of the female role will take a while to be assimilated culturally."[20] Yet Armendariz Velasquez's assertion that "female performers have always tended to be more reserved but all that is changing" foresaw and provided models for performers like Courtney Love, who is often noted, though not entirely correctly, for what has been called her unprecedented feminine rock aesthetic.[21]

Alicia Armendariz Velasquez (*left*) and Theresa Covarrubias (*right*) of the Chicana band Goddess 13. Photo by Pablo Prieto. Used by permission.

One of the best preserved and most accessible documents of Armendariz Velasquez's fearless performance style as Alice Bag is the Bags's recording of "We Don't Need the English" on the band's 1979 *Yes L.A.* album.[22] With characteristic sardonic humor, Alice and the band loudly refuse the notion that the only authentic punk scene is to be found in Great Britain:

> We don't need the English, telling us what we should be
> We don't need the English, with their boring songs of anarchy,
> telling us what to wear . . .

The song opens by rejecting "the English, with their boring songs of anarchy," a direct reference to "Anarchy in the U.K." by Über–punk band, the Sex Pistols. The song concludes by metaphorically banning the English from the "Canterbury," an infamous, rundown apartment complex in Hollywood that served as a breeding ground for Hollywood punks.[23] Though she did not write the song, the lyrics hold a different valence when we consider that Armendariz Velasquez was bilingual in a city that often denigrated Spanish-speaking ethnic minorities and that she taught bilingual education for the Los Angeles Unified Public School District.

Although Armendariz Velasquez emerged as a performer in the 1970s Hollywood punk scene (unlike Covarrubias, who grew out of the East Los Angeles punk scene), she came to her Chicana consciousness in the early 1990s.

After performing as a Lovely Elvette with the Chicano El Vez and the Memphis Mariachis, with Cholita, and with other L.A.-based bands, Velasquez formed a folk group, Armendariz Las Tres, with Teresa Covarrubias and Angela Vogel, former member of the East Los Angeles band the Odd Sqad.[24] When Vogel left the band, the two remaining members formed the duo, Goddess 13.

East Los Angeles's The Brat

What attracted Teresa Covarrubias, who was born to a working-class Mexican American family, to the punk musical subculture was its do-it-yourself attitude, what she calls the "non-pretentiousness of it." Covarrubias discovered punk in the mid-1970s when her older sister, backpacking through Europe, began sending her punk fanzines from Germany and England.

> What really attracted me to punk, was the notion that "Gee, I could do that." 'Zines had all these paste-up things and all these crazy little articles, and these girl bands and guy bands, and it just seemed like so open. It didn't seem like . . . you had to play really well. It seemed like a from-your-gut type thing, and I just fell right into it. You know, it was really raw, and it was in your face, and I really liked that, it kind of got me going.[25]

Inspired by this low-tech sensibility, one that she says "emerged" from the gut and seemed open to young men and women, she decided to form a New Wave band, with Rudy Medina, called The Brat. The Brat became synonymous with East L.A. punk. In contrast to Armendariz Velasquez's family, which was fully supportive of her musical lifestyle, Covarrubias's family discouraged her. Although she found a space within the band to critique gender norms, performing songs like "Misogyny," she found that sexism did exist in the punk scene, especially among her own bandmates. At times, they dismissed her creative opinions because she did not play an instrument. During those times, she explains:

> Because I couldn't get what I wanted, I started acting out in really self-destructive ways . . . because I just felt like I had no say . . . even now, women don't have a lot of faith in themselves, especially if you are going outside of the norm, when you're treading new ground. Everybody's always telling you what you can't do. . . . People look at you and you're brown and you're a woman, and they think, "She can't do that." It's like they immediately assume less.[26]

Fortunately visual documentation exists of Covarrubias's performances of "Misogyny." In 1992 the television program *Life and Times* dedicated an entire segment, "Chicanas in Tune," to Covarrubias and Armendariz Velasquez. "Misogyny" was originally written while Covarrubias was with The Brat. The "Chicanas in Tune" clip captures Covarrubias's 1980 punk/New Wave mode and documents her performance as she swings to the beat in a shimmering early-1960s-style dress. Her voice is forced to compete with the guitar, but she holds the attention of her enthusiastic audience. The lyrics critique the position of women within patriarchal culture:

> A woman is a precious thing
> Far beyond a wedding ring
> You have kept her under your thumb
> Creating the light haired and dumb
> You don't love her
> You abuse her
> You confuse her
> You just use her
> A woman's mind is a priceless gift
> You talk to her as if it's stripped
> Women's beauty is in her mind
> All you see is the sexual kind
> You don't love her . . .
> Blatant is misogyny
> Scattered in our history
> You will find it hard to kill
> The strength from within a woman's will
> You don't love her . . .

The narrator breaks down the elements of misogyny by exposing how they are practiced in everyday life: "You don't love her / you abuse her / you confuse her / you just use her." She critiques the strictures of matrimony that reduce women to property, to be possessed much like a wedding ring. Again the narrator exhorts the listener to understand that a woman's strength lies in her mind and will and that it is a waste to value women only for their sexuality. Moreover the power of the narrator's critique lies in her acknowledgment of the blatancy and frequency of women's abuse. Violence against women is so prevalent and in the open that its practices can be tracked throughout history and across geography, though its effects often go unacknowledged.

Though The Brat released a successful EP in 1980 called *Attitudes,* they eventually broke up and morphed into Act of Faith. The group released a compact disc in 1991, called *Act of Faith,* and then broke up again. Covarrubias has continued to write and perform, apart from her duties as an elementary school teacher in the Los Angeles Unified School District.

Mex Goddesses

Although Armendariz Velasquez was described as part of a group of young punk songstresses that in the 1970s "blanch[ed] at being described as women's libbers—a tame, middle-aged scene by their standards [although they]. . . . could accurately be described as nihilistic feminists,"[27] her optimistic, if realistic, critique of gender relations becomes apparent later. Covarrubias, as a racialized "brown" woman at Hollywood punk shows in the 1980s, approached the limits of punk's liberatory potential when she encountered "a punk elite" that was "really particular about what you looked like . . . If you didn't look right, they could be rude. . . . There were a couple of times that they would tell me, 'You don't belong here.'"[28] She and Armendariz Velasquez melded and channeled the emancipating sensibility of punk and of women-of-color feminism into the musical projects Las Tres and Goddess 13, projects that forged a sound that disrupted the exclusivity of white feminism and anti-Mexican punk. This sound, according to Armendariz Velasquez, spoke to women of color about their experiences as women.[29] "Happy Accident" by Armendariz Velasquez typifies the ways the group highlighted violence against women in their performances. The song's narrative centers on a battered woman's response to her partner's violent abuse:

> Please believe me
> I didn't mean it
> All I saw was
> the look in his eyes
> and I feared for my life
> once again.
>
> I didn't know
> it was coming
> all I know
> is he done it before
> sent me crashing to the floor
> but no more. . . .
> Oh and

I can't say that
Oh no, no
I regret it
'cause after all I had tried to leave every other way
And if I had the chance
to do it all again
I don't think it
would have a different end
I'm quite happy with this accident.

I didn't know
it was loaded
Yes, I knew where he kept all his guns
and I just grabbed the one
that was closest
So, if you ask
why I'm smiling
You may think
that a prison cell's tough
but I'm much better off
than before.

Oh and
I can't say that
Oh no, no
I regret it
'cause after all it'd be him or me
you'd be talking to.

Though the narrative is bleak, the mid-tempo beat and clave accent create a "Chicana *trova* sound."[30] The contrast between the rhythmic sound of the music and the lyrics creates a punk-like disruption. The limited options the woman possesses in response to the domestic violence that has "sent [her] crashing to the floor" end up freeing her from one situation but containing her in another. She finds that a "prison cell's tough / but I'm much better off than before." This tragic, all too real scenario speaks to the alarming rate of incarceration for women of color.[31]

Las Tres recorded a live performance at the Los Angeles Theater Center in 1993 and had recorded enough material to shop a compact disc to labels. However the tapes never saw the light of day because the two women could not afford to buy the masters from the recording engineer. The band had been in hiatus since the mid-1990s, but they reunited for El Vez's 2002 Quinceañera Show and for the Eastside Review, a reunion of East Los Angeles boogie and rock 'n' roll bands from the 1940s which performed at the Los Angeles Japanese American Cultural Center in October 2002.

Vexed

Because "the Vex became a center for artistic activity of all kinds," punk musicians began to interact with visual and performance artists.[32] Theresa Covarrubias remembers that The Brat "did a show there with local artists. . . . It was through the Vex that I realized there were a lot of artists and poets in East L.A."[33] Equally important for young Chicanas gathering at the Vex, whatever their artistic medium, themes of sexuality, antiwar protests, and antiracism ran throughout the narratives. In fact, Reyes and Waldman claim that bands like The Brat produced enough original, exciting material to generate interest in the band throughout the L.A. punk underground. It was not long before punk fans from the West Side, maybe some of those who sneered at Theresa when she traveled to their part of town, came to see The Brat perform at the Vex.[34]

It can be argued that Chicana/o youth, marginalized by the West Side rock scene, enticed West Side youth, who otherwise refused to see Chicano culture as cosmopolitan or worthy of their interest, and succeeded in creating integrated places in the most unexpected ways. As Sean Carrillo claims: "The punk scene had done the impossible. It accomplished what few cultural movements before had been able to do: it attracted all people from all over town to see a Latino band, and it brought musicians from all over the city to . . . deep in the heart of East L.A."[35]

Covarrubias and Armendariz Velasquez found punk to be an alternative oppositional movement to the Chicano movement, from which they felt excluded because of their position on gender issues. For these Chicanas from East L.A., punk subculture was not the end of their identity formation, but it was a path to a new way of being in the world and to exposing the world to their reality.

Pistols Go Chicano, Hendrix Goes Tex Mex:
Plotting New Connections

Understanding U.S. punk within a U.S. Latino/Latin American context produces exciting new questions, problematics, and contradictions in the analysis of popular music. Equally important, it challenges the dominant paradigm framing Chicano Studies. To conclude, I'd like to return to *Pretty Vacant* to explore how the film problematizes both Popular Music Studies and Chicano Studies. *Pretty Vacant* turns on three narrative strands that finally intersect at the climax of the film. The first strand involves Molly's avoidance of her father and his attachment to a nostalgia for Mexico that does not incorporate her (so refreshingly different from Moctezuma Esparza and Gregory Nava's representation of Selena as a devoted daughter). Molly's dad has bought her an airplane ticket for the annual family reunion in Mexico that she does not want to attend. The second strand invokes Molly's discovery of a well-kept secret that will allow her, as a producer of 'zines and a beginning filmmaker, to rewrite rock 'n' roll history by inserting herself, and Tejano culture, in her films. The third strand involves Molly's preparation for a performance of her all-girl band called "Aztlán-a go-go," in which she is the drummer. Molly's father eventually catches up to her, and she ends up going to Mexico. But what she finds is not her father's version of *México viejo,* but a dynamic, exciting youth culture composed of *rockeros/as* (young people who listen to and make *rock en español*) who are also concerned with social change.

Broadcast in Los Angeles on Public Television in May 1998, the film successfully uses humor to deal with usually painful issues, including a daughter's fight against patriarchal constraints, the frustration of having one's history erased, and the refusal to recognize the artistic and intellectual talents of racialized young women in the struggle to create the conditions for the emergence of a world free from gendered, racialized, and economic oppression. The film also provokes questions it does not necessarily address: as the daughter of a Mexican maid and a working-class Tejano, informed by the Chicano movement in its Texas manifestation, what can Molly—who lives at the geographic meeting place of Mexico and the United States, and who lives at the cultural intersection of Steve Jordon (who is known as San Antonio's "Chicano Jimi Hendrix of the accordion") and the Sex Pistols (Jordon stands for the symbolic intersection of San Antonio's and London's working-class culture)—tell us about this particular cultural moment, about new formations of politics of representation, and how does she speak to unequal economic conditions? What can Molly's character, who sees herself in both a local and international milieu, and who recognizes herself as a gendered, racialized, and classed subject, tell us about transnational popular music and its potential for a feminist cultural politics, one that Gloria Anzaldúa, Norma Alarcón, and Sonia Saldívar-Hull specify as a border feminist politics insofar as it "is a feminism that exists in a borderland not limited to geographical space . . . that resides in a space not acknowledged by hegemonic culture" and that illuminates the "intersections of the multiple systems of exploitation: capitalism, patriarchy, and white supremacy"?[36]

The Molly character offers us a few important insights: that disempowered youth still make their presence felt in the realm of alternative though not always oppositional culture; that rock returns to the United States from Mexico as *rock en español* in the hands of Chicana/o and Mexican youth who themselves are transformed by the music; that Chicana feminism cannot be contained by nationalism and national boundaries; that all forms of resistance to the values of the dominant culture have yet to be incorporated and that resistance exists, albeit not in mass movements, but in local sites; and that 'zines, popular music, and independent film enable conversations to occur across distant geographical locations between young people whose interests are not represented by corporate media. Finally the character of Molly reminds us that Chicana feminist thinking has enabled the production of this film, and it helps us to locate sites of resistance to gendered norms and to the desires of the dominant culture in the most unexpected places.

Remapping Punk

Pretty Vacant takes place on the west side of San Antonio during the early 1990s. It is a setting far removed from both the time and place of the Sex Pistols' initial fame in the 1970s. Yet it is Molly's investment in rewriting 1980s pop culture that drives her to revise and complicate circuits of musical diaspora as mapped out by the work of British scholars such as Paul Gilroy's *The Black Atlantic* (Molly literally recreates this Gilroy-style mapping in relation to Tex-Mex and its transatlantic meeting with the Sex Pistols in the film) and Dick Hebdige's *Subculture: The Meaning of Style* by documenting the "Tejanoization" of the Sex Pistols' music. Always subverting stereotypical expectations of what constitutes Chicanas' interest, the most recent issue of her 'zine is dedicated to punk music. She sets out to prove a secret that will forever transform rock 'n' roll history: that her favorite British punk band, the Sex Pistols, had been Chicano-fied by their visit to San Antonio. Molly believes that the Sex Pistols heard Steve Jordon's funky *conjunto,* called "El Kranke," and that they were going to do a cover of the song for their performance. Her current edition of *Ex-Voto* is dedicated to her two musical obsessions Esteven Jordon (Jimi Hendrix of the Accordion) and the Sex Pistols. She is determined to prove that Chicano music influenced the Pistols during their performances in San Antonio. As a band that gives her inspiration for thinking about the world in new ways and for plotting new connections, Molly does research on the legendary final performance of the Sex Pistols at a cowboy club in San Antonio called Randy's. According to Molly, it was their last and best performance.

Snooping around the backstage area, she finds a piece of paper hidden behind the stage. "Get this—the Sex Pistols' play list! And, even more amazing? Scribbled at the bottom?—Listen to this—'El Kranke,' someone wrote 'El Kranke!' one of Steve Jordon's songs! Shit man, the Pistols were gonna end the show that night with some *conjunto*!"[37]

Inventing her alternatives around British punk is a response to her limited options circumscribed by Chicano patriarchy and U.S. racism. Her attraction to British Punk is not about Great Britain, but instead it is about her desire for an Other—she exoticizes Britain from a Tejana point of view: it is her imaging of Britain as a place where oppositional discourses and styles are produced, styles that she can later mine for their symbolic potential. But this imaging of Great Britain is not that far off. It is the inverse of European youth having their image of the U.S. framed by oppositional discourses articulated by some hip-hop production. Molly mentions that the "Clash (acclaimed anti-capitalist punk British band popular in the '80s), for instance jazzed up their music with this reggae influence. A direct reflection of their exposure to the Caribbean diaspora and its musical expression there in London."[38]

Such discourses emerging in the "third world" found their way to Great Britain through the musical milieu of progressive black British immigrants and white British youth. Via the imported British records, Tejana Molly tunes in to the embedded oppositional discourses layered within the music—but the process of layering discourses within the sounds and lyrics of the music does not end there. Molly narrates the further layering of the British sound with *conjunto*—with its own oppositional history in "Tejas." She explains: "I was going on the assumptions that the Pistols probably heard the *conjunto* on KCOR or Radio Jalapeño on the bus ride down from Austin. But the point is, it worked."

For Molly, her 'zine *Ex-Voto*, her band, and short films are the places where she engages what Norma Alarcón describes as the "struggle for histories actual and imaginary that give substance and provide an account of her/their position within culture and the political economy."[39] Molly's art practices are emblematic of both Chicana feminist art practices and theoretical writings of the 1980s. She self-publishes the 'zine *Ex-Voto* "'cause no one was addressing my needs," just as Chicana feminists formed organizations like MALCS (Mujeres Activas en Letras y Cambio Social) and writers and artists created venues for their own work. Molly's 'zine catalogues the influences on her proto-feminist subjectivity. She is still in formation. She combines the cut-and-paste aesthetic of punk with Chicana *rasquache* to create a form that expresses her social location, where she prints essays titled, "Never Mind Che, Here's La Molly," ironically riffing off the song "Never Mind the Bollocks, Here's the Sex Pistols," while at the same time implicating Che Guevara, or at least the memory of him, in gendered power relations and disrupting the iconic Che as the signifier of social revolution. That she publishes the letters responding to 'zine articles written about "Emma Temayuca, the history of *retablos*, Love and Rockets, María Félix movies, Dolores Huerta, Ester Hernández, the Ramones, and Sor Juana Inéz de la Cruz" speaks to the way in which the circulation of popular art forms is used to create community outside of the bounds of ethnicity.

The Emergence of Chicana DIY Feminist Politics

Molly *is* linked to an earlier generation of Chicana politics, but the filmic representation of that connection is done in a complex, anti-essentialist manner through the composition of a scene that carefully locates Molly spatially and temporally. On her way to work at an independent record store called Hogwild where she clerks, Molly leads us through local shots of San Antonio's *mexicano* neighborhoods, the Alamo, and the city's freeways. At the record store, Molly informs us:

> I was born twenty-one years ago on January 23rd, 1973, a Saturday, the same day Raza Unida met for their first—and only—national convention, and across the Atlantic, David Bowie released *Ziggy Stardust*: both movements didn't last, a radical Chicano political party and Bowie's particular strain of androgynous rock, but both had their influences on me to this day.[40]

Molly's birthday, January 23, 1973, is significant in the development of Chicana politics. In "Mujeres Por La Raza Unida," Evey Chapa details the development of the Chicana Caucus in relation to the January 23rd National Raza Unida meeting, a caucus that was formed by women who felt that more needed to be done to ensure women's participation in the party's electoral politics and positions of power. Chapa explains,

> We used the already evident commitment of many *mujeres* to the Raza Unida Party, . . . to implement the strategies for the development of Mujeres por La Raza Unida . . . a mini-meeting was held in Cristal [Crystal City, Texas] attended by those who felt that words are not enough, that action is the only possible recourse. We formulated a strategy to discuss and survey the *mujer* issue with *mujeres* themselves. We canvassed opinions throughout the state . . . for five months they planned . . . On August 4, 1973, in San Antonio, Texas, the first

Conferencia de Mujeres por La Raza Unida was held. It was attended by almost two hundred women from twenty different counties.[41]

The formation of the Chicana caucus within a larger political organization was an important move, but by the time Molly comes of age, the historical conditions that supported mass movements for social transformation and civil rights had changed. Yet Molly is a subject born out of the difficult struggles that did win important social advances. And that recognition allows her to narrate herself as being born of two movements, one concerned with social justice and organized around the more traditional electoral politics of the male domain, and the other concerned with the critique of traditional masculinity and located in the cultural sphere of popular music. Molly recognizes the value of both types of organizing. The lasting effects that the two movements had on her was to direct her to the realm of cultural politics, a place where she engages her own cultural work. She finds ammunition for imagining cultural transformation beyond the frame of cultural nationalism in the sphere of oppositional punk popular culture. In the domain of oppositional popular culture, she imagines affiliation with other marginalized youth who also desire a different world. Yet while working in the realm women have traditionally been relegated to—that of the domain of culture reproduction—Molly does not reproduce traditional Chicano, patriarchal cultural nor the status quo values of the dominant culture. She creates something new, like her flesh-and-blood analogues—an alternative public sphere that includes her. Though corporate media chose not to give coverage to most oppositional movements during the Reagan–Bush era—the historical moment when the globalization of capital accelerated and conservative political ideology dominated the public sphere—Molly's obsession with 1980s alternative popular culture speaks to the ways young people fashioned oppositional consciousness then and now out of available resources found in the most unexpected places.

The film *Pretty Vacant* was released around the same time as *Selena* (1997) —the first Hollywood hit film to feature a Mexican American female pop star protagonist. Unlike *Selena*, with its melodramatic narrative based on the real-life Selena's tragic death, *Pretty Vacant* engages questions of representation brought up by Chicana feminist theorists. Like the Latina punks Hopey and Maggie, whose lesbian relationship Jaime Hernández depicts with great sensitivity in the *Love and Rockets* series, Mendiola's Molly represents a grassroots feminist punk—still in formation—that draws inspiration from the signs of British punk, the *Love and Rockets* series itself, Tejano culture in general, and *rock en español* to construct an "alternative" location away from patriarchal Aztlán, yet still oppositional to the racism of the dominant culture, a place from which to imagine new ways of being in the world, ways that speak to similar but structurally different conditions of working-class feminists, both straight and queer.

Again I ask why are this film and its flyer so provocative? The numerous forms of cultural politics invented by Chicanas who have engaged in subversive art and identity-formation have been underexamined, despite the fact that we have much to learn from their aesthetic and feminist practices. We have yet to understand fully how they set the stage for a future generation of artists and musicians.

What is equally fascinating is the potential for dialogue between Chicana feminist singer-songwriters in the United States and *rockeras* from Mexico, who, of course, are positioned differently by their respective nation-states in terms of racial hierarchies and class location, and whose concerns are certainly not identical. In examining the flow of youth culture back and forth between Mexico and the United States, thorny and complex questions of race and class privilege emerge. Yet, as the musical culture demonstrates, the point of connection, of affiliation between Chicanas and Mexicanas interested in transforming gender relations, stems from the shared recognition of their subordinated position within patriarchal culture. Their discursive interventions concerning gender and class relations point toward the possibility for transnational affiliation around critiques of violence against women, and specifically against *mestizas* and women of color. The work of Julia Palacios and Tere Estrada on the history of women in Mexican rock, found in this collection, sets us in that direction.

Selected Discography

Act of Faith. *Act of Faith*. 1991. Produced by Time Bomb Music Company.
The Bags. "We Don't Need the English." 1979. *Yes L.A.* (compilation). Produced by Dangerhouse Records.
The Brat. *Attitudes*. 1980. Produced by Fatima Records.
Las Tres. *Las Tres Live at the LATC*. 1993. Produced by Panocha Dulce–Black Rose–Bhima Music.

On How Bloque de Búsqueda Lost Part of Its Name

The Predicament of Colombian Rock in the U.S. Market

HÉCTOR D. FERNÁNDEZ L'HOESTE

> Maybe it's naive, but I would love to believe that once you grow to love some aspect of a culture—its music, for instance—you can never again think of people of that culture as less than yourself.
> —David Byrne

> Transnationalism is the American mode of expansion. It means "freedom of action" rather than "power of control."
> —Samuel Huntington

In a recent *New York Times* article, David Byrne, the lead singer and ex-member of Talking Heads, expressed his dislike for the term *world music,* a label favored by recording houses and music stores nationwide.[1] According to Byrne, the term is simplistic and reductive since it groups, in a single category, all bands or music that lie beyond the English-speaking domain of the U.S. music market. Among other arguments, he suggests that the label is used to designate Otherness. In this way, all the cultures of the underdeveloped world are grouped and their characteristics are synthesized into a single difference. To Byrne, this routine, in which all chance of distinction is practically lost, is extremely problematic. The following article shows the marked contrast between Byrne's statements and the story of a group under his aegis, which, to a considerable extent, exemplifies his role as accomplice to cultural appropriation and magnifies the degree to which the artist, thanks in part to ethnocentrism, is unable to overcome the disposition to think of others *as less than him-*

self. Despite Byrne's good intentions, the case of the Colombian band Bloque illustrates the risks implicit in today's transnational, globalized music market.

Rock in Colombia: A Cultural Phenomenon in Spite of Itself

As in most Latin American nations, rock arrived in Colombia in the late 1950s.[2] For Colombia, a country that in those days exhibited minimal rates of migration and experienced a provincial, insular reality, rock represented increased contact with Latin American neighbors and cosmopolitan centers. Rock was, in a way, a revolving door to the global community. Although the country was geographically close to the United States, given its commercial isolation, it was perceived by inhabitants of the industrialized world as exotic and distant. When Gabriel García Márquez titled his masterpiece *One Hundred Years of Solitude,* the choice was not accidental. It is important to consider that the expansion of Colombian rock parallels the country's accelerated urbanization and a demographic spurt that would make it the second largest Spanish-speaking nation in the world. Hence the context of Colombian rock is a drastically fluctuating one, perhaps more changeable than that of other nations in the Americas. This essay proposes to give an accounting of the experience of rock in Colombia, though it cannot provide an exhaustive periodization; rather, my object is to suggest that a combination of aspects render the case of Colombia exceptional within the Western hemisphere. These aspects, in turn, are crucial in the consideration of Byrne's relationship to the band Bloque.

In geopolitical terms, given its hazardous topography, Colombia is a notably broken enclave. Regional differences are very marked, more so than in the average Latin American context, and they are profoundly reflected in local and national culture. The *patria chica* (small homeland), the sense of affiliation to a region—be it the Caribbean, the Andes (eastern, central, or western), the Eastern Plains, etc.—is a very important aspect of identity in Colombia and, in many cases, compensates for the deficiencies in the construct of the Colombian nation. Having now endured as a nation for more than fifty years, the political instability and social unrest that characterize Colombia are merely the consequence of the central government's failure to implement a legitimate project of nationhood; this aspect, unfortunately, has remained a constant. Accentuated regionalism exacerbates feelings of disparity and colors the social divisions prevalent, as in most Latin American countries, within Colombia's borders. Consequently it is impossible to allude to any process that entails identity formation without also contemplating and considering regional differences. Although in other cases it might prove feasible to talk of a *rock nacional* —Argentina and Mexico, countries with a more consolidated, and at times inflexible, official culture, come to mind—in the Colombian case, this is particularly problematic. In Argentina, in particular, where the label *nacional* was first elaborated, rock was perceived as an authentic celebration of national identity. In Colombia, however, such an association between rock and nationalism has been, at best, individualized. Regional differences have shaped, to a large extent, the celebration of rock as a cultural practice.

As elsewhere, the media and the private sector have played a key role in the rise of rock in Colombia. Thus centralism, typical of most Latin American nations, played a tangible role. Disc jockeys such as Jimmy Reisback, who worked for the Caracol (Cadena Radial Colombiana) network, played U.S. rock as a novelty as early as 1958.[3] Radio Quince, a chain with stations in the main Colombian cities—Bogotá, Medellín, Cali, Barranquilla, and Bucaramanga—dedicated its broadcasting almost exclusively to music for a younger audience; rock represented a substantial component of that programming. In the 1960s the *Club del Clan*, a hit TV program copied from Argentine and Puerto Rican versions, generated a cult-like following and contributed enormously to the music's growing popularity. In cinema, Argentine, Mexican, and Spanish imports accelerated the process of rock's popularity. Films such as Palito Ortega's *Amor en el aire* (*Love in the Air,* 1967), César Costa's *Juventud rebelde* (*Rebellious Youth,* 1961), *El cielo y la tierra* (*Heaven and Earth,* 1962), and *La juventud se impone* (*The Young Take Over,* 1964), as well as a host of pictures with Rocío Dúrcal, teen idol Marisol, and the twins Pili y Mili contributed largely to the movement's acceptance. In 1966 Nestlé, the Swiss conglomerate, organized Milo a Go-Go, a promotion tour for a milk-based drink, which most Colombians recall as the first national rock-oriented event.

Throughout this initial phase, following a general trend in the Americas, rock was chiefly a matter of imitation. If there was Tom Jones in the U.K. and Sandro in Argentina—both sexy, hunky singers—then in Colombia there was Óscar Golden. As for juvenile-oriented singers, Mexico watched teen idols Enrique Guzmán and César Costa, while Argentina listened to Palito Ortega. Colombia had its own versions: Juan Nicolás Stella, Álvaro Román, Harold, and Luis Fernando Garcés. Whereas Rocío Dúrcal was, for Spain, a young, provocative female singer, in Colombia there were Vicky and Lyda Zamora. In the United States there was Woodstock and in Mexico there was Avándaro; Colombians—*antioqueños* mainly, people from Medellín and the surrounding province—had Ancón. In that small town on the outskirts of the province, Colombians staged their own rock festival on June 18–20, 1971. Nevertheless, local differences did add an additional twist to the equation: after Ancón, the local clergy immediately denounced the event as malignant and, on the radio, Father Fernando Gómez Mejía, through his program *La Hora Católica* (*The*

Catholic Hour), assured listeners that even the devil had attended. Eventually given the local bourgeoisie's reactionary spirit and their voicing of concern to the provincial government, the rock concert became the principal cause for the downfall of Álvaro Villegas, Medellín's mayor at the time.[4]

Although events centered mainly in Bogotá and Medellín—in the case of "national" radio networks, programming was generally determined in the capital city—the movement's growth was marked considerably by regional and social differences. In Medellín, a city known, among other things, for the death of Argentine idol Carlos Gardel—the most important tango singer ever—and home to a traditionally conservative population, rock was embraced by youth as an alternative to a socially repressive order. Here rock acquired a distinctly lower-middle-class flavor. In Cali, a city renowned as the breeding ground for Colombian salsa, Latin sensibilities were not as eager to embrace a genre closely identified with foreign culture. After all, in the 1950s and 1960s, Cali had not yet benefited from the substantial government and private investment spurred by the Pan-American games and was then the fourth largest Colombian city. In many aspects, it was still a very provincial, peaceful town. Despite their propensity for U.S. products (unlike the Andean provinces, which seem to favor things European), cities such as Barranquilla and Cartagena incarnated the hegemony of tropical music, the body of genres associated with the Caribbean's musical tradition; thus rock was seen strictly as a thing of the upper classes. Bred on a diet of Afro-Caribbean rhythms, the people of the Atlantic coastal provinces perceived the occasional rock band as a snobbish eccentricity. Consequently only Bogotá, with its solid middle class, reliant on government bureaucracy, and Medellín, the only provincial capital with a comparable economic base, managed to develop a consistent following for rock. This close association between rock and the purchasing power of the middle-class sectors of these cities affected not only its establishment but also its development within the national context. Until the 1980s, with the arrival of Argentine and Spanish imports and the consolidation of a rock tradition in Spanish, the history of Colombian rock is, largely, a narrative that delineates the rivalry between these two cities.

In the 1960s a festive culture marked rock's popularity in Colombia. The music was associated primarily with dance and fun. While Bogotá celebrated bands such as Los Speakers, Los Flippers, and Los Danger Twist, whose repertoires consisted mostly of Spanish covers of English songs, Medellín embraced Los Yetis. At times, differences were more than skin deep. The capital's bands failed to include aspects of the local culture and were interpreted by many as concessions to the U.S.-European metropolitan order. Los Yetis, in turn, were influenced by *nadaísmo*, a poetic movement centered in Medellín, which represented an important literary event in the Colombian culture of the 1960s. *Nadaísmo* was a daring bet in a culture that enforced tradition and order; characteristically irreverent and iconoclast, the movement lambasted the academic world, the Church, and the government. The movement was also ideologically radical in the sense that it opposed the threat of all political systems—fascists and communists, equally dogmatic—to freedom. The music of Los Yetis, simple and rough, combined the logic of the *nadaístas* with hippie spirit and psychedelic aesthetics. In this respect, it is possible to claim that their limited production—two albums—contains elements of an autochthonous nature. Only at the end of the 1960s, once the prevalence of imitation was extinguished, is it possible to speak broadly of a local consciousness in national production.

During the 1970s, ironically, the movement went dormant. In this period, it is feasible to say that Colombian rock paralleled the evolution of Mexican rock—that is, much of the activity went underground. Demonization by the press and police persecution began to take their toll. The burgeoning popularity and accelerated pace of events of the 1960s never materialized into concrete proposals. In Mexico, the ballad was responsible, in part, for the movement's hibernation; in Colombia, local genres played a similar role. Record labels failed to see rock as a worthy investment and the wider class appeal of other genres was simply too alluring. While they could record a *vallenato* record in seventy hours and sell twenty thousand copies, a rock album demanded at least twice the number of hours in a recording studio and hardly reached three thousand copies.[5] Still by the beginning of the decade, folk singers and duets à la Simon and Garfunkel had established themselves firmly as figures: Pablus Gallinazus, Ana y Jaime, Norman y Darío, and José y Darío (in both of the latter cases, with Iván Darío López, an ex-member of Los Yetis). Although a great number of bands existed, most did not record. Gallinazus and Ana y Jaime, main exemplars of the *canción protesta*, the local variety of *nueva canción*, were among the lucky ones to make a recording. In Medellín, Judas and Últimos Tiempos shared most of the attention. The former attempted to prolong the hard-rock sound favored by Colombian hippies; the latter, also performing in Spanish, released several singles at the end of the decade. Musically, given their social backgrounds, the sound of bands from Medellín became increasingly aggressive, an unappealing path for the recording market. To achieve a higher social status, many bands embraced heavy metal, which, within a conservative, bucolic environment, bore dubious connotations. In Bogotá, cushioned by the government's presence—and its funding of the local economy—things took a different turn. Bands like Génesis, with Humberto Monroy, Edgar Restrepo, and Juan Fernando Echavarría, and

Malanga, with Chucho Merchán, Augusto Martelo, Amparo Cárdenas, Víctor Mencila, and Alexis Restrepo, began incorporating elements of Colombian music into their work. Certainly this concern for the integration of autochthonous elements bears the influence of the *canción protesta* movement. These experiments represent, to a fair extent, the first widely recognized attempts to develop a genuinely Colombian sound in rock; in this respect, their significance is critical. Although the bands eventually dissolved, their members bore considerable impact on the future orientation of a musical tradition. In the case of Génesis, Echavarría widely toured Latin America, researching indigenous instrumentation which was eventually integrated into his efforts in Colombia. Chucho Merchán, of Malanga, moved to London, where he launched a successful career which spanned more than twenty years. Although he played with Pete Townsend, the Pretenders, and Phil Manzanera, he is best known as the bassist for Eurythmics. Eventually, once the *rock en español* movement flourished, Merchán served as a key bridge between Bogotá and London.

While musicians from Medellín might have implemented similar formulae, their lack of access to the national media—television and radio in Colombia were, at the time, extremely centralized in Bogotá; in some respects, they still are—seriously hindered their efforts at national projection. Television, in particular, worked under an almost unique scheme: the government was owner and operator of the technological infrastructure but private production companies were responsible for the programming. As a result, for most of the national audience, rock appeared as something as distant as the capital itself, hidden amid the Andes; for many, *bogotanos* practically monopolized the artistic scene. Although seemingly irrelevant, this greatly affected the population's sense of its capacity to play a key role within official culture. Identity configuration and cultural participation, already disproportionately inequitable on account of social differences, achieved bizarre levels of misrepresentation. Slowly but surely, many of the artists in Medellín previously associated with the rock movement, facing harsh economic realities—or simply choosing a new, more productive style—drifted to other genres, mainly pop ballads and tropical rhythms. The band Afrosound, for instance, which initially sounded like a Colombian version of Santana, made an easy transition toward the latter variety. A few, like Piro, a symphonic rock band from Medellín, persevered with their approach.

Historically recording English-language rock in Colombia was not the norm, although in the 1980s this began to change. In contrast to Mexico, where in the 1960s and early 1970s English was embraced by many rockers as a vehicle of transgression, in Colombia English lacked a comparable valence of resistance. This was likely because the Colombian state was weak and played only a limited role in nationalizing Spanish-language forms of popular discourse. In turn, English lacked appeal as a confrontational tool. By contrast, the Mexican state had long sought to co-opt popular discourse as part of a nationalizing project. Hence in Mexico, English was used by *rockeros* as a means of contesting hegemonic culture. In both instances, however, left-wing sectors regarded English as an instrument of imperialism. During the 1980s, the use of English in Colombian rock was associated with purists, who equated it with true rock, or with upper-middle-class groups, who embraced it as a status symbol. Nash, a hard-rock band from Medellín, and Ship, its equivalent from Bogotá, both epitomized English-language rock during the late 1970s and early 1980s. Eventually while preserving its hard-rock style, the band Judas adopted Spanish and reemerged as Carbure. In punk, which arrived in 1979, lower-class sectors identified a way to counteract the emergence of heavy metal. By the early 1980s, the changing face of Colombian cities and the severity of the nation's economic crisis provided an ideal gritty setting for countless punk-rock bands. Two important events also influenced the Colombian scene: the avant-garde cultural outburst of activity in Spain following the death of Franco and the introduction there of a Democratic Socialist government—the period known as *movida* (move); and the prohibition of English music on Argentine radio during the Falkland Islands (Malvinas) War in 1982. The Spaniards were a novelty, but Argentine rock was well known and circulated readily among college students (that is, the middle and upper classes). Hence the recording boom in Argentina, a byproduct of the Malvinas conflict, had a direct impact on many Colombian rockers. Additionally the fact that the imported music was introduced as *rock nacional,* insinuating a link between it and national culture, appealed greatly to the Colombian public. Although Argentina was not the first country to boast local rock production (Mexico was), undoubtedly, Argentine rock was the first to gain wider commercial access and closer identification as a form of national culture. In Colombia, the private sector—in truth, the four or five conglomerates that control the national economy—had excelled in the advancement of a nationalist mentality by competing alongside a weak central government over the use of national symbols. A nationalist mindset, the bourgeoisie judged, lessened provincial differences and facilitated market penetration. To paraphrase Mexican author Roger Bartra, Colombian nationalism not only came to signify the meaning of Colombian identity but also the manner in which the average individual was dominated by the official, centralist apparatus.[6] There was a marked contrast between the Argentine band Soda Stereo's first visit to Colombia—in Bogotá, they played before a relatively small, standing audience in one of the pavilions at Corferias, the grounds of the International Fair—and their second tour, before a packed Santamaría, the bull-fighting ring in the capital's downtown district. The Chilean band Los Prisioneros, with their trashy music and sharp lyrics, became a special favorite; during their tour, they packed the Campín, Bogotá's soccer stadium, with sixty thousand spectators. The private sector was an avid witness. Like the political regime, they realized the huge potential of the phenomenon; unlike the government, their budget was not tied to nepotism. Two of the country's main conglomerates, the Santo Domingo group and the Ardila Lülle organization, owners of the soft drink and beer markets, actively sponsored bands and concerts. Since both groups also owned the main radio networks (Caracol and RCN, respectively) and, in the 1990s, the new private television networks, their support radically altered the possibilities for success of any artist.[7] In other words, like Televisa in Mexico, Globo in Brazil, or Venevisión in Venezuela, media conglomerates affected greatly—inhibited, mostly —the pace of cultural change. Whereas the most conventional artists—usually the favorites of the system—received heavy exposure, genres linked to sectors with limited purchasing power and groups with new, unconventional formulas had scant access to the media.

Throughout the 1980s, rock gained wider social acceptance and the viability of a Spanish-language rock movement was no longer contested. Just as it is possible to propose an understanding of Colombian rock out of the rivalry between two cities, it is also feasible to suggest its development from social tension between genres. In mid-1980s Medellín the antagonism between the groups Parabellum (hard-core) and Kraken (metal), and IRA (hard-core) and Masacre (metal) incarnated the opposition between the working class and more affluent sectors of society. Parabellum represented a successful attempt at hard-core rock, establishing a bridge between metal and punk; yet class animosity in Medellín, nurtured by the city's abrupt topographical layout and the rise of criminality as a means of social ascent, was stronger. Recording their first album in 1987, Kraken emerged as the first example of a new, heavy metal sound, more aligned with national reality, openly rejecting the thematic proposal of imported rock. Whereas U.S. and British metal bands had to toy with evil in their lyrics, in Medellín such imaginative rapture was unnecessary: reality was more than enough. Kraken's career would continue into the 1990s, when a major label would recruit them. In contrast, many of the key punk bands of Medellín, associated with the youth of the working-class sectors, appeared in the soundtrack of *Rodrigo D.* (1989), the film by Víctor Gaviria chronicling the plight of *sicarios*—young, paid assassins at the service of the drug cartels. Later, the film was severely attacked by punks since, according to them, it reductively equated their movement to the *sicarios*. The true spirit of punk, they claimed, had little to do with drug-sponsored political warfare. Near the end of the decade, Estados Alterados (Altered States), Medellín's main new wave group, gathered a considerable following. Since new wave appropriated aesthetic elements from the gay community, the Medellín crowd suffered from the effects of homophobia. Still at the beginning of the 1990s, Estados Alterados was the first Colombian group to have a video on the Latin version of MTV. In a nutshell, for multiple reasons, Medellín's musical progression was the product of tension between genres, which reflected, in an almost literal manner, social conflict.

In Bogotá, Darkness, a heavy metal band, La Pestilencia, a punk ensemble, and Compañía Ilimitada, a rock duo, caught most of the attention. Unlike the provincial bands, whose discourse was particularly regional, the bands from Bogotá attempted the thematic inclusion of the many sectors involved in Colombian culture and national conflicts. Compañía, whose band members came from an upper-class Bogotá prep school, was instrumental in the revival of Colombian rock, since its proposal involved a greater fusion of musical elements from across the country: *cumbia*, salsa, reggae, Andean music, etc. To a certain extent, it is possible to state that, consciously or not, many bands from the capital were particularly concerned with the development of music that would be perceived as nationally representative, inclusive in terms of its musical diversity, and consequently sponsoring a new form of cultural, centralist hegemony. Musical projects from the province, on the other hand, were more peripheral and embraced a more local perspective. Their national transcendence was interpreted, almost exclusively, as a consequence of the quality of their proposal.

La Pestilencia, a group of almost mythical proportions within the saga of Colombian rock, represents an exception to my argument. It is perhaps the only major band to actively nourish itself from the scene of both cities; thus, La Pestilencia is an archetypical exception to the norm. The critical nature of their music makes it hard to ignore them. Initially they were influenced by the Bogotá tendency toward a totalizing discourse; later they favored a more focused approach, attentive to more specific issues. Their first albums, *La muerte, un compromiso de todos* (*Death, Everyone's Commitment*, 1986), *Las nuevas aventuras de La Pestilencia* (*The New Adventures of La Pestilencia*, 1993), and *El amarillista* (*Tabloid Journalist*, 1996), trace their departure from seminal punk, through the influence of hard-core and heavy metal, to embody a personal rendition of the genre seriously committed to the dissection of social reality. Their thematic array runs the gamut: cultural colonialism, ecologic concerns, Malthusianism, and communicative alienation, among other themes. In 2001, under the auspices of Mercury Records, they released *Balística* (*Ballistic*).

If the 1980s represented a period of consolidation for Colombian rock, the 1990s were, for sure, the time to experiment and test international waters. In 1990, under the name of El Hotel Regina y la Orquesta Sinfónica de Chapinero, two cultural critics from Bogotá, Eduardo Arias and Karl Troller, along with the band Hora Local, recorded the performance piece ¡Gaitanista!—a mock homage to the Clash. Motivated by a strong concern for identity, the album involved significant exploitation of commercial culture. Although some decried the influence of Argentine Patricio Rey's playful Redonditos de Ricota, the album is, by far, the quintessential example of *bogotano* stabs at national cultural hegemony. Their subsequent production confirmed this tendency. In 1992, Ekhymosis, the Medellín band led by Juan Esteban Aristizábal, who would later launch a successful solo career under the name Juanes, released its first album, *Niño gigante* (*Giant Child*). The album included a rock version of the Colombian national anthem, which, just as in the Argentine case—with Charly García's adaptation—generated a matching scandal. When rock radio stations played it to fulfill government mandates (that the anthem be broadcast everyday), the consequent uproar and attacks promptly restricted its commercial diffusion. A year later, Aterciopelados, the best-known Colombian band in U.S. circles, debuted with *Con el corazón en la mano* (*With Heart in Hand*). In the case of the *antioqueños*, hard rock evolved into a more experimental Colombian sound, incorporating traditional instruments and rhythms; for Aterciopelados, however, grunge would give way to a hybrid version of techno, even if the music would always incorporate elements from Colombian traditions, from *guasca* (peasant music from the Andes) to *cumbia* (folkloric music from the Caribbean).

Thanks to the relative affluence of middle-class sectors of the capital, Bogotá's music scene produced groups with a more mellow, pop-oriented sound. Pasaporte and Poligamia were two such groups who enjoyed airplay on the radio and catered to the tastes of the middle and upper classes. The Colombian government, eager to benefit from the musicians, supported their efforts and even granted financial backing through the Ministry of Culture. In an odd twist, the Gaviria administration (1990–94), a champion of Colombian neoliberalism and right-wing policies that emulated British Thatcherism, financed the recording of a first album by La Derecha (the Right Wing), one of the most promising groups of the period, which, despite its potential, dissolved soon afterward. In many respects, the variety of genres and the proliferation of individualized musical projects confirm the lack of cohesiveness in Colombian society. It is exceedingly hard to suggest a common, collective spirit in Colombian rock. Rock in Colombia is Colombian by association, simply because it has been created in the country; it is far from being "national" in its cultural disposition and background, for it lacks true concern for a cohesive body politic. The country's fragmented identity, the intermittent nature of rock production, and the lack of a successful official culture render such correlation impossible. In Colombia, nation and state allude to very different spaces: the break between the people (nation) and the theoretical and physical presence of the state (rule of law, political identification, and infrastructure) is more marked than elsewhere in Latin America. That is why, to this day, many question the essence of so-called *rock nacional* in the Colombian context. Since the state itself is being contested, it seems rather impulsive to celebrate anything as *nacional.*

Hence it is seemingly logical that Colombia's best-known rock figure—despite owing substantial credit to pop—does not come from Medellín or Bogotá. Shakira, the daughter of a businessman of Lebanese descent born in New York and a Colombian woman, enjoyed a meteoric rise at the end of the 1990s. Shakira is from Barranquilla, a city where rock bands had represented—at best—a quaint curiosity. Her ascent confirms the genre's increasing popularity and the gaps in the dual hegemony of the national rock tradition. Though some of her early career was in the capital, for practical purposes, Shakira bypassed Bogotá's influence in her artistic development; instead she moved to Miami. Having sold millions of records, in Spanish as well as in Portuguese, throughout Latin America, Shakira released a successful English album, *Laundry Service,* at the end of 2001. Six months later, the recording was certified double platinum in the United States, multiple platinum in Latin America, triple platinum in Spain, and platinum in Canada. Furthermore according to the arts section in the February 16, 2001 edition of the Colombian newspaper *El Espectador,* in an indication of true globalization, the album's first hit, "Whenever, Wherever," was number one in Germany, Australia, Denmark, Canada, Italy, Norway, Turkey, Lebanon, and New Zealand. Shakira's product, characteristically generic and nationally anonymous, seems to fit equally well in Europe and the United States. She may sometimes talk about Colombia, but, unlike other acts—Aterciopelados, for instance, decorated an album with the national flag—her music and videos do not emphasize national aspects.

At the same time that Colombian music was becoming a successful export, crucial societal changes reflecting the impact of globalization were taking place at home. Without a doubt, one of the most important achievements of rock's acceptance is the establishment of the Rock al Parque concert series. The event, which has enjoyed remarkable regularity, entails one of the largest rock celebrations in Latin America, with massive attendance of bands and public. During the 1990s, Bogotá benefited from two consecutively efficient administrations, that of Antanas Mockus, an academic of Lithuanian descent who served as president of the National University, and that of Enrique Peñalosa, a

Duke University graduate with a degree in urban planning from a French university. They virtually changed the face of the city. Although their styles were different, they supported the celebration of huge, open-air concerts at three main venues in the capital. Bands from all over Latin America flocked to Bogotá and authenticated the event as a cradle of new talent. Mockus's method, in particular, suggested a revamping of the relationship between the individual and the urban environment. Rock profited from the event because its image became synonymous with urban flair, and previous concerns—such as rock as a purveyor of corruption and violence—were laid to rest. These are, in short, several circumstances and events that contribute to the definition of the national variety of rock as Colombian and distinguish it from the music production on the rest of the continent. Although some aspects of Colombian rock may reflect a similarity in conditions from other Latin American countries, it is their unique arrangement that grants Colombian rock its specificity.

The Case of Bloque: The Perils of Identity in Transnational Circuits

Amid all these incidents, the case of the band Bloque exemplifies the interaction between bands of the national variety and global circuits of communication. During the 1980s, Iván Benavides, singer and guitarist of the duo Iván y Lucía, a folk act in the spirit of *nueva canción*, was very popular within Colombian university circles. The duo was a college favorite and eventually appeared on television and recorded; their main single, "Alba," enjoyed mixed success. In the 1990s, Lucía Pulido, Ivan's partner, left for the United States to pursue vocal studies. Benavides then decided to form a band with a group of friends, becoming part of the *vallenato* experiment of Carlos Vives, a musician who would later become renowned in the Spanish-speaking world. *Vallenato* music, long a favorite in rural areas, was listened to mostly on the Caribbean coast and in lower-class homes throughout the country. From the beginning, Vives sought a more modern sound, adding electric guitar, percussion, and synthesizer to the traditional accordion ensemble. With a distinct urban flair, he successfully commercialized *vallenato* and heightened its social profile, bringing it to the middle and upper-middle classes. Aside from his own personal project, Vives created a label called Gaira Música Local, meant to sponsor groups that combined elements of traditional Colombian music with modern genres. Lucía Pulido, the band Distrito Especial—one of the favorites of the Bogotá night scene of the 1980s—and the group of friends who would eventually form the band Bloque were among the people Vives supported. Moisés Angulo, a TV actor who sang Caribbean tunes and the group Raperos de Urabá were also included. Aside from providing an opportunity to musicians with scant support from the recording labels, Vives reasoned, these artists could serve as opening acts during his tours with La Provincia (the Province), his group of musicians. As a result, Benavides's musicianship flourished. In fact, after a short while, the above-mentioned group of artists, headed by Benavides and Ernesto "Teto" Ocampo, his roommate, decided to record independently and pursue a separate identity. As part of La Provincia, Benavides had authored songs and co-produced the best-selling album *La Tierra del Olvido* (*The Land of Oblivion*, 1995). Now Benavides and "Teto" stopped being part of La Provincia and formed Bloque de Búsqueda, which alluded to the improvised team arranged by Colombia's National Police to capture the drug kingpin Pablo Escobar (the name means, literally, "search party"). The band, an eclectic mix of heritage and enthusiasm, directly integrated Caribbean elements and, in this respect, was unlike many previous Colombian rock bands. Through its musicians, it actively integrated the tropical tradition into the manufacture of rock. Mayte Montero, the female vocalist, had worked with such Colombian musical icons as Totó la Momposina and Joe Arroyo. Luis Ángel Pastor, the bassist, was an institution among Colombian tropical music bands. These musicians, it was clear, belonged to a different musical heritage; they were not just pretending to copy—as in the past—arrangements from other parts of the country. At the same time, the remaining band members came from Bogotá and belonged to the rock tradition. In the 1980s Carlos Iván Medina had formed Distrito Especial. Ocampo had studied in Los Angeles, where he met Pablo Bernal, another member. They were all familiar with the capital's night scene, where rock, salsa, *vallenato,* and jazz were played and blended. Hence the situation was a bit odd because, while playing under a different identity, many still collaborated with Vives. This type of compromise would eventually contribute to the band's problems.

Having landed a contract with a local recording house, they released a first album, titled after the band. The album, recorded in Bogotá and mastered in Miami, was received enthusiastically. Among others, it sparked the interest of David Byrne's New York City-based record label, Luaka Bop, which was a brand distributed by Warner Brothers. Excited by the discovery, Byrne offered the group a contract that opened the doors to the U.S. music market and, hence, to bigger horizons. At this point, things get a little confusing. Some accounts talk of a rupture between Benavides and Vives.[8] According to these versions, once the musicians tried to venture in an entirely independent way, many obstacles surfaced. On the other hand, other accounts claim that, precisely thanks to Vives's intervention, the musicians were able to dissolve their contract with the Colombian label Sonolux on amicable terms and sign with Byrne. In any case, at this point, Benavides and his friends were already under the management of Marusa Reyes, agent for the Mexican bands Caifanes and Jaguares. Having signed a contract with Byrne, Bloque de Búsqueda released a new recording in 1998, another album with the group's name as its title and with almost identical musical content—though remixed and mastered in Los Angeles—now with major distribution guaranteed. Since their identity was still linked to their previous professional relationship, at this point, to facilitate things, their name was shortened to simply Bloque. Sales, although not exorbitant, were satisfactory. The group went on a U.S. tour and was promoted as a powerhouse of Colombian rock. In the *Atlanta Journal-Constitution,* Steve Dollar raved about them and, in full-page coverage, used the band to explain the phenomenon of *rock en español.*[9] Unlike other *rock en español* bands, in which metropolitan influences prevailed, Bloque proposed a fusion of the elements of the African diaspora: funk, reggae, salsa, *cumbia,* and rock. The range of their mix was vast, and influences, though recognizable, were integrated with a deft touch: Jimi Hendrix, Led Zeppelin, Hector Lavoe, Rubén Blades, Ismael Rivera, Tom Waits, Caetano Veloso, Fela Kuti, James Brown, and Prince, among others.

The U.S. press was ecstatic. According to *New York Times* critic Jon Pareles, "The power of rock, too often taken for granted in the United States, is just gathering force across Latin America. Bloque, a band from Colombia, hotwires local traditions from across Colombia with funk, hard rock and jazz. It doesn't imitate American and English styles, it colonizes them." In his list of the year's ten best new groups, Bloque appeared as fifth; aside from the Brazilian Carlinhos Brown, Bloque was the only other non-English-speaking band on the list. Greg Kot, critic for the *Chicago Tribune* and correspondent for *Rolling Stone,* claimed, "The best new rock band on the planet is from Colombia. This co-ed octet mixes up Led Zeppelin crunch, tropical rhythms, rap vocals and Latin folk music with so much intelligence, savvy and joy that it sounds second nature. Iván Benavides is a front man who radiates charisma, sarcasm and urgency—imagine Midnight Oil's Peter Garrett with a sense of humor." In his review for *Rolling Stone,* he stated, "Nothing is too audacious for this band. . . . Bloque collapses tired notions about Latin rock and dances on the ruins." Bloque also drew critical review from the *Los Angeles Times:* "The ultimate live outfit, Bloque is the kind of band you wish would perform every weekend at the joint down the street. . . . The Colombian group's Los Angeles debut . . . was a revelation"; and the *Boston Globe:* "Bloque's music—political, angry, danceable, brilliant—is unlike anything yet recorded in the rock genre." From September to December 1998, the band was reviewed by specialized publications, such as *Spin* and *Rolling Stone,* and the press of major U.S. cities—every destination of the tour festively promoted by Warner Brothers.[10] Although this coverage does not determine the behavior of the market or the group's total sales volume, it does offer a good indication of the degree of acceptance of a musical product. The preceding quotes are not irrelevant; they represent the criteria of the establishment of the U.S. music press. Thus, the exuberance and benevolence of their criticism is, at the very least, a source for suspicion. The only other two contemporary Latin American rock imports to have sparked a similar response within the U.S. press are Argentina's Los Fabulosos Cadillacs and Mexico's La Maldita Vecindad, and these bands—it must be pointed out—arrived in the U.S. directly from Latin American beachheads via videos in MTV's Latin American version or through concerts and releases meant exclusively for the Spanish U.S. market. There are more conventional groups of Colombian rock, such as Aterciopelados, which have operated within this scheme: their entry into the U.S. market has been a consequence of their Latin American success. Unlike them, Bloque was marketed, from the start, as a *rock en español* band for the Anglo market, and, in terms of genre, as world music. At the end of the *New York Times* article, Byrne reveals, with a certain sense of pride and false modesty, that Bloque is one of the breakthroughs of his label. This reaction, in a market as competitive as the record industry is, at best, ambiguous.

The curious thing about this matter is that, during a recent visit to Colombia, I could not locate either the recording by Bloque or the one by Bloque de Búsqueda in the capital city's music scene.[11] Not even in the black market was it possible to find a trace; nor in Tower Records, located in the fashionable Zona Rosa district of Bogotá. It would have been logical to find the album on the Caribbean coast, given the strength of its music market, yet here too, the album was absent. (Cali, with its insular condition and its manifest preference for salsa was a less likely place to find the album, at any rate.) In short, a group hailed by the U.S. press as the avant-garde of Colombian rock is a virtual unknown in Colombia itself. Benavides has admitted to this fact; he attributes Bloque's limited national recognition to the lack of a press office during the time they were being touted as a runaway success in the U.S. In a recent article in *Cambio,* the newsweekly purchased by Gabriel García Márquez upon his return to journalism, Benavides appears next to a mixed group of musicians. Those musicians include Nelson Carlos Bicenty, lead singer for La Banda, whose music blends Andean music and Caribbean rhythms, and Armazón, a band that combines *carranguera*—the music of the bars of the Andes—with elements of rock and electronic sounds. The *Cambio* article describes Benavides as part of a new generation of musicians who want to commercialize traditional music without sacrificing its essence, a trend started and promoted by Carlos Vives's great success abroad. While mistakenly identifying Benavides as the lead singer of the group El Bloque, the article discusses Benavides's claims that the band tries to incorporate world trends into its music, and that, in this way, the members maintain connections to their roots yet do not live staring at their navels. His remarks coincide, to a certain extent, with Pareles's description of Bloque's ability to assimilate styles and genres with great ease. In any case, the article confirms the scant recognition of the artist and his band within a national context. It places the band, almost immediately, within a musical controversy over *colombianidad* led by ensembles of traditional music with chamber instrumentation, musicologists, and conservatory students. This restrictive musical tendency constitutes a repertoire, to say the least, that is a bit demanding for the preferences of the general public.

My contention is this: Bloque—or Bloque de Búsqueda—serves to illustrate the dynamics of transnationalization within the Latin American rock scene. Once they were transferred to the U.S. record industry, the band lost—aside from part of its name—a great deal of its image management. Distribution by an international house in a foreign market clearly has its implications. In a world where culture is increasingly internationally oriented and economies are global, the rendering of a Latin American identity abroad can be unlike the one projected at a national or regional level. In fact, the dynamics of this displacement are best illustrated by the change that Brazilian theorist Renato Ortiz associates with the shift from the multinational to the transnational. Under these conditions, the transnational recording companies cease to exhibit strong centers of power with numerous weaker branches. Rather, they produce with specific markets in mind, and become multi-faceted entities with specialized subsidiaries—as is the case of Luaka Bop, for Warner Brothers—which produces the same thing for everybody.[13] Such a trend tends, among other things, to dissipate any sense of otherness or distinction within the morass of the hegemonic market. Once the consumers of the industrialized world familiarize themselves with an act—no matter how singular—the opportunity to communicate difference is diminished, since the market assimilates the features pertinent to a particular product and identifies those features as mere permutation of the musical arrangement. In this way, in a medium where there is an increasing blurring of genre boundaries, music ceases to be indicative of ethnic or national origin and becomes simply an item of global consumption. This consumption is immediately associated with certain lifestyles and a homogenized segment of the market, which enjoys equivalents in many places of the world. In turn, the effectiveness of distinctive forms of representation of identity is lost. This is the first outcome of such a case.

Despite my interest in matters of identity, it must be clarified that I am not backing an essentialist argument. My understanding of identity does not refer to a single entity; rather, it implies a continually negotiated body of relationships in constant flux and indeterminacy. My emphasis on the relevance of regionalism in the preceding portion of this essay does not mean, for instance, that I support regionalism. Regionalism is, in this context, a small-scale version of nationalism. What moves me, therefore, is how each version of identity manages to attain legitimacy. It is evident that, as a category of interpretation, *colombianidad*, for example, faces a crisis. Therefore, my concern lies in the mechanics of transnationalization. When Bloque shortened its name, the change responded to the limitations of the music market. In the process, the band's original album was reduced from fourteen tracks to twelve. Three tracks with an ethnic sound too distinctive to be categorized as rock were discarded. In their place, two new themes were included, one of which was not even written by the band. Additionally, the instrumental portion of various tracks was enhanced. Aside from these changes, the musical arrangements are, to a great extent, very similar; perhaps there is a bit more electronic instrumentation. In terms of graphic art, the design of the U.S. release was still managed by Colombians. Without a doubt, the great difference lies in the media blitz and advertising campaign launched during the U.S. tour: the band was paraded and exhibited as a musical curiosity of the third world, in a fashion compliant with the success of *rock en español* in the Anglo market.

Once they operate in terms of global coordinates, the mass media weave an imaginary of a different kind. The difference does not lie in particular aspects of the depiction of this imagery, but in its role as mediator, in how the media articulate and materialize identities in the all-inclusive nature of this imaginary.[14] In the Colombian market, Bloque's profile is minimal; in the United States, thanks to Luaka Bop and David Byrne's support, which opens doors and controls distribution channels, it enjoyed better luck, not so much in terms of numbers but with respect to specificity. Regardless of his motivation, Byrne's efforts to popularize Bloque involved some manipulation. A music that initially signified difference turns into yet another vehicle for the economic interests of the industrialized world. Difference, Ortiz reminds us, is not the same as inequality, which is rampant in the music industry's distribution circuits. Having introduced to the market a vision compatible with a preconception of identity, the experience of consumption loses any potential for criticism. Something different might have happened had Sonolux, the Colombian label, gained access to the U.S. market on its own terms. It is particularly relevant to point out this difference, not because of any implicit sense of nationalism, but because it stands as clear evidence of the ways in which a Latin

American label (Sonolux) is less efficient. Sonolux, associated with Sony, still functions within a multinational scheme, targeting regional markets, and consequently less effectively in the U.S. music market.[15]

Second, this case leads one to reconsider the identity crisis resulting from the hypothetical homogenization of a globalized world. If globalization proposes the same for everyone, how are we to fabricate our individuality? Bloque's case problematizes this aspect and the fact that, with globalization, the world will not be homogeneous, but that certain *segments* of the population will be homogeneous. According to Renato Ortiz, globalization does not homogenize *all* markets, only certain market segments. These groups, which perceive things equally from any position in the world, are, by definition, deterritorialized. Overall homogenization is a fallacy for a very simple reason: one must take into consideration hegemony; one must consider the prevalence of a stronger, more influential nation-state that monopolizes power, and which offers and imposes guidelines on other nations. In other words, despite its overwhelming, leveling dynamics, globalization incarnates—intrinsically—the validation of an unequal order. Even if globalization involved the pursuit of egalitarianism, the very dynamics of such a process—the fact that there are powerful and weaker bodies involved—would generate difference. Hence, it is not feasible that, either in the short or long term, we are all to become copies of ourselves.

Third, having contemplated the evolution of the history of Bloque, one must consider the impracticality of a world model grounded in the concepts of center and periphery. As instruments of thought, these categories may still be valid, but, within globalization, if it does advance, these concepts will become increasingly inappropriate. The change from the multinational to the transnational, for example, clearly implies, beyond fragmentation, decentralization—that is, less reliance on a sole governing center. Therefore, the idea of a single center surrounded by peripheral bodies is less appropriate. As Ortiz correctly points out, to talk about center and periphery is akin to talking of colonialism, and colonialism presupposes the existence of a clear intent of domination by any nation. As a musical category, world music does *not* represent an attempt to colonize. It is a limited reading of the world, but its objective is not to colonize. Such a category of music offers an enhanced perception of the world, deformed but inclusive. Why? Because colonialism suggests the presence of an entity, a party *in the exterior,* taking hold of what remains outside. In world music, however, we are all meant to be *in the interior.* World music is a byproduct of the internationalization of capital, which extends the productive process—in this case, music distribution—to a world level while it displaces the local, regional, or national sphere. Just as with the integration of different product components from all over the globe (take, for example, the automobile industry) the same process is occurring in the music industry.

Fourth, it becomes evident that transnational corporations will redesign the nation as they see fit, since their geoeconomic and geopolitical interests may not agree with those of national states. Although capitalism still relies on national foundations, nation states as such might cease to function as the most important constituents in relationships of power. Even if we do not agree with the extreme position, forecasting the demise of the nation at the hands of local identities, in the one case, or global ones, in the other, we must concede that, in the future, the modern conception of the nation will be less relevant. At the very least, the nation as it is currently understood in Latin American circles will be dramatically transformed. Globalization does not mean the end of the nation. It does mean that it is on its way to a second or third tier of importance. As a category for the interpretation of identity, the "national" will become less and less significant. In terms of its national use value, the acceptance of Bloque's production seems to ratify this assertion. With increasing recurrence, a nationally groomed cultural form does not have to be validated by the local apparatus in order to incarnate national identity.

Then again, to mention the use value of a kind of music is to refer to its capability in the production of social collective bodies. In this aspect, Bloque's music has less substance. The group produces a demanding music, not meant for the mainstream. Bloque's greatest effectiveness comes from its support for Vives, who—despite criticism of his musical style—*is* a phenomenon of the masses and enjoys wide appeal. This is particularly significant, especially if one considers Benavides's participation in *La Tierra del Olvido,* the follow-up to Vives's groundbreaking *Clásicos de La Provincia* (*Classic Hits of the Province,* 1994), and the role of "Teto" Ocampo, Bloque's lead guitarist, as Vives's musical director. In Vives's latest releases, *El amor de mi tierra* (*Love for My Land,* 1999) and *Déjame entrar* (*Let Me In,* 2001), La Provincia, formerly in charge of arrangements, has assumed a lesser role; in fact, in the latter album, the ensemble is not mentioned in the credits. Yet, both albums continue to name Bloque's band members—Luis Ángel Pastor, Carlos Iván Medina, Mayte Montero, and Pablo Bernal—as participants, proof of a continuing relationship with the *vallenato* star. Thus, as an incarnation of *colombianidad,* the success of the band in the United States is, to a large extent, contradictory. In Colombia, the coincidence between national narratives and Bloque's proposal has been less tangible than in the case of Vives. In the U.S., outside of the Latino market, Vives is not widely known. Whereas Vives's habitat of significance has been limited to the Latino U.S. market or Latin America, Bloque's habitat of significance has been the Anglo market and has led, in spite of its smaller sales, to a more incisive penetration of the hegemonic mindset. Although Bloque confirms a conventional perception of nationality, their experience has borne greater influence in matters of identity.

Unfortunately, like many Colombian bands from the past, Bloque's story has a bad ending. As a result of friction among the band's members, during the U.S. tour replacement musicians were used occasionally, which is a practice frowned upon by the music label. Luaka Bop's demands that Mayte Montero be available during the entire length of the tour did not help either. The fact that Benavides settled in New York City, though perceived as an advantage by some, also turned out to be problematic. Although the band recorded a second album with Luaka Bop, its disintegration rendered hopeless any possibility of that album being released someday. By February 2001, Benavides, in collaboration with DJ Nova, a Bronx performer, had organized a new band called Lata. Writing for the *Village Voice,* Ed Morales described it as a combination of house, *son montuno, chandé* rhythms, and sampled shouts of mountain people; in short, vintage Benavides. According to Morales, the band's name—which means "tin," slang for something akin to a ruckus—also evokes a *lata de basura,* Spanish for "garbage can." Hence, it recalls an earlier comment by Benavides that Bloque's songs were an examination of the musical memory of the 1960s, when, while learning to dance to the rhythm of the "fucking Beach Boys," Colombians forgot to create their own modern music.[16]

Questions remain: In a world where cultural dissemination has been left in the hands of economic interests and publicity campaigns, who is responsible for a more authentic portrayal of identity? Is it at all possible to measure the degree of representational effectiveness of a cultural agent? In this respect, social theorist Octavio Ianni suggests that "the majority of the interpretations of reality in terms of the organization and dynamics of the national and world systems and subsystems contemplates the assumption that the prevailing organization and dynamics tend to be dictated by the more developed, modern, dominant, central, or hegemonic societies."[17] If we take into consideration the devalued standing of the national in today's world, this calculation gains complexity. Once again, an example serves as a better explanation. At the end of his *New York Times* article, David Byrne compares the significance of Bloque and Ricky Martin—a comparison of breathtaking proportions—to the impact of García Márquez and company during the Latin American literary boom. To me, this sort of compliment sounds as though the singularity of a group of Colombian musicians has been collapsed into categories of the "alternative" and the "worldly," consolidating a stereotypical, exotic, and fragmented perception of a distant identity, one best left unquestioned.

Selected Discography

Aterciopelados. *Con el corazón en la mano.* 1994. RCA International 74321-17384-2.

Bloque de Búsqueda. *Bloque de Búsqueda.* 1997. Sonolux/Sony Music DCC-82208.

Bloque. *Bloque.* 1998. Luaka Bop/Warner Brothers 9-47060-2.

Brown, Carlinhos. *Alfagamabetizado.* 1997. EMI H2-724383826926.

Shakira. *Laundry Service.* 2001. Epic EK63900.

Vives, Carlos. *Clásicos de la provincia.* 1994. EMI International H2-724352739820.

———. *La tierra del olvido.* 1995. EMI International H2-724352838028.

———. *El amor de mi tierra.* 1999. EMI International H2-7343-22854-1-6.

———. *Déjame entrar.* 2001. EMI International H2-7243-535956-2-3.

Let Me Sing My BRock

Learning to Listen to Brazilian Rock

MARTHA TUPINAMBÁ DE ULHÔA

> If Bob Dylan were Brazilian, "Hurricane" would have been [Legião Urbana's] "Faroeste Caboclo."
> —**Artur Dapieve**

In March 1998 I presented the results of my study on fans of Brazilian rock to the Research Seminar of the Institute of Popular Music (IPM) at the University of Liverpool.[1] I discussed aesthetic aspects of Brazilian rock, including examples chosen to demonstrate a brief panorama of the genre and some of its characteristics. I was curious to hear the reaction of a qualified audience on a subject rarely taken seriously in Brazilian academic circles, and, especially, its music circles. In Brazil, rock is not taken seriously because it is perceived as a product of the cultural industry made for popular consumption, one therefore lacking "artistic value" and unworthy of serious study. Moreover, even in the field of Brazilian popular music, there is some resistance to admitting that rock might have some kind of "national" character. In Liverpool, I perceived an echo of these same concerns. David Horn, with his characteristic gentility, waited outside the seminar to tell me that "it could be that the excerpts I used were very brief" but he was not able to detect many "Brazilian" characteristics in the examples that I chose. In other words, the sound qualities, notwithstanding the use of Portuguese, did not seem to demonstrate any apparent "national" quality. In my talk, I also mentioned the importance of "ideological rock"—that is, rock with lyrics that allude to Brazilian politics and a Brazilian sociocultural context (especially during the wave of disillusionment that overcame Brazilians in the 1980s following their brief enthusiasm when the 1964–

1985 military dictatorship ended). This prompted another question from a graduate student, who asked, "Why bring up the word 'ideology' to refer to a group of rock songs?" In this essay, I want to consider the two questions together, because a transnational genre like rock can be identified as "Brazilian rock," not only by the scholars and journalists writing on the subject, and the music industry, but more importantly, by legions of young Brazilian fans packing the rock shows and buying thousands of recordings.

At that time, I was more interested in methodological issues than in the question of what makes Brazilian rock Brazilian: my study on rock was only part of an ongoing project on Brazilian popular music genres' aesthetic categories. Needing to refine my technique, I went to Liverpool to meet Philip Tagg and to learn more about his work on the semiotics of music. In formulating his hypotheses on meaning, Tagg collects people's reactions to the music he is analyzing. Since music has its own logic and is not easily explained by words, Tagg relies on a kind of associative cognition—"lateral" thinking, in his words—asking people to tell him what other sounds and meanings they recall as similar to the "musemes" (basic musical elements that the listener hears) he offers.[2] My own approach had some points in common with his, except for one: instead of working with responses to selected tunes, I first collected the positions of fans, that is, their preferences and dislikes; then I interpreted and grouped answers into concepts that, together with musical analyses, led to parameters for establishing specific styles and genres.

The perspective I bring here takes into consideration Brazilian rock's evaluation by its qualified listeners, people who understand and participate in the genre: fans, musicians, producers, and critics. Toward this end, I used an ethnographic approach, conducting surveys and interviews complemented by bibliographic research and musical analysis.[3] It became evident that, from the perspective of Brazilian consumers of rock, the discriminating opinions they form are aesthetic and functional: Brazilian groups or individual musicians are evaluated as much by the sound they produce as by the message of the lyrics of the songs, as well as by the attitude and musical ability of the musician. The emphasis is on music and parameters of aesthetic evaluation, despite the "sociological" data, such as age group and gender, we collected. Obviously, this is only one among many possible modes of interpretation and analysis. Musicology, even in its most positivistic form, is a fairly hermeneutic discipline, given that all acts of listening, even the researcher's listening acts, are cultural: listening is limited and/or shaped by one's degree of musical competence.[4] In my own personal experience, I used to believe that much of the rock that I heard was simply noise, with the possible exception of the Beatles, who made an impression on me in my adolescence. Today, however, I realize that I have an appreciation for a great variety of bands, some of which are quite "thrash," while at the same time I have a clearer understanding of why I continue to consider other bands to be plain "trash." In my contact with rock music, and from trying to listen from a privileged perspective (that of the competent listener), I have actually expanded my own musical competence regarding rock, even though I have not covered all the aspects (not even the strictly musicological ones) of the genre in Brazil.

In Liverpool, the participants in the IPM seminar made several comments, opening up questions, each of which could generate a separate study. In this essay, however, I choose to focus more closely on the question of rock and national identity, because the notion of music as a symbolic commodity linked to nationality has been very significant in Brazil, whether in relation to samba, a regional genre that became a national symbol, or bossa nova, criticized for using "foreign" elements, or with the mediation of organic intellectuals such as Caetano Veloso in developing solutions that attempt to mediate between the global industry and local traditions. In fact, it is very intriguing to observe how strong the idea of nationality is in Brazil: even such a globalized genre as rock in Brazil has to be "Brazilian."

Historical and Musical Context

Rock and pop were introduced in Brazil in the wake of the increasing consolidation of the cultural industry, in which television was particularly important. The first television station in Brazil appeared in 1950, but initially it was an entertainment alternative primarily for the more privileged classes. Radio, in contrast, had been aimed at a wider public since the 1930s, and was more closely linked to government policies of national integration. Musical production was quite diversified, heeding the demands of a growing urban population. By the end of the 1950s, radio had popularized not only samba, but also an enormous variety of both domestic and foreign popular genres, including bolero, the Paraguayan *guarania* and polka, Mexican *corrido* and *ranchera* music, a great deal of U.S. music, and, not least, Brazilian carnival music. By the mid-1960s, however, television had become a strategic element in the implementation of national security policies devised by the military, which came to power in 1964. Many popular music programs were created by the various networks, including TV Record's two programs dedicated to bossa nova and a third program for more naive and romantic rock in the manner of the early Beatles. That show, *Jovem Guarda* (*Young Guard*), was conducted by Roberto Carlos (later considered the king of romantic music in Brazil). *Jovem Guarda* was a marketing success, involving the participation of its stars in films and the creation of an attractive youth-oriented style (with recognizable trademarks and slang). The show lasted from 1965 to 1968 and became a model for the marketing of mass-market pop music in Brazil.

After the 1964 military coup, feelings of national identity infused with "revolutionary" sentiment reoriented the political activities and artistic productions of groups on the Left, which eventually influenced popular music. Some of the protest songs written by these musicians, many of whom came from bossa nova, debuted at music festivals created by television stations. From these festivals, as well as from college music shows, arose the generation of artists (such as Chico Buarque de Hollanda, Edu Lobo, and Milton Nascimento) who formed what came to be known as MPB, Música Popular Brasileira, singer/songwriters with a project similar to that of the (subsequent) Nueva Trova Cubana and the Latin American Nueva Canción movements.[5] The adherents of MPB criticized the Jovem Guarda style for being far removed from politics and a mere imitation of a foreign model. One example of the conflicting perspectives of Jovem Guarda and MPB concerned the 1966 hit "Que tudo mais vá pro inferno" ("Everything Else Can Go to Hell"), in which Roberto Carlos, with his characteristic colloquial style and nasal vocals, sings to the accompaniment of guitar, bass, drums, and the Hammond organ typical of the period, in a sound more reminiscent of Nashville than of rock proper.[6] The lyrics mention the futility of having a "blue sky and the sun shining above" if the beloved is absent. Her absence torments him, and he wants her there to warm him up during the winter, and "everything else can go to hell." For politically active students of the time, this widely commercialized song, whose lyrics spoke of youthful sentimentalities so distant from the political context of the time, meant alienation and capitulation to U.S. imperialism.

In a music festival in 1967 two MPB songwriters, Caetano Veloso and Gilberto Gil, breached this ideological polarization (Brazilian versus foreign, artistic versus commercial) when they incorporated into their songs aesthetic elements from rock and pop, thus rejecting the requirement to refer either to ethnic roots or samba as the only options available for popular "Brazilian" music. These two musicians, together with Os Mutantes, Capinam, Tom Zé, and others, began the movement known as Tropicalismo.[7] Tropicalismo, like many vanguard movements, was short-lived, but it strongly influenced MPB, especially in its criticism of earlier forms of orthodox nationalism and its renewal of popular music by means of experimentalism and irony; in short, it represented a solution for the dilemma between "authenticity" and tradition in an industrialized, pop-culture world.

An emblematic example of Tropicalismo is the 1968 "Panis et Circencis" by Caetano Veloso and Gilberto Gil, with Os Mutantes. The arrangements and musical direction were by the classical composer Rogério Duprat (a sort of Brazilian George Martin), who introduced studio techniques of sound manipulation from contemporary music into popular music. In "Panis et Circensis," some effects nowadays accomplished electronically were done manually. These techniques included the placement of microphones, vocal effects simulating audio delay, the oscillator as a musical instrument, guitar distortions, and, at the end of the song, sounds from a dining room such as the tinkling of silverware, glasses, and conversation. The metaphoric language used in the lyrics—sunlit songs, loose tigers and lions in the gardens, the people in the dining room too busy being born and dying—demonstrate the composers' literary intentions.

In short, rock's entry into popular music in Brazil, symbolized by the electric guitar, was marked by the appearance of two distinct models of musical production: the Jovem Guarda of Roberto Carlos, a vanguard of mass popular music, and Tropicalismo, considered the more sophisticated option within a restricted type of musical production (MPB).[8] Jovem Guarda and Tropicalismo both related to the Beatles: Jovem Guarda, accentuating adolescent sentimentalism, and Tropicalismo, through songs with a certain degree of artistic aspiration.

Throughout the 1970s artists like Raul Seixas and groups like Secos e Molhados contributed to the definition of rock as a genre, incorporating transnational models. They also experimented separately with elements of Latin American culture, such as percussion instruments like the *berimbau* and congas, as well as Brazilian rhythms and politically engaged lyrics. In the 1980s a more cohesive Brazilian rock emerged, with many elements contributing to its consolidation: a new space in Rio de Janeiro for performances (the Circo Voador, or Flying Circus), where the theatrical rock band Blitz emerged; the creation of Radio Fluminense, a venue for new rock band demos (opening the way to single and, later, LP recordings of bands like Paralamas do Sucesso [Bumpers of Success]); a punk festival in São Paulo (introducing, among others, the band Ratos do Porão [Basement Rats]); a mega-rock event, the 1985 Rock in Rio (alternating acts like Queen, Iron Maiden, Yes, and Scorpions with Brazilians); and finally, the return to civil government, a new economic plan with greater possibilities for consumption, and a new kind of civic awareness. By the end of the 1980s *rock brasileiro, rock Brasil, rock nacional,* or even *BRock*—the capital letters emphasize nationality—as it has been variously called, had achieved a certain level of success.

The Musicology of Popular Music in Brazil—Making Sense of *BRock*

I distinguish between two aspects of the Brazilian rock phenomenon: the actual sound quality, that is, the musical expression (in semiotics, the signifier), and the semantic content (the signified) or meaning of this manifestation. Rock, in spite of its imperialist associations, can be considered Brazilian when Brazilians perform it under certain circumstances. Brazilian features might not be necessary, however, as the absence in the survey's answers of Lobão, a seminal figure in the 1980s rock scene of Rio de Janeiro, points out (see below). It all depends on the localized context.

Like all traditions, this one was also invented. When electric guitars were first heard in Brazil in the 1960s, they symbolized modernity and imperialism. This ideological position had to be contested; hence, Tropicalismo, which freed Brazilian popular music from being tied to traditional roots. During the 1970s, rock underwent several mediations and experiments, most of them incorporating regional tendencies. However, such mixtures did not mean rock was considered to be Brazilian music; only in the 1980s did the name *rock brasileiro* appear. With the democratization of Brazil in the 1980s, however, Brazilian popular music began to lose its nationalist overtones; music connected with protest (such as Chico Buarque's use of samba rhythms to signify the individual and anonymous hero) became "redundant," while regional rhythms and instruments were once again associated with entertainment. In this context, rock assumed the role of voicing criticism. This task was expressed mostly in the lyrics, since using Brazilian instruments or rhythms no longer automatically connoted nationalism.

If one considers only the music or its production without its reception context, one is bound to miss the point. The meaning of any genre is the result of consensus within its community, consumers included. Thus, its meaning is always changing. However, I do not want to imply that Brazilian rock is Brazilian simply because Brazilian fans and rock critics say it is so. Even if rock made in Brazil has apparent similarities with Anglo-U.S. rock, except for the language issue, if we listen closely and pay attention to nuances of reception, in which certain aesthetic elements are identified, selected, and privileged, we can understand how a segment of rock produced in Brazil can be considered Brazilian.

One clue was suggested by Philip Tagg when he heard the rhythmic structure of drums in "Que tudo mais vá pro inferno": the drum beats are similar to those in the Beatles' first songs—a partial Cuban clave rhythm, alluding, according to Tagg, to the popular radio and dance sounds heard in England in the 1950s that featured cha-cha and rumba, sounds that were part of the musical acculturation of the Beatles and their generation. What does Tagg's observation have to do with this discussion? What, one might ask, is the relation between Cuban music, the Beatles, and rock in Brazil? In truth, a great deal. First, it speaks of the hybrid character of popular music, which results from exchanges, loans, and appropriations. Second, it speaks to how the diffusion of globalized popular music can take place, how the local can incorporate the global, and how the global can absorb the local. Despite apocalyptic predictions by those who follow the Frankfurt School's diatribes against the cultural industries, music is not simply imposed, unless one culture is completely supplanted by another. In order for any music to be adopted and appropriated, a minimum degree of identification is necessary. Couldn't those fragments of Cuban sounds hidden in the texture of the drums be a point of contact between rock and Latin American music, facilitating the understanding of a seemingly new genre and its subsequent incorporation into local music? For Brazilians to go beyond mere imitation or translation of North American hits into Portuguese, and to begin composing original songs, it was imperative that they recognize something familiar, something that expressed their own desires. Jovem Guarda, for example, meant being modern and up-to-date with global standards.

Another aspect to consider is the apparent simplicity of popular music. A pop song should be easily memorized and, moreover, be composed of short and redundant or repetitive fragments. Also, in order to reach a large and heterogeneous public, the music should use elements understood by people at different levels of musical competence and in varied social contexts. Because an excess of musical elements can impede fluid communication, the rhetorical musical figures (musemes) from the repertoire of cultural connotations end up being "made over" or disguised, mixed together in the fabric of the accompaniment. Listeners readily identify the artist or the group, who stands out in the song as a figure would stand out in a painting. What lies behind this artist or group, in the background and hidden within the arrangement, is not always noticeable, and on many occasions is perceived only unconsciously.[9] In addition to perceiving sounds as positive or negative, listeners hear a style that they can identify as "heavy," "pop," or "vibrant." In order to understand why listeners do or do not like a sound, why they consider it beautiful or not, it is necessary to go deeper into the process of musical analysis.

People use music to communicate sometimes complex and profound contents. When words fail, music explains. But, how do we understand the messages transmitted? In reality, we understand music by means of an indirect process containing successive steps of decodification. Upon hearing a piece of music, we refer to our own repertoire of musical symbols, that is, other familiar musical pieces, and the meaning this repertoire acquired in our daily living. For example, upon listening to John Lennon's "Imagine," we can be aware of the sound of violins, also present in the soundtracks of romantic Hollywood films (many of them based on nineteenth-century European Romantic repertoires), or we can notice a particular sinuous melody reminding us of the popular serenades and traditional Brazilian songs of earlier decades. In other words, we indirectly make a connection with a shared cultural context. However, the connection between music and culture is not a direct one. Music is explained by other music, with one musical text making references to another musical text and not immediately to a sociocultural context. Nevertheless, despite this self-reflexivity—one song points toward another song in a successive fashion—no means of communication is as suggestive as music. As an example, we can take music and cinema: when we hear any fragment of a soundtrack, even without images, we already have a notion of the type of film, whether drama, comedy, epic, etc. With rock, it is the same. We only need to hear a few seconds, just one melodic fragment (for example, a riff like the one that begins "Satisfaction," by the Rolling Stones), a certain timbre (guitar distortion), a singer's voice (the almost spoken nasal quality of Bob Dylan, or the colloquial and smooth qualities of Paul McCartney), or a rhythmic/instrumental structure (the sharp double attacks on bass drums of the heavy metal band Sepultura), to identify rock, and the specific kind of rock involved.

Indirectly—by association or sound analogy (to Tagg, "anafony")—when we hear the rock fragment, we are able to relate it to incidents of our life and/or to everything that rock in general might mean: youth, noise, excitement, entertainment, sociability, and so on. This process, which Tagg describes well, occurs with any sample from any musical genre. In popular music, by nature more fragmented than concert music, this immediate act of pointing at something else and, therefore, to "paramusical" meanings, is more evident. It is even more palpable if we consider music as a commercial "product," a "thing" manufactured in a production line, therefore forsaking the need to be "artistic" and autonomous. This is the case, despite the fact that popular music is as much an art form as classical music (we relate to popular music affectively: it touches, moves, and irritates us) and not merely a disposable consumer product (although I do not deny the fetishistic character of the product, and the felt necessity to own the CD or wear the T-shirt that declares "I Went to the Show").

The cultural conventions that attribute meaning to given musical structures are historical, that is, they situate techniques, aesthetics, and ethics within a specific time and place. Nevertheless, these same musical structures have a certain autonomy.[10] We believe that a song is beautiful or unpleasant, even if we do not clearly identify the instrumental technique, the chords in the arrangement, or even its social function. Music communicates at different levels; depending on our musical and cultural competence, we will understand and appreciate a song more fully. This explains why musicians trained strictly in the classical tradition consider rock to be a purely social phenomenon. It might also clarify why non-Brazilian audiences might find it difficult to acknowledge the "Brazilianness" in certain repertoires. To clarify this question, I considered it important to survey rock fans in order to understand how they constructed the Brazilianness of Brazilian rock.

Categories of Aesthetic Evaluation of Brazilian Rock: Sound, Lyrics, Musician

In the survey, fans of Brazilian rock mapped out the territory and marked off the aesthetic limits acceptable for the genre by evaluating their favorite groups and artists. Survey responses were grouped by successive selection in three categories of a somewhat prescriptive quality: sound, lyrics, and artist. For example, with regard to sound, the scale distinguished among a sonic mass with highly specific poles. A sound might be light, smooth, and dance-like, but it should not become too slow or saccharine. On the other side of the spectrum, a hard sound, full of energy, can be distinguished from mere noise. To a great degree, the specifications for Brazilian rock expressed by fans and musicians indicate a valorization of technological innovation, the adoption of northeastern Brazilian rhythms, irreverence (for example, the use of musical quotations in an ironic fashion), and "fidelity" to the roots of rock, which means adhering to the standard performative aspects of rock while not discarding new riffs and grooves. Table 1 shows a synthesis of the concepts related to sound, suggesting an acceptable sound continuum going from hard rock and hard-core to entertainment and swing.

The musical element most connected to the category of sound was texture; the range of textures ran from "thick" or "dense" to "thin." Texture refers to how the vocal and instrumental parts of a musical structure are combined in a given moment. It depends as much on the number as on the type of interactions between the sonic components of the piece. The textural density is influenced by the spacing between the sounds and the quality of the timbre of instruments and voice, often modified by recording effects and the arrangement of the mix. In rock, in order to obtain a texture that is more or less dense, the way in which spacing and timbre are used matters more than the number of instruments. The heavier rock songs tend to have a sonic mass of great density in terms of lines tending toward polyphony (independence of the musical

Table 1. Fans' Responses to Brazilian Rock in Terms of Sound

Positive Responses	Negative Responses
Innovation	Foreign copies
Mixture with Northeast rhythms	Sameness
Original	Pasteurized
Pure	Stereotypical patterns
Musically irreverent	
A classic	Commercial
Vital	Noise
Energetic	Heavy
Heaviest	
Light and compelling	Too slow
Soft sound with sensuous touch	Saccharine
Danceable (swing)	

parts), dissonance of the timbre, rhythmic emphasis, and high volume; lighter rock tends to have a less dense texture along with a more homophonic integration of parts, an emphasis on melody, lower volume, and slower tempo. The same texture, or the same band, could be mentioned in a positive or negative light, as in the case of Sepultura, rejected by some and admired by others. Sepultura was admired for its dense and heavy sound, as well as for the group's capability to successfully mix Brazilian rhythms with the texture of heavy metal. On the other hand, some negative positions dealt with the incomprehensibility of lyrics. In this case, the informants expressed their preference for bands with a lighter sound, in which lyrics were sung in a much slower Portuguese.[11]

Another predominant aesthetic norm was that there should be a mixture of international and Brazilian rhythms. Raul Seixas (1945–1989) was the first songwriter to mix rhythms, scales, and accents from northeastern Brazil with rock. His 1972 song "Let Me Sing, Let Me Sing" is a good example of this alternation between rock and the dry narrative style of the Northeast. Figure 11 shows the traditional rock texture (even the "honky-tonk" piano style) of this song, whereas Figure 12 shows regional references, including modal inflection and the use of the keyboard accordion, triangle, and zabumba (bass drum) typical of traditional *baião* music.[12]

Rock texture in Raul Seixas's "Let Me Sing."

Baião texture in Raul Seixas's "Let Me Sing."

Besides the music, the verses change language, with the English refrain mentioning blues and rock 'n' roll and the Portuguese strophes elaborating on global and local symbols in a metaphoric way. The refrain asks the listener to let him sing his rock 'n' roll and blues, and leave. The verses change to Seixas's characteristic esoteric language, mentioning on the one hand that he has come to deal with the listener's problems since the Messiah has not come yet, and, on the other, that he desires to see the girl from Ipanema again because the dream is over. The strophes are all constructed around three pairs of verses, the third one being a repetition of the second. The first one masquerades the character of the following ones. It seems he is pouring out some sort of verbal nonsense: What does "The Girl from Ipanema" have to do with the listener's problems, or the fact that "the dream is over," and "the Messiah has not come yet"? The other six-line strophe describes the exact weight of the vocalist, claims he is not going to sing like the grasshopper, but won't give up singing what he has to sing. After another refrain insisting that the singer should be permitted to do what he wants (sing his blues and go), the *baião* texture returns with lyrics that, at first, are not very clear: he doesn't "want to own the truth, since truth doesn't have an owner," as the first two-line verses say. But then, "If green is the green of truth, two and two are five, not four anymore." What does this green mean? Finally, it becomes clear, and we understand "green" to be U.S. dollars. Thus, this particular example of rock may be interpreted as a protest song, criticizing the Girl from Ipanema, that is, bossa nova and globalization, and U.S. imperialism (if U.S. dollars are what counts, two and two are five . . .). Finally, the threat is dismissed and the singer says he doesn't have anything to say, since he only wants to enjoy his little rock song and "there's no danger he'll scare anyone."[13]

The lyrics represent the second parameter of fans' aesthetic evaluation of Brazilian rock. The lyrics should "speak the language of youth," they should be "sincere," "critical of society," "political," and, lastly, "intelligent" or "intellectual." Songs with "romantic," "beautiful," or "profound" lyrics represent another standard. When groups or artists of Brazilian rock were rejected because of their lyrics, it was generally because lyrics were considered vulgar, superficial or silly, lacking in poetry, or because fans were unable to understand the words. In general, the more successful groups are those with at least a few songs with comments of a political or social nature; thus, even artists from the past, like Seixas, can still be considered relevant and contemporary. Legião Urbana was especially lauded by respondents because of lyrics "that speak about society in addition to having a diversified style of sound," and are "romantic without being sentimental," "intelligent and politically oriented," besides using "urban language in their authentically poetic songs" that "avoid being aggressive." The group Raimundos (an overt reference to the Ramones) was strongly criticized for lyrics considered "vulgar" and full of "coarse language." However, it was precisely the use of profanities that delighted younger adolescents.

In terms of the third parameter of aesthetic evaluation, the musician, opinions can be grouped into two subcategories: the posture or image of the musician (which should be "true," "authentic," and "politically oriented," as opposed to "artificial" or "superficial"), and the musician's interpretive skill (in terms of "voice," "virtuosity," and stage presence, as opposed to "singing out of tune").

The combination of these three parameters can characterize a Brazilian rock band as "good." For example, Sepultura might alter its texture to adapt some musical content and then be considered competent. On their 1996 album *Roots*, they mix their sound with the drums and percussion work of Bahian musician Carlinhos Brown in the song "Ratamahatta," but use an acoustic guitar to accompany an indigenous healing song from the Xavante tribe ("Itsari," featuring members of the tribe). Another artist respected for heeding the aesthetic demands of the genre in Brazil, mainly for his "integrity" as a rock musician, is veteran rocker Lulu Santos (b. 1953), himself an admirer of Sérgio Dias (a legendary member of Os Mutantes), Quincy Jones, and the Police. He is known for his virtuosity on the guitar, his catchy melodies (ballad-like, easy to memorize), and his lyrics, which connect with the daily life of urban youth, as well as his stage presence. All contribute toward his prestige as a Brazilian rock musician of the pop style.

The Results: What Makes Brazilian Rock Brazilian

Most listeners can immediately notice a connection between Brazilian rock and its Anglo-American model. At IPM, for example, when I played some examples, Mike Broken identified echoes from the Beatles' *Sergeant Pepper*, and of several late-1960s female vocalists in a Tropicália piece, the influence of the Police in Paralamas do Sucesso, and a bit of Los Angeles rock but "with a leaning towards punk" in Lobão. Brazilian fans acknowledge the musical relationship with the mainstream model, but they also pick up on explicit or subtle references to their own cultural identity. The local element is especially evident in the melodic aspects, which in Brazil are greatly influenced by the characteristic articulation and intonation of the spoken language. Another distinguishing characteristic of Brazilian rock is its lyrical quality, deeply rooted in certain Brazilian musical traditions like the *modinha* (a sentimental song of the eighteenth and nineteenth centuries), and also, more obvious to the non-Brazilian ear, the use of regional rhythms, instruments, and scale systems. One should keep in mind this hierarchy—language patterns, lyric quality, rhythms, instruments—in which the latter are more evident, whereas the former occupy the background. Additionally, in musical terms, Brazilian rock is often more pop-oriented than is Anglo-American rock; and, it should be noted, Brazilian critics and fans are very aware of the difference between these two categories (pop and rock). An illustrative example is the group Titãs's (Titans) most "thrash" album, *Titanomania*, which did not sell well at all, either among the "heavy" crowd ("because they are not virtuosi instrumentalists") or among the band's usual fans, who could not, as one respondent put it, "recognize the pop style."

The bands most mentioned in the survey started recording in the 1980s as part of the "boom" mentioned above. They are Paralamas do Sucesso, with its mix of Brazilian and Latin American rhythms; Legião Urbana (Urban Legion), appreciated especially for its lyrics; Barão Vermelho (Red Baron), considered an "authentic" group; Sepultura, admired and rejected; and the previously mentioned Titãs. Other 1980s bands noted in the survey, but mostly for negative reasons, were: Kid Abelha (Honeybee Kid), a pop rock band; Engenheiros do Hawaii (Engineers of Hawaii), a band from the state of Rio Grande do Sul that tends toward pop style; and Ratos do Porão, a punk band from São Paulo state, criticized for its language. Some "oldies" were Lulu Santos, who started in the 1970s with soft rock and was admired for his shows; Rita Lee (1970s), the "mother of Brazilian rock"; Os Mutantes, the previously mentioned experimental group (in which Rita Lee was an early member); and Raul Seixas, the "father of Brazilian rock" (1970s). It is interesting to note that participants from all age groups included certain artists, like Seixas (deceased), Lee (out of the spotlight for some time), and Os Mutantes (as avant-garde band with several albums in the 1960s). <u>This suggests that fans recognize the historical importance of these musicians in the development of Brazilian rock.</u> *[margin note: historical importance]*

From the 1990s, younger fans appeared to favor Mamonas Assassinas (Killer Castor Beans), a group that performs rock parodies of commercial hits. After they died in a plane crash, fans temporarily transferred their interest to Raimundos, a band that employed lyrics with mixed meanings and dirty language. Also from the 1990s fans mentioned Skank (Portuguese for "skunk"), a group that began as reggae but later shifted to pop; Planet Hemp, with rap and reggae; and Baba Cósmica (Cosmic Drooling), though it was cited primarily in a negative way. Mixture and fusion also seem to increase in the 1990s. Bands like Raimundos mixed guitar distortion with regional rhythms. Other bands with a tendency toward mixture are Sepultura, especially on *Roots* (1996), which fuses the percussion style of Bahia in northeastern Brazil with heavy metal textures; and Chico Science and Nação Zumbi, who bring together traditional *carnaval* rhythms and postproduction studio techniques from rock in what has been called *"mangue bit"*—an experimental blend of techno and cybernetic elements (the "bit") with regional rhythms, particularly from the *maracatu,* a traditional genre from the northeastern city of Recife (hence the *"mangue"*). Another recent group with this tendency is Mestre Ambrósio (Master Ambrose), who emphasize traditional performance styles while mixing them with rock.[14]

The results of the research are complex, given the number of variables considered. Nevertheless, some aspects are noteworthy, among them the absence of certain figures. For instance, Lobão was missing from most answers, and was mentioned only five times in the entire survey. Well integrated into the cultural life of Rio de Janeiro (even playing in the drum corps [*bateria*] of a samba school), Lobão is well respected among musicians and appears frequently in the media, often challenging the establishment. The problem, it appears to me, is that Lobão altered his style in the 1990s, adopting a lighter line and becoming more integrated into the more prestigious MPB. On the other hand, other groups who changed their style, like Barão Vermelho, were praised because "they have and continue to have an active presence in Brazilian rock, always bringing innovations to their style, yet keeping in touch with their past: it's a very raw and basic style of rock." Nevertheless, even though Lobão was not cited in the surveys, he was recognized by the students conducting the surveys, themselves fans and specialists of rock, as an important figure of Brazilian rock because of his references to local contexts, and they included him in a basic repertoire of the genre. For example, his song "Vida Bandida" ("Criminal Life") contains the shouted phrase "sangue e porrada na madrugada" (blood and guts in the dawn), which the drums answer, bringing to mind the rhythmic function of the *tamborim,* one of the instruments of the *bateria* (see figure 13).[15] Another "musematic" reference is to the way the title of the song is shouted, sounding like the shots frequently heard in and around the *favelas* (hillside shantytowns) of Rio de Janeiro: "Vida, viDAAH, viDA banDIIHdaa!" These "musemes" (in this case, the rhythmic and performative aspects of samba and the similarity of the shouted phrase to the sharp, punctuated sound of gunshots) suggest the semantic content of the song, which refers to Rio's slums, often the stage for drug-related violence and home to most members of the samba schools.

Thus, despite the fact that fans often did not list him, Lobão represents an integral part of the history of Brazilian rock. Fans might fail to mention him, but musicians cannot ignore his work; similarly, critics have noted his historical role. Such is the sense in which the term "reception" is considered here. It

Excerpt of "Vida bandida" showing the samba museme.

is a qualitative term, a construction based on several sources, pointing toward consensus, informing a criterion for listening.[16]

Case Study: "Faroeste Caboclo"

Here, I will focus on a song by Legião Urbana in order to synthesize some of the elements important in general reception studies, as well as in the specific case of Brazilian rock. The story of the way in which the song "Faroeste Caboclo" ("Caboclo Western") came to be received in Brazil is illuminating. Composed in 1979 by Renato Russo (1960–96) when he belonged to a punk group in Brasilia called Aborto Elétrico (Electric Abortion), the song was written "in two afternoons without changing a comma." Such speed, according to Russo, can be explained because "the song has a rhythm which is very easy in the Portuguese language." It is based on the improvisational style of the northeastern *repente*.[17] *Repente* also refers to a particular style of vocal challenge based on a *mote* (from the French *mot*, meaning the motif that will be the focus of improvisation over a traditional metric formula). When it is very "wordy," *repente* is called *embolada* (tongue-twisting).[18] The song was not recorded until 1987, some eight years later, in an anthology of the first ten years of the band that would later become Legião Urbana.[19] Interestingly, "Faroeste Caboclo," with 159 verses and more than nine minutes in length, became the biggest hit on the album, and even today is widely played on the radio. I have seen the song performed innumerable times, with fans singing along to the entire song, which flies against the usual logic of pop music production that emphasizes repetition and easy memorization. The melodic style, with long sentences amid short intervals or repeated notes, follows the melodic contours of spoken Portuguese, with a tone that is more narrative than colloquial, impressing a dramatic inflection on the singing.

The lyrics tell the story of a migrant from northeastern Brazil to the nation's capital (Brasília) and his involvement and eventual violent death before television cameras. It is an authentic epic, yet a modern and cinematographic one, with its own soundtrack.[20] Throughout the story, musical texture changes according to the plot. The folk guitar and a light vocal style (folk rock) are reserved for moments of the story in which Santo Cristo, the protagonist, shows his soft and weaker side. One can infer the nature of marijuana fields in the countryside through the association with reggae. The melodic lines and the bass, in contrary movement (rock), emphasize moments of the story in which Santo Cristo suffers more: on his first trip to prison, when he loses his girlfriend to his rival, and, finally, when he dies. A heavier, faster, and more voluminous texture (hard rock) emphasizes the growing level of violence in the story, while a strident texture (punk) is associated with the evil character in the story, Jeremias, the bandit, who steals the protagonist's girlfriend and shoots Santo Cristo in the back.[21]

The story begins when João de Santo Cristo leaves the farm after a soldier has killed his father. He feels alienated and longs for the distant things he's seen on TV. At fifteen, he is sent to a reformatory. As a result, the hatred he feels for life increases. Santo Cristo goes to Salvador (the capital of the northeastern state of Bahia), where he finds a cattle owner who gives him a bus ticket to Brasília, the capital city. Upon arriving, he is dazzled by Brasília's lights. In Brasília, he becomes a carpenter's apprentice and meets a distant relative, who smuggles goods from Bolivia. Santo Cristo doesn't earn enough money from carpentry, so he decides to start a marijuana plantation. This section is accompanied by a soft sound texture (folk rock): folk guitars with plucked and arpeggiated strings, occasional bass notes, florid guitar lines in upper register, and a soft, relaxed vocal timbre.

Santo Cristo becomes rich, but because of the bad influence of the city's *boyzinhos* (young playboys), he starts stealing. This point in the story marks a transition signaled by a shift to a reggae texture. Next, there is a faster pace in the script, with frequent shifts between a rock texture (in which drums play in all four beats with emphasis on the 2nd and the 4th, and melody and bass move up and down in contrary motion), a hard rock texture (where the accompaniment doubles in speed—while the voice sings one 4/4 measure, the accompaniment plays two measures), and Russo singing in a louder, tenser, and harsher voice. The climax is signaled by a punk texture, with the shouted lyrics delivered in a guttural voice over guitars and bass playing rhythmic and distorted chords.

Santo Cristo is caught in his first robbery attempt, goes to "hell" (jail, signaled by the shift to rock), and becomes a bandit (hard rock). He meets Maria Lúcia, with whom he falls in love, and decides to return to his life as a carpenter (flashback to folk rock). Time goes by and, one day, a rich man comes, willing to hire Santo Cristo to be an urban guerrilla. He refuses and the man threatens to kill Santo Cristo (hard rock). Santo Cristo quits work and starts smuggling with his cousin (folk rock). Jeremias, a rival smuggler, decides to fight over territory (punk). Santo Cristo then orders a Winchester gun from his cousin (hard rock). The next scene is a description of Jeremias's criminal character (punk). The story cuts to Santo Cristo missing Maria Lúcia and going home, having decided to marry her (hard rock). Arriving home, he finds out that Jeremias has married Maria Lúcia (rock). Santo Cristo challenges Jeremias to a duel (hard rock). A television crew films the duel, in which Jeremias shoots Santo Cristo in the back (punk). Santo Cristo remembers his childhood; he recognizes Maria Lúcia, who brings him his Winchester (rock). Bleeding, he calls to Jeremias and shoots him; Maria Lúcia repents and dies with Santo Cristo (folk rock). In the end, João de Santo Cristo becomes a hero because he knows how to die; sadly, he was unable to complete his mission: to talk with the president and help all those who suffer (rock).

Rock critic Artur Dapieve compared this song to Bob Dylan's "Hurricane" (see the essay's epigraph).[22] Dylan's song employs folk guitar accompaniment with fiddle improvisations, a "musematic" reference to grassroots, folk-rock, and so on. The story unveils a linear narrative in which the black middleweight boxer Rubin "Hurricane" Carter is falsely tried, although he "could-a been the champion of the world." Comparing the recordings of Legião Urbana's "Faroeste Caboclo" and Bob Dylan's "Hurricane," we can note strong similarities of melodic contour, texture, and rhetorical structure between both songs. It is only when we listen more carefully that we come to note the differences of prosody, which, in the end, are the strongest indications for a differentiated semiotic interpretation. To the non-Brazilian listener, "Faroeste Caboclo" might appear to be a Brazilian simulacrum of several characteristics of English-speaking rock. The textures employed do not have anything specifically "Brazilian" about them. However, as the study of classic texts of ethnomusicology indicates, all listening is cultural. In reality, the issue is musical competence, not in the technical sense of music theory, but rather in the conception that Gino Stefani has given to the term. Music is understood at various levels, from the recognition of a repertory and specific styles (the rock canon) to the level of social practices, which may be fixed geographically and historically (the very much alive *repente* tradition).[23] In "Faroeste Caboclo" the sonority of the various textures of rock acts as a kind of musical backdrop for a specifically Brazilian narrative, without, however, requiring the inclusion of "typical" Brazilian rhythms and instruments. The Brazilianness resides between the lines, as it were, in the tradition of the epic qualities of the *repente* style from the northeast (in which the extended melodic line is similar to Bob Dylan's style), in the references to Brasília and its culture (itself a symbol of modernity), and in the rhythm and intonation of Brazilian Portuguese (irrelevant for a non-speaker).

Conclusion

This study still needs to be located within the wider context of studies on popular music. In reviewing the literature on rock, I noticed an emphasis on production and consumption. For instance, Simon Frith discusses rock as a product that is directed toward a certain segment of the market, a young segment (where "youth" is understood as a category of age and ideology).[24] The question, according to him, is how to determine the criteria for evaluating rock as a product of mass culture and discover the possibilities of expression available to rock as a means of mass communication. For this reason, he attempts to interpret the process of signification in rock in terms of industrial production and consumption by a mass market. In later studies, Frith shifted his focus to the aesthetics of pop song, urging us to pay attention to the pleasure of the music itself, arguing that more than representing social values, pop tastes help shape them.[25]

Another perception within sociology, complementary to the study of the Brazilian record industry, is that Brazilian rock can be seen as a regional form of production and consumption of a global genre. As Stuart Hall comments, globalization, in its strategy of creating niches within the market, exploits aspects of local differentiation.[26] In Brazil, nationalist ideology is central, hence the label *rock brasileiro*. In fact, nationalism and identity are arenas for deeply symbolic struggles. MPB, for instance, enjoys the prestige of being quintessentially "Brazilian." Eventually, Brazilian rock, after consolidating itself as a differentiated voice in the 1980s, also achieved this status.

My survey introduces a new perspective into the relationship between national identity and popular music, namely, the perspective of reception and musical competence. From a global perception, rock is considered rock if it is measured by its sound, that is, its textures and timbres. To a globalized ear, the difference has to be marked by the typical and the stereotypical. In that sense,

Brazilian rock is just a local version of the hegemonic model. From a local perception, however, Brazilian rock is more Brazilian when it uses global elements to narrate a story that, given its epic nature, could be atemporal, but which resonates deeply in symbolic history. In songs like "Faroeste Caboclo" Brazilians tell their own story: the story of a modernizing country caught in exploitation and manipulation. It is not a story with a happy ending, demonstrating that, after all, the enjoyment we experience from pop music often goes beyond mere pleasure.

Selected Discography

Chico Science e Nação Zumbi. *Afrociberdelia.* 1996. Chaos 850.278/2–479255.
Carlos, Roberto. *Jovem Guarda.* 1966. CBS 137432.
Legião Urbana. *¿Que País é Esse?* 1987. EMI 068 748 8201.
Sepultura. *Roots.* 1996. Roadrunner RR8900–2.

Guatemala's Alux Nahual

A Non-"Latin American" Latin American Rock Group?

PAULO ALVARADO

> Beautiful song, for sure. But I'm afraid an exec in my position can't risk his reputation endorsing a band nobody's heard about.
> —José Behar, Vice-Director, CBS Los Angeles,
>   speaking about Alux Nahual's song "De la noche a la mañana"

This essay examines the story and phenomenon of the Guatemalan rock group Alux Nahual, which over two decades wrote, produced, performed, and recorded nine albums of original rock music.[1] I was a founding member of the band, participating full-time during its first sixteen years of existence and then intermittently for its last four. The group emerged in Guatemala City in 1979, released its debut album in 1981, and performed abroad for the first time in 1983. We then went on to play in the rest of Central America, as well as a number of cities in the United States and Mexico, besides extensively touring our own country. In 1994 we achieved an all-time high of some fifty gigs. Our last concert took place in 1999; it was performed for a full-house audience, which was a frequent event. On some occasions, our audiences numbered as many as fifteen thousand people.

Although a Latin American band, insofar as origin and milieu are concerned, Alux Nahual created and performed something far different from what is usually categorized as "Latin" rock music. Very seldom were Afro-Caribbean rhythmic patterns used, and neither vernacular instruments nor regional dance and song forms played an important part in the way the music took shape. This essay intends to help open up a debate by questioning what is going on in this form of categorization, and by pointing out the discrimination inherent in requiring that the music of "tropical" cultures must be "dance" or "world" music.[2]

A Brief Overview of Guatemalan History

With somewhat less than 42,000 square miles and around twelve million inhabitants, Guatemala is the northernmost of five countries constituting what is properly called Central America, the neck of land between Mexico and Panama. Originally the name given to a considerably more extensive territory that included a large part of southern Mexico, the state of Belize, and the other four Central American states, Guatemala was established as a Captaincy General (one degree less than the Viceroyalty) after the arrival of Spaniards headed by Pedro de Alvarado in 1524. It remained as such for the better part of three centuries, until the upheavals of the early nineteenth century brought about not only the political separation of Latin America from Spain but also the fragmentation of the newly emancipated regions.

In the twentieth century, Guatemala's most salient feature has been its subservience to the United States, both politically and economically. The country's government has been in the hands of the military or military-controlled civilians, while an elementary agriculture-based economy built on cheap labor, latifundism, and inordinate concentration of property and the means of production have generated patterns of extreme inequality. As a result, the country is institutionally very precarious. There is a scarcity of public services, no social security, and two-thirds of the population is illiterate.[3] Official recognition of the nation's indigenous identities and cultural products has been nominal.

In 1954 a ten-year "revolutionary" effort to modernize the country, led by Presidents Juan José Arévalo (1945–51) and Jacobo Arbenz Guzmán (1951–54), was cut short by a U.S.-sponsored coup that overthrew the government of Arbenz Guzmán, one of the very few democratically elected governments in Guatemalan history. This, in turn, initiated a succession of presidents fraudulently elected or forced upon the people. Civil war spanning three and a half decades began in 1960 when a group of young military officers rebelled against the army and in turn started a guerrilla insurgency. Over the years, the human cost of the military response targeting insurgents and the civilian population alike has been unduly high: more than two hundred thousand people have been killed and hundreds of thousands more have been displaced.[4] The institutionalization of violence reached its peak between the end of the 1970s and the beginning of the 1980s, before the inception of nominally democratic regimes in 1985. Alux Nahual came together in its embryonic form as a high-school band in 1977, at the height of the violence, and by 1981 had recorded their first album.

Music in Guatemala

The history of music in Guatemala, like that of other Latin American countries with significant indigenous populations (45 to 55 percent in this case), can basically be described in the simplest of terms as one of cultural imposition on one hand and cultural resistance on the other. In the former instance, European music chiefly used for religious purposes has been both imported and imitated since the sixteenth century, while in the latter case autochthonous music, little of which might nowadays be presumed to be pre-Columbian in origin, has also survived. An examination of Guatemalan manuscripts of music written up to the end of the 1800s yields hardly anything but liturgical and devotional music produced after European fashion.[5] Most towns and villages hold marches for their patron saints' days and other cyclic gatherings, underscored by music. But other than the extraordinary Semana Santa (Holy Week) processions that take place every year, with day-long musical accompaniment by marching bands characteristically performing funeral tunes, music does not "happen" in the streets, as it often does in other Latin American countries. Music in Guatemala tends to be linked to ritual and commemoration, not to spontaneous communication. If music is required for a particular occasion, musicians or ensembles will be hired to *amenizar* (cheer up) the event, but they generally keep to themselves. Only sporadically might someone from the "audience" mix in with the performers in order to display artistic abilities.

The archetypal musical manifestation of Guatemala is, without contention, the marimba. Although its origin is uncertain (many maintain that it is pre-Hispanic, while others contend that it was brought over by African slaves), it is used extensively all over the country under the most varied of circumstances, from the lone village musician seemingly playing for himself on a street corner, to nationalistic festivals sponsored by supermarket chains, in which dozens of players simultaneously perform the music's traditional catalog of tunes. Essentially, Guatemalan marimbas are large xylophones with bulky resonators that bear only partial resemblance to the marimba in a conventional Western symphony orchestra. The finest are highly sophisticated, handmade "double" instruments (two segments, *bajo* and *tenor*, being used concurrently) played by up to seven musicians at a time. The repertoire takes account of rhapsodic virtuoso pieces by erudite composers, but is mainly made up of marches and songs which were, and continue to be, written in the style of dance forms from the first half of the twentieth century, such as foxtrot, cha-cha, and *cumbia*, as well as *son* (not to be confused with Cuban *son*), one of the few ongoing musical forms that is typically Guatemalan. Despite its "collective" nature and ubiquity, however, the marimba has steadily been losing its place to more recent devices, and aside from the *marimba orquesta* (with saxophones, bass, and drums, popular in the 1960s and 1970s), it has not proved to be a source of inspiration for rock musicians.

The Guatemalan Rock Music Scene

The emergence of rock and roll in the United States during the mid-1950s found an echo in Guatemala after 1960, when local groups with names such as the Jets, the Marauders, S.O.S., and Apple Pie began to surface.[6] This gradually led to other bands, with names such as Caballo Loco, Cuerpo y Alma, Plástico Pesado, and, by the end of the 1970s, groups such as Santa Fe, Siglo XX, Banda Azúcar, and Caoba. Though perfectly capable of producing their own music, these rock groups chiefly devoted themselves to copying foreign hits, which they performed primarily, if not exclusively, at social gatherings rather than at concerts. As a result, and in keeping with the age-old music-for-entertainment tradition, they were not able to withstand the assault brought about by the *disco-móviles* (mobile discothèques) that, during the late 1970s, forced even the strongest bands to break up. This paved the way for "tropical" groups better suited to the necessities of social partying. Along with the tropical bands came the Caribbean dance forms that came into fashion during the 1980s, notably merengue.

Arguably, those first rock bands were children of their age. Rock was still thought of as a music produced in English—even though few Guatemalans have a good command of English, which is taught poorly except at only the most expensive private schools. Singers went so far as to imitate the sound of the words phonetically, without understanding them.[7] One of the pioneers of Guatemalan rock-pop music was the multi-instrumentalist and vocalist Luis Galich, of the group Santa Fe, who started writing and performing in Spanish as far back as 1971. Yet he was pretty much alone in his quest. No one into rock was interested in Spanish-language music, which was often branded as too "romantic" and considered to be the opposite of rock. Galich argues that Spanish-language music seemed to lack the required expressive strength. In fact, few rock musicians were interested in playing anything but English-language covers; local musicians were considered "incapable" of writing good songs in Spanish.

Guatemalan musicians and audiences were led to believe by record companies and radio stations that rock had to be in English. Former record company representative "Pupo" Castañeda remembers: "Back in the sixties and seventies nobody *trusted* lyrics in Spanish. True, by the early eighties we already had an acquaintance with non-Anglophone [rock] endeavors from Spain, Argentina, Peru, and Mexico, many of which had been active for a long time. However, with the exception of the more 'romantic' songs, no label or radio station showed any real interest in this music, largely due to the fact that they thought of it as an *inferior version* of a definitely Anglo-Saxon product."[8] As to who was consuming what kind of music and under what circumstances, perhaps it is more important to first ask "Who was able to buy the music?" Essentially, the consumer audience for foreign rock was limited to the upper and middle class, who could purchase LPs on their visits abroad. These sectors lived in the city and often had their cars fitted with radio/cassette players; they were in a position to organize expensive balls and parties. The music they listened to came from outside of the country and was often brought in by hand. Gathering to listen to this music was understood to be, and accepted as, an element inherent to their class socialization.

But as a rule, the Guatemalan upper classes did not produce rock music. Instead, it was lower-middle-class musicians who gave rise to rock in more "popular" quarters. Obviously, residents of the poorer barrios were just as willing to consume such music, but they had to make do with what was handed down to them. The musicians from those neighborhoods would reproduce or transform the music and then would end up playing it at parties for those who could afford to pay them for doing so. As Rico Molina, bassist for Apple Pie, recalls: "We were awed by what foreign bands played. We reasoned that we just wouldn't be able to write songs as good as theirs. So we went for what we heard on the radio or learned the songs on the LPs we could get hold of. We built our own electric guitars and treasured any mike we could lay our hands on."[9]

Certain names have come to be associated prominently, if not exhaustively, with the early stages of rock music in Guatemala. The first was an event that could be regarded as Guatemala's Woodstock: the primal festival that assembled various rock groups and several thousand fans in November 1969 at "Plaza Berlín" on the southern outskirts of Guatemala City. Three days later the police abducted and tortured members of the group S.O.S. and proscribed future performances by the band. A second important name was "Radio Juventud" (c. 1970–73), perhaps the most committed rock station ever in this country. Thirdly, there were the performance spaces that would come to play a vital role in rock's survival: clubs such as La Manzana and La Montaña Púrpura, as well as the schoolyards of *institutos* (public secondary schools in downtown Guatemala City), where parties often evolved into unplanned concerts.

Not surprisingly, rock, like everything else in the country, was not spared by the ever-present social unrest. Gigs were interrupted by the police, with people in the audience being searched and arrested. Worse still, musicians would suddenly and mysteriously "disappear" without a trace—or they might be found dead, but not from a drug overdose. "During the 1970s, wearing long hair, smoking pot, 'unruly' behavior—for the police, all of this was synonymous with being a *guerrillero*," remembers "Maco" Luna of the rock group Cuerpo y Alma, a band that started out by covering Deep Purple and Black Sabbath songs, but that was exploring the possibilities of a more idiosyncratic "*son*-rock" sometime before the group folded.[10] By 1979, a shyly budding *rock chapín* (that is, *rock guatemalteco*) had been all but annihilated. Only a few bands survived into the early 1980s, including Pirámide, Panivers, Rocks, and Terracota. The sole exception to this unfortunate pattern was Alux Nahual.

Ultimately, the 1990s witnessed the emergence of many new bands with origins in the middle and upper classes, who may have felt encouraged by the country's relative political liberalization. Included among these are Bohemia Suburbana, La Tona, Piedras Negras, Estrés, Viernes Verde, Viento en Contra, Malacates Trébol Shop, and such singers as Ricardo Andrade, José Chamalé, and Armando Pineda.

A History of Alux Nahual

Alux Nahual materialized at the time of one of Guatemala's most macabre political administrations of the past forty-five years. It was during the time when keeping a group together to play parties had stopped being good business; when even *meeting up* was considered subversive.[11] The systematic elimination of national leaders that had begun during the 1960s had reached its apex, and entire sectors of Guatemalan society—professors at the national university, journalists, peasant organizations, and union leaders—had been annihilated.[12] It was also a time when the notion of *rock en español* was only a figment of somebody's imagination. Three of the band's founding members (brothers Alvaro and Plubio Aguilar and myself) happened to be students at the Deutsche Schule, the private school that had been established by the German coffee-farming bourgeoisie. We had tried to form a band before graduating, but it wasn't until two years later, in 1979, that we managed to team up again and perform for the first time under the name Alux Nahual. The original "Alux" consisted of Alvaro (vocals, acoustic guitar), Plubio (bass), their cousin Ranferí Aguilar (lead guitar), and myself (cello, keyboards). This basic group of four constituted the core around which other members came and went. These included Dr. Jack Schuster (violin), who played with the group during the first half of its life, Oscar Conde (flute), who became a member in 1983, and Lenín Fernández (drums), who would be the fourth and final drummer to join the band, in 1986. A Michigan-born scientist who came to Guatemala with a postgraduate degree in entomology, Schuster was more than ten years older than the other members and personified the heterogeneity of Alux Nahual's human resources and musical influences. His old-timey fiddle playing and occasional stints at bowed psaltery or autoharp contrasted sharply with Fernández's jazz percussion, or with my own musical training as a classical cellist. The Aguilar brothers were self-taught guitarists and, like myself, had finished school fluent in Spanish, English, and German. Alvaro studied chemistry at college, where he met Dr. Schuster, and Plubio studied computer science. Ranferí had also been our fellow student before moving to South America for several years. Abroad, he gained training in classical guitar, but he joined Alux as our electric guitarist. Oscar Conde was invited to take part in the recording of our second album and stayed with the band thereafter. At different points in time, both he and I had been enrolled in architecture, but Oscar went on to become a graphic designer and also made a name for himself as a songwriter for other artists, while I pursued a career as a composer of contemporary works and as a performer of chamber music. After the departure of former drummers Pablo Mayorga (1980–83) and Ranferí's brother Orlando (1980–86), who for a period of time were featured in the band playing two drum sets together during our concerts, it was one-time theology student Lenín who replaced them and gave the final touch to Alux Nahual's most permanent configuration.

Alux started off, quite naturally, by covering songs by well-known rock and pop artists, which was the way in which foreign influences became integrated into our style. In fact, at the outset, a large part of Alux's fans were attracted to the group by our ability to reproduce the riffs and "sound" of those we imitated: not only the everyday instrumentation of America's "Horse with No Name" or the guitar solo from Led Zeppelin's "Stairway to Heaven," but more particularly a violin/violoncello (originally viola) combination like that of Kansas's "Dust in the Wind," or the acoustic feel of acts such as Seals & Crofts. In the long run, however, it was the varied musical tastes of the musicians for progressive rock, in addition to an affinity for a variety of singer-songwriters, among them Elton John (U.K.), Joan Manuel Serrat (Catalonia), or Chico Buarque (Brazil), that would provide the foundations upon which Alux would create its own music for almost twenty years.

Normally, access to recordings of rock music was restricted to what happened to be in stock in the handful of record stores in Guatemala, but trips outside the country (particularly to the United States) by members of the group or friends, helped us "discover" new or unknown musicians and trends. Occasionally, also, certain underground radio programs gave us an inkling of what was going on overseas. But to this very day, exceedingly few Anglo rock artists have ever performed in Guatemala, which grants those locals who play this kind of music a very distinct value because of the original music's scarcity. At the beginning, therefore, and also quite predictably, the programs for our concerts included foreign hits—always in English, a practice we abandoned as Alux became better known. From the start, however, all of our shows also highlighted our own pieces (especially those by lead vocalist Alvaro Aguilar, with a lot of collective arranging going on), and these were always performed in Spanish. One such piece was "La fábula del grillo y el mar" ("The Fable of the Cricket and the Sea"):

> Buenas noches, señoras y señores,
> yo soy el hombre que vino a cantar
> a veces mi voz se pierde en la noche,
> a veces la gente viene a escuchar
> Voy a pedirles en este momento,
> que me presten por un rato su atención
> para que no sean palabras al viento
> lo que diga con esta canción
> voy a contarles una historia,
> un cuento: la fábula del grillo y el mar.
>
> (Good evening, ladies and gentlemen
> I am the man who came to sing
> sometimes my voice gets lost in the night
> sometimes people come and listen
> I'm gonna ask you now
> to give me a moment of your attention
> so that what I say with this song
> won't only be words gone with the wind
> I'll be telling you a story,
> a tale: the fable of the cricket and the sea.)

Ruling out sporadic bouts of enthusiasm, the role of Central American record companies in the dissemination of Alux's music in particular (and regional rock in general) has been of modest significance. As little more than concessionaries for foreign labels, their major role was and continues to be the distribution of musical products from the United States and Mexico. A typical example is that of the leading Guatemalan label, Dideca (Discos de Centroamérica), whose feeble understanding of local rock and dismal public relations have disappointed most of those who have ever had anything to do with them. Dideca earned its reputation and built its fortune principally by focusing on recordings of traditional marimba music, but the company has been in no hurry to encourage and champion innovative local artists.

Now, if this brief account of Alux Nahual seems somehow commonplace, its ordinariness can be misleading when viewed out of context. Besides an appallingly narrow artistic atmosphere and the second-to-highest illiteracy rate in all of the Americas, Guatemala boasts a repressive social system of the most tragically effective kind. So much so that while the band was never obsessed with contesting the social structure from which we came, even our primitive shots as musical creators aroused suspicion in conservative quarters and gained us ridiculous denouncements as a *protesta* group. Of course, this was not the sole privilege of Alux; since 1954 "subversion" has always been implied when it comes to most any cultural going-on. Henchmen of the status quo have been quick to point fingers (or, alas, machine guns) at any *desestabilizador* in literature, music, journalism, social science, ecology, or at any kind of activism that might easily be stamped as "communist" or "leftist." It has never been necessary to be involved in politics per se to become a political target in Guatemala. Then again, and with the indubitable benefit of hindsight, it is easy to pick on the band's unhappiest moments and dub us a *grupo fresa*.[13] This was certainly a criticism that local, self-appointed, "alternative" critics of the group engaged in, perhaps in an effort to disqualify Alux Nahual's music even as it was being appropriated by Central American working-class youth. A song like "Hombres de maíz" ("Men of Maize") would appear to exemplify these contradictions:

> No me importan los llantos
> ni los caminos largos
> si, cuando llega la noche,
> tengo flores en las manos
> no me importa el gobierno
> ni los revolucionarios
> pero si esto es vivir,
> prefiero morir así, cantando
> Vida: gracias por darme alma y piel
> una guitarra fina y una mujer sencilla
> Dichosos hombres de maíz

que viven en las montañas
y tienen flores en abril
y rocío en la mañana

(I don't mind the tears
or the lengthy roads
if I've got flowers in my hands
when night falls
I don't care for the government
or for the revolutionaries
but if this is to be alive,
I'd sooner die while singing
Thank you life, for giving me soul and skin
a good guitar and a simple woman
Lucky men of maize
who live in the mountains
and have flowers in April
and raindew in the morning.)

Maco Luna asked me about this song: "How come Alux was saying, 'thank you, life, for a good guitar,' when so many musicians had to manufacture their own instruments and have someone lend them amps and stuff?" It is true, Alux is remembered for its "massive" concerts, with tons of speakers, lighting equipment, and theatrical backdrops. Yet, probably because of our very naiveté, we also spent years practicing in makeshift rehearsal spaces, borrowing drum sets, making do with toy keyboards, and relying upon patched-up violin and cello pickups. Perhaps more pointed still was the question asked of us by the art critic Sergio Valdés: "How was it possible that Alux Nahual was singing 'Lucky men of maize, who live in the mountains and have flowers in April and raindew in the morning' precisely at the time when entire Indian villages were being razed by counterinsurgent forces?"

It seems to me that if Alux Nahual's musical proposals were approached and embraced decidedly by so many, it was because we had somehow managed to "pull it off." Guatemala has chronically suffered from a lack of heroes, idols, and leaders.[14] In this context, successful artists have not become leaders in a politically effective sense, but they may have helped shape political points of view by providing the public at large with icons to hang onto or with which to identify. I don't have any qualms about admitting that we were insufficiently class-conscious to leverage our position as musicians into *líderes de opinión*. But at the same time, I believe that it is fair to stress that while none of us pretended to possess an acute social awareness, which, in fact, we did not have, it is also fair to say that Alux Nahual's music had very little in common with disposable pop songs and attitudes either.

By 1982–83 the group had produced two albums and was enjoying huge turnouts at our larger-scale concerts, which confirmed our popularity. It became clear that Alux Nahual had come to the forefront of the popular music scene in Guatemala. At that point, we started to catch the attention of audiences in other Central American countries—as well as that of Central American immigrants and refugees living in the United States. When "Aquí está tu tierra" ("Here's Your Homeland") was issued as a single in 1983, about a year before the group's third album was released, the song became the first (and one of the very few) of the band's cuts to hit the Central American charts[15]:

> Vives en una gran ciudad
> y tienes el cambio a tu favor
> ya casi no recuerdas tu pueblo,
> aquél pequeño y soñador
> y los caminos que bajan al valle
> no te llaman la atención más
> pues donde vives son más anchas las calles
> y es más grande la ciudad.
> . . . .
> ¡Vuelve cuando puedas
> . . . aquí está tu tierra!
>
> (You live in a great city
> and the exchange rate is in your favor
> you barely remember your home town
> little and wistful
> and the paths that lead down into the valley
> no longer appeal to you
> Because where you live streets are wider
> and the city is bigger.
> . . . .
> Come back whenever you're able to
> . . . here is your homeland!)

At the end of 1983 we played in El Salvador for the first time. Shortly afterward, we performed in Honduras, and, a couple of years later, in Costa Rica. The subsequent albums were *Centroamérica*, released in 1986, and the following year, *Alto al fuego* (*Cease Fire*). With Central America deadlocked in a series of devastating civil wars that affected the entire region, the title track from *Alto al fuego* became a veritable "anthem," not just for Guatemalans but for all Central American youth:

> Y . . . se retiraron los ejércitos extranjeros,
> pero se quedaron los contras y los guerilleros
> cada quien quería izar una nueva bandera
> y cambiar los sueños de libertad
> por las chequeras
> ¡Alto al fuego, cese el fuego,
> en todo el territorio centroamericano!
> . . . .
> Y . . . ya no queremos volver
> a escuchar de las guerras,
> sólo queremos paz y trabajar las tierras
> cada quien sabrá
> buscar un nuevo camino
> y forjar con sus manos un mejor destino
> ¡Alto al fuego, cese el fuego,
> en todo el territorio centroamericano!
>
> (And so the foreign armies have left
> but the *contras* and the guerrillas remained
> Every one of them wanted to hoist a new flag
> and swap dreams of freedom
> for checkbooks
> Stop the fire, cease fire
> On all Central American ground!
> . . . .
> And so we don't want
> to know again of wars
> all we want is peace and to work the land
> Every one of us shall learn
> to look for new ways
> to build a better future with our hands
> Stop the fire, cease fire
> on all Central America ground!)

The topically significant titles turned out to have been well timed, since peace treaties were signed by the five Central American states between 1987 and 1989 in an effort (led by Costa Rican president and Nobel Prize–winner

Oscar Arias) to put an end to armed conflicts within the region. Alux was chosen to perform on the occasion of the "Esquipulas III" peace talks that were held in San José, Costa Rica, in 1988. Under Vinicio Cerezo, Guatemala's first legally elected civilian president in more than thirty years, talks commenced between the government and guerrilla leaders. These talks culminated in a long-awaited peace treaty in 1996. Alux was once again invited to perform before the multitude that congregated to witness the momentous signing of this document.

The band would also play for some sixteen thousand who gathered in the Monja Blanca stadium of San Salvador a short while before the 1992 peace accords that ended the Salvadoreans' own civil war. After the fighting was over, we were invited to visit the recently legalized "Radio Vencerémos" and were able to verify what we had earlier heard: "Alto al fuego" had been part of the radio station's programming for years. We then recalled what we had been told by employees of the Guatemalan military's TV Channel 5. General Héctor Gramajo (appointed Guatemala's minister of defense in 1985) had authorized the airing of the video clip of "Alto al fuego" because one of his children liked the song and stood up for it. In that way, "Alto al fuego" had developed into an emblematic song of El Salvador's guerrilla movement, while at the same time it was being used by none other than the Guatemalan Army's education TV station!

To go as far as to boast that Alux Nahual played any significant role in the peace talks would demonstrate a serious loss of perspective. The band did, however, successfully reflect the wishful feelings of the urban middle class we came from and it idiosyncratically voiced the rejection that a very large number of people felt for the stupidity of war. Thus, the band had gone from being a bountiful, if belated, exponent of the elaborate symphonic rock of the 1970s to the main Central American rock music reference of the 1990s. It had taken a long time for us to understand that it was not enough to be enthusiastic if you wanted to clear a path in a milieu that was methodically indifferent to anything musically innovative. Ultimately, however, Alux Nahual reached the point when it was no longer possible to start afresh, and so the band turned to reaping the benefits derived from years of surmounting all kinds of absurd obstacles.

The years 1994–95 grew into a long season of innumerable recitals in Guatemala and abroad. An ensuing discographic effort in 1996, aimed at penetrating the North American market and reaching other Latin American consumers, resulted in a final recording, and the period 1997–99 saw the band's members increasingly devoting themselves to independent ventures. A few months short of the group's twentieth anniversary, Alux disintegrated. We continue to work, separately, as musicians or in music-related activities.

Alux Nahual and the Music Market

Our first record was put out by Dideca at the end of 1981, and by the end of 1987, as Guatemala caught up with the wave of *"rock en tu idioma"* promoted by the transnational recording industry, Alux had four more records under its belt, including *Alto al fuego.* The album was, reportedly, the first long-playing record by a Central American rock group to sell ten thousand copies.[16] Two more records were issued under Dideca, the last one a "greatest hits" compilation called *Leyenda,* which has sold more than twenty thousand copies. Without question, Alux Nahual outsold all other Central American rock groups, despite the continued indifference and even open opposition from a portion of the media and a general unresponsiveness by the labels.[17] Estuardo Castañeda, a former record company representative with Dideca (1979–85), reasons that to a certain degree the hostility from critics might have been due to the fact that, for folks in the media, whom he typifies as socially hung up and resentful, we were *niños bien* from privileged backgrounds. For example, not long before the crucial 1987–88 period, the head of one of Guatemala's largest broadcasting corporations, Arcaso, was reputedly heard proclaiming that "he would not include Alux's music even if paid to do so." All the same, this unfriendliness toward Alux was not especially unique; it was part of a conduct generally observed vis-à-vis all national artists up to the end of the 1980s.

What is significant to point out, however, is that Alux Nahual succeeded with audiences in Central America, not because of record company marketing strategies or critical acclaim, but, in many ways, despite the resistance the band faced from within the media. In fact, no full-scale campaign to advertise our recordings was ever mounted by our recording labels.[18] Yet the band was enormously popular with a growing and diversifying fan base. This growing reception by fans was conspicuously highlighted in a show that we opened for the Mexican all-girl pop trio Flans in 1988, when that band was very much in fashion. The event took place in a location that up to that time had not been used for concerts, and it attracted some fifteen thousand people. To our utter surprise (we were the "warm-up" band), the audience knew all the lyrics to the songs from *Alto al fuego,* which had been released barely two months earlier and without any publicity. Instead of the illustrious threesome, they demanded that we carry on the show instead! Indeed, Alux Nahual's power to draw a big crowd turned us into the favorite choice of music impresarios who wanted to make good when hiring a local act to open concerts for foreign artists playing in Guatemala. What was seen as the group's ability to interpolate between rock and pop had come to be appreciated as a plus for shows that featured mostly lighter musical propositions, such as the Spanish groups Mecano and Hombres G, the Mexican performer Emmanuel, and Argentinian Miguel Mateos—all of whom we played with as opening acts. And, after a while, we began to notice that the remarks on the part of those internationally renowned artists with whom we shared the stage had one point in common: "This is *not* the kind of opening act we get all the time when we're on the road. The audience knows their songs! These guys are actually loved by their public!"

Eventually, after years of prodding our record company in vain, we started to seek attention elsewhere. New contacts were established, acquaintances made, and plans drawn up. Alux performed in several cities in the United States, where we were greeted with enthusiasm, and not only by the resident Central Americans—whom we expected to attend the shows in any event—but by astonished gringos as well, who anticipated just another Latin dance band. In 1991 we played in a six-city tour that found us performing alongside the dance bands Orquesta Hermanos Flores (El Salvador), Banda Blanca (Honduras), and FM de Zacapa (Guatemala). Yet, while those ensembles were required to do two sets every night for the audience to dance to, Alux was allowed to concentrate on one "central" show for the public to *listen to*. And therein lay the dilemma for audiences and record executives alike: If we were indeed a rock group from Latin America, why didn't our music sound like *rock latino?* Why weren't we doing at least some sort of salsa-rock dance tracks? Why didn't we play something more akin to Mexico's new generation of rock bands and offer a mixture of mariachi and Metallica?

The case of the group's ambiguous musical identity bore a curious resemblance to a difficulty we had encountered in the early years, when we were embarking on our first gigs outside the capital of Guatemala. Since the name of the band was in K'iché, this suggested (especially to audiences in the countryside) that we were a marimba and not a rock group.[19] Not until the end of the 1980s did artistic entrepreneurs from rural towns begin to contract Alux for rock concerts, in some instances two or even three times in one year. These gigs succeeded in filling halls and open-air theatres with audiences of up to three thousand people, where formerly only tropical and disco-dancing parties had been able to pack venues—and this in provincial towns that generally had fewer than 150,000 inhabitants.[20] The singularity of a "national rock" band being able to tour the Guatemalan countryside at that time, and play to audiences familiar with our songs, stood in clear contrast to the efforts aimed at promoting Alux in the United States. Whereas Alux Nahual *meant* and *stood for* something in the mind's eye of Guatemalan and Central American youth, the band bore little relevance for those beyond the region's geographical borders.

It all basically boiled down to one central issue: Alux Nahual could choose to remain a Central American band or, if we wanted to "internationalize" ourselves, we would need to be transmuted into a Miami, Los Angeles, or Mexico City–based band—and change our style to that of a "planned" rock concept.

The evidence to support this point goes beyond my experience with Alux Nahual. As of this writing, no Central American rock artist has ever won recognition outside the region. In the case of Alux, one reason for this, I would argue, is because the group did not conveniently match any marketable music category: our music neither fit the growing *rock en español* trend, nor were we sufficiently "exotic" (except for our name, perhaps) to be picked up within the "world music" genre. Moreover, we did not write music that was for dancing. With the exception of the hit single "Fiesta privada" ("Private Party"), the "dance tracks" we did try to write were of little or no consequence. It would be difficult to claim that Alux's music had a "groove" feeling. This fact alone goes a long way toward explaining why radio never played a major role in making Alux's music known, and why the band never did seriously interest run-of-the-mill company reps in other regions.

Yet one way or another, Alux Nahual's music did get passed on. Initially, the music was passed "from hand to hand," as some kind of underground progressive rock. Later on, such enthusiasts as late-night-radio disc jockeys and freelance supporters disseminated our music across the airwaves, and eventually we were promoted by shrewd soft-drink company salespeople and opportunistic charity organizations. Perhaps what best sums up the issue in a simple, paradigmatic manner is the end result of a meeting in 1990 held by members of Alux Nahual with José Behar, vice-director of what was then CBS of Los Angeles. We had gone to his office to try and promote our song "De la noche a la mañana" ("All of a Sudden"). As is typical for record executives, Behar told us to simply leave the demo and he would listen to it "later." We insisted that he listen to it then and there, however. He consented, and decided to sit back and relax while the song sounded on the stereo in his office. It was then, when the music had ended, that he smiled and declared approvingly, "Beautiful song, for sure. But I'm afraid an exec in my position can't risk his reputation endorsing a band nobody's heard about."

Why Should Alux Nahual Be So Different, Anyway?

In Latin America the vast majority of *canciones* aired by radio stations or accepted in the catalog of record companies have been pre-cast structurally and harmonically. This is so often the state of affairs that artists very commonly add the description "*canción*" in brackets following the title (much as they might add "tango" or "bolero" or "6x8," to designate what rhythmic pattern is at hand), because the structure of the song falls into some fairly identifiable category.[21] Such a convention presumably enables the listener to be assured of what to expect from a given piece of music before actually listening to it, based on a precodified auditory experience.[22] This takes us to the dichotomy of music-for-entertainment versus music-for-listening that always problematized Alux's repertoire in its relations with the mass media. Over time, when we were asked to offer a definition of our music, we arrived at such expressions as *"rock en español, con mensaje"* to try and ease the interviewer's obligation to categorize us. Accordingly, it was never easy to attach labels to the bulk of Alux Nahual's songs, either in terms of timbre, form-structure, or style (such as R&B, hard rock, soft rock). Even our lighter tunes departed from accustomed radio configurations and, although wholly "singable," did not depend on catchy, repetitive lyrics. That is to say, we never intended or were able to write groovy rhythmic dancetracks, but we did manage to come up with poetic images and melodic lines that sounded good when accompanied merely by guitar or piano.

Many of Alux's most remarkable songs were, in effect, composed after a comparatively simple fashion, with the author submitting ideas raw to the rest of the group for the purpose of receiving feedback as to the words, musical structure, and instrumentation. In that way, important and identifying gestures came into being during rehearsals. However, this was not merely because musicians were picking up indications given by the songwriter and embellishing their corresponding musical lines following the stock-in-trade of rock and roll practice for each instrument; more accurately, it was the result of not thinking about what "type" of piece was being "learned" and allowing enough freedom for each musician to contribute to it in an unexpected or unorthodox way. Very often, a band member would come to rehearsal saying, "Listen to this song or idea that I have, what do you make of it?" Some songs were pretty much finished and needed only additional touches here and there. But most underwent extensive discussion, with debates often going on for days on end without anybody actually getting down to rehearse the music, before a majority had agreed on the general subject and treatment of the piece. The point here is that, basically, rock music on the radio is radio-ready music. The result, for Alux Nahual, was that many of our songs were rendered ineffective for airplay or nightclub use because they failed to incorporate standardized elements or did not go where they were "supposed" to go. Over time, interests shifted and several members began to focus their energies more on production and marketing than on artistic innovation. Heated arguments developed over how to find the balance between standardization and originality that would be acceptable to everyone.

Examining one of Alux Nahual's most easily recognizable and differentiating feature, its instrumentation, will help to illustrate the purported divergences of the group when compared with most other Latin American rock groups. With acoustic guitar, violin, flute, and cello, all relatively well featured against electric guitar, bass, and drums, Alux could hardly be called an exemplary *latino* rock band. But, more interestingly, these "softer" instruments never functioned within the band as mere sporadic orchestral backdrops. Other groups might record with such instruments, but they were hardly discernible and would often be dispensed with when the groups performed live.[23] Even when Alux displayed few instrumentally bravura passages, there was a lot of elaborate timbre exchange and layering. Together with the customary rock elements such as power chords, a pounding rhythm section, loud vocals, and basic rhythmic patterns, these other instruments (for example, cello) were integral to the "sound" of the band itself. In other words, the instruments that did not conventionally "belong" to rock did not serve simply to mirror stylistic traits (for example, violin = country music, or flute = Jethro Tull) within the scope of episodic solos, but were constituent parts of the main musical lines and structures of songs. Typically, also, Alux's "romantic" *baladas* eschewed the bass and drums deemed indispensable for disco material, upsetting the immediacy of the usual verse-and-refrain sequences by emphasizing instrumental sections. This is the case with all the best-loved of Alux's slow-tempo tracks, such as "Mujer" ("Woman"), which uses only acoustic guitar and cello accompaniment to the vocals, "Lo que siento por ti" ("My Feelings for You"), "Libre sentimiento" ("Free Feeling"), and "De la noche a la mañana" ("All of a Sudden"). Additionally, it is worth noting that although we did at times exploit regional instruments to evoke certain associations (such as the Guatemalan *chirimía–tamborón* combination),[24] we neither incorporated them on a regular basis nor did we develop "folk" idioms (dear to Andean musicians in South America, or Tex-Mex bands in the North, for example), which might have allowed music industry representatives to more readily tag our group with a *folclórico* label or promotional slant.

Since Alux Nahual came from an "unheard-of place" yet did not sound at all like "Latin rock," foreign radio-station owners and broadcasting DJs were unable to mark it as such; the band would have had to fit some other stereotype. Even though we did not go out of our way to refuse "tropical" elements in our music, none of us were interested in including them simply to appeal to the patronizing sensibilities of North Americans or Western Europeans. Thus, we failed to fit into any real category—whether World Music (although we came from an "exotic" country, we were hardly exotic sounding), Latin rock (lacking a tradition of African-inspired dance, our efforts at fusion incorporated few dance rhythms), or *música tropical*. Dazzled by the belief (as with so many other things, brought in from another culture) that rock should fulfill certain prerequisites or give up being rock at all, Alux Nahual was correspondingly judged as inflicted with "faults" that were ultimately viewed as "intolerable" by the recording industry, mass media, and intellectuals. For one, we came from the "wrong" social provenance. Alux did not emerge from popular quarters or shantytowns, neither were we exiles or members of a clandestine fraternity in search of a liberating means of expression. To the contrary, all we had to show for ourselves was a lineup of half-a-dozen well-behaved, highly educated, middle-class schoolboys. Secondly, we had the "wrong" social manners. Even though members of the group had begun meeting in the late 1970s, none of us wore our hair down to our waist, none of us smoked pot, none of us had been arrested by the police. None of us ever fled our homes to share ramshackle lodgings with young poets and painters while issuing philosophical statements from the corner of a bar. We never sought the shelter of the media or of a religious congregation, either of which would have provided the group with an automatic audience. Third, we had the "wrong" social look. Regardless of the many free shows or low-priced gigs we performed everywhere throughout rural Guatemala, despite the concerts in aid of humanitarian causes and all sorts of benefit performances, we neither learned to dress up in trendy clothes nor to make ourselves up elegantly to facilitate the marketing of our likenesses. In fact, we hardly gave ourselves away as artists, or even as musicians. And, perhaps the worst of all: we had the "wrong" socio-musical behavior. The vocalist did not shout obscenities into the mike, the guitarist did not perform drunk, the drummer did not destroy his drums at every other concert, and no one stage-dived onto the public. In a word, Alux was not a *trespasser* of habits, whether social or musical, and therefore could not qualify as a "true" rock band! As David de Gandarias, composer and drummer for the 1960s rock band S.O.S., once remarked: "Alux Nahual did *not* misbehave."

Alux Nahual, Tropicalism, and World Music

What kind, what variety, what genre of music "should" have been produced by a Latin American rock group such as Alux Nahual in order to enable it to jump the regional barrier? Should we have written "tropicalized" Latin rock instead of our idiosyncratic interpretations of progressive rock-pop? And is it an essential argument or, rather, an *essentialist* one, which calls for dance music to be produced automatically by a musical ensemble from the third world because "they got rhythm in their blood over there"? It is beyond the scope of this article to delve into a discussion of the prejudices implied in the dominant conceptualization of World Music and how it marginalizes the music of other (that is, non-Western) cultures. It should be enough to remember that the World Music designation came into being around 1982–83, and was embraced by Western record companies, stores, and the media to facilitate the marketing of non-Western (and non-mainstream Western) music. The irony is that "world" music, more often than not, is tantamount to "local" or "regional" (allegedly less "synthetic," more "authentic," or even "environmental") music. Done in the name of a more politically correct attitude (meant to avoid the use of such loaded expressions as "exotic" or "primitive"), the promoters of the World Music marketing category ended up fabricating a global(izing) title for what is really a very restrictive category. While seeking to expand Alux Nahual's marketing possibilities from the limited level of consumption inherent to an underdeveloped, mostly rural economy to a transnational market based on mass consumption, we became conscious of the asphyxiating, limiting range of alterity this process tolerated. Alux wasn't, or was not considered to be, within that range. There is little doubt, now, that Alux would have had to be far more easily categorized in order to stand an actual chance of classifying for big-league distribution. For, in the end, it is the industry, not the artist or the public, that decides what kind of music we "need."

At the end of the day, Alux Nahual remains pertinent for a great many Central Americans. The band's recordings are sought after. Its songs continue to be played on radio. And, more relevantly, our music has been performed by musicians belonging to a generation so young that its members barely made it to our farewell concerts. For many, Alux stands out as a model of what *can* be achieved in this part of the world, in terms of successfully engaging in a collective artistic enterprise. I suppose such an enterprise was fundamentally original in purpose because it defied commercial conventions. Happily, we were able to keep on rockin' for a long period of time while also maintaining our artistic integrity.

Selected Discography

Alux Nahual. *Alto al fuego.* 1987. Dideca LP 87776.
———. *Alux Nahual.* 1981. Dideca LP 81486.
———. *Antología II.* 2002. Dideca CD 76621630 7929.
———. *Centroamérica.* 1986. Dideca LP 86726.

———. *Conquista.* 1982. Dideca LP 82533.
———. *Hermanos de sentimiento.* 1984. Dideca LP 84595.
———. *La historia del duende en concierto.* 2002. Acorde CD.
———. *Leyenda.* 1992. Dideca CD 92010.
———. *Leyenda II.* 1995. Dideca CD 95044.
———. *La trampa.* 1989. Dideca LP 89826.

My Generation

Rock and *la Banda*'s Forced Survival Opposite the Mexican State

HÉCTOR CASTILLO BERTHIER

¡*Que viva el rock!* Long live rock!: An emblematic, sonorous, identifying shout, synonym of joy, of hanging out, of the utopian union of dreams and hopes, of the desire to be together, of the pleasure of the concert, the performance, the thrill of the re-encounter of the people, of *la banda,* of the barrio, of the identity of thousands of young people, of *los chavos,* ready to come together within one of youth's principal forms of expression—if not the most vital of all—the music that abets chaos: Rock.

In postrevolutionary Mexico, one of the most reproachable conflicts between the authoritarian state and civil society was the massacre of several hundred students on October 2, 1968, at Tlatelolco, in Mexico City. On June 10, 1971, a second massacre took place against students and others. The time was right for another cornerstone, only this time for Mexican rock: the September 1971 Festival at Avándaro, Mexico's version of Woodstock. One might ask: How is it possible that young people—just a few months after the 1971 massacre—could assemble to listen to rock music? Does it not seem illogical? There are many possible answers to these questions, and there is no single way to interpret these events. What is clear is that in 1971, just as in 1968, a student movement with a well-defined political profile developed, but, curiously, the music that defined both movements was not, generally speaking, rock. Rather, it was the music of political struggle, more commonly called *música de protesta,* with which the student demonstrators identified. This was music played by the folkloric groups that had been launched into vogue by the Cuban Revolution and spurred on by the rise of military dictatorship in Argentina and the socialist effervescence in Chile.

There was very little original rock music in Mexico in 1968, and even less in 1971. However, the young *rockeros* who arrived at Avándaro were disenchanted by politics and social mobilizations. Avándaro represented, for them, a kind of mandatory "complacency"—one of the few political terms they knew and understood very well. They arrived at Avándaro imbued with the pacifist spirit of the U.S. hippies. They sought *la buena onda* (cool vibes), "peace and love," and, above all, a collective encounter as a way of understanding themselves—their tastes, their music, their coexistence—as part of a larger phenomenon, of living a life linked to rock 'n' roll. The journalist Ricardo Garibay once said that at Avándaro a parenthesis had been opened between the tens of thousands of young people who did not want to incorporate themselves into politics, who were searching for new ways—totally unknown and without apparent direction at that moment—of being and participating in their *patria*— yet who had become, in Carlos Monsiváis's famous expression, "foreigners in their own country." That parenthesis had not been closed, nor is it certain when it ever would be.[1]

But which homeland did Garibay have in mind? That of the murdering and corrupt politicians who had completely undermined and discredited the word "politics" for young people and the rest of the population? Which nation? The one represented by a ruling political party (the Partido Revolucionario Institucional, or PRI) that was omnipotent and authoritarian, and had no intention of favoring democratic progress? Foreigners from across which border? The border of the Río Bravo—or Rio Grande, according to one's geographical perspective—across which hundreds of thousands of migrants traveled in search of a better place to live, even if it meant being an *ilegal* with no rights or protections? Of all the possible Mexicos in that moment, with which one did youth identify themselves?

Mexico has its "Avándaro generation," which for more than three decades has been struggling from within, evolving politically and musically. The new heirs of that generation—*my* generation, or what is left of it—participate ever more actively in the new social movements, led by youth, environmental activists, and others, in favor of indigenous peoples and against imperialism— both new and old. The new *rockeros* also express themselves in favor of democracy and against authoritarianism and corruption. This vision of political consciousness was not explicit at Avándaro in 1971, but that event did favor the gestation of a new political consciousness linked explicitly with rock music, and that has come to incorporate many sectors of youth. The parenthesis spoken of by Garibay has not yet closed. It remains open for many, growing and widening more and more toward objectives never previously thought nor intuited. This essay seeks to outline some of the main characteristics and social outcomes resulting from the opening of that parenthesis more than thirty years ago.

Youth, *la Banda*, and the Mexican State

Rock in Mexico has never been static; it has always been versatile and dynamic, and it has suffered all possible metamorphoses through time. Thus, the first *rocanroleros* transformed rock 'n' roll into sweet and *ñoña* songs—to use a term coined by the rock chronicler Federico Arana to suggest a saccharine-tasting, anodyne music—whereas today Mexican rock is characterized by a contestatory, rebellious, and irreverent presence. Indeed, an outstanding feature of contemporary Mexican rock is its zeal for being linked to "noble causes," such as solidarity with the indigenous and the poor, support for AIDS awareness, the struggle against drug abuse, and the prevention of violence against street children. This linkage with grassroots activism can be attributed to the popularity of rock among university students and, especially, rock's close connection with youth from the economically marginalized sectors of urban society—groups I characterize in this essay as *banda* (pl. *bandas*). Within a situation of profound economic crisis, young people have found a form of defensive association in *bandas,* enabling them to face the conditions of their daily lives, while at the same time, rock has become the vehicle for self-expression and feeling "alive" in a generally hostile urban environment.

The concept of *banda* is socially and culturally complex. At one level, the term refers to a form of voluntary association among groups of *chavos* (kids), generally averaging thirty members who range in age from twelve to twenty-four years old and whose collective and territorial identity is forged in relationship to their immediate urban environment, or *barrio* (neighborhood). Although female members and even *bandas* formed exclusively by women exist, in general, *bandas* are predominantly formed by male youth. At another level, however, *banda* is also a space of social contention; it empowers youth who have very limited economic, social, or even moral resources, who do daily battle just to stay alive. *Banda* implies not being alone. *Banda* allows for unity within the marginalized urban zones—the *cinturones de miseria* (poverty belts) that continue to proliferate throughout the Mexican capital—as well as a defense from the world outside.[2] Indeed, some zones are difficult, if not impossible, for police to enter.[3] *Banda* is also a school, the school of the "street kids,"[4] which teaches them to search for the means of survival at any price (legal or illegal). *Banda* not only creates a spoken language but also a physical one. Clothing, hair, and ways of walking and dancing are all characteristics of this identity, although there is an enormous variation, depending on social context: overcoats and leather jackets, military boots, multicolored hairstyles, earrings, chains, sneakers, and T-shirts printed with knives and skulls are all characteristic of *banda* fashion. Above all, *la banda* implies rock. Rock is the preferred (though not exclusive) music of *banda*, and the ever-present *tocadas* (concerts) constitute a world of popular cultural socialization, of evasion, catharsis, and a reinforcement of one's own, hostile, aggressive identity.[5] As the Mexican cultural critic Carlos Monsiváis writes, "Of the social inventions of the 1980s none is so ubiquitous, so lively, and so despairing as *banda*, the grouping of young people marginalized by the economy and redeemed by their sheer numbers."[6]

To get a better idea of the dimensions of this phenomenon, a 1988 study found that in Mexico City alone there were around 1,500 youth *bandas*; in other words, approximately 40,000 to 45,000 *chavos* participated in *bandas* throughout the capital.[7] Since that time, Mexico City has continued to grow—reaching upwards of nineteen million people in 2001—and the *cinturones de miseria* that now define much of the urban landscape, and that nurture the social phenomenon of *banda*, have likewise proliferated. The formal urban job market is practically inaccessible to these youth, as is acquiring an education beyond secondary, or even primary, school. Their social identity is neither that of workers nor students, and much less that of *ciudadanos* (citizens). Instead, these young people identify themselves simply as *banda*, holding up the name of their group (which is often tied semantically with the name of their barrio) as their principal form of self-identification.

Rock's shift, from the upper and middle classes that sheltered it during the 1950 and 1960s to its appropriation by the *banda* of the lower-class, urban barrios during the 1970s and 1980s, has been accompanied by the undeniable and irremediably authoritarian presence of the Mexican state: the corporatist politics of a one-party system and the rhetoric of a so-called "revolutionary family" to which all Mexicans belong. Although this authoritarianism has diminished since the ruling PRI was finally voted out of power in the presidential elections of 2000, its presence is still felt in the periodic censorship of the communications media and in the frequent repression of spaces for youth culture. The history of the state's corporatist relationship with youth is long and complicated, and must be understood in order to grasp the meaning of contemporary youth's status as social actors, and thus the relationship of rock music to the phenomenon known as *banda*.

The origin of a corporatist politics aimed explicitly at youth dates back to at least 1938, when under President Lázaro Cárdenas the official party was renamed the Partido de la Revolución Mexicana (PRM), adopted the motto, "For a workers' democracy," and pledged to fight for "the union of all popular sectors against capitalism's aggression."[8] The political effervescence during Cárdenas's presidency was palpable; nevertheless, the PRM was quickly transformed into a hegemonic party that based its power on the construction and control of three principal social sectors: labor, peasants, and the military.[9] In the context of socialist economic and educational policies, in 1938 the Confederación de Jóvenes Mexicanos (Mexican Youth Confederation) was created, followed one year later by the Central Única de la Juventud (Youth's Sole Union), which gave rise to the creation of a specialized government office to attend to youth matters. Thus it was that the Oficina de Acción Juvenil (Juvenile Action Office) was created in 1942 under the tutelage of the Secretaría de Educación Pública (Secretary of Public Education, or SEP), which had the objective of "creating a National Directive Youth Advisory Board, integrated by representatives of the country's diverse juvenile *centrales* [unions]."[10]

During the "stabilizing development" era of President Miguel Alemán (1946–52), which sought to shift attention to foreign and domestic capital investment and away from the socialist economic impulses of Cárdenas, a new phase, characterized by the creation of the Instituto Nacional de la Juventud Mexicana (National Institute of Mexican Youth, or INJM), was inaugurated in 1950. The principal directives of this new agency were to "prepare, direct, and orient Mexican youth in all basic national problems in order to achieve the democratic ideal, and their material and spiritual prosperity." More significantly, the new agency was entrusted to "carry out the study of problems, formulate adequate solutions, and propose appropriate initiatives to the corresponding social or official organisms, or fulfilling them as appropriate."[11] Due to budget limitations, the Institute was initially oriented only toward Mexico City, but after 1958 the INJM's presence was extended to diverse regions of the country through the creation of Casas de la Juventud (Youth Houses).[12] Up to this point, the government's objectives seemed clear: to affiliate young people with the INJM; to promote certain technical skills; to sponsor cultural activities and civics courses; and, through all of this, to develop new social networks whose members could be gradually and systematically incorporated into the official ranks of the PRI.[13]

By 1977, the INJM had undergone a name change to the Instituto Nacional de la Juventud (National Youth Institute) or Injuve. This change reflected an attempt to modify the Institute's image and change its programs in an effort to incorporate young people who had remained aloof or reluctant to participate. The INJM, and later Injuve, sponsored numerous social-research seminars, symposiums, congresses, forums, and roundtables aimed at analyzing youth themes and juvenile problems. Yet very little is known about the real impact that Injuve had on society. For some, this period was dedicated to the athletic and physical development of thousands of young people, who would later be recruited as bodyguards, or *guaruras,* and incorporated into the federal and judicial police. For others, the project served simply to underwrite the Frente Juvenil Revolucionario (Revolutionary Juvenile Front), the principal youth segment of the PRI. What seems apparent, in any event, is that the programs of the Injuve were far removed from the socioeconomic realities and cultural interests of an urban youth population that had become increasingly diverse. As Pérez Islas comments, "A separation between youth and institutions had been established, a fact that, joined with the weakening of the economic [development] model . . . left the new generations to walk on their own. While Injuve was organizing *vueltas ciclistas* [bicycling contests], and promoting military service and athleticism, many youth were turning to rock, marijuana, and alternative culture."[14] This marked separation profoundly influenced youth's perceptions of public institutions: Injuve, like other "official programs," was something foreign and thus without transcendence in their daily lives.

Chavos Banda and the Crisis of the Mexican State

This mounting sense of Injuve's failure in addressing and thus channeling the needs of urban youth coincided with the emerging concept and image of the *chavos banda,* above all in the capital. The street had always been the privileged meeting place for Mexico's youth. In the 1930s and 1940s, rebellious youth were called "Tarzans," while in the 1950s they were called *pachucos,* and in the 1960s, *rebeldes sin causa* (rebels without a cause). In the 1970s, these youth were known as *flotas,* and by the 1980s the term *bandas* was being used. The first *bandas* were the Panchitos and the B.U.K. (Bandas Unidas Kiss). Another group took the name PND (Punks Not Dead), which was the title of a song by the English group the Exploited; the song was emblematic for the group and was transformed into a sort of "anthem" by this and other *bandas.* Other names included: Mierdas Punk (Punk Shits), Mugrosos (Filthies), Vagos (Vagrants), Verdugos (Executioners), Virginidad Sacudida (Discarded Virginity), Ratas Punk (Punk Rats), Niños Idos (Gone Children), Sex Leprosos (Sex Lepers), Apestosos (Stinkies), and Manchados (Tainted). Many key elements are immersed in the images called up by the groups' names: hate, neglect, ignorance, poverty, rejection, dissatisfaction, social resentment, revenge, vindictiveness. Soon, news of the *bandas*' violent confrontations began to fill the mass media. Now baptized as *chavos banda* (youth gangs), government authorities and the media collectively highlighted the negative aspects of the phenomenon without offering any means of addressing the problems underlying it. The *chavos banda,* however, found ways of responding in turn. "We make them afraid because we're ugly, dirty, fucked-up . . . and maybe they're right, but we're like this because the main drug which screws us up is the damned society."[15]

An important social actor in the attacks on *banda* at that time (and to some degree, still today) has been the Catholic Church. In a socially conservative society such as Mexico, claims that the *chavos banda* were linked to Satanism no doubt rang true. From the pulpit, and through such publications as *Rock y Satanismo*,[16] *Atalaya* (*Lookout*), and *Despertad* (*Awake*), with a monthly distribution of 11,350,000 copies), the Church accused rockers of forming satanic cults and of carrying out black masses. Parents were alerted to the "lost future" their children would have if they embraced rock. As a result, many *bandas* adopted names of the devil such as Abadón, Luzbel, Lucifer, Belcebú (Beelzebub), Herejía (Heresy), Blasfemia (Blasphemy), Sacrilegio (Sacrilege), Cadáveres, and Brujería (Witchcraft), which of course further stoked the consternation of priests and parents, certain that their worst prophesies had come true.[17]

The sociological and anthropological studies as well as the journalistic reports and books that first described and studied teenage *bandas* mythified them immediately. They idealized the *bandas*' meeting methods, their sense of union, and, in fact, they created the image of a "new social actor" that was really nonexistent in any organized fashion.[18] This image of the *chavo banda* served a useful purpose, however, and after photographs of *chavos* with their group, "their gang," appeared, the *bandas* acquired a new dimension that the PRI quickly capitalized upon by creating a new government institute oriented toward youth, the Consejo Nacional de Recursos para la Atención de la Juventud (National Advisory Board of Resources for the Attention of Youth), or CREA.

During its ten years of existence (1977–87), CREA established a creative approach toward working with urban youth, including the organization of a variety of cultural events, which came to include free rock concerts. This diverse cultural programming favored the emergence and consolidation of numerous musical groups, writers, journalists, and poets, who encountered a "free space" in the cultural activities sponsored by CREA. In turn, during this period there was an increase in the number of independent publications and recordings, contests, recitals, and concerts for youth, all of which allowed young people to believe that the government had become more attentive and open to listening to its youth.

Yet the PRI's goal, as before, remained unchanged: the corporatist incorporation of youth into the ruling party's institutions. Many *chavos* began to question CREA for its political role, while cynical voices began calling the institution *No-Crea*—a double entendre that means both "doesn't create" and "don't believe." CREA was commonly criticized for trying to be "the minor league of the party" (that is, the PRI), and certain directors took such pride in that role that any pretense of CREA as a semi-independent government institution was abandoned in favor of promoting the organization as an explicit tool of the ruling regime. One example was how the PRI hoped to politically integrate the *chavos banda* into the party by utilizing the Consejos Populares Juveniles (Popular Juvenile Advisory Board), or CPJ. The councils attempted to organize marginalized youth for civic participation projects, supposedly on an independent and democratic basis. In the CPJs, everything was permitted: graffiti, mohawks, torn shirts, and, above all, rock. Such permissiveness exposed the existential marginality of such groups and their desires for social integration, but at the same time the CPJ's direct affiliation with an increasingly politicized CREA underscored the manipulative policies of a government whose principal goal was to ensure the votes of millions of young people in future elections.

By the late 1970s and early 1980s, rock had begun to leave the spaces and consciousness of the periphery and had begun its slow but steady return toward the middle classes. A seminal moment in this process was the appearance, in October 1980, of the Tianguis del Chopo, a vast rock flea market where attendees were invited to bring their "old records" to exchange them with others. Co-organized by Ángeles Mastretta, director and coordinator of cultural events at the Museo del Chopo, and Jorge Pantoja, of the Pro-Music and Art Organization, the *tianguis* "brought together collectors, producers, musicians, and fans interested in record production and collection of any sort," and especially of music that was considered "rare, un-cataloged, or out-of-print."[19] The idea was originally conceived as an attempt to "slow down the black market's grasp on collection material," but it also provided an outlet for the music of independent labels and producers, as well as for the promotion of old-fashioned, vinyl records and of bands lacking commercial exposure. Initially, attendance was such that the number of *rockeros* who arrived to exchange material greatly exceeded the organizers' expectations, thereby creating the demand that the *tianguis* should be installed every Saturday. These rock fans and connoisseurs, in coming together in "El Chopo," set the trend, almost unknowingly, for the birth of what would be the most important distribution of rock at the national level. "During many years," writes Maritza Urteaga, "El Chopo was the key informational and educational space, given that there were no other sources of information from abroad; and, from that perspective, it was more a space for the bartering of information than a market [for consumption]."[20] As a result of nearly a decade of government censorship and repression of rock, information about records, magazines, photographs, posters, and even movies that had to do with rock culture had became cult material for an entire generation of youth. These fans thus discovered in El Chopo a whole new type of underground exchange. Equally important, the Tianguis del Chopo was a space for the integration and interpellation of diverse collectivities of *chavos* who made up this meeting ground. "One doesn't go to the *tianguis* just to get material; one goes to get warmth, reaffirmation, and this is only possible by acting out *banda*, forming part of one of the numerous *rockero* tribes who arrive every Saturday to enjoy affection by way of a third object: rock, a recording, a performance."[21] Indeed, legions of *chavos* arrived at the *tianguis* from all over the country—from Sonora, which had almost specialized in heavy metal; from Guadalajara, represented by the BUSH (Bandas Unidas del Sector Hidalgo); from Aguascalientes, which had had a university rock radio station for over fifteen years; from Guanajuato, where the RULG (Rockeros Unidos de León, Guanajuato) organized support marches for *rock nacional*; and from Zacatecas, Chiapas, Oaxaca, Tampico, Tijuana, and many other regions. Mexico City had indeed become the nation's rock capital.

Two key rock performers deserve mention here, for each created a bridge between the youth of the *bandas* and the middle classes, who were returning to national rock after a hiatus of more than a decade. The first is Alex Lora, founder and lead performer of El Tri, Mexico's longest-running rock group (if one considers its earlier incarnation, Three Souls in My Mind). Lora is the country's most famous *rockero*, with more than thirty years performing and forty-one records to his name (twenty-two with Three Souls in My Mind, and nineteen with El Tri). As a group, El Tri is appreciated not only by *banda*, but also by the middle classes and even some people from the upper class. The group can be found playing at the National Auditorium as well as in *hoyos fonquis* (transient performance spaces of different types: abandoned warehouses, bullfighting arenas, old cinemas).[22] Lora and El Tri should be given credit for the consistency and coherence of their rock 'n' roll attitude—and their willingness to hold on to the musical scene with a rock that is *jodido* (literally, "screwed up"), urban, and played from the heart, disregarding conventional musical quality but clearly demonstrating the group's endurance within the rock genre. Juan M. Servín, an anthropologist, describes a performance by El Tri somewhat disparagingly in this way: "Going to an El Tri concert is for those who love in an unconditional way, for the homesick, or for fools who haven't lost hope that in the course of a concert something might occur that will revitalize a vicious circle."[23] Despite criticism, El Tri continues to press forward, with *la banda,* its *banda,* and with its battle cry: ¡Viva el rock and roll!

The second key performer was Rodrigo "Rockdrigo" González, whose music created one of the first links between the middle classes and the plebeian *bandas.* The novelist and rock critic José Agustín described Rodrigo González in 1983 as someone who had "achieved what is, for me, an extraordinary accomplishment: making Spanish sound perfect, truly natural in rock and roll.... With Rodrigo's lyrics (intelligent, malicious, provocative, poetic), it can be affirmed that Mexican Spanish is perfectly suitable for rock.... From the beginning I thought that Rodrigo González was our version of Bob Dylan with a sense of humor."[24] This notion that Rockdrigo had developed a simplified, "do-it-yourself" rock performance generated the label of *rock rupestre* (*rupestre* being the term used to describe prehistoric paintings and drawings, but here used to connote autochthonous urban expression), a label that has become a part of Mexican rock's lexicon. Rockdrigo's particular brand of rock and roll was a far cry from the technological paraphernalia and stage pretensions of typical rock. Based solely on acoustic guitar, voice, and sometimes harmonica, Rockdrigo's style indeed often sounded like that of Bob Dylan, Donovan, or Paul Simon, but in fact it had its origins with such Mexican musicians as Jaime López, Roberto Ponce, and Emilia Almazán. Rockdrigo's sound (and attitude) has gone on to influence such well-known musicians as Nina Galindo, but more significantly, his influence continues to be heard in the countless street performers who still interpret his music. In effect, Rockdrigo broke down the barrier of prejudice about the lack of "authenticity" in Mexican rock, while proving that people from different social strata could enjoy the same music. Tragically, he was killed in the 1985 earthquake that leveled Mexico City.

By the late 1980s, Spanish had been fully reclaimed as Mexican rock's official language, and lyrical content now spoke of the reality of *banda*s' social surroundings and concerns. Themes such as marginalization, unemployment, pacifism, ecology, human rights, and poverty were increasingly reflected in Mexican rock lyrics, and it became customary to *hacerla de pedo* (to answer back). Respect for religious morals was lost, while sexuality—forbidden by parents, the media, and official censorship—was denounced, and the enemies of the youth movement were identified: authoritarianism, corruption, and the PRI itself.

It was in this context that the first leaders of the Consejos Populares Juveniles affirmed that their organization was attempting to harness the energy of the *chavos banda* from the marginalized zones of the capital. As Fabrizio León writes, "The CPJ emerged out of the need for an organization to give a different image to the problem of gangs, as well as for the *bandas'* own defense.... The CPJ organizes the *bandas* and, as spokespeople for them, we analyze and investigate the relevant causes and effects [of their situation], in order to be able to counteract their marginality with whatever cultural and political means we have."[25] One example of the discourse embraced by the CPJ and other similar groups in their simultaneous strategy of representation/cooptation is the following text, entitled "Society of the Street Corner," which appeared in a pamphlet from Ciudad Juárez (edited by the government organization *Solidaridad*) in 1993:

> During every stage, in a different way, radio, press, television have devalued us.
> They've depicted the young as a threat, as an incarnation of evil, like the Devil.
> Society is threatened by our presence, it's menaced, it's terrorized.
> Through us, society, unable to assimilate criticism of its differences, purges its guilt, finds scapegoats.[26]

From their relationship with the government, however, the CPJs began to transform themselves into semi-political groups which became the self-assigned "leaders" of the youth movement more broadly, but whose numbers, in truth, were actually very small and had limited social reach. These organizations attempted explicitly to incorporate the political participation of young people, who, on various occasions, were transformed into "shock groups" (also called *porros*) utilized by the PRI and distinct governmental dependencies; consequently, the reputation of the CPJs vis-à-vis the real *banda* was increasingly discredited.

The government's concern with the problem of marginalized youth, at least with respect to the PRI's corporatist project (at that historic moment, in crisis) was once again in evidence during the 1988 presidential campaign of Carlos Salinas de Gortari, whose patently fraudulent "victory" marked the decisive turning point for the collapse of the ruling party. For example, during his campaign, an entire work morning was dedicated to assimilating the discourse of the *chavos banda*—discussing their needs, their social rancor, and their demands—and in turn devising a series of programs and promises aimed at the youth vote. As Carlos Monsiváis wrote, "Salinas de Gortari has presented himself as 'the candidate of youth,'... but beyond this, he does not give them much opportunity to speak.... A few pleasures are satisfied, but they are not given a voice on television or in the press."[27] At one campaign event, Salinas de Gortari spoke about youth before an auditorium filled by *chavos banda,* brought by the CJP, where he affirmed:

> The country's modernity creates the challenge of finding mechanisms of agreement between the government and youth, which will transform rebellion, dissatisfaction, and criticism of young people into factors of productive innovation and social change. . . . The mass promotion of sports will be integrated into the government's program, which I propose to head, and will become a key priority in the work of the State.[28]

As president, Salinas de Gortari erased CREA by decree, replacing the organization with the Comisión Nacional del Deporte (Conade), into whose flow chart the Dirección General del Deporte (General Athletics Committee) and the Dirección General de Atención a la Juventud (General Youth Attention Committee) were integrated. Sport thus was elevated, once again, as a "generator of change" for youth. Mexico's government is transformed every six years by new presidential elections, and social programs for young people are no exception.

Near the end of Gortari's mandate, Ernesto Zedillo, the PRI's 1994 presidential candidate, also met with a group of *chavos banda.* The newspaper *La Jornada* summarized the encounter: "In the middle of the concrete jungle, before a surprised Ernesto Zedillo, an astounded María de los Ángeles Moreno [senatorial candidate for Mexico City], and an open-mouthed Fernando Solana [another senatorial candidate], a group of *chavos banda* spoke with the PRI presidential candidate. They showed up 'to talk to the Big Cheese,' 'bitch to bitch,' to tell him: 'Your party has busted us up.'" According to the article, the PRI had chosen "tamed" *chavos banda* for the interview, all of whom belonged to the youth sector of the party. Nonetheless, the event's organizers lost control over who entered and "some very offensive *chavos banda* put the pressure on and managed to step in 'in order to tell their truth.'" The truth, it turned out, came harshly: "'You only seek us when you need votes. When you provide resources, it is only to keep us quiet, and later, once you have settled things down, we don't even show up in the papers.'"[29]

One of the most recent proposals concerning Mexican youth appears in the National Development Plan 1995–2000 (PND); it was endorsed by the National Sport Commission and the Dirección General de Atención a la Juventud (Causa Joven), which was transformed into the Mexican Institute of Youth (IMJ) in early 1999. In the PND, Mexican youth are identified as "one of society's vulnerable groups" who require "special support for their integration" into society. The national population was growing by about 1.7 million

Graffiti painted on the side of a garbage dump (popularly known as "El Tanque" [The Tank]) in the Alvaro Obregón district of Mexico City. 1990. The text reads (*left to right*): Banda Come Together; Zero *Razzias* [Police Raids]; We're Not Crazy, It's Just How We Are; No Repression!; Death to the PRI Government." Photo by Héctor Castillo Berthier. (Archivo Fotográfico de Circo Volador.) Used by permission.

Mexicans annually, the plan went on, and by 1995 the population of youth between fifteen and twenty-nine years of age would represent 30.6 percent of the total inhabitants of the country, a little more than 27 million people in actual numbers. If one considers that there are currently 35 million children in the country, the PND concluded, one might well say that during the next two decades Mexico will reach maximum historical levels of its young population.[30]

With the arrival of the so-called "first democratic government" in Mexico City in 1997,[31] avenues and plazas were renovated through a program called "The Street Belongs to Everyone." Moreover, between 1998 and 2000, in several free festivals held in the Zócalo (Mexico City's central plaza), rock performers like Charly García, Manu Chao, La Maldita Vecindad, Santa Sabina, Real de Catorce, La Tremenda Corte, Panteón Rococó, and Salón Victoria shared the stage with Madredeus, Joaquín Sabina, Los Lobos, the Buena Vista Social Club, Milton Nascimento, and even Los Tigres del Norte (a *norteño* band made famous for its so-called *narcocorridos*), in an end-of-the-millennium party that was meant to celebrate a new kind of city spirit. The events included rock acts from many countries, and, given the fact that they are not rockers, the presence of Los Tigres, the Buena Vista Social Club, and Milton Nascimento served to validate the rockers' working-class status. The latter agreed to share the stage in the hope that the democratic wind that was beginning to blow in the Mexican capital might reach the general population in an all-inclusive manner, without bias, thus strengthening social coexistence and the reencounter of social identities.

Yet not everything changed with the arrival of democracy. The current political process, in which district political leaders are elected rather than appointed, has created a potent political cocktail, in which Mexican rockers are positioned among bureaucratic functionaries, followers of conservative agendas (who think rock is diabolical), and even orthodox Leninists (who still think of rock as another form of imperialist penetration). Consequently, the true strength of Mexican rock does not lie in its acceptance or rejection by the media, the politicians, the church, or parents. It is there, period. It bears its own shape and markets; it has autonomous mechanisms of reproduction and embraces the everyday, and it even allows itself the luxury of having some of its current successful groups—like Panteón Rococó, Real de Catorce, and, from Monterrey, La Verbena Popular—reject commercial offers from major labels in order to continue along their line of work, independent and better linked to the heart of their natural audience—*banda*.

Circo Volador: A Utopia Becomes a Reality

Faced with the obsolescence of a state rooted in outdated principles and the effervescence of a civil society that was becoming increasingly mature and participative in all spheres of national life, youth and other newly politicized social groups sought out new ways to insert themselves into civic life. The streets were filled, little by little, with marchers voicing new demands; radio and newspapers began disseminating new stories. A still authoritarian political environment now had to accept the imminent presence of these new social actors.

A singular example of this process is, without doubt, the Circo Volador project, of which I was a founder. Born out of an academic report, commissioned by the Mexico City government in 1988, on "*Bandas* and Popular Youth in Mexico City," the Circo Volador is, in effect, a rock outreach center that strives, not without political and economic difficulties, to offer marginalized youth a safe and creative space. Housed in a former movie theater complex, Circo Volador's cavernous space provides excellent opportunities to stage concerts, art exhibits, and conferences directed by the youth themselves. At the same time, the project has sought to transform the negative stereotypes held by politicians and the media toward *la banda* and its rock music culture. The story of the creation of the Circo Volador is in itself a fascinating tale that reveals the contradictions and complexities of the government's ongoing relationship with marginalized youth in Mexico City, as well as the utopian possibilities that grassroots activists—and *rockeros*—have collectively tried to enact.

The principle challenge was how to approach the enormous universe of young people in a simple, everyday manner and how to create a social space that would be accessible to all social groups, yet with a distinct orientation toward youth. At the same time, what needed to be avoided was the creation of a large bureaucratic infrastructure that would introduce dozens of sociologists, anthropologists, psychologists, and official promoters of culture aimed at some grandiose notion of social intervention. Those of us who were interested in such a project decided to petition the government for use of the government-run radio station Estéreo Joven (105.7 FM), which at the time was a public radio station under the direction of IMER (Instituto Mexicano de la Radio). Estéreo Joven was a bland, inefficient, spiritless, insignificant station, dedicated to filling its transmission time with pro-government capsules, biased information, and an arbitrary combination of music (supposedly oriented toward youth) that combined Frank Sinatra with "hits" from commercial radio. At that moment in time, a private radio station, Rock 101, had initiated a well-publicized new programming format under the title *Rock en tu Idioma* (Rock in Your Language), which was dedicated to transmitting new rock, mostly from Spain and Argentina. The targeted audience, however, was mostly young middle- and upper-class youth, not *banda*.

The government granted the petition to create a new program dedicated to *banda* on Estéreo Joven, which coincided with, and directly reflected, the PRI's internal crisis—thus the regime's efforts to increase its appeal among youth. What is evident is that Estéreo Joven radically transformed its image after the 1988 elections by incorporating new producers and voices, and by allowing Mexican *banda* rock to be played on the station for the first time. In fact, the music of the *chavos banda*, until that time, had been absent from both commercial and official radio. A two-hour program called *For Gangs Only?: A Closer Space for Rock*, was subsequently transmitted on Estéreo Joven every Saturday night from 11 p.m. to 1 a.m., a time when many *chavos* were gathering and listening to music and radio in the buildings, workshops, warehouses, and vacant lots, on the streetcorners and rooftops of their neighborhoods. Significantly, *For Gangs Only?* was the only program on the radio that bypassed the requirement to transmit the national anthem at midnight. Through its music and an open microphone for call-ins, a deepening appreciation of "street corner culture" now became possible, both for social researchers like myself and, equally important, for the thousands of young people who at last could hear their own music, language, and everyday concerns reflected in the mass media. Radio personnel would go into the barrios to look for and meet with the listeners who called in, who in turn registered their cultural interests with respect to music, magazines, fanzines, poetry, drawings, ways of dressing, murals, graffiti, and so on—all of which was kept in an expanding database that would later form an important part of the Circo Volador center. Another strategy was to sponsor homegrown rock groups, such as what happened with the huge music competition "Rock en la Selva de Asfalto" (Rock in the Concrete Jungle).

Citing the work and experience that had accumulated during the project's first six years, the Secretary of Social Development for Mexico City was asked to provide a physical space where a Center of Art and Culture, especially designed for young people, could be established. Thus, the founding of the Circo Volador, installed in what had been the old Francisco Villa Cinema, an enormous space that had been constructed in the late 1960s in the Jamaica neighborhood. Jamaica is a poor zone in the eastern part of the city, inhabited by mostly lower-middle-class people, who face a multitude of daily exigencies, but with a smattering of middle-class as well. The once publicly operated cinema had been closed in the mid-1980s, after which it had sat abandoned for more than nine years, until it was turned over to Circo Volador in 1994. A slow but steady process of rehabilitation was initiated, employing the collective participation of several hundred young people, as well as diverse sources of financing, including donations from companies, foundations, and public agencies.

Since the center's inauguration in 1998, Circo Volador has faced three recurrent problems in relationship with governmental authorities. The first is that the vast majority of public functionaries lack preparation and awareness of who young people really are and the complex problems they face. The authorities seem to fear large gatherings of youth and are distrustful of youth's capacity to question the system. In 1997, for example, when the Circo Volador Art and Culture Center—with seating capacity for 3,000—was on the verge of opening its doors, the District head issued an "operating license" that restricted the size of events to no more than 70 persons. The center was told: "Remember the word 'youth' is prohibited in [the political district of] Venustiano Carranza."[32]

A second recurrent problem has to do with endemic administrative problems between private citizens and their government. For many years in

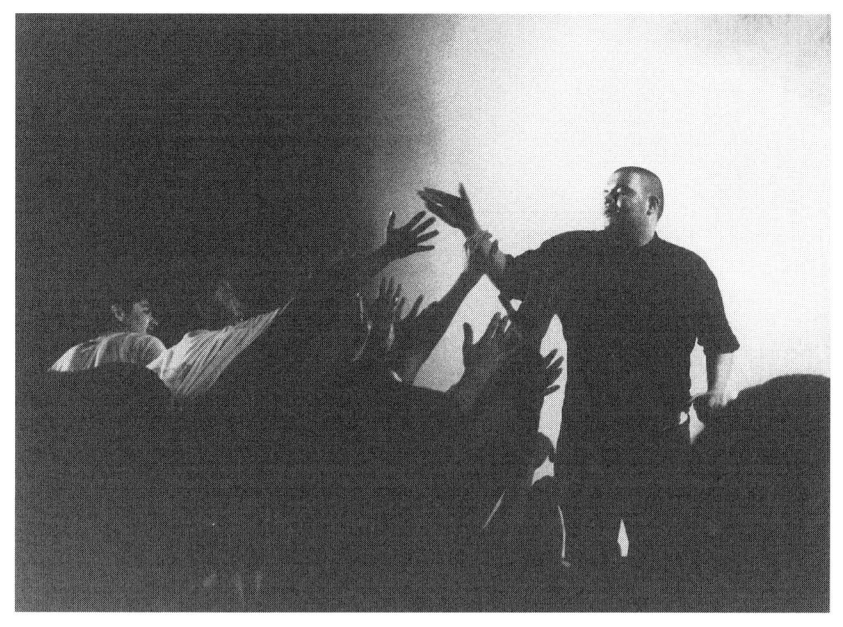

"Pato" of Control Machete during the filming of their video "Andamos armados" ("We're Walking Armed") in the facilities of the Circo Volador. Photo by Genaro Delgado. 1996. (Archivo Fotográfico de Circo Volador.) Used by permission.

Mexico, all offices overseeing the administration of local government lacked a firm legal structure and were therefore easily corrupted. This system has created distortions and traps for those individuals who need government services, including the issuing of permits. Indeed, the problems reach into every sphere of life in Mexico. Corruption, in sum, is endemic at all levels of the Mexican government.

A third problem has to do with what might be called "political time," that is, the scheduling of elections, alliances between political parties, the public image of political functionaries, and the constant negotiations among power groups who struggle over the control of public administration. During "political years," the effect of all this is that ordinary citizens can find it exceedingly difficult to move forward with any type of project that requires governmental approval or support.

In fact, the Circo Volador opened its doors for the first time in September 1997, while the PRI still controlled via direct appointment Mexico City's mayoral office, as well as power at the local, district level. In December 1997, free elections brought a different administration to power for the first time, under the direction of the Partido de la Revolución Democrática (PRD), a political party identified with the Mexican Left. During the three years of government by the PRD, not a single major problem with operations at the Circo Volador occurred. Additionally, the Center received support from a program of shared investment with city government and the Dutch agency NOVIB, allowing the implementation of diverse activities to attend to young people from lower- and working-class sectors. Nevertheless, in those three years, it proved impossible to renew the Center's license, because the local Code for Business Establishments required a parking area for 230 vehicles. It was useless to point out to authorities that the young people who attended events at the Center did not have automobiles and that the Circo Volador faces a metro station that connects the eastern and northern parts of the city, which is where most working-class young people live. "The law is the law" was the reply. Although it lacked a formal license, Circo Volador continued to operate until September 2000. In that political year, however, local assembly elections were held for the first time in Mexico City, and, in the Venustiano Carranza district, where the Center is physically located, the PRD lost the election to the Partido Acción Nacional (PAN)—a political party linked to conservatives on the Mexican Right. On September 13, it was summarily announced that the Center would be closed. The reason given was that once the new PAN delegates took office and discovered that the Center was operating without adequate parking and without the necessary license, there could be serious legal problems.

The PAN delegates took control in October 2000, and, for the Center, the long administrative and legal process began again. It took fifteen months—more than 850 hours, if one counts the time spent dealing with the new PAN public officials—to finally obtain the Center's current operating license. The license reads, "New license for the operation of services for entertainment or events, a cultural center, theatre, cinema, concert hall, and temporary exhibition center." Circo Volador also acquired a parking area, which no one uses, and which now requires (by law) the employment of a young person, dressed as a valet, to receive the public that arrives by metro, bike, or skateboard.

The Center's relationship with the authorities is and has been very difficult; there are too many legal vacuums, excessive bureaucracy, corruption, and ignorance, and the official interlocutors with whom an intelligent relationship can be established are few. In Mexico, even with the arrival of incipient democracy, relations of power are still resolved in the streets with massive protests, tumultuous mobilizations, and the blocking of access to buildings. The "politicians" are accustomed to this; transcending this premodern inheritance from an earlier authoritarianism has not yet become possible.

The Circo Volador continues to sponsor workshops in photography, sound production, jewelry making, music, theater, performance, painting, and graffiti. It also holds conferences, roundtables, and expositions. Rock concerts, with new groups every weekend and monthly festivals at very low prices, are a central element of the project. Between 1998 and 2000 around 120,000 young people visited the space, and more than 6,000 participated in the workshops, roundtables, conferences, and other activities. Five hundred young people have received training as cultural guides, and, for that reason, the phrase used in their presentations has a profound meaning: a utopia becomes reality.

Conclusion

Because of its physical and human dimensions, Mexico City appears as an enormous "social laboratory" with an intense and contradictory way of life. The overwhelming opulence of some sectors coexists with the misery of the so-called *cinturones de miseria* that lack public utilities and where houses are often literally carved out of caves in the hillsides or fashioned from makeshift tin and cardboard boxes. These are the zones where deficient urban planning intersects with the daily arrival of rural migrants, themselves pushed out of the countryside by extreme poverty. The city is home to some 19 million people, the majority of whom carry out a daily struggle to cope and survive in the face of enormous obstacles. For youth living in these poverty belts, which no longer simply ring the metropolitan area but are embedded within it as well, the daily struggle is accompanied by the cries of rock 'n' roll.

Since its beginnings, Mexican rock has connoted rebellion, nonconformity, generational struggles, and the search for new forms of expression. As a cultural practice, Mexican rock has generated a diversity of symbolic identities for urban youth of all social classes. Indeed, rock has shown itself to be "transclassist," in the sense that it mimics the essence of the numerous social strata through which it passes, changing its image and its message as it traverses the different listening spaces of varied social groups. Arguably, the assimilation of Mexican rock has been an osmotic process: from its origins among the middle classes in the 1960s, Mexican rock later spread to the lower sectors of society, where it was transformed and converted into a complex and socially committed proposal of youth identity. For these youth, the *banda*, the *tocadas* (concerts) constitute a world of cultural socialization, of evasion, of catharsis, and of reinforcement of one's own identity in confronting a hostile, aggressive world.

Among the factors that have permitted the social permeability of rock across different social strata is the element of "transnationality," the fact that rock is not linked to just one country: rock is not the sole property of the industrialized nations. Perhaps the main achievement of this long process in Mexico is that rock has been assimilated, nationalized—in a word, Mexicanized. Today, Mexican rock is a reality, and *banda*, synonymous with a notion of the *público popular,* does not want to close a parenthesis opened over thirty years ago. This work is not, nor could it pretend to be, exhaustive; the quantity of information about the topic far surpasses the modest reaches of this essay. There are many projects yet to be done that would document and strengthen this narrative and, without a doubt, this is a propitious time to develop them, since rock lives, vibrates, and is a fundamental part of Mexico's present-day youth culture. That is why we have no other choice than to repeat, yet again, that festive and hopeful phrase: Long live Mexican rock!

Selected Discography

Atoxxxico. *Tú tienes la razón.* 1992. TOAJ 005.

Caifanes. *La historia.* 1997. BMG-Ariola CDLX2 743215011125.

Los Dug Dug's. *15 éxitos.* 1985. RCA PECD 470.

González, Rodrigo. *Hurbanistorias.* 1986. Pentagrama PCD 042.

La Maldita Vecindad y los Hijos del Quinto Patio. *La Maldita Vecindad y los Hijos del Quinto Patio.* 1989. Ariola CDM 3040.

Molotov. *¿Dónde jugaran las niñas?* 1997. Universal MCADN-75031.

Panteón Rococó. *A la izquierda de la Tierra.* 1999. Real Independencia RICD-01.

Real de Catorce. *Real de Catorce.* 1987. La Mina CDP-1169.

Three Souls in My Mind. *15 grandes éxitos.* 1982. Cisne Raff CD-DCD-3001.

Neoliberalism and Rock in the Popular Sectors of Contemporary Argentina

PABLO SEMÁN, PABLO VILA, AND CECILIA BENEDETTI

During the 1990s an important portion of youth in the *sectores populares* did with rock (and from rock) very weird things. They glorified thieves and slums, as if they were heroes and revolutionary paradises, and *rock nacional* became more nationalist than ever before. The Argentine popular sectors, impoverished yet modernized (an apparent paradox that, as we shall see, is not one) have made their mark in both the listening and creation of rock music. We call this phenomenon *rock chabón*.

Rock chabón is the result of the presence of new voices and listeners of rock in Argentina. This presence is that of the popular sectors, which have cultural and social experiences different from the middle classes, who, with a few exceptions, have until now dominated the production of rock.

In this article we will show *rock chabón*'s specificity by analyzing one of its most important characteristics: it acts as a form of social criticism that has its roots in the idea of the "good old times," and it takes a moral stance that is situated far away from the individualist values that frame the sensibilities of the middle classes. On one hand, *rock chabón* banks on the populist imaginary, while, on the other, it relies on community social groupings such as neighborhood associations, soccer club fans, the cult of the family, and the like. *Rock chabón*'s songs evoke that world, and its listeners like the songs because they portray their own experience in a positive light; yet, at the same time, the songs help to construct such an experience. This is the major difference between *chabón* and mainstream *rock nacional*. As an important part of the difference, the audiences of *rock chabón* play a much more prominent role in the creation of a "joint" performance than was customary with the previous *rock nacional*.

What we define as *rock chabón* is not a musical subgenre since it embraces different styles. Nor is it an articulated movement in the sense of a social movement within *rock nacional*. Although the interventions of musicians and fans sometimes may present the homogeneity and affinity of organized actions, *rock chabón* presents a structure that is much more fluid, something that could be called a cultural current or a structure of feeling.[1] In short, *rock chabón* is a cluster of themes and attitudes that are present in the songs of an ample spectrum of musical groups belonging to diverse social sectors (but with a strong presence of popular sectors), in the aesthetic preferences of a public mostly composed of subordinated people, and in the interaction between these two analytic moments.

Concurrently, *rock chabón* appears to be clearly identified with particular issues, prominent among them, social criticism. In this regard *rock chabón* is, once more, the heir to a tradition and a very different version of that tradition. As we will see below, if on the one hand *rock chabón*'s bands and public are among the most important supporters of human rights organizations like Las Madres de la Plaza de Mayo, on the other, they sustain a nationalist stance that does not have anything to do with the previous history of the genre.

Rock Chabón and Neoliberal Argentina

The appearance of *rock chabón* can be better comprehended if we take into account the sociological context of the 1990s, characterized by the implosion of formal industrial employment, the increase of unemployment (from a historical figure of less than 5 percent to an astonishing 20 percent) and non-qualified occupations, and the deterioration of the living conditions of the popular sectors and the lower middle class. In this regard, it is worth pointing out that the idea of poverty as a transitional stage (that is, the hope of moving up the socioeconomic ladder) only recently ceded its predominance in the representations of the working-class sectors among whom the *rock chabón* dynamic emerged.[2]

Rock chabón is the rock of those youths who, longing for the world of their elders (a world characterized by full employment and perspectives of social improvement, and symbolically expressed by Peronism), find an alternative to their exclusion from the neoliberal socioeconomic model developed in Argentina of the early 1990s in this form of musical expression. They think, with good reason, that they cannot find such an alternative in any of the traditional political venues in contemporary Argentina, that is, within the major political parties that support, in doctrinaire fashion, the very economic model that marginalizes them. At the same time, perhaps with the exception of the newly developed *cumbia villera*, there is no other cultural expression in general (that is, theater, television, etc.) or musical expression in particular that interpellates and narrativizes this new Argentine social group. Therefore, *rock chabón* is a musical practice that collaborates in the construction of an identity of "marginalized young people belonging to the popular sectors" through the diverse alliances these youngsters establish between their different, imagined, narrative identities and the identities set forth by *rock chabón*. *Rock chabón* is the music of impoverished and modernized youths because the neoliberal model has offered them a fertile context in which to both identify and construct themselves through rock. Let us consider the characteristics of these two determinations at the core of *rock chabón*.

First, as some of us have noted elsewhere,[3] *rock chabón* could be characterized as "pro-Argentinean, from-the-outskirts, and neo-oppositional." These characteristics acquire their full meaning if *rock chabón* is understood in its interdependence and interaction with the populist cultural matrix to which these three characteristics belong. In a nutshell: We believe that such populist inheritance is a crucial component in the "confrontational" plots of this kind of rock. Therefore, we want to show how the social subject historically constituted by populism in Argentina occupies an important place in the interpellations and narratives that sustain this type of rock. As a matter of fact, more than the presence of the "real" subject of one of Peronism's most important discursive formulations (the "worker"), what is prominent in many narratives of *rock chabón* is the inclusion of the first nostalgic account of the worker's absence from the social landscape of the nation's popular sectors.

Populist narrative successfully offered—along with the semantic construction *pueblo* ("common people," as millions of Argentines identify themselves) and a series of very structured storylines of national belonging—not only identities and rights that referred to egalitarian principles but also the legitimacy of protest to support those perspectives. In this way, a set of expectations was framed in terms of a conciliatory ideology, but also contained elements of extreme social contestation, something that differentiates Peronism from other Latin American forms of populist expression. Most importantly, the effects of Peronist social and political interventions impacted everyday life, creating social identities, expectations, habits, and cultural resources that, as Elizabeth Jelín shows,[4] crystallized in a notion of personal dignity, "pride and self respect."[5]

At the same time, the effectiveness of populist formulations and narratives persists beyond the disappearance of the socioeconomic conditions that sustained the Peronist political regime. The hegemony of the globalization process did not kill the populist imaginary. As Pollak points out regarding imaginaries (or cultural narratives) in general:

> Its memory . . . can survive its disappearance, assuming the form of a myth that, because it cannot anchor itself in the political reality of the moment, nourishes itself on cultural, religious or literary references. Then, the faraway past can become the promise of a future and, sometimes, a challenge thrown toward the status quo.[6]

We think that in the case of *rock chabón* populism has to be viewed as a working subtext that is simultaneously mediated by other texts. It is precisely through this process that the populist interpellations and narratives are transformed into something different from what they were—that is, they become the pro-Argentinean, from-the-outskirts, and neo-oppositional kind of rock that characterizes *rock chabón*. For many young people (fans and musicians alike), those semantic concepts and nationalist imaginings are vital references for their presence in the rock world and Argentinean society as well, a society that has changed in relation to what their parents had envisioned. For these young people, moving up the social ladder by means of education and employment is neither a possibility nor a dream. It is, instead, a facet of a past that is often characterized as "glorious."

Second, if we point out that *rock chabón* is, on the other hand, a product linked to the era of neoliberalism, it is because of three combined circumstances. First, the possibilities of diffusion and legitimation of rock have increased with the consolidation of a leisure industry that, in turn, had to rely on an Argentine vernacular rock, once it consolidated itself as a first-order musical expression in the 1980s. This occurrence (which opened up the possibilities for rock to reach the popular sectors), combined with the fact that the neoliberal process itself created a crisis in the life-world and sensibilities of the popular sectors, which in turn paved the way for contemporary youth to implement, with greater frequency than their predecessors, musical trajectories very different from that of their parents. Moreover, a third circumstance linked to neoliberalism helped to implant rock in the popular world: the monetary regime of a fixed exchange rate made the otherwise very costly musical and recording equipment cheaper, in such a way that to start a musical group using electric instruments was no longer a middle-class luxury. The popular sectors lost jobs and welfare but nevertheless acquired guitars, drums, and portable recording studios.

The Historical Confrontational Character of *Rock Nacional*

The *rock nacional* movement was always characterized, from its very beginnings in the mid-1960s, by its oppositional stance.[7] Most of its discourses revolved around the definition of rock as a resistant "attitude" toward something that was generically defined as "the system," which was understood alternatively as an oppressive bureaucratic apparatus, capitalism, and the cultural industry. At the same time, those discourses opposed rock to a music considered "commercial," an opposition that implicitly questioned art commercialization in particular and cultural industries in general.

In tandem with this general development of the genre, *rock nacional* produced stylistic variants that addressed specific aspects of different young people's cultural and social milieus. These variants represented and helped create a very heterogeneous constituency. Throughout this process, some of these variants either came from or (more commonly) responded to the public of the poorest sectors of society. These musical traits relate to what is known as "heavy rock" (or Spanish blues), which for many years established itself as the industrial workers' rock, or "outskirts rock."

Therefore, since the 1960s, an intense internal debate that sought to establish which stylistic variant "really" represented the identity of urban youths was always part of the history of the movement. In this regard, by the mid- to late 1980s (the nearest "pre-history" of the story we want to address in this article), the debate over *rock nacional* shared much in common with previous polemics about the proper narratives and interpellations for addressing contemporary Argentinean urban youth. These advocated either the maintenance, at any price, of the initial libertarian proposal, or its accommodation (in different ways) to the times and the adolescent cohorts. At least among the most important *rock nacional* musicians, there was a vindication of rock's true role: "walking always on the borders of the system, composing songs that, with luck, help to change somewhat the collective unconscious, the *coco* (head) of the people."[8]

All these changes occurred within the framework of a sociopolitical process that did not radically modify the social situation (either symbolically or materially) of young people from the popular sectors. However, that would change, six or seven years later, under the auspices of the neoliberal agenda advanced by President Carlos Menem. In this sense, the *rock nacional* variant we are analyzing constitutes, at one and the same time, a new development of a very well entrenched trend and a polemical reaction to the entire history of the *rock nacional* movement; it is an integral part of the *rock nacional* historical-cultural field, while it succeeds in shattering what appeared to be a unanimous consensus about the fundamental characteristics and meanings of the genre. In this sense, as a result of its new social location, it generates a discontinuity: *rock chabón* protests against other problems, from a different cultural sensibility than the historically dominant *rock nacional* and, many times, it also struggles against *rock nacional* itself.

Rock Chabón as "Neo-Contestatarian Rock"

The reason for our adoption of "neo-contestarian," instead of the classic appellative "contestatarian," is that the former locates the meaning of *rock chabón* as an identitarian practice and a phenomenon directly situated in the context of the profound and regressive restructuration of Argentinean society. The national rock of the 1960s can indeed be characterized as "contestatarian," in the sense that it was reacting critically against the imperatives of social integration (seen, at the time, as both inevitable and alienating), or against the military dictatorship overthrown in the early 1980s. Instead, the rock of popular sector youth of the 1990s is "neo-contestatarian," in the sense that its discourses are used to narrate and revile the disintegration and dual reintegration of society. Neo-contestatarian *rock chabón* is opposed to what is perceived as the dismemberment of a world that previous rockers rejected, and because of this, it redefines its own place by invoking the figures of the past. It assumes other topics—other heroic figures, another territory, another political program, other utopias, and other enemies—than those of the traditional protest song in general and of the contestatarian source of *rock nacional* in particular.

While 1970s rock sanctified madmen and beggars, whose separation from the world was supposed to incarnate a supposed relativistic lucidity, 1990s rock deposits its radicalism in characters who, like the "matador," are (imaginarily) of the past and who revolt desperately *against* the world rather than separating themselves *from* the world. As such, it is in the domain of heroes narrated by *rock chabón* where the neo-contestatarian mixture best reveals its architecture and evinces its efficiency. The heroes of *rock chabón*, as neo-contestatarian, arise from a singular mixture. The song "Matador" is a paradigmatic case of this singular architecture:

> Me llaman el matador nací en Barracas
> si hablamos de matar mis palabras matan
> No hace mucho tiempo
> que cayó el León Santillán

ahora sé que en cualquier momento
me la van a dar
agazapado en lo más oscuro de mi habitación, fusil en mano, espero mi final
de pronto el día se me hizo de noche
llega la fuerza policial
Me llaman el matador
de los cien barrios porteños
no tengo por qué tener miedo
mis palabras son balas
balas de paz
de justicia
soy la voz de los que hicieron callar
por el solo hecho de pensar distinto.

(They call me the matador, born in Barracas
if we speak of killing, then my words kill
Not long ago
León Santillán fell [was killed]
now I know at any moment
they'll get me, too
crouched in the darkest spot in my room,
rifle in hand, I await my end
Suddenly the day turned into night
the police force arrives
They call me the matador
of one hundred *porteño* neighborhoods
I don't have any reason to fear
my words are bullets
bullets of peace
of justice
I am the voice of those who were quieted
just because they thought different.)

In the lyrics of this song, a scene is presented in which there is a confusion of various characters. On one hand, there is the anti-dictatorial rebel, portrayed in the plural and indefinite tense, as the voice of those who were quieted for thinking differently. On the other hand, there is the contemporary marginal urban dweller. Also forming part of the portrait is the traditional *malevo* (tough guy) from the barrio, the matador of one hundred *porteño* neighborhoods that tango depicted so well. Included in this mixture of characters are the different struggles that these characters embody or incarnate—in other words, struggles against the police and military dictatorship.

This new hero of *rock chabón* is, at the same time, marginal, traditional, and quasi-Guevarista. This last characteristic is reflected not only in the lyrics of the song (the fact that the matador's bullets are explicitly bullets of justice and peace) but also in the explicit images that were utilized for its television promotion by means of a video clip in which Che Guevara's face fluttered on a flag carried by the *murga* (festive band) that stars in the clip. Here, the union of heroic references attempts a synthesis that in Argentina, prior to *rock chabón*, would have been impossible to imagine: the fusion in one and the same character of traces of the national and popular mythology (like the *malevo*) with those of classical revolutionary mythology (like Che Guevara). In addition, the description of the enemy evinces an effort of analogous composition. The police are characterized as the "*fuerza policial*" (police force) (the form by which police themselves want to be recognized by common delinquents)—and also as the "enemy of thinking differently" (the way the police are acknowledged, in terms of ideological and political conflict, by the radical middle classes).

Another example, whose homology with the previous song speaks more of a cultural climate than of individual occurrences, is that offered by Ciro Pertussi (leader of Attaque 77) describing one of their songs, "Héroe de nadie" ("Nobody's Hero"), in an interview:

> It speaks of a character, "Fatigue," who fights every day in the concrete jungle. Over time he becomes "the madman of the machine gun," a delinquent of the neighborhood, where he is considered a hero by some, a type of Robin Hood who protects those inhabitants. A history that mixes sinister aspects with fiction after his confusing death.

This kind of stance reaches one of its most illustrative points on *Postal 97*, an LP by Dos Minutos. On this record, all the songs attempt to sketch the social environment of the group and its fans. In the heterogeneity of scenes that form part of that description there are songs that, like "1987," "La balanza" ("The Scale"), or "Gatillo fácil" ("Hair Trigger"), criticize the police from a position that, in relation to police abuses and human rights violations, is quite similar to the one adopted by many of the young people we interviewed. In the different songs on the record, one can see, given the regularity of police abuse, the constant danger in which the youths live ("a bullet escaped, fired by that man, right there, disguised in blue" ["Hair Trigger"]).

In this way, what is considered inadmissible from the perspective of leftist political parties (since the poor, idealized by their ideologies, do not break the law but are its victims) is glorified by Dos Minutos. Oppressed peoples and delinquents can belong to the same group, since all acts of theft presuppose a just expropriation, an alternative that, in practice, is preferable to the acceptance of the illusion or the impossible road of honest work as a means of progress. What the old protest rock deplored—the workplace, routine, petit bourgeois aspirations—is something that *rock chabón*'s new form of protest places firmly in the past, comfortably installed among the simple dilemmas of other social groups.

Therefore, we could say that the world idealized by *rock chabón* is not a utopia of the sort that emerges from John Lennon's "Imagine." *Rock chabón* has a much simpler program: it reads the positive side of what it perceives as profoundly negative, it sustains the legitimacy of what other voices would subject to criticism, and it attempts to create certain margins of freedom in relation to what is repressed in different ways by poverty and police control.

Also, *rock chabón* accomplishes all this by way of another important differentiation regarding traditional protest rock. In this sense, *rock chabón* differentiates itself from old protest rock by its decidedly hedonistic proposition. In old contestatarian songs, thought and profound reflection were often opposed to dancing and having fun. And although these last two elements were evident in some songs, it could not be said that they were central to *rock nacional* as a genre. On the other hand, *rock chabón* assumes as its own the values of the body in movement. In this way, something that was marginal in the traditional narrative of *rock nacional* becomes central when the "marginals" occupy center stage. Thus, it is in virtue of its national and popular key that *rock chabón* activates and places at the center of its musical proposition danceable folkloric rhythms such as *candombe* and *murga*, rhythms that interpellate the body as well as the head—simultaneously Argentinizing and "marginalizing" them. This is so because these rhythms are not only "Argentine" but also a cultural marker of the popular urban sectors. Through this very counter-interdiction of the body, the popular sectors' rock 'n' roll is no longer a synonym for mental vacuity or a lack of sentiments.

On the contrary, it seems that *rock chabón* gets the best of both worlds at once, because without abandoning the oppositional stance of *rock nacional*, it addresses thorny topics within the framework of a festive activity like the (now) danceable concert. Consider the following testimony, stated by La Renga's saxophonist, to Cecilia Benedetti in 1996:

> In general terms, it is like the band has a certain consciousness, we tend to want things to change a little, also to try, like . . . You work all week

long, you bust your ass, everybody exploits you, you're so hungry you shit yourself. The [economic] adjustment gets worse and worse, the social situation is more terrible, in Rosario they eat cats, in Tierra del Fuego they kill workers, a mess, do you understand? It's like the people also deserve a moment of rest, which doesn't mean that they forget about the other things that happen, do you understand? It's not that we set this goal for ourselves, but what it ended up being is that people come to see La Renga to forget things for a while, but at the same time, if it's time to say things or see what we can do, we do it too. It's like this, people are fed up, the day of the concert arrives, and they enjoy themselves, they feel like they're in the company of people who think more or less the way they do.

Evidencing the short distance that separates musicians from their public in this kind of rock (because, among other reasons, many members of the audience eventually become part of the bands themselves), some interviewees in our study repeat, virtually word-for-word, what the musicians themselves express:

> **Cecilia:** And what was it like, the sentiment before (before La Renga became a massive phenomenon)?
> **José:** It was like a brotherhood, where everyone went and got together to have a good time, to listen to La Renga, to vent ourselves in the concerts, and we would greet each other and more or less we knew everybody else.
> **Cecilia:** To vent yourself of what?
> **José:** The fact that the government, life, bosses, yourself, they all throw shit at you.
> **Cecilia:** Do you feel that the band is addressing the situation we are living?
> **Freddy:** In part. Also, to bail out a little. There are lyrics that stray from reality.
> **Abel:** Los Piojos have a bit of that, but it isn't that they talk to you about reality and all that but rather that they try to amuse you a little. They are lyrics that transmit something but also they are generally fun lyrics.
> **Tolo:** They give you a peek at it and sometimes they pull you out. They make you forget . . .
> **Pepe:** Maybe it's a last resort, you know, they pull you out and they stick you in their music.[9]

It's important to note here that, within these rhythmic preferences and in accordance with its hedonistic proposition, _rock chabón_ lauds the use of marijuana. If in other moments of _rock nacional_'s history, and in conjunction with global trends, drugs were the medium for the construction of a fantasy, the road to introspection, and even the way to individual liberation, we find in the discourses of _rock chabón_ the exaltation of marijuana within a festive code, but one that is gregarious and unifying as well. The song "Verano del 92" ("Summer of '92"), by Los Piojos, is a good example of what we are saying:

> Juan Pedro Fasola
> nuestro gran amigo
> qué ganas de verte
> tenemos todos acá
> hace tanto tiempo
> que no te sentimos
> contando aquel cuento
> de la buena pipa
> ahí va
> voy a quemar la piedra de tu locura
> así no hay amargura y se va el dolor
> Fasolita querido
> a ver cuándo venís por acá
> Fasolita querido
> que te quiero ver
> te quiero contar
> lo mal que se vive lo bien que se está
> uoh oh oh oh oh
> suba al árbol que está oscureciendo
> suavemente en la hoja tírese.
>
> (Juan Pedro Fasola
> our good friend
> all of us here
> would really like to see you
> it's been so long
> since we've heard you
> telling that story
> about the good old pipe
> here it goes
> I'm gonna burn the stone of your madness

that way there's no bitterness and the pain leaves
dear little Fasola
let's see when you show up around here
dear little Fasola
I really wanna see you
I wanna tell you
how bad we live, how good we feel
whoa oh oh oh oh
climb the tree 'cause it's getting dark
fill in the paper gently.)

The lyrics to this song (like many others in *rock chabón*) is full of double-entendres about the drug world. These double-entendres, among other things, serve to enact the boundaries of identity of *rock chabón*'s followers; that is, they separate those who "truly understand" from those who don't. In this case, for instance, the song's title refers to a summer in which there was a great scarcity of marijuana, that Juan Pedro refers to Pedro Juan, the border city between Paraguay and Brazil where the joints are very good, and the enigmatic phrase "suavemente en la hoja tírese" alludes to the inscription on the paper used to make joints: "tírese suavemente en la hoja."

As is customary in this kind of rock, the young audience validates the lyrics with its own *cantito*, like the one popularized at the concerts of La Renga: "Quiero que legalicen la marihuana / para fumarme un porro por la mañana / quiero tomarme un vino y una cerveza / para ver a La Renga de la cabeza" (I want them to legalize marijuana / to smoke a joint in the morning / I want to drink wine and beer / to come and see La Renga that drives me crazy). Moreover, banners showing marijuana leaves and addressing different themes (usually unrelated to marijuana issues but rather addressing some of the other topics dealt with in this article) are always present in *rock chabón* concerts.

As we stated previously, *rock chabón*, by way of music that appeals to the body more than to the head, proclaims values that result from the dislocation of youth from the work world. Thus, if national rock from the 1970s and 1980s was a rock of young people who worked but who did not like the monotonous and alienating character of their jobs, *rock chabón* is the rock of the children of working-class people, themselves jobless, desperately willing to work as their parents did—even in monotonous and alienating jobs.

This rock, which on the one hand identifies itself with common populist places, but on the other does not talk at all about the work world, addresses several conditions simultaneously. While it stands as the music of those for whom rock's rebelliousness resonates, it is also the rock of the children of adults who experienced a populist epoch and transmitted their values to their progeny. As Chizo, the singer of La Renga pointed out: "In our families, politics were never spoken of much. We're children of working-class migrants from the countryside. From home to work, Peronists, bah. Good or bad, Peronism marked the workers very strongly." Additionally, this is also the rock of youths who lived the experience of the expiration of those values and the radical transformation of the job market, with its characteristic informality, instability, devaluation, or absolute absence, and, also, a world of consumption and comfort that is always more readily promised than accessible. Consequently, *rock chabón* can be conceived precisely as a mode of inhabiting a tension: the one present between a world not yet left and another that still is not possible to enter. This is evident in a song by Divididos, "Te da asco el overol y con un gin lo extrañás" (The overalls make you sick and you show you miss them with a gin).[10]

In this way, *rock chabón* discusses in depth something that was only marginally approached before by *rock nacional*. It vindicates the notion of vagrancy, attributing to it, not without bitterness, a normative value. Even though this aspect was also present in the early stages of *rock nacional* ("La Balsa" ["The Raft"], a song that helped inaugurate the genre in the 1970s, alluded to this situation), *rock chabón* develops it to levels never seen before. In this respect, the song "Nothing to Do" ("Nada que hacer"), from Dos Minutos' *Postal 97* album, is paradigmatic:

> No tengo nada que hacer
> ya comí, ya bebí, ya fumé
> voy a ver TV
> sesenta canales nada para ver
> salgo a caminar el barrio sigue igual
> voy a visitar a mis amigos
> tomaremos algunas cerveza
> y hablaremos de cosas de la vida
> también hablaremos de toda esta malaria
> en que el pueblo está hundido
> y el tiempo pasará
> y todo seguirá igual
> la luna ya apareció
> mañana otro día más
> nada que hacer
> nada que hacer.

(I have nothing to do
I ate already, I drank already, I smoked already
I'm going to watch TV
Sixty channels, nothing to see
I go out to walk, the barrio stays the same
I'm going to visit my friends
we'll drink a few beers
and we'll talk about life
we'll also speak of all this destitution
in which the people have sunk
and time will pass
and everything will stay the same
the moon has appeared
tomorrow is another day
nothing to do
nothing to do.)

Here, "nothing to do" is also related to a world these young people do not like (in the original, unpublished lyrics to "La Balsa" that world was referred to as a "shitty world"). However, in "Nothing to Do," the point of destiny is not an idealized new world, as in "La Balsa," where the task is to build a vehicle (the raft), go out, and reach that world. Instead, the tremendous force of the lyrics is that "Nada que hacer" means precisely that: "to do nothing," because it seems that nothing can be done, except either to kill time while unemployed and do all the things a chronically unemployed person might do (watch television, eat, smoke, drink, visit friends), or to discuss how bad things are in the country, without any glimpse of what to do to change things for the better.

Likewise, that corner in which they are perceived as doing nothing is, for the actors of *rock chabón*, a place for the construction of affection. There, the shared drinking establishes an ethos allowing the creation of communities and of distinguishing those communities from their "natural enemies" (that is, the police and *caretas* [pretenders]). At the same time, the same groups, which often are formed as an outcome of attending concerts, configure a valued and cultivated sociability. This sociability, which is an alternative to a culture of workers, is defined more by the community of pleasures and hostilities than by working origins and common interests springing from a similar class situation.

As we mentioned before, as in the contestatarian forms that preceded it, *rock chabón* also uses the police as a target of its hostility. This hostility is expressed in many song lyrics, as in "Demasiado tarde" ("Too Late"), by Dos Minutos:

> Estás en el kiosco,
> tomás una cerveza
> corre el tiempo, seguís con la cerveza
> a lo lejos se ve una patrulla
> alguien grita: allá viene la yuta [policía]
> Descarten los tubos [botellas]
> empiecen a correr
> la yuta está muy cerca
> no da para correr.
>
> (You are in the *kiosko* [neighborhood store]
> you drink a beer,
> time goes by, you keep on drinking
> Far away, there is a police car
> Somebody shouts: the pigs are coming
> Throw away the bottles
> Start running
> The cops are too close
> There is no time to run.)

The substance of opposition to the police is not in the violation of a felt humanity, nor is it the human rights destroyed by state violence (a central theme in rock lyrics of the 1970s and 1980s). Even when some of these elements are present in its lyrics and postures, *rock chabón* anathematizes the police in terms of their "bitter," "falsifying," "snitching," and "cowardly" character. The police continue to be portrayed as harassing, as they were in the rock songs of the 1970s and 1980s, but the human rights violations that can be imputed to them do not arise from according them a repressive project or a totalitarian ideology opposed to a humanist, revolutionary, or libertarian one. In this regard, both traditional *rock nacional* and *rock chabón* sing against the police, but they have a different police activity in mind when they sing their songs. In the case of the rock of the 1970s and 1980s, the police activity that most young people criticized was the anti-political activity, like the repression of political rallies, whereas the police activity denounced by *rock chabón* is repression against poor people in general (for theft, burglary, and the like) and poor young people's activities in particular (such as violence in the streets and the soccer stadiums). Therefore, it is not by chance that the following *cantito* is sung at both soccer games and *rock chabón* concerts: "Policía, policía / que amargado se te ve / cuando vos venís a Obras / tu mujer se va a coger" (Officer, officer / what a sour look you have / when you come to Obras [the name of a soccer stadium] / your wife is fucking someone else).

From a humanist and liberal perspective, the hostility against the police is born from a confrontation that gives the impression of being limited or merely tactical. This apparent tactical stance disappears if we propose that the relations of hostility are constituted under the aegis of a matrix with other coordinates to define morality. In that regard, the following lyrics from Dos Minutos', "You're Not the Same," are a good example:

> Carlos se vendió al barrio de Lanús
> el barrio que lo vió crecer
> ya no vino nunca más
> por el bar de Fabián
> y se olvidó de pelearse
> los domingos en la cancha
> Por las noches patrulla la ciudad
> molestando y levantando a los demás
> ya no sos igual
> ya no sos igual
> sos un vigilante de la Federal
> sos buchón (alcahuete)
> sos buchón
> Carlos se dejó crecer el bigote
> y tiene una nueve para él
> ya no vino nunca más
> por el bar de Fabián
> y se olvidó de pelearse
> los domingos en la cancha
> El sabe muy bien que una bala
> en la noche, en la calle, espera por él.

> (Carlos sold out the Lanús neighborhood
> the neighborhood where he was born
> he never returned any more
> to Fabián's bar
> and he forgot to fight,
> Sunday afternoons, in the soccer stadium
> During the nights he patrols the city
> harassing and incarcerating other people

You are not the same,
you are not the same
You are a federal cop,
you are a snitch,
you are a snitch
Carlos grew a moustache,
and has a 9-mm on him
He never returned any more,
to Fabián's bar
and he forgot to fight,
Sunday afternoons, in the soccer stadium
He knows pretty well that a bullet
during the night, in the street, is waiting for him.)

In this song, the neighborhood affiliation appears as the positive identity the protagonist abandons, earning him the negative marker of "being a cop," a cop whose destiny, according to the song, is to be killed and, it seems, for "good reasons" (During the nights he patrols the city / harassing and incarcerating other people).

As a part of this different morality of the youth of the popular sector in the 1990s, we could mention, first, the idea of *aguante* (resilience), a moral and physical value that designates the capacity of resisting and challenging any pretense of imposition and adversity. To have or not to have *aguante* is what distinguishes the police from those who declare themselves to be and are their enemies. Secondly an important part of such morality refers to the rights of the people, of the needy, of the nation's neglected. From this position of legitimacy and from that moral and physical quality, the *"chabones"* condemn the surveillance, imposition of discipline, and repressive violence that are produced by the police. It is from this narrative that a discourse of human rights is embraced, despite the fact that this does not signify the centering of the subject of *rock chabón* in a liberal world vision. Still it is an embrace that generates a constant support by the followers of *rock chabón* for human rights organizations such as Las Madres de la Plaza de Mayo.

It is a change that implies a non-liberal political perspective. The protest rock of the 1960s and 1970s could affirm: "People who advance can be killed, but their ideas will remain" (as León Gieco did in "Iron Men"), because the rock movement then understood struggle as a contest of ideas in which the enemy was violent and without vision. *Rock chabón,* instead, proposes the efficacy of the body in a struggle in which that body is not a pure physical object but the testimony of a moral attitude. In this sense, the posture of *rock chabón* is not the same as the one advanced by the revolutionary militants of the 1960s and 1970s either. Those militants understood violence and the seizing of weapons as a (non-desired) side-effect of the political circumstances, as an effect of the drowning of democracy or an imposition of the enemy. The epic scenario of *rock chabón* is neither the idealistic struggle, nor the revolutionary war, but the street fight for territory. But much more than the absence of a liberal perspective, what we have here is the testimony of a cultural discontinuity that helps one to understand the cultural specificity of *rock chabón*: the fact that the phenomenon is irreducible to the category of a political ideology. *Rock chabón* expresses and constructs the sensibility of certain popular sectors in which the connotation of the category "person," which governs the liberal imaginary of modern Western societies (the citizen, the separation between politics, family and religion, and so on), is not necessarily the same.

In some of *rock chabón*'s narratives we find a gregarious point of view and a sense of justice that models politics in relationship to "the household" in a logic of reciprocity and hierarchy. This kind of discourse is the basis for a rebellious attitude that will always be poorly understood if it is equated with social protest perspectives of other societies and, most of the time, in the longings of the social science researchers.

Instead it is this kind of perspective that allows us to understand how a singer like Ricardo Iorio (whose songs and attitudes are an undeniable part of *rock chabón*) can declare and practice his support of Las Madres de la Plaza de Mayo while also making, a couple of months later, xenophobic nationalistic statements. The apparent contradiction is overcome if we understand that both his support of the Madres and his nationalism arise from a matrix in which the "household" and the "mother" are sacred, and thus the Madres and the nation are its metaphors. This discontinuity is also apparent as a symptom: the middle-class youth who like the rock of the 1980s think that the *rock chabón* of the 1990s is right-wing nationalism. What is important is that both the positive idealization that imagines the followers of *rock chabón* as revolutionaries and the negative one that imagines them as "fascists" superimpose an ethnocentric reading of the social and the political in the description of the world of the popular sectors. This last issue, that of nationalism and the barrio, is precisely, one of the most important characteristics of *rock chabón.*

Finally we believe that what makes *rock chabón* a completely new phenomenon in the Argentine political-artistic scene is that its neo-contestatarian key is proposed, most of the time, first as a neighborhood one, and then as national one. We have already seen the example of "Nothing to Do," which does not propose that nothing is done in general, but rather, situates things in the context of the neighborly activity of thousands of unemployed or semi-employed youths of modern-day Argentina. Or we can mention the song "Más de un millón" ("More than a Million"), in which Argentina, the homeland, is mentioned as a place that is sinking. In this sense, the privileged territory of *rock chabón* is, as it never was in other moments of national rock, on one side, the working-class barrio, what's local; and on the other side, and almost as a continuity of the first, a particular version of the motherland.

It is in this sense that *rock chabón* glorifies, in varied dimensions, an origin that establishes the parameters of its protest. We believe that just as its heroes are special, its territories (principally, the working-class barrio) are equally so. In them, tradition and the warmth of customs, are vindicated against the cold and harsh reality of the cosmopolitan city. This aspect, which was already partially present in traditional *rock nacional*, is resignified when one notes that for *rock chabón*, the nation is a positive value in ways and degrees unknown for the contestatarian rock of the 1970s.

Rock chabón anchors itself in the local allegiance to the barrio, within an imaginary structure in which an existing national allegiance contains it: the nation, an entity from which the barrio receives feedback, giving it a special content, but also embracing it. In the performances (by both musicians and audience), the musical choices, and the lyrics that define the contour of their heroes and utopias, *rock chabón* becomes patriotic as an expression of its popular roots. It is precisely here where the most important difference with traditional national rock resides. The national rock of the 1960s–1980s was characterized by musical references to tango and folklore. In this regard, *rock nacional* was always fusion music, but that fusion was mostly done from the point of view of the organic, middle-class intellectuals of the genre. Therefore the musical fusion was accomplished, in most cases, using middle-class expressions of tango and folklore. In this regard, for the traditional *rock nacional*, tango was equated with Astor Piazzolla (practitioner of a highly "intellectual" version of tango) and not with Alberto Castillo (a very "non-intellectual" one), and folklore with Domingo Cura (a folklorist highly influenced by jazz), but not with José Larralde (a very traditional folklore musician). It is thus that *rock chabón* acknowledges musical references in tango as well as folklore musicians, especially in those musicians that rock, even in its period of being most open to the world of tango and folklore, never acknowledged.

Something similar occurs during performances. In concert, *rock chabón* bands continuously appraise the nation, "la patria," in ways that were unimaginable twenty years ago. The trajectory of the group Divididos makes a paradigmatic example of the turn that we are pointing out. Its current members used to form part of a group (Sumo) that, in the 1980s, sang in a reggae rhythm that was not precisely "Argentinean" the following: "Yo quiero a mi bandera, yo quiero a mi bandera, planchadita, planchadita, planchadita" (I love my flag, I love my flag, well-ironed, well-ironed, well-ironed), a song with clearly pacifist and anti-chauvinist connotations. In the 1990s, as Divididos, they perform their shows with Argentine flags as part of the scenery and celebrate a gaucho-like manner of speaking. Renewing the canons of rock intertextuality, they have begun to create covers of Argentine folklore classics, such as Atahualpa Yupanqui's "El Arriero" ("The Muleteer").

In turn, audiences validate this effort through the display of their own banners, like the one often displayed at La Renga concerts: "Morir queriendo ser libre / volveremos" (Dying wanting to be free / We will return)—the sentence written over a drawing of the Malvinas/Falkland Islands. With such a message, the banner references relationships with two very different texts: La Renga's song "Hablando de la libertad" ("Speaking of Liberty") and the motto of the ex-fighters of the Malvinas/Falkland Islands War. The battle cry, with the drawing underneath, forges a new sense for the song—that it refers simply to liberty—linking the image to the struggle to recover nationally sovereign territories from the hands of foreigners. Here the dichotomy of powerful/not powerful and the continuity in defending what is Argentina's reappear. Likewise a war against a foreign invader (Britain), which culminated in defeat, a war silenced by government officials, is vindicated.[11]

Many banners at *rock chabón* concerts (independent of their inscriptions) are based on the colors of the national flag. In this way, the banners establish a direct relationship among the public, the bands, and the nation that does not require any words to be expressed. At the same time, those Argentine banners and their messages, "performed" as they are in the particular setting of a rock concert, reinterpret the meaning of the nation, which acquires new meanings through the ideas expressed in *rock chabón* musical culture: the adhesion to a rock band, the vindication of the barrio, the opposition between those who hold power and those who do not possess it, and the like. Thus the notion of what constitutes the motherland and to whom it belongs is disputed with hegemonic sectors:

Cecilia asks why Los Piojos's fans like the group's lyrics.

> **Ricky:** They defend local stuff. They don't like foreign stuff.
> **Cecilia:** And what do you think about nationalism?
> **Ricky:** It is nationalism but in the sense that we love this country and are against this country's politics. I don't know a single person who supports it. And Los Piojos represent music in our sense.

Another good example in this regard is a banner found in La Renga concerts: "La patria se hizo canción 'La Renga Quilmes Cuco Colice Edgardo

Zurdo'" (The homeland became the song "La Renga Quilmes Cuco Colice Edgardo Zurdo"). This banner recontextualizes the refrain of "Me hice canción" ("I Became a Song"), re-forming it upon introducing the homeland as a subject. The homeland is transformed into an artistic expression and La Renga, given its creations, into a supporter of national identity.[12] Other "rags" enhance the significance of these representatives of national identity: "Esquivando charcos en este infierno encantador la mentira es la verdad y la ciudad dormida y sin sueño La Renga Diego Divididos Los Piojos Esto sí es Argentina" (Evading puddles in this enchanting hell the lie is the truth and the city asleep and without a dream La Renga Diego Divididos Los Piojos This really is Argentina). This banner constructs a phrase from songs of different *rock chabón* bands: La Renga ("Esquivando charcos" ["Evading Puddles"]), Los Redondos ("El infierno está encantador esta noche" ["Hell Is Charming Tonight"]), Divididos ("Qué ves" ["What Do You See"]), and Los Piojos ("Cruel"). The important thing here is not the meaning of the phrase that evolves, but rather that the verses remit to identifiable songs of bands that belong to the *rock chabón* genre; the ability consists in being able to combine the verses, which is a manner of uniting all these bands in the same line of rock.[13] The names of the bands (except Los Redondos), the name of Diego (alluding to Diego Maradona), and a verse of the song "La rubia tarada" ("The Dumb Blonde") by the punk-rock band Sumo appear later. Sumo no longer exists, but it is considered a precursor of the rock trend to which the rest of the bands ascribe. In this last song, Argentina is represented as "drinking a gin in the poor neighbor's bar" and in opposition to the upper-middle-class kids who frequent the discothèques and upscale nightclubs. Thus this banner expresses that it is rock that is distinctly national, and, more specifically, the musical propositions of *rock chabón*.

According to these banners, the homeland is no longer in the crystallized and homogeneous cultural forms that generally constitute the cultural patrimony that is preserved by the hegemonic sectors,[14] but in manifestations in continuous movement that combine the vernacular and the foreign. To propose *rock chabón* bands as a specific version of national identity implies constructing this sense of belonging outside the dominant logic, relying on cultural expressions that are viewed as one's own, as resources of identification and collective memory.

Painted on cloths with the colors of the national flag, the songs reproduced there acquire use value: they allow public expression of the sentiments, thoughts, and convictions of those who go to (and "participate in" using the plain sense of the term) the concerts. The national flags re-create *rock chabón* as "national" as well as a contestatarian cultural manifestation: vindicating those who are subordinate, remembering the great oblivions, evoking inequalities, disputing sacred notions promoted by the dominant sectors. Additionally they recreate rock as a space for the construction of differential identities.

A similar "nationalization" of the genre occurs with the lyrics. In this regard, figures appear in the narratives of *rock chabón* that, in the imaginations of musicians and various cultural traditions and national policies, are identified with "the nation's people," the true "essence" of the homeland. In this manner, the group Almafuerte sustains in one of its songs: "Desheredados, gauchos, indios, empobrecidos reencarnan" (The disinherited, gauchos, Indians, impoverished people reincarnate). Also the group Divididos comes to prioritize these national figures by opposing them to *rock nacional* itself, using northern folkloric rhythms in which the lyrical interpellation is overdetermined by the musical one: "Nace un hijo negro / cachetazo al rock" (A black son is born / a big smack to rock).[15]

Rock chabón can sing "a black son is born, a big smack to rock," warning of the tension that has always existed between "blacks" (*cabecitas negras*), the poor of Argentina, and traditional *rock nacional,* a privileged expression of middle-class youth. At the same time, if the Divididos song favors rock, it does so by restoring it as "black" music, music that originates from (and is directed to) the base of society.

Equating today's poor with yesterday's massacred is a discourse explicitly retaken by *rock chabón*. This is an articulation highly prized by a non-liberal school of Argentine historical revisionism, and, above all, is one of the central narratives of the imaginary woven by Peronism—that of the nationally oppressed, which was constructed as a symbolic continuity from the gauchos of the nineteenth century to the *cabecitas negras* of the middle of the twentieth. Not only is this discourse recaptured, but it is also projected onto the present. Thus "El pibe tigre" ("The Tiger Kid"), a song by Almafuerte that is the paradigm of this articulation, is the story of a company employee who ends up being swindled by his bosses. The characteristic thing here is that the directors are negativized, not for their capitalist nature, but because they are not nationals (they are "foreigners," "gringos," "de las multinacionales," and "fleeing with their money out of the country").

Another example in the same direction would be La Renga's song "Vendepatria clon" ("Sellout Clone"):

> Desde el norte si ahí empieza
> hasta el sur donde termina
> del mar a la cordillera

ya no va a ser la Argentina
¿Y cuándo compren todo
qué más van a querer?
Contemplando en mi simpleza
peleando con mi ignorancia
olí que el aire de mi tierra
va teniendo otra fragancia.
¿Y cuándo compren todo
qué más van a querer?
El que más amó la tierra
no es que no la merecía
clonaron más vendepatrias
de lo que uno se imagina.

(From the north, yeah, it starts there
toward the south where it ends
from the sea to the mountains
it's not going to be Argentina any longer.
If they buy it all
what else are they going to want?
Contemplating on my simplicity
fighting with my ignorance
I smelled that the air of my land
is acquiring another aroma.
If they buy it all
what else are they going to want?
The one who loved the land the most
it isn't that he didn't deserve it
they cloned more national sellouts
than one would imagine.)

The lyrics of this song criticize the *"vendepatrias"* (a very old nationalist leitmotif), those who have recently sold the country through the privatization process, but no reference is made to who is "buying" the country and for what reasons they are doing so. In this regard, the lament is about losing "our" land (it's not going to be Argentina any longer) and the words "patria," "tierra," and "Argentina" appear repeatedly during the song.

A song that would have been impossible to imagine in the national rock of the 1970s and 1980s is "San Jauretche," and it summarizes some of the most important issues we have addressed so far in this section of the article:

Perdimos el tiempo justo
de ser una gran nación
el ser chico hoy nos duele
en el alma y la ambición
hubo un día en que la historia
nos dio la oportunidad
de ser un país con gloria
o un granero colonial
pero faltó la grandeza de tener buena visión
por tapados de bisón y perfumes de París
quisieron de este país
hacer la pequeña Europa
gaucho, indio y negro a quemarropa
fueron borrados de aquí
yo le pido a San Jauretche
que venga la buena leche
Sarmiento y Mitre entregados
a las cadenas foráneas
el sillón y Rivadavia
hoy encuentran sucesores
que les voy a hablar de amores
y relaciones carnales
todos sabemos los males
que hay donde estamos parados
por culpa de unos tarados
y unos cuantos criminales
yo le pido a San Jauretche
que venga la buena leche
si dos años nos dejamos
nos dejamos de robar
dijo uno muy sonriente
la cosa puede cambiar
como dijo Don Ricardo
cleptocracia es lo que hay
bolsiqueros de esta tierra
por favor tómenselas
Yo le pido a San Jauretche
que venga la buena leche.

(We missed the right time
to be a great nation
today, being a small country hurts
in our souls and our ambition
there was a day when history
gave us the opportunity
to be a country with glory
or a colonial granary
but the greatness of vision was missing
for coats of bison and perfumes from Paris
they wanted to make
this country a little Europe
gaucho, Indian, and black people, at short range
were erased from here
I ask San Jauretche
let the good vibes come
Sarmiento and Mitre sold out
to the foreign enterprises
the armchair and Rivadavia
today find successors
I'm not going to tell you about love
and carnal (familial) relations
we all know the problems
present where we're standing
Some idiots are to blame
and a bunch of criminals
I ask San Jauretche
let the good vibes come
if for two years we stop
we stop stealing
one person said all smiling
things can change
as Don Ricardo said
"kleptocracy" is what there is
raiders of this land
please leave right away
I ask San Jauretche
let the good vibes come.)

The name of the song refers to one of the most important revisionist historians of the country, Arturo Jauretche, one of the founders of FORJA (Fuerza Orientadora Radical de la Joven Argentina), the group that, in the 1930s, harshly denounced the Argentinean oligarchy for "selling" the country to the British Empire and became part of the Peronist movement of the 1940s. To transform Jauretche into a "saint" and to make a song about him is a "first" in *rock nacional* history, showing the strong Peronist cultural framework that is behind the genre. At the same time, the lyrics address, one by one, the most important topics of the Peronist (and nationalist) credo: the need to industrialize the country; to abandon the colonial relationship with first world countries that rely on Argentina's specialization in the production of agricultural commodities alone; the pro-European stance of the Argentinean oligarchy; the murder of the Indian, black, and gaucho aboriginal populations to pursue a pro-imperialist national project; the denunciation of the most important Argentine "founding fathers" (Sarmiento, Mitre, Rivadavia) as having sold out to the British; and so on. Additionally the lyrics link those historical facts of Argentina's dependency to the present of the country, denouncing President Carlos Menem (who claims he is a Peronist president) as the inheritor of the worst pro-imperialist tradition—that is, the current "sellers of the country"—as well as making fun of major figures of Menem's entourage and their part in robbing the country.

At the same time, the lyrics of the song pay homage to *rock chabón* itself, referring to the denunciation of Menem's neoliberal project by Ricardo Mollo (the leader of Divididos and a constant reference for the entire genre) in his song "Salir a asustar" ("Going Out to Scare"), in which he uses the word "cleptocracia." From the point of view of the music, if the theme of the lyrics is nationalism, the music addresses the same issue as well, through the use of a folk rhythm, *chacarera*, clearly discernible in the violin part (played by the well-known *chacarera* performer Peteco Carabajal), and in the piano part, as well. As we can see, most of the issues discussed thus far appear well summarized in only one song.

Conclusion

In this essay we wanted to show how *rock chabón* helps in the construction of a particular type of identity in contemporary Argentina, that of "marginalized young people belonging to the popular sectors." *Rock chabón* allows such a construction through the interaction of the different alliances those youngsters establish between their diverse imagined narrative identities and the identities that *rock chabón* sets forth.

We think that a good way to end this article is quoting the *cantito* that is most frequently repeated at La Renga concerts, because it synthesizes the most important points we have addressed in this chapter:

> Vamos La Renga
> con huevos vaya al frente
> que se lo pide toda la gente
> Una bandera que diga Che Guevara
> un par de rocanroles
> y un porro pa'fumar
> Matar un rati para vengar al Walter
> y en toda la Argentina empieza el carnaval.
>
> (Let's go La Renga
> with balls come on out
> because everybody is asking for that
> A banner that says Che Guevara
> a couple of rock 'n' roll songs
> and a joint to smoke
> To kill a cop to avenge Walter
> And carnival starts all over Argentina.)

This *cantito* is usually the one that cheers the band so they will appear onstage.[16] Here, the majority of the topics we mention are alluded to. Elements originating from the universe of entertainment—rock 'n' roll, marijuana, Carnival—are mixed with others that belong to the traditional political sphere of the Left: a revolutionary leader (Che Guevara), the police. These elements, in turn, frame themselves within a notion of the "motherland," Argentina. In this sense, what the *cantito* expresses is that the concert never stops being a leisurely environment, but at the same time, in the *cantito*, links are established with political questions originating from the past that are connected to other important ones of the present. Ernesto "Che" Guevara, whose political posture facing the capitalist system led to his death, is vindicated, but also resurrected is a fan (Walter Bulacio), a follower of Los Redondos who was killed by police for the "crime" of attending a rock performance. At the same time, the possibility of killing a policeman to avenge this death is celebrated as well.

The music of this *cantito* is also emblematic of themes we have been discussing. First it is taken from a chorus favored by soccer fans who, like the ones following the Boca Juniors Club (the most *popular*—in the double sense of having many followers and of originating in the popular sectors) used to sing the following: "la doce (la hinchada) quiere quemar el gallinero [referring to Boca's arch-enemy River Plate], que se mueran los cuervos [San Lorenzo] y la guardia imperial [Racing Club]" (the twelve [the fans] want to burn the barn [referring to Boca's archenemy River Plate], may the crows die [San Lorenzo] and the Imperial Guard [Racing Club]). Secondly the music comes from a very well known popular song from the late 1940s and early 1950, that is, the Peronist decade par excellence.

We firmly believe that *rock chabón* is a novelty in the Argentine popular music scene for different reasons. On one hand, because for the first time in the history of *rock nacional*, the popular sectors themselves jumped up to the stage and started to produce music for people "like themselves." At the same time, *rock chabón* introduces a new thematic take on the genre, rescuing many issues that were not part of the previous tradition of *rock nacional*, since they belonged to the cultural matrix of Peronism. Finally because if, on one hand, *rock chabón* continues a well-entrenched *rock nacional* tradition—that is, it also is an oppositional music—on the other hand, it promotes a very different kind of opposition to the system. Its "neo-oppositional" character is mainly expressed by its appraisal of a completely new string of popular heroes (the urban marginalized, delinquents, and the like); by the festive celebration of marijuana consumption; by the sad portrayal of a postindustrial/post-Populist Argentina, with its growing unemployment, violence, and lack of a future; by its constant criticism of repressive institutions like the police; and by its nationalist discourse about the "patria." All these topics are expressed, in different degrees, by both the artists and the audiences. The artists accomplish this through their performances, lyrics, and music; the audiences, through their active participation in the concert with the banners and *cantitos*.

In showing the tremendous participatory character of the genre, it is important to note that the above *cantito* is usually sung in the middle of "El Blues de Bolivia" ("Bolivia Blues"). The trumpet creates the *cantito*'s rhythm and only the audience sings. Thus the boundary between the band's songs and those of the audience is dissolved.[17] Michel De Certeau qualifies consumption as another production—dispersed, silent, and invisible—that does not refer to people's "own products but to the way in which these products are used."[18] We think that the banners and the *cantitos* constitute vehicles for the expression of modes of consumer appropriation, of the kind of "Other" production mentioned by De Certeau. These objects multiply the voices expressed in the concert.[19] The areas unoccupied by the musicians—the outskirts of the performing area, the moments prior to the show—are appropriated by the consumers, who blend their adhesion and fidelity toward the band or their barrio with criticism of the social system, a criticism that, being an idiosyncratic marker of *rock nacional* in general, acquires new meanings when the popular sectors appropriate rock, as in the case of *rock chabón*.

Selected Discography

Almafuerte. *Mundo guanaco*. 1995. DBN 51327.
———. *En vivo, Obras 2001*. 2001. DBN.
Attaque 77. *El cielo puede esperar*. 1990. DBN 50803.
———. *Un día perfecto*. 1997 BMG 54474-2.
———. *Radio insomnio*. 2000. Polygram 76923-2.
Divididos. *La era de la boludez*. 1993. Polygram 521020-2.
2 Minutos. *Valentín Alsina*. 1994. DBN 522560-2.
———. *Volvió la alegria, vieja!* 1995. DBN 528285-2.
Patricio Rey y sus Redonditos de Ricota. *Gulp!* 1985. DBN 50013.
———. *Oktubre*. 1986. DBN 50014.
Los Piojos. *Ritual*. 1999. DBN 51631.
La Renga. *La Renga*. 1998. DBN 526034-2.

A Detour to the Past

Memory and Mourning in Chilean Post-Authoritarian Rock

WALESCKA PINO-OJEDA

> It does not require much theoretical sophistication to see that all representation—whether in language, narrative, image, or recorded sound—is based on memory. Re-presentation always comes after. . . . But rather than leading us to some authentic origin or giving us verifiable access to the real, memory, even and especially in its belatedness, is itself based on representation. The past is not simply there in memory, but it must be articulated to become memory.
> —**Andreas Huyssen,** *Twilight Memories: Marking Time in a Culture of Amnesia*

> Music has allowed the expression . . . of the secret connection that links the integrating *ethos* with *pathos,* the universe of feeling.
> —**Jesús Martín Barbero,** *De los medios a las mediaciones: Comunicación, cultura y hegemonía*

> A decisive aspect of modern-day Chile is the compulsion to forget. A memory block is a frequent occurrence in societies that have lived borderline experiences. In them, this denial regarding the past generates the loss of discourse, the difficulty of speech. There is a deficiency of common words to name that which has been lived.
> —**Tomás Moulián,** *Chile actual: Anatomía de un mito*

The phrase that best characterized Chilean youth in the 1990s was "¡No estoy ni ahí!" (I don't give a damn!). In no time, this phrase was deployed to characterize youth as a lost generation; it was interpreted as their "death sentence" as citizens and became the slogan that best signaled their complete lack of political commitment. This reaction by an older generation toward youth might best be understood as the former's inability to comprehend the lack of interest by youth in the nation's recent past. Therefore political apathy and amnesia became the label stamped by others to identify this generation, whose childhood took place in the 1970s and whose adolescence witnessed the timid steps toward post-dictatorial democracy.

Of course, any behavior looks apathetic in comparison with the effervescence or driving force for change which characterized 1960s youth. In Chile, such creative energy was materialized in the Nueva Canción (New Song) movement, whose aesthetic agenda, initiated in the 1950s, reacted against the overwhelming invasion of commercialized mass culture by introducing and researching indigenous/folk popular art forms. This was in fact an anthropological and political-artistic movement, whose principal leaders were, however, two self-taught artists, Chile's Violeta Parra and the Argentine Atahualpa Yupanqui. The work of the Nueva Canción movement was able to reach a generation of middle- and upper-middle-class youth, who, from the universities, attempted to recuperate and communicate popular culture missing from the official mass media.[1]

Nevertheless this project did not end with changes in the media. In the political sphere, a government socialist project began to take shape and became institutionalized in 1970, when Salvador Allende won the Chilean presidential elections, making history as the first socialist government elected by popular vote. Art and politics had never before found themselves so allied: in 1970, Quilapayún recorded the "Cantata Popular Santa María de Iquique" and Víctor Jara his "Canto libre" ("Free Chant"). In 1971 Pablo Neruda received the Nobel Prize in literature, the rock group Los Jaivas recorded its first album (*El volantín* [*The Kite*]), and Congreso, another important rock group, released *El Congreso* (*Congress*). All this ended on that *other* September 11 (1973), when the Chilean Right, supported by the military and the C.I.A., expressed their "distress" through a coup d'état that gave General Augusto Pinochet absolute power for seventeen years. The Pinochet era opened with persecution, disappearances, exile, and death, from which neither politicians, academics, workers, or artists were exempt.[2] The authoritarian regime was legitimated through policies that censored the recent cultural history of the country. It also consolidated, through free-trade economics, a doctrine implemented with absolute discipline by the students of Milton Friedman—the so-called Chicago Boys—an economic experiment whose market-led restructuring became known as "neoliberalism."

Under the constraints of terror at the end of the 1970s, another musical movement, Canto Nuevo, attempted a new alliance between aesthetic language and social commitment. Canto Nuevo was an urban music with political themes incorporating elements of jazz, pop, and bossa nova, as well as the folklore inherited from Nueva Canción. Like the latter, Canto Nuevo was cultivated by artists from an established middle class, members of universities or academies, and a young collectivity firmly committed to current political social movements. Consequently it represented not only the sentiment of antidictatorial political and intellectual groups, but also continuity with music that had been interrupted when its followers were persecuted, exiled, or assassinated after 1973. This musical scene developed in the early 1980s in tandem with the fragile blossoming under the dictatorship of rock music, which had also been repressed. Juan Pablo González offers the following synopsis of the rock scene at that time:

> The revival of the early forms of rock during the 1980s is associated with the rise of a generational movement. This new generational identity is expressed, for instance, as a criticism against the idealism of the generation of the 1960s. . . . The revival of rock was generalized in Chile by 1984 . . . This access to the masses was reached because of rock's capacity to respond to the contemporary socio-cultural environment in which the Chilean youth live. The growth and modernization of Chilean cities have augmented their pollution, violence, materialism, and insecurity. The repressive practices of the military government have created a tremendous feeling of frustration and rebellion among young people. This situation has shaped new rock in Chile. Ranging from commercial to vanguard trends, there have been techno-pop groups such as Aparato Raro, new-pop groups such as Emociones Clandestinas, Valija Diplomática, Cinema, Engrupo, UPA, Paraíso Perdido, and De Kiruza, and experimental groups such as Primeros Auxilios, Electrodomésticos, Viena, and Fulano.[3]

It was in this context that Canto Nuevo groups, such as Santiago del Nuevo Extremo, Ortiga, the duet Schwenke y Nilo, Sol y Lluvia, and soloists, such as Capri, Isabel Aldunate, and Eduardo Peralta, among others, worked side by side with rock musicians. This coexistence, however, became increasingly conflictive, to the degree that rock sidelined politically committed music and finally replaced it. As Mattern states:

> The dilemma of *Canto Nuevo* lay in the tension it faced between its crucial role of political remembrance and maintenance of democratic identity and, on the other hand, its tendency to become confined, in terms of mass appeal, to politically impotent nostalgia. Ironically, the

role of *Canto Nuevo* in keeping memories alive also partly defined its failure. By looking backward it defined itself at least initially in nostalgic terms which failed to connect with the contemporary concerns of many youth.[4]

It is from this new phase of rock music that the aggressive project of the band Los Prisioneros emerged and, in the mid-1980s, instigated the movement toward post-authoritarian rock. Jorge González, leader of the group, explains the success of this musical project in the following terms:

> What I was singing about in "Muevan las industrias" ["Put the Industries to Work"] and in "El baile de los que sobran" ["The Dance of the Ones Left Behind"] would never have had the power to move people if we had not had an eagerness . . . to tell about these situations. That is what gives it meaning; if not, probably, any of the litanies of the Canto Nuevo would have been more important than those songs, because no way were we the most confrontational group. There were a lot of groups which were more direct in political and social terms, but they were such a drag. Because what they were talking about was boring and sad even to them. We felt bad too, but behind this sad situation we were excited and it made us dream, maybe because we were younger and had no ideology.[5]

On the other hand, when referring to this tension, Joe Vasconcellos, one of the musicians who linked Canto Nuevo and contemporary rock, maintains: "Conversing with rock musicians . . . they told me there was an internal trauma in themselves related to the lyric aspects, because everyone wanted to get as far away from Canto Nuevo as possible."[6] Therefore it is the convergence of these paths which paved the way for post-authoritarian Chilean rock: an attempt to overcome boredom, an expression of the "desire to dream," and an avoidance of the traumatic feeling produced by the "art of metaphor" characteristic of Canto Nuevo. Thus the challenge was how to face a past, defined by its epic character, which had coalesced into monumental pieces of music with perfect aesthetic coherence and ideological commitment but had ended in one of most brutal tragedies in the sociopolitical history of the country. This essay will formulate one possible response.

In *El grito del amor: Una historia temática actualizada del rock* (*A Cry of Love: An Updated Thematic History of Rock*), Fabio Salas offers a meticulous synthesis of rock's development in the Chilean context.[7] He highlights the 1960s' work of the group Los Macs, who, like most of their contemporaries, were strongly influenced by British rock. This group recorded the first rock song in Chile, "La muerte de mi hermano" ("My Brother's Death"), composed in 1965 in response to the U.S. invasion of the Dominican Republic.[8] The following decade initiated a new era, in which Chilean rock musicians began to explore, from their local perspectives, the diverse strains of rock being produced in international circles. In the 1970s three groups had the greatest influence in the development of this trajectory. Los Blops created an existentialist, urban rock, exemplified in their best-known song, "Los momentos" ("The Moments"), which became a Chilean classic. Occasionally they participated in the Nueva Canción movement, as when they recorded "El derecho de vivir en paz" ("The Right to Live in Peace") with Víctor Jara. The group Congreso initiated its career in 1969 and continues to be one of the most important ensembles, above all due to their work in the fusion of folklore and jazz. Contemporaries to Congreso, Los Jaivas recorded in 1969 what became their first hit "Todos juntos" ("All Together"), and in 1981 set monumental Latin American poetry to music in Neruda's poem, "Alturas de Macchu Picchu" ("Heights of Macchu Picchu"), while exploring the electronic sound of classical and indigenous instruments. The dictatorial period (1973–90) instilled a process of self-absorption, which found its ideal expressive medium in poetry. Thus the movement that emerged in the late 1970s with the name Poesía Joven (Young Poetry) is intimately associated with the Canto Nuevo movement. Salas explains the atmosphere at the time:

> Chilean youth culture is characterized after 1973 by its dispersion and heterogeneity . . . [and] a rather characteristic *sui generis* existentialism, represented as isolation, displacement, lack of commitment, and exacerbated individualism. This condition even supercedes social class difference, spreading throughout the community.[9]

In this context, the appearance of Los Prisioneros in the mid-1980s represents more than a break from the dominant aesthetic and collective mood, since they were already introducing features that would later become mainstream in post-authoritarian rock. The isolation and displacement to which Salas alludes in current rock adopts an agenda that emphasizes remembering, updating the past, but not in order to attempt its recuperation (an unattainable goal in any case), through one's own biography: "The mode of memory is *recherche* rather than recuperation."[10] Thus I understand music as narrative, as an "analyzable real practice," which carries along superficial as well as deep residues of the symbolic system from which it emerges and toward which it is directed.

Public Intimacies, Denial, and Neglected Spaces

The "I" that passes through present-day Chilean rock finds itself traversed by consumerist music from the 1960s to the 1980s, configuring the symbolic-acoustic scene of the childhood and adolescence of these artists. For this reason, we are presented with images emerging from the homes of these artists, from the orality of a mass medium such as radio, but performed out of the private nature of the family context; a collective message, yet detailed with specificities of the domestic: the child's home and its own laws of everyday life. For this reason, it is particularly important to keep in mind what Martín Barbero advises in approaching a study of the popular: one must include "not only that which is culturally produced by the masses, but also that which they consume, that which they are fed; and the need to think of the popular in culture not as something limited to what has to do with its past—and a rural past—but also mainly as the realm of the popular linked with modernity, *mestizaje,* and the complexity of the urban."[11] Therefore these memories are set, first, in the intersection between the re-creative act (Huyssen) and the consumerist one (Martín Barbero); next, in the crossroads of the rural-urban and its consequent temporal mix; and, finally, at the threshold where the mass cultural apparatus (radio and television) converges by operating within the peculiarity of the domestic space. This act of remembering appears at first personal and subjective, but, in fact, it deals with public memory—though hidden. It brings into the present moment images of privacy, which are, nonetheless, shared.

An interesting parallel in Chilean literature of the 1990s can be found in the work of Pedro Lemebel, who produces a similar effect through his chronicles, and re-creates the impact, the horror generated in witnessing pronouncements on television which deny collective pain. His chronicle "Karin Eitel (o 'la cosmética de la tortura, por Canal 7 para todo espectador')" ("Karin Eitel [or 'the Cosmetics of Torture, on Channel 7 for All Viewers]'") is a good example.[12] Similarly we might recall the allusions by Rubén Blades in his song "Desapariciones" ("Disappearances") regarding the raids carried out by agents of repression, especially when he states, "estaban dando la telenovela / por eso nadie miró pa'fuera" (the soap opera was on TV / that's why no one looked out to see). Despite its ring of truth, the lyric insinuates apathy in witnessing the fate of neighbors who are disappearing, while at the same time it shows a premeditated, self-protecting indifference, the alienation of the television audience, which does not necessarily prevent gunshots and explosions from being stored in collective memory; it deals then with collective registers acquired in the domestic scene, which, for that very reason, are neither discussed nor

"Un pueblo que olvida no merece ni el cadáver de la libertad" (A people that forgets deserves not even freedom's corpse). Graffiti in Barrio La Victoria, Santiago, Chile. 1992. Photo by Héctor Castillo Berthier. (Archivo Fotográfico de Circo Volador.) Used by permission.

filed in the public arena. Chilean post-authoritarian rock expresses precisely the memory that is not factual, but rather the social relations in force while the actions were taking place.

Another aspect of my reading relates to an idea explored by Tomás Moulián, namely, the loss of a discourse produced by the denial of the past. However I am inclined to argue that what post-authoritarian rock accomplishes is more than denial. It is a cryptic operation, to borrow a term from psychology, which has a direct relationship with the experience of mourning, purging, and freeing oneself from loss and traumatic experiences, finding its antithesis in melancholy, in commemorative nostalgia that obstructs the catharsis rendering mourning possible.[13] The preceding claim leads me to propose that Chilean rock, rather than staging a compulsive forgetfulness—inasmuch as it is a defining feature of the "modern-day Chile" studied by Moulián—stages an unresolved mourning, presented in the form of nostalgia engendered by local sociopolitical reality (the dictatorial experience), as well as by the effect of the economy's transnationalization and the globalization of culture. In fact, what now exists is an obsession to remember that could certainly be explained as a fin de siècle syndrome. I would prefer, however, to locate it more specifically as a response to the crisis of a modernity which celebrates the present as a utopia of the "always-new," of the new-as-utopian, as described by Huyssen, which makes itself all too evident in the world of consumerism. It is here where competition appears that renders merchandise obsolete as soon as it is released.[14] Moreover it is a commemorative exercise being articulated not from the realm of the hegemonic, but rather from the realm of non-sanctioned memory, the past that is not filed away in historical memory's official domain. Thus the space of "what happened back then" that rock hopes to recreate, which rummages around in mnemonic twists, is not institutionalized by official memory, be it from a left- or right-wing position: it's a detour rather than a denial. In the case of Chile, these official spaces are represented by "*la canción comprometida*" (political song, for example, Nueva Canción and Canto Nuevo), or the folklorized popular song used for conservative and patriotic purposes. Consequently these mnemonic instances are not yet included in the map of the "lettered city," to quote Ángel Rama's concept. Such corners are the least traumatic ones; hence the domestic carries double meaning: as a space that allows the individualization of the past beyond its historical standardization, and as a meaning-authorized enclave, of a certain permanence before the abyss of the ungraspable present; a home that is physical and metaphysical at the same time: "The depth of the past is summoned in order to give depth to the domestic intimacy which industrial goods have stereotyped."[15] Hence it deals with recovering a reality that has, in some way, remained unserialized: the family kitchen, the living-room and public parks, as evident in the following statement by Jorge González, leader of Los Prisioneros:

> In my childhood . . . in the 1970s, all music sounded sad. . . . In Chile some long drawn-out songs were big hits. The ones sung by Bread, for example, or the Carpenters. The saddest music was what they put on the radio. And the *cumbias* sounded like that, like something nostalgic, gloomy; like something out of the public parks where people went to drink, and they ended up drunk and began to cry.[16]

This nostalgia emanates from a generation whose childhood took place in the 1970s, an era of ideological absolutism. Mass culture, interestingly, offers an escape from that absolutism and, therefore, a discursive meaning to commercialism. The enormous proliferation of the image of the domestic sofa of the 1960s in advertising and television programs can be explained in this context. During the 1990s, for example, there was a Chilean TV program called *El sillón rojo* (*The Red Armchair*). Thus mass culture is recovered inasmuch as it occupies a space scorned by the lettered elite, allowing it to remain at the margins of any institutional cultural project.[17]

These exclusions are purged in present-day Chilean rock through the recreation of forms originally from mass-popular culture and the urban popular (also described as "urban folklore"), which represent the mixing of the rural-urban and have found a niche in the slum belts of big cities. In this sense, encrypted memory is that of the popular, as the *canción comprometida* (committed song) of the Left understood it in the 1960s—that is to say, popular music produced by "the people." Instead what is evoked is rock 'n' roll, the twist, and the romantic ballad. For a Chilean audience, these foreign musical forms offer a different route from the one presented by the Nueva Canción and Canto Nuevo, which are—as already explained—aesthetic-political choices accepted and deciphered in mainstream Chilean music. We are dealing with the recovery of that which Martín Barbero has described as the "unrepresented popular," or "the group of actors, spaces, and conflicts that are socially accepted but not interpellated by the parties of the Left . . . as are women, young people . . . [and] spaces such as the house, family relations, social security, the hospital."[18]

During the 1990s, the group Los Tres produced the most sustained formula in this exploration of the urban popular sector, due mainly to the participation of Roberto Parra (brother of Nueva Canción artists Violeta and Nicanor Parra). The consequent recovery and diffusion of Parra's musicological poetics allowed them to delve into the hybridity of the rural-urban, the small-town folk in direct contact with urban areas, and, in Parra's case, the culture originating in ports, fishermen's coves, bars, and brothels. Roberto Parra's music represents an entire range of spaces neglected by political or intellectual agendas dealing with the popular; his poetics center on a culture of *"bajos fondos,"* those clandestine spaces which, given their licentious character, allow the transgression of taboos. In the case of Parra, having resided in these places, his production adopts features of greater authenticity; thus, his poetics is sustained by autobiographical elements and distances itself from all academicism or party legitimation of the popular.[19] Parra's work with the popular subverts the mythology of the *"roto chileno"* (an individual of rural origin, a sort of rogue who survives in the city through his skills, who knows how to milk the system), as well as that of the naive peasant, or the idealized worker and proletariat. Parra's autobiographical musical drama, *La negra Ester,* offers an appreciation of this "other" popular space. The recovery of this work brought about by Los

Tres goes beyond merely incorporating some of his songs into their repertoire ("La vida que yo he pasado" ["The Life I've Had"] and the adaptation "Quién es la que viene allí" ["Who's That Girl Coming?"]) or having recorded the CD *La Jane Fonda*. It extends to the assimilation and re-creation of a musical gamut including the *"cueca chora"* (as opposed to the Hispanicized *cueca*, legitimized as a national dance), foxtrot, U.S. bluegrass, and the Charleston, forms that Parra brought together and baptized as *"jazz guachaca."* In Chilean jargon, this phrase refers to second-class, hybrid, Latin-Americanized jazz, taken from filmic mass culture, gangster movies, brothels, and port bars. In the Chilean context, these musical manifestations point to an encounter with a sort of subaltern transnationalism, located primarily in the seaport zones close to Santiago. In short, Parra deals with popular-folkloric forms (*la cueca*), but also other forms presented in mass media, as well as those created in convergent points of the popular, manifestations kept alive in clandestine entertainment spaces, acquired and consumed not in the workplace, but in spaces of leisure.

Re-Awakening the 1960s

Beginning in the mid-1980s, the type of rock established through the recovery of mass popular culture returned to singers and composers favored by the broadcast and print media of the 1960s. One of the principal media outlets was *Ritmo* (*Rhythm*), a magazine that featured most popular singers and provided basic guitar arrangements for songs. In 1996 Los Prisioneros compiled most of their work on the album *Ni por la razón ni por la fuerza* (*Neither by Reason Nor Force*), including a cover of "La noche" ("The Night"), a hit by 1960s Italo-Belgian pop icon Salvatore Adamo, which the group originally recorded in 1989. Los Prisioneros offer a perfect copy of the original version, not only in terms of instrumentation, but also with respect to vocal performance. This gesture not only expresses an homage to the singer, who, together with the Spaniard Rafael and the Argentine Sandro, "had greatly influenced them," according to Claudio Narea (the group's guitarist) on the album's jacket, but, above all, it also expresses an inclination that reveals the group's social origin, as Jorge González expounds:

> There is something that surprises me with regard to other musician friends; while they were getting to know Adamo because their nanny would play his music in the kitchen, in my case, it was because my mom listened to him. So this is a very big difference; a distinct closeness that defines you. If Los Prisioneros had not come from where we did, it wouldn't have gone so well.[20]

González's claim allows us to notice the zeal behind the recovery of this music, not only in the framework of individual tastes and memories acquired in a childhood context, but also to point out the existence of a collectivity identified with these cultural forms. Thus it brings the past into the present, but, above all, into a radically different context: that of rock, a space initially reserved for the consumption of the upper-middle class.[21] Therefore, the reactivation of Adamo's song twenty-five years after being fashionable faces a triple taboo: recovering a product stigmatized as ideologically alienating and lacking in "cultural" value; being inserted in a musical code marked by rebellion (rock); and being recorded amid the musical climate of Canto Nuevo, in which openly denunciatory or existential songs were considered imperative. Therefore, rather than being read as an escapist act, marginalized from national reality prior to the transition to democracy, the group's gesture makes evident the extent to which the "I" confronts a process in which it refuses to respond to ideological demands that frame, simplify, and erase the symbolic web from which it has emanated.

It is worth keeping in mind that the group emerged in 1984 from one of the many poorer neighborhoods around the capital, when its three members were sixteen years old and when protest music was represented by the Canto Nuevo movement. In that environment, the presence of Los Prisioneros not only influenced the political-intellectual dissident elite, but their music also spoke to a socially different sector of the younger generation, coming from the marginalized zones in Santiago's periphery. In this sense, the recuperation of a popular singer, such as Adamo, is a good example of the detour I have described.

Los Prisioneros's initial hit was "La voz de los ochenta" ("The Voice of the 1980s"), in which the guitar's sound is intercepted by monotonous drumbeats re-creating the rhythm of the legendary twist of the 1960s, when Chilean youth celebrated the Nueva Ola (New Wave), their local version of rock. (In the 1980s, in an interesting twist of events, British bands would adopt the English translation of this label.) The rant of "The Voice of the 1980s" assures us that:

> Algo grande está naciendo
> en la década de los ochenta
> ya se siente la atmósfera
> saturada de aburrimiento
> Los hippies y los punk tuvieron la ocasión
> de romper el estancamiento
> . . . .

Las juventudes cacarearon bastante
Y no convencen ni por solo un instante
Deja la inercia de los setenta
Adiós barreras, adios setentas
En plena edad del plástico,
seremos fuerza, seremos cambio
No te conformes con mirar
en los ochenta tu rol es estelar
tienes la fuerza, eres actor principal.

(Something big is being born
in the eighties
you can feel it in the atmosphere,
saturated in boredom
The hippies and the punks had the chance
of breaking the stagnation

. . . .

The youth bragged a lot
and they don't persuade at all
Leave behind the inertia of the seventies
Goodbye barriers, goodbye seventies
Amid the age of plastic,
we will be strength, we will be change
Don't settle for just watching,
in the eighties, the starring role is yours
You have the strength, you're the main actor.)

The aggressive tone of the so-called generational directive that promoted the displacement of hippies and punks of the previous decades contrasts with the spellbinding sound of homemade technology in this song, an aspect that, paradoxically, locates it clearly as punk rock, where voices that are almost infantile practice irreverence. However this "homegrown" rock centers on subject matter sustained by the impulse of change, shouts, and rhythms, suggesting a progressive and perfecting movement in which the subject itself reasserts its protagonism. The group offered something different in 1986 with "El baile de los que sobran" ("The Dance of the Ones Left Behind"), where the synthesizer that imitates an accordion's timbre of melancholy tones displaces the guitar's metallic sound. Accompanying it is the insistent barking of a street dog, the vagabond mutt of the big city. The song's urban sound is not produced by the booming of bus loudspeakers that invade the capital's downtown, like those employed by the group Santiago del Nuevo Extremo, one of the clearest exponents of the Canto Nuevo in their song "A mi ciudad" ("To My City"); rather, it comes from the tramp sniffing around poor barrios. "The Dance of the Ones Left Behind" describes young people without a place in society. Adopting a tone between confessional and descriptive, the narration introduces a subject that, despite identifying with the audience, sometimes strays away from those "left behind." The "voice" of the 1980s has been replaced by dance. The articulation of a message has given way to a rhythm that must be followed, danced, but that others now sing. The actors of this dance are "left behind," basically because:

> El futuro no es ninguno de los prometidos
> En los dulces juegos.
> A otros les enseñaron secretos que a ti no.
> A otros dieron de verdad esa cosa llamada educación.
> Ellos pedían esfuerzo, ellos pedían dedicación
> ¿Para qué? Para terminar bailando y pateando piedras.
> Únanse al baile de los que sobran.

> (The future is not promised
> in sweet games
> Secrets were shown to others but not to you.
> Others were truly given that thing called education.
> They asked for effort, they asked for dedication
> For what? To end up dancing and kicking stones.
> Join the dance of those left behind.)

The expulsion from a project with a future is presented as a premeditated erasure, substantiated by lack of access to the secret of success. Since others were indeed endowed with the privilege of education, success lies, clearly, beyond the grasp of the vocalist and his friends. The image of "kicking stones" is presented as a third world equivalent of the Anglo-Saxon rolling stone, where the rebellious and vagabond spirit belongs to an urban youth expressing its frustration before "a boring democracy with no identity and no change in sight," as Vikki Riley claims, alluding to Australian punk rock.[22] The kicking of rocks by Los Prisioneros evinces neither the fall nor the progressive displacement from a higher ground, as in the case of Sisyphus, the mythic hero, who, though condemned to push a rock continuously, manages to envision the peak he climbs; on the contrary, kicking stones proposes dust, the clumsiness of a road filled with obstacles, an empty surface of imperfections that suggest the impossibility of a higher ground.

It is here that we find Los Prisioneros' gesture of rebellion, namely, in their attempt to include a marginal social and generational sector on the stage of Chilean rock at the end of the dictatorial era, which is not only manifest in songs with ill-feeling toward the status quo, but is also present in the very act of incorporating into their repertoire (in 1989) the "uncommitted" romantic ballad, habitually reserved for the domestic space, and a "de-politicized" form, one institutionally reserved for the consumption of young sectors still absent from political forums, or else for the proletariat sector, still "unprepared" for this arena.

Other Chilean rock groups have also returned to singers popular with the working classes in the 1960s. In 1995 Los Tres produced the album *La espada y la pared* (*A Rock and a Hard Place*), which includes a song by Nueva Ola star Buddy Richard, "Tu cariño se me va" ("Your Love Is Leaving Me"). In this regard, Tito Escárate in conversation with band leader Alvaro Henríquez, states:

> **TE:** We should remember that, at some point, that movement (Nueva Ola) represented a phenomenon of bad taste, completely ignored by the cultural elite.
> **AH:** When we made the cover of the Buddy Richard song, "Your Love Is Leaving Me," this prejudice vanished and all the new-wavers started to come out. I was asking myself: "Could this be because we did it?" I don't believe that just one person does things: it is always a group of people who make things happen.[23]

The success of Sandro, the Argentine singer, was contemporary with the Chilean Nueva Ola. Just like Adamo and Buddy Richard, the prejudice mentioned by Escárate and Henríquez also fell upon the Argentine singer because his enormous popularity was found mostly in the most marginalized social sectors: housewives, domestic help, and high school students exempt from the influence of rock and pop in English. In 1999 BMG of Argentina released the album *Un tributo a Sandro: Un disco de rock* (*A Tribute to Sandro: A Rock Recording*). Artists from various Latin American countries participated in this homage, among them Los Fabulosos Cadillacs, León Gieco, and Virus, all from Argentina, but also Colombia's Aterciopelados, as well as Javiera y Los Imposibles, from Chile. The album's subtitle, "A Rock Recording," appears as a necessary clarification, not only to situate the artists on the album and the revival of a sexual icon of the 1960s, but also to offer a reading in which Sandro himself is presented as a *rockero*. It was a daring attempt by Los Prisioneros to recover, in the late 1980s, one of the top-ten songs from 1960s radio. In the Chile of that earlier moment, most energy was directed toward the urban protest song; in the mid-1990s, Los Tres reiterate and re-semanticize this music, giving it new legitimacy and initiating a parallel project of genealogical elaboration for Chilean rock, an act reinforced by the homage to Sandro. As a result, the nostalgic gesture of going back to childhood and overstepping social boundaries and cultural ideological prejudices begins to metamorphose into an act of self-legitimation, constructing a personal *rockero* identity through a tradition that remained outside the canon. In a nutshell, this is a musical production emerging from the masses, consumed by the same, but scorned by the political and academic intelligentsia, who established itself as a voice and representative of these same marginalized groups.

The work of the group Javiera y Los Imposibles is perhaps the most paradigmatic one in the process of incorporatiing mass-consumed music from the 1960s, 1970s, and 1980s. In terms of striking a balance between lyrics and music, their 1998 album *La suerte* (*Luck*) is perhaps the most successful. Traditional rock shares space with evident echoes from the 1960s ("Tango," "Dulce veneno" ["Sweet Poison"]), especially some belonging to the film industry of the period. Of the twelve songs that make up the album, Javiera Parra, the group's lead vocalist, wrote the lyrics for nine of them. The thematic thread that unites this album is a feminine voice that communicates a condition of existential discomfort, expressed in suicidal lyrics, a mood akin to the poetry of the Argentine Alejandra Pizarnik, or to certain zones of Violeta Parra's work. "Dulce veneno" is, in this way, the most successful composition in poetic-musical terms:

>Agárrate bien firme
>Que la caída es libre
>
>. . . . .
>Me pincharé feliz
>Tendré un dedo halagado
>Si en esa mano helada
>En cambio hay una daga
>No buscaré consuelo
>Me haré un nido en el pelo.
>
>(Hold on tight
>Because it's a free-fall
>
>. . . . . . .
>I'll gladly pinch myself
>I will have a praised finger
>If that icy hand
>has a dagger instead
>I won't seek consolation there
>I'll make a nest in my hair.)

In the album's musical arrangement, one can recognize a 1960s-type organ sound, a guitar—at times melodic, other times loud—and a feminine voice whose childlike reminiscences generate feelings of innocence, tedium, or drowsiness, all traits that contribute with carefully written, generously poetic lyrics to the macabre existentialist theme of the album. In "A Color" ("In Color"), the predominant characteristic is the pop sound of the 1970s, with some orchestral arrangements evoking the music imposed in that period by the San Remo Festival (held in Italy), with its obvious Chilean equivalent, the Viña del Mar Festival. Happy melodies reveal loving adolescent relationships in search of pleasure, all by way of clever lyrics, which give this album a sense of homage to the broadcast "color" of the times. "El muchacho de los ojos tristes" ("The Boy with Sad Eyes"), a remake of a very popular tune of the 1970s by the Spaniard Manuel Alejandro, introduces the musical line that defines the most recent album, *AM* (as in Amplitude Modulation). This album is the quintessential example of the nostalgia which characterizes, with some nuances, Chilean post-authoritarian rock. The CD's cover presents the family kitchen of the 1960s, with electronic appliances recently incorporated into the domestic life of the emerging Chilean middle class, as well as, of course, a radio on the family table. Unlike the two previous albums, *AM* is an anthology of some of the songs popularized by radio during the 1970s and 1980s. The original defining characteristics are the musical arrangements that allow for a cha-cha rhythm in, for example, "Detalles" ("Details"), a song by the Brazilian songwriter and singer Roberto Carlos.

To return to our initial thesis, we might ask ourselves: how do we explain that, as a space for resolution, Chilean rock memory chooses music stigmatized, precisely because of its service to conservative interests? In order to understand this, one must avoid facile Manichean dichotomies. In this respect, Martín-Barbero states: "[Néstor] García Canclini has taught us to pay attention to plot: not all assimilation of things hegemonic by the subaltern is a sign of submission, just as mere rejection is not a sign of resistance. Not all that comes 'from above' are values of the dominant class, since there are things which respond to logic other than that of domination."[24] I would venture that this generation is in a process of rupture with previous ideological polarities by engaging in a cryptic experience that definitively seals segments of a traumatic past and reinstates in its place the yearning for a home, a nostalgia that works as a pleasurable substitute that leaves mourning in suspense. In a similar vein, Moulián reminds us:

> Santiago has stopped being a small-town city, as it was as late as 1973. At that time, it appeared to be a politically vibrant but unsophisticated

city, with no complexity in its urban plot. It was an extensive village, with a strange mix of intensity and pastoral feeling. It was simultaneously a city whose public space was invaded by political iconography, but also a city that was reserved, inward looking, with great formal timidity.[25]

It is precisely the weight of the political iconography idealized by their parents that dissuades today's youth from searching in official memory and to look instead in the family home. Both iconographic and auditory "committed" images constitute a monument with which today's youth do not want to deal, not just because of mere generational rejection, but also because of the burial of memories, a mourning that has not yet taken place. On the other hand, and now in a more conscious way, the most evident characteristic of this generation is a frontal rejection of worn-out binaries, expressed in a clear attempt to distance themselves from polar ideologies (Left vs. Right), hierarchical categorizations of cultural practices (elite culture and subculture), as well as values based on spaces of coexistence (the public arena vs. the private one; urban space vs. rural). In the end, it all boils down to questioning and exercising disobedience toward lettered culture and its attendant standardization, domestication, and hierarchization of knowledge.

> The clergy, the owners of written culture, confronts the emergence of the peasant masses as a cultural pressure group—guardian of "folkloric culture." . . . The clash is situated basically in the conflict between the ecclesiastic culture's rationalism—a marked separation of right and wrong, of true and false, saints and demons—and the relativity, the ambiguity that permeates all folkloric culture because of its belief that now they are good and later they will bad, in a changing and fluctuating status. . . . Thus, Manichean dualism and schematism appear paradoxically not as originally popular modes, but as impositions from the erudite tradition.[26]

Within this framework, the popular recovered, re-created, and represented in Chilean fin de siècle rock is that which is neither read nor chosen by institutional culture with the aim of homogenizing it within the Manichean epistemology mentioned above by Martín Barbero; rather, it is that which has emerged and developed precisely on the margins of that polarity. Another aspect leading to separation, which engenders disobedience toward canonical cultural forms in this generation, is explained by the fact that a large proportion of its members, for different reasons, have been part of the transnational stage: on one hand, because of their participation in the nomadic practice of exile as children and, on the other, because they belong to the generation of the multinational communication media boom. We are, therefore, facing itinerant subjects, not merely due to the geographic mobilizations provoked by exile; they are international subjects, collecting other experiences and speaking several languages. And this is so not only because of MTV's influence, but also because, as children of exiles, they grew up in France, the United States, Australia, Sweden, Italy, and elsewhere. Their awareness of the "globalized" world comes about not only because of the Internet and communication media, but also because of their personal biographies, given that a large number of these musicians are children of exiles who have returned.

An important exception to this rule is the work of Los Miserables. In their recordings "De Rusia con amor" ("From Russia with Love") and "El cuervo" ("The Crow"), they evoke from the 1960s the only gesture that ties them to leftist political ideology of the mass culture of the period. In 1997, seven years removed from the newly established democratic government, Los Miserables launched their album *Cambian los payasos, pero el circo sigue* (*The Clowns Change, But the Circus Stays the Same*), with its cover title wrapped around the central image of a donkey ornamented with small skulls and images of circus contortionists. In the liner notes of the compact disc, some of the cover's images are repeated and new ones are added, among them a photographic arrangement picturing then-President Eduardo Frei as a clown, further illustrating the album's title.

The sound of Los Miserables leans toward strident chords of electric guitar. The aggressive chords are accompanied by voices that virulently shout lyrics speaking of vengeance and discord, which explain the group's name. This collectivity presents itself as the most aggressive of them all, especially since they describe themselves as inspired by a philosophy they've coined as "hate-o-cracy." In the current sociopolitical context, Los Miserables appears as the visible voice of a young collective body that abhors all political institutionalism, whether left- or right-wing. Its presence in Chilean society is felt in open spaces that are being appropriated and politicized with hate and vengeance as the motto. The body politic is not identified as the headquarters of a party, but rather the soccer fans, brothers with whom favoritism toward a particular team is shared; the selected scenario is the soccer stadium; and the targets of confrontation are the enemy fans and—above all—the police force, intimidated by the exhibition of naked torsos, provocative words, spellbound projectiles, colored smoke in which the carnivalesque blends with the hellish. The appropriation of the soccer stadium as a space for unleashing resentment and giving free rein to confrontations does not seem gratuitous, especially if we remember that, for the coup d'état, stadiums were converted into prisons, torture chambers in which uniformed authority caused horrific pain and innumerable deaths. This overlapping of semantic spaces, as suggested by Patricio Guzmán in his documentary film *Chile, la memoria obstinada* (*Chile, Obstinate Memory*, 1997), is exactly the space in which young people challenge the police, who have the duty of containing them, and who now, in a reversal of roles, appear frightened—facing the considerable anger of fans. Los Miserables have inserted themselves in the current political-music scene based on a rebellion with a memory; the "struggle" takes place in a space that is different, yet nonetheless charged with historical feeling that helps to contextualize the vengeful refrains. The disc begins and ends with a war anthem of the soccer fans, "La banda" ("The Band"), that brings to mind the voices of old college anthems in the rhythm of a *batucada*. In the manner of a coalition of the people circulating through the streets and calling for participation, the chorus of the song states:

> De una banda del pueblo soy,
> soy miserable
>
> . . . .
>
> Vamos hermano, vamos cantando
> que la paciencia del pueblo se va acabando
> y si tú como nosotros quieres revolución
> vamó hermano a cantar esta canción.
>
> (I am part of a band of the people,
> I am miserable
>
> . . . .
>
> Let's go, brother, let's start singing
> 'cause the people's patience is wearing thin
> and if you want revolution, as we do,
> c'mon, brother, sing this song.)

Perhaps this is the only group that still uses words like "people" and "revolution." The rejection of political bodies involved with the government is not justified by a denial of politics; on the contrary, Los Miserables' songs incorporate the leftist terminology from before Boris Yeltsin and the fall of the Berlin Wall. Che Guevara's image and Fidel Castro's voice resound as a backdrop for songs such as "Discordia" ("Discord"), which states:

> El libre mercado, invasión indecente
> libertad pá el dinero y no para la gente
> El pueblo siempre avanza, seguro pero lento.

Hay que cambiar la historia, la magia que desborda
sacar la tierna furia, organizar discordia.

. . . .

Tenemos digno ejemplo y mucha inteligencia
Ejemplos de guerrilla batiendo a los corruptos
el capitalismo jamás será justo
si nos unimos todos esto puede cambiar
yo soy un hombre bueno y hay muchos en este lugar

(Free market, indecent invasion,
freedom for money and not for the people.
The people always go forward, slowly but surely.
History must be changed, the magic that overflows
bring out the tender fury, organize discord

. . . .

We have a good example and great intelligence.
Examples of the guerrilla beating the corrupt
capitalism will never be just
if we all unite, all this can change
I'm a good man and there are many in this place.)

As evidenced by this song, the rock of Los Miserables does not stray from the classical poetics of the musical form, as rebellion and escapism do not suppose an alternative that leads to the void. Rather, as Robert Walser sustains in *Running with the Devil: Power, Gender, and Madness in Heavy Metal Music*:

> What seems like rejection, alienation, or nihilism is usually better seen as an attempt to create an alternative identity that is grounded in a vision or the actual experience of an alternative community. Heavy metal's fascination with the dark side of life gives evidence of both dissatisfaction with dominant identities and institutions and an intense yearning for reconciliation with something more credible.[27]

The emancipating utopia is no longer transmitted via folkloric rhythms singing the virtues of revolution with epic language; rather, it has been replaced with shouts of fury, in which hatred toward the "corrupt" unmasked by the guerrilla does not deny the existence of trustworthy leaders, nor the generosity of many others trying to accomplish the same goal. The awareness of a past and the desire for a future that is still seen as possible explain the "hate-o-cratic" attitude of these lyrics, since they trust neither the project nor the leadership needed to carry it out. Thus the relationship is accomplished through programs from the past and some of its leaders, which brings about a nostalgic recuperation of revolutionary Russia, an aspect achieved via the inclusion of a James Bond song of the 1960s: "From Russia with Love." The guitar-led melody transports the listener to a state in which the past seems to be re-created without the interference of the last three decades. The romance between the astute British hero and the Russian spy who falls in love, while providing a title to the film and its main theme, loses all sense of romanticism and privacy in order to awaken the nostalgia for what revolutionary Russia could have been: what is achieved is a nostalgic and loving salute to such a Russia.

Can one still defend the claim that Chilean rock music responds to an escapism and apathy that do nothing more than mock the civic irresponsibility of this generation that refuses to go to the polls? Cultural theoretician José Joaquín Brunner suggests otherwise:

> Consequently, one could ask if, behind this disappearance of the masses, there is not something different, much more interesting and revealing than mere "apathy." For example, whether it doesn't reflect, precisely, the breakdown of ideologies. Or whether that absence announces a new phenomenon of political decentering, which, upon becoming local and concrete, growing closer to the people's actual problems, will drift amid the loss of its massive base, of its character of collective spectacle.[28]

Given the apocalyptic perspective that interprets the current moment as a collapse of ideologies, it seems useful and legitimate to confront it with what Brunner describes as "political de-centering," to understand that such language no longer manifests itself in the same way, nor is it in the same spaces: it is in concerts, soccer games, spaces reserved for entertainment, for supposedly de-politicized activities. New pockets of political activism are found there. Apparently this desire to democratize culture certainly passes by and, at times, stops at the need to democratize politics. Although the decade of the 1960s is presented as the chosen past space because of its coincidence with childhood and private memory in a general historical sense, as Huyssen reminds us: "The neoconservative attack on all utopias as inherently and insidiously totalitarian and terrorist . . . has as its obvious goal the rewriting, if not the erasure of the effects of the 1960s, that decade of the recent past which most emphatically rekindled the utopian spirit."[29] It is not too illogical to suggest that, upon recuperating this time period, there is a search for the domestic past, while, at the same time, "the utopian imagination [which] has been transformed in recent decades, re-emerging in formerly unpredictable places such as the new social movements of the 1970s and the 1980s and being articulated from new and different subject positions."[30] That is to say, these subjects are located, not in the institutional political arena or in confrontation with such institutionalism, but rather on the margin, distrustful of governing politics and of governing practices. Chilean post-authoritarian rock evinces not de-politization, but rather the de-centering of institutional political discourse, and it does this by imposing the domestic space, the private memory that confronts, complements, or contrasts official memory, recovering and re-creating stigmatized musical forms. Memory and mourning coexist in this musical form that, in the new millennium, has begun to purge pain in the form of "tribute." This can be observed in the recently edited CDs, *Víctor Jara: Tributo Rock* and *Después de vivir un siglo: Tributo a Violeta Parra* (*After Living a Century: Tribute to Violeta Parra*). This provides sufficient reason to believe that what is evident is not amnesia but the emergence of new memories, or perhaps, the abandonment of the detour in favor of a better-known route to the past.

Selected Discography

Después de vivir un siglo: Tributo a Violeta Parra. Various artists. 2001. Warner Music Chile 092742458-2.

Javiera y Los Imposibles. *La suerte.* 1998. MGM Chile 74321 56291-2.

———. *A color.* 2000. Columbia Chile.

———. *AM.* 2001. Columbia Chile 5099750007129.

Los Miserables. *Cambian los payasos, pero el circo sigue.* 1997. Alerce Productions CDAE 0298.

Los Prisioneros. *Ni por la razón ni por la fuerza.* 1996. EMI Latin 72438 5257629.

Los Tres. *La espada y la pared.* 1995. Sony Music CNIA2-476096.

Un tributo a Sandro: Un disco de rock. Various artists. 1999. BMG B00001QEI3.

Vasconcellos, Joe. *Transformación.* 1997. EMI Odeón Chilena 72438 2106029.

Víctor Jara: Tributo Rock. Various artists. 2001. Alerce Producciones CDAE 0416.

The Nortec Edge

Border Traditions and "Electronica" in Tijuana

SUSANA ASENSIO

Electronic popular music, also known as Electronica, represents the ultimate paradigm of transnational music. Although it is produced all over the world and embraces virtually all kinds of music, styles, genres, and influences, Electronica follows fairly similar procedures everywhere: it is electronically manipulated and thus able to transform every unit of sound, every rhythm, in an endless flow of musical variations. Precisely because of the diversity of audiences it reaches and the re-processing of sounds it allows, Electronica creates a continuous feedback between the local and the global. Thus new styles are continuously being re-created within already established trends, transforming these trends and expanding their publics both on and off the dance floor. The international phenomenon of Electronica challenges traditional definitions of the global and the local, in which geographical limits and cultural "ethnoscapes" were clearly recognizable. In an effort to explore the nature of local responses to Electronica, this essay explores the case of "Nortec," a recent *propuesta* (proposal) in Electronica that appeared sometime during 1999 in Tijuana, a border city situated in the northern Mexican state of Baja California Norte, and that has since come to influence a burgeoning electronica scene throughout other parts of Mexico.[1]

Tijuana is one of the so-called twin cities, sharing its border with San Diego and thus serving as a point of departure for the countless Mexicans each year who seek work in the United States. As the largest of the border cities, Tijuana's social networks and cultural life are influenced both by the fact that almost half of the city's population is mobile, and by its status as a principal conduit for international drug traffic. Drug dealers, prostitutes, and the continuous flow of U.S. residents who cross the border both to shop and in search of vice, have all contributed to a negative image of Tijuana. Toward the end of the 1990s, however, an incipient Electronica scene emerged which implicitly challenged these negative associations. What would become known as the Nortec Collective asserted itself, and the Nortec style has gained international recognition, precisely by asserting its right to participate in global dance culture while simultaneously celebrating a sense of pride in originating in a place called Tijuana. Soon after its founding, Nortec, a term coined by joining the musical genre terms *norteño* and *techno,* became enormously popular in local venues throughout the so-called Tijuana Circuit—the name given to the triangle formed by Tijuana, Ensenada, and San Diego. The newly created Norteño Techno not only fit into the general dance music scene, but also expressed the cultural roots of the collective with a strongly local message transmitted by global means. Nortec musicians initially were made up mainly of electronica producers and DJs, but the collective soon grew to include graphic and fashion designers, photographers, painters, and architects involved in Tijuana's cultural life.

Nortec began as a musical *propuesta* based on a mixture of *norteño* (the generic term for popular country styles from the North of Mexico) and *banda sinaloense* (brass band music typical of the Mexican Pacific Coast) with electronic popular sounds and techniques. The foundational bands of the Nortec collective were performers from Tijuana like Panóptica (Roberto Mendoza was a former member of Artefakto and Fussible, and the founder of Noarte, a cultural organization in the city), Fussible (formed by Pepe Mogt and Jorge Ruiz, also from Artefakto), Bostich (Ramón Amezcua), and Clorofila (formed by Fritz Torres and Jorge Verdín), as well as some bands from Ensenada, like Terrestre (Fernando Corona), Plankton Man (Ignacio Chávez), and Hiperboreal (Gabriel Beas). Also included in the Nortec movement are Balboa, from Mexico City, and the DJ Tolo, founder of Tlahuilia Records in Tijuana, with whom some of the groups released their first works. After their first musical successes, the members of the collective expanded their horizons to embrace all of Tijuana—not just its musical traditions. Several graphic arts and fashion designers joined the project with the idea of forging a uniquely modernized *norteño* image of Tijuana. For example, these artists offered an ironic reappropriation of some of the most common stereotypes held about the city—its guns, marijuana, guitars, and cowboys. At the same time, local architect Raúl Cárdenas launched a project to dignify the makeshift reality of construction in the peripheral areas of the city. In sum, from the start Nortec was much more than simply a musical phenomenon. Rather, the artistic and social responses associated with Nortec reflected a much broader project aimed at fashioning a new cultural discourse. Several years later, Nortec has gained international attention and audiences, and many other local and non-local artists have become involved in the project. Yet, despite its "universal sound," the Nortec *propuesta* remains fundamentally rooted in local traditions: Nortec reflects a differential trend within Electronica that seeks to reconcile the musical traditions of the border with new sound technologies, while situating itself within the expansive, global genre of techno music.

In the Electronica of Nortec we find the most representative traditions of *norteño* and *banda sinaloense,* together with influences from Tijuana's popular music scene, which embraces rock sounds and punk philosophies. All these influences have been recycled using electronics to create a meaningful *propuesta*, which is at once representative of Tijuana's distinctiveness and of the border experience more generally. In order to fully understand this *propuesta*, however, it is necessary to outline in brief a history of Tijuana, its situation as a border city, and its musical scene during the years preceding the birth and success of Nortec.

Revisiting La Frontera: Tijuana and the Border

> All borders, by their very historical, political, and social constructions, serve as barriers of exclusions and protection, making "home" from the "foreign."[2]

In Mexico, because of its internal differences as well as the polarization between Mexico City and the rest of the country, identities seem to be switching to smaller "ethnoscapes" reflective of a multisided *mexicanidad,* a "Mexican-ness" in continuous reformulation. As an alternative for the term "neighborhood," which implies spatial boundaries and ethnic homogeneity, Appadurai introduced the term "ethnoscape" to invokes ideas of instability, fluidity, and disjunction.[3] The border areas of the country have become especially fertile ethnoscapes, as communities and individuals in continuous flux redefine their identities with respect to the political domination emanating from Mexico City, on one hand, and the overriding presence of the United States, on the other. For those on the border, the principal emblem of these identities "in construction," as well as its main watchtower, has been *la frontera,* a significant geographical and ideational space that has taken on special prominence for both countries in the past two decades. This border space is now characterized by the fact that it is a place where thousands of people cross back and forth between the two countries, as well as between the Mexican periphery and its central and southern provinces. Complex new hybrid identities have developed out of these ongoing emigrations and immigrations. Some authors have even catalogued this territory as a "third country,"[4] a unique space for creativity and experimentation, one that is captured through the work of border artists such as Guillermo Gómez Peña.

The definition of any region, nonetheless, must remain flexible in a geographical as well as in a temporal sense, for economic, social, political, and cultural borders rarely appear at the same point.[5] Borders, as liminal spaces, are not passive elements that simply delimit the boundaries of the nation-state, but rather are active agents of change in the sociopolitical processes that affect the countries that straddle such spaces. The Mexican–U.S. frontier has evolved over time into a differential, hybrid space in perpetual configuration and one that remains culturally relevant. In particular, two developments have had a definitive impact on the border: the twin cities structure, and the phenomenon of *maquiladoras*. Each of these, as we shall see, play a crucial role in defining the socioeconomic and cultural context in which Nortec emerged.

The so-called "shared cities," or "twin cities," phenomenon refers to the several pairs of closely situated cities that straddle each side of the border: Tijuana–San Diego, Laredo–Nuevo Laredo, Ciudad Juárez–El Paso, and Matamoros–Brownsville.[6] The cities of Tijuana and San Diego exemplify the interrelated yet independent nature of the twin city phenomenon in general. As David Lorey explains, following World War II San Diego benefited from the expansion of area military bases, "while Tijuana grew apace as a tourist center for both military personnel and southern Californians interested in the gambling and the nightlife."[7] In all of these cities, specific traits appear which distinguish them from the nation-state, of which they are periphery and limit, but also from the nearby foreign city, with which they act as osmotic membrane and filter.

A second defining characteristic of the border is the rise of the *maquilas,* or *maquiladoras,* foreign assembly plants that import duty-free components and raw goods from the United States and transform them into finished products that are then exported back across the border.[8] From a total of twelve plants in 1965, *maquila* operations had multiplied to 2,200 plants by 1996, with the majority concentrated in Tijuana and Ciudad Juárez.[9] Although providing employment, the low wages and repressive work environments of the plants restrict the possibility of social mobility while simultaneously creating a "pull" factor for emigrants from poorer parts of Mexico looking for work.

The close proximity of Tijuana and San Diego and the *maquila* phenomenon together have helped to create an environment that is socially dynamic, yet one that can also be extremely dangerous. Nortec's appeal, arguably, was precisely in that it chose to describe the border experience in an alternative way. The "philosophy" of Nortec was successful for several reasons. First, Tijuana became its emblem and nerve center, yet the cultural discourse of Nortec resonated for other places whose "borders" were not necessarily geographical. Second, Nortec embodied a manifesto clearly oriented toward the future but without putting aside local tradition or popular culture. Finally, Nortec did not seek to erase or even to denigrate explicitly the negative realities of Tijuana, but rather incorporated these associations (both real and stereotypical) into its philosophy with a subtle irony. The best example of this ironic appropriation comes from the graphic dimension of the movement, the main elements of which are discussed below.

From Rock to Electronica, and from Tijuana to the World

In spite of all the contradictions and particularities of Tijuana, or maybe because of them, the varied rock scene that arose in the city during the 1980s did not succeed completely. Most local groups did not make it beyond the local network of venues and clubs; and by the end of the decade, that same network was being used for other purposes, leaving rock bands with an insufficient number of places in which to perform.[10] Some bands in the city transformed their music into a kind of postindustrial rock by melding the sounds of punk from the early 1980s with minimalist and industrial influences of groups like Kraftwerk, and then incorporating more and more electronic sounds.[11] This was the musical environment in which Nortec appeared. The main novelty of the movement was the incorporation of local musical traditions into electronic dance music, and the ironic yet positive view of Tijuana that the Nortec pioneers chose to represent in their music to the public. Technology was the means to master an uncertain future in these new projects, allowing for the incorporation of local traditions to transmit a message of empowerment and re-enchantment.

As electronica music, Nortec did not emerge out of a vacuum. Postindustrial or electronic rock was already well known throughout Mexico, and groups such as Deus ex Machina, Artefakto, Década Dos, and Ford Proco had been recording a mixture of industrial rock and Electronica (the so-called "industrial music") for several years. But at the time of Nortec's emergence, this movement was suffering from a crisis of musical identity within Mexico. One of the most respected groups, Artefakto, broke up in 1998, but its members soon became active in Nortec.[12] In 1999 one of Artefakto's former members explained:

> The industrial-electronic-rock hybrid . . . kept us dazzled and trapped until the mid-nineties, but after 1995 . . . we didn't like it anymore; nothing had happened since the eighties, the sound of most groups in the scene became a cliché, with boring rhythms and distorted voices, machine gun sequences. . . . Being mature means not only learning from your experiences, but also being open to new possibilities and accepting that at some point we all have to conclude certain chapters in our lives in order to be able to write new ones.[13]

Even though it was produced in Mexico, Electronica was not viewed as particularly "Mexican," which differentiated it especially from the support given to *rock nacional*. In Artefakto's last CD (*Interruptor,* 1997), songs appear randomly in English and Spanish. One of the Spanish tracks on the record ("Sumisión") deals with the lack of hope in a world controlled by other people:

> Tras el día y tras la noche
> Ya no distingo por pagar
> En unos días o en unos años
> O hasta cuando sea normal.
> Mira esas caras,
> No te dicen nada al voltear,
> Ignorancia absoluta es quien te da el poder
> Es quien te deja hoy obrar,
> Es quien te deja manipular,
> Es absurdo y ridículo,
> Imperdonable e inexplicable.
> Cuánto tiempo más vamos a esperar,
> Cuánto quieres más
> y cuánto nos queda?
> Y soñamos con cambiar,
> A nuestro dolor controlar.
> Cómo podremos seguir más?
> Déjanos sentir vivos otra vez,
> Miéntenos aunque sea una vez más.
>
> (After the day and after the night
> I don't differentiate my debts anymore
> In a few days or years
> Or even when it's normal.
> Look at those faces,

> They tell you nothing as they pass
> Absolute ignorance gives you power,
> And allows you to act,
> And to manipulate,
> It is absurd and ridiculous,
> It is unforgivable and inexplicable.
> How much longer are we going to wait,
> How much more do you want
> and how much more do we have left?
> And we dream of changing,
> controlling our pain.
> How will we be able to continue?
> Let us feel alive again,
> Lie to us just one more time.)

It is easy to recognize in the track the manipulation of sounds, especially the use of filters, which serve as an apocalyptic aesthetic evoking loss, destruction, and the lack of a place in the world, the void described by Martín Barbero as "the unfulfilled promise of modernity."[14] It is the hopeless atmosphere of the postindustrial 1990s or, as the title of Ford Proco's last release reads, "the mud-and-honey vertigo."[15]

Despite the ambiguity of the term "postindustrial," and the fact that this type of development simultaneously overlaps with other types,[16] the term has distinct connotations. It is here referred to as an unbounded period of time linked to specific urban environments: those affected by global changes in their economic, work, and social structures, in the distribution of goods, and thus, in their forms of expressive culture. We can relate this postindustrial period to the advent of the computer age and the changes in industrial economies. Although these conditions are specific to each particular place and appear at different times, they are ordinarily followed by punk-like movements that express their reactions against the situation created by a lack of hope. The aesthetic legacy of the "no-future" philosophy was the "do-it-yourself" artistic approach, which can also be found in Tijuana's Nortec.

Other Mexican bands outside the city were likewise expressing in their lyrics and "paratexts" a lack of hope.[17] Most of them were part of the postindustrial electronic, rock, and punk scenes. The Mexico City group Deus ex Machina pointed out the future's alienating character in a bilingual text that accompanied their 1992 release:

> DEUS ex MACHINA. This is the spirit of a time that has not come yet, but to which we vertiginously soar. An obscure vision of the future, a tragic

and aggressive image. Deus ex Machina is cyberpunk because it peeks at the future to find a senseless and manipulated atmosphere, genetically disturbed where reality becomes a fantasy by a digital process, allowing the individual to sink into virtual horizons.[18]

Showing a ferocious nihilism, the band openly celebrated a "no-future" aesthetics throughout their material. Their sounds were digitally manipulated to transmit a sense of obscurity and devastation, while the image on the cover of their CD shows a hybrid of a Mexican Indian morphing into a robot. Although the lyrics are difficult to understand due to the electronic manipulation of the vocals, their track "Crisis of Identity #1749" suggests a continuum of hopeless expressions:

> Negra conciencia
> falsa cordura enferma
> normalidad convertida en genocidio
> causa del efecto de la causa
> violencia no basta
> deseas tu destrucción
> necesidad emocional
> consumo irracional
> escape de la realidad
> juegos de crimen y corrupción
> violencia no basta
> deseas la destrucción
> adicción a la sumisión
> ansiedad en la máquina social
> te conformas con la marcha
> o te aplastan al pasar.
>
> (Black conscience
> sick false awareness
> normality transformed into genocide
> cause of an effect of a cause
> violence is not enough
> you wish for your destruction
> emotional necessity
> irrational consumerism
> escape from reality
> crime games and corruption
> violence is not enough

you wish for destruction
addiction to submission
anxiety in the social machine
you go along with the rest
or they crush you as they pass.)

Interestingly, the same sounds expressing devastation were later converted into dance floor hits in Tijuana. This was the beginning of the recycling process. The "no-future" trend was about to be transformed into an "all-future" one.

Carlos Gaviria understands the expression "no-future" as the "representation of the ideology of a society that no longer makes objects to last a lifetime, but to exist during the time imposed by the industrial logic, that is, the logic of publicity."[19] It is precisely that industrial logic which brought disenchantment when it failed in its project of modernity, not only in Mexico, but all around the world. This lack of hope, this disenchantment, crystallized aesthetically during the postindustrial era into practices of recycling and the appropriatiation of urban objects and spaces through technology. Following Echevarren, "no-future" would thus be the label of an ideological as well as an aesthetic vision characterized by the lack of hope: "[These] attitudes and behaviors . . . show that the struggle for a better future, for changing the world and justifying any claim is over."[20] The aesthetic crystallization of this thought took place in the cultural tendency of recycling, based on a new appropriation of the environment epitomized by the phrase "do-it-yourself," or "DIY." Polhemus points out that the most interesting novelty brought by punk cultures was their response to the lack of hope. In his book about street styles Polhemus explains how the punk generation "grew up in the shadow of the hippies' ever optimistic, utopian dream." With a "cynical shrug," punk marched in a different direction entirely and in the process "changed the world." Punk's insistence that both music and style should derive from a DIY approach to life gave rise, Polhemus emphasizes, "to endless, bizarre variety."[21] In turn, the "do-it-yourself" approach from the punk era was transformed with the new technologies into a recycling machine oriented to the future.

Mexican Electronica from the late-1990s was, thus, profoundly different from that of the early-1990s, as represented by Artefakto and Deus ex Machina, in that it transmitted a new positive message, a hopeful alternative. While certain groups like Artefakto and Deus ex Machina disappeared from the music scene altogether (the former members of Artefakto gave rise to the Electronica groups Fussible and Panóptica, part of the Nortec collective), others like Ford Proco converted fully into Electronica and abandoned their former rock influences. Limits, borders, and differences no longer had a disengaging effect. Instead, they were configuring a place for integration and hybridization. As the booklet contained in Nortec's first CD release explained:

> Nortec distills the essence of the local borderland, with a transcultural amalgam of *norteño* Mexican folklore and a catalytic global Electronica creating new, strangely familiar sounds and dances. An evolutionary system of binomials, of identity itself, they are the point of departure of a transition between protest and *propuesta*, they are agents of change that, parallel with the visual, architectural, and graphic arts, plot a narrative of new processes, behaviors, and generational forms, scouting in content like an omnipresent aleph that, no matter where you go, points forward, to *nortec*.[22]

Traditional Roots Updated: Ethnicity in a Global Age

> The affirmation of particular traditions leads to diverse ways of insertion into the global scene, or into its margins . . . but it is never simple or just a mere opposition.[23]

As a project, Nortec was created to recycle, mix, and re-create the urban and the traditional in Tijuana, moving beyond the former machinist and apocalyptic visions. Pepe Mogt, of the group Fussible, described Nortec as "a style of electronic music born in Mexico" that combines influences of the North (in particular, Tijuana and Ensenada) with those from the capital, Mexico City. "Most of all," Mogt argues, "Nortec recycles sounds from the city, re-using some and deleting the rest." Describing it as "a genre that can be incorporated into other existing genres," he emphasizes its uniqueness by calling attention to its "personal sound, an abstract Electronica with acoustic sounds and Mexican grooves manipulated electronically."[24] Two principal musical influences define the local component of Nortec: *banda sinaloense* and *conjunto norteño*. *Banda sinaloense* refers to brass-band ensembles (which derive originally from the northwestern state of Sinaloa) whose distinct character, the so-called "Sinaloan flavor," is the result of the "contrast of clarinet and brass timbres, the juxtaposition of *tutti-soli* (that is, an alternation between the whole *banda* and the individual instrument groups), and the improvisation of countermelodies on one of the front-line instruments, a technique that is nowadays often used while accompanying vocalists. There is [also] a strong emphasis on volume and pulse."[25]

From Sinaloa, *banda* music traveled to other parts of Mexico, and although Sinaloa is not a border state, its identity is nevertheless linked to Tijuana and the border imaginary due to a number of common circumstances. For example, Sinaloa is said to be the place where most of Mexico's marijuana is produced, while Tijuana is the main traffic center for its distribution to the United States. Moreover, the distribution of *maquiladoras* extends to Sinaloa along the coast, thus introducing certain elements of the border experience (such as an intensive social fluidity and an influx of migrants from other states) to Mexican cities that are far beyond from the border itself. Lorey thus argues that "border phenomena are experienced as far from the international boundary as . . . Sinaloa, Durango, Jalisco, and the Yucatán Peninsula . . . where the *maquiladora* production has pulled people into the border world."[26]

Spreading along the line established by the *maquilas*, Sinaloan *banda* arrived in Tijuana, often in the form of *technobandas*, an updated formation of *banda sinaloense* which incorporated modern instruments. Reaching across the border, Mexican American youth in Los Angeles latched onto *technobanda* as a means of preserving their provincial identities within a modern and "foreign" setting. As Helen Simonett writes, during the 1990s, "a whole new generation of young fans in the metropolitan area of Los Angeles began to appropriate musical styles of the Mexican working-class, but also to re-signify them as symbols of their own cultural identity."[27] The most characteristic sounds of these bands were the percussion of *tarolas* (snare drum) and the brass wind instruments (for example, tuba, trumpet), and these were the favorite samples picked up by Nortec for their mixes. The rhythmic use of *tarolas* and *tamboras* (a double-headed bass drum) made audiences dance, which was fundamental to the rapid spread of the music. Soon clubs were packed with audiences who responded more to the music than to Nortec's cultural and ideological project per se. Tijuana's youth first danced to the sounds of Nortec and only afterward acknowledged the traditions involved in the creative process. As a twenty-three-year-old clubber put it: "I'm not a big fan of that music [referring to *banda* and *norteño* music], but now that I hear it this way, combined, it sounds so cool . . ."[28]

In addition to the vertical axis drawn by *banda* from Sinaloa to Tijuana, a second, horizontal axis is the one that integrates *norteño* music along the U.S.–Mexican border. Known often as Tex-Mex on the U.S. side of the border, this music is mainly performed in Mexico by *conjuntos norteños*, small bands built around the central element of an accordion. The roots of *norteño* music can be traced back to the polka music of Czech and German immigrants who settled in northern Mexico and south Texas in the mid-1800s. The accordion-based dance music flourished among the Mexican population in the border region and developed into a particular style. In the 1950s innovative *norteño* groups integrated a vocalist and updated their instrumentation by adding electric bass and percussion. Two decades later, *norteño* music had spread along the border and into the Mexican and U.S. interior. The importance of this music to the Nortec phenomenon is that it is a specific border tradition shared by both sides. Referring to the Mexican American *orquesta,* (an ensemble related to Mexican *norteño* bands), Manuel Peña points out that Mexican Americans found themselves "caught in a double bind, an untenable position between two class and cultural worlds." In response to this dilemma of trying to "reconcile their Mexican past and their American future . . . [a] pervasive biculturalism emerged as a 'solution,' expressed in bilingualism and such forms of expressive culture as the *bimusical orquesta*." Peña emphasizes that "almost by definition, this biculturalism remained dynamic."[29]

Both *banda* and *norteño* represent the bicultural character of the border. Both are considered as straddling the line between traditional and popular music. Although neither originated in Tijuana, both are regarded as representative of Tijuana's musical traditions, for each is representative of cultures along the border. It is precisely this hybrid that, for the Nortec collective, defines Tijuana. Hence by combining Electronica with the punk philosophies of appropriation, recycling, and a DIY approach to music, Nortec became a natural way for producers and DJs to represent the city, and, by extension, the cultural experience of the border.

New Marketing Strategies for a New "Glocal" Age

> Border music is simultaneously national and transnational in that it affects everyday life in the local . . . region and thematizes the limits of the national perspective in American studies.[30]

Legend says that it was Pepe Mogt, a member of Fussible, who started the Nortec movement when he went looking for raw sounds from local *banda* musicians in Tijuana to blend together with techno. He began to record live performances and musicians in the streets, but the tracks did not mix well with Electronica because of background noise. So he went to various studios, where he was able to acquire outtakes from *banda* and other recordings, which he then distributed among his friends. After several weeks, many came up with different examples of what later would be called Nortec. The tracks all sounded different and yet they shared a common "flavor." This initial group of producers played the first three tracks for local DJs and the response was overwhelming. Different clubs began to ask for the music and the news spread rapidly: "People from all over Mexico started calling and saying, 'Can you come

Image created by Angeles Moreno to represent Nortec. Used by permission.

here and play Nortec?' I didn't know what to say; there were only three songs," Pepe Mogt later recalled.[31]

The initial samples of Sinaloan *banda* and *norteño* sounds led to a further exploration of the city and its realities. "Now it is not about recording sequences from the keyboards, but capturing and salvaging the sounds of the city," stresses one of the members of Fussible.[32] The traditional music samples served as a point of departure for a further exploration of the Tijuana reality. "Nortec is an expression of a way of life, the way we live in Tijuana," emphasized Ramón Amor Amezcua, aka Bostich.[33] The link with mainstream Electronica came from different sources, the most important of which was radio. During the 1990s, San Diego radio stations began placing their transmitters south of the border to circumvent U.S. regulations. Local musicians in Tijuana discovered late-night broadcasts of electronic music popular in the United States, and later explored works from contemporary European composers like Luciano Berio and Krzystof Penderecki. Some of these Tijuana groups, including Bostich, subsequently produced albums in various electronic styles, but their sound was derivative of foreign models—until the inclusion of local music in 1999 and the subsequent development of Nortec.

The foreign and national musical press soon began reporting enthusiastically about Nortec, describing it as a new Mexican genre. An article in the *Los Angeles Times,* for instance, labeled Nortec a "revolutionary new movement" while arguing that it had been "years—arguably decades—since Latin music experienced the creation of a new, original genre."[34] But at the local level Nortec was being experienced more as a holistic cultural movement, and the musicians associated with it insisted on identifying their work as an artistic expression linked to Tijuana's complex reality. Tijuana was explicitly identified as their source of inspiration.[35] For instance, one of the landmark tracks of the movement, Fussible's "Odyssea 2000" was inspired by a Tijuana nightclub that once hosted raves but that later featured live *norteño* and *banda* performances. Ironically, this stress on the local scene was the perfect entranceway into the global Electronica market.

In interviews carried out with various members of the Nortec collective, the thing they point out is the differing responses to the music, depending on where it is played. For example, in Rosarito and Ensenada, clubbers mix with more traditional audiences to dance *cumbia, quebradita* or techno-like style to Nortec tracks. In Mazatlán (Sinaloa), the homeland of *banda sinaloense,* the first responses were not positive, as local clubbers saw *banda* music in opposition to Electronica; however, as Nortec began to gain popularity, the response became more positive. In London, the track "Odyssea 2000" by Fussible reached number one on the BBC, but the group was identified as "South American" instead of Mexican. In New York City, Nortec was linked to Latino popular music, especially to the local rock scene, which inevitably stressed predominant Mexican stereotypes rather than the group's border identity.[36]

In any event, the popularity of the movement grew spectacularly during the year 2000, especially among those who had access to the Internet.[37] Part of the music's success is related to the multimedia nature of the phenomenon, that is, the close relationship between sounds and innovative graphic designs. The designs intended to represent Nortec gave the movement a recognizable and idiosyncratic image that appealed to the various dimensions of the phenomenon. Various artists from Mexico and beyond designed colorful icons intended to evoke the border, and thus the local within the national and transnational: these ranged from guns to guitars, accordions to marijuana leaves, makeshift shacks to oversized *norteño* hats. Surprisingly, however, the percussion and brass winds—the most characteristic sounds of the movement—were not so widely distributed as graphic icons. Some of the images created for Nortec come from San Diego, such as those produced by Jorge Naranjo and Gerardo Yepiz. Others come from Tijuana, such as those by Fritz Torres and Angeles Moreno. Even the Argentinian designer Jorge Sánchez has contributed to the creation of images for Nortec. Nonetheless all of them share some common traits: the mix of traditional and avant-garde designs, the recurrence of the *norteño* hat, and an ironic view in which positive and negative stereotypes intermix within the same image.

As the movement developed rapidly, more and more artists began to contribute to the initial musical proposal. The movement became richer and more

Image created by Gerardo Yepiz (Tijuana–San Diego) to represent Nortec. The image represents Luis Donaldo Colosio, with a *norteño* hat. The Mexican presidential candidate of the Partido Revolucionario Institucional (PRI) was assassinated in Tijuana on March 23, 1994. The image normally appears with the message "Regresaré" (I will return) at the bottom. Used by permission.

complex, and also more representative of the city's cultural life. In July 2000 the first Nortec Festival was held in Tijuana. It consisted of many live sessions by different producers, exhibitions by graphic designers, colloquia and conferences about electronic popular music and its connections with the twentieth century avant-garde, turntable-ism workshops, and computer music demonstrations. The exhibition of graphic designs was promoted by the American Institute of Graphic Arts of Baja California (Instituto Americano de las Artes Gráficas de Baja California), and many of the most representative images of Nortec were presented there for the first time. Besides its status as musical movement, Nortec was intended to be a point of encounter and reference for the expressive culture of the northwestern border region. As has also happened with hip-hop and techno, Nortec's message succeeded once it reunited the musical, visual, and graphic avant-gardes.

The link with architecture arose from the fact that the mobile population in Tijuana often builds provisional homes by recycling materials from the city, including the incorporation of garage doors brought to the border from San Diego. Although makeshift, these homes have left a distinctive mark on the economically peripheral areas of Tijuana. Seeking to acknowledge and valorize this aesthetic reality, architect Raúl Cárdenas initiated a project within the

CD cover of *Bostich + Fussible* (Mil Records, 2000) showing the "provisional" constructions in Tijuana. Designed by TOROLAB/Raúl Cárdenas. Used by permission.

city's cultural center to celebrate these constructions as characteristic of Tijuana: they would symbolize the "do-it-yourself" philosophy of the recycling practice that was also present in the Nortec movement. These constructions, in turn, became part of the graphic designs used on the cover of the 2000 release by Bostich and Fussible, thereby reiterating the local roots of the movement.

Beyond the Border: Electronic Re-enchantments

> It is impossible to understand what the vertigo of velocity means to a young person today, or the ecstasy of drugs, if we don't put it in a dialogue with the profound disenchantment in which we are living nowadays.[38]

Martín Barbero writes about how modernity has broken the enchantment of the world by rationalizing it, thus taking away the magic and mystery.[39] He also tells us about how the recuperation of this sense of magic ironically comes in many cases via technology.[40] Technology offers the potential power to change the world, which makes it a balsam of re-enchantment for a vast number of young people. The technological possibilities in music are immense: the production of new sounds, sampling, filtering, changing of frequencies and amplitudes. All these possibilities are now available with a personal computer minimally equipped and connected to the Internet.

While all of these processes have been developed in different ways in music, each also is linked idiosyncratically with the spaces from whence they appear and with which they interact. For instance, Detroit's initial techno was linked by its pioneers Derrick May, Kevin Saunderson, and Juan Atkins to the new technologies appearing in the music industry during the 1980s, and to the particular industrial history of the city. The message brought by this new genre was "to cross the race, class, intellectual, and sexual boundaries."[41] Detroit is described as a place "where the burned-out cliché of urban decay and bleak desolation exists only for those that haven't acquired The Vision®."[42] This "Vision," for techno followers, means the ability to transform a formerly hostile environment into someplace livable. In the opinion of these "techno godfathers," this music could not have been created in any other city in the world but Detroit. Similarly, the House movement in Chicago and New York used new technologies during the 1980s to transform disco music into a fresh phenomenon able to attract youth to the dance floor again. One thing common to both of these movements is that technology served to fulfill the hedonistic pleasure of dance. Following John Gill, this hedonism is crucial to understand the success of dance music. Dance music, he writes, has become "the one form of music which, even in its most degraded form, is bound up in something that closely resembles Roland Barthes's notion of *jouissance*, that is, rapture, bliss, or transcendance"; it is "a music whose whole point is both to describe and to induce rapture."[43]

As a site of origin for a new musical phenomenon, Tijuana presents a very specific case, for it is a border city, a "no-place," a place of transit with few permanent elements.[44] Moreover Tijuana represents a case of double marginality, both as border (with the United States) and as periphery (within the global economy, within the Mexican nation). Like hip-hop and its musical expression rap (born in the Bronx), *mangue bit* in Brazil (born in Recife, a northwestern Brazilian city built on the swamps), and techno (forged in Somerville, a marginal area of Detroit), Nortec was also born in marginality. Indeed all of these musical movements occurred in what May Joseph calls "the global peripheries."[45] Taking these cases into account, we can no longer discuss the "localization" of "global practices" in particular places; instead we have to acknowledge that every transformation is not only different, but has unique meanings, aims, and practices, which make it understandable only through the dialogue and interdependence between multiple imaginary as well as real centers and peripheries.

Nortec incorporates in its discourse not only avant-garde technologies, but also the most traditional and rudimentary ones. From the most simple techniques, like cut-and-paste, bricolage, and recycling, to the most advanced, like electronic transformation and digital filters, Electronica styles incorporate into their discourses all the technologies available in the place where their re-enchantments occur. In Nortec, the "music from the streets" was again the territorialized source serving as the basis for development of a differential electronic sound. Through the mixture of recognizable traditional elements and distinctive new ones, the ascription of the movement and its significance became more complex and, at the same time, meaningful for broader audiences. The music acquired a hybrid dimension that makes it paradigmatic for many other Latin American cities: it suggests transition and overlapping sociocultural processes, yet it de-dramatizes these conflicts by exposing the disjunctures and contradictions as creative and evocative qualities.

Significantly, in the music of Nortec messages are no longer where they used to be, namely, in the lyrics of the songs. The messages, instead, have become more complex and have expanded to the images and the paratexts, as is common with other experimental electronic music movements. Although some of the tracks produced by the Nortec collective include lyrics, most of the information regarding the movement comes from other sources, such as CD booklets and Web pages put together by producers, record labels, and fans. These paratexts are a complement to the listening, but they also influence and mediate the way the music is understood. In Nortec sounds do not exist any longer per se, but as a means of transmitting messages, as new forms of communication that appeal to the intellect and the body through technology.

Nortec is thus justified as an aesthetic *propuesta* of a future worth living. This *propuesta* stresses the regeneration of hope and experience, and while Nortec has kept its local audiences first in mind, the message has in turn become universal. Through the use of global technologies and techniques, the Nortec collective has succeeded in connecting the experiences of a particular place with general international trends. Local traditions are empowered and universalized as positive sources of inspiration. Taken into international arenas, local significance is not diminished but rather enhanced through what Roland Roberson terms a new, "glocal" form of communication.[46]

An important element of the glocal, moreover, is derived from the new significance ascribed to modern cities as part of the symbolic imaginary of non-territorialized social groups, such as those constituted around Electronica. Non-territorialized groups, or what Andy Bennett describes as "neo-tribes,"[47] share similar characteristics of being cosmopolitan even when the space in which they inhabit may be located in the marginalized peripheries. In Nortec, the role of the urban environment was clearly defined from the start. For example, live samplings of urban sounds, such as those from performances by local musicians playing in venues around the city, were manipulated electronically in the studio along with prerecorded sounds in a search for a proper "groove."[48] The use of the urban environment, however, was approached differently from that evoked by rock bands during the 1980s: it is not just a physical space to conquer, but a symbolic place to be embraced. Rosana Reguillo discusses the case of Latin American cities of the 1980s and 1990s in a similar way:

> During the 1980s we discussed the territory, the neighborhood as epicenter of practices and nucleus of the processes of construction of identity for middle- and low-class youths in cities. But during the 1990s the generalized crisis, the changes brought by globalization, and the local specificity of its manifestations point to a displacement of the notion of identity from that referred to the *locus*, to this new one articulated around many and varied elements at the same time.[49]

Nowadays, the "city" is many cities at the same time: it incorporates rural traditions through emigration and enables the coexistence of different overlapping worlds that operate simultaneously in a shared space. Cities function as sites in which different elements clash with synergetic consequences. Tijuana made Nortec possible precisely because it provided the necessary international character while offering the specificity of local culture and sounds. As has happened with other cultural projects, both cosmopolitanism and differentiability reinforced each other, allowing local audiences to recognize the phenomenon as their own while international audiences explore its exotic distinctiveness.[50]

The history of Nortec has been documented almost before the process has had time to sediment. There are ongoing discussions, conference papers, press articles, radio programs, and a vast number of Web pages that follow news related to the movement. In less than three years, the scope of the project has become tremendously complex, especially given its short duration. Several CDs by the Nortec collective are now on the market, along with other compilations in which some of the original producers collaborated. As of 2002 these included *The Spaced Tj: Dub* (1999), *Fono* (1999), *Tijuana Bass Sampler* (1999), *Nortec Sampler, Vol. 1* (1999), *Nortec Sampler, Vol. 2* (2000), *Bostich + Fussible: Nortec Remixes* (2000), and *The Tijuana Sessions* (2001). Audiences in many Mexican and U.S. cities, but also in Berlin (Love Parade, 2000), Tokyo (2000), and Barcelona (Festival Sonar 2001) have listened to Nortec, both on recordings and live. The Internet, moreover, has emerged as the main means of disseminating information and music from the collective, and thus reaches untold audiences around the world, together with journals, magazines, and newspapers.

Most Electronica in "developed" countries is enriched by experimental discourses; new frontiers are created with every inclusion. By contrast, Electronica is recycled, hybridized, and reterritorialized in places like Latin America, where a dialogue with local traditions is established. Electronica can be appropriated and given expressive form in places where it has had no distinct significance before. Whether Nortec becomes a new mainstream form or simply stands as an exotic product for international markets, its short history already shows that it has accomplished an important task, namely, that of providing a new sensibility and modern expression to the chaos of coexisting cultures, socioeconomic anxieties, and diverse aesthetic influences in one very particular place: Tijuana.

Selected Discography

Artefakto. *Interruptor.* 1997. Opción Sónica OPCD55.
Bostich. *Tijuana Bass Sampler.* 1999. Produced by Mil Records.
Bostich and Fussible. *Bostich + Fussible: Nortec Remixes.* 2000. Mil Records OPCD132.
Deus ex Machina. *Deus ex Machina.* 1992. Opción Sónica OPCD04.
Ford Proco. *Vértigo de lodo y miel.* 2000. Nimboestatic AT003/NIM005CD.
Fussible. *Fono.* 1999. Opción Sónica OPICD108.
Nortec Sampler. 1999. Produced by Mil Records.
Nortec, Vol. 1. 1999. Mil Records PALMCD 2045-2 (LP).
Nortec, Vol. 2. 2000. Mil Records (LP).
Nortec Collective. *The Tijuana Sessions,* vol. 1. 2001. Mil Records–PALMCD.
The Spaced TJ: Dub. 1999. Produced by Mil Records–Tlahuilia (EP).

Esperando La Última Ola / Waiting for the Last Wave

Manu Chao and the Music of Globalization

JOSH KUN

> It is not only by shooting bullets in the battlefields that tyranny is overthrown, but also by hurling ideas of redemption, words of freedom and terrible anathemas against the hangmen that people bring down dictators and empires.
> —Emiliano Zapata

Subcomandante Manu

In 1994, only months after the EZLN, the Zapatista Army of National Liberation, first emerged out of the Lacandón jungle to occupy San Cristobal de Las Casas and hold a deeply cracked mirror up to the face of contemporary Mexico, the Franco-Spanish band Mano Negra released their final album, *Casa Babylon*. Recorded while the band was touring Latin America, the album touched on everything from ragga to salsa, but it began in Chiapas, with a tribute to guerrilla insurgent leader Subcomandante Marcos and his Internet- and fax-issued "Declaration of War" against Mexican political lies. The opening track of the album was named "Viva Zapata," in which chants of "El pueblo, unido, jamás será vencido" unfurled over an escalating funk groove. It was the first recorded musical testimony to Marcos's new-school Zapatismo.[1]

The EZLN's campaign for indigenous dignity—built on demands for indigenous land rights, self-government, political equality, and self-education—was a perfect Mano Negra cause.[2] Born in 1987 out of the ashes of the post-Punk Parisian underground bands Hot Pants and Los Carayos, and led by Manu Chao (the French son of anti-*franquista* Spanish exiles), Mano Negra positioned themselves as anarchic, polylinguistic ringleaders of an international, postcolonial underclass. They were themselves a band of ex-Europeans, a wandering gaggle of Europe's Others—Spanish refugees, North African immigrants, *gitanos*. Showcasing the hybrid, wild-style carnival mix of rock, cowpunk, Algerian rai, and Afro-Cuban rhythms they called *"patchanka,"* early Mano Negra songs like "Sidi H' Bibi," "Indios de Barcelona," and "Peligro" flipped between English, Spanish, Arabic, and French to unpack Europe as an exploding bomb of immigrant sounds and boiling third world anger. "There's going to be war on the streets," Chao threatened on "Indios de Barcelona": "Gringo better take a trip trip trip."[3]

The liner notes to Mano Negra's debut album, *Patchanka*, were littered with immigration documents and passport stamps. Next to the lyrics for "Killin Rats" (where Chao decries political "rats" like Adolf Hitler, who "set the world on fire") is a faux-CIA wanted poster with Chao's photograph: "Wanted for subversive lyrics, corrupting songs, outrageous guitar-playing, sexually explicit voice committed in this album." From their very beginnings in Paris, Mano Negra flaunted their ambivalent relationship to European nationalism (musicians who needed immigration papers and passport stamps to belong as citizens) and their desire for musical subversion by singing threatening, seditious, "wanted" songs that critiqued the European political order—in order to "provincialize Europe" to use Dipesh Chakrabarty's term—from the stage of a nightclub.[4]

Mano Negra eventually left Europe altogether for its former colonies in Latin America, beginning in 1992, when they started playing working-class port towns from the deck of a traveling ship as part of their Cargo Tour. The trip produced the most oft-cited piece of Mano Negra lore: when asked what anarchy meant by an Argentinean talk show host, the band trashed the studio. A year later, they were doing free shows with local street musicians in train stations across Colombia. It all just fed the Afro-Latin *menudo* of *Casa Babylon*'s Latin American critical fury. "Goodbye Paris," Chao sang on "Drives Me Crazy": "I'm leavin' you. Nothing they said about you is true." On "Señor Matanzas," the band chanted down Latin American military dictators. On "Sueño de Solentiname," they dreamed of Guanajuato, Guatemala, and Panama during the same night of unrest, asking the "beloved world" to relieve them of a suffering that has no cure. And on "Bala Perdida," the world's urban centers seethed with "*guajira* blood" and "explosive cargo," where people "boil night and day on the avenue." "When they ask for liberty," Chao laments, "they don't give it to them." Chao had always treated Mano Negra's songs as if they were agit-pop comic books. On *Casa*, he recycled themes ("the last wave" before the end of the world) and characters, like Super Chango (the Yoruban thunder god reborn as a Latin American answer to Batman) or the kicked-around "little monkey" of the urban jungle who "speaks his mind" and takes over cosmopolitan capitals as "King of the Bongo" and one of the "King Kong Five."

Long considered a masterpiece of kinetic aural globalism, *Casa Babylon*'s gleeful Spanish and English merger of rock, funk, dancehall, and rap (with hints of zouk, mariachi, and rai) has grown over the years into a sort of unofficial template for Latin American *rockeros* looking for models of New World collision. When I interviewed Monterrey, Mexico's Plastilina Mosh, years ago, their ex-*trashero* guitarist and rapper Jonas couldn't stop beaming about Chao, crediting *Casa Babylon* as the inspiration for Plastilina's 1998 break-beat and monster truck lounge session *Aquamosh*. And in 1995, Tijuana NO drummer Alex Zuniga wouldn't let me out of his house in Playas de Tijuana until I had seen his copy of a Mano Negra book, which, along with essays, lyrics, and polemics, contained all of Chao's art collages from the band's album covers: *lotería* cards, bar codes, cabaret playbills, newspaper clippings, and kitschy images of ethnographic natives.

But Mano Negra's audience was never just limited to one city, one continent, or one region. The audience the band sang about and sang for covered a wide, internationalist terrain populated by immigrants, exiles, political dissidents, and refugees from Tijuana to Gibraltar, from Paris to Algiers. In their seven years as a group, Mano Negra's music became a galvanizing node in a dissenting globalist circuit of musical activists that grew to include Tijuana NO in Mexico, Bad Brains in D.C., and the Basque separatists Negu Gorriak in Spain. Of course, their message also eventually reached back to Chiapas. In February 1999, Mano Negra was included in an EZLN communiqué issued by Subcomandante Marcos and addressed to "Musicians of the World." Marcos offered his gratitude to a long list of bands who have pledged their support for the Zapatista struggle in dedicatory songs, benefit concerts, and political protests—artists who have all used their music to echo the Chiapas cry for dignity and justice, "Ya basta." He even sent Lacandonian shout-outs to ticket sellers and roadies. Marcos wrote, "Viejo Antonio said . . . that music holds roads that only the knowledgeable know how to walk and that it . . . builds bridges that bring closer worlds that otherwise you wouldn't even dream about."[5]

The memo had come five years too late. By the end of 1994, Mano Negra's multinationalism had toppled beneath the weight of its own musical Babel, and Manu Chao went missing-in-action, existing only as pseudo-legend for the next four years: an insurgent Parisian-Basque nomad who travels the Americas without an identity, is wanted by goon squads across the planet, and hangs out, whenever he can, in Tijuana. He resurfaced in 1998 with a long-awaited solo album, *Clandestino*. "To run is my destiny, to make fun of the law," it began. "Lost in the heart of the Great Babylon, they call me the clandestine one because I don't have papers." Chao recorded *Clandestino* on an eight-track recorder and a six-string guitar, while traveling from Africa to Latin America to Europe. He sampled radio broadcasts from his temporary homes across the planet and also sampled the voice of Subcomandante Marcos on "Luna y sol." "For us, rebellious dignity. For us, the negated future. For us, the future, nothing," Marcos says, right after Chao sings, over and over again, "Everything is a lie in this world."

Though it fashioned itself as an album without maps, an album that moved freely back and forth across North Africa, Europe, and the Americas, *Clandestino* did have two geographical centers, both of them border cities: Gibraltar (the connective node between Europe and Africa), and Tijuana (the *maquiladora* metropolis that is, with its sister city San Ysidro, the busiest crossing point between the United States and Mexico). Chao has called the cities "two central points of the planet's fever."[6] They are both cities that lie pulsing but undetected at the heart of the global economy, cities that are at once sites of transnational global commerce and sites of transnational dislocation and low-wage economic poverty, where entire populations pursue menial labor on the streets and in *maquiladora* factories to keep exported goods flowing across the very borders they are not allowed to cross. *Clandestino* even begins with Chao as a lawless *mojado* crossing the border to El Norte, "lost in the heart of the great Babylon" and branded "clandestino" because he isn't carrying papers. Fifteen songs later, on "El Viento," the border returns, but this time Chao morphs into the wind and crosses unseen. His "tequila, sexo y marijuana" tribute to the border metropolis, "Welcome to Tijuana," is more fun than revelatory, but it doesn't matter. Tijuana has left its mark all over *Clandestino* through sound: the plastic whistle of a falling bomb issued from a toy keychain popular with Tijuana street vendors.

But like Mano Negra's global rebel yells, Chao's new "clandestino" identity is rooted wherever political guerrillas are causing trouble, and he shifts personas between being *peruano*, *boliviano*, and *africano*, between being EZLN and Caravane des Quartiers. When he becomes "El Desaparecido," we hear familiar traces of Santiago, Buenos Aires, and Ciudad Juárez, but we also hear Chao turning disappearance into <u>an act of shape-shifting resistance</u>. "When they *desaparecide* look for me," the post-European trickster boasts, "I'm never there."

Clandestino's true subject, however, was not Chao himself but the populations and communities he met on his travels, populations and communities across Europe, Africa, and the Americas who were all, in different ways, negotiating and surviving experiences of displacement, dislocation, and dispersement, whether through exile, migration, genocide, or politically legislated xenophobia. The characters in Chao's global musical dramas are people without a place or people fighting to keep their place in a world where placelessness has become a dominant feature of the contemporary political order (according to the U.N., over 125 million people currently live outside of their country of origin).[7] Chao's subjects are disenfranchised world citizens who have found themselves caught between the contradictory pulls of globalization: increased prosperity for some, increased labor exploitation for others; increased freedom of movement for some, increased barriers and expulsions for others. As George Lipsitz has characterized it:

> The rapid movement across the globe of people, products, ideas, and images seems to undermine foundational certainties about the meaning of local and national identities, the value of personal and collective histories, and the solidity of social relationships and social networks. New forms of economic activity produce both astounding wealth and appalling poverty—sometimes in the same locations. New technologies liberate us from tiresome tasks yet create unprecedented environmental dangers. In some respects, global marketing brings the people of the world closer together than ever before, yet consuming the same products, enjoying the same products, or working for the same employers does not seem to make us any less divided, as old antagonisms and new enmities create violent conflicts on every continent.[8]

It is precisely this crisis that Chao's music speaks to, but he speaks with an acute attention to place—to border cities like Tijuana and Gibraltar, but also to urban centers where marginalized and displaced populations struggle for new forms of community across policed civic maps. In a recent study of music and the European racial imagination, Philip Bohlman has written of music as the key soundtrack to the lives of "the placeless" in Europe. "Throughout European history, race has been a problem of defining and enforcing distances between those who belong and those who do not," he argues. "The ultimate act of racializing is the denial of place, that is, the removal of conditions of belonging." Bohlman proposes that it is through listening to Europe's "sound-mixes" that we are able to map the pasts and futures of the placeless.[9] Chao's *Clandestino,* which he recorded as a continuous minimalist song cycle built on a limited number of the same recycled melodies and rhythms, is precisely that, a migratory song-mix born from placelessness, a song-mix that explores the racialization of Europe's and America's displaced others, from the Peruvians and Africans of "Clandestino" to the Mexican and Central American *indocumentados* of "Welcome to Tijuana."

Chao's 2001 follow-up to *Clandestino* is *Próxima Estación: Esperanza,* which continues the cycle of some of *Clandestino*'s melodies and rhythms, but creates something altogether different—a celebration of the joys and pleasures needed to survive the politics of pain and violence. Where *Clandestino*'s patron saint was Subcomandante Marcos, *Próxima* bows to Bob Marley, and Chao recorded it wherever inspiration hit: Brazil, Spain, Africa. As a sequel to *Clandestino*, *Próxima* further established Chao as one of globalization's most eloquent voices of protest, an artist who participates in the workings of global capitalism (both solo albums have been released and distributed through the multinational label Virgin Records) as a vehicle of giving voice to globalization's underbelly—its low-wage laborers, its displaced populations, its migrants, its victims. And he does it with music born from the exchanges and hybridities not of the corporate transnational sphere that Guillermo Gómez Peña has called the "mainstream bizarre" of franchised, commodified difference (a transnational muticulturalism "devoid of 'real' people of color"), but from the vernacular, everyday sphere of grassroots transnational multiculturalism, where differences are performed and negotiated through cultural exchange, conflict, and encounter within, not outside of, the global capitalist apparatus.[10]

In this sense, Chao makes music with what Chela Sandoval has called a "differential consciousness," in that he has dedicated his career to using music to forge "a global decolonizing alliance of difference in its drive toward egalitarian social relations and economic well-being for all citizenry: an oppositional global politics, a cosmopolitics for *planeta tierra*."[11] In *Próxima*'s accompanying CD booklet, there is a photograph of Chao wearing an Algerian soccer jersey and he is standing on the beach in Playas de Tijuana, the Tijuana beach community where the rusty border wall protrudes out into the ocean after running out of land to divide up. Chao is facing the sea and a group of white seagulls drenched in orange sunshine fly over his head.

The first time I spoke with Chao, in 1999, by phone from Paris right after he finished *Clandestino*, he was still "waiting for the last wave"—that recurring glimpse of the apocalypse held over from *Casa Babylon*—and "waiting for the last song." Like a troubadour Che Guevara, a guitar-picking Marcos, or a NAFTA/GATT Gregorio Cortez, he was ready to face the end alone, waiting for the last revolutionary drum, the last sign that maybe he wouldn't be swallowed whole by the twenty-first century. By the second time we spoke, in a Los Angeles bar in 2001, that doubt had turned to hope on *Próxima Estación*. I learned that he had stopped traveling, had rented an apartment in Barcelona, and for the first time in years, had a place that he was comfortable calling his own.[12]

The Monkey Speaks His Mind

JK: Though you were born in Europe and spent much of your life performing in Europe, in recent years—especially since the release of Casa Babylon—your attention has moved to Latin America. How did that shift happen?

MC: When I was living in Europe, I already had a lot of contact with South America. When I was a child, in my home, my father used to be in contact with a lot of people from Argentina, Uruguay, and Chile who were in exile from the dictatorships and came to Europe for political reasons. My father's place was a meeting point for all these people. Plus, my grandfather lived for ten years in Cuba. There were a lot of relationships and a lot of records.

JK: Tijuana is central to *Clandestino*. What is your attraction to it as a place?

MC: When you travel a lot, you feel that there are certain places in the world that are hot points. Tijuana is one of them. It's a symbol of what is the biggest problem of the end of the century: the border and problems of immigration. Just like on the record I talk a lot about Gibraltar, a hot point between Africa and Europe; Tijuana is a hot point between the United States and South America. There's the same kind of problems and you can feel the condensation of the troubles of the world there. Another big world problem is the political mafia, and Tijuana is a good example of that, too [laughs]. Tijuana is a place of contradiction. For a lot of people coming from South America trying to cross the border, it can begin to be like a kind of jail. And for the other side, you come there just to have a good time. That's the hypocrisy of this border: from one side it's so easy to cross over, just to have fun one night, see some prostitutes, get drunk, spend your money, and on the other side it's completely the opposite.

JK: But this separation often gets misunderstood as an actual dividing line. On the one hand, the border is a physical geopolitical reality but on the other it's a fiction.

MC: It's an abstraction. A guy from Tijuana has more in common with a guy in San Diego than a guy in San Diego has with a guy in Boston or a guy from Tijuana has with a guy from Oaxaca. They're more *hermanos*, despite the border. Because not one *frontera* is actually a cultural border; there are always economic borders between those who have money and those who don't.

JK: So many young Latin American rock bands, say Tijuana NO or Plastilina Mosh, talk about Mano Negra as the biggest influence on what they do. Why do you think Mano Negra was so influential for them?

MC: Maybe we came to South America at the right time, when all the bands were a little bored with the music always coming from the outside. Everybody started thinking it was possible to use his own culture without shame. And we came at that moment, when it was time to change and they saw a band that used to change any kind of music using a lot of cultures without shame and they liked it. They saw it was possible. A lot of bands really took to *Casa Babylon*—the way it was recorded, its songs, the sense of freedom it has, the idea that you can use anything without a problem.

JK: Can you talk about the importance of Marcos and the Zapatistas to your music?

MC: Four years ago, when we started with *Casa Babylon,* the Zapatista movement was beginning, for us anyway. At that moment, we felt very involved with these guys. We liked the message, we liked what they were talking about, the way they see the world. It was like, finally, someone we could trust. Because all of the messages from the Zapatistas were the exact same things I was thinking. There just aren't that many examples of messages like that coming to you in the world. So four years later, with this album, I'm still not deceived by them. They're still an example. They have a good analysis of what modern society is and how it works. They understand the power of the economy for us all. Economy runs the world; politicians mean nothing. Also, they never said that they were fighting for power. They fight for dignity. They don't want to be presidents of Mexico. They don't want political responsibilities. They don't want the power. They want dignity. That changed a lot of things.

JK: Does "clandestino" refer to any one community in particular or is it a general category for you?

MC: There's more and more people who have to live like *clandestinos* in the world. It's not easy to live that way. A lot of friends of mine in Europe have to live like *clandestinos*. It's the same in the U.S. for many Latinos. Years ago it was more a matter of being political refugees, but now it's not just people coming for political reasons. They come for social reasons. They have to feed a family and in their countries it's not possible anymore. Why is it not possible? Because the first world has taken everything. So they go to the first world to

340 • JOSH KUN

try to make a living, but the first world says "No, you can't come in." That's a problem and one day, the third world is gonna get really angry and we'll see what happens.

[margin note: but they're being placated]

JK: So "clandestino" becomes a symbol of all *indocumentados,* refugees, exiles . . .

MC: It's the same problem. When I'm in Mexico or South America or Colombia, I talk to the guys on the beach waiting for the boat, or in Algeria I talk to the guys waiting for any opportunity to get into Europe. It's the same—they have the same life, the same kind of problems, and they try to cross the border for the same reasons. And it's getting worse everyday. The laws of the governments are getting tougher and tougher.

JK: What kind of social future will this lead to?

MC: There's gonna be hard times. Things have to change quickly. This problem of *clandestinidad* from borders really close by is making rage grow in the third world. And then you have to decide how to act on that rage either positively or negatively. A lot of people try positively and others, because they're lost and because they have rage, they do it negatively. It's not the right solution—they use violence, bad interpretations of religion, other bad things. It's like, if the first world treats us bad we're gonna treat them bad right back. And they're right, but we have to find better solutions.

JK: Part of what I love about *Clandestino* is the way it links different revolutions, different communities, and different geographies to common causes.

[margin note: transmit!]

MC: The world is wonderful for that. There's plenty of universes. Brazil is a universe. New York is a universe. And at the same time it's a little little little planet. There's so much difference, yet at the same time so many links. It inspires me when you can be in Africa and talking to a guy about African religions and after that you're talking with a guy in Ireland or Galicia about Celtic religions and they're so different but there are also so many big links and connections. I like traveling for that reason.

JK: On *Clandestino,* there's a feeling of constant movement and migration. And in your own life, you travel constantly. What's the importance of migration and travel to current global culture?

MC: Migrations and travel have been happening throughout the history of mankind. People travel, people move. The gypsies who live in Spain migrated from India. The French who they say are so French migrated from the East or I don't know where. There have always been migrations. Human societies are like rivers and that's why borders don't mean anything. If you close a river, the water no longer runs and it builds and builds and nothing good can come of it. If there's riches in the North, then bring the people North. Or if not, make riches available in the South and they'll be better off there than in the North—they'll have the possibility of feeding their children.

JK: If you could imagine a revolution between all the *clandestinos* you sing about—*africanos, bolivianos, mexicanos,* Arabs—how would it look?

MC: The only thing I know is that we are in a race against time. I don't know from where these changes are going to come, but I know they have to come soon because if not, what is growing the most right now is not unity between these communities but the radicalization of each one. In that sense, I'm somewhat pessimistic. Instead of uniting, everybody thinks they can find the solution themselves: that this God values more than that God, this flag more than that flag. No, no: the problem is worldwide and the people have to understand that quickly.

JK: During *Clandestino,* you were very much a migrant. Now you are living in one place. Does this record reflect more of a settler's mindset?

MC: For the last three years, the biggest change in my life has been that I now have an apartment. For seven years, I had been living without an apartment and just traveling. Now my apartment is in Barcelona and I have my neighborhood there. What it allows me to do is to be more organized. When you're traveling all over the world, it's more difficult to bring your studio. But I'm still always traveling a lot. This album [*Próxima Estación*] was recorded and finished a year and a half ago. It was recorded the same way as *Clandestino,* with my eight-track and me just traveling around. Some are songs that were not on *Clandestino* because there wasn't any space, like "Mi Vida." I never stop to make an album and record it. I'm always recording. Both albums were recorded in the same way with the same kind of production. It's me and my friend Renaud Letang. It's a record made by two people.

JK: But this record sounds bigger than *Clandestino*. There are horns. There's more of the old Mano Negra patchanka sound.

MC: Yeah. It's more up-tempo. *Clandestino* was really a kind of blues album. This one is more *patchanguero*. And it's because of the horns.

JK: You also sound happier here. Some of the songs are just lighter emotionally, like "Papito."

MC: Yeah. It's because we want to change. *Próxima Estación* is the little sister of *Clandestino,* but she's come out much happier.

JK: And more hopeful, which was what was absent on *Clandestino*. The last time we heard from you, you were "lost in the twentieth century," you were "waiting for the last wave" to wash you away. Where does this new hope come from?

MC: My best teacher of hope has been the third world. In South America, you learn a lot about hope. Where you see the people with the most hope in the world are the people who are in the worst situations. In the first world, sometimes we lose this kind of hope. We hope for things that are more general, less precise. In South America or in Africa, every morning when they wake up they need hope. In the third world, when you are faced with a bad situation, there is not time for depression. If you're depressed, you die. You need hope every morning when you wake up to feed your children, to make a living. It's an everyday hope. It's the hope you need to survive. So they have a sense of hope that is more evident than ours in the first world.

JK: Even though you are European by birth, I have always thought of you as a sort of ex-European, as a voice of the part of Europe that Europe has never wanted to claim.

MC: Europe is a strange place. I'm European. I was born in France and raised in France and Spain. I cannot hide that and I do not want to hide that. Europe is an old lady. One day I was talking with a guy from Chiapas, we met in Paris, and we were talking about Mexico and he said, "Man, come to Mexico, things are moving, new things." So I asked him, "How do you see Europe?" and the guy said, "Sorry, but it's like a rusty boat. South America is like a little speed boat, but Europe is like an old rusty boat." Almost like a kind of Titanic! That's the difference: Europe is old, the people are old.

JK: If Europe's the Titanic, then you're the music playing as it sinks.

MC: There are two Europes. There is the economic Europe and the other Europe that economic Europe tries to kill. The actual Europe is so different from the Europe they try to create. A good example is in France, where for years there were racist and nationalist parties coming out and earning like 40 percent of the vote and wanting to close Europe, with big walls, so Africa cannot come anymore, so the Turks cannot come into Germany, to close everything. When France won the World Cup, they were all Africans. France was so proud to win the World Cup but all the people on the team were exactly the kind of people that Europe doesn't want anymore. After the World Cup, the racist parties in France fell down. People were so proud to win the World Cup, but it was all black people. So maybe they're not so proud. But they help the country. They bring us money. Everybody in the world knows France is the champion. But all black people! From North Africa, places that are not French.

JK: Can you talk a little about your songwriting process? It seems to me that more and more you're really writing songs that are fragments of a larger whole, like short chapters in an ongoing novel.

MC: My process is to not have process. Every song is a new adventure. My process is to be recording at all times and to have no concept of what I am doing. That's what saves me. If you go to record an album and you have two months in the studio, you need to have a concept, you need to know what you're gonna do. If you're just traveling with an eight-track, you just record when you want to record, when there is an idea. What I love about my job is that I get to work with coincidence. I'm not the boss. The boss is the moment. My job is to catch that moment, that instant. It's a difficult job. I'm still learning how to do it. I'm looking for professors for that because they never taught us that in school. If you have a nice idea at five in the morning, tomorrow is gonna be too late. Maybe you'll just change a comma or something, but it's finished, it's out. My eight-track allows me to work when it's hot. The idea is there, I record it. It's in the moment. I write the lyrics in the moment; I record them, it's really fresh. I love to work like that. I really learned to work like this on *Casa Babylon*. The real border between what I'm doing now and what I was doing with Mano Negra came before *Casa Babylon*. That was the same kind of recording. There was no band. Mano Negra had split up. We were just in a studio somewhere and said, "Let's see what happens."

JK: On *Próxima Estación*, like on *Clandestino*, you repeat themes and melodies, recycle rhythm tracks and even lyrics. "Calavera no llora," one of my favorite lines from your song "Bienvenido a Tijuana," even shows up here.

MC: I call those my little dwarfs, my little sounds, my little universe. A lot of it has to do, again, with coincidence. There is a song on the album sung by Valeria ("Homens"). She's from Rio de Janeiro. She's a *capoerista* there and she has a little hip-hop band. I used to live with this family there. It was my little town, my little place. She was rehearsing with her band and I was working with my eight-track and they were not happy with their rhythm, so I had the "Bongo Bong" rhythm with me and I said, "Try it with that." And they were happy, so we recorded it, in that moment.

JK: You mentioned Chiapas earlier, and clearly a lot has happened in Chiapas since *Clandestino* was released. Is any of *Próxima*'s hope also hope for what changes might be happening with Chiapas with the Fox presidency?

MC: These guys in Chiapas always give me hope. They are a little light on this planet that I believe in, and there are not too many things left to believe in. The message from Chiapas, I always understood it, has always been so pure. And after so many years it is still pure. That's incredible. I really believe that what happened in Chiapas was the precursor of what happened in Seattle, of this kind of protest all over the world, this protest against globalization. And what amazes me is how fresh they still are. They haven't changed. I really believe in them. I try to help them, but I don't think I help them enough. In December of last year, we played there, in La Realidad, in San Cristobal, we met Marcos, we met with La Subcomandancia. I let them know how much I believe in them. Because it's not so often you really believe in something and you really get in the kitchen. Usually you are deceived. That happened to me back when I was a big fan of rock and roll bands. I was ready to give my life to them, but when I became more well-known and had the opportunity to meet them, 80 percent of the time I was deceived. When I'm really happy is when I'm in places like Chiapas, when I'm not deceived. It confirmed that they are following the good path.

JK: Marcos has always said that much of the EZLN's goal is to restore truth to Mexico, to expose the lies of Mexico. On *Clandestino* you sang "Everything in this world is a lie," and you've been organizing a series of concerts you call "Festival of Lies." Isn't their commitment to truth, their protest against the lies of globalization, also what attracts you to them?

MC: I really appreciate their way of talking and that whole discourse. They say, "We are a movement and all we want is to disappear. Our aim is to disappear, when nobody needs us anymore." They don't fight for power, they don't fight for fame. They fight for the dignity of so many communities. They fight for the day they can disappear, when nobody needs to hear what they have to say.

JK: The name of the touring band you've put together since recording *Próxima Estación,* Radio Bemba, means "word of mouth" or "rumor." Is there more truth in what gets passed along mouth to mouth? Is there more truth in this unofficial, oral communication?

MC: No. Don't trust us, because we're lost. I'm still lost. I'm still looking for any solutions. I'm still lost in the century. Don't believe the hype [laughs]. I talk about this with my friends all the time. In South America, it's amazing how many people come to us looking for answers. It's our tradition to do press conferences before every show, but press conferences not just for press, for anyone who wants to come and talk. But everywhere the questions were 10 percent musical and 90 percent political or social. It's like, I'm a musician. That's the job I've chosen in my life. I want to be a musician. This kind of political thing, political responsibility, I didn't choose it. It's there and I'm gonna take it. But it's very difficult because the border between giving your ideas and demagoguery is really thin. That's why maybe on *Próxima* there are less politics. Because I don't want to make a living on that. If people ask for my ideas, I give them. But we live in a world where rebellion is such a weapon of marketing that now I want to be careful. It would be really easy for me to make an album that was full of political things. But that would stink.

JK: But for music to be political you don't have to shout "Viva Zapata." Pleasure can be political, too.

MC: That's what I'm proud of about *Clandestino*. It's not a political album. There was just one political thing on it, Marcos and the EZLN. It was just a political affirmation, nothing more. What I always say is that the only revolution I can handle is my own revolution. My revolution is to try to radiate positive vibrations everywhere I go and give hope to people and give good energy to people and to have my kitchen clean. That's the only revolution I believe in. When they ask me about solutions, I say the only solution that I have is to have my own kitchen clean. If everyone would do the same, there would be a huge revolution, and it would be a wonderful revolution because it wouldn't be recuperable. My job is to clean my kitchen. Your job is to clean your kitchen. I believe in that.

JK: Earlier this year I saw you play in Tijuana and then the next day in Los Angeles. When you played L.A., to a crowd that was as much industry as it was fans, your energy was very different from the TJ show, where the crowd embraced you with a fever and intensity that I had never seen before.

MC: I still have that vision of the guy standing on a piece of cardboard on top of the audience. It was incredible. They were totally different shows. Most of all because the place in Tijuana was messy. It was a war. Because of the sound. You could not work on the sound, so you had to work on the energy. The L.A. place was so different. All we were thinking about was the sound and getting the sound right. We used to try to have good sound in Tijuana, but now it's like, forget it. It's impossible. So let's just have a good show and explode.

JK: In Tijuana, you were food. In L.A., you were entertainment.

MC: I respect both. I'm a musician. I'm an entertainer. That's my job.

Afterword

A Changeable Template of Rock in *Las Américas*

GEORGE YÚDICE

Rock as a Structure of Feeling

Rockin' Las Américas is the first comprehensive study of the various rock and rock-inflected musics in Latin and Latino America. While it (or any study, for that matter) cannot be exhaustive, it does cover a vast terrain and nearly half a century. It offers a social and cultural history of rock in several countries, dealing with a range of activities from various genres of music, television shows, youth groups, club cultures, the music industry, and style cultures including clothing, body decorations, and visual and textual preferences. It is thus about a group of behaviors that constitute no one style but a recognizable structure of feeling, an attitude that transcends music per se, as the Brazilian rockers Lobão and Cazuza have asserted,[1] or a template, as Reebee Garofalo suggests. There is also a structure of feeling that binds the essays. They all seek recognition for musical expressions that were repressed and historically remain overlooked, whether those of early rock in Mexico (Zolov) and Cuba (Pacini Hernandez and Garofalo), or Latina participation in the development of rock and punk in the United States (Habell-Pallán). This will to provide recognition is also consistent with the premise that something about these expressions is or was *transgressive*, the very reason for their repression or exclusion.[2] Transgression here is a contestation of normative national identities promoted by Latin American elites, whether of the Right or the Left, or the repudiation of normative ethno-racial formations—for example, Chicanas in the development of punk—that were presumed not to fit the white, middle-class images of youth culture traditionally projected by the U.S. media and the culture industries.

The will to provide recognition necessarily brings these essayists to consider the paradox that an imported music like rock might nevertheless be construed as an *authentic* expression and not the derivative mimicry of which it was originally accused and is sometimes still considered. Since rock originated in the United States and many of its first Latin American manifestations were covers of U.S. pop hits, it is useful to think through this paradox from the purview of the "misplaced ideas" paradigm elaborated by the Brazilian literary and cultural critic Roberto Schwarz.[3] Mimicry tends to be understood from the perspective of idealizing discourses based on lack, which would require subjects to repeat norms to approximate an ideal that is necessarily misplaced in colonial and postcolonial societies like Brazil and, by extension, Latin America. For Schwarz, however, such discourses are not *inauthentic*, for first world ideas are a necessary feature of the periphery's constitutive disjuncture, which can be characterized as combined and unequal development.

In this analogy, rock would seem to be "out of place" in authoritarian third world societies, where transgression is *not* aimed at a disciplined (in the Foucauldian sense) population, with rule of law and effective (rather than merely formal) citizenship for all. In the cases of the United States and Britain, by contrast, it is assumed that youth culture and music in the 1960s were an expression of revolt against the disciplinary technologies of the modern era (education, cultural formation, and other normalizing institutions). U.S. and British youth were not acting politically against the raw power of military dictatorships (as in Brazil and the Southern Cone) or authoritarian governments (as in Mexico) in which social control was achieved through state violence rather than institutionalized social and cultural discipline alone.

Schwarz points out, however, that out-of-placedness is fitting and commensurate with combined and unequal development in Latin America. Indeed, a music that lends itself to all kinds of fusions and appropriations embodies its hybrid character rather well. Rock attitudes were appropriate vehicles for expressing an opposition that straddled both anti-discipline and anti-authoritarianism. As several contributors to this volume observe, in Latin America long-haired men were often beaten and jailed, as if their physical demeanor were an act against dictatorship.

To understand the significance of rock in the 1960s, the heyday of Latin American authoritarian governments, it is necessary to historicize the social and cultural significance of music in the period preceding it. What characterized Latin American modernization was precisely the attempt to construct, within the contradictory ideological terrain of combined and unequal development, authentic national identities that would provide the hegemonic glue, so to speak, needed to bind disparate populations brought into contact as Latin American countries restructured to enter the post-depression world economy. Popular music, much more than education and other disciplinary institutions, was the material with which ruling populist parties and elites sought to galvanize a disparate population from the 1930s to the 1950s. And that music was the music of the subaltern and working classes: the samba, son, and merengue of African-derived Brazilians, Cubans, and Dominicans; the tango of immigrant workers in Argentina and Uruguay.[4] Moreover, "people's culture" was disseminated from radio, recordings, cinema, and so on—not outside the market but within culture industries that were controlled and sometimes subsidized by the state. The most salient examples are samba and carnival in Brazil, and radio and cinema *rancheras* in Mexico.

This is the cultural-political stage onto which rock was thrust in the 1950s, necessarily clashing with what had been sanctioned as authentically national, both for the traditionalist and classist values of elites and the popular imagery spawned by populists and the media. But all of this was to change in the 1960s, as a revolt was in the air against a nationalism that was no longer credible. Indeed, rock's most salient characteristic—its capacity to sonically mobilize (often erotically charged) impulses—would find great receptivity among youth who could not identify with the traditional or populist imagery that dominated the airwaves. This was certainly the case with the Brazilian youth who ushered in the U.S. and British-inspired musicians of the Jovem Guarda and the hybridizing Tropicalistas in the mid- to late 1960s, and the Mexicans who took to the Onda Chicana as "a vehicle for the continued transgression of public space and the reconstitution of community in the wake of the government's repression," as Zolov makes clear.

Although Mexican intellectuals could not stomach the use of English in Onda Chicana lyrics, the language of the other side of the border nevertheless empowered youth who found in English a repudiation of discredited nationalist values.[5] When Zolov asks, "What did youth *hear* in this music?" he suggests that the sounds themselves were able to mobilize not just ideas but feelings about the most important questions youth harbored about themselves and their environment. These involve recognition of their own values (since youth tend to be more idealistic than older generations, who have resigned themselves to the status quo), how their identity will play out socially, and to what degree they will subject themselves to disciplinary institutions. Indeed rock was an excellent vehicle for the combined anti-Oedipal and libidinal impulses that were central to the contestatory youth identities of the 1960s and 1970s, which in Latin American contexts took a pointedly political character.

This antidisciplinary character is clear among youth from working and marginal classes and identity formations (as evidenced in the essays by Zolov, McCann, Trigo, Habell-Pallán, Castillo Berthier, Semán et al., Pino-Ojeda, and Asensio), but also among the middle-class youth who were radicalized by the repressive tactics of Latin American authoritarian regimes from the 1960s to the 1980s, or by the exclusionary character of U.S. society. Consider the Brazilian youth of the 1960s for whom the British pop-inspired *iê-iê-iê* (yeah-yeah-yeah) generation of rock musicians must have sounded like a sensorial detour from the national symbols of samba, *fútbol*, and carnival. As Bryan McCann writes, "Their music certainly inspired repugnance among those zealous of protecting Brazil's national cultural heritage." To the degree that this was the case, rock conveyed an opposition to that conservative approach to national heritage. McCann adds, however, that "there was nothing unsettling about seeing their [Jovem Guarda] faces on the covers of magazines or on the TV program they inaugurated in 1965." What McCann touches on here, as does Habell-Pallán in comparing Chicana *punkeras* with white, middle-class U.S. punk-rockers or Mexican *rockeros*, is that sound and associated imagery *differentiate* and *negotiate* recognition and identity across a stratified society. McCann interprets the different musical sounds available in the 1960s and 1970s on a continuum from lesser-to-greater rebelliousness that seems to coincide with the gradated color of the fans: Jovem Guarda musicians may introduce the foreign, but they are white and clean-cut. The Tropicalistas were more rebellious, insofar as they ignored the normative injunctions of the Right and the Left, seeking instead to register the hybrid sonic and ideological contradictions inherent in combined and unequal modernization. Finally McCann finds a more "authentic" liberation in Black Rio's musicians, who wield black *pau*er through erotically charged soul music.[6]

The important point for me here is not so much the distinction between dilution (Jovem Guarda) and concentrated potency (Black Soul), as one might make in comparing Pat Boone to Chuck Berry, but the fact that the differentiation between them is sonically crucial to questions of *recognition* and *identity*. The difference between the two criteria—dilution vs. authentic potency, recognition and identity—is important and worthy of greater discussion.

Youth Culture and Youth Rebellion

The youth cultures that emerged among the middle and working classes in the United States in the 1950s can be characterized by their dissatisfaction with the status quo of both suburbia and the inner city, captured, for example, by the film *Rebel Without a Cause*. Moreover, this dissatisfaction was harnessed to a libidinal connection to rock and roll, which sonically distinguished youth from the normative cultural values of their parents. In the 1960s, this differentiation became even greater as rock became harder and associated with a "turned on" (versus a "square") culture, opposition to the Vietnam War, and some of the contestatory energy of the new social movements.

But with rock, rebelliousness and opposition did not remain indissolubly linked. By the end of the 1960s it was becoming evident that the culture industries had found ways of tapping profitably into the identificatory value of countercultural music and such anti-normative paraphernalia as fashionably faded and worn-out blue jeans and work shirts. Consumerism thus both made visible the hipness of styles of clothing, bodily decoration, and musical sounds, and channeled the rebellious impulses expressed through them. Perhaps the earliest critique of this development was Herbert Marcuse's notion of repressive desublimation, according to which countercultural "liberation" was but a more potent capture of subjectivity by consumer capitalism.

Nevertheless in the historical conjuncture of post-1960s U.S. and British societies, consuming (and producing consumable) style became a terrain of struggle for differentiation and recognition in its own right. If, for critics such as Richard Hoggart and Christopher Lasch, the dissipation brought about by consumerism could only be held at bay by cultural *resilience* (that is, the maintenance of traditions), the scholarly work on subcultures that arose in the 1970s posited that resistance could be pursued *within* the medium of styles shaped by consumer culture. The stylewise practices of youth and minority subcultures were held up and valorized against normative cultural references. In *Subculture: The Meaning of Style*, Dick Hebdige offered the most influential account of the period, noting that sound (for example, punk or reggae) and objects—any sign, for that matter—could be put to "illegitimate" uses to "express, in code, a form of resistance to the order which guarantees their continued subordination."[7]

But perhaps more than resistance, what we see at work is the differentiation that style enables, distinguishing this group from that. As such, stylistic differentiation is a variation on the Gramscian commonplace that culture is a site of struggle. In pre-1960s U.S. society, such a struggle was reined in by the continual reestablishment of hegemony. But at a certain historical threshold identified with the general acceptance of multiculturalism and the premise that diversity is good, normative cultural hegemony is no longer compelling, including that of Anglo normativity, and style becomes the means by which differences proliferate, a situation that resonates with Laclau and Mouffe's positing of "social complexity" in advanced capitalist social formations as a multiplicity of struggles that challenge domination.[8] If this analysis is correct, then there is nothing *inherent* in particular signs (rock music, for example) that operate as differentiators; they are, rather, *contingent* on a range of historical relations, such as the links that rock has with black culture, eroticism, and rebellious impulses, and the usefulness that identification with marginality has for deploying opposition.

But when contingency focuses on another facet of the sign, say the white masculinism of rock, it is opened up for contestation on the basis of gender and race, as Habell-Pallán observes: "Chicana/o punk, like punk everywhere, embodied a sonic response to the 'excesses of seventies rock.'" The *punkeras* Covarrubias and Armendariz Velasquez "melded and channeled the emancipating sensibility of punk and women-of-color feminism into the musical projects . . . that forged a sound that disrupted the exclusivity of white feminism and anti-Mexican punk."

This view of the differentiating power of pop musics is characteristic of societies where the social has become "unsutured" through the proliferation of identities spurred by consumer-capitalist-assisted democracy. In such societies, the "identification between social agents and classes" dissolves and thus also any global social identity.[9] This does not mean that the social control effected by discipline disappears, but that consumable style is harnessed to contestation as part of the performative ethos of such societies.

Taking Root in Latin America and the Caribbean

When rock took root in Latin America in the 1950s and early 1960s, social conditions were quite different from the authoritarian period that would follow and were characterized by significant gains in worker mobilization and student solidarity in the context of rapid modernization. At that time, leftist intellectuals were able to insert certain demands into state policy, as part of their espousal of popular causes. This was the case in the populist and developmentalist Brazilian governments of Getúlio Vargas, Juscelino Kubitschek, Jânio Quadros, and João Goulart (the last toppled by a military coup in 1964). The development projects of the 1950s and 1960s were a catalyst for popular mobilization. Strong labor and socialist movements emerged to contest the state's articulation of high and popular culture. In the mid-1950s came the reformism of the Instituto Superior de Estudos Brasileiros (ISEB), the Marxist Centros Populares de Cultura, the left-wing Catholic consciousness-raising movement, and the Northeastern Popular Culture Movement. Like liberation theology, these movements made an "option for the poor," that is, for the popular classes.

The 1960s thus represent the crystallization of a common cultural consciousness among so-called popular sectors and leftist intellectuals, with the potential to create an alternative hegemony. But in the Southern Cone, Brazil, and Mexico, hegemony did not function as an equilibrium between political and civil society, as is typical of modern democracies. Political society was clientelist; corporatist rather than civil society reigned. Renato Ortiz, for example, writes of the "precariousness of the very idea of hegemony among us," pointing to the pact between state-aligned elites who promoted import-substitution industrialization and developmentalism, and an equally state-aligned popular nationalism that sought state welfare, delivered in corporatist and clientelist forms since the 1920s and 1930s.[10]

The origins of "popular culture" in Latin America can be traced to this paradoxical state, which shaped those sectors most responsible for supporting that culture: education, radio, film, and anthropological institutions. In the mid- to late 1960s, the governments of Brazil, Argentina, Uruguay, and Mexico, taken over by authoritarian political actors, resorted to outright repression. The 1964 coup in Brazil and the 1968 massacre in Tlatelolco in Mexico, preceded by a spate of workers' strikes, resulted in the banishment of leftist political opposition and, in Brazil, a more radical armed guerrilla movement. Political repression was part of the strategy for modernizing Brazilian society, aided by investment and promotion in modern communication technologies and television. The military formulated clear policies to resignify and transform the very notion and reality of the popular, away from a perspective rooted in class and cultural struggles and toward a notion of popularity defined by consumer markets.

Rock music takes root in the conflicted terrain between government modernization projects and the control mechanisms put in place to rein in the Left and the emerging counterculture. Both in Brazil and Mexico, by the end of the 1960s and the beginning of the 1970s, government took control of the media, with the result that oppositional Música Popular Brasileira (MPB) artists and even ironic musicians like the Tropicalistas were exiled. In the Mexican context, as Zolov writes, after the Woodstock-like rock festival Avándaro, "repression . . . halted the flow of recordings and other marketable commodities." The result was that opposition went underground, in part. Moreover, *cultural* opposition or resistance developed punk-like affinities for marginality, which were an expression of repudiation of social and political control. According to Heloisa Buarque de Hollanda, the most astute commentator on Brazilian *cultura marginal* of the 1970s, this period was characterized by "explosions in discourse and behavior and in cultural production—to the sound of rock and grenades thrown by the war (*guerrilha*) against dominant culture and its legitimized forms of power and knowledge."[11]

In the heyday of *rock nacional*, in the 1980s, rock preserved the contestatory power of critiques of authoritarianism, often disguised by allegory and metaphor, and served as a conduit for the democratic energies of the new social movements. In Brazil, the democratic opening was emblematized by Ira!'s "dias de luta" (days of struggle). Taking the title from this song, Ricardo Aleixandre published a four-hundred-page survey of Brazilian rock in the 1980s, a period that counterposed a new expression and sense of musical maturity against the prevailing social, political, and cultural status quo. Particularly important is Alexandre's wide-ranging critical net, capable of grasping the myriad attitudes expressed in the music: the musicians' personal immaturity, their overweening pretensions, their confusions and internecine fights, as well as their innocence, romanticism, and musicianship.

More generally, it is inaccurate in this context to contrast rock with the *nueva canción* or protest song; on the contrary, there emerged many interesting collaborations, such as that of Charly García and Mercedes Sosa in Argentina, or the more subdued explorations of Alux Nahual in Guatemala. Indeed, by the mid-1970s Latin American rock had already diversified into many forms; in Brazil alone there is a stunning range, from the visceral sound of "Made in Brazil," to the progressive rock of Os Mutantes and Módulo 1000, to the psychedelic-baroque style of A Braca do Sol, to the rockabilly of the Ruy Maurity Trio, to the erudite fusions of progressive rock and the regional sounds of O Terço. "Musicians like Walter Franco, Jards Macalé, Lô Borges, Tim Maia, Hilton and Beto Guedes, among others, also contributed to closing the gap between rock and national pop, thus opening the way to a new generation in the 1980s."[12]

Given this proliferation, it is no longer possible to equate rock with a single contestatory ethos. The most compelling 1980s bands of Brazilian *rock nacional*—Titãs, RPM, Legião Urbana, Paralamas do Sucesso, Ritchie, Barão Vermelho, Engenheiros do Hawaii, Blitz, Lobão, Kid Abelha, Gang 90, Capital Inicial, Lulu Santos, Sepultura—are all well known for their eclecticism and fusions. Titãs, perhaps the consummate band of the 1980s, mixed reggae, funk, hard rock, punk, Jovem Guarda, *música brega* (kitschy, bubble-gum pop),[13] and high-art *poesia concreta*.

There were, however, marginal cultural and musical movements that do not fit paradigms of popular opposition or of multicultural fusions. This was the "antipolitics" of the lumpen *chavos banda* discussed by Zolov and Castillo

Berthier, marginal poets and singers in Brazil,[14] and subsequently the punk bands associated with the *sicarios* in Colombia and featured in the film *Rodrigo D*. In their contribution to this volume, Semán, Vila, and Benedetti provide one of the best treatments of marginality and music, noting with an expert historical eye the conjunctural change that ushered in *rock chabón*, the preferred music of Buenos Aires's lumpenized working classes. As they write, the crisis in lifeworld and sensibilities unleashed by neoliberalism created circumstances in which youth "implement, with greater frequency than their predecessors, musical trajectories very different from that of their parents," such that roguery (*malevos*) and revolution are brought together as never before. As if expressive of a new conjuncture, *rock chabón* brings together marginal identities, traditional allegiances (populism), and a quasi-*guevarista* antipolitical politics.

It is this detailed and insightful attention to the contexts and particular groups in which rock emerges that makes *Rockin' Las Américas* so valuable. The essays not only give us a sense of what the musics sound like, but more importantly, how their fans and enemies received those musics, against the backdrop of significant social changes. Indeed the final two essays, which address hybrid genres and border crossings, ingeniously offer the reader both the very local, Tijuana (*norteño*) formation of the "universal sound" of techno (Asensio), and the global context in which Manu Chao localizes his music with local musicians and traditions (Kun).

Together, the essays in this volume, which delve into the social and historical emergence of rock musics in each region of the Americas, manage to convince the reader that a socio-musical structure of feeling inheres throughout at the same time as that structure of feeling takes on myriad expressions. This is the best place to begin to think about and resonate to the music.

APPENDIX
Rock in Latin America, 1940–2000

Meant as a guide for the reader, the timelines on the following pages, created by Héctor Fernandez L'Hoeste, depict the development of rock in Spanish and Portuguese throughout the Americas. They include groups from most of the countries discussed in the essays—Argentina, Brazil, Chile, Colombia, Cuba, Guatemala, Mexico, Puerto Rico—as well as some representing the Latino community in the United States. The graphics are not meant to be comprehensive, and considerations of space and layout limit a fully accurate portrayal of the music's evolution. The location of each group or musical act on the chart corresponds to a period—or to the beginning of a phase—of high visibility. The timelines are divided into four sections: 1940–1969, 1970–1979, 1980–1989, and 1990–2000.

Timeline of Latin American Rock and Roll Artists (1940–1970)

- Pachuco Boogie Boys (USA) — c. 1940
- Lalo Guerrero & Los Cinco Lobos (USA) — c. 1944
- Jovem Guarda (Brazil)
- Club del Clan: Sandro, Los Shakers (Argentina)
- Santana, Daniel Valdez, Ruben & The Jets (USA)
- Nueva Ola Movement: Los Ramblers, Luis Dimas, Cecilia (Chile)
- Roy Brown, Noel Hernández (Puerto Rico)
- Thee Midnighters (USA)
- Los Locos del Ritmo, Los Teen Tops, Los Rebeldes del Rock, Enrique Guzmán, Angélica María (Mexico)
- Los Gallos, Dada, Los Kent (Cuba)
- Los Dug Dug's
- Los Yaki, Javier Bátiz y Los Finks (Mexico)
- Los Relámpagos (Guatemala)
- Sputniks, Rock-fox (Brazil)
- Los Marauders, Los Jets (Guatemala)
- Los Gatos, Almendra, Manal (Argentina)
- Roberto Carlos, Os Mutantes (Brazil)
- Con Safos, Yaqui, Tierra (USA)
- Gloria Rios (Mexico)
- Los Pacíficos (Cuba)
- Eastside Sound: The Premiers, Cannibal and The Headhunters (USA)
- Luis Bravo, Los Llopis, Los Armónicos, Los Hot Rockers (Cuba)
- Los Mac's (Chile)
- Chucho Avellanet, Bobby Capó, Charlie Robles, Los Hispanos, Lucecita Benítez, Lissette (Puerto Rico)
- Los Zafiros (Cuba)
- SOS, Apple Pie (Guatemala)
- Ritchie Valens (USA)
- Los Speakers, Los Flippers, Los Danger Twist, Los Yetis, Oscar Golden, Vicky (Colombia)

Timeline axis: 1940, 1942, 1944, 1946, 1948, 1950, 1952, 1954, 1956, 1958, 1960, 1962, 1964, 1966, 1968, 1970

Timeline (1970–1979)

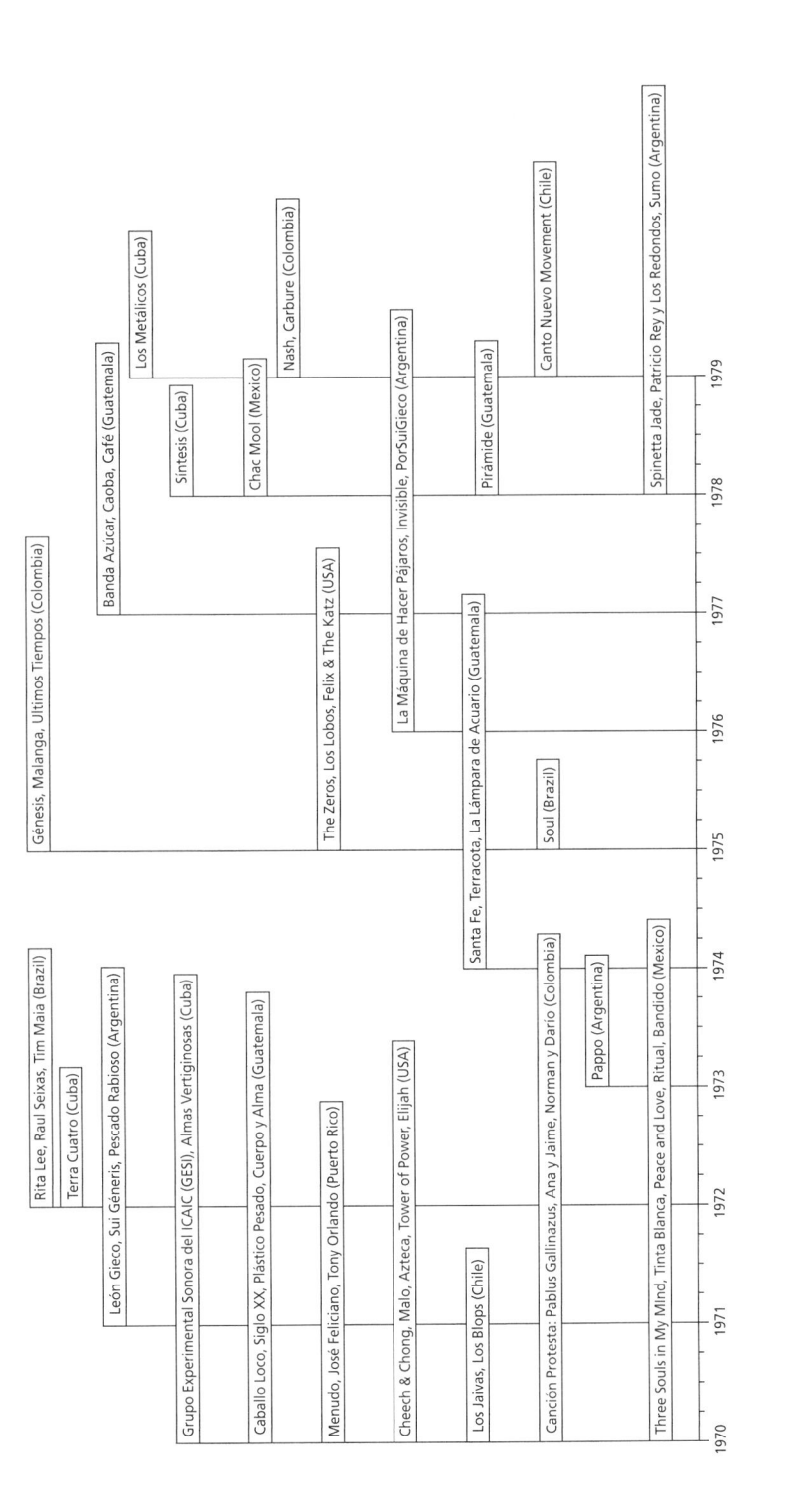

- Rita Lee, Raul Seixas, Tim Maia (Brazil)
- Terra Cuatro (Cuba)
- Génesis, Malanga, Últimos Tiempos (Colombia)
- Banda Azúcar, Caoba, Café (Guatemala)
- Los Metálicos (Cuba)
- León Gieco, Sui Géneris, Pescado Rabioso (Argentina)
- Grupo Experimental Sonora del ICAIC (GESI), Almas Vertiginosas (Cuba)
- Síntesis (Cuba)
- Caballo Loco, Siglo XX, Plástico Pesado, Cuerpo y Alma (Guatemala)
- Chac Mool (Mexico)
- Menudo, José Feliciano, Tony Orlando (Puerto Rico)
- Nash, Carbure (Colombia)
- Cheech & Chong, Malo, Azteca, Tower of Power, Elijah (USA)
- The Zeros, Los Lobos, Felix & The Katz (USA)
- La Máquina de Hacer Pájaros, Invisible, PorSuiGieco (Argentina)
- Los Jaivas, Los Blops (Chile)
- Santa Fe, Terracota, La Lámpara de Acuario (Guatemala)
- Soul (Brazil)
- Pirámide (Guatemala)
- Canción Protesta: Pablus Gallinazus, Ana y Jaime, Norman y Darío (Colombia)
- Pappo (Argentina)
- Canto Nuevo Movement (Chile)
- Three Souls in My Mind, Tinta Blanca, Peace and Love, Ritual, Bandido (Mexico)
- Spinetta Jade, Patricio Rey y Los Redondos, Sumo (Argentina)

1970 1971 1972 1973 1974 1975 1976 1977 1978 1979

Timeline (1980–1989)

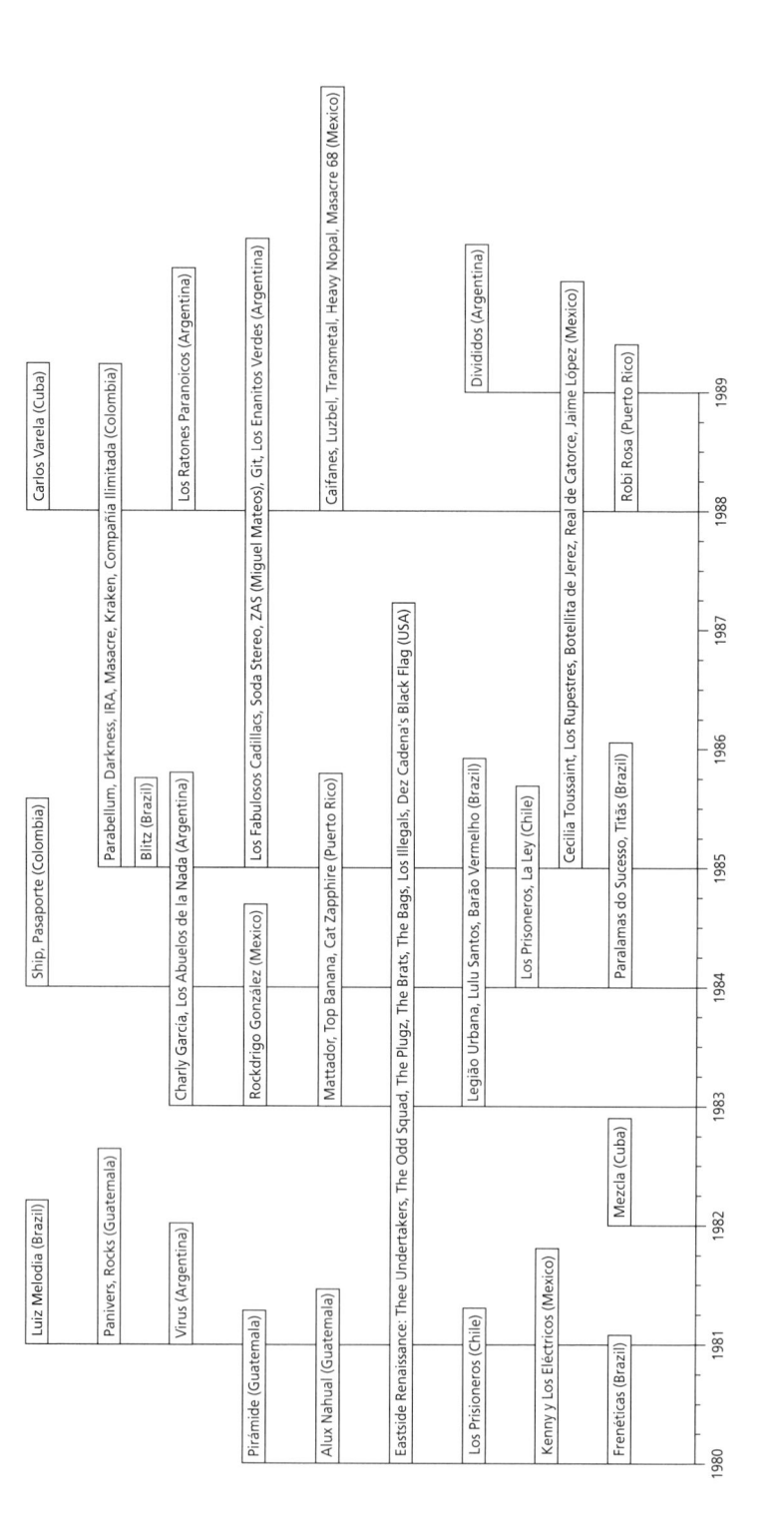

- **Luiz Melodia (Brazil)** — 1980
- **Panivers, Rocks (Guatemala)** — 1980
- **Vírus (Argentina)** — 1980
- **Pirámide (Guatemala)** — 1980
- **Alux Nahual (Guatemala)** — 1980
- **Eastside Renaissance: Thee Undertakers, The Odd Squad, The Plugz, The Brats, The Bags, Los Illegals, Dez Cadena's Black Flag (USA)** — 1980
- **Los Prisioneros (Chile)** — 1980
- **Kenny y Los Eléctricos (Mexico)** — 1980
- **Frenéticas (Brazil)** — 1980
- **Mezcla (Cuba)** — 1982
- **Ship, Pasaporte (Colombia)** — 1983
- **Charly García, Los Abuelos de la Nada (Argentina)** — 1983
- **Rockdrigo González (Mexico)** — 1983
- **Mattador, Top Banana, Cat Zapphire (Puerto Rico)** — 1983
- **Legião Urbana, Lulu Santos, Barão Vermelho (Brazil)** — 1984
- **Los Prisioneros, La Ley (Chile)** — 1984
- **Paralamas do Sucesso, Titãs (Brazil)** — 1984
- **Parabellum, Darkness, IRA, Masacre, Kraken, Compañía Ilimitada (Colombia)** — 1985
- **Blitz (Brazil)** — 1985
- **Los Fabulosos Cadillacs, Soda Stereo, ZAS (Miguel Mateos), GIT, Los Enanitos Verdes (Argentina)** — 1985
- **Cecilia Toussaint, Los Rupestres, Botellita de Jerez, Real de Catorce, Jaime López (Mexico)** — 1985
- **Carlos Varela (Cuba)** — 1988
- **Los Ratones Paranoicos (Argentina)** — 1986
- **Caifanes, Luzbel, Transmetal, Heavy Nopal, Masacre 68 (Mexico)** — 1987
- **Divididos (Argentina)** — 1988
- **Robi Rosa (Puerto Rico)** — 1988

Timeline (1990–2000)

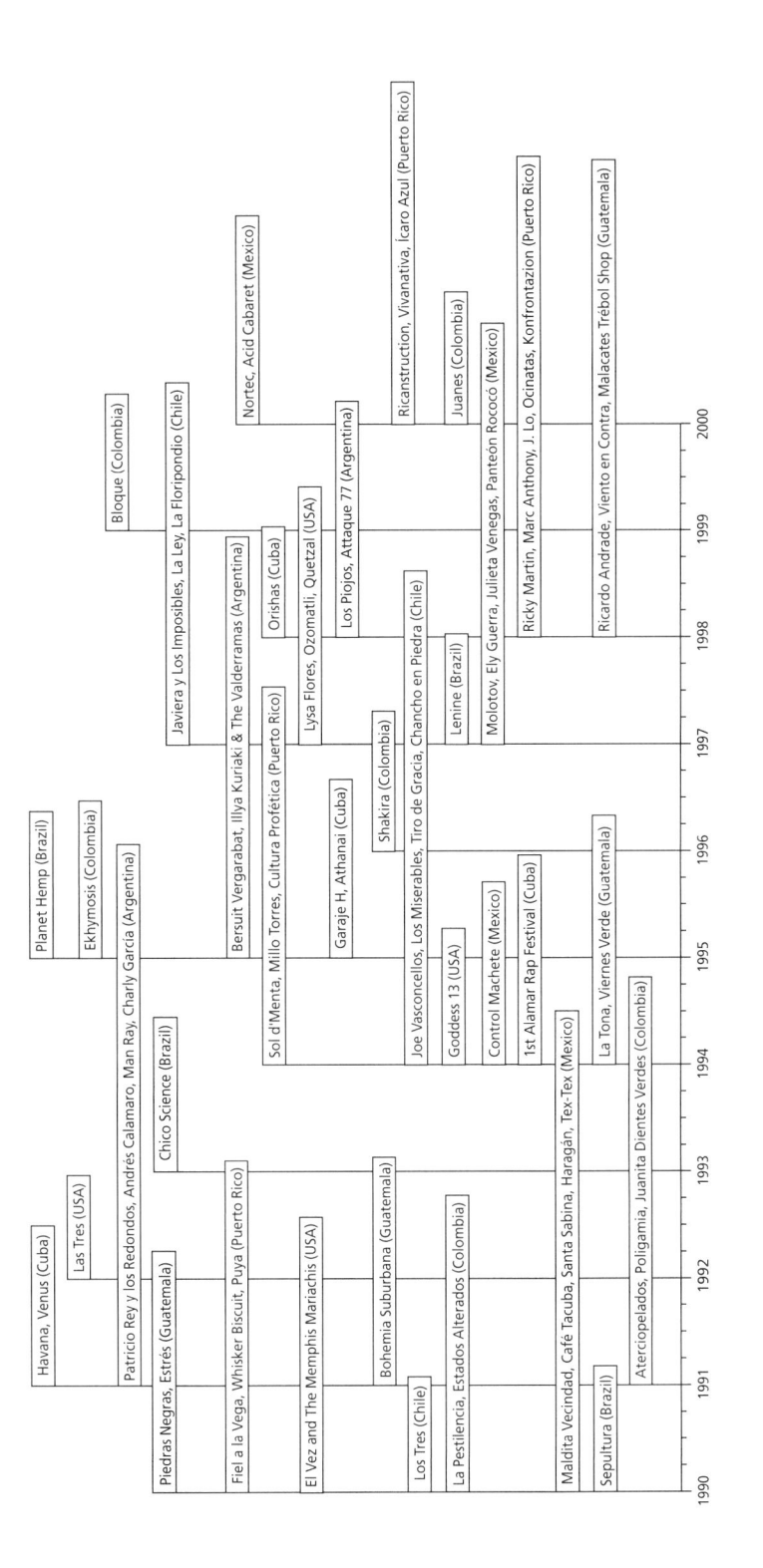

- Havana, Venus (Cuba)
- Las Tres (USA)
- Patricio Rey y los Redondos, Andrés Calamaro, Man Ray, Charly García (Argentina)
- Planet Hemp (Brazil)
- Ekhymosis (Colombia)
- Piedras Negras, Estrés (Guatemala)
- Chico Science (Brazil)
- Fiel a la Vega, Whisker Biscuit, Puya (Puerto Rico)
- Javiera y Los Imposibles, La Ley, La Floripondio (Chile)
- Bloque (Colombia)
- El Vez and The Memphis Mariachis (USA)
- Bersuit Vergarabat, Illya Kuriaki & The Valderramas (Argentina)
- Nortec, Acid Cabaret (Mexico)
- Bohemia Suburbana (Guatemala)
- Sol d'Menta, Millo Torres, Cultura Profética (Puerto Rico)
- Orishas (Cuba)
- Los Tres (Chile)
- Garaje H, Athanai (Cuba)
- Lysa Flores, Ozomatli, Quetzal (USA)
- La Pestilencia, Estados Alterados (Colombia)
- Shakira (Colombia)
- Los Piojos, Attaque 77 (Argentina)
- Ricanstruction, Vivanativa, Icaro Azul (Puerto Rico)
- Maldita Vecindad, Café Tacuba, Santa Sabina, Haragán, Tex-Tex (Mexico)
- Joe Vasconcellos, Los Miserables, Tiro de Gracia, Chancho en Piedra (Chile)
- Juanes (Colombia)
- Sepultura (Brazil)
- Goddess 13 (USA)
- Lenine (Brazil)
- Control Machete (Mexico)
- Molotov, Ely Guerra, Julieta Venegas, Panteón Rococó (Mexico)
- 1st Alamar Rap Festival (Cuba)
- Ricky Martin, Marc Anthony, J. Lo, Ocinatas, Konfrontazion (Puerto Rico)
- La Tona, Viernes Verde (Guatemala)
- Ricardo Andrade, Viento en Contra, Malacates Trébol Shop (Guatemala)
- Aterciopelados, Poligamia, Juanita Dientes Verdes (Colombia)

NOTES

Mapping Rock Music Cultures across the Americas

1. Eric Zolov, *Refried Elvis: The Rise of the Mexican Counterculture* (Berkeley: University of California Press, 1999).

2. See Christopher Dunn, "Tropicália, Counterculture, and the Diasporic Imagination in Brazil," in *Brazilian Popular Music & Globalization*, ed. Charles Perrone and Christopher Dunn (New York: Routledge, 2001), 72–95; and Charles A. Perrone, *Masters of Contemporary Brazilian Song: MPB, 1965–1985* (Austin: University of Texas Press, 1989).

3. See Robin Moore, "From the *Canción Protesta* to the *Nueva Trova*, 1965–1985," *International Journal of Qualitative Studies in Education* 14, no. 2 (2001): 177–200.

4. See Reebee Garofalo, ed., *Rockin' the Boat: Mass Music and Mass Movements* (Boston: South End Press, 1992); and Timothy Ryback, *Rock Around the Bloc: A History of Rock Music in Eastern Europe and the Soviet Union* (New York: Oxford University Press, 1990).

5. There are two acceptable ways of spelling "rocker" in Spanish, *rockero* and *roquero* (pronounced identically). For consistency, throughout this manuscript we have adopted the first spelling. In an indication of shifting linguistic politics, the 2001 edition of the *Diccionario de la lengua española*, published by the Spanish Royal Academy (RAE), which is the self-designated guardian of official Spanish, for the first time introduced a definition for *roquero(a)*, as "pertaining to or related to rock [music]." The term *rock*, which had not appeared in earlier editions of the dictionary, is singled out as an English word (i.e., *voz inglesa*). Although the 2001 edition of the dictionary was prepared in collaboration with Spanish-language academies throughout the world, including that of the United States, the Royal Academy's version of the language remains steeped in the tradition of Spain, and thus ignores and, in many cases, contests language favored in the Americas. Thus despite the prevalence of the spelling *rockero* in Latin America, there are signs that the media are beginning to follow the dictates of the RAE and are adopting the new standard.

6. Much of the conceptual work for the volume was accomplished at the Rockefeller Foundation's Ballagio Study Center in Italy during summer 2002. Not all of the contributors here were present at Bellagio, nor are all the Bellagio participants represented in this volume. The volume editors are indebted to all the valuable comments presented in Bellagio, and we have noted those places where we have integrated participants' comments into the final text of this Introduction. We also want to acknowledge the helpful criticisms of earlier drafts of this Introduction offered by Reebee Garofalo, Emmy Bretón, and Bryan McCann.

7. The term "Latin America" dates to the period of French imperial expansion in the 1860s and was employed primarily for Spanish and Portuguese contexts. Yet many argue that "Latin America" is not a linguistic domain, but rather a geopolitical category, and thus should also encompass English- and Dutch-speaking nations such as Jamaica, Guyana, Trinidad and Tobago, and even the Dutch enclaves of Aruba, Bonaire, and Curaçao. As for the term "America," in most Western languages it alludes to the entire hemispheric mass—from Alaska to Tierra del Fuego. Thus the U.S. population lives a contradiction: whereas it annually celebrates the arrival of

Europeans to America on October 12, it does not acknowledge that Columbus never actually set foot on U.S. soil.

8. This paragraph borrows language offered by Reebee Garofalo during our meetings in Bellagio.

9. Black music was subsequently marketed racially, under a series of terms, such as "soul," a category that morphed into "funk" in the 1970s, and later "rap," "urban," and "hip-hop."

10. See Reebee Garofalo, "Whose World, What Beat: The Transnational Music Industry, Identity, and Cultural Imperialism," *World of Music* 35, no. 2 (1993): 16–32; and John Tomlinson, *Cultural Imperialism: A Critical Introduction* (London: Pinter Publishers, 1991).

11. Roger Wallis and Krister Malm, *Big Sounds from Small Peoples: The Music Industry in Small Countries* (London: Constable, 1984).

12. Dave Laing, "The Music Industry and the 'Cultural Imperialism' Thesis," *Media, Culture, and Society* 8 (1986): 331.

13. Although the transnational recording and film industries were not solely U.S.-owned (Polydor Records, EMI, and Capitol, for example, were all important producers and distributors of European rock), their influence was so powerful that when the British Invasion arrived, it was largely mediated by U.S.-based cultural industries; this meant, for example, that many fans associated groups such as the Rolling Stones with the U.S. scene. Even the British could not escape being refracted through the prism of U.S. cultural hegemony!

14. Thus it is understandable that in most Latin American countries the very first manifestations of rock involved Spanish covers of North American hits; through this scheme—essentially, an import-substitution arrangement—the cultural industry emulated (intentionally or not) the dynamics of other sectors of the productive apparatus.

15. This was a trend that dated to the 1920s and that greatly accelerated after World War II.

16. The term "middle sectors" is from John Johnson, *Political Change in Latin America: The Emergence of the Middle Sectors* (Stanford, Calif.: Stanford University Press, 1965).

17. Initially this was the goal of the Social Progress Trust Fund, under the Eisenhower administration; subsequently President Kennedy proposed the Alliance for Progress.

18. Stephen Rabe, *The Most Dangerous Area in the World: John F. Kennedy Confronts Communist Revolution in Latin America* (Chapel Hill: University of North Carolina Press, 1999).

19. This is, to a certain degree, a generalization, necessary for making a larger point. Certain musicians, such as Pablo Milanés, did not hesitate to use tropical rhythms, such as salsa, in order to convey a political message. The question of salsa's "appropriateness" as a political idiom, nevertheless, was itself a subject of debate (see, e.g., Brittmarie Janson Pérez, "Political Facets of Salsa," *Popular Music* 6, no. 2 [1987], 149–59).

20. Fernando Reyes Matta, "The 'New Song' and Its Confrontation in Latin America," in *Marxism and the Interpretation of Culture,* ed. Cary Nelson and Lawrence Grossberg (Urbana: University of Illinois Press, 1988), 447–60.

21. During the colonial period, millions of enslaved Africans were transplanted to the Americas. They have retained a strong demographic and cultural presence in areas where plantation agriculture predominated—the entire Caribbean basin and Brazil—but in other countries, such as Mexico, Peru, Argentina, and Uruguay, which once

had significant populations of Africans and peoples of African descent, they have largely been erased from historical memory. This process of erasure began during the second half of the colonial era with the recovery of indigenous populations as a cheap source of available labor, but it was fully enacted in the nineteenth century through racist nationalist ideologies and immigration policies that favored those with European ancestry—a process often referred to as "whitening." The result has been a construct dating to colonial times in which skin color has been inscribed as the primary— though not exclusive—marker of status within a codified racial hierarchy, with "whites" at the top and people of African and indigenous descent at the bottom. Mestizos—individuals of mixed indigenous and European heritage—constitute the largest population group in many Latin American countries, but they occupy an intermediate position along this racialized spectrum.

22. See Peter Wade, *Blackness and Race Mixture: The Dynamics of Racial Identity in Colombia* (Baltimore: Johns Hopkins University Press, 1993); and Wade, *Race and Ethnicity in Latin America* (Chicago: Pluto Press, 1997).

23. See Peter Wade, *Music, Race, and Nation: 'Música Tropical' in Colombia* (Chicago: University of Chicago Press, 2000).

24. This paragraph incorporates language suggested by Reebee Garofalo.

25. Dunn, "Tropicália," 72–95.

26. "No me importa el gobierno ni los revolucionarios / pero si esto es vivir, prefiero morir así, cantando."

27. While there is no exclusive source to date the origin of this term, most texts covering Argentine rock agree on its usage by the late 1960s. See Pablo Alabarces, *Entre gatos y violadores: El rock nacional en la cultura argentina* (Buenos Aires: Ediciones Colihue, 1993); Alfredo Beltrán Fuentes, *La ideología antiautoritaria del rock nacional* (Buenos Aires: Centro Editor de América Latina, 1989); and Osvaldo Marzullo and Pancho Muñoz, *El rock en la Argentina: La historia y sus protagonistas* (Buenos Aires: Editorial Galerna, 1986).

28. The importance of the concept of "feeling" is reflected in the fact that the English-language word "feeling" has often been adopted phonetically to describe artistic sentiment, for example, *filin*. However, our generalized usage of the term "feeling" should not be confused with the U.S. jazz-influenced style of romantic Cuban bolero music known as *filin*.

29. Charles A. Perrone, "Changing of the Guard: Questions and Contrasts of Brazilian Rock Phenomena," *Studies in Latin American Popular Culture* 9 (1990): 65–83.

30. See, e.g., Néstor García Canclini, *Hybrid Cultures: Strategies for Entering and Leaving Modernity* (Minneapolis: University of Minnesota Press, 1995); Jean Franco, "What's in a Name? Popular Culture Theories and Their Limitations," *Studies in Latin American Popular Culture* 1 (1982): 5–14; and William Rowe and Vivian Schelling, *Memory and Modernity: Popular Culture in Latin America* (London: Verso, 1991).

31. These bands were initially categorized under a World Beat marketing rubric; see Deborah Pacini Hernandez, "Amalgamating Musics: Popular Music and Cultural Hybridity in the Americas," in *Musical Migrations: Transnationalism and Cultural Hybridity in Latin/o America*, ed. Frances Aparicio and Candida Jaquez (New York: St. Martin's Press, 2003).

32. In certain countries, such as the Dominican Republic, *música tropical* was also well entrenched among the upper classes as a symbol of their cultural nationalism. The reader should not confuse the term *música tropical* with the term *tropicália;* the latter term was specific to the Brazilian rock movement from 1967 to 1969.

33. See Jorge Duany, "Popular Music in Puerto Rico: Towards an Anthropology of Salsa," *Latin American Music Review* 5, no. 2 (fall 1984): 187–216; Félix Padilla, "Salsa

Music as a Cultural Expression of Latino Consciousness and Unity," *Hispanic Journal of Behavioral Sciences* 2, no. 1 (1989): 28–45; and Angel Quintero Rivera, *Salsa, sabor y control: Sociología de la música "tropical"* (México: Siglo XXI, 1998).

34. Central to the rise of Los Angeles as a production site for Mexican rock has been the role of veteran Argentine rocker Gustavo Santaolalla, who migrated to L.A. in 1978. He has excelled as a producer, earning wide acclaim and even a Latin Grammy, and counts among his successes such performers as La Maldita Vecindad, Café Tacuba, Los Caifanes, Molotov, Bersuit, and Juanes.

35. See Arlene Dávila, *Latinos Inc.: The Marketing and Making of a People* (Berkeley: University of California Press, 2001).

36. The language in this paragraph incorporates suggestions by Michelle Habell-Pallán.

La Onda Chicana: Mexico's Forgotten Rock Counterculture

1. Two recent additions to the acclaimed documentary series *Mexico Siglo XX* focus exclusively on the history of rock in Mexico and include previously unviewed footage from the famed Avándaro festival. There have also been several re-releases of music from La Onda Chicana period, though distribution is limited. A Web site created by a fan in the United States, Ray Brazen, has become an important source of images and information on Avándaro, and of one of the featured groups from the period, Los Dug Dug's (Ray Brazen, http://www.raybrazen.com [accessed 19 August 2003]). The recent reissue of Federico Arana's encyclopedia volume, *Guaraches de ante azul: Historia del rock mexicano* (Guadalajara: María Enea, 2002), is an invaluable source for Mexico's rock history. There is also a forthcoming encyclopedia coordinated by Arturo Lara Lozano (*Enciclopedia del rock mexicano* [Mexico City: Universidad Autónoma de México, Atzcapotzalco]). In an important sign of the rediscovery of La Onda Chicana, the recent Mexican film *Y Tu Mamá También* (2001) features on its soundtrack one of the era's most renowned songs, "Nasty Sex," by La Revolución de Emiliano Zapata. On the thirty-second anniversary of the Avándaro music festival, the "lost" tapes were released as a double-CD collection (with voiceover narration by Armando Molina, one of the festival organizers) titled *Avándaro: Por fin . . . 32 años después* (Ludell/Bakika, 2003).

2. José de Pascual Janet, "Jóvenes de ayer y de hoy," *Jueves de Excélsior,* 24 January 1957, 19.

3. "Ley federal de radio y televisión," *El Diario Oficial,* 19 January 1960. These statements were part of the "principles" established by the law, which had 105 Articles.

4. Ibid.

5. During the period 1962–66, Los Loud Jets (known abroad as the "Mexican Jets" and the "Mexican Jumping Beans") toured Latin America, the United States (where they appeared on the *Ed Sullivan Show*), the Netherlands, Western Europe, and Asia.

6. Carlos Beltrand Luján, former sales agent for Discos Orfeón, interview with author, Mexico City, 18 May 1994.

7. Víctor Roura, *Apuntes de rock: Por las calles del mundo* (Mexico City: Nuevomar, 1985), 32.

8. This is not to discount the evolution of a critical discourse among youth themselves, which in fact laid the basis for the later countercultural movement known as La Onda. The only point I wish to emphasize here is that there was little precedent of artistic independence established for later groups to build upon.

9. Joaquín "Chas" López, interview with author, Mexico City, 7 April 1993.

10. Armando Nava, interview with author, Mexico City, 5 June 1993.

11. While many of these bands sang in English during live performances, the conservative strictures of the mass media (reflective of a reactionary nationalism imposed by the state) required them to record using Spanish lyrics, in effect maintaining the concept of the *refrito* despite its increasing disparagement by youth.

12. Margo Glantz, *Onda y escritura en México: Jóvenes de 20 a 33* (Mexico City: Siglo XXI, 1971), 9.

13. Carlos Monsiváis, "México 1967," *La cultura en México,* 17 January 1968, 5.

14. "Los cerebros de la 'Revolución Bolchebeatle,'" 6 September 1968, Departamento de Investigaciónes Políticas y Sociales, Archivo General de la Nación, Gallery 2, box 2925, folder 32, no. 3-5.

15. Thomas Hughes to Secretary of State, "Mexican President's Decision to Use Force against Students May Exacerbate Differences," 29 August 1968, National Archives and Records Administration, College Park, Md., Record Group 59, box 2158.

16. Quoted in Elena Poniatowska, *Massacre in Mexico,* translated by Helen Lane (New York: Viking Press, 1975), 82.

17. Despite the polemical conflicts between protest song and rock throughout Latin America, many of the essays in this volume demonstrate that by the late 1960s native rock movements had nevertheless succeeded in gaining a place of respect within student protest culture; in many instances, the fusion with native song traditions was already underway.

18. Another important factor is that the student movement, reeling from accusations by the press that "foreign influences" were to blame for the revolt, took an especially nationalist turn after mid-August. This was reflected, for example, in the symbols and images used by the students during marches, but also in the rise to fame of folk performers such as Oscar Chávez. I am indebted to Gerardo Estrada for this important insight.

19. Quoted from the video *Mexico*—Part II (WGBH, 1988).

20. Quoted in José Agustín, *La contracultura en México: La historia y el significado de los rebeldes sin causa, los jipitecas, los punks y las bandas* (Mexico City: Grijalbo, 1996), 88–89.

21. Jim Hougan, "Mexico Raises a Counterculture," *Nation,* 25 September 1972, 239.

22. Polydor Records, for example, promoted La Revolución de Emiliano Zapata in Southern California and parts of Texas.

23. See the discussion in Eric Zolov, *Refried Elvis: The Rise of the Mexican Counterculture* (Berkeley: University of California Press, 1999), 186–87.

24. Victor Roura, "El buen ROCK aguanta el español," *México Canta,* 12 October 1973, 31.

25. Mario Mora, "La Revolución de Emiliano Zapata: Traducción integra en español del primer L.P.," *México Canta,* 27 August 1971, 6–9.

26. O'Malley noted this potential when she wrote, "Despite the long effort to make Zapata a part of the official hagiography, he is still a vital and unfixed political symbol. It remains to be seen whether he will finally be a symbol of the Revolution or of revolution" (Ilene O'Malley, *Myth of the Revolution: Hero Cults and the Institutionalization of the Mexican State, 1920–1940* [Westport, Conn.: Greenwood Press, 1986], 58). Of course, Zapata remains a potent symbol for both official and unofficial nationalist ideology. This was true during the student movement in 1968, when students waved placards featuring Zapata (thus asserting the right to rally in his name), and it remains true for the case of the Zapatistas in Chiapas and for the ramifications on urban popular culture that this movement has had.

27. In June 1971 scores of students were attacked by a paramilitarist group identified as the *halcones,* which signaled the limited space for independent protests

under the new Echeverría regime, despite the President's promised *apertura*. The use of stage microphones at Avándaro was restricted to authorized personnel; the large presence of the police and military clearly helped to suppress all political comments.

28. Enrique Marroquín, "'Dios quiere que llueva para unirnos,'" *Piedra Rodante*, 30 October 1971, 12.

29. Ironically however, the marginalization of native rock in the name of combating "cultural imperialism" did nothing to stem the inflow of foreign rock, which by this time was widespread (transnational subsidiaries had figured out how to evade high tariffs by pressing disks within Mexico).

30. These thoughts arose from a comment made by Martha Ulhôa during the conference at Bellagio. Blues was introduced into the Mexican rock scene by Javier Bátiz and his Famous Finks (see the essay in this volume by Julia Palacios and Tere Estrada). The question of "listening"—of how music is perceived (and thus embraced/rejected) through its relationship to preexisting musical referents—is an important one that merits further exploration in order to understand the nature of La Onda Chicana's "popularity," both then and now.

Between Rock and a Hard Place: Negotiating Rock in Revolutionary Cuba, 1960–1980

1. Louis A. Pérez, *Cuba and the United States: Ties of Singular Intimacy* (Athens: University of Georgia Press, 1997), 221–23.

2. Humberto Manduley López, "El rock en Cuba: Historia de un hijo descarriado," *Revolución y Cultura* 4 (1994): 9.

3. Ruby Hart Phillips, cited in Pérez, *Cuba and the United States*, 211.

4. Gary R. Mormino and George Pozzetta, "Ybor City and the Beginning of a Latin Community, 1886–1900," in *The Immigrant World of Ybor City: Italians and their Latin Neighbors in Tampa, 1885–1985* (Urbana: University of Illinois Press, 1987), 63–79.

5. Pérez, *Cuba and the United States*, 217.

6. Ibid., 227.

7. Cristobal Díaz Ayala, *Música cubana: Del areíto a la Nueva Trova* (San Juan, P.R.: Editorial Cubanacán, 1981), 213.

8. Humberto Manduley López, interview by authors, Havana, 1997.

9. Of the seven recording companies operating in Cuba, only RCA Victor and Seeco were U.S.-owned (see Díaz Ayala, *Música cubana*, 233–57); for the pressing plant, see ibid., 223.

10. Ibid., 210.

11. Liliana González Moreno, "Rock en Cuba: Juicio, hibridación y permanencia," *Actas del III Congreso Latinoamericano de la Asociación Internacional para el Estudio de la Música Popular*, http://www.hist.puc.cl/historia/iaspmla.html.

12. Humberto Manduley López, "Rock in Cuba: History of a Wayward Son," *South Atlantic Quarterly* 96, no. 1 (Winter 1997): 9.

13. González Moreno, *Rock en Cuba*, 2.

14. Alfredo Prieto, interview by Deborah Pacini Hernandez, Boston, November 1995.

15. Humberto Manduley López, interview by authors, Havana, August 1997.

16. Ernesto Juan Castellanos, ed., *Los Beatles en Cuba: Un viaje mágico y misterioso* (Havana: Ediciones Unión, 1997). Valdez's statement is on p. 128; Villar's remarks are on p. 112. All translations from the original Spanish are by Deborah Pacini Hernandez.

17. Manduley López, interview.

18. Karen Lee Wald, "Lennonism in Cuba at Last," *Z Magazine*, June 2001, 57.

19. See, e.g., Peter Wicke, "The Times They Are A-Changin': Rock Music and Political Change in East Germany," in *Rockin' the Boat: Mass Music and Mass Movements,* ed. Reebee Garofalo (Boston: South End Press, 1992), 81–92.

20. Rodolfo Rensoli, interview with authors, Havana, January 1999.

21. López Sacha is quoted in Wald, "Lennonism in Cuba," 59. ICAIC is Cuba's national film institute, the Instituto Cubano de Arte e Industria Cinematográficos.

22. Prieto, interview.

23. The BBC Latin America Saturday show called *Ritmos* also played British popular music, including the Beatles (Guille Vilar, *De Los Beatles a Los Panchos,"* in *Los Beatles en Cuba: Un viaje mágico y misterioso,* ed. Ernesto Juan Castellanos [Havana: Ediciones Unión, 1997], 14.)

24. Ernesto Juan Castellanos, "Epílogo: La censura de Los Beatles: ¿Mito o realidad?" in *Los Beatles en Cuba,* ed. Ernesto Juan Castellanos (Havana: Ediciones Unión, 1997), 149.

25. Pedro M. Cruz, "Primer programa de los Beatles en la Radio Cubana," in *Los Beatles en Cuba: Un viaje mágico y misterioso,* ed. Ernesto Juan Castellanos (Havana: Ediciones Unión, 1997), 120.

26. Ibid.

27. Ibid.

28. Castellanos, "Epílogo," 145–48.

29. Athletes and merchant marine sailors provided working-class Cubans with access to recordings from abroad.

30. Vilar, *De Los Beatles,* 114.

31. González Moreno, *Rock en Cuba,* 4.

32. Vilar, *De Los Beatles,* 114.

33. Wald, *Lennonism in Cuba,* 59.

34. Cruz, *Primer programa de los Beatles,* 119.

35. Manduley López, interview.

36. Manduley López, "Rock in Cuba: History of a Wayward Son," 136.

37. González Moreno, *Rock en Cuba,* 5.

38. Manduley López, *Rock in Cuba,* 136.

39. Yolanda Valdés, "Los Pacíficos: Primera manifestación de la música de los Beatles en Cuba," in *Los Beatles en Cuba: Un viaje mágico y misterioso,* ed. Ernesto Juan Castellanos (Havana: Ediciones Unión, 1997), 128.

40. Lorenzo DeStephano, "Los Zafiros/The Sapphires: Music from the Edge of Time," http://www.lorenzodestefano.com/zafiros.htm.

41. Manduley López, interview.

42. Pablo Menéndez, interview by Deborah Pacini Hernandez, Havana, August 1994.

43. Yvonne Daniel, *Rumba: Dance and Social Change in Contemporary Cuba* (Bloomington: Indiana University Press, 1995), 93.

44. Carlos Moore, *Castro: The Blacks and Africa* (Los Angeles: Center for Afro-American Studies, 1988), 259–60.

45. When the nightclubs were reopened a year later, the decision was made to make them profitable. Without generous state subsidies, these nightclubs were once again effectively restricted to foreign visitors and those Cubans who were able to pay the higher entrance fees.

46. Menéndez, interview.

47. Ibid.

48. Guille Vilar, "El GESI es también una ética," 2001, http://www.lajiribilla.cubaweb.cu/sumario/porautores.html.

49. Clara Díaz, "Nace la Nueva Trova," 2001, http://www.lajiribilla.cubaweb.cu/sumario/porautores.html.

50. See Charles Perrone and Christopher Dunn, *Brazilian Popular Music and Globalization* (New York: Routledge, 2001), 19–20.

51. Mariana Martins Villaca, "La política cubana y el movimiento de la Nueva Trova," paper presented at the IV Congreso de la Rama Latinoamericana de la Asociación International para el Estudio de la Música Popular (IASPM-LA), Mexico, April 2002. See also Robin Moore, "From the *canción de protesta* to the *nueva trova*, 1965–85," *Qualitative Studies in Education* 14, no. 2 (2001): 177–200.

52. Jaime Sarusky, "Leo Brouwer: Una huella duradera en el siglo XX," 2001, http://www.lajiribilla.cubaweb.cu/sumario/porautores.html.

53. Ibid.

54. Menéndez, interview.

55. Ibid.

56. Liner notes to *En busca de una nueva flor*, 1979, Discos Nueva Cultura Latinoamericana LP 0035.

57. After her visit, Dane was invited to help with the organization of the Festival de Canción Protesta by inviting socially progressive musicians from the United States such as Bob Dylan, Joan Baez, and Janis Ian to perform; none of them accepted (Pablo Menéndez, interview with authors, 1997).

58. Menéndez, interview.

59. Jaime Sarusky, "Pablo Menéndez: Un joven 'conservador,'" 2001, http://www.lajiribilla.cubaweb.cu/sumario/porautores.html.

60. Leonardo Acosta, "¿Cómo y por qué surgió el GESI?" 2001, http://www.lajiribilla.cubaweb.cu/sumario/porautores.html.

61. Sarusky, "Leo Brouwer."

62. Silvio Rodríguez is quoted in Jaime Sarusky, "La época, la música, lo humano," *Revolución y Cultura* 5: 50.

63. Menéndez is quoted in Sarusky, "Pablo Menéndez."

64. Brouer is quoted in Sarusky, "Una huella duradera."

65. Menéndez, interview.

66. Rodríguez is quoted in Sarusky, "La época, la música, lo humano," 52.

67. Ibid.

68. Ibid.

69. See Sarusky, "Pablo Menéndez."

70. See Carmelo Mesa-Largo, *Cuba in the 1970s: Pragmatism and Institutionalization* (Albuquerque: University of New Mexico Press, 1989).

71. Menéndez notes that the recording was edited without GESI's permission, so he disowns it as a GESI production (see Sarusky, "Pablo Menéndez").

72. Martins Villaca, "La política cubana y el movimiento de la Nueva Trova."

73. Humberto Manduley, "Queda la música," 2001, http://www.lajiribilla.cubaweb.cu/2001/n13_julio/357_13.html.

74. González Moreno notes that Luis Bravo produced two LPs in three years, but she does not provide dates (*Rock en Cuba*, 5).

75. González Moreno, *Rock en Cuba*, 6–9.

76. Rodríguez, cited in Sarusky, "La época, la música, lo humano,": 51.

77. Carlos Alfonso, interview by authors, Havana, August 1997.

78. Menéndez, interview.

79. Alfonso, interview.

80. Ibid.

81. Ibid.

82. Leonardo Acosta, "La timba y sus antecedentes en la música bailable cubana," *Salsa Cubana* 2, no. 6 (1998): 10.
83. Ibid.
84. Liner notes to *En busca de una nueva flor,* 1979.
85. Alfonso, interview.
86. Menéndez, interview.
87. See Deborah Pacini Hernandez and Reebee Garofalo, "Hip Hop in Havana: Rap, Race, and National Identity in Contemporary Cuba," *Journal of Popular Music Studies* 11/12 (1999/2000): 18–47.
88. González Moreno notes that thirty-five recordings identified as rock were released by Cuban and foreign labels in the 1990s, although her discography lists only twenty of them (*Rock en Cuba,* 5).
89. Reebee Garofalo, "No More Babaloo," *The Real Paper,* 9 August 1980), 8; Peter Manuel, "Marxism, Nationalism, and Popular Music in Revolutionary Cuba," *Popular Music* 6, no. 2 (1987): 163.
90. Guille Vilar, interview.
91. Judy Cantor, "Portrait of the Artist as a Communist Bureaucrat," *Miami New Times,* 24 June 1999.

Black Pau: Uncovering the History of Brazilian Soul

1. Manoel Jacinto Coelho, *Universo em Desencanto: Imunização racional, racional superior,* vol. 15 (Rio de Janeiro: Editora Gráfica Brasileira, 1973), 122.
2. The best overview of Rio de Janeiro's music scene in the 1950s is Ruy Castro's history of bossa nova (Castro, *Chega de saudade: A história e as histórias de bossa nova* [São Paulo: Companhia das Letras, 1990]).
3. "O equilíbrio precário de um gênio da música," *Jornal do Brasil,* 16 March 1993. Despite Roberto Carlos's enormous success, there is no good history of his career or of the Jovem Guarda in general.
4. The TV shows, running concurrently in 1967, were *O Fino da Bossa,* hosted by Elis Regina, *Jovem Guarda,* hosted by Roberto Carlos, Erasmo Carlos, and Wanderléa, and the short-lived *Divino, Maravilhoso,* hosted by Caetano Veloso and Gilberto Gil.
5. Nelson Motta, *Noites tropicais: Solos, improvisos e memórias musicais* (Rio de Janeiro: Objetiva, 2000), 211.
6. In contrast to most Brazilian musical phenomena other than samba, Tropicália has been the subject of extensive and excellent analysis. See in particular, Caetano Veloso, *Verdade tropical* (São Paulo: Companhia das Letras, 1997); Charles Perrone and Christopher Dunn, eds., *Brazilian Popular Music and Globalization* (Gainesville: University of Florida Press, 2001); and Christopher Dunn, *Brutality Garden: Tropicália and the Emergence of a Brazilian Counterculture* (Chapel Hill: University of North Carolina Press, 2001).
7. Virgínia Cavalcanti, "Tim Maia," *Manchete,* 20 March 1972; "A falsa imagem pesa mais do que os meus 110 quilos," unsourced newspaper clipping of the early 1970s; both in Arquivo Tim Maia, Museu da Imagem e do Som—Rio de Janeiro (hereafter cited as MIS).
8. Cavalcanti, "Tim Maia," 57; Macksen Luiz, "O sonho de Tim Maia," *Jornal do Brasil,* 22 November 1970.
9. Maia, as quoted in *Folha de São Paulo,* 16 March 1998, 7.
10. Motta, *Noites tropicais,* 204.
11. The authorship of "Réu Confesso" is disputed. Maia registered the composition

in his own name and was later sued by Neusa Maria da Costa, who claimed to have written the tune and submitted it to Polydor.

12. On the reactions of Roberto Carlos and Erasmo Carlos to Maia's success, see Pedro Alexandre Sanches, "Cantor ia sempre além," *Folha de São Paulo, Ilustrada,* 16 March 1998, 6.

13. "Tim Maia, ídolo dos guetos," unsourced newspaper clipping of February 1978, in Arquivo Tim Maia, MIS.

14. See, e.g., "Tim Maia, ídolo dos guetos," Arquivo Tim Maia, MIS.

15. Motta, *Noites tropicais,* 217.

16. "Tim Maia, réu confesso," *O Jornal,* 11 December 1973, and unsourced newspaper clipping of 18 March 1972, both in Arquivo Tim Maia, MIS.

17. On Ilê Aiyê and *bloco afro* in general, see Antonio Riserio, *Carnaval Ijexá* (Salvador: Corrupião, 1981), as well as Milton Araújo Moura, "World of Fantasy, Fantasy of the World," and Piers Armstrong, "Songs of Olodum," both in *Brazilian Popular Music and Globalization,* ed. Charles Perrone and Christopher Dunn (Gainesville: University of Florida Press, 2001).

18. Gilberto Freyre, *Casa grande e senzala* (Rio de Janeiro: José Olympio, 1933).

19. Florestan Fernandes, *The Negro in Brazilian Society* (New York: Columbia University Press, 1969).

20. George Reid Andrews, *Blacks and Whites in São Paulo* (Madison: University of Wisconsin Press, 1992).

21. Fernandes, *The Negro.* For an illuminating summary of Fernandes's importance and subsequent historiographical developments, see Michael Hanchard, *Orpheus and Power: The Movimento Negro of Rio de Janeiro and São Paulo, 1945–1988* (Princeton, N.J.: Princeton University Press, 1994), 32–42.

22. On the early soul dances, see the interview with Carlos Alberto Medeiros in *Artefato* 2, no. 10 (1978): 12–14.

23. Lena Frias, "O orgulho (importado) de ser negro no Brasil," *Jornal do Brasil,* 17 July 1976, 2.

24. See, e.g., "E depois do black pau?" *Jornegro* (São Paulo), July 1978, 5.

25. Medeiros, *Artefato.*

26. Frias, "Orgulho," 5.

27. Ibid., 4.

28. Livio Sansone, "From Africa to Afro: Use and Abuse of Africa in Brazil," *South-South Exchange Program for Research on the History of Development,* lecture no. 3 (1999): 26–33.

29. See e.g., the interviews and analysis in Carlos Benedito Rodrigues da Silva, "Black Soul: Aglutinação espontânea ou identidade étnica?" in *Movimentos sociais, urbanos, minorias étnicas e outros estudos,* ed. L. A. Silva (Brasilia: ANPOCS, 1983), 245–62.

30. "Agora falando, soul," *Jornegro* (São Paulo), May 1978, 4.

31. Frias, "Orgulho," 5.

32. John French, "The Missteps of Anti-imperialist Reason: Pierre Bourdieu, Loïc Wacquant, and Michael Hanchard's Orpheus and Power," working paper, Duke/University of North Carolina Latin American Studies Colloquium, 1999, 27–30.

33. Livio Sansone, "The Localization of Global Funk in Bahia and in Rio," in *Brazilian Popular Music and Globalization,* ed. Charles Perrone and Christopher Dunn (Gainesville: University of Florida Press, 2001), 148–52.

34. "Agora falando, soul," *Jornegro,* 4.

35. Medeiros, *Artefato,* 12.

36. Leila Gonzales and Carlos Hasenbalg, *Lugar de negro* (Rio de Janeiro: Marco Zero, 1985), 31–46.

37. Hanchard, *Orpheus*, 119–27.
38. Frias, "Orgulho."
39. See, e.g., "Turismo ve só comércio no Black Rio," *Jornal do Brasil*, 15 May 1977; and "Black Rio assusta maestro Julio Medaglia," *Folha de São Paulo*, 10 June 1977.
40. Gilberto Freyre, *Estado de São Paulo*, 30 May 1977.
41. Author communication with Sérgio Lupper, July 2001. Hanchard recounts the similar, if more dramatic, tale of one of his informants, and considers its implications (Hanchard, *Orpheus*, 182 n 27). For Hanchard's treatment of Brazilian soul of the 1970s in general, see *Orpheus*, 111–19. Fabienne Souza Borges da Costa was expelled from the Escola Cócio Barcelos in September 1977. When Fabienne sued, the courts upheld her expulsion (*Jornal do Brasil*, 14 September 1977).
42. Cristóvão Bastos, interview with author, Rio de Janeiro, June 2001.
43. Dunn, *Brutality Garden*, 72–95.
44. For details on Maia's last years, see, among other obituaries, Sérgio Martins, "Artista estava a anos-luz de seu folclore," *Folha de São Paulo, Ilustrada*, 16 March 1998.
45. See http://www.edmotta.com.
46. João Batista de Jesus Felix, "Chic Show e Zimbabwe e a construção da identidade nos bailes black Paulistanos," M.A. thesis, University of São Paulo, FFLCH, 2000, 9.
47. Hermano Vianna, *O mundo funk carioca* (Rio de Janeiro: Zahar, 1988); George Yúdice, "The Funkification of Rio," in *Microphone Fiends: Youth Music and Youth Culture*, ed. Andrew Ross and Tricia Rose (New York: Routledge, 1994), 195–215.

Boricua Rock: Puerto Rican by Necessity!

1. Raymond Williams, *The Long Revolution* (London: Chatto and Windus, 1961), 61.
2. Juan Flores, *From Bomba to Hip-Hop* (New York: Columbia University Press, 2000).
3. Javier Santiago, *Nueva ola portoricensis: La revolución musical que vivió en la década del 60* (Santurce, P.R.: Publicaciones Del Patio, 1994).
4. See Ana Maria García's film *Cocolos and Rockeros: For Rock or Salsa?* (Du Art Film and Video, 1992); Ángel G. Quintero Rivera, *Salsa, sabor y control: Sociología de la música tropical* (Coyoacán, Mexico: Siglo XXI Editores, 1998), 149–50, 176–81, on why young migrant Puerto Ricans in New York City in the late 1960s and early 1970s chose salsa and not rock; and Peter Watrous, "Much of Latin Pop, Aging and Sterile, Isn't Keeping Pace," *New York Times*, 6 August 2000, sec. 2, 27–28.
5. Cf. Jorge Duany, "Rethinking the Popular: Recent Essays on Caribbean Music," *Latin American Music Review* 17, no. 2 (1996): 176–92.
6. Quintero Rivera, *Salsa, sabor y control*, 181.
7. Ibid., 25 (translation mine).
8. Harold Hopkins, telephone interview by author, 20 July 2001.
9. Paniagua, telephone interview by author, 20 July 2001.
10. Kevin Benson, telephone interview by author, 6 June 2000.
11. In a *Contemporary Music Journal* survey (August 2001) of Midwestern U.S. alternative rock radio stations, Puya was fourth on several program playlists.
12. Paniagua, interview. In the late 1980s a Boricua band named Top Banana was signed to CBS, with no significant results. More recently, Sol D'Menta signed first with Polygram and later Sony, but was later dropped by both labels.
13. Josh Norek, telephone interview by author, 20 August 2001.
14. Paniagua, quoted in Rodrigo Salazar, "Puya, ahorake?" *Urban Latino* 33 (2001): 32–33. On April 19, 1999, during U.S. Navy bombing practices, an off-target bomb killed a civilian security guard and injured four others on the island of Vieques. This

incident sparked a fury of public protest, as island and mainland Puerto Ricans and their supporters united in demanding that Navy bombing exercises stop.

15. Hopkins, interview.

16. Christopher Alan Waterman, *Jùjú: A Social History and Ethnography of African Popular Music* (Chicago: University of Chicago Press, 1990), 54.

17. Edgardo Soto Torres, "El cantar de una generación," *Diálogo,* May 1999, 24.

18. Edgardo Soto Torres and Elías Geigel, "El rock de Puerto Rico: Desafío músical a un pueblo dormido," *La Banda Elástica* 35 (2000): 52.

19. Juan M. García-Passalacqua, "Fieles a Puerto Rico, una generación que no es X," *El Nuevo Día,* 2 August 1998, 10.

20. García-Passalacqua, "Fieles a Puerto Rico." See also Elidio La Torre Lagares, "Deconstruyendo mi generación: Una manera de entender a Fiel a la Vega," *El Nuevo Día,* 3 May 1998, 4–5.

21. Ed Morales, telephone interview by author, 3 June 2000.

22. Soto Torres, "El cantar de una generación," 24.

23. Ibid., (my emphasis).

24. For an analysis of Fiel a la Vega's sociopolitical lyrics, see José Anazagasty Rodríguez, "Colonial Capitalism, Hegemony, and Youth Praxis in Puerto Rico: Fiel a la Vega's Rock en Español," *Latin American Music Review* 23, no.1 (2002): 79–105.

25. According to Soto Torres, Auger is influenced by American artists such as Bob Dylan and Bruce Springsteen, as well as by *nueva trova* and *nueva canción* artists such as Silvio Rodríguez (Cuba), Rubén Blades (Panama), and, especially, Puerto Rico's own musico-politico provocateur, Roy Brown (Edgardo Soto Torres, telephone interview by author, 15 September 2001). Fiel has also worked with significant Puerto Rican *nueva canción* artists of the 1970s, such as Haciendo Punto en Otro Son and Moliendo Vidrio. See also Javier Santiago, *Nueva ola portoricensis,* 313–18.

26. Tito Auger, telephone interview by author, 4 September 2001.

27. Soto Torres, interview.

28. Soto Torres and Geigel, "El rock de Puerto Rico," 53.

29. Guillermo Echevarría, telephone interview by author, 18 June 2000.

30. Flores, *From Bomba to Hip-Hop,* 17, 20, 22, 28.

31. Ibid., 164.

32. Soto Torres, interview (my translation).

33. Edgardo Soto Torres, "Boricua Rock," e-mail message to author, 4 September 2001.

34. Not4Prophet (né Alano Baez), telephone interview by author, 18 May 2000.

35. Not4Prophet, quoted in Rosa Fernández, "Ricanstruction," *Jersey Beat* (n.d.).

36. Not4Prophet, interview.

37. Ibid.

38. Not4Prophet, quoted by Tamara, "Ricanstruction," *Profane Existence* (n.d.), 38.

39. Not4Prophet considers Albizu Campos the "Malcolm X" of Puerto Rico (interview).

40. Not4Prophet, interview.

41. Ibid.

42. According to the band's manager, Vagabond, the cited lyric is from Ricanstruction's as-yet-unreleased recording of the same name: *Love+Revolution* (Vagabond, telephone interview by author, 6 April 2002).

43. Soto Torres, interview.

44. Jorge LaBoy, interview by author, New York City, 26 May 2000.

45. Flores, *From Bomba to Hip-Hop,* 58.

46. Morales, interview.

47. La Secta All Star's first independently produced recording, *La Secta All Star*

(2001, Fonovisa), sold 10,000 units in its first week of release. Also see Randy Luna, "Puerto Rican Indies Shun Major's Help," *Billboard,* 11 August 2001, 45.

48. Susan McClary, *Conventional Wisdom: The Content of Musical Form* (Berkeley: University of California Press, 2000), 153.

49. Peter Wicke, *Rock Music: Culture, Aesthetics, and Sociology* (Cambridge: Cambridge University Press, 1990), 25.

50. Simon Frith, "The Magic That Can Set You Free: The Ideology of Folk and Myth of the Rock Community," *Popular Music* 1 (1981): 168.

The Politics and Anti-Politics of Uruguayan Rock

1. Lawrence Grossberg, "The Media Economy of Rock Culture: Cinema, Post-Modernity, and Authenticity," in *Sound and Vision. The Music Video Reader,* ed. Simon Frith, Andrew Goodwin, and Lawrence Grossberg (London: Routledge, 1993), 205; and Simon Frith, "Music and Identity," in *Questions of Cultural Identity,* ed. Stuart Hall and Paul du Gay (London: Sage, 1996), 122–23.

2. George Lipsitz, *Time Passages: Collective Memory and American Popular Culture* (Minneapolis: University of Minnesota Press, 1990); and Simon Frith, *Sound Effects* (New York: Pantheon, 1981).

3. Grossberg. "The Media Economy of Rock Culture," 199.

4. Ibid., 200.

5. Ibid., 201.

6. The concept of *transculturation* stands as one of the major contributions of Latin American thought to the field of cultural studies, perhaps only second to dependency theory, the star of the social sciences in the 1960s. The term *transculturation* was coined circa 1940 by Fernando Ortiz in his now classic *Contrapunteo cubano del tabaco y el azúcar* (*Cuban Counterpoint: Tobacco and Sugar*) to capture the complexities of Cuban cultural history and circumvent the doubly ideological term *acculturation*. Acculturation was overly impregnated by a cultural relativism that became an alibi for referring to "those phenomena which result when groups of individuals having different cultures come into continuous first-hand contact, with subsequent changes in the original cultural patterns of either or both groups," according to the authorized definition from the "Memorandum for the Study of Acculturation" (Robert Redfield, Ralph Linton, Melville J. Herskovits, "Memorandum for the Study of Acculturation," *American Anthropologist* 38 [1936]: 149–52). In the introduction to Ortiz's book, Bronislaw Malinovsky accepts *transculturation* to mean "an exchange between two cultures, both of them active . . . from which a new reality emerges, transformed and complex" (x–xi). Actually, this definition differs very little from the standard one, although Malinovsky denounces on etymological grounds the ethnocentric bias of the latter, which implies that "the 'uncultured' is to receive the benefits of 'our culture,'" a variant for assimilation (Ortiz, *Contrapunteo cubano del tabaco y el azúcar,* x–xii). Ortiz's "transculturation" does emphasize fusion and synthesis ("neoculturation"), but it also foregrounds the idea of a transitive process of successive "deculturations" (or "exculturations") and "acculturations" (or "enculturations"), characterized by confrontation and struggle. During the 1970s, Angel Rama reformulated the concept in *Transculturación narrativa en América Latina* (*Narrative Transculturation in Latin America*) within the framework of dependency theory, injecting it with a continental dimension. Although Rama applies the term exclusively to literature, after him, *transculturation* became one of the most important tools in the field of Latin American cultural studies, an interdisciplinary mega-concept capable of interweaving anthropological, sociological, political, and literary studies. See Renato Ortiz. *Mundialização e cultura* (São Paulo: Editora Brasiliense, 1994), 155; and Martín Hopenhayn, *Ni*

apocalípticos ni integrados: Aventuras de la modernidad en América Latina (Santiago de Chile: Fondo de Cultura Económica, 1994). See also Fernando Ortiz, *Cuban Counterpoint: Tobacco and Sugar,* trans. Harriet de Onís (New York: Knopf, 1947), and Ángel Rama, *Transculturación narrativa en America Latina* (Mexico: Siglo XXI, 1982).

7. Karl Marx, *The Grundrisse. Foundations of the Critique of Political Economy* (London: Penguin Books, 1973).

8. Magdalena Herrera, *El País* [edición digital], http://www.iracundomania.com/2000.html.

9. Osvaldo Fattoruso, in Roberto Elissalde and Guillermo de Alencar Pinto, http://www.geocities.com/gaston20ar/shakers.bio.html.

10. Ibid.

11. Antonio D. Plácido, *Carnaval: Evocación de Montevideo en la historia y la tradición* (Montevideo: Imp. Letras, 1966), 57; Ildefonso Pereda Valdés, *El negro en el Uruguay: Pasado y presente* (Montevideo: Instituto Histórico y Geográfico, 1965), 171.

12. Tótem, *Tótem,* 1995, Sondor CD 49642.

13. In Uruguay the regime promoted a perverse mechanism of ideological control and social submission. The terror was effected through the victims' complicity, but it also served the victims as an alibi for setting aside any and all responsibility in their own victimization. See Carina Perelli and Juan Rial, *De mitos y memorias políticas* (Montevideo: Ediciones de la Banda Oriental, 1986).

14. Gerard Béhague, "Popular Music in Latin America," *Studies in Latin American Popular Culture,* no. 5 (1986); Hugo García Robles, *El cantar opinando* (Montevideo: Alfa, 1969).

15. Mauricio Ubal, "Carnaval: Arte y zafra," *Brecha,* no. 30:25, http://www.brecha.com.uy.

16. Rumbo, *Rumbo,* 1980, Sondor 48783.

17. Jaime Roos, *Brindis por Pierrot,* 1985, Orfeo 90787.

18. La Chancha Francisca, *La berenjenas también rebotan,* 1989, Orfeo 980970-1.

19. G. Baltar and L. E. Behares, "Rock uruguayo: Lo dicho y la escucha," *relaciones* 38 (1987). (Web site for this journal is http://fp.chasque.apc.org:8081/relacion; however issues dating this far back are not linked.)

20. A. M. Echeberría and V. Varela. "Jóvenes violentos," *relaciones* 91 (1991). (Web site for this journal is http://fp.chasque.apc.org:8081/relacion; however issues dating this far back are not linked.)

21. "Viviendo en Uruguay," Los Traidores, *La lluvia ha vuelto a caer,* Orfeo 91154-1.

22. Benjamín Arditi, "Expansividad de lo social, recodificación de lo 'político,'" in *Imágenes desconocidas: La modernidad en la encrucijada postmoderna,* ed. Fernando Calderón et al. (Buenos Aires: Clacso, 1988), 168.

23. "Miscelánea IV," [Tabaré Riverock Banda], *Rockanrol del Arrabal,* 1989, Orfeo 90993-4.

24. Jorge Nasser, "Níquel," in *A ritmo de rock,* ed. Cecilia Martínez and Tabaré Couto (Montevideo: La República, 1988), 58.

25. Cuarteto de Nos, "Eres una chica muy bonita," *Otra Navidad en las trincheras,* 1994, Ayuí A/E126K.

26. Juan Flores, *From Bomba to Hip-Hop: Puerto Rican Culture and Latino Identity* (New York: Columbia University Press, 2000), 194–95; Román de la Campa, "Norteamérica y sus mundos latinos: Ontologías, globalización, diasporas," *Revista Iberoamericana* 71, no. 193 (2001): 753–69.

27. Jean Franco, "Globalización y la crisis de lo popular," *Nueva Sociedad,* no. 149 (1997): 62–73.

28. Patricia Turnes, "Peyote Asesino for export: Nada terraja," *Brecha,* no. 662, http://www.brecha.com.uy/.

29. Ibid.
30. La Vela Puerca, "Alta magia," *Deskarado*, 1997, produced by Obligado Producciones.
31. Peyote Asesino, "Perkins," *Terraja*, 1995, Orfeo 91524-4.
32. Peyote Asesino, "Cama biónica," *Terraja*, 1995, Orfeo 91524-4.
33. Peyote Asesino, *Terraja*, 1995, Orfeo 91525-4.
34. La Vela Puerca, "El bandido Saltodemata," *Deskarado*, 1997, produced by Obligado Producciones.
35. Peyote Asesino, "UR Gay," *Terraja*, 1995, Orfeo 91524-4.
36. "La mugre de tus orejas," *Rocanrol del arrabal*, 1989, Orfeo 90993-4.

"A contra corriente": A History of Women Rockers in Mexico

1. Tim Padgett, "Julieta Venegas: Turning Rock 'n' Roll into a Mexican Idiom," *Time* (Latin American edition "Special Issue"), 15 October 2001.
2. These data are approximate, since it is difficult to determine how many rock groups exist in Mexico's capital, given that bands are created and dissolved in a short time. In the year 2000 the organization Rock Mexicano registered around three hundred Web pages of rock groups with diverse styles, mostly from Mexico City and its metro area. Women participated, either as vocalists or instrumentalists, in thirty-five of these groups.
3. José Gutiérrez Maya, *La historia del rock and roll en México* (Mexico City: Disco Recuerdo, 1998), 16.
4. Ela Laboriel, interview by Tere Estrada, San Miguel Chapultepec, Mexico City, 15 January 1996. The Laboriel family was originally from Honduras. The family is also black, which is not common in Mexico. Of the Laboriel children, Ela, Francis, and Johnny became singers, and Abraham is currently a renowned musician in the United States.
5. Parménides García Saldaña, *En la ruta de la onda* (Mexico City: Editorial Diógenes, 1972), 101. Parménides García Saldaña was an outstanding young journalist and writer who helped initiate the trend called Literatura de La Onda in the 1960s.
6. Martha Agüero, interview by Tere Estrada, Houston, Texas, 19 March 1999. Agüero recalls that when they signed a contract to tour in the United States, they were restricted to mainly performing Mexican folkloric music.
7. Silvia Garcel, interview by Tere Estrada, Cuicuilco, Mexico City, 26 February 1999.
8. Ibid.
9. Ibid.
10. Ela Laboriel, interview.
11. A little later, Julissa was consecrated as the woman who dared to be different, through her role in the movie *Los Caifanes* (1967), in which she played a *"fresa" chava* (middle-class gal) who has the opportunity to explore another world and ventures to see what is there. She won a Diosa de Plata award as best actress in 1967 for her work in this film.
12. Ela Laboriel, interview.
13. Commentary from *Actualidades de América*, March 1962, 28, quoted in Gutiérrez Maya, *Historia del rock and roll en México*, 24.
14. According to some critics, Angélica María left her good-girl image behind with the movie *Cinco de chocolate y uno de fresa* (1967), in which Los Dug Dug's played and for which José Agustín, the writer, wrote the screenplay and song lyrics.
15. ITESM Monterrey Cine Club, Estrellas del Cine Mexicano, Angélica María, http://www.mty.itesm.mx/dcic/carreras/lcc/cine_mex/estrellas/angelica_maria.html.

16. First, she was billed as part of Martha y los Ventura (1968–1970); later, in 1970, she became a soloist, calling herself Martha Ventura, but that didn't last long. She was the last icon of the rock and roll balladeers.

17. For further discussion of this "invasion," see the chapter by Eric Zolov in this collection. Javier Bátiz is one of the most important guitar players in Mexico and was brought from Tijuana, by the Tena brothers of Los Rebeldes del Rock, to sing in El Harlem, a *café cantante*. He was key in the introduction of blues and soul in Mexico City, rhythms that were, until then, virtually unknown. Baby's real name was María Esther Medina Núñez, but they called her "Baby" because she was the youngest of six children.

18. Baby Bátiz, interview by Tere Estrada, Narvarte, Mexico City, 28 October 1992.

19. Comments by Baby Bátiz on the program "Rockeras: Diálogos en confianza," Canal 11, Mexico City, 7 January 2000. The expression *"mucha onda"* (hip feeling) referred to singing with a nasal and hoarse voice.

20. Besides Baby, other women arrived from the northern border as members of new groups, among them Los Stukas with their singer Jenny Silva, Blanquita Estrada with Los Rockin Devils, and Marisela Durazo, who would emerge with Tequila.

21. Mayita Campos, interview by Tere Estrada, Observatorio, Mexico City, 7 November 1992.

22. The show had only one performance, in Acapulco in 1969, before it was cancelled by authorities. Alfredo Elías Calles, grandson of Mexico's "strongman" president from the 1920s, was a patron of *rockero* groups in Mexico during the 1960s and 1970s. He ran several elegant discos in Mexico, such as Tiberios in Acapulco, and was constantly bringing groups from Tijuana.

23. Carlos Monsiváis, "De la construcción de la sensibilidad femenina," *Fem* 18 (December 1986–January 1987): 18.

24. Chela Lora, interview by Tere Estrada, Altavista, Mexico City, 30 October 1995.

25. Ela Laboriel, interview.

26. When the Avándaro Festival took place, Baby Bátiz and the other members of Soul Force were stuck in traffic about fifteen kilometers away and never arrived.

27. Marisela Durazo, interview by Tere Estrada, Houston, Texas, 3 November 1992.

28. Carlos Monsiváis, *Amor perdido* (Mexico City: Editorial Era, 1977), 247–58.

29. According to Ela Laboriel, this spectacle began when someone who was filming a movie invited the *chavas* (gals) to climb on a truck to dance and take off their clothes for money (Ela Laboriel, interview).

30. Alfonso Miranda, interview by Tere Estrada, Mexico City, 22 February 1999.

31. For discussion of the significance of this term, see the essay by Eric Zolov in this volume.

32. Laura Abitia, interview by Tere Estrada, Roma, Mexico City, January 1999.

33. Ibid.

34. Norma Valdez, interview by Tere Estrada, Copilco, Mexico City, 20 December 1992.

35. Baby Bátiz, interview by Tere Estrada, Narvarte, Mexico City, 28 October 1992.

36. Ela Laboriel, interview.

37. Laura Abitia, interview.

38. Cecilia Toussaint in the show "Sólo para bandas," Estéreo Joven radio station, México, May 1991.

39. Ibid.

40. Ibid.

41. Kenny Avilés, interview by Tere Estrada, Del Valle, Mexico City, 14 November 1995.

42. Ibid.
43. Fernanda Tapia, interview by Tere Estrada, Mexico City, 27 October 1995.
44. Dominique Peralta, interview by Tere Estrada, Anzures, Mexico City, 16 January 1996.
45. For discussion of the concept of *chavos banda*, see the essay by Héctor Castillo Berthier in this volume.
46. Ángela Martínez, interview by Tere Estrada, Narvarte, Mexico City, 15 March 1996.
47. Ibid. For further discussion of the Tianguis del Chopo, see the chapter by Héctor Castillo Berthier in this volume.
48. Ibid.
49. Zappa Punk, interview by Tere Estrada, Centro, Mexico City, 28 March 1996.
50. Ibid.
51. Ibid.
52. Primer Encuentro de Mujeres en el Rock, Museo Universitario del Chopo, November 1991, Mexico City.
53. Zappa Punk, interview.
54. Rita Guerrero, "Contra el vicio de no comprometerse," interview by René Aviña, *Rock & Pop,* (December 1994): 52.
55. Rita Guerrero, Rockeros.com, Santa Sabina, interview with Rita Guerrero, http://www.rockeros.com/santasabina.
56. Rita Guerrero, "Rita y Julieta: El dulce sabor de la sangre," interview by Hugo García Michel, *La Mosca en la Pared* 2, no. 19 (December 1997).
57. In January 2000, Gloria Trevi and her agent, Sergio Andrade, were arrested in Brazil after ten months of police persecution and charged with corruption of minors, kidnapping, and rape.
58. Roberto Ponce, "Frida, Ely Guerra, Sasha Sokol y Julieta Venegas: Creación versus mercancía, voluntad versus drogas. La novísima generación de compositoras busca su identidad musical en el mundo 'pop de los hombres,'" *Proceso,* 31 August 1997, 70.
59. Ibid., 72.

Soy punkera, ¿y qué?:
Sexuality, Translocality, and Punk in Los Angeles and Beyond

1. I am grateful to the editors for inviting me to participate in the Rockefeller Foundation Bellagio Research Residency team. Thanks to the following institutions that have funded portions of this project: the Rockefeller Foundation Humanities Postdoctoral Fellowship; Smithsonian Institution's Latino Initiative Fund; the Woodrow Wilson National Fellowship Foundation Career Enhancement Junior Faculty Postdoctoral Grant; and the UC President's Postdoctoral Fellowship. Portions of this draft have been presented at the following meetings: NACCS 1998; ASA 1999; MLA 2000; and LASA 2000. I thank Lisa Lowe for her wonderful early comments, Rosa Linda Fregoso for Tejana insight, George Mariscal for clarifying the nuances of Chicana/o cultural nationalism, and Jocelyn Guilbault for her excellent suggestions.

2. José D. Saldívar, "Postmodern Realism," in *Columbia History of the American Novel,* ed. Emory Elliott (New York: Columbia University Press, 1991), 521. See also William A. Nericcio, "A Decidedly 'Mexican and American' Semi[ero]tic Transference: Frida Kahlo in the Eyes of Gilbert Hernandez," in *Latino/a Popular Culture,* ed. Michelle Habell-Pallán and Mary Romero (New York: New York University Press, 2002), 190–207.

3. See the writings by David Reyes and Tom Waldman, *Land of a Thousand Dances:*

Chicano Rock 'n' Roll from Southern California (Albuquerque: University of New Mexico Press, 1998); George Lipsitz, *Dangerous Crossroads: Popular Music, Postmodernism, and the Poetics of Place* (New York: Verso, 1994); Steven Loza, *Barrio Rhythm: Mexican American Music in Los Angeles* (Urbana: University of Illinois Press, 1993); José D. Saldívar, *Border Matters: Remapping American Cultural Studies* (Berkeley: University of California Press, 1997); Frances Aparicio and Candida F. Jaques, eds., *Musical Migrations: Transnationalism and Cultural Hybridity in Latin/o America* (New York: Palgrove Press 2003); Curtis Marez, "Becoming Brown: The Politics of Chicana/o Popular Style, *Social Text* 48 (1996): 109–32.

4. The interviews I conducted with former Chicana *punkeras* are part of a longer book manuscript in-progress.

5. Reyes and Waldman, *Land of a Thousand Dances,* 135.

6. Ibid.

7. In fact, Chicana/o youth had historically been at the forefront of formulating stylized social statements via the fashion and youth subcultures—beginning with the Pachucos, and continuing on through Chicana Mods. For an excellent discussion of how Chicana artists "made do" with limited resources, see Laura Pérez, "Spirit Glyphs: Reimagining Art and Artist in the Work of Chicana Tlamatinime," *Modern Fiction Studies* 44, no. 1 (1998): 36–76.

8. For an insightful essay on Chicana youth culture of the 1940s, see Catherine Ramírez, "Crimes of Fashion: The Pachuca and Chicana Style Politics," *Meridians: A Journal of Transnational Feminisms* 2, no. 2 (2002): 1–35.

9. For a history of Chicanos in Los Angeles, see George Sanchez, *Becoming Mexican American: Ethnicity and Acculturation in Chicano Los Angeles, 1900–1945* (New York: Oxford University Press, 1993).

10. Reyes and Waldman, *Land of a Thousand Dances,* 135–36.

11. Ibid..

12. Alicia Armendariz Velasquez, interview by author, Los Angeles, 12 August 1998.

13. For more on Marisela Norte, see Michelle Habell-Pallán, "No Cultural Icon: Marisela Norte," in *Women Transforming Politics,* ed. Kathy Jones, Cathy Cohen, and Joan Tronto (New York: New York University Press, 1997), 256–68.

14. For a detailed analysis of Chicana cultural production and Chicana feminist discourses, see Sonia Saldívar-Hull, *Feminism on the Border: Chicana Gender Politics and Literature* (Berkeley: University of California Press, 2000).

15. Angie Chabram-Dernersesian, "I Throw Punches for My Race, but I Don't Want to Be a Man: Writing Us Chica-nos (Girl, Us)/Chican*as*—into the Movement Script," in *Cultural Studies,* ed. Lawrence Grossberg, Cary Nelson, and Paula Treichler (New York: Routledge, 1992), 81–95.

16. David Jones, "Destroy All Music: Punk Rock Pioneers of Southern California" (manuscript).

17. Kristine McKenna, "Female Rockers—A New Breed," *Los Angeles Times* (Calendar Section), 18 June 1978, 78–82.

18. Ibid., 78.

19. Ibid.

20. Ibid., 82.

21. Ibid., 78.

22. Sincere thanks to Jim Fricke, program curator at the Experience Music Project, for allowing me to access the *Yes L.A.* compilation.

23. For varied testimonies of Canterbury's history, see Marc Spitz and Brendan Mullen, *We Got the Neutron Bomb: The Untold Story of L.A. Punk* (New York: Three Rivers Press, 2001).

24. For a discussion of another Chicano artist who finds resources in the most unexpected places, see Michelle Habell-Pallán, "El Vez Is 'Taking Care of Business': The Inter/National Appeal of Chicana/o Popular Music," *Cultural Studies* 13, no. 2 (1999): 195–210.

25. Teresa Covarrubias, interview by author, East Los Angeles, 8 August 1998.

26. Ibid.

27. McKenna, "Female Rockers—A New Breed," 82.

28. Reyes and Waldman, *Land of a Thousand Dances,* 139.

29. *Life and Times: Chicanas in Tune,* video produced by Esther Reyes for Community Television of Southern California, 1994 (originally broadcast on KCET-TV, Los Angeles).

30. Las Tres, *Live at the LATC,* 1993 (audiocassette). Thanks to Antonia García-Orozco for inventing the notion of Chicana Trova in relation to Nueva Trova—that is, Chicana Trova is sung in English and lyrically calls for consciousness-raising through a form of folk music that can be played on accessible instruments.

31. See Tiffany Lopez, *The Alchemy of Blood: Violence as Critical Discourse in U.S. Latina/o Literature* (Durham, N.C.: Duke University Press, forthcoming); on incarceration and women of color, see Angela Davis, *The Prison Industrial Complex,* 2000 (compact disk; AK Press B00002JXEI).

32. Reyes and Waldman, *Land of a Thousand Dances,* 136.

33. Ibid.

34. Ibid., 140.

35. Sean Carrillo, "East to Eden," in *Forming: The Early Days of L.A. Punk,* ed. Sean Carrillo, Christina McKenna, Claude Bessy, and Exene Cervenka (Santa Monica: Smart Art Press, 1999), 42.

36. Sonia Saldívar-Hull, "Feminism on the Border: From Gender Politics to Geopolitics," in *Criticism in the Borderlands: Studies in Chicano Literature, Culture, and Ideology,* ed. Héctor Calderón and José D. Saldívar (Durham, N.C.: Duke University Press, 1991), 204, 211.

37. *Pretty Vacant,* directed and produced by Jim Mendiola, 1996 (distributed by Subcine: Independent Latino Film and Video). Molly recuperates the great Tejano "punk" accordion player Steve Jordan into her conceptual map of Chicano culture. According to Rosa Linda Fregoso, Jordan has generally been left out in accounts of Tejano oppositional culture—unlike "Little Joe," a Tejano musician associated with the movement—because of his heroin addiction and unconventional lifestyle (see Mendiola's *Speeder Kills* [produced by Faith Radle, 2003] for another filmic narrative that thematizes punk and Chicana identity).

38. *Pretty Vacant,* 1996.

39. Norma Alarcón, "Cognitive Desires: An Allegory of/for Chicana Critics," in *Chicana (W)rites on Word and Film,* ed. María Herrera-Sobek and Helena María Viramontes (Oakland: Third Woman Press, 1996), 187.

40. *Pretty Vacant,* 1996.

41. Evey Chapa, "Mujeres Por La Raza Unida," in *Chicana Feminist Thought,* ed. Alma García (New York: Routledge, 1997), 179.

On How Bloque de Búsqueda Lost Part of Its Name: The Predicament of Colombian Rock in the U.S. Market

1. David Byrne, "Crossing Music's Borders in Search of Identity: 'I Hate World Music,'" *New York Times,* 3 October 1999, B1.

2. Although Cuban critic Leonardo Acosta traces his first attempts at rock production back to 1957, with Los Hot Rockers, the group he formed with pianist Raúl

Ondira and lead singer Tony Escarpenter, their production is not documented. Hence, the Mexican rock and roll movement of the late 1950s appears to be the first one with a documented production (see Leonardo Acosta, *Fiesta Havana 1940–1960 : L'âge d'or de la musique cubaine* [Paris: Vade retro, 1999]).

3. Omar Urán, Patricia Valencia, and Gilberto Medina, *Medellín en vivo: La historia del rock* (Medellín: Corporación Región, 1997).

4. Many years later, in an ironic twist of events, rock concerts became the key reason for the appeal of Bogotá Mayor Andrés Pastrana to the capital city's middle-class masses. Pastrana went on to become president; his string of City Hall–sponsored concerts engendered Rock al Parque, the largest public-funded tradition of rock concerts in the Americas. In 2002, the Instituto Distrital de Cultura y Turismo published a volume chronicling these concerts, which are celebrated yearly and enjoy a regular attendance of up to 150,000. On the other hand, in 1971, Colombian mayors were not elected, but appointed. The democratic election of mayors and governors was instituted as the result of reforms in the 1980s. For further mention of the original Ancón Festival, see Pilar Riaño-Alcalá, "Urban Space and Music in the Formation of Youth Cultures: The Case of Bogotá, 1920–1980," *Studies in Latin American Popular Culture* 10 (1991): 87–106.

5. *Vallenato*, a music born of the mix of mestizo folklore and German migration to Colombia's Caribbean coast, is a best-selling folk genre. The data are from Federico López, owner of Lorito Records, a Colombian indie label, cited in Urán, Valencia, and Medina, *Medellín en vivo*, 52.

6. Roger Bartra, *The Cage of Melancholy: Identity and Metamorphosis in the Mexican Character*, trans. by Christopher J. Hall (New Brunswick, N.J.: Rutgers University Press, 1992).

7. In 2002 Caracol was sold to a Spanish media conglomerate. In truth, the move was designed to increase its profile at the international level.

8. Relevant information is available on Web sites dedicated to Colombian rock; see http://www.calle22.com or the rock section of http://www.colombia.com.

9. Dollar's review of Bloque's album stated: "The verdict: A great album in any language. Promiscuity is a virtue in Bloque's polycultural rock songs" (*Atlanta Constitutional Journal*, 7 January 1999). The review followed an earlier *Constitutional Journal* article, on January 3, in which Dollar celebrated *rock en español* in the United States.

10. These quotes, as well as many others pertaining to U.S. press coverage of Bloque, were judiciously incorporated in the Luaka Bop Web site. Though the singularity of the source may be problematic, it also highlights the way in which information was managed. See http://www.luakabop.com/bloque/cmp/main.html.

11. I have managed to verify this from the middle of 1999 to the first semester of 2000. If one considers that a U.S. album usually takes up to six months to be released in the Colombian market, the length of time contemplated in this search is rather prudent.

12. "Sonidos nuevos," *Cambio*, 19 April 1999, 116–18.

13. Renato Ortiz, *Los artífices de un cultura mundializada* (Santa Fe de Bogotá: Siglo del Hombre Editores, 1998).

14. I am alluding to Jesús Martín Barbero's definition of "mediation" (see Martín Barbero, *Communication, Culture, and Hegemony: From the Media to Mediations* [London: Sage, 1993]).

15. Aside from its ties to the Ardila Lülle group, one of the four consortiums that command the Colombian economy, Sonolux has collaborated with Sony for more than a decade. Recently thanks to the success of another artist, singer Charlie Zaa, this

relationship has strengthened. Once again, the company's Web site contains information in this regard; see http://www.sonolux.com.

16. A full quotation is on the Luaka Bop website, http://www.luakabop.com/bloque/index.html.

17. Octavio Ianni, *Las teorías de la globalizacion* (Mexico City: Siglo XXI Editores, 1996), 54.

Let Me Sing My *BRock*: Learning to Listen to Brazilian Rock

1. Part of this essay was developed during my 1997/98 stay in Liverpool, for a postdoctoral leave, under the auspices of the Brazilian National Research Council (CNPq). I want to thank Sara Cohen for the opportunity of discussing my work at IPM's Research Seminar.

2. For a selection of Tagg's writings, seewww.theblackbook.net/acad/tagg/index.html

3. My 1996–97 research, funded by CNPq, was assisted by three students: Mônica Neves Leme, Rita de Cássia Swenke Brandão, and Leonardo Barbosa Martins de Oliveira. Additionally, approximately forty students from the Villa Lobos Institute at the University of Rio de Janeiro participated as informants (most were fans and many played in rock bands), critics (transcribing and analyzing specific styles of rock), and pollsters (administering surveys).

4. Based on Gino Stefani, "A Theory of Musical Competence," *Semiotica* 66, no. 1–3 (1987): 7–22.

5. Regarding MPB, see Charles Perrone, *Masters of Contemporary Brazilian Song: MPB, 1965–1985* (Austin: University of Texas Press, 1989).

6. On Jovem Guarda and Roberto Carlos, see Martha de Ulhôa Carvalho, "Tupi or Not Tupi MPB: Popular Music and Identity in Brazil," in *The Brazilian Puzzle: Culture on the Borderlands of the Western World,* ed. Roberto Da Matta and David Hess (New York: Columbia University Press, 1995), 159–79.

7. Several aspects of Tropicalismo are discussed in Charles Perrone and Christopher Dunn, eds., *Brazilian Popular Music and Globalization* (Gainesville: University Press of Florida, 2001). See also Christopher Dunn, *Brutality Garden: Tropicália and the Emergence of a Brazilian Counterculture* (Chapel Hill: University of North Carolina Press, 2001).

8. I follow here the formulations of Pierre Bourdieu, in which symbolic culture is negotiated according to its availability; it can be exclusive (in terms of numbers or difficulty) for a smaller circle of initiates or industrially manufactured for a larger public.

9. See Antoine Hennion, "The Production of Success: An Anti-Musicology of the Pop Song," *Popular Music* 3, no. 3 (1983): 159–93.

10. See Carl Dahlhaus, *Foundations of Music Theory* (Cambridge: Cambridge University Press, 1993).

11. For an analysis of Sepultura in the context of globalization, see Keith Harris "'Roots'? The Relationship between the Global and the Local within the Global Extreme Metal Scene," *Popular Music* 19, no. 1 (2000): 13–30. Idelber Avelar, "Defected Rallies, Mournful Anthems, and the Origins of Brazilian Heavy Metal," in Perrone and Dunn, *Brazilian Popular Music and Globalization,* also discusses Sepultura in connection to place and politics.

12. "Let Me Sing, Let Me Sing," by Raul Seixas and Nadine Wisner, with Raul Seixas, in *Os Grandes Sucessos de Raul Seixas* (1993 [1972], Philips/PolyGram M-811024-2).

13. As Christopher Dunn observes: "Seixas is somewhat unique among his generational cohort in that he seemed to have entirely ignored bossa nova, jazz-

samba, Tropicália, and even the rock innovations of Os Mutantes, and consciously positioned himself outside the MPB camp" (Dunn, *Brutality Garden*, 171).

14. See Larry Crook, "Turned-Around Beat: Maracatu de Baque Virado and Chico Science"; and John Murphy, "Self-Discovery in Brazilian Popular Music: Mestre Ambrósio," both in Perrone and Dunn, *Brazilian Popular Music and Globalization*.

15. "Vida Bandida," by Lobão and Bernardo Vilhena with Lobão, in *Lobão—Vida bandida* (1987, RCA 1100028).

16. This perspective owes more to literary, reader-oriented theories and concepts like "horizons of expectation" and "informed readership" (listening) that are based on shared convention, than to communication theory.

17. Carlos Leoni Rodrigues Siqueira Junior, *Letra, música e outras conversas* (Rio de Janeiro: Gryphus, 1995), 73.

18. An early example of this "rapid-fire verse" *embolada* style can be found in the Library of Congress Endangered Music Project (*The Discoteca Collection*, RCD 10403): the 1938 recording of the *coco* "Tamanquêro eu quero um pa" performed by Sebastião Alves Feitosa and José Alves Silva.

19. "Faroeste Caboclo" by Renato Russo, with Legião Urbana, in *Que país é esse?* (1987 [1979], EMI 068 748 8201).

20. As Renato Russo mentions: "It's that hero mythology, James Dean, a rebel without a cause" (Siqueira Junior, *Letra, música e outras conversas*, 73).

21. Antônio Marcus Alves de Souza interprets "Faroeste Caboclo" as a manifestation of modernity, as he classifies all Legião Urbana's work. The story of Santo Cristo has three phases: (1) that of adolescence, in which he discovers the urban world, a phase marked by the search to "lose one's self" in the chaotic city; (2) the promise of happiness, possibility; and (3) the encounter with the tragic barriers that lead to the apotheosis of death "legitimated by the means of mass communication" (*Cultura, rock e arte de massa* [Rio de Janeiro: Diadorim, 1995], 109–11).

22. In Artur Dapieve, *BRock: O rock brasileiro dos anos 80* (Rio de Janeiro: Editora 34, 1985), 136.

23. See the 2001 record/project *Canções do Brasil: Palavra Cantada* for the *coco embolada* "Eu nunca posso perder" performed by Frank and Nazah, two kids from the Brazilian Northeast (more information may be found at http://www.palavracantada.com.br).

24. Simon Frith, *Sound Effects: Youth, Leisure, and the Politics of Rock 'n' Roll* (London: Pantheon, 1983).

25. Simon Frith, *Performing Rites: On the Value of Popular Music* (Oxford: Oxford University Press, 1996).

26. Stuart Hall, "The Question of Cultural Identity," in *Modernity and Its Futures*, ed. Stuart Hall, David Held, and Tony McGrew (Cambridge: Politic Press/Open University Press, 1992).

Guatemala's Alux Nahual: A Non-'Latin American' Latin American Rock Group?

I'd like to thank my brothers, Dr. Felix Alvarado and Professor Manuel Alvarado, for their kind and unselfish help reviewing my article.

1. Pronounced Ah-loosh Nah-wahl in Mayan K'iché, the name might be freely (and somewhat tautologically) translated as "Spirit of the Genie." Regionally, *alux* is understood as a type of specter, elf, or goblin, while *nahual* is a more abstract term signifying an alter ego or guardian spirit.

2. If I write in the first person, it is because, as a co-founder and active musician in the group, I must bear in mind that I have a privileged but ambiguous insider/outsider status in relation to Alux Nahual.

3. 1997 Yearbook of Educational Statistics (Guatemala City: Ministry of Education, 1998).

4. David Holiday, "Guatemala's Precarious Peace," *Current History,* February 2000, 78–84.

5. Most of these manuscripts have been preserved in the archives of the Metropolitan Cathedral. Few early scores by such Guatemalan composers as José Eulalio Samayoa (1781–1866) were conceived of as secular works. Likewise, Guatemalan concert music continues to follow European models. There are rare exceptions, such as the music of Joaquín Orellana (b. 1937), whose output began to depart from Western standards only in the 1970s.

6. "Rico" Molina, the bassist for Apple Pie, recalls starting off with a group called Los Relámpagos in 1964 that was originally going to be called Lightning, or even Blitz.

7. Germán Giordano, guitarist with Caoba during the late 1970s, remembers what happened when certain performers momentarily forgot their phonetically memorized lyrics: they would simply replace them with "English"-sounding mumbo-jumbo; nobody in the audience could tell the difference.

8. Estuardo "Pupo" Castañeda (representative for Dideca, 1979–85), January–April 2002.

9. Ricardo "Rico" Molina (bassist for Apple Pie, 1967–75), November 2001.

10. Marco Antonio "Maco" Lunes (bassist and vocalist for Cuerpo y Alma, 1969–73), November 2001.

11. This was a period of heightened state violence, under General Romeo Lucas García (1978–82); the violence was continued by General Efraín Ríos Montt (1982–83), who launched a scorched-earth campaign that was then carried on by General Oscar Mejía Víctores (1983–85).

12. Probably one consequence of this violence is the attitude of non-solidarity that is prevalent to this day. In its power to summon youth together, Guatemalan rock may be helping to confront and transcend this fear.

13. Literally, "Strawberry Group," that is, "superficial, light, trivial, petit-bourgeois."

14. The epitome of this absence of heroes is the national soccer team, one of the very few from the American continent that has never qualified for the World Cup, despite the widespread popularity of *fútbol* in Guatemala.

15. Radio "charts" in Central America are popularity logs based on the number of phone calls a station receives requesting a song to be aired.

16. Dideca presented Alux Nahual with a Disco de Oro for having sold ten thousand records in 1989, although it is likely that the mark had not actually been reached at that point. On the other hand, the company's sales reports to the group have only accounted for records sold in Guatemala and Costa Rica.

17. The very first discs (now over two decades old) continue to be in demand, yet as late as 2001 Dideca was unwilling to make any more copies of them. Finally in 2002, Dideca marketed a CD six-pack of the first LPs. Our two final albums were released under Sony Music, one of which, *Americamorfosis,* has sold some ten thousand copies. However, Sony no longer makes these albums available. A noteworthy "homage" to Alux Nahual, produced in two separate volumes, was inspired and guided by producer Giacomo Buonafina and came out under the name *Espíritu del duende, un tributo* (1998–99). It contains new (often widely differing) versions of our songs by twenty-two artists from Mexico and Central America.

18. Sony Music can be credited with sponsoring a couple of promotional tours and releasing Alux's last two CDs outside of Central America, but no major marketing campaign (typical for musical imports) was ever seriously attempted.

19. The indigenous language K'iché (formerly Quiché, in Hispanicized spelling) is one of more than twenty languages currently spoken in Guatemala. Local rock groups have seldom used names in a vernacular tongue, preferring either Spanish or English.

20. Reception was better in the cool, mountainous, northwestern communities of Quezaltenango, Huehuetenango, and San Marcos than in the warm, tropical lowlands such as Escuintla and Mazatenango.

21. Meant for listening, rather than for dancing, *canciones* have a story to tell, an experience to recount.

22. Many tropical musical groups go so far as to have somebody yell "Cumbia!" or "Mambo!" during the introduction of a song.

23. See for example, the twenty-fifth anniversary live recording (1994) of the Chilean rock group Congreso, which includes flute, cello, and acoustic guitar. When it comes to the more striking musical statements or solos, it is the jazz-like sax or funk electric bass that stand out, not these other, "softer" sounds.

24. The *chirimía* is a double-reed aerophone of Moorish origin played almost exclusively by indigenous musicians, while the *tamborón* is a drum of large diameter. The combination was used in the opening measures of *Conquista* (1982).

My Generation:
Rock and *la Banda*'s Forced Survival Opposite the Mexican State

1. Ricardo Garibay, "Dar juntos la batalla: Urgencia del diálogo entre la juventud y el poder," *Excelsior,* 28 October 1971, 6, cited in Eric Zolov, *Refried Elvis: The Rise of the Mexican Counterculture* (Berkeley: University of California Press, 1999), 215.

2. Mexico City could be viewed as a single unit; however, politically as well as geographically, this "unit" is divided into two sections, the Federal District (D.F., made up of sixteen political delegations) and the Metropolitan Zone (which includes seventeen nearby municipalities of the state of Mexico), each of which holds approximately 50 percent of the city's population (9.5 million people each).

3. Despite this, the side streets of working-class *colonias* are part of the policeman's beat, and that is where young people are detained and subjected to extortion in order to obtain their freedom.

4. See William Foote White, *Street Corner Society* (Chicago: University of Chicago Press, 1971).

5. Although for *banda* with more substantial incomes, the *sonideros* (music joints), raves, and even discos offer other musical recreation choices.

6. Quoted in José Luis Paredes Pacho, *Rock mexicano: Sonidos de la calle* (Mexico City: Aguirre y Beltrán, 1993), 6. When one mentions *banda* with reference to rock—above all, when young people use the word to speak of themselves—one is speaking of the general public: *banda* is a synonym for rock's natural audience. But a second social connotation exists, discussed below, which has to do with the phenomenon of the so-called *banda* followers.

7. Héctor Castillo Berthier, *Juventud, cultura y política social: Un proyecto de investigación aplicada en la ciudad de México, 1987–1997* (Mexico City: Instituto Mexicano de la Juventud, 2000), 86.

8. Stephen Goodspeed, "El papel del jefe del ejecutivo en México," *Problemas Agrarios e Industriales de México* 7, no. 1 (1955): 120.

9. The official military sector was eliminated in December 1940 when it was decreed that military personnel could only be affiliated with the party as individuals.

10. José Antonio Pérez Islas, "Historia de un amor como no hay otro igual," in *México joven: Políticas y propuestas para la discusión,* ed. Rafael Cordera, José Luis Victoria, and Ricardo Becerra (Mexico City: Universidad Nacional Autónoma de México, Secretaría de Asuntos Estudiantiles, 1996), 83–84.

11. *Diario Oficial de la Federación,* 25 February 1950, 9, cited in Castillo Berthier, *Juventud, cultura y política social,* 68.

12. The first Casa de la Juventud was built in Guadalajara, Jalisco, and was inaugurated on December 6, 1960; similar projects followed in Aguascalientes, Tabasco, San Luis Potosí, Querétaro, and Zacatecas. These installations included classrooms, an auditorium, a library, medical services, an exhibition salon, gymnasium, pool, a sports recreation area, and areas for agriculture and livestock (Pérez Islas, "Historia de un amor").

13. On January 18, 1946, during the second day of the Assembly of the National Executive Committee of the PRM, the name change was agreed upon in an effort to blunt the more radical tendencies within the party. That is when the Institutional Revolutionary Party (PRI) officially came into existence, with the motto "democracy and social justice." The motto was ambiguous, but no longer displayed the explicit "red" tint that its immediate predecessor had shown.

14. Pérez Islas, "Historia de un amor," 85.

15. Alicia Ziccardi, Sergio Zermeño, and Héctor Castillo Berthier, "Popular Youth and *Banda* in Mexico City," *Presencia* (Rio de Janeiro) 14 (1988).

16. René Laban, *Musica, rock y satanismo* (Mexico City: Arcoiris, 1989).

17. In 2001 there continued to exist a renowned Christian rock sung by metal groups like Puño de Hierro (Iron Fist), Poder Oculto (Occult Power), and Santo Oficio (Holy Office). This relationship is not new; in fact, since the early 1970s many churches have integrated electronic instruments and percussion into their musical and choral groups. As Father Víctor Pérez Valera commented during a radio interview in May 2001: "Young people would find this music and its sounds inside the House of God." But, at that time, there were some limits on the full participation of teenagers, since the lyrics of many of the songs were written by the priests. Thirty years later, things have changed: the current tendency is to create "religious music" outside the churches, with commercial recordings and concerts. This trend is exemplified by the group Gamaliel Morán, whose lyrics for "Freedom Lives" state: "The world seduces you by disguising its ideas. . . . You act like a sheep walking to the slaughter. . . . The whole truth is found in Him / Just give Him your faith and freedom lives / By being His slave, you'll be even freer" (1997, CanZión Producciones CECZ039).

18. See Castillo Berthier, *Juventud, cultura y politica social*.

19. Abraham Ríos Manzano, *Tianguis cultural del Chopo: Una larga jornada* (Mexico City: PACMYC and Tianguis Cultural del Chopo, 1999), 21. The name derives from a combination of the commonly used Nahuatl term for "marketplace," *tianguis*, and the Chopo Museum, where the rock gathering first took place. Shortly after its initiation, the gathering was forced to relocate and the *rockeros* eventually established a permanent location alongside the capital's central railway station (no longer in operation). Still, the original name stuck, and, ever since, the flea market has been known as the "Tianguis del Chopo," or simply, "El Chopo."

20. Maritza Urteaga, *Por los territorios del rock: Identidades juveniles y rock mexicano* (Mexico City: Editorial Causa Joven [SEP], 1998), 115.

21. Ibid.

22. The term *hoyos fonquis* comes from an early seventies expression, "You smell *fonqui*," which described the foul body odor of participants, since many of these spaces were deteriorated and offered inadequate, insalubrious conditions that were sometimes dangerous for the attending public. For further discussion, see the essay by Julia Palacios and Tere Estrada in this volume.

23. *Códice Rock* 21 (1999): 11.

24. José Agustín, quoted in *Rockdrigo González*, ed. Modesto López (Mexico City: Pentagrama, 1999), 117.

25. Fabrizio Leon, *La banda, el consejo y otros panchos* (Mexico City: Grijalbo, 1984), 51.

26. "Sociedad de la esquina," *Programa Solidaridad,* vol. 10, 1993, 5.
27. Carlos Monsiváis, "Entrevista a Carlos Monsiváis," *Banda Rockera* (3rd anniversary issue), 1988, 10.
28. Castillo Berthier, *Juventud, cultura y política social,* 73.
29. "La Banda le habló 'al chile' al Candidato," *La Jornada,* 20 May 1994, 1.
30. *Plan Nacional de Desarrollo 1995–2000* (Mexico City: Comisión Nacional del Deporte y Dirección General de Atención a la Juventud, 1997).
31. In 1824 the Mexican government created the Distrito Federal (Federal District of Mexico City), which maintained a municipal status until 1928. During the following sixty-nine years, under the organic law of the Federal District and federal territories, the Mexican president was charged with the city's management. In 1997 the head of government for the Federal District of Mexico City once again became an elected official, a change described by the media as "the first democratic government of the city."
32. Raúl Torres Barrón, head of the Venustiano Carranza district, when asked by the author in June 1997 about the authorities' interpretation of a "massive gathering" of youth. At that point, after two years of bureaucracy, Circo Volador had finally received an operating license, but with an attachment that stated that "massive gatherings" (that is, rock concerts) attended by more than seventy persons were strictly forbidden.

Neoliberalism and Rock in the Popular Sectors of Contemporary Argentina

1. Raymond Williams, "Marxismo y Literatura," in *Homo Sociologicus* (Barcelona: Ediciones Península, 1980).
2. Alberto Minujín and Gabriel Kessler, *La nueva pobreza en la Argentina* (Buenos Aires: Ariel, 1995). See also José Nun and Juan Carlos Portantiero, *Ensayos sobre la transición democrática en la Argentina* (Buenos Aires: Punto Sur, 1987).
3. Pablo Semán and Pablo Vila, "*Rock Chabón*: The Contemporary National Rock of Argentina," in *From Tejano to Tango: Latin American Popular Music,* ed. Walter Aaron Clark (New York: Routledge, 2002), 70–94.
4. Elizabeth Jelín, "La matriz cultural Argentina, el peronismo y la cotidianidad," and "Imágenes sociales de la justicia: Algunas evidencias," in *Vida cotidiana y control institucional en la Argentina de los 90,* ed. Elizabeth Jelín, 25–40, 117–36 (Buenos Aires: Grupo Editor Latinoamericano, 1996).
5. Jelín, "La matriz cultural," 40.
6. Michael Pollak, "Memoria, esquecimento, silencio," *Estudos Históricos* 2/3 (1989): 11.
7. Pablo Vila, "Rock Nacional: Crónicas de la resistencia juvenil," in *Los nuevos movimientos sociales,* vol. 1, *Mujeres: Rock Nacional,* ed. Elizabeth Jelín (Buenos Aires: Centro Editor de América Latina, Colección Biblioteca Política Argentina, no. 124, 1985), 83–148; Pablo Vila, "*Rock Nacional* and dictatorship in Argentina," *Popular Music* 6, no. 2 (1987): 129–48; Pablo Vila, "Argentina's *Rock Nacional:* The Struggle for Meaning," *Latin American Music Review* 10, no. 1 (1989): 1–28; Pablo Vila, "*Rock Nacional* and Dictatorship in Argentina," in *Rockin' the Boat: Mass Music and Mass Movements,* ed. Reebee Garofalo (Boston: South End Press, 1992), 209–29; Pablo Vila, "El rock nacional: Género musical y construcción de la identidad juvenil en Argentina," in *Cultura y pospolítica: El debate sobre la modernidad en América Latina,* ed. Néstor García Canclini (Mexico City: Consejo Nacional para la Cultura y las Artes, 1995), 231–71; Pablo Vila, "A Social History of Thirty Years of *Rock Nacional* (1965–1995)," in *The Universe of Music: A History,* ed. Malena Kuss (New York: Schirmer Books/ Macmillan, forthcoming).

8. Charly García, quoted in Vila, "Argentina's Rock Nacional."
9. Following a well-established practice in anthropology and sociology, all the names are synonymous.
10. "Sábado," *Acariciando lo áspero,* 1990.
11. Cecilia Benedetti, "Rock nacional y consumo: El caso de La Renga," Tesis de Licenciatura en Ciencias Antropológicas, Universidad de Buenos Aires, 2001.
12. Ibid.
13. Ibid.
14. M. Rotman, "Diversidad y desigualdad: Patrimonio y producciones culturales de los sectores subalternos." Paper presented at the III Reunión de Antropología del MERCOSUR, Posadas, November 1999, 23–26.
15. Almafuerte, "Zamba de la resurrección," *Almafuerte,* 1995; Divididos, "Haciendo cola para nacer," *Acariciando lo áspero,* 1990.
16. Benedetti, "Rock nacional y consumo."
17. Ibid.
18. Michel de Certeau, *La invención de lo cotidiano* (Mexico City: Universidad Iberoamericana/Iteso, 1996).
19. Benedetti, "Rock nacional y consumo."

A Detour to the Past: Memory and Mourning in Chilean Post-Authoritarian Rock

1. Cf. Osvaldo Rodríguez Musso, *Cantores que reflexionan: Notas para una historia personal de la Nueva Canción chilena* (Madrid: Lar, 1984); Eduardo Carrasco, *Quilapayún: La revolución y las estrellas* (Santiago de Chile: Las Ediciones del Ornitorrinco, 1988); Luis Cifuentes, *Fragmentos de un sueño* (Santiago de Chile: Ediciones Logos, 1989).
2. The most representative case of the dictatorship's impact on Chilean Nueva Canción is the death of Víctor Jara, who, after being taken prisoner in the Estadio Chile, now renamed after him, was assassinated by the repressive apparatus. Other musicians left for exile: Inti-Illimani to Italy, and Quilapayún, Isabel and Ángel Parra, Patricio Manns, and Los Jaivas to France.
3. Juan Pablo González, "Hegemony and Counter-Hegemony of Music in Latin America: Chilean Pop," *Popular Music and Society* 15, no. 2 (1991): 68.
4. Mark Mattern, "Popular Music and Redemocratization in Santiago, Chile, 1973–1989," *Studies in Latin American Popular Culture* 16, (1997): 106.
5. Tito Escárate, *Canción telepática* (Santiago: LOM Ediciones, 1999), 23.
6. Ibid., 95.
7. Fabio Salas, *El grito del amor: Una historia temática actualizada del rock* (Santiago: LOM Ediciones, 1998).
8. Rubén Scaramuzzino and Bruno Galindo, eds., *Diccionario del Rock Latino* (Madrid: Sociedad General de Autores y Editores, 2000), 22.
9. Salas, *El grito del amor,* 197.
10. Andreas Huyssen, *Twilight Memories: Marking Time in a Culture of Amnesia* (New York: Routledge, 1995), 3.
11. Jesús Martín Barbero, *De los medios a las mediaciones: Comunicación, cultura y hegemonía* (Naucalpan, Mexico: G. Gili, 1998), 47.
12. Pedro Lemebel, *De perlas y cicatrices* (Santiago: LOM, 1998).
13. Cf. Idelber Avelar's study, *The Untimely Present: Postdictatorial Latin American Fiction and the Task of Mourning* (Durham, N.C.: Duke University Press, 1999).
14. Huyssen, *Twilight Memories,* 6.
15. Martín Barbero, *De los medios a las mediaciones,* 189.

16. "Jorge González canta cumbias, pero ya no es masivo: Amor por lo popular," http://www.chilerock.uchile.cl/reportajes/gm/cuerpo.html.

17. It is exactly this disdain, this lack of consideration toward symbolic products produced by "civil society," which has generated what is currently understood as the crisis of the intellectual. George Yúdice develops this argument in his article, "Intellectuals and Civil Society in Latin America," *Annals of Scholarship* 11, no. 1–2: 157–74.

18. Martín Barbero, *De los medios a las mediaciones*, 28.

19. In this sense, Roberto Parra's work is significantly distanced from that of his two siblings, the poet Nicanor Parra, who as a response to the traditional literary language proposes the idea of "anti-poetry," which presents what he describes as "the language of the tribe"; and the poet and musician Violeta Parra.

20. Escárate, *Canción telepática*, 37.

21. See González, "Hegemony and Counter-Hegemony of Music in Latin-America," for a discussion of class issues in Chilean rock.

22. Vikki Riley, "Punk Rockers of the World Unite," in *From Pop to Punk to Postmodernism*, ed. Philip Hayward (North Sydney: Allen and Unwin, 1992), 115.

23. Escárate, *Canción telepática*, 335.

24. Martín Barbero, *De los medios a las mediaciones*, 87.

25. Tomás Moulián, *Chile Actual: Anatomía de un mito* (Santiago de Chile: LOM–Arcis, 1997), 125.

26. Martín Barbero, *De los medios a las mediaciones*, 122.

27. Robert Walser, *Running with the Devil: Power, Gender, and Madness in Heavy Metal Music* (Hanover, N.H.: University Press of New England, 1993), 9.

28. José Joaquín Brunner, *Bienvenidos a la modernidad* (Santiago de Chile: Planeta, 1994), 90.

29. Huyssen, *Twilight Memories*, 86.

30. Ibid.

The Nortec Edge: Border Traditions and 'Electronica' in Tijuana

1. I have chosen to use the Spanish term *propuesta* when discussing Nortec because it is the closest approximation of what this phenomenon is all about. *Propuesta* simultaneously embraces a notion of cultural activity with social action and consciousness. The English term "proposal" captures these multiple meanings, though only in part.

2. Hastings Donnan and Thomas M. Wilson, "An Anthropology of Frontiers," in *Border Approaches: Anthropological Perspectives on Frontiers*, ed. Hastings Donnan and Thomas M. Wilson (New York: University Press of America, 1994), 1–14.

3. Cited in Helena Simonett, "Strike Up the Tambora: A Social History of Sinaloan Band Music," *Latin American Music Review* 20, no. 1 (1999): 59–104.

4. José David Saldívar, *Border Matters: Remapping American Cultural Studies* (Berkeley: University of California Press, 1997), 8.

5. David E. Lorey, *The U.S.–Mexican Border in the Twentieth Century* (Wilmington, Del.: Scholarly Resources, 1999), 8.

6. Basilio Verduzco Chávez, Nora Bringas Rábago, and Basilia Valenzuela Varela, *La ciudad compartida: Desarrollo urbano, comercio y turismo en la región de Tijuana–San Diego* (Guadalajara and Tijuana: Universidad de Guadalajara / El Colegio de la Frontera Norte, 1995); Milo Kearney and Anthony Knopp, *Border Cuates: A History of the U.S.–Mexican Twin Cities* (Austin: Eakin Press, 1995).

7. Lorey, *U.S.–Mexican Border*, 125.

8. Ibid., 105.

9. Ibid., 107.

10. Rafa Saavedra, "Terminal Norte: Los espacios para el rock tijuanense," in *Oye cómo va: Recuento del rock tijuanense,* ed. José Manuel Valenzuela and Gloria González (Tijuana: Centro Cultural Tijuana / Instituto Mexicano de la Juventud, 1999), 140–46.

11. Roberto Mendoza, "Electrónica en la frontera," in *Oye cómo va: Recuento del rock tijuanense,* ed. José Manuel Valenzuela and Gloria González (Tijuana: Centro Cultural Tijuana / Instituto Mexicano de la Juventud, 1999),137.

12. Artefakto was from Tijuana. Its members later formed other electronic music groups, namely, Fussible and Panoptica, and thus participated in the creation of Nortec.

13. Roberto Mendoza, first a member of Artefakto and, later, of Fussible, http://www.noarte.org/artefakto/news.htm (accessed March 1999). All translations from the Spanish throughout this essay are my own.

14. Jesús Martín Barbero, *Pre-textos: Conversaciones sobre la comunicación y sus contextos* (Cali: Universidad del Valle, 1995), 177.

15. Ford Proco, "Vértigo de lodo y miel," *Nimboestatic,* 2000, Nimboestatic AT003/NIM005CD. Ford Proco is a group devoted to industrial electronic music following the tradition of groups like Kraftwerk.

16. Néstor García Canclini, *La globalización imaginada* (Mexico City: Paidós, 1999).

17. "Paratexts" are those texts present in any written text that are not acknowledged as the main text but give important information to understand it; these text may include anything in the text from the title to the acknowledgments. With respect to books, they are defined and discussed by Gerard Genette in *Paratexts: Thresholds of Interpretation,* trans. Jane E. Levin (Cambridge: Cambridge University Press, 1997). I have applied the term to musical texts in which the line is not clear-cut, because the "texts" are diluted between the lyrics and the written part of the booklets. The "musical text" thus exists within a sound dimension (that is, melodies, rhythms, lyrics) and the "paratexts" are the remainder, including notes, addenda, presentation of the work, or any given explanation accompanying the musical text. The paratexts guide, mediate, and prepare the reception of the (musical) text (see Susana Asensio, "Nuevos lenguajes de la era post-industrial: Paratextualidad y electrónica," *Actas del VI Congreso de la SibE. Faro 2000* [Faro: SibE, 2000]).

18. Deus ex Machina, *Deus ex Machina,* 1992, Opción Sónica OPCD04.

19. Martín Barbero, *Pre-textos,* 130–31.

20. Roberto Echevarren, *Arte andrógino: Estilo versus moda en un siglo corto* (Montevideo: Ediciones Brecha, 1997), 116.

21. Ted Polhemus, *Street Styles: From Sidewalk to Catwalk* (London: Thames and Hudson, 1994), 91, 93.

22. CD booklet, Bostich + Fussible, *Nortec Remixes,* 2000, Mil Records OPCD137.

23. García Canclini, *La globalización imaginada,* 51.

24. Pepe Mogt, from Fussible, interviewed by Winton Borrero, June 2000, http://www.mundorocklatino.com.

25. Simonett, "Strike Up the Tambora," 86.

26. Lorey, *U.S.–Mexican Border,* 9.

27. Helen Simonett, "Narcocorridos: An Emerging Micromusic of Nuevo L.A.," *Ethnomusicology* 45, no. 2 (2001): 331.

28. Neil Strauss, "The Pop Life: On the Mexican Border, Crossing Genres," *New York Times,* 8 March 2001.

29. Manuel Peña, *The Mexican American Orquesta: Music, Culture, and the Dialectic of Conflict* (Austin: University of Texas Press, 1999), 27.

30. Saldívar, *Border Matters,* 3.

31. Quoted in Strauss, "Pop Life."

32. Enrique Lavin, "Nortec for Dummies," *CMJ,* 19 February 2001, 8.
33. Ibid.
34. Ernesto Lechner, "Border Crossings: Mexican Nortec Mixes It Up," *Los Angeles Times,* 10 February 2001.
35. Ramón Bostich, interview with author, New York City, March 2001.
36. Pepe Mogt and Ramón Amezcua, interviews with author, New York City, June 2000 and March 2001. In techno clubs in New York, the performance of Nortec members was set on a stage decorated with many of the Mexican stereotypes—chiles, jalapeños, colored piñatas—with which the musicians performing did not identify at all (Pepe Mogt and Ramón Amezcua, interview with author, New York City, December 2001).
37. Most of the publicity and the news related to Nortec happens on the Web. People from Tijuana, Mazatlán, Tokyo, or London can be updated at the same time about the developments of the collective, listen to their new tracks, and download images. Because of this, however, it is virtually impossible to address a particular type of "standard" audience for the movement. Electronica audiences are normally young, but tremendously varied and heterogeneous regarding class, origin, ethnicity, and education.
38. Martín Barbero, *Pre-textos,* 178.
39. Ibid., 177.
40. Ibid., 186.
41. From p. 2 of the booklet of Derrick May's 1997 CD, *Innovator* (Transmet TMTCD4).
42. Ibid., 10.
43. John Gill, *Queer Noises: Male and Female Homosexuality in Twentieth-Century Music* (Minneapolis: University of Minnesota Press, 1995), 134.
44. Marc Augé, *Non-lieux: Introduction à une anthropologie de la surmodernité* (Paris: Seuil, 1992).
45. May Joseph, Introduction to *Performing Hybridity,* ed. May Joseph and Jennifer Natalya Fink (Minneapolis: University of Minnesota Press, 1999), 8.
46. Robertson uses the term "glocal", which combines the global and the local, to emphasize that each is in many ways defined by the other, and that they frequently intersect rather than being polarized opposites. Robertson adopted this blend of local and global from its use in Japan to describe the adaptation of global farming techniques to fit local conditions and its subsequent use as a marketing buzzword to refer to the indigenization of global phenomena (see Roland Robertson, "Time-Space and Homogeneity-Heterogeneity," in *Global Modernities,* ed. Mike Featherstone, Scott Lash, and Roland Robertson [London: Sage, 1995]).
47. Andy Bennett, "Subcultures or Neo-Tribes? Rethinking the Relationship between Youth, Style, and Musical Taste," *Sociology* 33, no. 3 (1999): 599–617.
48. Pepe Mogt, Fussible, interview with William Borrero, June 2000, http://www.mundorocklatino.com.
49. Rosana Reguillo, "El año 2000, ética, política y estéticas: Imaginarios, adscripciones y prácticas juveniles. Caso mexicano." In *"Viviendo a Toda": Jóvenes, territorios culturales y nuevas sensibilidades,* ed. Humberto J. Cubides, María Cristina Laverde, and Carlos Enrique Valderrama (Bogotá: Siglo del Hombre Editores, 1998), 57.
50. When the collective released their first compilation for the United States, they printed a manifesto entitled "Ten Things to Do before Listening to Nortec Collective, The Tijuana Sessions, Vol. 1." The first was to "forget what you know about Tijuana." The manifesto continued: "Forget cheap prostitutes, marines on shore leave, unpaved

roads, semi-automatic spraying narco-bosses, donkey shows. Forget danger, fear, worry. Forget Perry Como singing 'South of the Border.' Forget CNN. Forget 'Tiawanna.' Forget TJ. . . . Know that there is a different Tijuana and know that the Nortec collective . . . are musicians, graphic designers, architects, filmmakers, visual artists, and fashion stylists. Their Tijuana is a border metropolis of almost New York, L.A., and London. It is Americas' most important switching point, where cultures clash, languages, styles, laborers, and sounds (lots and lots of sounds) all migrate into each other without the proper documents, clashing and connecting, merging and marrying, like few other spots on the planet" (Nortec printed flyer, 2001).

Esperando La Última Ola / Waiting for the Last Wave: Manu Chao and the Music of Globalization

1. Special thanks to Tom Tompkins of the *San Francisco Bay Guardian*, Yon Elvira of Virgin Records, and the publicity department of Ark 21 Records for helping make these conversations come to fruition. Thanks are also due to Cecilia Bastida and Alex Zuñiga for their insights and guidance. My deepest gratitude goes to Manu Chao himself, who graciously, and repeatedly, offered up his time.

2. For a variety of approaches to the EZLN and the Chiapas revolution, see Elaine Katzenberger, ed., *First World, Ha Ha Ha!: The Zapatista Challenge* (San Francisco: City Lights Books, 1995); John Womack, *Rebellion in Chiapas* (New York: New Press, 1999); and Subcomandante Marcos, *Shadows of Tender Fury: The Letters and Communiqués of Subcomandante and the Zapatista Army of National Liberation* (New York: Monthly Review Press, 1995).

3. General biographical overviews of Mano Negra and Manu Chao can be found in Ruben Scaramuzzino and Bruno Galindo, eds., *Diccionario de Rock Latino* (Zaragoza: Zona de Obras, 2000).

4. Ileana Rodríguez, "Reading Subaltern Texts, Disciplines, and Theories: From Representation to Recognition," in *The Latin American Subaltern Studies Reader*, ed. Ileana Rodríguez (Durham, N.C.: Duke University Press, 2001), 9.

5. Subcomandante Marcos, "To: Musicians of the World," e-mail communiqué, 20 February 1999.

6. Charlynne Curiel, "Manu Chao: Tijuana, un punto de fiebre en el planeta," in *Oye cómo va: Recuento de rock tijuanense*, ed. José Manuel Valenzuela Arce and Gloria González Fernández (Tijuana: Centro Cultural Tijuana–Instituto Mexicano de la Juventud, 1999), 193.

7. George Lipsitz, *American Studies in a Moment of Danger* (Minneapolis: University of Minnesota Press, 2001), 8.

8. Ibid., 3.

9. Philip V. Bohlman, "The Remembrance of Things Past: Music, Race, and the End of History in Modern Europe," in *Music and the Racial Imagination*, ed. Ronald Radano and Philip V. Bohlman (Chicago: University of Chicago Press, 2001), 645.

10. Guillermo Gómez-Peña, "The New Global Culture: Somewhere between Corporate Multiculturalism and the Mainstream Bizarre (a Border Perspective)," *Drama Review* 45, no. 1 (Spring 2001): 6.

11. Chela Sandoval, *Methodology of the Oppressed* (Minneapolis: University of Minnesota Press, 2000).

12. Portions of the interviews that make up the next section of this essay appeared in Josh Kun, "Subcomandante Manu: An Interview with Manu Chao," *Color Lines* 2, no. 4 (Winter 1999–2000): 42–43.

Afterword: A Changeable Template of Rock in *Las Américas*

1. See "Lobão X Cazuza," *Bizz* (September 1985), http://danilobaio.usonline.com.br/bandas%20%20lobao%20cazuza.htm.

2. The one very interesting exception is Paulo Alvarado's account of his band Alux Nahual, which he claims was not considered marketable enough precisely because it did not fit prevailing categories, including those defined in relation to transgression or resistance. As middle-class white boys, they had, he notes, the "wrong social manners," the "wrong social provenance," the "wrong social look." This made them unmarketable and unpresentable as a subversive rock group representing the political impulses of the oppressed, which is what would make a group internationally identifiable.

3. Roberto Schwarz, *Misplaced Ideas: Essays on Brazilian Culture* (New York: Verso, 1992).

4. And not only populist parties. In Cuba, for example, the Afrocubanist movement was not only an oppositional rejection of the collusion of Cuba's political leaders with U.S. imperialism (see Robin Moore, *Nationalizing Blackness:* Afrocubanismo *and Artistic Revolution in Havana, 1920–1940* [Pittsburgh: University of Pittsburgh Press, 1997]), but also a means to create a new historical bloc whereby blacks, mulattos, and whites could identify with one another.

5. The glaring exception in this history is Cuba after 1959: there were few or no public expressions of opposition by youth. Cuban revolutionary symbology and fervor in the 1960s did not mesh well with the simultaneous countercultural expression of Western youth. On the contrary, as Pacini and Garofalo observe, even relatively timid incorporations of rock by the likes of Pablo Milanés and Silvio Rodríguez were repressed. In contrast to the other authoritarian governments, Cuban officials and revolutionary intellectuals were laboring intensely to create a socialist disciplinary society. There was no place for the flabbiness of spirit that capitalist consumer culture was presumed to inculcate in youth.

6. The *pau* (pronounced "pow") in *black pau* is a pun: the word, which literally means "wood" or "stick," is also the Portuguese slang word for cock. The suggestion is that black power, indeed, black music itself, derives from black male sexuality.

7. Dick Hebdige,*Subculture: The Meaning of Style* (1979; reprint, London: Routledge, 1991), 18.

8. Ernesto Laclau and Chantal Mouffe, *Hegemony and Socialist Strategy: Towards a Radical Democratic Politics* (London: Verso, 1985), 159–71.

9. Ibid., 58.

10. Renato Ortiz,*Cultura brasileira e identidade nacional* (São Paulo: Brasiliense, 1985); quote is from p. 65.

11. Heloisa Buarque de Hollanda,"O destino dos bons rios," *Jornal do Brasil*, caderno B, 14 May 1983, http://acd.ufrj.br/pacc/destino.html.

12. Fernando Rosa, "Anos 70, o rock 'Made in Brasil,'" *Senhor F—A revista do rock*, http://www.senhorf.com.br/sf3vs/secreta/introd/anos70.htm.

13. Giba Assis Brasil (n.d.) defines *brega* as follows: "In Brazil there is a concept—BREGA—that epitomizes both the songs of Julio Iglesias and the interior decoration of maids' quarters, Barbara Cartland's books and 3-D reproductions of Leonardo's *Last Supper*. In sum, it is bad taste, the lower end of the culture industry" ("Raul Seixas: Três explicações," http://www.nao-til.com.br/nao66/rscarta.htm).

14. See Carlos Alberto Messeder Pereira and Heloísa Buarque de Hollanda, *Patrulhas ideológicas* (São Paulo: Brasiliense, 1980).

BIBLIOGRAPHY

Acosta, Leonardo. *Fiesta Havana, 1940–1960: L'âge d'or de la musique cubaine.* Paris: Vade Retro, 1999.
———. "Cómo y por qué surgió el GESI?" *La Jiribilla: Revista Digital de Cultura Cubana,* no. 13 (July 2001). http://www.lajiribilla.cubaweb.cu/2001/n13_julio/362_13.html.
Agustín, José. *La contracultura en México: La historia y el significado de los rebeldes sin causa, los jipitecas, los punks y las bandas.* Mexico City: Grijalbo, 1996.
———. *Rockdrigo González.* Mexico City: Pentagrama, 1999.
Alabarces, Pablo. *Entre gatos y violadores: El rock nacional en la cultura argentina.* Buenos Aires: Ediciones Colihue, 1993.
Aleixandre, Ricardo. *Dias de luta: O rock e o Brasil dos anos 80.* São Paulo: Editora DBA, 2002.
Anaya, Benjamín. *Neozapatismo y rock mexicano.* Mexico City: La Cuadrilla de la Langosta, 1999.
Anazagasty-Rodríguez, José. "Colonial Capitalism, Hegemony, and Youth Praxis in Puerto Rico: Fiel a la Vega's Rock in Español." *Latin American Music Review* 23, no. 1 (2002): 79–105.
Andrews, George Reid. *Blacks and Whites in São Paulo.* Madison: University of Wisconsin Press, 1992.
Aparicio, Frances R. *Listening to Salsa: Gender, Latin Popular Music, and Puerto Rican Cultures.* Hanover, N.H.: University Press of New England [for] Wesleyan University Press, 1998.
Aparicio, Frances R. and Cándida Jáquez, eds. *Musical Migrations: Transnationalism and cultural Hybridity in Latin/o America.* New York: Palgrave Macmillan, 2003.
Arana, Federico. *Guaraches de ante azul: Historia del rock mexicano.* Guadalajara: María Enea, 2002.
Arditi, Benjamín. "Expansividad de lo social, recodificación de lo 'político.'" In *Imágenes desconocidas: La modernidad en la encrucijada postmoderna,* edited by Fernando Calderón and Aníbal Quijano. Buenos Aires: Clacso, 1988.
Armstrong, Piers. "Songs of Olodum." In *Brazilian Popular Music and Globalization,* edited by Charles Perrone and Christopher Dunn. Gainesville: University of Florida Press, 2001.
Asensio, Susana. "Nuevos lenguajes de la era post-industrial: Paratextualidad y electrónica." *Actas del VI Congreso de la SibE* (Faro 2000). Faro: SibE, forthcoming.
Augé, Marc. *Non-Places: Introduction to an Anthropology of Supermodernity,* trans. by John Howe (London: Verso, 1995).
Ayestarán, Lauro. *La música en el Uruguay.* Montevideo: SODRE, 1953.
———. *El folklore musical uruguayo.* Montevideo: Arca, 1967.
Baltar, G., and L. E. Behares. "Rock uruguayo: Lo dicho y la escucha." *Relaciones* 38 (1987).
Bartra, Roger. *The Cage of Melancholy: Identity and Metamorphosis in the Mexican Character.* Translated by Christopher J. Hall. New Brunswick, N.J.: Rutgers University Press, 1992.
Bayce, Rafael. "El rock, ¿importa?" *Relaciones* 42 (1987).

Béhague, Gerard. "Popular Music in Latin America." *Studies in Latin American Popular Culture* 5 (1986).

Beltrán Fuentes, Alfredo. *La ideología antiautoritaria del rock nacional.* Buenos Aires: Centro Editor de América Latina, 1989.

Bennett, Andy. "Subcultures or Neo-Tribes? Rethinking the Relationship between Youth, Style, and Musical Taste." *Sociology* 33, no. 3 (1999): 599–617.

Bessy, Claude, Sean Carrillo, Christine McKenna, and Exene Cervanka. *Forming: The Early Days of L.A. Punk.* New York: Smart Art Press/Distributed Art Publishers, 2000.

Bhabha, Homi K. "Of Mimicry and Man: The Ambivalence of Colonial Discourse." In *The Location of Culture.* London: Routledge, 1994.

Britto García, Luis. *El imperio contracultural: Del rock a la postmodernidad.* Caracas: Nueva Sociedad, 1991.

Brunner, José Joaquín. *Bienvenidos a la modernidad.* Santiago de Chile: Planeta, 1994.

Capagorry, Juan, and Elbio Rodríguez Barilari. *Aquí se canta: Canto popular, 1977–1980.* Montevideo: Arca, 1980.

Carbone, Alfonso. *La enciclopedia de rock.* Montevideo: Coopren, 1988.

Carvalho, Martha de Ulhôa. "Música Popular in Montes Claros, Minas Gerais, Brazil: A Study of Middle-Class Popular Music Aesthetics in the 1980s." Ph.D. diss., Cornell University, 1991.

———. "Tupi or Not Tupi MPB: Popular Music and Identity in Brazil." In *The Brazilian Puzzle: Culture on the Borderlands of the Western World,* edited by Roberto Da Matta and David Hess. New York: Columbia University Press, 1995.

Castellanos, Ernesto Juan. *Los Beatles en Cuba: Un viaje mágico y misterioso.* Havana: Ediciones Unión, 1997.

Castells, Manuel. *The Rise of the Network Society.* Oxford: Blackwell, 1996.

Castillo Berthier, Héctor. *Juventud, cultura y política social: Un proyecto de investigación aplicada en la ciudad de México, 1987–1997.* Mexico City: Instituto Mexicano de la Juventud, 2000.

Castro Ruy. *Chega de Saudade: A história e as histórias de bossa nova.* São Paulo: Companhia das Letras, 1990.

Clarke, John, Stuart Hall, Tony Jefferson, and Brian Roberts. "Subcultures, Cultures, and Class: A Theoretical Overview." In *Resistance Through Rituals: Youth Subcultures in Post-War Britain,* edited by Stuart Hall and Tony Jefferson. London: Routledge, 1991.

Dapieve, Artur. *BRock: O rock brasileiro dos anos 80.* Rio de Janeiro: Editora 34, 1995.

Dávila, Arlene. *Latinos Inc.: The Marketing and Making of a People.* Berkeley: University of California Press, 2001.

De la Campa, Román. "Norteamérica y sus mundos latinos: Ontologías, globalización, diásporas." *Revista Iberoamericana* 71, no. 193 (2001): 753–69.

De la Parra, Fito. With T. W. and Marlane McGarry. *Living the Blues: Canned Heat's Story of Music, Drugs, Death, Sex, and Survival.* Nipomo, Calif.: Canned Heat Music, 2000.

Díaz, Clara. "Nace la Nueva Trova." *La Jiribilla: Revista Digital de Cultura Cubana,* no. 13 (July 2001). http://www.lajiribilla.cubaweb.cu/2001/n13_julio/350_13.html.

Díaz Ayala, Cristobal. *Música cubana: Del areíto a la nueva trova.* San Juan, P.R.: Editorial Cubanacán, 1981.

Diez de Medina, Rafael. *La estructura ocupacional y los jóvenes en Uruguay.* Montevideo: CEPAL, 1992.

Diverso, Gustavo. "Rockeros: También nueces: En busca de la contra-cultura." *Relaciones* 42 (1987).

Duany, Jorge. "Popular Music in Puerto Rico: Towards an Anthropology of Salsa." *Latin American Music Review* 5, no. 2 (Fall 1984): 187–216.

———. "Rethinking the Popular: Recent Essays on Caribbean Music." *Latin American Music Review* 17, no. 2 (1996): 176–92.
———. "Después de la modernidad: Debates contemporáneos sobre cultura y política en Puerto Rico." *Revista de Ciencias Sociales*, 5 June 1998, 218–41.
Dunn, Christopher. *Brutality Garden: Tropicália and the Emergence of a Brazilian Counterculture.* Chapel Hill: University of North Carolina Press, 2001.
Echeberría, A. M., and V. Varela. "Jóvenes violentos." *Relaciones* 91 (1991).
Echevarren, Roberto. *Arte andrógino: Estilo versus moda en un siglo corto.* Montevideo: Ediciones Brecha, 1997.
Escárate, Tito. *Canción telepática: Rock en Chile.* Santiago: LOM Ediciones, 1999.
Estrada, Tere. *Sirenas al ataque: Historia de las mujeres rockeras mexicanas, 1956–2000.* Mexico City: Instituto Mexicano de la Juventud, 2000.
Favaretto, Celso. *Tropicália: Alegoria, alegria.* São Paulo: Ateliê. 1996.
Flores, Juan. "Puerto Rican and Proud, Boyee!: Rap Roots and Amnesia." In *Microphone Fiends: Youth Music and Youth Culture,* edited by Andrew Ross and Tricia Rose. New York: Routledge, 1994.
———. *From Bomba to Hip-Hop: Puerto Rican Culture and Latino Identity.* New York: Columbia University Press, 2000.
Franco, Jean. "What's in a Name? Popular Culture Theories and Their Limitations." *Studies in Latin American Popular Culture* 1, no. 1 (1982): 5–14.
———. "Globalización y la crisis de lo popular." *Nueva Sociedad* 149 (1997): 62–73.
Fried, Gabriela, Gabriela DelSignore, Luis Eduardo Morás. *Jóvenes: Una sensibilidad buscada.* Montevideo: Nordan, 1991.
Frith, Simon. "The Magic That Can Set You Free: The Ideology of Folk and Myth of the Rock Community." *Popular Music* 1 (1981): 159–68.
———. *Sound Effects: Youth, Leisure, and the Politics of Rock 'n' Roll.* London: Pantheon, 1983.
———. "Music and Identity." In *Questions of Cultural Identity,* edited by Stuart Hall and Paul du Gay. London: Sage, 1996.
———. *Performing Rites: On the Value of Popular Music.* Oxford: Oxford University Press, 1996.
García Canclini, Néstor. *Hybrid Cultures: Strategies for Entering and Leaving Modernity.* Minneapolis: University of Minnesota Press, 1995.
———. "El debate sobre la hibridación." *Revista de Crítica Cultural* 15 (1997): 42–47.
———. *La globalización imaginada.* Mexico City: Paidós, 1999.
García Robles, Hugo. *El cantar opinando.* Montevideo: Alfa, 1969.
García Saldaña, Parménides. *En la ruta de la onda.* Mexico City: Editorial Diógenes, 1972.
Garofalo, Reebee. *Rockin' Out: Popular Music in the U.S.A.* Upper Saddle River, N.J.: Prentice Hall, 2002.
———. "Whose World, What Beat: The Transnational Music Industry, Identity, and Cultural Imperialism." *World of Music* 35, no. 2 (1993): 16–32.
———, ed., *Rockin' the Boat: Mass Music and Mass Movements.* Boston: South End Press, 1992.
Gill, John. *Queer Noises: Male and Female Homosexuality in Twentieth-Century Music.* Minneapolis: University of Minnesota Press, 1995.
Gilroy, Paul. *The Black Atlantic: Modernity and Double Consciousness.* Cambridge: Harvard University Press, 1993.
González, Juan Pablo. "Hegemony and Counter-Hegemony of Music in Latin America: Chilean Pop." *Popular Music and Society* 15, no. 2 (1991): 63–78.

González Guver, M., and M. Esmoris. "Rock y cultura juvenil." *Relaciones* 44/45 (1988).
González Moreno, Liliana. "Rock en Cuba: Juicio, hibridación y permanencia." *Actas del III Congreso Latinoamericano de la Asociación Internacional para el Estudio de la Músical Popular,* Bogotá, 2000. http://www.hist.puc.cl/historia/iaspm/pdf/Gonzalezliliana.pdf.
Grossberg, Lawrence. "Another Boring Day in Paradise: Rock and Roll and the Empowerment of Everyday Life." In *Dancing in Spite of Myself: Essays on Popular Culture.* Durham, N.C.: Duke University Press, 1997.
Guerreiro, Goli. *Retratos de una tribu urbana: Rock brasileiro.* Salvador: Centro Editorial e Didático da UFBa, 1994.
Habell-Pallán, Michelle. "El Vez is 'Taking Care of Business': The Inter/National Appeal of Chicana/o Popular Music." *Cultural Studies* 13, no. 2 (1999): 195–210.
Habell-Pallán, Michelle, and Mary Romero, eds. *Latino/a Popular Culture.* New York University Press. 2002.
Hanchard, Michael. *Orpheus and Power: The Movimento Negro of Rio de Janeiro and São Paulo, 1945–1988.* Princeton: Princeton University Press, 1994.
Harris, Keith. "Roots? The Relationship between the Global and the Local within the Global Extreme Metal Scene." *Popular Music* 19, no. 1 (2000): 13–30.
Hebdige, Dick. *Subculture: The Meaning of Style.* 1979; reprint, London: Routledge, 1991.
———. *Cut'n'mix: Culture, Identity, and Caribbean Music.* London: Comedia, 1987.
Ianni, Octavio. *Teorías de la globalización.* Mexico City: Siglo XXI Editores, 1996.
Jameson, Fredric. *Postmodernism: Or, The Cultural Logic of Late Capitalism.* Durham, N.C.: Duke University Press, 1991.
Jameson, Fredric, and Masao Miyoshi. *The Cultures of Globalization.* Durham, N.C.: Duke University Press, 1998.
Joseph, May. Introduction to *Performing Hybridity,* edited by May Joseph and Jennifer Natalya Fink. Minneapolis: University of Minnesota Press, 1999.
Kearney, Milo, and Anthony Knopp. *Border Cuates: A History of the U.S.–Mexican Twin Cities.* Austin: Eakin Press, 1995.
Laban, René. *Musica, rock y satanismo.* Mexico City: Arcoiris, 1986.
Laing, Dave. "The Music Industry and the 'Cultural Imperialism' Thesis." *Media, Culture, and Society* 8 (1986): 331–41.
Leon, Fabrizio. *La banda, el consejo y otros panchos.* Mexico City: Grijalbo, 1985.
Lipsitz, George. *Time Passages: Collective Memory and American Popular Culture.* Minneapolis: University of Minnesota Press, 1990.
———. *Dangerous Crossroads: Popular Music, Postmodernism, and the Poetics of Place.* London: Verso, 1994.
———. *American Studies in a Moment of Danger.* Minneapolis: University of Minnesota Press, 2001.
Lorey, David E. *The U.S.–Mexican Border in the Twentieth Century.* Wilmington, Del.: Scholarly Resources, 1999.
Lozano, Arturo Lara. *Enciclopedia del rock mexicano.* Mexico City: Universidad Autónoma de México–Atzcapotzalco, forthcoming.
Madeira, Angelica. "Rhythm and Irreverence (notes about the rock music movement in Brasília)." *Popular Music* 15, no. 4 (1991): 57–70.
Manduley López, Humberto. "El rock en Cuba: Historia de un hijo descarriado." *Revolución y Cultura,* no. 4 (1994): 9–11; also published (in two parts) in *Diario de Querétaro,* 16 August 1995 and 24 October 1995.
———. "Rock in Cuba: History of a Wayward Son." *South Atlantic Quarterly* 96, no. 1 (Winter 1997): 135–41.

———. "Queda la música." *La Jiribilla: Revista Digital de Cultura Cubana*, no. 13 (July 2001). http://www.lajiribilla.cubaweb.cu/2001/n13_julio/357_13.html.
———. *El rock en Cuba.* Havana: Editorial Atril, 2001.
Manuel, Peter. "Marxism, Nationalism, and Popular Music in Revolutionary Cuba." *Popular Music* 6, no. 2 (1987): 161–78.
———. "Rock Music and Cultural Ideology in Revolutionary Cuba (1985)." In *World Music, Politics, and Social Change,* edited by Simon Frith. Manchester: Manchester University Press, 1989.
———. "Puerto Rican Music and Cultural Identity." In *Ethnomusicology* 38, no.2 (1994): 249–80.
Manuel Alvarez, Luis, Cristobal Díaz Ayala, José Mandry, and Edgardo Soto Torres. *Acangana!: One Hundred Years of Puerto Rican Music.* San Juan, P.R.: Fundación Banco Popular, 2000.
Marcial, Rogelio. *Jóvenes y presencia colectiva: Introducción al estudio de las culturas juveniles del siglo XX.* Zapopan, Jalisco: El Colegio de Jalisco, 1997.
Marcondes, Marco Antonio, ed. *Enciclopédia da música popular brasileira: Erudita, folclórica e popular.* São Paulo: ArtEditora, 1977.
Martín Barbero, Jesús. *Pre-textos: Conversaciones sobre la comunicación y sus contextos.* Cali: Universidad del Valle, 1995.
———. *De los medios a las mediaciones: Comunicación, cultura y hegemonía.* 5th ed. Mexico City: Editorial Gustavo Gili, 1998.
Martínez, Rubén. *The Other Side: Fault Lines, Guerrilla Saints, and the True Heart of Rock 'n' Roll.* London: Verso, 1992.
Martins, Carlos. *Música popular uruguaya, 1973–1982: Un fenómeno de comunicación alternativa.* Montevideo: CLAEH/EBO, 1986.
Martins Villaca, Mariana. "La política cubana y el movimiento de la nueva trova." Paper presented at the *IV Congreso de la Rama Latinoamericana de la Asociación International para el Estudio de la Música Popular* (IASPM-LA), Mexico, April 2002.
Marzullo, Osvaldo, and Pancho Muñoz. *El Rock en la Argentina: La historia y sus protagonistas.* Buenos Aires: Editorial Galerna, 1986.
Martínez, Cecilia, and Tabaré Couto. *A ritmo de rock.* Montevideo: La República, 1988.
Mattern, Mark. "Popular Music and Redemocratization in Santiago, Chile, 1973–1989." *Studies in Latin American Popular Culture* 16 (1997): 101–13.
McClary, Susan. *Conventional Wisdom: The Content of Musical Form.* Berkeley: University of California Press, 2000.
McGowan, Chris, and Ricardo Pessanha. *The Brazilian Sound: Samba, Bossa Nova, and the Pop Music of Brasil.* 2nd exp. ed. Philadelphia: Temple University Press, 1998.
Monsiváis, Carlos. *Amor perdido.* Mexico City: Editorial Era, 1977.
Moore, Robin. *Nationalizing Blackness:* Afrocubanismo *and Artistic Revolution in Havana, 1920–1940.* Pittsburgh: University of Pittsburgh Press, 1997.
———. "Transformations in Cuban Nueva Trova, 1965–95." *Ethnomusicology* 47, no. 1 (Winter 2003): 1–41.
Motta, Nelson. *Noites Tropicais: Solos, improvisos e memórias musicais.* Rio de Janeiro: Objetiva, 2000.
Moulián, Tomás. *Chile actual: Anatomía de un mito.* Santiago de Chile: LOM Ediciones/Arcis, 1997.
Muñoz, C., and G. DelSignore. "La subcultura neodionisíaca: Una generación ausente y solitaria." *Relaciones* 73 (1990). http://llfp.chasque.apc.org:8081/relacion.
Ortiz, Renato. *Cultura brasileira e identidade nacional.* São Paulo: Brasiliense, 1985.
———. *Mundialização e cultura.* São Paulo: Editora Brasiliense. 1994.
———. *Otro territorio: Ensayos sobre el mundo contemporáneo.* Buenos Aires: Universidad Nacional de Quilmes, 1996.

———. *Los artífices de un cultura mundializada*. Santa Fe de Bogotá: Siglo del Hombre Editores, 1998.
Pacini Hernandez, Deborah. "Dancing with the Enemy: World Beat and the Politics of Race and Authenticity in Cuban Popular Music." *Latin American Perspectives* 25, no. 3 (1998): 110–25.
———. "A Tale of Two Cities: A Comparative Analysis of Los Angeles Chicano and Nuyorican Engagement with Rock and Roll." *Centro, Journal of the Center for Puerto Rican Studies* 11, no.2 (2000): 71–93.
Pacini Hernandez, Deborah, and Reebee Garofalo. "Hip Hop in Havana: Rap, Race, and National Identity in Contemporary Cuba." *Journal of Popular Music Studies* 11/12 (1999/2000): 18–47.
Padilla, Félix M. "Salsa Music as a Cultural Expression of Latino Consciousness and Unity." *Hispanic Journal of Behavioral Sciences* 2, no. 1 (1989): 28–45.
———. "Salsa: Puerto Rican and Latino Music." *Journal of Popular Culture* 24, no. 1 (1990): 87–104.
Paredes Pacho, José Luis. *Rock mexicano: Sonidos de la calle*. Mexico City: Aguirre y Beltrán, 1993.
Pereira, Carlos Alberto Messeder, and Heloísa Buarque de Hollanda. *Patrulhas ideológicas*. São Paulo: Brasiliense, 1980.
Perelli, Carina, and Juan Rial. *De mitos y memorias políticas*. Montevideo: Ediciones de la Banda Oriental, 1986.
Pérez, Louis A. *Cuba and the United States: Ties of Singular Intimacy*. Athens: University of Georgia Press, 1997.
Perrone, Charles. *Masters of Contemporary Brazilian Song, MPB 1965–1985*. Austin: University of Texas Press, 1989.
———. "Changing of the Guard: Questions and Contrasts of Brazilian Rock Phenomena." *Studies in Latin American Popular Culture* 9 (1990): 65–83.
Perrone, Charles, and Christopher Dunn, eds. *Brazilian Popular Music and Globalization*. New York : Routledge, 2001.
Polhemus, Ted. *Street Styles: From Sidewalk to Catwalk*. London: Thames and Hudson, 1994.
Quintana, Darío, and Eduardo de la Puente. *Todo vale: Antología analizada de la poesía rock argentina desde 1965*. Buenos Aires: Distal, 1996.
Quintero Rivera, Ángel G. *Salsa, sabor y control: Sociología de la música tropical*. Coyoacán, Mexico: Siglo XXI Editores, 1998.
Radano, Ronald, and Philip V. Bohlman, eds. *Music and the Racial Imagination*. Chicago: University of Chicago Press, 2001.
Rama, Angel. *Transculturación narrativa en América Latina*. Mexico City: Siglo XXI, 1982.
Rama, Germán. *Los jóvenes de Uruguay: Esos desconocidos*. Análisis de la Encuesta Nacional de Juventud. Montevideo: CEPAL, 1991.
Reguillo, Rosana. "El año 2000, ética, política y estéticas: Imaginarios, adscripciones y prácticas juveniles: Caso mexicano." In *'Viviendo a Toda': Jóvenes, territorios culturales y nuevas sensibilidades*, edited by Humberto J. Cubides, María Cristina Laverde, and Carlos Eduardo Valderrama, and Mario Margulis. Bogotá: Siglo del Hombre Editores, 1998.
Remedi, Gustavo. *Murgas: El teatro de los tablados: Interpretación y crítica de la cultura nacional*. Montevideo: Ediciones Trilce, 1996.
Reyes, David, and Tom Waldman. *Land of a Thousand Dances: Chicano Rock 'n' Roll from Southern California*. Albuquerque: University of New Mexico Press, 1998.
Reyes Matta, Fernando. "The 'New Song' and Its Confrontation in Latin America." In *Marxism and the Interpretation of Culture*, edited by Cary Nelson and Lawrence Grossberg. Urbana: University of Illinois Press, 1988.

Riaño-Alcalá, Pilar. "Urban Space and Music in the Formation of Youth Cultures: The Case of Bogotá, 1920–1980." *Studies in Latin American Popular Culture* 10 (1991): 87–106.
Ríos, Mary. *Guía de la música uruguaya.* Montevideo: Arca, 1995.
Roberts, John Storm. *The Latin Tinge: The Impact of Latin American Music on the United States.* New York: Oxford University Press, 1999.
Rodrigues da Silva, Carlos Benedito. "Black Soul: Aglutinação espontânea ou identidade étnica?" In *Movimentos Sociais: Urbanos, Minorias Étnicas e Outros Estudos,* edited by Luiz Antonio Machado da Silva. Brasilia: ANPOCS, 1983.
Rodríguez, Edgar. *Rock en Ichkaansihó.* Mérida, Yucatán: Conaculta/Instituto de Cultura de Yucatán, 2001.
Rodriguez-Rodriguez, Aixa L. "Music as a Form of Resistance: A Critical Analysis of the Puerto Rican New Song Movement's Oppositional Discourse." Ph.D. diss., University of Massachusetts–Amherst, 1995.
Roland, Eduardo. *Contra cualquier muro: Los grafiti de la transición (1985–1989).* Montevideo: UNO/Vintén, 1989.
Roman-Velázquez, Patria. "Discothèques in Puerto Rico: Salsa vs. Rock." In *Popular Music: Style and Identity,* edited by Will Straw. Montreal: Centre for Research on Canadian Cultural Industries and Institutions, 1995.
Rosa, Fernando. "Anos 70, o rock 'Made in Brasil.'" *Senhor F: A revista do rock.* http://www.senhorf.com.br/sf3vs/secreta/introd/anos70.htm.
Ross, Andrew, and Tricia Rose, eds. *Microphone Fiends: Youth Music to Youth Culture.* New York: Routledge, 1994.
Roura, Víctor. *Apuntes de rock: Por las calles del mundo.* Mexico City: Nuevomar, 1985.
Rowe, William, and Vivian Schelling. *Memory and Modernity: Popular Culture in Latin America.* London: Verso, 1991.
Ryback, Timothy. Rock *Around the Bloc: A History of Rock Music in Eastern Europe and the Soviet Union.* New York: Oxford University Press, 1990.
Salas, Fabio. *El grito del amor: Una actualizada historia temática del rock.* Santiago: LOM Ediciones, 1998.
Sansone, Livio. *From Africa to Afro: Use and Abuse of Africa in Brazil.* Amsterdam: SEPHIS, 1999.
Santiago, Javier. *Nueva ola portoricensis: La revolución musical que vivió en la década del 60.* Santurce, P.R.: Publicaciones del Patio, 1994.
Sarusky, Jaime. "La época, la música, lo humano." *Revolución y Cultura* 5 (September–October 2000): 50–54.
———. "Pablo Menéndez: Un joven 'conservador.'" *La Jiribilla: Revista Digital de Cultura Cubana,* no. 13 (July 2001). http://www.lajiribilla.cubaweb.cu/2001/n13_julio/364_13.html.
———. "Leo Brouwer: Una huella duradera en el siglo XX." *La Jiribilla: Revista Digital de Cultura Cubana,* no. 13 (July 2001). http://www.lajiribilla.cubaweb.cu/2001/n13_julio/355_13.html.
Semán, Pablo, and Pablo Vila. "Rock chabón e identidad juvenil en la Argentina neo-liberal." In *Los noventa: Política, sociedad y cultura en América Latina y Argentina de fin de siglo,* compiled by Daniel Filmus. Buenos Aires: FLACSO/EUDEBA, 1999.
Scaramuzzino, Ruben, and Bruno Galindo, eds. *Diccionario de rock latino.* Zaragoza, Spain: Zona de Obras, 2000.
Sheriff, Robin. "'Negro is a Nickname That the Whites Gave to the Blacks': Discourses on Color, Race, and Racism in Rio de Janeiro." Ph.D. diss., City University of New York, 1997.
Simonett, Helena. *Banda: Mexican Musical Life Across the Borders.* Middletown, Conn.: Wesleyan Univeristy Press.

Siqueira Junior, Carlos Leoni Rodrigues. *Letra, música e outras conversas.* Rio de Janeiro: Gryphus, 1995.
Soto Torres, Edgardo. "El cantar de una generación." *Diálogo* (May 1999): 23–24.
———. "Fiel a la Vega: Sin Censura." *Revista Alterna* 1, no. 1 (June 2000): 9–16.
———. "Rock boricua en la ruta independiente." *Diálogo* (September 2001): 20
Soto Torres, Edgardo, and Elías Geigel. "El rock de Puerto Rico: Desafío músical a un pueblo dormido." *La Banda Elástica* 35 (2000): 52–53.
Souza, Antônio Marcus Alves de. *Cultura, rock e arte de massa.* Rio de Janeiro: Diadorim, 1995.
Tagg, Philip. "Analyzing Popular Music: Theory, Method, and Practice." *Popular Music* 2 (1982): 37–65. Also available at http://www.theblackbook.net/acad/tagg/articles/pm2anal.html].
———. "Musicology and the Semiotics of Popular Music." *Semiotica* 66, no. 1–3 (1987): 279–98. Version with updated bibliography and notes available at http://www.theblackbook.net/acad/tagg/articles/semiota.html.
Tomlinson, John. *Cultural Imperialism: A Critical Introduction.* London: Pinter Publishers, 1991.
Trigo, Abril. "Words and Silences in Uruguayan Canto Popular [Popular Song]." *Studies in Latin American Popular Culture* 10 (1991): 215–38.
———. "Candombe and the Reterritorialization of Culture." *Callaloo* 16, no. 3 (1993): 716–28.
———. "Rockeros y grafiteros: La construcción al sesgo de una antimemoria." *Hispamérica* 70 ww(1995): 17–40.
———. *¿Cultura uruguaya o culturas linyeras? (Para una cartografía de la neomodernidad posuruguaya).* Montevideo: Vintén Editor, 1997.
Ulhôa, Martha Tupinambá de. "Nova história, velhos sons: Notas para ouvir e pensar a música brasileira popular." *Debates* 1 (1990): 78–101.
———. "Música romântica in Montes Claros: Inter-gender Relations in Brazilian Popular Song." *British Journal of Ethnomusicology* 9, no. 1 (2000): 11–40.
Urán, Omar, Patricia Valencia, and Gilberto Medina. *Medellín en vivo: La historia del rock.* Medellín: Corporación Región, 1997.
Valenzuela Arce, Jose Manuel, and Gloria Gonzalez Fernandez, eds. *Oye cómo va: Recuento de rock tijuanense.* Tijuana: Centro Cultural Tijuana—Instituto Mexicano de la Juventud, 1999.
Veloso, Caetano. *Tropical Truth: A Story of Music and Revolution in Brazil.* New York: Knopf, 2002.
Vianna, Hermano. *O mundo funk carioca.* Rio de Janeiro: Zahar, 1988.
Vila, Pablo. "Rock Nacional and Dictatorship in Argentina." *Popular Music* 6, no. 2 (1987): 129–48.
———. "Argentina's Rock Nacional: The Struggle for Meaning." *Latin American Music Review* 10, no. 1 (1989): 1–28.
Vilar, Guille. "El GESI es también una ética." *La Jiribilla: Revista Digital de Cultura Cubana,* no. 13 (July 2001). http://www.lajiribilla.cubaweb.cu/2001/n13_julio/348_13.html.
Wade, Peter. *Blackness and Race Mixture: The Dynamics of Racial Identity in Colombia.* Baltimore: Johns Hopkins University Press, 1993.
———. *Race and Ethnicity in Latin America.* Chicago: Pluto Press, 1997.
———. *Music, Race, and Nation:* Música Tropical *in Colombia.* Chicago: University of Chicago Press, 2000.
Wald, Karen Lee. "Lennonism in Cuba at Last." *Z Magazine,* June 2001, 56–60.
Wallis, Roger, and Krister Malm. *Big Sounds from Small Peoples: The Music Industry in Small Countries.* London: Constable, 1984.

Walser, Robert. *Running with the Devil: Power, Gender, and Madness in Heavy Metal Music.* Hanover, N.H.: University Press of New England, 1993.

Waxer, Lise, ed. *Situating Salsa: Global Markets and Local Meanings in Latin Popular Music.* New York: Routledge, 2002.

Wicke, Peter. *Rock Music: Culture, Aesthetics, and Sociology.* Cambridge: Cambridge University Press, 1990.

Zolov, Eric. *Refried Elvis: The Rise of the Mexican Counterculture.* Berkeley: University of California Press, 1999.

Zona de Obras, coord. *Diccionario del rock latino.* Madrid: Sociedad General de Autores y Editores SGAE, 2000.

CONTRIBUTORS

Paulo Alvarado is a Guatemalan composer, producer, and cellist who has achieved recognition and won several awards in his country for his chamber and orchestra music, songs, and scores for the theater and contemporary ballet. In these capacities, and as a founding member of Alux Nahual, he has performed in ensembles ranging from the rock group to the early music group *La Cantoria de Tomás Pascual* and the Contemporary String Quartet. He regularly presents his own music in public (utilizing multimedia and choreographic installations, as well as at recitals of his songs), has produced and is featured on more than a dozen long-playing recordings and has written more than 450 essays and musical criticism for the Guatemalan newspaper *Prensa Libre*. He is currently preparing an edition of his chamber music and working on the soundtracks for several films.

Jorge Arévalo Mateus has an M.A. in ethnomusicology from Hunter College. He is a Ph.D. candidate in ethnomusicology at the CUNY Graduate Center in New York City, where he is specializing in popular and traditional music in the Americas. He has also worked as a music archivist and exhibit curator in various New York City–based cultural institutions, including several years at the Woody Guthrie Archives, the Louis Armstrong House and Archives, and the Raíces Latin Music Museum. He is an accomplished musician (guitar) who has recorded and performed widely in the New York City area.

Susana Asensio has a doctorate from the University of Barcelona–CSIC in ethnomusicology and has published widely on music and migration and the relationship between music and marginalized subjects. She has recently taught and conducted postdoctoral research at both Columbia University and New York University.

Cecilia Benedetti is a doctoral candidate in the humanities at the University of Buenos Aires, where she also studied anthropology. She has taken an active role in various projects related to cultural processes in the city of Buenos Aires.

Héctor Castillo Berthier has a doctorate in sociology from the Universidad Nacional Autónoma de México (Mexico City), where he currently holds an appointment in the Institute of Social Research. He has published widely on questions of urban society, including *Juventud, cultura y política social: Un proyecto de investigación aplicada en la ciudad de México, 1987–1997* (2000), and has a weekly radio program dedicated to rock cultural expression. He is also the founder of Circo Volador, a music-oriented organization for working- and lower-class youth (http://www.circovolador.org).

Tere Estrada is a musician and author of *Sirenas al ataque: Historia de las mujeres rockeras mexicanas, 1956–2000* (2000). She holds a B.A. in sociology from the Universidad Nacional Autónoma de México (Mexico City) and wrote a thesis entitled "Lenguaje e identidad en el rock mexicano, 1985–1990."

Héctor Fernández L'Hoeste received his Ph.D. in hispanic languages and literature from SUNY Stony Brook (1996). He is associate professor of Spanish at Georgia State University in Atlanta, where he teaches Latin American culture. His publications include *Narrativas de representación urbana* (1998), a chapter of which centers on Argentine rock. His articles on Latin American cinema, literature, and media theory have appeared in journals such as *Hispania, Chasqui,* and *Film Quarterly.* He has also authored pieces on the topic of Latin American graphic humor, which have been published in *Imagination Beyond Nation* (1998), the *International Journal of Comic Art,* and in conference proceedings.

Reebee Garofalo is a professor in the College of Public and Community Service at the University of Massachusetts, Boston. He has written numerous articles on racism, censorship, the political uses of music, and the globalization of the music industry. He is the author of *Rockin' the Boat: Mass Music and Mass Movements* (1991), and is currently working on a second edition of *Rockin' Out: Popular Music in the USA.* He is also co-editor of *Policing Pop* (2003).

Michelle Habell-Pallán is assistant professor of American ethnic studies and faculty affiliate of Latin American studies at the University of Washington. During 2002–2003 she was a Rockefeller Foundation Postdoctoral Fellow at the Center for Chicano Studies (University of California, Santa Barbara), and in 2001 was awarded a Woodrow Wilson National Foundation Research Fellowship. She is coeditor of *Latino/a Popular Culture* (2002) and has published several articles on U.S. and Canadian transnational Latina cultural production, including "'El Vez Is Taking Care of Business': The International Appeal of Chicano Popular Music," in *Cultural Studies* (April 1999). Her book, tentatively titled, "The Travels of Chicana and Latina Popular Culture," is forthcoming from NYU Press.

Josh Kun is assistant professor of English at the University of California, Riverside. He writes a weekly arts column for the *San Francisco Bay Guardian* and the *Boston Phoenix.* His essays and articles on popular music have appeared in *Los Angeles Weekly, SPIN Magazine, Village Voice,* and in numerous scholarly publications. He has been writing about *rock en español* and Latin Alternative music since 1993, and was the host of the first commercial, English-language Latin rock radio show in Los Angeles (*The Red Zone* on Y107 FM). He now hosts *Rokamole,* a weekly Latin rock music video and culture show on KJLA–LATV. He has served as an on-air Latin rock consultant for television (ABC, UPN, FOX Latin America) and radio (BBC's *The World*), and since 2000 has hosted the annual Latin Alternative Music Conference in New York City.

Bryan McCann received his Ph.D. from Yale University and is assistant professor of Latin American history at Georgetown University. His recently published book is entitled *Hello, Hello Brazil: Popular Music in the Making of Modern Brazil* (2004).

Deborah Pacini-Hernandez is associate professor of anthropology and teaches Latino studies courses at Tufts University. She is the author of *Bachata: A Social History of a Dominican Popular Music* (1995), numerous articles on Spanish Caribbean and U.S. Latino popular music, and is a coeditor of the *Journal of Popular Music Studies*.

Walescka Pino-Ojeda received her doctorate in Latin American literature and critical theory from Washington University. She is currently a lecturer in Spanish at the University of Auckland in Auckland, New Zealand, where her research involves literature, cinema, and music in Latin America. Her most recent publication is *Sobre castas y puentes: Conversaciones con tres escritoras latinoamericanas: Elena Poniatowska, Rosario Ferré, and Diamela Eltit* (2000).

Pablo Semán teaches at the Universidad Nacional de General San Martín in Argentina and is a postdoctoral fellow at CONICET (Consejo Nacional de Investigaciones Científicas, Educativas y Tecnológicas). His research involves diverse forms of popular culture. His most recent publication is "Brazilian Pentecostalism Crosses National Borders" (in collaboration with Ari Oro), which appears in *Between Babel and Pentecost: Transnational Pentecostalism in Africa and Latin America Pentecostalism and Transnationalism: Africa/Latin America*, edited by André Corten and Ruth Marshall-Fratani (2001).

Abril Trigo is associate professor of Latin American cultures in the Department of Spanish and Portuguese at Ohio State University. He has published extensively on Latin American cultural studies, with particular emphasis on the historical formation of national imaginaries and their articulation to popular culture in the Río de la Plata. His publications include *Caudillo, estado, nación: Literatura, historia e ideología en el Uruguay* (1990), and *¿Cultura uruguaya o culturas linyeras? (Para una cartografía de la neomodernidad posuruguaya)* (1997). He recently finished *Migrant Memories*, a book on migrant theory based upon the ethnographic study of a migrant community in the U.S., and is a coeditor of *Latin American Cultural Studies Reader* (2004). Currently, he is working on *Políticas de la transculturación en la América Latina globalizada*, a book-length essay on eco-cultural formations in Latin America and a critique of the political economy of culture in the periphery.

Martha Tupinambá de Ulhôa is professor at the Instituto Villa Lobos of the Universidade do Rio de Janeiro in Brazil. She holds an M.F.A. degree in piano performance from the University of Florida and a Ph.D. in musicology from Cornell University. She has published on various aspects of Brazilian music, both in Brazil and abroad. Her current research centers on a semiotic musical analysis of popular Brazilian songs.

Pablo Vila is associate professor of sociology at the University of Texas at San Antonio. His research involves culture and identity along the U.S.–Mexico border and popular music in Argentina. His most recent publication is *Crossing Borders, Reinforcing Borders: Social Categories, Metaphors, and Narrative Identities on the U.S.–Mexico Frontier* (2000).

Eric Zolov received his Ph.D. in history from the University of Chicago (1995) and is associate professor of Latin American history at Franklin & Marshall College. He is the author of *Refried Elvis: The Rise of the Mexican Counterculture* (1999), and coeditor of *Latin America and the United States: A Documentary History* (2000) and *Fragments of a Golden Age: The Politics of Culture in Mexico since 1940* (2001). His current research focuses on the impact of the Cuban revolution on Mexican politics and U.S.–Mexican relations during the 1960s.

INDEX

Aborto Elétrico (Brazil), 215
Abuela Coca, La (Uruguay), 136–37
Adamo, Salvatore (Italy/Belgium), 299–300
African American music, 58, 66, 72–73, 94; doo-wop, 50, 52, 74–75; Philly Soul, 77–78; United States soul music, 69–70, 76–77, 82–84
African influences, 12–14, 18–19, 64, 80, 121, 192
Agustín, José (México), 29
Alejandro, Manuel (Spain), 305
Alemán, Miguel, 245
Alfonso, Carlos (Cuba), 61–65
Allende, Salvador, 6, 11, 291
Almafuerte (Argentina), 282
Almas Vertiginosas (Cuba), 61, 359
Almendra (Argentina), 16, 120, 358
Alux Nahual (Guatemala), 14, 232, 238, 354, 360, 384n1, 385n18; formation of, 222, 225–26; popularity of, 230–31, 233, 239, 385n16; style of, 16, 220, 226–29, 234–37
Alvarez, Santiago (Cuba), 49
Alves, Francisco (Brazil), 78
American Bandstand, 9, 27, 93. *See also* television
Ancón rock festival (Colombia), 9, 181–82
Andean music, 12–13, 150, 187–88, 193, 299
Apple Pie (Guatemala), 223, 358
Arbenz Guzmán, Jacobo, 6, 221
Argentina, 41, 303–4, 353; "Dirty War" period in, 1, 14; neoliberalism in, 262–65; populism in, 263–64, 272–73; in *rock chabón*, 266, 268, 278–83, 285–86; rock music in, 21, 119, 140, 185, 224, 242. *See also* Argentine rock
Argentine rock, 1, 21, 224, 264. *See also individual band names; rock chabón; rock nacional*
Armendariz Velasquez, Alicia (U.S.), 162, 164–72, *167*, 352, 360–61
art, 60, 291; and architecture, 313–14, 325, 334; visual, 162, 172, 176, 178, 313–14, 325, 334
art rock, 13–14, 63

Aterciopelados (Colombia), 18, 188, 193, 303, 361
Attaque 77 (Argentina), 268, 361
Avándaro rock festival (Mexico), 9, 11, 23, 38–41, 149, 150, 241–43, 353, 366n1, 378n26, 378n29
Avellanet, Chucho (Puerto Rico), 93, 358
Avilés, Kenny (Mexico), 153, *154*

Bags, The (U.S.), 162, 165. *See also* Chicanos/as
Bahia, 70, 80, 209–11. *See also* Brazil
ballads, 51, 105, 110, 147, 183
Banda Azúcar (Guatemala), 223, 359
banda sinaloense, in Nortec, 321–23
bandas, 243, 246, 250–52, 254–59, 325, 386n6. *See also chavos banda*
Bandido (Mexico), 34, 37, 359
Barão Vermelho (Brazil), 213–14, 354
Bátiz, "Baby" (Mexico), 147–48, 151–52, 378n17, 378n26
Bátiz, Javier (Mexico), 147–48, 368n30, 378n17
Beatles, 6, 28–29, 51, 65, 93; Cuban government and, 1, 43, 47–49; influence of, 13, 118, 130, 204–6, 212; popularity of, 44, 119, 144
Benavides, Iván (Colombia), 190–94, 197–98
Black Jeans, Los (Mexico), 147
black music, 4–5, 80, 88–90, 364n9; Afro-Caribbean music, 94, 97, 105, 143, 182, 220; Afro-Cuban music, 52–53, 63–64; Afrosound (Colombia), 184; *batuque*, 136; tropical music, 110, 182, 184, 191–92, 221, 223, 237–38, 364n19, 365n32, 386n22. *See also* African American music; African influence; race
black power/consciousness movements, 73, 88, 105, 110; in Brazil, 69–70, 78–79, 81–83, 85, 90. *See also* race
Blades, Rubén (Panama), 13, 192, 295, 374n25
Blitz (Brazil), 204, 354, 360
Bloque (de Búsqueda), 20, 180, 190–95, 197–98, 361, 382n9, 382n10

409

blues, 41, 53–54, 99, 106, 147–48, 265, 368n30. *See also* rhythm and blues
Bogotá, Colombia, 9, 182–84, 186–87, 189–91
bolero, 121, 143, 202
Boricua rock (BR) (Puerto Rico), 91–93, 97–98, 102, 104–13, 361, 373n12
bossa nova, 71, 73, 79, 89, 119–21, 202, 292
Brat, The (U.S.), 162–63, 168–70, 172, 360. *See also* Chicanos/as
Bravo, Luis (Cuba), 46, 51, 358
Bravos, Los (Spain), 61
Brazil, 84–85, 218, 350; culture in, 89–90, 350, 352–53; government of, 6, 70, 74–75, 81, 200–202, 204, 352–53; music in, 41–42, 55, 69–73, 78, 136, 202–3, 205, 209, 215, 328; race in, 14, 70, 79–82, 85–86, 90; rock in, 1, 71–72, 200, 202, 204, 354; *rock nacional* of, 204, 354. *See also* Brazilian rock; Brazilian soul
Brazilian rock, 200, 204, 211; Brazilianness of, 205–6, 208, 212–13, 217–19; case study of, 215–18; influences on, 212–15. *See also individual band names*
Brazilian soul, 68, 76–77, 359; commercialism of, 84–87; as hybrid, 69–70, 79; legacies of, 69, 71, 88–90; relation to politics, 82–84, 87
British rock, 27, 48, 110, 205–6, 212, 293–94; British Invasion, 15, 44, 50–51; British punk, 167, 175
Brouwer, Leo (Cuba), 55–56, 58, 60
Brown, James, 82, 88, 192. *See also* African American music
Brown, Roy (Puerto Rico), 94, 358, 374n25
Brunner, José Joaquín, 310
Buarque de Hollanda, Chico (Brazil), 59, 120, 203, 205
Byrne, David, 20, 179–80, 191–93, 195, 198

Caballo Loco (Guatemala), 223, 359
Café Tacuba (Mexico), 18, 22, 95, 361, 366n34
Cafés cantantes (youth clubs), 1, 29, 145–46, 148. *See also* Venues
Caifanes, Los (Mexico), 192, 360, 366n34
candombe, 118, 120–25, 136, 269. *See also* black music
Canto Nuevo, 291–94, 297, 300, 302, 359; *canto popular,* 125–26, 129–30, 134. *See also* political song
capitalism, 8, 86, 197, 351–52; opposition to, 17, 265, 337; relation of rock to, 9, 102, 115–16, 265. *See also* industrialization; neoliberalism
Cárdenas, Lázaro, 39, 245
Caribbean music, 13, 191–93, 223
Carlos, Roberto (Brazil), 72–73, 75, 78, 202, 204, 305, 358
carnival music, 120, 122, 125–27, 129, 134, 202. *See also* black music
carranguera, 193
Casa de las Américas, 55
Cassiano, Genival (Brazil), 69, 76–78
Castro, Fidel, 6, 11, 43, 65
Catholic Church, 26, 143, 150, 181–83, 247, 306
censorship, 25, 36, 48–50, 59–61, 82, 146, 244
Central America, 220–21, 230–32; Central American rock, 233, 235, 237–38
cha-cha, 44, 143, 206, 305
charango, 11–12. *See also peñas;* political song
chavos banda, 16, 40, 246–47. *See also* bandas
Chicanos/as, 34–35, 162–63, 175–76, 358, 380n7; feminism of, 164–65, 173–74; in *Pretty Vacant* (film), 172–78, 381n37. *See also* Latinos
Chico Science (Brazil), 214, 361
Chile, 6, 290, 298–300; government repression in, 291–92, 295–97, 307–8, 389n2; military regime in, 6, 12, 291; music in, 11–12, 41, 148, 242, 291–92, 303, 358–59. *See also* Chilean rock
Chilean rock, 12, 17, 41, 299–302; aggressiveness of, 307–9; influences on, 293–94, 304–5; post-authoritarian, 296–97, 303–6, 310–11. *See also* individual band names
choro, 87, 89
Circo Volador (Mexico), 254–59, 388n31
cities, 18, 19, 44, 108, 336; border, 315, 335, 338; music of, 105–7, 115–16; sounds of, 301–2, 323–24, 329–30
class, 25, 45, 81, 202, 225, 263, 279, 292, 352–53; appeal of rock and, 46, 182, 350; audience for rock and, 16–17, 183, 255–56; and connotations of rock, 8–9, 27; development of rock and, 8–9, 130, 145; effects on music preferences, 19, 47, 69, 93, 119, 186, 188, 190, 265, 349; and language of rock lyrics, 15–16, 185; music venues and, 53, 82, 88, 150; punk and, 104, 163, 165; rock and, 131, 224, 261, 264, 300; rock audiences and, 40, 108, 136, 151; of *rock chabón,* 272–73, 281; rock in Mexico and, 41, 244, 248, 254, 259; social mobility of, 262, 264;

youth culture and, 119, 265, 350–51. *See also* working class
Club del Clan (Argentina/Colombia/Puerto Rico), 9, 118–19, 181, 358. *See also* television
Cold War, 6, 8
Colombia, 7; government, 180, 183, 188; music in, 190, 303; national identity in, 194–95, 197; regionalism of, 180–82, 184, 187–88, 191–92; rivalry among musical genres in, 186–87; rock in, 1–2, 142, 180–85, 187–93
Colombian rock, 187–93
commercialism, 135, 203, 207, 297, 351; of Bloque, 190, 193, 195; criticism of, 70, 84–87; to increase marketability, 190, 195; and lack of promotion of rock, 100, 152, 233; and promotion of rock, 82–84, 93, 151–52, 181, 233–34; resistance to, 10–11, 91–93, 98, 102, 254, 291. *See also* media
communists, 15, 52–53, 55, 228. *See also* Cuba; Left
Congreso (Chile), 291, 294, 386n23
Control Machete (Mexico), 361
Costa, César (Mexico), 147, 181
Costa Rica, 230
counterculture, 9, 34, 125, 130, 351; of La Onda, 37–39, 148–50; rock in, 115–16; values of, 149–50. *See also* hippies; youth
Covarrubias, Teresa (U.S.), 162, 164–65, 167, 167–70, 172, 352, 360–61. *See also* Chicanos/as
covers, 9, 27–30, 32–34, 110, 119, 144–46, 226–27, 280; English-language, 28, 51, 118–19, 143, 223, 385n7; Spanish-language, 15, 26, 93, 143, 148, 182, 299, 303, 310–11, 364n145. *See also* refritos
Cuba, 6, 11, 15, 66; cultural policies in, 46–47, 52–53, 59–61; economy of, 8, 17, 65; GESI and government of, 57–61; government's response to rock, 47–50, 54–55, 61, 64–65, 67; music in, 44, 52–53, 55–57, 60, 62, 65, 93, 205–6; relations with U.S., 43–45, 64; revolution in, 10, 44, 47, 53–56, 60; rock in, 7, 43, 49, 51, 394n5. *See also* Cuban rock
Cuban rock, 51–52, 54–58, 60–67. *See also* individual band names
cultural imperialism, 22, 185; resistance to, 39–40, 43–44, 58–59, 151; rock seen as, 7, 9–11, 15, 43–44, 58–59, 205
cultural nationalism, 8, 35, 177, 185

culture industries, 18–20, 30, 135, 265, 349, 351, 364n13. *See also* commercialism; media
cumbia, 13, 187–88, 192, 297, 325; rock and, 18–19, 40. *See also* black music
Cura, Domingo (Argentina), 279

Dada, Los (Cuba), 61, 358
dance, 13, 89, 122, 125, 143, 146, 299; Brazilian soul, 70–71, 80, 82; music's suitability for, 10–11, 136, 325; to rock, 46, 83, 182, 269; soul, 84–85, 87, 90
dance music, 18–19, 46, 58, 70, 88–89, 221–23, 236, 299, 313; Cuban, 44, 52–53, 61–62; expected from Latin bands, 234, 238–39; influence on rock, 40–41, 205–6, 334; Mexican, 40, 143, 322–23; techno as, 322, 328
democracy, 70, 75, 221–22, 291; Mexican, 31, 242, 253–54; returning to Latin America, 16, 128–30, 232; youth movements supporting, 31, 242
Deus ex Machina (Mexico), 316, 318–20
"Dirty War" period (Argentina), 1, 14, 266, 275, 277–78
disappearances, political, 154, 295–96
disc jockeys (DJs), 49, 153–54, 181, 313, 323
disco, 88–89, 223, 328
distribution/dissemination, 44, 47, 93, 192–93, 195–97, 227–28, 349; alternative means of, 108, 164, 235, 239, 248–49; limited, 101, 121, 171. *See also* media; music industry; record companies
Divididos (Argentina), 273, 279–80, 282, 360
División del Norte, La (Mexico), 34
do-it-yourself (DIY) approach, 18, 51, 162–63, 168, 175, 318, 320, 327
Dominican Republic, 6, 294
Dos Minutos (Argentina), 268–69, 273–77
drugs: dances associated with, 89–90, 151–52; Maia's use of, 68, 75, 79, 88–89; and rock chabón, 271–72, 288; traffic in, 186–87, 313, 322; use, 13, 59, 155
Dug Dug's, Los (Mexico), 28–29, 366n1, 377n14
Dylan, Bob, 13, 54, 93, 148, 217

Echeverri, Andrea (Colombia), 142
Echeverría, Luis, 11, 33, 39, 367n27
El Salvador, 108, 230, 232
El Vez and the Memphis Mariachis (U.S.), 168, 361. *See also* Chicanos/as

electronica, 5, 317–18, 320, 323, 331; Nortec and, 312–14, 316, 321, 324, 329

English. *See* language

EZLN (Zapatista Army of National Liberation), 332, 334, 339, 344–45, 367n26

Fabulosos Cadillacs, Los (Argentina), 18, 136, 193, 303, 360

Fania All Stars (U.S./Puerto Rico), 64, 95

fans, 95, 118, 201, 233–34, 329, 345–46; of Brazilian rock, 200, 208–9, 211–14; of rock, 51, 93, 248–49. *See also* rock, audiences of

fanzines, 27, 36–37, 161, 167–68, 174–75

festivals, music, 95, 118, 203, 326, 361; of protest music, 55, 59, 370n57; rock, 1–2, 9, 149–50, 181–82, 189–90, 204, 224, 253–54, 259. *See also* Avándaro rock festival (Mexico)

Fiel a la Vega (Puerto Rico), 91, 98–102, 113, 361

films, 25, 29, 52, 59, 70, 108, 119; in rise of rock, 27, 143, 181; U.S., 24, 46, 364n13

folk music, 150–51, 183, 237, 377n6; folk protest, 118; folklore in political songs, 242, 291, 297; and folkloric music, 52–53, 280, 282; folk-rock, 93, 94, 100, 216–17; use of folkloric music in hybrids, 106, 125, 279, 286, 294; *vallenato* as, 18, 190–91, 382n5. *See also* protest music; traditional music

Frei, Eduardo, 307

Friedman, Milton, 291

funk, 14, 40, 53–54, 90; influence of, 87, 192, 334; in musical hybrids, 79, 88–89, 98, 136, 158, 354. *See also* African American music; black music

García, Charly (Argentina), 111, 188, 253, 354, 360–61

García Canclini, Néstor, 305

Gardel, Carlos (Argentina), 182

gender: feminism, 164–65, 169–70, 173–76; gender politics, 139, 168, 173–74; gender politics in rock, 20–21, 152–53, 158; gender roles, 142–44, 147, 158–59; men's dominance in music, 20–21, 83, 104–5; in punk scene, 104–5, 165, 170, 352; and sexual harassment, 146–47, 151–52; sexuality, 26, 83, 86, 143–44, 149–50, 156, 158, 165–66. *See also* patriarchy

Gieco, León (Argentina), 277, 303, 359

Gil, Gilberto (Brazil), 13–14, 55, 74, 88, 203–4. *See also* black music; Brazil

globalization, 18, 196, 218; effects of, 194, 197, 264, 336; influence on music, 135–40; of music, 180, 189, 206; opposition to, 116–17, 132, 138, 337, 344

Globo television network (Brazil), 19, 76. *See also* television

González, Rodrigo "Rockdrigo" (Mexico), 18, 250, 360

Goulart, João, 352

Grupo Experimentación Sonora del ICAIC (GESI), 12, 56–61, 63, 65, 359. *See also* Cuban rock; Political song

Guatemala, 6, 9, 14, 20, 220–26, 385n5; government of, 221–22, 225, 228, 232. *See also* Guatemalan rock

Guatemalan rock, 223–25. *See also individual band names*

Guerra, Ely (Mexico), 142, 158, 361

Guerrero, Rita (Mexico), 157–58

Guevara, Che, 107, 176, 268, 287, 308, 337

Guzmán, Alejandra (Mexico), 158

Guzmán, Enrique (Mexico), 26, 147, 181, 358

Haley, Bill, 6, 24, 50, 144

hip-hop, 18, 41, 89, 106, 135–37, 328. *See also* African American music; black music; rap

hippies, 6, 32–33, 48, 183. *See also* counterculture; *jipis*

Hollywood. *See* Los Angeles

Honduras, 230

Hoyos fonquis, as rock venues, 151–52, 387n22

hybridity (musical), 55, 135, 298, 313; Abolição's, 79–80; Bloque's, 191–92; GESI's music as, 56–58, 60–61; jazz in, 94, 294; Maia's music as, 76–78; Mano Negra as, 333–34; Nortec as, 321–23, 329; *norteño* music as, 322–23; of other artists, 64, 73, 158, 337; popular music as, 58, 125, 206, 349; reasons for adopting, 12, 18; Ricanstruction as, 106, 110; rock as, 21, 113, 136–37, 187, 213–14; rock in, 65, 73, 88, 95, 99, 121, 130, 193, 209; *rock nacional* as, 279, 354; samba in, 73, 88; Síntesis's music as, 63–64; soul in, 68–69, 88; traditional music in, 18, 95, 97–98, 120, 122–24, 126–29, 191, 193, 209, 294; urban music as, 94, 106

identity, 35, 164, 263, 314, 322; and *bandas*, 243–44; Colombian, 180, 188–89; and culture of cities, 329–30; meaning of rock and, 105, 123, 304, 309, 349–50; national, 6, 139, 203, 218, 280–81, 286, 349; play of multiple positions in, 92, 104; Puerto Rican, 92, 94, 99–100, 104, 106–7, 113; and *rock chabón*, 272, 280–81, 286; tension of, 95–96, 198, 352; transnationalization of, 194–95
imperialism, 6, 33, 242, 286. See also cultural imperialism
indigenous culture, 14, 29, 33, 332. See also traditional music
industrialization, 7, 262–63, 286, 315–16, 320, 322; Import Substitution Industrialization, 10, 16, 353
Institute of Popular Music (IPM), 200, 202
instruments, musical, 69, 89, 222–23, 286, 322–23, 341–42; acquisition of, 49–51, 264; of Alux Nahual, 225–26, 237; in Brazilian rock, 73, 209–12, 216–17; *charango*, 11–12; in Chilean rock, 294, 301; diversity of, 76–77, 79–80; electric, 11, 62, 73, 143, 151, 205; in GESI's music, 56–58; horns, 62, 77, 136, 313, 321, 325, 341–42; improvised/accessible, 51, 229, 381n30; marimba, 222–23, 228, 358; in Nortec, 321, 325; of *nueva canción*, 11–13; percussion, 122, 125, 325; in rock, 61–63, 73, 96, 136; of *technobandas*, 322; traditional, 77–78, 188, 204, 220, 386n24
intellectuals, 16–17, 22, 24, 30, 33, 39, 60, 304, 352–53
international melodic music, 117–19
internationalism, 112, 307; and localism, 18, 329. See also transnationalism
Internet, 66–67, 325, 328, 330–31
Inti-Illimani (Chile), 59, 150
Iracundos, Los (Uruguay), 117–20
Irakere (Cuba), 62, 64

Jaivas, Los (Chile), 12, 41, 291, 294, 359
Jara, Víctor (Chile), 12, 150, 291, 294
Javiera y Los Imposibles (Chile), 303–5, 361
jazz: in hybrids, 62, 69, 79–80, 94, 97, 106, 120, 136, 158, 294; influence of, 58, 61–62, 87, 120–21, 125, 191, 292; race and, 53–54
jipis, 32–33, 37. See also counterculture; hippies
Jovem Guarda (Brazil), 15, 72–75, 203, 206, 349–50, 354, 358

Kenny y Los Eléctricos (Mexico), 153, 360
KonFrontazion (Puerto Rico), 102–5, 113, 361
Kraken (Colombia), 186, 360
Kubitschek, Juscelino, 352

Laboriel, Ela (Mexico), 143–44, 146, 149, 152, 377n4, 378n29
language: of agit–rock, 137–38; Alux Nahual's, 225–27; bilingualism, 97, 111; in Brazilian rock, 209–12, 215–16, 218; in Brazilian soul, 83, 85; of Chicana Trova, 381n30; Cuban government discouraging English, 47, 53, 55; of Electronica, 317; English in La Onda Chicana, 23, 34–36, 39, 41, 349; English-language covers, 28–29, 51, 223; in Guatemala, 385n19; of Jovem Guarda, 72; Maia's, 75; Mano Negra's, 333–34; of media conglomerates, 19–20; Portuguese, 15, 19–20; profanity in rock, 26, 138, 211–12; Puya's, 95, 97–98; of rock, 15–16, 118–20, 151, 184–85, 223–24, 243; "rock en tu idioma" movement, 16, 152–53, 233, 255; rock in English, 10, 28, 32–33, 47; rock in Spanish, 23, 47, 52, 61, 63–64, 101, 123, 367n11; of *rock nacional*, 15; Shakira's, 189; slang, 15–16; spanglish, 137–40; Spanish–language covers, 15, 26, 93, 143, 148, 182. See also lyrics; *rock en español*
Latin alternative music, 91–92, 97–98; Alux Nahual compared to typical, 220, 237–38; expected to be dance music, 234, 238–39; marketing of, 111–12. See also world music
Latinos/as, 91–92; marketing to, 20, 111–12, 135, 234; in U.S., 20, 111–12, 135, 137, 162, 193. See also Chicanos/as
Lee, Rita (Brazil), 213, 359. See also Brazil
Left, the, 9, 12, 17, 228, 353; Brazilian, 1, 74, 75, 203; Marxism, 75, 105; music preferences of, 1, 10–11, 13, 16; response to rock, 6, 10–11, 30, 39, 150–51, 155, 185; socialism, 6, 8, 291, 352; terminology of in Chilean rock, 308–9. See also communists; revolution; students; youth
Legião Urbana (Brazil), 211–13, 215–18, 354, 360, 384n21
Ley, La (Chile), 360–61
Lobão (Brazil), 212, 214–15, 354
Lobos, Los (U.S.), 253, 359. See also Chicanos/as

Locos del Ritmo, Los (Mexico), 26, 28, 358
López, Jennifer, 111
Lora, Alex (Mexico), 249. *See also* Three Souls in My Mind
Los Angeles, 19, 162–63, 165, 167, 172, 322, 366n34. *See also* Chicanos/as
lyrics, 68, 136–37, 236; aggressiveness of, 307–9; of Brazilian rock, 200, 205, 209–12; contents of, 73, 187, 261, 301–2, 304; everyday concerns in, 18, 107, 250; hopelessness in, 317–20; language of, 15–16, 23, 140, 308–9; local concerns in, 64, 99–100, 200; in *murga*-rock, 126–29; poetics of, 121, 204, 294, 304–5; politics in, 51, 64–65, 97–98, 101–2, 108, 110, 125, 203–4, 295–97; punk content of, 102–3, 108; relation to music, 171, 329, 391n17; resistance through, 14, 107–8; of *rock chabón*, 266–70, 270–77, 280, 282; socio-ecological topics of, 107–8, 150, 169, 250; sources of, 68, 136, 294; vulgarity/profanity in, 26, 138, 211–12. *See also* language

Madres de la Plaza de Mayo, Las, 262, 277–78. *See also* "Dirty War" period (Argentina)
Maia, Tim (Sebastião Rodrigues) (Brazil), 68–69, 87, 90, 354, 359, 371n11; background of, 71–72, 74–75; career of, 71–72, 75–76, 88–89; criticisms of, 70, 89; diversity in arrangements by, 77–78. *See also* black music; Brazil
Maldita Vecindad y Los Hijos del Quinto Patio (Mexico), 22, 193, 253, 361, 366n34
mambo, 44, 143
Manal (Argentina), 358. *See also* Argentine rock
Mano Negra (France/Spain), 136, 332–34, 339, 341. *See also* Manu Chao
Manu Chao (France/Spain), 253, 332, 334–46
Marcos, Subcomandante, 332, 334–35, 339, 344–45. *See also* EZLN
María, Angélica (Mexico), 29, 147, 358, 377n14
marketing, 44, 193, 202–3; of Boricua rock, 98–100, 112; and categorization of music, 235–39, 394n2; homogenization of segments, 194, 196; independent, 103, 108, 112; to Latin American consumers, 19–20, 111–12; and marketability, 28, 36, 123, 353. *See also* distribution/dissemination

Marley, Bob, 80, 110
Martin, Ricky (Puerto Rico), 111, 198, 361
Martín Barbero, Jesús, 295, 298, 305–6, 327
Mary Jets, Las (Mexico), 144, *145*
Medellín, Colombia, 181–84, 186–87
media, 7, 299, 331; access to, 18, 184; control of, 186, 353; government and, 24–25, 31, 46–47; music classification and, 19, 236–39; popular culture and, 8, 299, 349; power of, 30, 45–46, 195, 349; selective coverage of rock by, 99–100, 158, 233; in spread of rock, 44, 93, 181; transnational, 92–93, 307. *See also* press; radio; record companies; television
Menem, Carlos, 265, 286
Menéndez, Pablo (U.S./Cuba), 53–54, 56–59, 63–65. *See also* Cuban rock
merengue, 13, 19, 105–6, 136, 143, 223. *See also* black music
Metallica, 95
Mexican Americans, 34–35, 322–23. *See also* Chicanos/as; Latinos/as
Mexican rock, 21–22, 33–34, 40–41, 143, 224, 227, 243, 254, 259–60; bands in, 377n2, 378n20; and class, 249–50; criticisms of, 23, 30, 242. *See also individual band names*
Mexico, 8, 22, 25, 254, 353; border with U.S., 312–16, 321–22, 326; culture of, 15, 23–24, 29, 33, 142, 144, 344; democratic government in, 253–54, 257–58; government and *bandas*, 247, 250–52; government relations with youth, 242, 247–48, 252–58; government repression in, 26, 37–39, 40, 249; identities in, 35, 314; music in, 11, 40–41, 152, 154, 220, 258, 318–19, 320–21; Nortec in, 313–14, 321–23; political parties of, 154, 155, 245, 257–58, 387n13; politics in, 33, 244–46; regionalism of, 249, 321–23; relations with U.S., 23, 151, 178; resistance to government of, 332, 344; rock in, 1, 7, 9, 15, 142–43, 147–48, 173, 183–85, 242–43; stereotypes of, 392n36, 392n50; student movement in, 31, 241–42; women in rock in, 144, 158–59; youth of, 29–30, 147, 154, 243–44, 246–48, 252–53. *See also* Mexican rock; Partido Revolucionario Institucional (PRI)
Mexico City, 27–29, 31–32, 249, 253–59, 314, 377n2, 386n2, 388n31
Mezcla (Cuba), 64, 360. *See also* Cuban rock
Miami, in culture industries, 19–20, 158

Milanés, Pablo (Cuba), 12–13, 54–56, 60, 93, 364n19. *See also* political song
military regimes, 12, 14, 353; in Argentina, 1, 14, 266, 275, 277–78; in Brazil, 74–75, 81–82, 84–85, 200–204; in Chile, 291, 294, 303, 307–8, 389n2; in Guatemala, 221–22, 232, 385n11; in Uruguay, 123, 125–26, 128–30, 376n13
milonga, 121, 130
Miserables, Los (Chile), 307–9, 361
modernity, 81, 320; disenchantment with, 140, 297, 318, 327; and modernization, 8, 10, 31, 219, 221, 350, 352; rock and, 8–9, 21, 25, 27, 120–21
Molotov (Mexico), 22, 95, 361, 366n34
Monsiváis, Carlos, 29–30, 242, 244, 251
Montevideo, Uruguay, 120, 122, 129
Motown, 13, 69, 83. *See also* African American music; record companies
MTV Latin America, 19, 140, 158, 187, 193. *See also* television
MTV Latino, 111–12. *See also* television
murga, 120, 125–27, 269
murga-rock, 126–29
music education, 51, 55–57, 146, 148, 226
music industry: categorization by, 194, 239; limits imposed by, 93, 99, 105; marketing by, 111, 135, 239; resistance to commercialism of, 91–93, 98, 104; "rock en tu idioma" movement in, 19, 153; transnationalization in, 19, 194; U.S. hegemony in, 364n13. *See also* commercialism; marketing; record companies
music preferences: analysis of, 201–2; class and, 19, 47, 93, 186, 188; race and, 14, 19, 53–54, 65–66, 93; regionalism and, 182, 186, 193, 249
música de protesta. *See* political song
música folclórica. *See* folk music
Música Popular Brasileira (MPB), 55, 203, 214, 353. *See also* Brazil
música romántica. *See* ballads; bolero
Mutantes, Os (Brazil), 203–4, 213, 354, 358

Nascimento, Milton (Brazil), 59, 78, 120, 203, 253–54
nationalism, 9, 195, 333; Brazilian, 1, 74, 203, 205, 218; Colombian, 180–81, 185–86; Mexican, 23, 27, 35, 39–41; opposition to, 130, 349–50; Puerto Rican, 93–94, 99–100, 105, 107, 113; rock and, 15, 123–24; in *rock chabón*, 262–64, 278–83, 286, 288. *See also* cultural nationalism

neoliberalism, 16–17, 132, 188, 262–65, 286, 291, 355; privatization, 16, 283. *See also* capitalism; globalization
New Wave (as punk), 16, 119, 164, 166, 168, 187
New Wave (Nueva Ola), 300, 303, 358
New York City, 94, 105, 107–8, 112, 325
Nicola, Noel (Cuba), 56, 57, 63
nihilism, 104, 107, 319–20
Nortec, 5, 312, 328–29, 361; appearance in, 316, 323–25, *326*; architecture in, 326–27, *327*; culture of, 313–14, 325–27, 392n37; do-it-yourself approach to, 318, 327; recycling ideology in, 321–22, 326–27
norteño music, 40, 321–24
North America, 95, 232. *See also* United States
Not4Prophet (Alano Baez) (U.S./Puerto Rico), 105–10, *106, 109*
nueva canción, 11–13, 59, 99–100, 291, 294, 297, 354, 358, 374n25; and *canción protesta*, 183, 359; in Colombia, 183–84, 190; compared to other genres, 125, 203, 292; in politics, 10–12, 94. *See also* political song
Nueva Ola/Onda (New Wave), 15, 300, 303, 358. *See also* Jovem Guarda (Brazil)
Nueva Trova. *See* political song
Nuyorican music, 94, 105. *See also* New York City; Puerto Rico. *See also individual band names*

Onda, La, as counterculture, 29–32, 148–50, 366n8
Onda Chicana, La: Avándaro festival in, 38–41; bands of, 36–38, 366n1; decline of, 22–23, 39–40, 150; definition of, 34–35; English in, 15, 34–36, 41; rise of, 33, 349
Ortega, Palito (Argentina), 118, 181
Ortiz, Renato, 194–96, 353
Ozomatli (U.S.), 361

Páez, Fito (Argentina), 111, 120
Panóptica (Mexico), 313, 320
Panteón Rococó (Mexico), 253–54, 361
Paralamas do Sucesso (Brazil), 204, 213, 354, 360
Pareles, Jon, 192, 194
parental authority, 26–27, 32, 144, 156. *See also* patriarchy
Parra, Fito de la (Mexico), 36
Parra, Javiera (Chile), 304–5

Parra, Nicanor (Chile), 298, 390n19
Parra, Violeta (Chile), 150, 291, 298
Partido Revolucionario Institucional (PRI), 244; nationalist culture of, 23–24, 35–37, 40–41; opposition to, 31, 242; youth and, 31, 242, 245–48, 251–52, 255, 257. *See also* Mexico
patriarchy: gender politics in rock and, 20, 104–5, 178; opposition to, 6, 9, 24, 156, 169, 173, 178. *See also* gender
Patricio Rey y Los Redondos (Argentina), 18, 188, 359, 361
Peace and Love (Mexico), 34, 37–38, 153, 359
peñas, 150–51. *See also* political song
Peronism, 262–64, 273, 282, 286, 288
Peru, 11, 224
Pestilencia, La (Colombia), 16, 187, 361
Peyote Asesino (Mexico/Uruguay), 135–40
Piazzolla, Astor (Argentina), 279
Pinochet, Augusto, 6, 291
Piojos, Los (Argentina), 271, 280, 361
Plastilina Mosh (Mexico), 334, 339
plena, 106, 112
police, 87, 154, 386n3; repression of rock by, 17, 145, 224–25; in *rock chabón*, 268–69, 274–77, 287; torture and repression by, 307–8. *See also* military regimes
political song: *la canción comprometida* as, 297–98; Movimiento Nueva Trova as, 60–61, 63; Nueva Trova as, 1, 12, 63–65, 93, 203, 374n25, 381n30. *See also nueva canción*; Protest music
politics: and Alux Nahual, 229–31; anti-politics and, 17, 131–32, 138–39; in Brazilian rock, 205, 211–12; feminism and, 173, 175–76; of language, 15–16, 111, 184–85; in Mexico, 244–48, 254, 258; in *murga*, 125–27; musicians avoiding, 30–31, 38, 72, 203; in other genres, 125, 275, 292–93; in Puerto Rican rock, 93–102, 107, 110; punk and, 104, 154–55, 157; rejection of/indifference to, 242, 290–91, 305–6, 308, 310–11; relation to Brazilian soul movement, 82–85, 87; in rock, 48–49, 121–22, 154–55, 292–94, 298, 307–9, 333, 345; of *rock chabón*, 278, 280, 282–83, 285–87; youth and, 14, 251–52, 262–63. *See also* gender
pop music, 11, 75, 111, 117–19, 212, 218, 292, 303–4, 352; incorporation of, 95, 122–23, 305; rock and, 213, 233–34, 354

populism, 33, 39, 261, 263–64, 272–73, 349, 352. *See also* Cárdenas, Lázaro; Echeverría, Luis; Peronism
PorSuiGieco (Argentina), 359
Portuguese. *See* language
Presley, Elvis, 7, 24–25, 46, 50–51, 51
press, 24, 100, 192–93. *See also* media
Prisioneros, Los (Chile), 186, 293–94, 297, 299–303, 360–61
producers, record, 83–84, 95, 108, 164, 323–24, 329
protest music, 12–13, 55, 203, 205, 303–4; in Mexico, 40, 150, 241–42; rock and, 228, 354; in Uruguay, 118, 123, 125; vs. *rock chabón*, 266, 269, 277–78. *See also* Canto Nuevo; *nueva canción*; political song
Puerto Rican rock, 92, 96, 113. *See also* Boricua rock (BR); *individual band names*
Puerto Rico, 91, 101–2, 105, 108; government, 101–4; identity of, 99–100, 104, 106–7; independence movement in, 93–94, 96–97, 104, 113; lack of national status for, 92–93, 96–97; nationalism of, 99–100, 107, 112; rock in, 93, 110, 112. *See also* Puerto Rican rock
punk, 154, 171, 185, 204, 301, 353; bands, 16, 102, 155, 187; characterizations of scene, 165, 186–87; Chicana, 162–65; culture of, 107, 163, 177, 323; Do-It-Yourself ideology of, 162–63, 168, 175, 320; hopelessness in, 17, 318–19; incorporation of, 95–96, 105–6, 110, 131, 136, 216–17, 316, 323, 354; in *Pretty Vacant* (film), 174–78, 381n37; Puerto Rican, 95–96, 102, 104–6, 109–10; women in, 155, 162, 170, 352
Puya (Puerto Rico), 91, 94–98, 112–13, 361

Quadros, Jânio, 352
Quilapayún (Chile), 59, 291

race, 12–13, 58, 282, 336; Afro-Brazilians, 70, 74; Afro-Cubans, 45, 52–53; Afro-Uruguayans, 121–24; in Brazil, 69–71, 80–82; and Brazilian racial democracy rhetoric, 79–80, 85–86, 90; and Brazilian soul movement, 70–71, 82–83, 85; dance music and, 13, 70–71, 88; Maia and, 72, 74, 79, 89; in music preferences, 14, 19, 54, 65–66, 72, 93, 108; in punk scene, 104, 165, 170; and racism, 85–87, 90, 149, 178; "whitening," 12–13, 50–51, 53, 364n21. *See also* black power/consciousness movements; African influence

radio, 89, 100, 186, 202, 305, 324; audience for rock on, 255–56; censorship of, 47, 59, 146, 185; Cuban, 45–47, 49, 59; Cubans listening to U.S., 49, 51; effects of airplay on bands, 97, 235–37; English music limited on, 47, 55, 185; programs on, 46, 49, 181, 224, 255–56, 345, 369n23; rock on, 43, 47, 71, 110, 153–54, 181, 223–24, 227

Raimundos (Brazil), 212–13

rap, 65–67, 71, 90, 136, 334, 361; incorporation of, 18, 89, 98, 106, 110, 136. *See also* hip-hop

Ratos do Porão (Brazil), 204, 213

Real de Catorce (Mexico), 253–54, 360

Rebel Without a Cause (film), 24, 351

rebellion, 7, 47, 103–4, 107, 259, 350, 351; anti-authoritarianism, 14, 107, 292, 353–54; in Chilean rock, 302–3, 307–8; portrayal in Mexico, 24–26, 31–32; youth, 27, 31–32, 348

record companies, 27, 90; BMG Ariola, 158; BMG of Argentina, 303–4; Brazilian, 75–76; CBS records, 83–84; Columbia Records (CBS), 7, 64; controlling image of musicians, 144, 191–94; in Cuba, 368n9; Dideca (Discos de Centroamérica), 228, 233–34, 385n16; dropping Boricua bands, 373n12; effects of lack of interest by, 101, 164, 183, 227–28, 235; EGREM, 52, 64–65; EMI Latino, 99; EMI–Odeón Argentina, 119–20; Fermata Records, 75; independent, 98–99, 164, 190–91; influence on music, 87, 147, 239; language of rock and, 223–24; Luaka Bop, 191–92, 195, 198; MCA Records, 94–95, 98; Melody Records, 153; Mercury Records, 187; Mexican, 26, 32; multinational, 75–76, 83–84, 98–99; national, 46, 75–76, 185, 195–97; Polydor Records, 36, 68, 75–76, 83, 367n22; RCA Argentina, 118; RCA Records, 7, 29; relations with musicians, 26, 32, 89, 101, 152; rock and, 65, 183; Sonolux, 191, 195–95; Sonolux/Colombia, 382n15; Sony Records, 139–40, 385n16, 385n18; Stax, 13, 69, 77, 83; transnational, 34, 95, 158, 195–97, 233, 239; Universal Music Latina, 139–40; Virgin Records, 337; Warner Brothers, 87, 191–93; Warner Records, 75–76. *See also* music industry

refritos, 15, 25–26, 28, 367n11. *See also* covers

reggae, 14, 18, 41, 80, 106, 130, 187, 192, 216, 354; and rastafarianism, 105–6. *See also* black music

Regina, Elis (Brazil), 75, 78

religion, 222, 387n17; and spirituality, 106–7, 150. *See also* Catholic Church

Renga, La (Argentina), 269–70, 272–73, 280–81, 286–88

Revolución de Emiliano Zapata, La (Mexico), 33–34, 36–37, 366n1, 367n22

revolution, 8, 44, 59; cultural, 34–35, 37; and revolutionary consciousness, 10–11, 24, 40, 107. *See also* Cuba, revolution in; rebellion

rhythm and blues, 64, 71, 75, 88–89, 94, 148. *See also* African American music; black music; blues

Ricanstruction (Puerto Rico), 105–10, 113, 361

Right, the, 6, 9, 39. *See also* militarism; police

Rio de Janeiro, Brazil, 68–69, 71, 73, 78, 84–86; music scene in, 69, 71, 79–80, 89–90, 214

Ríos, Gloria (Mexico), 20, 143, 358

rocanrol (Mexico), 25–27, 243. *See also* *refritos*

rock: acceptance of, 2, 43, 55, 64–65, 67, 94, 186; access to, 50, 184, 227; aesthetics of, 131, 162–63; aggressiveness of, 183, 301, 307–9; analysis of elements of, 208–11; Anglo, 100, 227; appeal of, 7, 9–10, 24–25, 38, 43, 54, 63–64, 182, 350; arrival in Latin America, 180, 352; audiences of, 7–9, 17, 93–94, 163, 172, 255–56; class and, 8–9, 16–17, 24–25, 38, 40, 93, 151, 244, 248, 254, 265, 300; classification of, 14, 234; consumption of, 7–9, 18, 205, 218; for dancing, 46, 66, 83, 143, 234; defenses of, 57–58, 63, 67; definitions of, 4–5; demonization of, 150, 181–83, 247; diversity of, 4–5, 65; globalization's influence on, 135–36, 140; government repression of, 39–40, 47–48, 53, 61, 249, 292, 350, 353; incorporation of, 55, 60, 62–63, 73–74, 95, 126–29; influence of, 62, 71, 88, 95, 125, 191–92, 204, 334; lack of interest in, 65, 71; language of, 15–16, 35–36, 152, 223; Left's opposition to, 10–11, 155; local, 16, 20, 40–41, 121, 185, 234–35, 264; meaning of,

116–17, 349; men's dominance in, 20–21; mimicry in, 16, 23, 120–21, 181–83, 223, 226; nationalism and, 14–17, 24–25, 349; opposition to, as corrupting, 9, 24–25, 49, 247; opposition to, as cultural imperialism, 5–7, 10–11, 13, 39–40, 43, 155, 205; opposition to, as foreign, 25, 27, 59; as oppositional, 48–49, 116, 263, 265, 272, 347–49; outreach through Circo Volador project, 254–59; politics and, 12, 22–23, 54–55, 93; pop and, 213, 233–34, 354; post-authoritarian, 293–94, 296, 303–6, 310–11; private sector sponsoring/exploiting, 93, 181, 186; as problematic in Latin America, 1–2, 5; race and, 53–54, 66, 93; regional, 21, 190, 227–28, 234–35; in relation to other genres, 186–87, 292–93, 354; repression of, 1–2, 29, 224–25; resistance to, 19; rights to, 1, 12, 17–18, 20; social activism and, 152, 243; symbolizing modernity, 8–9, 205–6; transnationalism of, 194–95, 204, 234–35, 259–60; uses of, 143, 156; value of, 113, 116–17, 140, 265, 348–49; values and, 47, 115–16, 143–44, 349, 351. *See also* countries of origin; *rock nacional*; women, in rock

rock chabón, 18; content of, 266–74, 282–83, 287–88; nationalism of, 262–64, 278–83, 286, 288; as neo-oppositional, 278–79, 288, 355; *rock del arrabal*, 130–34, 140; *rock nacional* compared to, 261–62, 266, 273–75, 277–79, 282–84, 286, 288

rock critics, 26, 36, 100, 142, 146–47, 192, 194, 217, 233, 324–25. *See also* Monsiváis, Carlos

rock en español, 110–11, 153, 173–74, 184, 192, 225; for Anglo audience, 193, 195; classifications of, 19, 235; marketing of, 111–12, 193, 233, 255. *See also* Latin alternative music

rock festivals. *See* festivals, rock

rock nacional, 64; Argentine, 14, 181, 185, 261, 266, 279; Brazilian, 204, 354; characteristics of, 15–16; coinciding with neoliberalism, 16–17; Colombian, 180–81, 188–89; Cuban, 64; as oppositional, 265–66, 269, 354; Puerto Rican, 100, 110, 112–13; *rock chabón* compared to, 261–62, 266, 273–75, 277–79, 282–84, 286, 288; Uruguayan, 123–24

rock styles: agit-rock, 135–40; blues-rock, 99; Christian, 387n17; classic, 110; grunge, 188; hard, 154–55, 354; hard-core, 19, 95–96, 186–88; heavy, 265; heavy-metal, 19, 95–96, 98, 131, 154–55, 183, 185–87, 209; house movement, 328; metropolitan, 115–16, 116; symphonic, 13, 16, 58

rockeras. *See* women, in rock

Rodrigo D No Future (film), 17, 186–87

Rodríguez, Silvio (Cuba), 1, 11, 43, 54–55, 60, 374n25; GESI and, 12, 56, 58–59; influence of, 61, 93

Rolling Stones, 29, 93

rumba, 44, 53, 143, 206. *See also* black music

Sabina, Joaquín (Spain), 253
Salinas de Gortari, Carlos, 251–52
salsa, 13, 19, 62, 93, 110, 182, 193, 364n19; incorporation of, 18, 95–98, 106–7, 109, 187; influence of, 94, 136, 191–92
Salvador, Brazil, 80
Salvador, Dom (Brazil), 69, 79–80
Salvador, Emiliano (Cuba), 56–57
samba, 14, 19, 71, 73, 77, 79–81, 87–89, 136, 202, 214
Sandro (Argentina), 181, 303–4, 358
Santa Sabina (Mexico), 157–58, 253, 361
Santana, Carlos, 36, 93, 358, 361
Santaolalla, Gustavo (Argentina/Mexico), 95, 140, 366n34
São Paulo, Brazil, 70–71, 80–81, 86, 88–90
Schwarz, Roberto, 348
Seixas, Raul (Brazil), 204, 209–11, 213, 359, 383n13
Sepultura (Brazil), 95, 209, 212–14, 354, 361
Serú Girán (Argentina), 14
Sex Pistols, 104, 160–62, 167, 174
Shakers, Los (Uruguay), 118–20, 130, 140, 358
Shakira (Colombia), 142, 189, 361
Síntesis (Cuba), 62–63, 63–64, 359
ska, 18, 41, 130, 136
slums, 78–79, 130–34
social activism, 54, 152, 155, 164–65; Alux Nahual's, 229–30; in Brazil, 55, 70–71, 85, 352; Chao's, 333–36, 339–40, 345; Puerto Rican, 96–97, 105–7, 113; rock and, 228, 243, 250, 286, 354; in *rock chabón*, 277–78, 282; and youth movements, 242–43, 255. *See also* black power/consciousness movements
Soda Stereo (Argentina), 16, 111, 185–86, 360
S.O.S. (Guatemala), 223–24, 358
Sosa, Mercedes (Argentina), 59, 150, 354

soul, 13–14, 40, 68, 75, 80, 150, 158; U.S., 14, 73, 75–77, 82–84, 147–48. *See also* African American music; black music; Brazilian soul
Spain, 47, 61, 65, 185, 224, 265, 332–34, 336–38, 341
Spanish. *See* language
Spinetta, Luis Alberto (Argentina). *See* Almendra
Sputniks (Uruguay), 71–72, 358
students, 24, 30, 352; Mexican government and, 32, 37–39, 41, 241; protests by, 31, 241–42, 367n18, 367n27; rock and, 22–23, 32, 243. *See also* youth
Sui Géneris (Argentina), 41, 359

Tagg, Philip, 201, 205–6
tango, 18, 120–21, 125, 130, 182, 279
tariffs, on record imports, 25, 27, 368n29
techno music, 188, 328. *See also* Electronica; Nortec
Teen Tops, Los (Mexico), 26, 28, 147, 358
television, 45–46, 90, 119–20, 135; Caracol network, 181, 382n7; control of, 25, 186; media conglomerates and, 19, 186, 382n7; music festivals and, 118, 203; music shows on, 202–3, 371n4; *Orfeón a Go Go*, 27, 146; rock on, 9, 27, 43, 47, 146, 181; Telesistema/Televisa, 9, 153. *See also* media
Thee Undertakers (U.S.), 163, 360
Three Souls in My Mind (TRI) (Mexico), 16, 34, 40, 249, 359
Tianguis del Chopo (rock flea market), 156, 248–49, 387n19
Tijuana, Mexico, 28, 335, 338; as border town, 312–16, 328, 392n50; Nortec and, 313, 323–27, 327, 330–31, 392n50
Tijuana NO (Mexico), 22, 334, 339
Titãs (Brazil), 213, 354, 360
Tlatelolco, student massacre at, 32–33, 241. *See also* Mexico; rebellion
tours, rock concert, 95, 118–19, 192–93, 195, 220, 230, 234, 353
Toussaint, Cecilia (Mexico), 152–53, 360
traditional music: Alux Nahual rarely using, 220, 237; Argentine, 279, 286; Brazilian, 76–78, 205; in Brazilian rock, 212–14, 218; Colombian, 183–84, 188, 190–94; influence of, 41, 120; Mexican, 313, 323; in Nortec, 313, 316, 324, 329; not in *sambalanço*, 73–74; in Nueva Canción, 291; Puerto Rican, 94–95; in rock, 1, 18, 40–41, 63–64, 188

transculturation, 121, 124, 130, 135–36, 375n6
transnationalism, 165; effects of, 306–7, 335–36; of music, 95, 194–95, 204, 312; vs. multinationalism, 196
Tres, Las (U.S.), 168, 170–72, 361
Tres, Los (Chile), 298–99, 303, 361
Trevi, Gloria (Mexico), 158, 379n57
Tri, El, 249–50. *See also* Three Souls in My Mind
tropical music. *See* black music
Tropicália (Brazil), 1, 14–15, 42, 55–56, 74, 76–77, 203–5, 350, 353

United States, 135, 181–82, 189, 350–51; CIA of, 6, 291; Cuba's relations with, 44–45, 47, 53, 64, 66; cultural blockade of Cuba by, 15, 48; culture of, 8, 164, 351–52; influence on music in Latin America, 35–36, 40–41, 47, 53–54, 61–62, 71, 73–74, 92, 147–48; Latin American music in, 191–92, 322–23, 325; Latin music in, 220, 234; Latinos in, 20, 34–35, 111–12, 135, 137, 162, 193; as market, 95, 191, 195–95; media of, 19–20, 324; Mexican border with, 312–16, 321–22, 326; Mexico's relations with, 23, 178, 242, 314; music in, 89, 94, 112, 162, 328; Puerto Rico's relations with, 92–93, 96–97, 99–104, 373n14; race relations in, 84, 149; relations with Latin America, 5–6, 16, 221, 294; rhythm and blues of, 64, 71; rock in, 8, 24, 27–28; rock's independence from, 21, 63; State Department of, 6, 31. *See also* cultural imperialism; Los Angeles; New York City; United States music
United States music, 75–76, 83, 202, 227; rock, 13, 43, 48, 61–62, 147–48, 212, 227
Uruguay, 120–22, 134–36; government of, 123, 125–26, 128–30, 353, 376n13; rock in, 117–19, 130–34, 140. *See also* *individual band names*

vallenato, 18, 190–91, 382n5
Van Van, Los (Cuba), 61–62
Varela, Carlos (Cuba), 64–65, 360
Vargas, Getúlio, 81, 352
Vasconcellos, Joe (Chile), 293, 361
Vela Puerca, La (Uruguay), 135–40
Veloso, Caetano (Brazil), 55, 74, 76, 87–88, 192, 203–4
Venegas, Julieta (Mexico), 142, 158, 361

venues, music, 66, 70, 90, 102, 150–51; in Cuba, 53–54, 65–66, 369n45; for rock, 29, 44, 51, 150–52, 204, 224–25; for rock in Mexico, 29, 146, 150–52, 249, 254–59, 316, 386n5. *See also* cafés cantantes; *hoyos fonquis; peñas*
Vieques, Puerto Rico, 97–98, 100–101, 104, 108, 373n14
Viglietti, Daniel (Uruguay), 55, 59
violence, 277–78; state, 221–22, 275, 385n11, 389n2; against women, 165–66, 169–71; youth, 186–87, 246–47. *See also* "Dirty War"; disappearances; military regimes; police
Virginidad Sacudida (Mexico), 156
Vives, Carlos (Colombia), 190–91, 197
vocals, 62–63, 89, 103, 147, 191, 304–5; in Brazilian music, 78, 215; electronic manipulation of, 318–19; Maia's, 68–69, 76–78
Vogel, Angela (U.S.), 164, 168, 361

Waits, Tom, 192
Waldman, Tom, 162–63
Walser, Robert, 309
women: counterculture values of, 148–50; as dancers, 143, 146; music venues for, 150–51; in punk scene, 154, 162, 168, 352; on radio, 153–54; in rock, 20, 105, 155–56, 158–59, 166; in rock, difficulties of, 149, 151–53, 158, 164; in rock, in Mexico, 142, 144, 157, 178, 377n2, 378n20; at rock festivals, 149–50; violence against, in punk lyrics, 169–71. *See also* gender; patriarchy
working class, 46, 178, 265, 352–53; music preferences of, 19, 130; in punk, 155–56, 165; *rock chabón* and, 269–70, 275–76, 278–79, 288; and *rock del arrabal*, 130–34; youth *bandas* of, 243, 246, 249–50. *See also* Class
world beat, 64, 98, 123
world music, 179, 196–97, 221, 238–39

Yaki, Los (Mexico), 9, 29, 149, 358
Yetis, Los (Colombia), 182–83, 358
youth, 102, 143, 163, 290–92, 306–10; Chicano/a, 380n7; culture of, 27, 29–30, 33, 147, 173–74, 177, 294, 350–51; government and, 251–54, 292, 302–3, 349; in Mexico, 23, 31–32, 242–44, 246–47, 251–59; music preferences of, 44, 53, 62, 71, 118–19, 265; politics and, 17, 244–46, 251–52, 290–91, 308, 310; rebellion of, 302–3, 307–8, 348–49; rock and, 116, 131–32, 145–47, 182, 248–49, 262–63, 265, 349
Yupanqui, Atahualpa (Argentina), 150, 291

Zafiros, Los (Cuba), 4, 51–53, 358
Zapatistas. *See* EZLN
Zappa Punk, La (Patricia Moreno Rodríguez) (Mexico), 155–56, *157*, 159
Zé, Tom (Brazil), 203
Zedillo, Ernesto, 252